THE MAMMOTH READER

Super-size Stories & Incredible Information

WEST SIDE PUBLISHING

Contributors: Jeff Bahr, Fiona Broome, Robert Bullington, Eric Erickson, Mary Fons-Misetic, Lawrence Greenberg, Erika Cornstuble Koff, Shanon Lyon, Susan McGowan, Laura Pearson, JR Raphael, Jason Rip, Russell Roberts, Cheri Sicard, Sue Sveum, Wesley Treat, Donald Vaughan, James A. Willis, Kelly Wittmann, Anna Zaigraeva

Cover Illustrator: Adrian Chesterman

Interior Illustrator: Art Explosion, Jupiterimages, Nicole Lee, Robert Schoolcraft

Fact Verification by: Hollie Deese

Louis Weber, CEO
Publications International, Ltd.
7373 North Cicero Avenue
Lincolnwood, Illinois 60712

ISBN-13: 978-1-60553-914-0
ISBN-10: 1-60553-914-7

Manufactured in USA.

8 7 6 5 4 3 2 1

Contents

❖ ❖ ❖ ❖

Step Right This Way!

❖ ❖ ❖ ❖

Hello and welcome to *The Mammoth Reader,* the most entertaining and informative book around! Admittedly, introducing a compendium such as *The Mammoth Reader,* the third book in our annual Armchair Reader™ series, is a bit like being a carnival barker. This volume is so filled to the brim with interesting curios that perhaps I should be perched on a wooden box, beckoning thrill-seekers and the curious to "Step right this way!"

But no. Instead, I'm sitting at my desk, softly tapping on my keyboard and enjoying the relative quiet of the office as our staff of busy editors and art directors go about making wonderful new books. I may lack a megaphone and 10-cent tickets, but I'm still excited about *The Mammoth Reader*—it's like a sideshow tent chock-full of fascinating facts, articles, and lists. Inside, you'll find nuggets of information about a wide array of topics, covering science, celebrities, art, animals, food, history, sports, and plenty of just plain ol' weird stuff. We have it all, from the Watermelon War and tiger-taming ladies to Gold Rush ghosts and how to talk like a trucker. There's stuff to elicit a laugh or a sigh, facts that will make you scratch your head, and tidbits that you'll definitely be telling your friends and family later on.

Perhaps the carnival sideshow simile is a bit much for some readers. Let me take another approach: Scientists have proven that you have to take care of your brain as you would your body to stay alert and functioning at maximum capacity. Well, reading *The Mammoth Reader* is an excellent way of getting a mental workout. You'll find yourself enlightened, more informed, and connecting to the world around you on a deeper level. At the very least, you'll be a lot better at pub quizzes. Here's just a little taste of what is inside:

• Charles Dickens wrote his classic novels facing north.

• In the ancient Mediterranean world, olive oil—not soap—was used for bathing.

• Ex-President Theodore Roosevelt took a bullet in the chest during a 1912 political rally, but he made his scheduled speech anyway.

• Major league baseball umpires are required to wear black underwear while working.

• Want to take the kids on a vacation? Try Virginia Beach, Virginia, a lovely 165-acre city park built on top of a sanitary landfill. You can even fish in Lake Trashmore!

• In the late 1950s, Chinese leader Chairman Mao Zedong proclaimed that all sparrows be killed as part of his "Great Leap Forward" program. His justification: The sparrows ate too much grain. In response, the Chinese people killed at least eight million sparrows—which, ironically, led to an increase in locusts and the destruction of crops.

• Have you ever taken a whiff of a cow's udder? Or taken a gander at a king monkey cup or watermeal? All three are actually odd (and oddly named) plants.

• Contrary to popular belief, swallowing a wad of gum doesn't mean it'll stay in your system for seven years. It just won't get digested, and will come out looking like it did when you were chewing it. Ew.

Please enjoy,

Allen Orso

P.S. Please let us know what you think of the Armchair Reader™ series. You can contact me personally at www.armchairreader.com.

The Blue People of Kentucky

❖ ❖ ❖ ❖

*Skin, the largest organ of the body, comes in
many colors. But who ever heard of blue?*

There exists a rare blood disorder called *methemoglobinemia* that
affects a very small percentage of the population. The disorder happens
when a Caucasian person's blood carries a higher than normal level of
methemoglobin, a form of hemoglobin that does not bind oxygen. Too
much methemoglobin can make the blood dark brown and give the skin
a distinctly bluish tint. A person can get this disorder via exposure to
certain drugs in the antibiotic and bromate family, but the most famous
occurrences of methemoglobinemia were caused by genetics.

The Blue Fugates

In the early 1800s, a man named Martin Fugate lived in the Appala-
chian Mountains with his wife, who was said to have carried the reces-
sive gene that causes methemoglobinemia, or metHB for short. One
carrier of metHB won't make a blue person, but two will: The Fugates
married into the Smith family, who also carried the gene. In 1832, a
blue baby was born. Now, a blue baby or two might not make news, but
because of serious inbreeding among the clans, eventually there was
a concentration of these "Blue Fugates" near Troublesome Creek, an
area in the hills near Hazard, Kentucky.

In the 1960s, a hematologist named Madison Cawein diagnosed
them with metHB and treated them with an injection of the
chemical methylene blue, effectively replacing the missing enzyme
in their blood. The results were amazing, though temporary: The
Fugates who were treated were restored to a pinkish hue that lasted
as long as they took regular doses of the chemical.

A Shade of the Past

Now that people get around more easily and inbreeding is more of a
social taboo, the gene that carries metHB is becoming even rarer than
before. The "blue people of Kentucky" are increasingly harder to find,
though with nature's infinite combinations, it's still possible to encounter
a blue man or woman at Troublesome Creek.

That Sweet 'Stache

❖ ❖ ❖ ❖

From its ancient beginnings to its 1970s heyday, folks have continued to "split hairs" over the merits of the mighty mustache.

A 'Stache Is Born

The ancient Egyptians drew pictures of dudes with pencil-thin lip hair as early as 2650 B.C., while Confucius and his pals were sporting mustaches in the mid-sixth century B.C. But the 'stache's popularity didn't really start growing until eighth century A.D., when King Charlemagne epitomized French chic by proudly bearing a mustache, while other Middle Agers were still grooming their beards.

Forbidden 'Stache

But 'stache growth was cut short in 1447, when English parliament officially banned the broom. A century later, King Henry VIII introduced a tax on facial hair of any kind (even though he personally sported both a beard and mustache).

When the Protestant Reformation began in the 16th century, priests grew facial hair as a sign of protest against Catholic priests, who kept clean-shaven because it was thought that whiskers would trap or otherwise damage pieces of the holy sacrament. Still, while Queen Elizabeth I probably appreciated the sentiment, she wasn't a fan of the lip fuzz—maybe because the 'stache was a style worn by England's French enemy (Frenemy?). So she reinstituted the facial-hair tax.

Well into the 1800s, the English deemed mustaches evil because of their interference with Communion, and in 1838, the King of Prussia nixed nose neighbors among his troops for fear it would compromise them in hand-to-hand battle (mustache yanking = painful).

Stylin' 'Stache

Nevertheless, by 1850, 'staches were back in a big way, both in Europe and in America, where New York dandies grew 'em in slim and styled above the lip, thanks to special pomades, waxes, and dyes.

The Civil War saw the rise of handlebar- and walrus-style soup strainers, which led to the rugged "Wild West" whiskers popularized by gold rushers and outlaws of the 1870s. New products such as mustache combs and cups (which featured a special ledge to keep lip hair dry while drinking) catered to the mainstream mustache. Hirsute Hollywood heroes furthered the fuzz fad from the 1920s through the '40s with Charlie Chaplin's "toothbrush," Groucho Marx's thick broom and brows, and Clark Gable's debonair duster.

Armed and 'Stached

By the time World War I broke out in 1914, the military mustache was protocol for Americans and British alike. American GIs kept their 'staches small and sleek (so gas masks could seal tightly against their faces), while British troops favored the handlebar and toothbrush. In general, mustache style was a symbol of rank among British troops: officers wore 'em waxed and pointy, while infantrymen's 'staches were bushy and droopy.

Post–World War II, the American facial-hair fad seemed to fade—likely a result of Hitler's hairy lip—even while the push-broom boom continued across Europe, with Salvador Dali and Albert Einstein among the many to sport serious 'stache.

Super 'Stache

The hippie movement of the '60s brought the mustache back to America's upper lips with its rebellion against clean-shaven culture. A decade later, the '70s 'stache took on a "tough guy" image thanks to Hollywood hunks such as Burt Reynolds and Robert Redford. By the end of the era, many a man bore broom. But as disco dwindled, so did the mustache, and by the time Tom Selleck's *Magnum P.I.* went off the air in 1988, the 'stache was being shaved.

Back in 'Stache?

But crumb catchers could be making a comeback: More and more celebrities are sporting them onscreen, and though most seem to be for comedic effect (think Borat), the seed has been planted—perhaps the 'stache will make a triumphant return.

The Times They Are A-Changin'

1902

- The first January 1 Rose Bowl game is played at UCLA in Pasadena, California. Michigan beats Stanford 49–0.

- The American Automobile Association (AAA) opens in Chicago. Cars are here to stay.

- Cuba gains its independence from the United States.

- Architect Daniel Burnham builds one of New York's first skyscrapers. The 285-foot-tall, 22-story building is dubbed the "Flatiron Building" for its iconic wedgelike shape.

- New York Central Railroad launches passenger rail service between Chicago and New York, with travel time a mere 20 hours.

- The first JCPenney store opens in Kemmerer, Wyoming.

- Foot traffic is now possible beneath the River Thames in London, with the opening of the Greenwich Foot Tunnel.

- Intercontinental communications becomes easier when the first telegraph cable is laid across the Pacific Ocean.

- Theodore Roosevelt is the first U.S. president to ride in a car. A noted outdoorsman, President Roosevelt is also the inspiration for a new toy, the Teddy Bear, sold for the first time in a Brooklyn toy store.

- Philanthropist Andrew Carnegie founds the Carnegie Institution for scientific discovery in Washington, D.C., with $10 million.

- Willis Carrier invents the first air-conditioning system. Summers become a little easier to handle.

- What happens when two journalists and sports enthusiasts have lunch in Paris? In the case of Henri Desgrange and Geo Lefevre, the idea for the Tour de France is born.

- The first movie theater in the United States—called Tally's Electric Theatre—opens in Los Angeles, California.

A New Breed of Nip and Tuck

❖ ❖ ❖ ❖

Cropping ears and tails to meet breed standards are long-standing practices. But does Pickles really need a nose job or breast reduction?

A Face-Lift for Fido

Today's pampered pets enjoy the same lavish luxuries as pampered humans: fancy spas, posh hotels, upscale boutiques. So if a person can get a little work done, why can't a Pekingese?

Two of the places leading the pack on pooch plastic surgery are Brazil and Los Angeles, already considered the top dogs when it comes to cosmetic enhancement. Most procedures for pets are medically motivated: face- and eye-lifts for chow chows and shar-peis, whose copious skin folds can irritate the eye and become infected; rhinoplasty for smush-nosed breeds such as Boston terriers, pugs, and bulldogs, who often have trouble breathing; and chin-lifts for excessive droolers prone to mouth infections, such as mastiffs and Newfoundlands. Broken teeth from too much bone chewing can be repaired with root canals and crowns, and a pronounced overbite can be corrected with braces (all covered by pet dental insurance, in case you're wondering).

Cosmetic Canines

That said, a growing number of pet cosmetic surgeries seem to be driven by the same insecurities that drive people to go under the knife themselves. Consider Neuticles, prosthetic testicles for neutered dogs to help preserve their "self-esteem" after the goods are gone. Other popular procedures include Botox injections to fix overly droopy ears and breast reductions for female dogs after they've given birth.

U.S. dog shows currently prohibit surgeries that alter a dog's appearance beyond traditional breed standards. But if Miss California can have a boob job, can Prissy the poodle's nip-tuck be far behind?

The Slowest Movie Monsters

❖ ❖ ❖ ❖

So you're chilling out on your front porch, when who shows up but Frankenstein's Monster or a zombie in the mood for some brain food. What do you do? Run away? Take refuge behind a wicker chair? It would certainly help to know if the monster was quick of foot or just your standard foot-dragging hideous beast. Thankfully, we've compiled this list of some of the slowest monsters in moviedom.

Creature from the Black Lagoon

Now this is just sad. In water he may be hot stuff, but on land the Gill-man moves like the Gill mannequin. Add to that the fact that he feels the need to scoop up every unconscious female in his path and stagger around under her weight, and this creature is a threat to nobody but herniated snails.

The Crawling Eye

The name says it all: crawling. In the eponymous 1958 horror flick, this giant eyeball with an octopus-like bevy of flailing arms spends most of its time high atop the Swiss Alps in a foggy cloud—except when it gets rambunctious and decides to descend in search of humans. Besides the fact that it's little threat to anyone except comatose mountain climbers, let's repeat the key word here: crawling. If the Eye shows up on your doorstep, all arm-waving and grouchy, point him to the nearest mountain peak, and watch him very slowly slither away.

Zombies

Zombies present an interesting challenge: There's no way of knowing which type of reanimated corpse has shown up. Is it the traditional zombie, he of the my-shoes-are-tied-together gait and vacant stare? Or is it a neo-zombie, one that moves like quicksilver lightning and is snacking on your arm before you can say "dinner's on me?" If it's the old-fashioned sort, feel free to text a few friends, catch some TV, and have a sandwich before you run. But if it's one of these newfangled zombies, you'd better tighten your athletic shoes.

Frankenstein's Monster

Frankie presents another challenge. In the first few Frankenstein movies starring Boris Karloff, the Big Guy moved quickly and fluidly. But then he developed the arms-outstretched, lurching walk that made him look like a starched clothesline battling a stiff wind. Now Mr. Used Body Parts is only a menace to those who tend to fall asleep when they're running.

The Blob

Question: What is slower than a gelatinous mass of, well, gelatin? *Answer:* A very *large* gelatinous mass of gelatin. The Blob is only capable of catching people (particularly nubile young women) who inexplicably trip when fleeing from nameless evil. Then the victim spends the next ten minutes or so looking behind them in frozen terror while waiting for the fiend to catch up. Sure, the Blob oozes and slimes his way over everything in its path, but it's pretty much a low-gear trip all the way.

Mindless Psycho Killers

You know who you are, Jason. You too, Michael Myers. While these guys have perfected the art of plodding persistence, their arsenal of machetes, axes, pitchforks, and other large sharp objects have slowed them down to the point of their victims being able to out-run them in broken flip-flops.

And now, the slowest movie monster:

The Mummy

This foot-dragging, wrapped-in-bandages excuse for a fiend is ridiculously slow. Initially the Mummy had some magical mumbo-jumbo he used to terrorize his victims, but by the sequels, he was reduced to drinking tea to survive. Ooh, a shambling, one-armed, tea-drinking monster—how incredibly scary! What's his awful power? Does he wear white after Labor Day? End sentences with prepositions? Trust us, unless you're immobilized, wrapped in bandages, you can outrun the Mummy.

HOW IT ALL BEGAN

Fry Daddy

Credit for America's French-fry fondness goes to our third president, Thomas Jefferson, who sampled the thinly sliced, fried potatoes as an ambassador to France. He brought the delicacy home, serving "potatoes, fried in the French manner" at an 1801 or 1802 White House dinner.

But the food didn't become standard American fare—or even known as "French fries"—until World War I, when U.S. soldiers stationed in France developed a taste for the salty spuds.

But whether or not the French fry actually originated in France is a subject of much debate. They may actually have developed in the river communities of Belgium as early as the 17th century, when folks replaced their standard fried fish with potatoes during the winter months as the river iced over.

This Spud's for You

Fried potatoes were definitely on the menu at the fancy-schmancy Moon's Lake House restaurant in Saratoga Springs, New York. History credits restaurant chef George Crum with inventing potato chips in 1853, but some say it actually may have been his sister Katie, who took credit for them in an 1899 interview (Crum never protested). In any case, the recipe was never patented, and the story goes like this:

Chef Crum was not only talented but also temperamental, and if an unhappy patron sent their food back to the kitchen, Crum returned the dish inedible. And that's what he intended to do with the fried potatoes that were sent back for being too thick and soft.

He sliced the potatoes extremely thin, fried them to a crisp, and coated them with salt. The patron (who, according to some sources, was Cornelius Vanderbilt) loved Crum's potatoes; almost overnight, baskets of the newly dubbed "Saratoga chips" began appearing in restaurants in Saratoga Springs and all over the coast.

Tourists applied the recipe idea in their own kitchens. In 1895, home cook William Tappenden took the chips (which at some point became known simply as "potato chips") from stovetop to store, delivering batches to retailers in his native Cleveland, Ohio. By 1921, potato chips were an American standard and had even made their way overseas, where the British—who already called fried potatoes "chips"—dubbed them "crisps."

Fast Facts

- Both poison oak and poison ivy are considered members of the cashew family.

- Adults have weaker taste buds compared to kids.

- You can increase the life of a rubber band by storing it in the fridge.

- Tooth enamel is the hardest substance in a human body.

- Kermit the Frog got his name from a friend of Jim Henson. Kermit Scott grew up with Henson and went on to become a philosophy professor at Purdue University.

- Up to 33 percent of all Americans are chronically underhydrated.

- More than half of all turns on roads are right turns.

- The 200 buffalo that roam California's Catalina Island are descendants of a few that were taken there for a movie shoot in the 1920s and left behind.

- Fire ants first entered the United States in 1920 at Mobile, Alabama, on a cargo ship from South America.

- The average person breathes 25,000 times on a normal day.

- There are almost 12,000 species of grasshoppers worldwide.

- Lake Michigan was once known as "Lake of the Stinking Water."

- The inability to remember a word is called lethologica. Try to remember that one.

The Franklin Syndicate

❖ ❖ ❖ ❖

*What does it take to fleece the public? Confidence, a
believable lie, and something everybody wants: money. Take
a closer look at the first big American pyramid scheme.*

In 1898, a low-wage clerk named William F. Miller was working at a
New York brokerage firm, desperately trying to support his family on
meager earnings. At only 19 years old, Miller was tantalizingly close
to the world of financial success but lacked the funds to participate.
One evening while leading his Bible study class, Miller hit upon the
idea of inviting the men in his group to invest $10 each in return for
a 10 percent return every week. Though skeptical at first, but knowing that their friend had some sort of job on Wall Street, the men
eventually agreed.

Robbing Peter to Pay Paul

Although Miller originally conceived his scheme as a means to raise
quick money to speculate in the stock market, he quickly realized that it was far easier to simply find new investors and pocket
the profits. These investors, convinced by the returns being paid
to the current investors, gladly contributed money and most often
chose to reinvest their dividends. Miller named his new enterprise
"The Franklin Syndicate" and set up a Brooklyn office. Because he
promised a 10 percent return every week (520 percent per year), he
quickly became known as "520% Miller."

144 Floyd Street

All of the syndicate's advertising featured the visage of Benjamin
Franklin and his quotation: "The way to wealth is as plain as the road
to the market." Indeed, many were beguiled into believing that the
road to wealth lay in Miller's office located in a house at 144 Floyd
Street. Miller soon began hiring clerks to accommodate the crush of
eager investors.

   At the peak of the syndicate's popularity, the house was a
beehive of financial activity with 50 clerks working into the night.

Miller, sitting at the top of the front porch stoop, received the cash, distributed receipts, and seemed to hardly notice as the money piled up behind him. His clerks opened correspondence, distributed dividends, and mailed advertisements. It was reputed that investors could receive or drop off money in any of the rooms, including the kitchen, parlor, or laundry.

People from as far away as Louisiana and Manitoba, Canada, sent money. The activity and evidence of so much money easily enticed even the delivery men and postal carriers to deposit their cash as well. The press of people eager to hand over their hard-earned wages was so great on one particular Friday that the stoop collapsed. At the end of each day, Miller and his clerks literally waded through knee-high mounds of cash.

Overwhelmed, Miller added Edward Schlessinger as a partner. Schlessinger helped open the Franklin Syndicate's second office in Boston. In return, he took a third of the profits away in a money-filled bag every evening.

Enter the Colonel

When the newspapers, particularly the *Boston Post* and a New York financial paper edited by E. L. Blake, began to cast doubts about the syndicate's legitimacy, Miller's advertising agent introduced him to an attorney named Colonel Robert A. Ammon. Charismatic, compelling, and utterly corrupt, Ammon incorporated the company, did battle with the press, and increasingly became the syndicate's chief behind-the-scenes operator.

When the *Post* alleged that the Franklin Syndicate was a swindle, Ammon and Miller took $50,000 in a bag to the paper's office to prove their liquidity. When a police chief referred to the Franklin Syndicate as a "green goods business" the two men repeated the display, whereupon the police chief apologized.

The Swindler Is Swindled

Miller, Ammon, and Schlessinger knew that the end was near, but only Ammon knew just how close it really was. Having fully duped Miller into believing he was acting in his best interest, Ammon prodded the young man to squeeze every last dollar from the enterprise before it collapsed.

On November 21, 1899, Miller placed $30,500 in a satchel and went to Ammon's office. Ammon advised his client to give him the money to protect it from the investors. Ammon also convinced Miller to surrender securities, bonds, and a certificate of deposit, all of which totaled more than $250,000. On Ammon's advice, Miller opened the Floyd Street office the following day, a Friday and the last best chance to gather additional funds. After work, Miller was pursued by a detective but eluded his pursuer by ducking through a Chinese laundry and fleeing to Ammon's office. Upon learning that Miller had been indicted in Kings County for conspiracy to defraud, the lawyer convinced his client to flee to Canada.

Die in Prison or Let Your Family Suffer?

It's unclear whether Miller returned two weeks later because he missed his wife and baby or because Ammon, nervous about scrutiny being cast on his own role in the syndicate, convinced him to come back. What is certain is that, with Ammon acting as his counsel, Miller was sentenced to the maximum ten years in Sing Sing prison. Knowing that Miller was the only man capable of implicating him, Ammon gave his client's family $5 a week and reminded Miller that without the allowance his family would starve. After three years, the District Attorney finally convinced Miller, sick from his years in prison and tempted by the possibility of a pardon, to turn evidence against Ammon.

Just Desserts?

- Ammon served five years—the maximum penalty for receiving stolen goods.

- Schlessinger fled with $175,000 in cash to Europe where he gambled and lived well until his premature death in 1903.

- Miller was released after five years in prison. He moved his family to Long Island where he operated a grocery until his death. When a man named Charles Ponzi was being tried for running a pyramid scheme 20 years later, a reporter from the *Boston Post* located Miller and asked him to compare his scheme to Ponzi's. Though there is no record that Ponzi knew of "520% Miller," the reporter concluded that the two men's schemes were remarkably similar.

Talk to the Expert

AMATEUR FEMALE BOXER

Q: What inspired you to take up boxing?
A: My grandpa was an amateur boxer in the '40s, so I grew up watching and have always been a fan. They sanctioned women's boxing in 1994, and I took it up in 1998. I never knew I would get that addicted.

Q: What's so addictive?
A: You never stop learning, and it's a personal challenge. It's really not about winning or losing against the opponent—it's about continually challenging yourself.

Q: It's a combination of mental and physical skills.
A: Exactly. A lot of people don't know that. They see a street fight and think that's what it is, and actually, it's a game of points. And there are different strategies you use in different moments, so it's not about just punching. It's actually pretty sophisticated.

Q: How do you prepare for a fight?
A: Practice, practice, and more practice! Each opponent has a different style—you never know what you're gonna face. So the only way to get around that is to train for all of those situations.

Q: Describe the feeling in the ring.
A: Everyone's a little nervous. There's never a fear of being injured—it's very safe. However, there's a fear of losing, there's a fear of not doing your best. You're also exposed; it's you versus another person. And if they win, it means they're better than you.

Q: What stereotypes have you run into?
A: For female boxers, it's very unexpected that women can box, period. It's a very traditional, old-school sport and even people within the game don't always support the women, because they view it as a man's sport. I also think people are surprised that you can be a professional, you can be feminine outside of the ring, and then also be a national champion.

On the Double

❖ ❖ ❖ ❖

Ever heard someone say, "There's another person inside of me, just waiting to get out?" For parasitic twins, that's pretty much true.

O Brother, Where Art Thou?

Parasitic twins are formed by the same biological defect that causes conjoined twins. Both begin promisingly like any other set of identical twins: A single egg is fertilized and begins dividing into two individual babies. But here the egg hits a snag and doesn't quite finish what it started.

With conjoined twins, both embryos continue to fully develop and both are typically born alive—albeit fused together at the chest or abdomen or, occasionally, the head. But in the case of parasitic twins, only one embryo continues growing normally. The other stops at some point and begins feeding off the blood supply of its twin like a parasite. Though conjoined twins can occasionally share a heart, they usually have their own brains. With parasitic twins, however, the parasitic embryo lacks both heart and brain and so it is never actually alive, although it can go on to grow hair and limbs and even fully functioning genitalia. (Creepy!)

If conjoined twins are rare (1 in 200,000 births), parasitic twins are even rarer (1 in 500,000 births). In fact, there have been only 90 documented cases of parasitic twins throughout medical history.

Stuck on You

Parasitic twins can be either internal or external—and both are pretty unnerving. In the case of external twins, the parasitic twin appears as an extra set of limbs or a faceless, malformed head growing out of the host twin's abdomen. Usually the limbs just hang there uselessly. But sometimes the nervous systems are attached, so the host twin can actually feel the parasitic twin being touched.

Internal parasites, known as *fetus-in-fetu,* happen when the host embryo envelops the parasitic embryo early in pregnancy. In this case, the parasitic twin continues to grow inside of its host's abdomen. As the parasite grows, the host appears to be pregnant (a weird sight on a man or an infant!). Usually doctors mistake this strange growth for a tumor—and are shocked when they go in to remove it and find they are actually performing a C-section to remove the patient's stillborn twin.

Sideshow Stars

The earliest known case of parasitic twins occurred in Genoa, Italy, in 1617 with the birth of Lazarus and Joannes Baptista Colloredo: Joannes was a fully formed torso growing out of Lazarus's stomach. Lazarus, aka "The Boy with Two-Heads," traveled Europe exhibiting himself, setting a precedent for future generations of parasitic twins to make a living on the carnival circuit.

One of the more fascinating carnival cases is Myrtle Corbin, a Ringling Brothers star in the 1880s known as a *dipygus,* or "double buttocks" parasitic twin. Everything from the waist down was double: two sets of legs, two backsides, and yes, two sets of reproductive organs. Though normally the extra set of limbs is ⌐ːless, that wasn't so for Myrtle: Her "sister" delivered two of her five children, making Myrtle the only case of dipygus twins to give birth.

Modern Marvels

More recently, an eight-limbed Indian toddler named Lakshmi Tatma made the news in 2007 when her village decided that she was a reincarnation of her namesake, the multilimbed Hindu goddess of wealth. Her parents turned down offers to sell her to the circus, opting instead for surgery to remove her extra arms and legs.

Modern medicine has also made it possible to uncover more cases of fetus-in-fetu. In 2006, the world learned of a 36-year-old Indian farmer who'd been plagued all his life by a very distended belly and a chronic shortness of breath, who went in to have a stomach tumor removed. During surgery, doctors discovered a hand (with fingernails) inside the man, then another, followed by a hair-covered head, teeth, and genitalia.

A similar thing happened to a seven-year-old boy in Kazakhstan in 2003, when the school doctor noticed movement in his swollen stomach. And in 2008, pregnant-looking girls in Greece and China were taken into surgery, where they "delivered" their identical twins.

"Psychics Predict World Didn't End Yesterday"
See the kind of insights $1.99 a minute can get you?

"Statistics Show Teen Pregnancy Drops Off Significantly After Age 25"
It only drops off slightly, however, after age 20.

"Fisherman Arrested for Using Wife as Shark Bait"
In his defense, she did say she wanted to take a swim.

"Bonnie Blows Clinton"
That is, the tropical storm and the city in North Carolina. What were *you* thinking?

"Clinton's Firmness Got Results"
This one actually is about the president—and his *policies,* you pervert.

"Specialist: Electric Chair Can Be 'Extremely Painful'"
This specialist's specialty: stating the painfully obvious.

"Students Cook & Serve Grandparents"
Dr. Hannibal Lecter, you're needed in classroom B . . .

"County to Pay $250,000 to Advertise Lack of Funds"
County also to pay another $250,000 to commission a study on how to overcome a limited budget.

"Volunteers Search for Old Civil War Planes"
They may have a tough time, being that planes weren't around back then.

"Missippi's Literacy Program Shows Improvement"
The newspaper staff, unfortunately, was not enrolled.

Batter Up! The Babe Ruth Quiz

How much do you know about the Sultan of Swat?
Try to answer these 18 hard-hitting questions!

1. On what day was Babe Ruth born?

February 6

2. What was Babe Ruth's real name?

George Herman Ruth Jr.

3. Who was the only one of Babe's siblings to live past infancy?

A sister named Mamie

4. From what minor league team did the Boston Red Sox purchase Ruth?

The Baltimore Orioles

5. Which major league team had first crack at buying Ruth before the Red Sox?

The Philadelphia Athletics

6. How old was Ruth when he was purchased by his first major league team, the Red Sox?

19 years old

7. Who was the Red Sox owner who bought Ruth?

Joseph J. Lannin

8. What was the maiden name of Helen, Ruth's first wife?

Woodford

9. Who was Ruth's first manager with Boston?

Bill Carrigan

10. How many home runs did Ruth hit in the major leagues between 1914 and 1916?

Seven

11. What instrument was Ruth often photographed holding in 1920 during the St. Mary's Industrial School Band's tour to raise money?

The tuba

12. How many games did it take Ruth and the New York Yankees to win their first World Series in 1923?

Six

13. Ruth was suspended by Yankee Manager Miller Huggins in 1925. How much was he fined?

$5,000

14. What did Ruth keep under his baseball cap to keep him cool?

A cabbage leaf, which he'd swap out every few innings

15. Ruth had names for his bats. What was the name for the bat he used to hit his 60th home run in 1927?

Beautiful Bella

16. Who succeeded Huggins as Yankee manager in 1929 after he passed away?

Art Fletcher

17. Off of what pitcher did Ruth hit his famous "called shot" home run in the 1932 World Series?

Charlie Root

18. Who did Ruth and his wife Claire want to play the lead in the film, *The Babe Ruth Story?*

Paul Douglas

FROM THE VAULTS OF HISTORY

- Alexander the Great (356 to 323 B.C.) and Nearch, the commander of his fleet, are the first known deep-sea divers. They descended 25 meters with the aid of a huge diving bell, which allowed the men to breathe while underwater.

- Mozart, born in Austria in 1756, learned to play keyboards when he was just age three. He was composing music for the piano by age five and wrote his first full symphony when he was nine. Mozart's dad tutored him, so the prodigy never attended regular school.

- King Solomon had more than 700 wives and approximately 300 concubines. Maybe he wasn't so wise after all.

- Walter Hunt invented the ubiquitous safety pin in 1849. He sold the patent for a measly $400.

- It's rumored that the last thing Elvis Presley ate before he died was four scoops of ice cream and six chocolate chip cookies.

- George W. Bush, Roy Orbison, and Darth Vader all have a new species of beetle named after them.

- Winston Churchill smoked an average of ten cigars per day. At his country home, he stocked around 4,000 cigars, mainly Cuban, in a room adjacent to his study.

- Writer Carson McCullers, noted for her bittersweet novel, *The Heart is a Lonely Hunter*, was something of a fan of alcohol. Her favorite drink while writing was a mixture of hot tea and sherry. McCullers named the concoction "Sonnie Boy" and, often claiming it was only tea, would drink it from a thermos all day long.

- Charlie Chaplin once lost a Charlie Chaplin look-a-like contest. (He didn't even make it to the finals.)

- Abdul Kassam Ismael, Grand Vizier of Persia in the tenth century, carried his library with him wherever he went. Four hundred camels trained to walk in alphabetical order carried more than 117,000 volumes.

The Fast Food Graveyard

❖ ❖ ❖ ❖

Some fast food restaurants seem to believe that we'll eat just about anything. But as this list of discontinued items attests, not everything passes mustard, er, muster.

McDonald's McDLT

Despite McDonald's attempt to get all acronym-y on us, the sandwich's full name was the McDonald's Lettuce and Tomato sandwich. Served inside two separate Styrofoam containers designed to keep "the hot side hot and the cool side cool," customers put their own sandwich together. Although it took a while, people soon caught on that putting lettuce and tomato on top of a burger patty was something they could do in the privacy of their own homes. The McDLT went to hamburger heaven in 1990.

Burger King's Veal Parmigiana Sandwich

When most people think Burger King, they probably don't think of veal. Yet in 1988, Burger King added a veal parmigiana sandwich to their menu. Actually, it was a reintroduction, since the sandwich was originally introduced in the 1970s. Of course, after they covered it in cheese and poured tomato sauce over it, it was kind of hard to tell just what you were eating. Maybe that's what did it in—the fact that a fast food place was selling *veal!*

McDonald's HulaBurger

This was an odd concoction created by McDonald's founder, Ray Kroc, in 1963. Originally intended as a meat-free option for Catholics during Lent, the HulaBurger featured a giant pineapple slice in place of a hamburger patty. It would eventually be replaced with the Filet-O-Fish.

Taco Bell's Seafood Salad

Let's face it—nothing hits the spot after a party than a late-night trip to Taco Bell.

That is, except for a brief period of time in the late '80s, when a peek at the Bell's menu would reveal an item guaranteed to induce a gag reflex: the Taco Bell Seafood Salad. The salad involved filling a tortilla shell bowl with lettuce, tomatoes, baby shrimp, and imitation crab meat. It was then topped with a variety of sauces and olive slices. It didn't last long.

Burger King Chicken Bundles

In what could best be described as chicken sliders, Burger King's Chicken Bundles were mini-sandwiches that were sold in packs of three. They were part of a 1987 marketing theme that included Burger Bundles. Neither really caught on, though, even after the burgers were renamed "Burger Buddies."

McDonald's McLean Deluxe

In 1991, McDonald's decided to add a healthy alternative to their menu. Enter the McLean Deluxe, which boasted a 91 percent fat-free patty. People were willing to put up with the sandwich's bland taste in favor of eating healthy, until it was discovered that carrageen, or seaweed extracts, was added to the meat. After that, sales plummeted; the McLean Deluxe was a thing of the past by 1994.

Burger King Yumbo

Back in the 1970s, Burger King wasn't content to merely be the home of the Whopper. Enter the Yumbo, a taste treat with a rather unfortunate name. The Yumbo was created using ham instead of beef, a couple of slices of American cheese, and a sesame seed bun. Once all those ingredients were assembled, the whole thing was melted together into one gooey mess.

McDonald's Arch Deluxe

In one of the greatest fast-food marketing ploys, in 1996 McDonald's decided to tout their new Arch Deluxe as "the burger with the grown-up taste." While initial response to the sandwich was huge, reality soon set in: Despite the "special" mustard-and-mayonnaise sauce, the Arch Deluxe was really just a plain ol' hamburger. It was quickly removed from menus, and to this day, it is considered one of the biggest fast-food flops ever.

Fast Facts

- Old-timers may remember Lorne Greene as Pa Cartwright from the long-running TV show Bonanza. Very old old-timers may remember him as a Canadian radio newscaster during World War II when he was known to listeners as "The Voice of Doom."

- Public ordinances in Carmel, California, forbid the wearing of high heels. Also banned are neon signs, fast-food restaurants, and eating in the street.

- The "ZIP" in "ZIP code" stands for "Zoning Improvement Plan."

- America's former VP once roomed with an MIB. Al Gore and actor Tommy Lee Jones lived together during their freshman year at Harvard.

- Perhaps anticipating the spike in the cost of jet fuel, American Airlines began cost-cutting more than 20 years ago when they reduced the amount of olives in First Class salads, saving themselves $40,000 a year. Nevertheless, AA's annual meal costs still exceeded $425 million at the turn of the century.

- At the time that Leonardo Da Vinci painted the Mona Lisa, the custom of Florentine ladies was to shave their eyebrows.

- Oil Springs, Ontario, is the site of the world's first producing oil well, remarkable because when the pumps were turned on in 1858, we didn't yet have cars.

- Other than the ice caps in the Antarctic and Arctic Oceans, the Great Lakes contain 20 percent of the world's freshwater. At some time, most of it flows over Niagara Falls.

- Anne Taylor, a 63-year old female schoolteacher from Bay City, Michigan, was the first person to go over Niagara Falls in a wooden barrel and live. She achieved the feat in 1901.

History's Little Mystery

❖ ❖ ❖ ❖

Where's Napoleon's, uh, "little Napoleon"?

Au Revoir, Napoleon

After his military defeat, French general Napoleon Bonaparte died in exile on the remote island of St. Helena in 1821. Seventeen people attended his autopsy, including Bonaparte's doctor, several of his aides, and a priest.

As one version of the story goes, at some point during the autopsy, Napoleon's penis was removed and put aside to keep for posterity. While there are some historians who find this implausible, the fact remains (pun intended) that about 30 years later, one of Napoleon's aides published a memoir in which he claims to have helped remove several of Bonaparte's body parts.

The Fate of the Relic

In 1924, a collector from Philadelphia named A. S. W. Rosenbach purchased a collection of Napoleon artifacts for about $2,000. Among the items he purchased was a "mummified tendon taken from Napoleon's body during the post-mortem." Upon further inspection and research, Rosenbach declared the tendon was definitely the leader's penis.

Three years later, Rosenbach put the item on display in New York, and thousands of people viewed the penis under a glass case. The descriptions weren't kind; some likened the relic to "a shriveled seahorse" or "beef jerky." All the accounts have one thing in common: The item was a bit on the small side.

Oddly, the French government was wholly uninterested in the collection. And to this day, it refuses to even acknowledge the possibility of the object's authenticity, further casting doubt on whether or not the object is actually Napoleon's "little general."

In the late 1970s, a urologist and professor from Columbia University purchased the penis for about $3,000 at an auction. Whether or not it's actually the genuine article is still up for debate. Until scientists get their, er, hands on it, the public will just have to speculate about this odd collectible.

E. T. Phone ... Canada?

❖ ❖ ❖ ❖

Do extraterrestrials prefer Canada? The nation ranks first in UFO sightings per capita, with a record high of 1,004 reported in 2008 and 10 percent of Canadians claiming to have encountered one.

What's That?

Though recorded instances of UFO sightings on Canadian soil date back to the 1950s, extraterrestrial encounters emerged most prominently on the global radar in 1967 with two startling occurrences. The first happened when a quartz prospector near a mine at Falcon Lake in Manitoba was allegedly burned by a UFO.

The second followed in October of that year at Shag Harbour, Nova Scotia, when several witnesses—including residents, the Royal Canadian Mounted Police, and an Air Canada pilot—reported strange lights hovering above the water and then submerging. A search of the site revealed only odd yellow foam, suggesting something had indeed gone underwater, but whether it was a UFO remains a mystery.

A Growing Phenomenon

Since then, the number of sightings in Canada has increased nearly every year. Most take place in sparsely populated regions—the rationale being that "urban glow" obscures the lights of spaceships and that country folk spend more time outdoors and thus have better opportunities to glimpse UFOs. It may also be that rural areas are simply more conducive to extraterrestrial activity. (We've heard of crop circles, but parking garage circles? Not so much.)

Most sightings reported are of the "strange light" and "weird flying vessel" variety, and indeed most have rather banal explanations (stars, airplanes, towers). Still, each year between 1 and 10 percent of sightings remain a mystery.

INSPIRATION STATION

Elton's Ode to Billie Jean

The long-lasting friendship between Elton John and Billie Jean King began in 1974, when avid tennis player Sir Elton became so enthusiastic about the women's champ and her team, the Philadelphia Freedoms, that he and Bernie Taupin wrote a song about them. Elton joked that he dedicated the tune, called—what else—"Philadelphia Freedom," to King in return for a track suit she gave him, but in truth it was her passionate fight for the rights of both female tennis players and women in general that inspired him. The already wildly successful musician was nervous about playing the song for King, a feminist icon, for the first time, but she immediately loved it. "Philadelphia Freedom" was released on February 24, 1975, and quickly shot to No. 1 on the Billboard Hot 100 Chart. John and King remain close friends after all these years, working together on charity projects and, of course, playing tennis.

Postcard Inspiration

Most postcards don't cost much and are eventually tossed in the trash—pleasant to receive but nothing of lasting value. The same certainly can't be said of the postcard J. R. R. Tolkien carefully wrapped in paper and labeled "the origin of Gandalf." Gandalf, as any fan of *The Lord of the Rings* trilogy knows, is the greatest and wisest of all the wizards in Middle-earth; just one look at the painting on the postcard, and it is easy to see where Tolkien got the idea for Gandalf. Painted in the late 1920s by Josef Madlener, *Der Berggeist* shows an elderly, somewhat mysterious-looking man with a long white beard and a wide-brimmed hat. Sitting on a large rock by a stream in a woodland setting, he gently pets a tame deer. While the scene is peaceful, the observer gets the sense that there is a lot going on under the surface and readily understands why this work was such nourishing fodder for Tolkien's fertile imagination.

Controversial Queen

❖ ❖ ❖ ❖

In establishing the identity of the Egyptian queen Nefertiti,
scholars find themselves up to their necks in conflicting info.

Like Cleopatra, Nefertiti is one of the most
famous queens of ancient Egypt. She's also often
referred to as "The Most Beautiful Woman in
the World," largely due to the 1912 discovery
of a painted limestone bust of Nefertiti depicting her stunning features: smooth skin, full lips,
and a graceful swanlike neck—quite the looker!
Now housed in Berlin's Altes Museum, the likeness has become a widely recognized symbol of
ancient Egypt and one of the most important
artistic works of the pre-modern world. But the
bust, like almost everything about the famous queen, is steeped
in controversy.

Conflicting Accounts

It wasn't until the bust surfaced in the early 20th century that
scholars began sorting out information about Nefertiti's life. Her
name means "the beautiful one is come," and some think she was a
foreign princess, not of Egyptian blood. Others believe she was born
into Egyptian royalty, that she was the niece or daughter of a high
government official named Ay, who later became pharaoh. Basically,
no one knows her origins for sure.

When the beautiful one was age 15, she married Amenhotep IV,
who later became king of Egypt. Nefertiti was thus promoted to
queen. No one really knows when this happened—other than it was
in the 18th Dynasty—but it's safe to say that it was a really long time
ago (as in, the 1340s B.C.). Nefertiti appears in many reliefs of the
period, often accompanying her husband in various ceremonies—
a testament to her political power.

An indisputable fact about both Nefertiti and Amenhotep IV
is that they were responsible for bringing monotheism to ancient
Egypt. Rather than worship the vast pantheon of Egyptian

gods—including the supreme god, Amen-Ra—the couple devoted themselves to exclusively worshipping the sun god Aten. In fact, as a sign of this commitment, Amenhotep IV changed his named to Akhenaten. Similarly, Nefertiti changed her name to Neferneferuaten-Nefertiti, meaning, "The Aten is radiant of radiance [because] the beautiful one is come." (But we're guessing everyone just called her "Nef.") Again, it's unclear as to why the powerful couple decided to turn from polytheism. Maybe there were political reasons. Or perhaps the two simply liked the idea of one universal god.

Disappearance/Death?

In studying Egyptian history, scholars discovered that around 14 years into Akhenaten's reign, Nefertiti seems to disappear. There are no more images of her, no historical records. Perhaps there was a conflict in the royal family, and she was banished from the kingdom. Maybe she died in the plague that killed half of Egypt. A more interesting speculation is that she disguised herself as a man, changed her named to Smenkhkare, and went on to rule Egypt alongside her husband. But—all together now—*no one knows for sure!*

During a June 2003 expedition in Egypt's Valley of the Kings, an English archeologist named Joann Fletcher unearthed a mummy that she suspected to be Nefertiti. But despite the fact that the mummy probably is a member of the royal family from the 18th Dynasty, it was not proven to be female. Many Egyptologists think there is not sufficient evidence to prove that Fletcher's mummy is Nefertiti. So, that theory was something of a bust.

In 2009, Swiss art historian Henri Sierlin published a book suggesting that the bust is a copy. He claimed that the sculpture was made by an artist named Gerard Marks on the request of Ludwig Borchardt, the German archeologist responsible for discovering the bust in 1912. Despite the mysteries surrounding Nefertiti, there's no question that she was revered in her time. At the temples of Karnak are inscribed the words: "Heiress, Great of Favours, Possessed of Charm, Exuding Happiness...Great King's Wife, Whom He Loves, Lady of Two Lands, Nefertiti."

Fast Facts

- Each rain forest tree contains 1,500–2,000 species of insects, and 80 percent of these are new to entomologists.

- When a male dung beetle goes courting, the female judges his worthiness as a suitor by the size of his dung ball. If it's acceptable, she'll ride atop it in a queenly fashion as he pushes it along. The ball of dung also serves to feed their offspring.

- Caffeine junkies won't like this: Coffee contains 1,000-plus chemicals per cup and of the 26 tested so far, 13 caused cancer in rats.

- The amount of poo a chicken can produce during its lifetime can provide enough electricity to keep a 100-watt light bulb beaming for five hours. Harnessing it might be a problem, depending on the "freshness factor."

- Depending on one's appetite and longevity, the average American during their lifetime will eat as much food as six to ten elephants weigh.

- New Mexico's David Shiffler may be the youngest paleontologist ever. Using his trusty yellow Tonka Toy backhoe, in 1995, the three-year-old unearthed part of a dinosaur egg estimated to be 150 million years old.

- Forty percent of people who visit other peoples' houses snoop in their medicine cabinets.

- Limburger cheese is generally considered to be the foulest-smelling of all cheeses. French cheese makers, who probably had plugged nasal passages, may have topped this classification. Vieux Boulogne cheese is so rank it is not permitted on public transit.

- Seven to eight percent of human males have deficient color vision, and most humans are color blind in dim light.

Outrageous Celebrity Demands

❖ ❖ ❖ ❖

Sometimes, the bigger they are, the harder they make it on everyone else. Check out what demands these celebs make in their contracts.

Madonna

The Queen of Pop requested a new toilet seat for every night of her 2006 Confessions tour. Spokesperson Liz Rosenberg dismissed criticism of Madge's bizarre contract: "Who wouldn't want a new toilet seat wherever they go?" (She has a point.) Madonna also insisted on special candles in all dressing rooms to ward off the evil eye, and requested white draping, white roses, and plenty of cases of Kabbalah water.

*NSYNC

It wasn't too much for this boy band to ask for a police escort to and from concert venues—the throngs of screaming girls made it a necessity. Some of the other requests, however, were clearly more for comfort than safety. In *NSYNC's contract, a $3,000 fine would be assessed if their confidential dressing room phone line was compromised—a sum payable in cash *before* the show began. For pre- and post-show noshing, the group requested, among other items, a case of Barq's Red Crème soda, two boxes of strawberry Pop Tarts, one box of chocolate Pop Tarts, and boxes of Cap'n Crunch and Oreo Cookie cereal.

Jennifer Lopez

If you're so lucky to be granted entry into pop diva Jennifer Lopez's dressing room, for heaven's sake, *don't spill anything.* Lopez demands an all-white room, including tablecloths, drapes, candles, and couches. On the menu in this pristine environment is apple pie à la mode and room-temperature Evian, but absolutely no tomato, apple, or grape juice. For decor, J-Lo asks for yellow roses with red trim, white lilies, and white roses. If she's going to a hotel afterward, the temperature must be set at 80 degrees, and there had better be sheets with at least a 250 thread-count or she's outta there.

Angelina Jolie

Journalists wishing to have a word with superstar actress Angelina Jolie have to sign on the dotted line first. For the 2007 movie *The Mighty Heart,* Jolie's lawyer made it clear that no personal questions may be asked while interviewing for the purpose of movie promotion, no part of the interview can be used in conjunction with any other story, and no "disparaging, demeaning, or derogatory" comments can be included. Many journalists, including the Associated Press, have refused to agree to terms they see as nearly censorship of the free press. No one, not even Jolie, is that important.

Amy Winehouse

It's not surprising what this hard-living, rehab-attending vocalist has on her backstage rider: two bottles of wine, a case of lager beer (but specifically no Stella Artois or Carling), one bottle of Smirnoff or Zubrowka vodka, one bottle of chilled champagne with flute glasses, one bottle of Courvoisier, four cans of Red Bull, 40 Marlboro Light cigarettes, and four lighters. After the show, "three good quality hot pizzas" must be delivered to the crew. If they're not up to par, the retainer states her band will refuse them and the contractors won't be refunded.

Prince

While Madonna and J-Lo are insisting on white, Prince is back in black wherever he goes. All-black dressing rooms replete with black M&Ms are must-haves for the musician. In 2007, the *Daily Mail* reported that Prince asked for a five-bedroom house to be built inside the grounds of a London stadium where he was performing. Don't look so surprised: His retainer once insisted that "all items in this dressing room must be covered in clear plastic until uncovered by [Prince]. This is ABSOLUTELY NECESSARY."

Say What?

"I quit flying years ago. I don't want to die with tourists."
—*Billy Bob Thornton*

"Vegas is everything that's right with America. You can do whatever you want, 24 hours a day."
—*Drew Carey*

"The quickest way to a man's heart is through his chest."
—*Roseanne Barr*

"Cocaine is God's way of saying you're making too much money."
—*Robin Williams*

"To succeed in life, you need two things: ignorance and confidence."
—*Mark Twain*

"I know a man who gave up smoking, drinking, sex, and rich food. He was healthy right up to the day he killed himself."
—*Johnny Carson*

"Most turkeys taste better the day after. My mother's tasted better the day before."
—*Rita Rudner*

"The Internal Revenue Service is the real undefeated heavyweight champion."
—*George Foreman*

"I honestly think it is better to be a failure at something you love than to be a success at something you hate."
—*George Burns*

"If you watch a game, it's fun. If you play it, it's recreation. If you work at it, it's golf."
—*Bob Hope*

"About all I can say for the United States Senate is that it opens with a prayer and closes with an investigation."
—*Will Rogers*

"When you are as great as I am, it is hard to be humble."
—*Muhammad Ali*

Immortality in the Ocean

❖ ❖ ❖ ❖

*By repeating its life cycle, a certain creature
can reverse the aging process.*

A Handy Talent

In the 1990s, scientists noticed something peculiar about
Turritopsis nutricula, a certain hydrozoan related to the
jellyfish: It seemed to be able to live forever. The tiny
creature, seen bobbing around blue Caribbean oceans,
is capable of returning to its juvenile polyp stage, even
after reaching sexual maturity and mating.

The hydrozoan evolved this ability
through a cell development process called
"transdifferentiation." Certain other animals
can do this in order to regenerate an
appendage—say, an arm or a leg—but this creature is the only one
capable of regenerating its whole body. First, it turns into a bloblike
shape, which then develops into a polyp colony. *Discover* magazine
described this process as similar to a "butterfly turning back into a
caterpillar." Actually, the creatures seem to only revert to this early
stage when in trouble, (e.g., they are starving or are in danger of
getting picked on by other sea creatures). Crazily enough, they can
repeat this process over and over again, whenever it is necessary. In
this way, despite the ongoing threat of hunger and bullies, they do not
have to die.

Panama or Bust

More recently, scientists have noticed that the *Turritopsis* are traveling great distances. Although they originated in the Caribbean, certain types of the hydrozoan have been turning up in the waters near
Spain, Italy, Japan, and Panama. They're being extremely resourceful
in finding a ride across the sea: According to *Discover,* "Researchers
believe the creatures are criss-crossing the oceans by hitchhiking
in the ballast tanks of large ships." In any case, one thing's for sure:
the *Turritopsis*—with its ability to turn back the clock—is bound to
become the envy of everyone in Hollywood.

MYTH CONCEPTIONS

Myth: If you shave hair on the face, legs, neck, etc., it will grow back thicker.
Fact: Nope. Shaving is simply the act of cutting the hair at the skin surface and has no effect on the part of the hair where growth and pigmentation occur—that happens way below the skin's surface.

Myth: Casino owners pump oxygen into their casinos to keep patrons awake, gambling, and giddy.
Fact: This is a myth. No casinos use this made-up method.

Myth: Sugar makes adults—and especially kids—hyper.
Fact: No evidence currently exists that shows feeding children a high-sugar diet will induce hyperactivity. In fact, some people get lethargic and tired after eating sugar.

Myth: Reading in dim light will ruin your eyesight.
Fact: There is no evidence to support this, though it is true that eyes have to work harder to see in dim light. Still, reading *War and Peace* at bedtime won't make you go blind—it might just make you sleepier.

Myth: Decaf coffee has no caffeine.
Fact: International standards say decaffeinated coffee must be 97 percent caffeine free. That means there's still a little punch in your decaf, folks.

Myth: You can tell what sex a baby will be by the height and position of the mother's belly.
Fact: This is purely an old wives' tale. There's no scientific proof that you can tell the sex of a baby until the baby's sex can be clearly seen.

Myth: You can cure a hangover with _____.
Fact: If you have a hangover, it's because you drank too much alcohol. No "hair of the dog that bit you" (i.e., more liquor), miracle pill, or strong coffee is going to help. Only time and proper hydration will cure what ails you.

Yep, Moonshine and NASCAR Are Kin

❖ ❖ ❖ ❖

*White lightning, hooch, mountain dew, hillbilly pop—whatever
you called it, it was the lifeblood of the South. It was illegal,
and it was the juice that jump-started NASCAR.*

Model "T" for Tripper

Henry Ford was an adamant teetotaler, but without him, the South's
illicit moonshine business could never have been so successful. The
mass production of Ford's Model T, and later his V-8, coincided
with the dawn of 1920s Prohibition. Southerners demanded bootleg
booze, and "whiskey trippers" were now equipped to deliver as many
as 100 gallons a night, at 30 cents a gallon. To crack down was futile:
Local cops often had kinfolk in the biz and, in any case, appreciated
"corn likker" as much as anybody else.

Despite the end of Prohibition in 1933, there was still a
demand for moonshine. Alcohol was technically legal but only
from legitimate, tax-paying distilleries. Selling untaxed liquor, or
moonshine, was illegal (as it is today). Moonshine was also cheaper
and stronger than the legal stuff.

Federal tax agents were sent in to hunt down the shiners, who
learned speed was their best defense. For an extra leg up, shiners
sought the help of "whiskey mechanics," who specialized in souping
up V-8s, sawing cylinders to boost horsepower, and tweaking the rear
suspension with heavy-duty springs and steel wedges to keep liquor
bottles in place while driving on twisty mountain roads.

Shiners vs. Shiners

Informal races soon cropped up among the shiners to see who had the
fastest cars and meanest driving skills. Tracks were plowed in the red
dirt fields; crowds dropped coins in a hat for the winner's purse. Local
entrepreneurs started cashing in as well, sponsoring races at horse
tracks and fairgrounds across the South.

The appeal was clear: Until then car racing had been the domain
of the American Automobile Association (AAA) and the wealthy

Northern elite. But stock car racing's everyman appeal is what struck driver and race promoter Bill France as a golden opportunity.

NASCAR Is Born

Southern stock car racing picked up momentum after World War II, and several regional organizations formed. AAA had been flirting with stock car racing for years, and it now decided it wanted to control the action, but France wanted races for regular working folk.

In late 1947, he called a meeting of representatives from every southern stock car group. Within three days, they had united as the National Association of Stock Car Auto Racing (NASCAR), named France president, and agreed to uniform racing rules. To gain respect as a legitimate organization, France felt they must distance NASCAR from its moonshine roots. Easier said than done, since most of his drivers had cut their teeth running whiskey. What he could do was make the races "strictly stock," meaning no souped-up cars allowed. Several drivers showed up at the first race in February 1948 with no car to drive, looking for willing spectators to hand over their keys.

Glenn Dunaway was one such driver. He finished first in a borrowed Ford coupe—that is, until a post-race inspection showed signs of "bootlegger souping," and he was disqualified. Sure enough, the car's owner had delivered a load of moonshine just a few days earlier.

Keep Shining

Many of NASCAR's earliest stars traced their roots to moonshining. Legendary driver Junior Johnson was eight years old when he started running whiskey in 1939; he gave it up in the late '50s, after a yearlong prison stint interrupted his racing career. Curtis Turner, another great, claimed he started running hooch at age ten.

Today, NASCAR is a multibillion-dollar industry with a family-friendly image. Yet glimmers of its whiskey-soaked history still "shine" through: As recently as March 2009, retired driver Carl Dean Combs was arrested in North Carolina for making and selling hooch.

WORD HISTORIES

Hopscotch: The earliest English name for this popular children's game was "scotch-hoppers." In fact, there is no history tying the game to Scotland or its people. Rather, the word *scotch* means the same as score or line. Simply, the outline of the game was drawn or "scotched" into the ground, and the kids got hopping.

Intexticated: Here's a new word to send shivers down the spines of parents. It applies to people who are preoccupied with sending or receiving text messages, particularly while driving.

Supercilious: This word applies to people who think they are better than their peers, showing haughty disdain. Interestingly, the word's origin perfectly describes the actions of these very people, with chins raised and eyebrows lifted. The Latin word *supercilium* can be broken down into two words that mean "eyebrow" and "pride."

Hoosegow: Now a slang term meaning jail, the word gets its original meaning from the Spanish *juzgado*, meaning court of justice. Mexican usage shortened it to *juzgao*, using the word in reference to a jail. It later became popular in the American Old West, spelled just the way it sounded to the American ear.

Pipe dream: Now here's one that is pretty much what it sounds like. Originating in an 1890 *Chicago Tribune* article, the term refers to dreams or wishes that are similar to those that would come from smoking an opium pipe—that is, fantastic and likely to go up in smoke.

Vacuous: This adjective means stupid or lacking in intelligence. In Latin it is *vacuus*, or "empty," which pretty much says it all.

Tobacco: Christopher Columbus may have discovered the earliest examples of the cigarette when he reached America in 1492. There, his men spotted natives with cylinders that were filled with sweet-smelling herbs. These tubes glowed, and smoke came out when the villagers sucked on one end. The natives called these cylinders *tobaccos*, but when Columbus returned to his homeland, he used the term in reference to the dried leaves inside the tube.

Lobbyist: According to the BBC, this is one who frequents the entrance hall, or lobby, of the British House of Commons, hoping to influence the members of Parliament as they come and go.

The Hosts of Horror

❖ ❖ ❖ ❖

What's better than staying up late and watching bad B horror films on TV? Having these local horror hosts to usher you in.

The Cool Ghoul

Starting in the 1960s, folks in Cincinnati tuned in to *Scream-In* (a play on the show *Laugh-In*), starring Dick Von Hoene's character, The Cool Ghoul. The host wore a bizarre costume: painted-on eyebrows, a long orange-red wig, and a jaunty cap that made him appear like some sort of demented hippie. The Ghoul continued to make public appearances until Von Hoene's death in 2004.

Dr. Paul Bearer

"I'll be lurking for you!" That was how Dr. Paul Bearer (aka Dick Bennick) signed off every one of his *Creature Feature* shows on WTOG-TV in St. Petersburg, Florida. The show ran from 1973 until Bennick's death in 1995, making Dr. Bearer the longest-running horror host in TV history. Dressed in a black suit with slicked-down hair parted in the middle, Bennick flipped audiences out with the glass eye he wore.

Vampira

Bearing a likeness to Morticia Addams from *The Addams Family,* Maila Nurmi made her Vampira character an icon. On May 1, 1954, *The Vampira Show* premiered on KABC-TV in Los Angeles, making Vampira one of TV's first horror hosts. The show was cancelled after only one season, but Vampira's look would go on to influence generations of horror fans.

Elvira, Mistress of the Dark

Perhaps no other horror host is more recognized than Cassandra Peterson's sexy vampiric character, Elvira. She began hosting *Elvira's Movie Macabre* in 1981, patterning her look after '50s horror host

Vampira, who later unsuccessfully sued Peterson for copying her likeness. Thanks to a ton of publicity and cross-promotion, Elvira, the first nationally syndicated horror show host, was a hit.

Marvin

Terry Bennett's character, Marvin, only lasted two years on Chicago's WBKB show *Shock Theatre* (1957–1959). But Marvin was notable for what he *wasn't*—neither monster nor ghoul, but a Beatnik who wore a black turtleneck and giant coke-bottle glasses.

Svengoolie

One of the strangest horror hosts, Svengoolie, debuted on Chicago-area WFLD television in September 1970 on the show *Screaming Yellow Theater.* Played by Jerry G. Bishop, Svengoolie was a hippie with a Transylvanian accent. The show was cancelled in 1973, but it was resurrected in 1979 in the form of *Son of Svengoolie,* with Rich Koz in the title role. In true zombie form, the cancellation of the show in 1986 couldn't keep a good ghoul down: On New Year's Eve 1994, Koz returned on Chicago's WCIU-TV's *Svengoolie,* rubber chickens and all.

Sammy Terry

Appearing periodically from 1962 through the 2000s, Bob Carter played Sammy Terry, first as part of the show *Shock Theater* and then on his own *Nightmare Theatre* on WTTV-4 in Indianapolis. The show featured several guests, including a rubber spider named George. Terry wore skull-like makeup and a hooded cloak, but when television transitioned to color, audiences saw that his makeup was a weird greenish-yellow color and his gloves appeared to be of the yellow latex dishwashing kind. Interestingly, most people found Terry to be even scarier in color.

Sir Graves Ghastly

"Turn out your lights. Pull down the shade. Draw the drapes." These were the instructions intoned by Sir Graves Ghastly, played by Lawson Deming on WJBK's *Sir Graves Ghastly Presents* in Detroit from 1970 to 1983. A vampire rocking a devilish goatee, a strange cast of characters often accompanied Sir Graves, including Reel McCoy, a gravedigger who would unearth the movie of the evening; and The Glob, whose weird face would appear in the moon over the cemetery.

FROM THE VAULTS OF HISTORY

A Boho Birth

Was the 12th-century French nun and scholar Héloïse the world's first recorded "hippie chick"? Was her son the first famous "boho baby"? The details of the lovechild's conception and birth seem to argue yes on both counts. Héloïse was known for her brilliant mind and insatiable intellectual curiosity at a time and place when women were rarely even taught to read. Her paramour, Pierre Abelard, was a forward-thinking philosopher and theologian. When they came together as pupil and teacher, sparks immediately flew, and premarital sex was not far behind. When Héloïse became pregnant, Abelard offered to marry her, but she declined with a "free love" argument and proposed a no-strings-attached relationship. "The name of mistress instead of wife would be dearer and more honourable for me, only love given freely, rather than the constriction of the marriage tie, is of significance to an ideal relationship," she wrote.

Abelard persisted, and Héloïse eventually caved in, but she insisted that their marriage remain a secret, seemingly embarrassed by the conventionality of it all. When their son was born in 1118, she even gave him a groovy, literally far-out name: Astrolabe. Fittingly, Héloïse is rarely left out of any college women's studies curriculum.

Still Good Friends

You'd think a guy who had two of his wives beheaded wouldn't be much fun as an ex-husband, but King Henry VIII and Anne of Cleves got along much better after they split than they did when they were briefly married. They both just realized that there was no chemistry there whatsoever, never consummated the marriage, and agreed to an amicable annulment in 1540. Anne decided to remain in England rather than return to her native Germany, and she stayed in touch with Henry's kids, even accompanying his daughter Mary on her triumphant accession parade into London in 1553. Talk about dodging a bullet—or in this case, an ax.

Anatomical Anomalies

❖ ❖ ❖ ❖

Mother Nature isn't always right. Here are a few examples.

But Can It Wag?

Many people don't know that every human embryo actually starts life outfitted with a tail, though we usually lose them before birth. The reason why there are only several dozen known cases of people born with "true human tails" is because almost as soon as the embryonic tail develops, its growth is suppressed by *apoptosis,* or programmed cell death. True human tails, when they are retained by newborns, range from one to more than five inches in length—and, yes, they are able to wag!

Breathe Easily–If You Can

Flying is a strenuous activity requiring vast amounts of oxygen and an efficient respiratory system. Birds have a flow-through system of ventilation, which doesn't let freshly oxygenated air mix with the depleted air leaving the body. Mammals, however, mix fresh air with depleted air when they breathe, which is very inefficient. This is unfortunate for bats, since these flying mammals must take to the sky with inferior ventilation systems. Too bad they can't swap lungs with flightless birds such as emus and penguins, who still have the avian flow-through system that is of little use to them on the ground.

Picasso's Dream Fish

The bony flatfish has evolved to lay flat on the seabed. The most sensible way to flatten itself would be back-to-stomach, like a ray, so that both eyes are on top of its head. However, most bony fish are flat sideways, which means lying down flat would leave one of their eyes pointing uselessly at the ground. But where there's a will, there's a way: The flatfish asymmetrically reshapes its skull during adolescence, so that one of its eyes migrates over the top of the head and winds up on the other side! The result is both comical and creepy.

Fast Facts

- Centuries ago, the Roman Catholic Church frowned on eating with a fork. "God in his wisdom has provided man with natural forks—his fingers," wrote Church leaders. Therefore, "it is an insult to Him to substitute artificial metallic forks for them when eating."

- As people mull the use of additives in food, they should be mindful that food researchers have said that the flavor of every natural food can be artificially duplicated in a test tube and adopted for commercial food products.

- Chewing gum has been prohibited in Singapore since 1992. In 2004, the ban was loosened to allow for medicinal gum but only if purchased from a druggist or dentist, and only if the chewer's name was registered.

- America's hens produce 5.5 billion eggs per year. To achieve this requires 240 million hardworking hens.

- In 1968, William Shatner of Star Trek fame did what some music critics have termed as his first comic turn—he recorded an album, featuring among other tunes, "Mr. Tambourine Man" and "Lucy In the Sky With Diamonds."

- Canadian inventors are not to be underestimated. They claim credit for the Geiger counter, paint roller, kerosene, zipper, and, most important, beer cases with tuck-in handles. They also lay claim to the concept of the Academy Awards (since Louis B. Mayer grew up in Canada) and the dotted white line painted down the middle of highways.

- Legal action can be taken by a spectator accidentally hit by a puck during a National Hockey League game. As to whom to sue, some complainants have even tried suing the hot dog vendor for blocking their view.

Behind the Music of Our Time

- In 1967, British radio deejays deemed The Rolling Stones' track "Let's Spend the Night Together" too racy. So the deejays simply flipped the disc over and played the b-side, "Ruby Tuesday." This propelled "Ruby Tuesday" to No. 3 on the British charts.

- Michael Stipe once said that the 1960s children's television musical group The Banana Splits (starring a dog, a gorilla, an elephant, and a lion) was a bigger influence on R.E.M. than The Beatles.

- Dean Martin knocked The Beatles out of the No. 1 spot on the charts in 1964 with his smooth single "Everybody Loves Somebody."

- Dr. Hook & The Medicine Show's song "Sylvia's Mother" was meant to be a parody of teen breakup songs, but the public took it seriously and sent it to No. 5 on the American charts.

- Singer Little Eva came across her 1962 hit, "The Loco-Motion," in an interesting way: She'd been babysitting the children of Carole King, who wrote the song.

- Danish pop group Aqua was sued by the Mattel toy company over their 1997 hit "Barbie Girl." The case was eventually dismissed with the presiding judge saying, "The parties are advised to chill."

- The theme for the television show *Beauty and the Beast*, "The First Time I Loved Forever," was cowritten by Melanie, best known for her 1971 hit "Brand New Key."

- In 1971, The Byrds set the standard for lyrical ickiness in "Chesnut Mare" when they hoped a horse would be "just like a wife."

- Before Donna Summer was discovered and became an international disco diva, she was in Germany performing in a production of the musical *Hair*.

- Chuck Berry's hit single "Maybellene" was originally called "Ida May."

- Both Steely Dan and The Soft Machine took their band names from the novels of William S. Burroughs.

Back from the Brink

❖ ❖ ❖ ❖

By the end of World War II, the population of the Japanese Akita had dwindled to near extinction, with only 16 dogs remaining. One man made it his mission to bring them back.

In 1944, 30-year-old Morie Sawataishi was an engineer working in northern Japan's snow country when he heard the disgusting rumor: People were killing their Akitas, selling the pelts to Japanese soldiers, and—as food became scarce—eating the meat. Morie couldn't believe it. When he was a boy, the Akita had been declared a national treasure. What had changed?

Dog Tired

Quite simply, Akitas were no longer hip. Even before the war, the Japanese had grown tired of their native snow dogs and wanted something novel and foreign. Akitas seemed old-fashioned, throwbacks to the 19th century, when the dogs were admired for their fearlessness (Akitas were known to corner bears).

In 1927, a preservation society was founded to protect the dogs, but that didn't boost the pups' popularity. They did get some good publicity from Hachiko, the Akita who arrived at a Tokyo train station every day to greet his master—even nine years after the man's death. The government erected a bronze statue of Hachiko in 1935, and he became a national symbol of loyalty. But by 1944, the statue had been melted down for metal. So much for loyalty.

Canine Contraband

Though Morie had never been what you'd call a "dog person," he felt compelled to do something. He heard murmurings about a puppy for sale, the granddaughter of a prizewinning Akita. Morie paid the breeder six times his salary for her.

Morie never named the dog, whom he kept hidden in a shed and walked only in the late night and early morning hours to avoid detection. As his work took him across snow country, he covertly inquired, who else had an Akita? By the time the war ended in 1945,

Morie had put together a list—only 16 purebreds remained, and two belonged to him (he had also bought a male for breeding).

Back in Pack

In the spring of 1946, with a litter of puppies on the way, Morie held the first postwar dog show at his home. Nearly 50 Akitas were present, but it was hard to believe they were of the same breed. Years of malnutrition and crossbreeding with foreign dogs had given them a hodgepodge of features. What's more, no one could agree on which features were ideal. Everyone felt ears should be erect and tails curved, but should bodies be lean or stocky? Heads round or sharp? Debates aside, Morie was just pleased to spark a dialogue and turn attention back to the breed.

Bred and Ready

"Attention" turned to "frenzy" in the early 1950s after an ad campaign featured a famous Japanese actress with her Akita (think Paris Hilton with her purse Chihuahua). American GIs clamored for the dogs. Suddenly, everyone in Japan was an "Akita breeder." Everyone except Morie, that is. Rather than sell his dogs for profit, he gave them away to people he knew, keeping and breeding the ones he thought had the strongest features and, most importantly, *kisho* (spirit).

For more than 60 years, Morie raised and trained Akitas—100 in all. His last dog, Shiro, died at age 15 in late 2007; Morie followed one year later at age 92.

- *The first Akita was brought to the United States in 1937 by Helen Keller, who was so moved when she heard the story of Hachiko while visiting Japan, that she asked for a dog just like him.*

- *The Akita takes its name from the Akita Prefecture, a district in Japan's snow country.*

- *The statue honoring Hachiko was recreated after the war in 1948.*

Sock of Ages

❖ ❖ ❖ ❖

*Every spring, hundreds of fervent fans trek to Rockford, Illinois,
home of the sock monkey, to pay homage to this all-American icon.*

Red Heel Is All the Rage

Dolls made from socks aren't anything new, but there's only one
"sock monkey," the iconic plush creature with giant red lips. The
history of the popular monkey weaves a tale (or "yarn," if you will)
dating back to 1872, when a machine was invented that guaranteed
a seamless toe and heel. As with any great idea, knockoffs soon
flooded the market. Though they had been making the iconic red
socks since 1890, in 1932, the Rockford-based Nelson Knitting
Company introduced the "De-tec-tip," a signature red heel, to help
distinguish their socks as the real deal.

Sock It to Me!

During the 1940s and '50s, the company regularly sent its Red Heel
socks to nuns in Wisconsin, who turned the socks into monkey dolls
and then sold them to raise money. The company went ape for
the idea and convinced Sears and Montgomery Ward to include a
monkey pattern with each Red Heel sold. By 1953, Nelson Knitting
Company had patented the design of the sock monkey, and patterns
were included with every pair of socks.

The sock monkey strode through the '70s, then waned
considerably until 2001, when photographer Dee Linder (known
as the Sock Monkey Lady) sparked new interest
with a Web site that showcased her photos of the
primates about town. In 2005, this resurgence in
monkey mania inspired Rockford to embrace its
history and launch the Sock Monkey Madness
Festival. Highlights of the two-day soiree include
an international film festival, a sock monkey
beauty pageant, monkey-making workshops,
and even a "hospital" to treat old and "overly
loved" monkeys.

Odd Ordinances

- Get your peanuts early if you're shopping in Lee County, Alabama. It's illegal to buy a bag of peanuts there on Wednesdays between sunset and sunrise.

- Drivers may not be blindfolded while operating a motor vehicle in Alabama.

- In Kentucky, it's illegal to have an ice cream cone in your back pocket. Thank goodness cargo pants have side pockets!

- You cannot give a moose any alcoholic beverages in Fairbanks, Alaska.

- In Anchorage, Alaska, you may not tie your dog to the roof of a car.

- It's perfectly legal to shoot a bear in Alaska. However, it is against the law to wake a sleeping bear to take a picture.

- It's not so surprising that it's illegal to cut down a Saguaro cactus in Arizona—but a 25-year prison sentence?

- It's against the law to manufacture imitation cocaine in Arizona.

- Whatever you do in Arizona, don't ride your horse up the stairs of the county courthouse.

- Bring your reading glasses and have your mind made up, because you only have five minutes to vote in Arkansas.

- Dogs are prohibited from barking after 6:00 P.M. in Fayetteville, Arkansas. Good luck enforcing that!

- Well, that's thoughtful: While it is legal for a man to beat his wife in Arkansas, the limit is one time per month.

- In stylish California, women may not drive in a housecoat.

- Prostitutes in San Francisco are not required to make change for bills over $50.

- In Wyoming, you need an official permit to take a picture of a rabbit at certain times of the year.

The King Is Dead...Wait, Not Yet

❖ ❖ ❖ ❖

*On January 20, 1936, England's beloved King George V—
grandfather of the reigning Queen Elizabeth II—died in
his sleep. Or was it actually murder? You be the judge.*

Case Files

On January 17, 1936, Queen Mary called the royal physician, Lord
Bertrand Dawson, to attend to her 71-year-old husband, King
George V, who couldn't seem to shake his bronchitis. Over the next
three days, the king slipped in and out of consciousness. On the
morning of January 20, the king held a ten-minute meeting with
his counselors and, at some point, summoned his private secretary,
Wigram, to discuss the nation's business. "How is the Empire?" he
asked, in what would allegedly be his final words. Exhaustion over-
came him before the conversation could continue.

That night after dinner, Dawson gave the king a shot of morphine
to help him sleep. At 9:25 P.M., Dawson issued a brief medical
bulletin to prepare the nation for the inevitable: "The King's life
is moving peacefully towards its close," it said. An hour and a half
later—five minutes before midnight—the king was dead.

For half a century, this is the story that the public (and
biographers) believed. But some startling details have come to light,
revealing what may in fact be a case of murder in the first degree.

Stop the Presses!

November 28, 1986, was a day that literally rewrote history. It was
on this day, nearly 50 years after the king's death and 41 after Dawson's, that the physician's personal diary was published in the Windsor archives. The sordid truth about the king's demise was exposed.

According to the doctor's notes, the king simply wasn't dying
quickly enough. Around 11:00 P.M. on January 20—an hour and
a half after Dawson released the bulletin announcing the king's
imminent passing—he realized it was not going to be a speedy
process. "The last stage might endure for many hours," he wrote,
"unknown to the patient but little comporting with the dignity and

serenity which he so richly merited." What's worse, the king's delay would mean that his obituary wouldn't run in the morning edition of the London *Times,* the paper considered most appropriate for national news, but rather in some "less appropriate" evening publication. How bourgeois!

Taking matters into his own hands, Dawson called his wife and asked her to contact the *Times* to have them hold publication; there was going to be some big news coming yet that night. Then, at 11:25 P.M., Dawson prepared a lethal cocktail of three-quarters of a gram of morphine and one gram of cocaine, and he injected it into the king's jugular vein. Thirty minutes later, King George was dead—just in time to make the morning news. "A Peaceful Ending at Midnight," read the *Times* headline.

In his notes, Dawson describes his actions as "a facet of euthanasia or so-called mercy killing," done to protect the reputation of the king. He also claims that both the queen and Prince Edward were in agreement that the king's life should not be prolonged if his illness was fatal. That said, his notes say nothing about his efforts to consult them of his decision. Most likely, he made it on his own.

Murder or Mercy?

Euthanasia is defined as "the intentional killing of a dependent human being for his or her alleged benefit." Euthanasia by action means "intentionally causing death by performing an action such as giving a lethal injection," while nonvoluntary euthanasia means doing it without the patient's consent. Murder, on the other hand, is to "kill unlawfully and with premeditated malice."

If the question is intent, then it's hard to argue that Dawson's actions make him a murderer, even though many in England, including the medical community, believe that's just what the prominent physician was. From a legal perspective, euthanasia is and always has been "unlawful" in England, as it is in most places throughout the world.

In fact, Dawson himself opposed euthanasia as a legal practice. Just ten months after the king's passing, Dawson spoke against a bill that would have legalized it, arguing that it should be a choice left to the individual doctor, not the federal government. In what can now perhaps be seen as an attempt to excuse his own actions, Dawson went on to say that a doctor "should make the act of dying more gentle and more peaceful, even if it does involve the curtailment of the length of life."

Although Dawson died in 1945 with a glowing reputation for his years of service to the royal family, today his name is a source of anger and disgrace. As recently as 1994, the *British Medical Journal* published an article deriding him for his selfishness and "arrogance," claiming that he committed a "convenience killing" of the king in order to return to his own busy private practice in London.

And About Those Last Words...

Now, it's true that King George asked Wigram, "How is the Empire?" and then drifted into sleep. But those words actually weren't the last ones spoken by the dying king. According to Dawson's notes, the king's last worst words were uttered just as the doctor injected him with the first dose of morphine: "God damn you."

- *In Switzerland, assisted suicide has been legal since the 1940s. According to a 1997 Reuters UK article, many terminally ill people from other countries travel to Switzerland to end their lives.*

- *In 1994, Oregon passed the Death with Dignity Act, becoming the first state to legalize physician-assisted suicide, in which a patient voluntarily enlists the help of a doctor to end his or her life. (Think Dr. Jack Kevorkian.) The law didn't go into effect until 1997.*

- *Speaking of Dr. Kevorkian (aka "Dr. Death"), the physician was released from prison in June 2007 following an eight-year sentence for second-degree murder, of which he was convicted after administering a fatal injection to Michigan patient Thomas Youk, who suffered from Lou Gehrig's disease. Prosecutors had previously failed on four different occasions to convict Kevorkian for assisting in the suicides of terminal patients.*

Fast Facts

- Of the nine Oscars awarded to MGM for Best Animated Short Subject, seven were for Tom & Jerry *cartoons.*

- Captain Marvel's face was patterned after actor Fred MacMurray.

- Ray Bolger and Jack Haley each received $3,000 a week to portray the Scarecrow and the Tin Woodsman, respectively, in The Wizard of Oz (1939). The film's star, Judy Garland, received just $500 a week.

- PEZ was developed in Germany in the 1920s, and originally was available only in peppermint. The name is an abbreviation of pfefferminz, the German word for peppermint.

- The ratio of colors in a bag of chocolate M&Ms is 30 percent brown, 20 percent each of red and yellow, and 10 percent each of orange, green, and blue.

- In 1900, there were approximately 8,000 automobiles on American roads. Fifteen years later, the number had exceeded 2 million.

- Please draw your attention to the center ring! The first known circus school was established in China during the T'ang Dynasty (A.D. 612–907). Classes included "duel sword dancing," "seven-ball jumping," and rope walking.

- Leonardo da Vinci dissected more than 30 corpses to better understand what made people tick, despite legal restrictions against doing so. From these morbid examinations, he produced an estimated 750 very detailed drawings of the human body.

- By 1800 B.C., asses were so important as beasts of burden that Damascus, an important Middle East trade center, was known as the "City of Asses."

The Times They Are A-Changin'

1912

- New Mexico and Arizona become the 47th and 48th states. They will be the last to join the Union until 1959.

- Albert Berry becomes the first skydiver, jumping from a moving airplane with a parachute.

- Juliette Gordon Low founds the Girl Scouts in the United States.

- Isabella Goodwin of New York City becomes the first female detective in the United States, becoming a role model for women sleuths in numerous movies and TV shows to come.

- U.S athlete Jim Thorpe wins gold medals in the pentathlon and decathlon events at the Stockholm Olympics. Following a NYC ticker-tape parade in his honor, the medals are stripped away after it is discovered that he once received pay for playing baseball, making him a professional athlete.

- Thank Helen Taft (wife of President William Howard Taft) for the beautiful cherry blossom season in the nation's capital. In March of this year, she plants the first cherry tree in Washington, D.C.

- The Republic of China is created.

- The volcano Novarupta erupts in Alaska. It is considered the largest eruption in the 20th century.

- Congress establishes the eight-hour workday, but most Americans are hard workers, putting in 10–12 hour days.

- On April 10, the British ship RMS *Titanic* sets sail on its maiden voyage to America. Shortly before midnight on the 14th, the ocean liner hits an iceberg in the North Atlantic and begins to sink. Only 711 people are rescued, and more than 1,500 passengers lose their lives.

- Lawrence Luellen of Boston creates a disposable paper cup called the Health Kup. Today it is better known as the Dixie Cup.

All About Andy

❖ ❖ ❖ ❖

The tomato soup cans. The portrait of Marilyn Monroe. That banana. There are some images in popular culture that are so ubiquitous, it's almost easy to forget who created them in the first place. Who's the man who put pop art on the map?

Andy Warhol is the guy behind some of the most recognizable art of the latter half of the 20th century. In fact, his pop art helped shape pop(ular) culture in general. Read on to discover more about the life and times (and art) of Andy Warhol.

Mama Warhola
Warhol (born Andrew Warhola in 1928) had a close relationship with his mother, who immigrated to the United States from Slovakia. She lived with him in New York City from 1952 to 1971. She sometimes created art with her son, credited as simply "Andy Warhol's Mother."

Warhol's Big Break
After attending college at Carnegie Mellon University in Pennsylvania, Warhol got work as an illustrator in New York City at magazines such as *Glamour*. Throughout the 1950s, he made a name for himself as one of the most sought-after illustrators in the industry. Warhol's extensive client list included *The New York Times, Harper's Bazaar*, Tiffany & Co., Fleming-Joffe leather company, Bonwit Teller department store, Columbia Records, *Vogue*, and NBC.

Those Soup Cans
Beginning in the 1960s, Warhol dedicated more time to art. He painted a series of pictures based on comics and advertisements, including the now-iconic Campbell's Tomato Soup can in 1962. The paintings were an instant megahit, and Warhol's career as a pop art icon was launched.

Short Films, Long Films

Warhol wasn't just a painter—he was a publisher, writer, music producer, and film director, as well. As an auteur, Warhol created more than 600 films, many of them just under five minutes. His longest work was a 25-hour-long piece called *Four Stars*, made in 1967–68.

The Fabulous Factory

By 1964, Warhol had his "Factory" in the city, a warehouse space entirely decked out in silver. Parties for the glitterati were thrown at the Factory, where the art world at large, cross-dressers, and folks on the fringe of society were eager to attend. When it wasn't packed with guests, Warhol used it for studio space.

In 1966, Andy also opened the Gymnasium, a nightclub in New York that featured exercise equipment on the dance floor.

Avant-Garde

Warhol was the first artist to exhibit video footage as art, essentially creating the "multi-media" medium in 1965. Warhol also regularly taped conversations with others or dictated his ideas into a tape recorder. There are approximately 3,400 of these audiotapes.

Plastic and Velvet

For a time, Warhol tried his hand at performance art. He had a multi-media show called "The Exploding Plastic Inevitable." Featured on the bill was the prefame (but now iconic) rock band The Velvet Underground.

I Shot Andy Warhol

In June of 1968, Valerie Solanas, a writer who had appeared in one of Andy's films, shot Warhol in the chest while in his studio. After a five-hour operation, the artist recovered. A movie about the event, called *I Shot Andy Warhol,* was released in 1996.

Most Famous Quote

Even if people don't know his body of artwork that well, they've probably heard Warhol's most famous line: "In the future, everybody will be world famous for fifteen minutes." It's now common to hear the phrase, "15 minutes of fame."

Plastic Panache

In the late 1940s, George Lerner was a well-known inventor with visions of fruits and vegetables. His idea? To create plastic mouths, eyes, and noses that could be pushed into pieces of produce to make funny faces.

Toy companies pooh-poohed the idea: In conservation-minded post-World War II America, the thought of turning food into a toy seemed wasteful. Eventually, a cereal company decided Lerner's pieces would make a good box prize and bought his idea for $5,000.

In 1951, Lerner met with Rhode Island toymakers and brothers Henry and Merrill Hassenfeld, who ran a small family-owned company eventually known as Hasbro. They loved his idea, and a deal was struck so that the Hassenfelds held the rights to the toys.

On April 30, 1952, the Mr. Potato Head Funny Face kit debuted. It sold for just under $1 and, as the first toy advertised on TV, it became an instant success, with sales hitting more than $4 million the first year.

Steel Boom

If playing with plastic produce is fun, why not a steel coil? In 1943, Philadelphia-based naval engineer Richard James accidentally knocked a torsion spring off his desk and watched it bounce around his office. Seeing potential for a toy, he set to work developing a steel formula that would allow the spring to walk down stairs. Richard's wife, Betty, searched the dictionary for a word to aptly describe the spring's movement. She ultimately landed on *slinky,* the Swedish word for "stealthy, sleek, and sinuous."

With a $500 loan, the Jameses produced a small number of Slinkys, which didn't sell until Gimbels department store agreed to let Richard do a demo shortly before Christmas 1945. It was a hit: All 400 Slinkys sold out in 90 minutes. To keep up with the growing demand, Richard devised a machine that could produce a Slinky every ten seconds.

In 1960, Richard left the company to follow a religious cult to Bolivia, leaving Betty with six children to raise and a business to run. Undaunted, Betty continued growing the company to the multimillion-dollar industry it is today. She eventually moved production to her hometown of Hollidaysburg, where the Slinky—now the state toy of Pennsylvania—is still produced.

The Bellyache Heard Around the World

❖ ❖ ❖ ❖

*Let's face it, it wasn't exactly the "Shot Heard 'Round the World."
But because it was Babe Ruth, the "Bellyache Heard Around
the World" carried some importance. But what happened?*

Sultan of Swat

Babe Ruth was, and remains, one of the most famous baseball players in history. It was Ruth's prodigious slugging in the early 1920s that saved baseball from the Black Sox Scandal. It was also his presence on the New York Yankees—a formerly mediocre team—that turned them into a collection of world-beaters.

In his first few seasons with the Yankees, Ruth set home run records and drove the team into the World Series three years in a row (1921–1923). The Yankees won the series in 1923, and even though they missed out in 1924, there was every expectation that they'd be back in 1925—after all, they had Babe Ruth. But no one counted on the Bellyache Heard Around the World.

Hot Dogs and Fables

Although he was reportedly fighting the good exercise fight on his farm in Sudbury, Massachusetts, Ruth, who never met a meal he didn't eat, had ballooned to 245 pounds over the winter. Prior to spring training in early February 1925, Ruth went to Hot Springs, Arkansas, to get in shape for the coming season. Besides its therapeutic mineral baths, Hot Springs was also known as a pre-Vegas Vegas. Before long, Ruth was fully caught up in two of his favorite pastimes: sex and food. To combat his stomach's protests over the large amount of chow he was shoveling in, Ruth gulped bicarbonate soda to settle his belly. However, there was no such remedy for whatever sexual diseases were floating around. As contemporary sportswriter Fred Lieb noted: "One woman couldn't satisfy him. Frequently it took half a dozen."

Needless to say, Ruth was badly out of shape when spring training started in St. Petersburg, Florida. By late March he was struggling with "lame legs." But that hardly stopped the Ruthian caravan of food and sex. As teammate Joe Dugan later commented, "He was going day and night, broads and booze."

As the Yankees made their way north from spring training to start the season, Ruth got progressively worse. Finally, on April 7, Ruth collapsed at the train station in Asheville, North Carolina. Rumors spread like wildfire that the Sultan of Swat was dead; a London newspaper vividly reported the death scene. Ruth revived, only to collapse again in the train bathroom, smashing his head against the sink. When the train reached New York, the unconscious Ruth (estimated at 250–270 pounds) was hoisted out through the train window. At the hospital, Ruth was delirious and convulsing. On April 17, he had a very hush-hush operation.

So What the Heck Happened?

For decades, the story given to explain Ruth's illness was one invented by sportswriter W. O. McGeehan, which combined rambunctiousness with aw-shucks innocence: Ruth had simply eaten too many hot dogs, peanuts, and soda. That's just so All-American it has to be true, right?

There are other stories. Long after Ruth's death, his wife Claire wrote that he had suffered a groin injury. Perhaps, but groin injuries normally don't cause their subjects to become delirious. Another possibility is gonorrhea—a rumor believed by several teammates and even Yankee General Manager Ed Barrow. Yet while Ruth's liaisons with anything wearing a skirt could certainly have given him a STD, surgery would have been an unusual treatment.

This leaves the possibility that Ruth had what one of his physicians called an "intestinal abscess." Ruth biographer Marshall Smelser speculated that Ruth likely had an obstruction of the intestine, requiring a temporary colostomy. In those days, such a personal and private procedure would not have received mention in the press.

Most likely, we'll never know the full truth. That year was Ruth's worst season in baseball, but soon he was back to boozing and whoring. As his roommate "Ping" Bodie allegedly said when asked what it was like to room with Ruth, "I ain't rooming with Ruth. I room with his suitcase."

Fast Facts

- The '80s rock band Duran Duran based its name on the character Durand Durand from the 1968 sci-fi flick Barbarella, starring Jane Fonda.

- Think of the frequent flyer miles! Robert Ripley, creator of Ripley's Believe It Or Not, traveled to 197 countries in his search for interesting oddities.

- The first commercially successful animated cartoon was Gertie the Dinosaur (1914), created by cartoonist Winsor McKay. It took 10,000 drawings to create—each hand-drawn by McKay and an assistant.

- Eww! When Marvel Comics published a comic book featuring the popular rock band KISS in 1977, a sample of blood from each band member was mixed into the ink at the printing plant.

- Thomas Edison nicknamed his first two children, a girl and a boy, Dot and Dash.

- Trepanning—cutting a hole in the skull—was one of the first medical treatments used by prehistoric man.

- One of the first pregnancy tests was developed in ancient Egypt. It required a woman to urinate on a mixture of barley and emmer wheat; if either grew, she was probably pregnant.

- That's a lotta ladies! The largest all-female movie cast was MGM's The Women (1939), starring Joan Crawford and Norma Shearer. It featured 135 speaking roles.

- The Earth is struck by more than 100 lightning bolts every second.

- Cranberries are as bouncy as a basketball when they're ripe.

- Papa John's began in a broom closet. Founder John Schnatter started making pizzas in a closet at the back of his father's tavern in 1983. He came in and out of the bar's back door while ferrying his pizza deliveries.

The Land of Misfit Cereals

❖ ❖ ❖ ❖

Beginning in the 1970s, nothing said "Saturday morning" like a TV blaring cartoons and a big, brimming bowl of sugary cereal. Well, that and fighting your siblings for the prize hidden at the bottom of the box. During the '80s, cereal makers started cross-promoting their products. Suddenly, bizarre cereals hawked by unlikely stars (and creatures) started popping up on grocery store shelves. Grab a spoon and dig into these misfit cereals.

Nerds

In 1983, Nerds candy was released. Fueled by the overwhelming response to the sugary nuggets, Ralston released Nerds Cereal in 1985. Like the candy, Nerds Cereal had two flavors, each in its own separate package, allowing the eater to decide which to enjoy first. The gimmick didn't translate to cereal, though, and while Nerds Candy continued to be successful, the cereal didn't fare as well and production stopped altogether.

Urkel-Os

Today, you'd be hard-pressed to get folks to admit they were fans of Steve Urkel, the ultra-nerd on *Family Matters*. But that didn't stop a cereal company from releasing Urkel-Os in 1991. While other novelty cereals used special shapes or colors to tie in the character on the box, Urkel-Os didn't even bother. Instead it simply featured banana and strawberry-flavored "O" shapes.

Bill & Ted's Excellent Cereal

It was a hit movie and a somewhat successful cartoon, so in 1990, it seemed only natural that Bill & Ted's Excellent Cereal would work, right? Dude, totally wrong! Despite cinnamon oat squares, marshmallow musical notes, and the promise of "A most excellent breakfast adventure," the cereal was an enormous flop. Some blamed it on poor marketing while others pointed out that the cereal resembled a certain popular dry dog food. Whatever the reason, the cereal was deemed "bogus" and vanished from shelves in 1991.

Ghostbusters

Who ya gonna crunch? Originally unleashed in the mid-'80s as a tie-in to the *Ghostbusters* movie, the cereal, which featured marshmallow ghosts and fruit-flavored "no" symbols, managed to hang around for a few years. The draw seemed to be in part because the cereal company, Ralston-Purina, continually updated the box's design. When it appeared as though kids were finally tired of the cereal, Ralston-Purina tried a last-ditch selling point, marketing it as "the first cereal box that glows in the dark."

WWF Superstars

Pro wrestling is known for big, sweaty guys. Now, why anyone would think that turning said feature into a cereal was a good idea is beyond us. No wonder this 1991 cereal was gone in less than a year! Conspiracy theorists also claim that the WWF Superstars cereal was nothing more than repackaged leftover GI Joe Action Stars cereal.

Monopoly

Finally, game pieces that kids *can* put in their mouths! In 2003, General Mills teamed up with Hasbro to create Monopoly cereal, complete with marshmallows color-coded to match the corresponding property cards from the board game. Lest there be any confusion, every cereal box was clearly marked "Monopoly: Cereal Edition."

Green Slime

In 2003, General Mills unleashed their Green Slime cereal on unsuspecting breakfast aisles. The cereal featured green "slime-shaped corn puffs," which actually resembled green Xs, as well as strange orange marshmallow things that were supposed to resemble the Nickelodeon blimp logo. One can only imagine what color the milk was afterward.

Nintendo Cereal System

When the original Nintendo game system took off in 1985, Nintendo brass got together and came up with a plan to further expand their growing empire. More games? Better controllers? Nope. Their hot new item was none other than the Nintendo Cereal System. The packaging for the cereal was unique: while most cereals came in brightly colored boxes, the Nintendo Cereal System box was primarily black. Also, the box was divided in half, one side filled with Super Mario Brothers cereal and the other with Zelda Adventure Series cereal. But the only difference between the two was the kind of marshmallows each featured—Mario had objects like mushrooms and Zelda had weapons like boomerangs.

While the cereal was around only around for less than a year, it has taken on a life of its own with nostalgia buffs. Unopened boxes of the cereal have been selling for more than $100 on eBay.

C-3PO's

George Lucas was a marketing genius when he kept the "garbage rights" to his little film *Star Wars* and immediately started slapping the film's name and characters on everything from action figures to bed sheets. Still, more than a few people thought Lucas had gone to the Dark Side when he teamed up with Kellogg's in the mid-'80s and released C-3PO's, "A new force at breakfast." This cereal's demise might have been due in part to no one understanding what the cereal was supposed to be shaped like, even though commercials plainly stated it was "twin rings fused together, for two crunches in every double O." Uh, tasty!

Mr. T Cereal

No, the A-Team didn't endorse it. And it wasn't anything more than corn-flavored "T" shapes, albeit with "a touch of brown sugar." Still, the commercials let us know that by eating Mr. T cereal, we were becoming part of a team "that knows how cool breakfast can be." But here's a little bit of trivia: In 1985's *Pee-Wee's Big Adventure*, Mr. T cereal was the breakfast of choice for Pee Wee Herman.

FROM THE VAULTS OF HISTORY

- In 1920, Russian transplant pioneer Serge Voronoff "successfully" transplanted monkey testicles to a human. Uh, congratulations?

- Future U.S. president Andrew Jackson was born in a log cabin in North Carolina to nearly illiterate parents. He did not learn the basics of reading, grammar, or math until age 17.

- If you have a good idea, but people aren't quite ready for it, try to stay positive: When Alexander Graham Bell patented the telephone in 1876, he sold only six phones in the first month.

- John D. Rockefeller gave away more than $500 million during his lifetime.

- Lewis Carroll, author of *Alice in Wonderland,* took a lot of laudanum, otherwise known as opium. He suffered from migraines and had a stutter; apparently, the drug eased these woes.

- By the time Queen Elizabeth I of England died in 1603 at age 69, she owned an estimated 80–100 pearl-studded wigs.

- Uri Geller, who enjoyed major fame during the 1970s, said his psychic powers came from the distant planet of Hoova.

- Russia's Catherine I made a rule that no man could get drunk at her parties until after 9 P.M.

- Charles Dickens wrote his famous novels facing north. He also slept facing north, claiming that it improved his writing ability.

- Napoleon Bonaparte designed the French flag.

- Richard the Lion-Hearted, king of England from 1189–1199, spent more than 95 percent of his reign away from his kingdom. A combination of war and politics kept him from spending more than six months in his country.

- British merchant Peter Durand invented the tin can for preserving food. The patent, No. 3372, was granted on August 25, 1810, by King George III.

Curious Cowboys

❖ ❖ ❖ ❖

These intriguing people gave folks something to talk about.

Bass Reeves

Bass Reeves has the honor of being one of the most successful U.S. marshals in the West's history, as well as the first black one. He was born a slave in Crawford County, Texas, in 1846. After the Civil War broke out, Reeves escaped and found refuge in Indian Territory (modern-day Oklahoma) among the Creek and Seminole tribes. After the war, Reeves eventually settled in law enforcement. He arrested more than 3,000 men and women during his 32-year career. When he retired in 1907 at age 61, he found he had too much time on his hands, so he joined the Muskogee Police in Oklahoma. Reeves finally hung up his saddle when he died on January 12, 1910.

Spade Cooley

Billed as the "King of Western Swing," Spade Cooley was a protégée of the King of the Cowboys, Roy Rogers. He even had his own immensely popular cowboy music television show, *The Hoffman Hayride,* which ran for a decade. However in 1961,when his wife informed the musician that that she wanted a divorce, Cooley beat her to death in front of their 14-year-old daughter. After serving eight years in prison, he agreed to play a special sheriff's benefit. On November 23, 1969, after performing in front of 3,000 people, Cooley thanked his fans, walked backstage, and died of a heart attack.

Charley Parkhurst

Parkhurst was described as one of the toughest stagecoach drivers in the West, even after losing an eye after getting kicked by a horse. Once, during a torrential rainstorm, Parkhurst safely delivered his coach and passengers as the bridge they were crossing collapsed underneath them. He died in 1879 of cancer, but his greatest feat was yet to be discovered: Parkhurst was really a woman. In fact, the doctor who performed her post mortem discovered that Charlotte Parkhurst had also conceived a child. This made Parkhurst technically the first woman to vote in the United States, albeit under the guise of a man.

Say What?

"When I was young, I used to think that money was the most important thing in life. Now that I am old, I know it is."
—*Oscar Wilde*

"I feel sorry for people who don't drink. They wake up in the morning and that's the best they are going to feel all day."
—*Frank Sinatra*

"My problems all started with my early education. I went to a school for mentally disturbed teachers."
—*Woody Allen*

"Never attribute to malice that which can be adequately explained by straightforward stupidity."
—*J. C. Collins*

"An intellectual is someone who has found something more interesting than sex."
—*Edgar Wallace*

"I used to keep my college roommate from reading my personal mail by hiding it in her textbooks."
—*Joan Welsh*

"I am not a vegetarian because I love animals; I'm a vegetarian because I hate plants."
—*A. Whitney Brown*

"Curiosity killed the cat, but for a while I was a suspect."
—*Steven Wright*

"If you steal from one author, it's plagiarism; if you steal from many, it's research."
—*Wilson Mizner*

"A Boy Scout troop is a lot of boys dressed as jerks, led by a jerk dressed as a boy."
—*Shelley Berman*

"Democracy means that anyone can grow up to be president, and anyone who doesn't grow up can be vice president."
—*Johnny Carson*

Abbreviation Originations

❖ ❖ ❖ ❖

Abbreviations save time—and we're not talking about the LOLs and OMGs found on the Web. Here's a look at how some of our language's most common (and legitimate) abbreviations came to be.

Prescription: Rx

We may understand that "Rx" stands for "prescription," but what do the letters stand for? The abbreviation comes from the Latin term *recipe,* which means to "take" or "receive." The "x," most accounts indicate, was initially written as a slash on the "R" itself. Of course, some people also swear that the symbol is a derivation of Jupiter's astrological sign, so take your pick.

Pound: lb.

This two-letter statement of weight may look strange to native English speakers, and it's no wonder: This abbreviation is also derived from Latin. The abbreviation "lb." is actually short for *libra pondo,* a Latin phrase meaning, "a pound by weight." Over time, the phrase was shortened from "libra pondo" to "pound." Despite the change, the original two-letter abbreviation stuck.

Missus: Mrs.

Wondering why the abbreviation for "missus" has that mysterious "r" in the middle? It's because it used to stand for something else. "Mrs." was developed as a bunched-up version of "mistress," which, back in the old days, didn't used to have the saucy connotation it does now. (It simply meant "wife.") Once again, this is a case of the language evolving, but the abbreviation staying the same.

Baseball Strikeout: K

A little sports history can teach you a lot about "K," the common abbreviation for "strikeout" in the game of baseball. Back in the late 1800s, a strikeout was referred to as having "struck." Since the letter "S" was already taken in the box score as shorthand for "sacrifice," the next logical choice for "struck" was its last letter.

Fast Facts

- The popularity of scrapbooking has resurged in recent years, and hobbyists should be aware they are joining an illustrious line of like-minded people. One fan was Samuel Clemens, aka Mark Twain, who invented a self-adhesive scrapbook that sold 25,000 copies. "Well enough," he commented on its sales, "for a book that did not contain a single word."

- The world's most expensive chocolates, priced by Harrod's at $10,000 a box, are individually handmade with organic cocoa and decorated with either gold, Swarovski crystal, or handmade silk roses. The 49 chocolates within the box are separated by gold and platinum dividers.

- Finland calculates traffic fines based on a percentage of the person's recently reported income. In 2002, a director of the Finnish company Nokia received a speeding ticket for $12.5 million.

- A squirrel's brain is about the size of a walnut.

- Helen Hayes made her first movie, Jean and the Calico Doll, in 1910. She made her last movie, the 1988 religious documentary titled Divine Mercy, No Escape, at age 88.

- King Alfonso XIII of Spain was tone-deaf. He always kept near him a person whose sole job it was to tell the king when the Spanish national anthem was played so he knew when to stand.

- King George I of England was a German national and could neither speak nor write English.

- The first U.S. coins were made using Martha Washington's silver service.

- A snake may have more than 300 pair of ribs.

- Speaking ill of the dead can get a person into legal hot water in many states, including Georgia, Colorado, and Idaho. Nor will most states put up with people spreading rumors about banks and other financial institutions.

The Astonishing Elephant

❖ ❖ ❖ ❖

Compassionate, astonishingly strong, intelligent, and resourceful, the elephant is one of Mother Nature's coolest characters. Check out these 22 pachyderm pointers!

1. For the past 32 years and counting, the Asian elephant has been on the endangered species list.

2. A female elephant is pregnant for 22 months—almost two years. Yikes.

3. Depending on the weather, an Asian elephant can guzzle 30 to 50 gallons of water every day.

4. The largest known specimen of the African savanna elephant is on display at the Smithsonian's National Museum of Natural History in Washington, D.C. It stood 13 feet tall and weighed 22,000 pounds when it was alive.

5. An elephant's trunk comprises 150,000 different muscle fibers.

6. Having a "fat day"? Forget it. The average male Asian elephant weighs between 10,000 and 12,000 pounds.

7. African savanna elephants are currently most common in Kenya, Tanzania, Botswana, Zimbabwe, Namibia, and South Africa.

8. The closest relatives to the elephant are the hyraxes (small chunky mammals that resemble fat gophers), dugongs and manatees, and aardvarks.

9. Although Asian and African elephants look alike, several physical characteristics distinguish them from one another. Asian elephants are generally smaller, with shorter tusks. They also have two domed bulges on their foreheads, rounded backs, less wrinkly skin, and their trunks have a finger-like projection at the tip.

10. Elephants supplement the sodium in their food by visiting nearby mineral licks.

11. African elephants speak their own special language. Communication takes place using rumbles, moans, and growls. These low-frequency sounds can travel a mile or more.

12. Ever wonder why an elephant has a trunk in the first place? It's because an elephant's neck is so short that it wouldn't be able to reach the ground. The trunk allows the elephant to eat from the ground as well as the treetops.

13. An elephant's trunk weighs about 400 pounds.

14. Just as humans are either right- or left-handed, elephants are either right- or left-tusked.

15. Between 1979 and 1989, Africa's elephant population plummeted from 1.3 million to 750,000, as a result of ivory poaching.

16. Elephants greatly enjoy taking baths, but in the meantime the red-billed oxpecker (a relative to the starling) picks ticks and other parasites off the elephant's skin.

17. Those big, floppy ears aren't just for decoration—they help the huge animals cool off. It's not always enough, though. Since elephants don't have a layer of fat under their skin to act as insulation, they must often retreat to the shade or find water during the summer's hottest days.

18. A group of elephants is called a herd. When two herds join forces (which happens during migration) it's called a clan.

19. The first time elephants were seen in Europe was in 280 B.C., when an army of 25,000 men and 20 elephants crossed from North Africa to Italy.

20. Adult elephants can't jump.

21. Under the right conditions, an elephant can smell water from approximately three miles away.

22. Elephants are noted for their social behavior. They sometimes "hug" by wrapping their trunks together as a way of greeting one another. Baby elephants may suck their trunk for comfort—sort of the equivalent of a human sucking his or her thumb.

If You See Only Five...

Buddy Flicks

❖ ❖ ❖ ❖

If you and your friend have ever had an adventure (and heck, even a trip to the mall can be an adventure), then you understand the appeal of buddy flicks. Here are five of the best.

1. *Butch Cassidy and the Sundance Kid* (1969)—Based on the true story of turn-of-the-century bank robbers Robert Leroy Parker and Harry Longabaugh, this film was the first to pair handsomer-than-thou actors Paul Newman and Robert Redford. It's a wonderful, often funny story of friendship in the face of adversity, and it was nominated for seven Academy Awards.

2. *The Blues Brothers* (1980)—*Saturday Night Live* alums John Belushi and Dan Aykroyd are Jake and Elwood Blues, two musicians who scheme to save the endangered Catholic home where they were raised. Directed by John Landis, it's a madcap adventure that boasts one of the wildest multi-car wrecks ever filmed.

3. *Stand By Me* (1986)—Based on a novella by Stephen King, *Stand By Me* revolves around four preteen friends in 1959, who set out to find the body of a missing boy. Occasionally humorous and often moving, it perfectly captures the importance of adolescent friendship and what it means to us in adulthood.

4. *Lethal Weapon* (1987)—In one of Hollywood's best "cop buddy" flicks, Mel Gibson and Danny Glover are perfect as a pair of mismatched L.A. detectives who stumble on a heroin-smuggling operation being conducted by ex-Vietnam Special Operations commandoes. Bullets fly and plenty of stuff blows up, but it's the developing relationship between the two cops that makes the movie work.

5. *Thelma and Louise* (1991)—Now, buddy movies aren't just for guys, as this Ridley Scott–directed movie demonstrates. The titular heroines go on the run after Louise (Susan Sarandon) kills a man while defending her best friend, Thelma (Geena Davis). It's a poignant drama with strong feminist themes, and a must-see for all buddy-flick aficionados.

Drink Up!

❖ ❖ ❖ ❖

*Impress your friends with some knowledge-quenching trivia
the next time you grab one of these favorite beverages.*

7UP

Thirsty? Here, have a Bib-Label Lithiated Lemon-Lime Soda. Not
quite as catchy, eh? Believe it or not, though, that's what 7UP was
originally called. Charles Leiper Grigg came up with the not-so-
memorable moniker when he first branded the drink back in 1929.
Luckily, he realized the drink would likely fizzle under the 12-syllable
name. He changed it to 7UP Lithiated Lemon Soda, and then eventually to plain ol' 7UP.

The reason for the "seven" is a bit of a mystery. Some theories
say there were initially only seven ingredients in the drink, while
others say that the original bottle held seven ounces. One thing that's
considered fact, though: The 7UP formula did once contain lithium
citrate. The mood-altering drug was a common ingredient in lemon-
lime sodas at the time, though it's long since been removed.

Dr Pepper

It may be just what the doctor ordered, but an MD didn't invent Dr
Pepper; rather, it was the brainchild of a pharmacist named Charles
Alderton. He came up with the concoction while working at a corner drugstore in Waco, Texas, in the late 1800s. Legend has it his
customers took to calling the drink "the Waco."
So where's the good doc come in? Alderton's
boss decided to dub the fizzy drink after a friend
named Dr. Charles Pepper.

Coca-Cola

Coke's inventor, however, *was* a doctor. Dr. John
Pemberton, a pharmacist from Atlanta, is credited with coming up with the original Coca-Cola
formula. He created the first Coke inside a kettle
he kept in his backyard. And yes, the rumors are
true: The drink did contain cocaine until 1905.

The Coca-Cola name itself doesn't have much of a backstory: Pemberton's bookkeeper simply thought it'd work well in a logo, supposedly saying: "The two Cs would look well in advertising." The man wrote out "Coca-Cola" in his now-famous cursive handwriting, and the rest is history.

Pepsi Cola

Pepsi Cola's first sip also came courtesy of a pharmacist—Caleb Bradham of New Bern, North Carolina. Bradham brewed up the beverage at his drugstore's soda fountain, mixing carbonated water with sugar, vanilla, oil, and reportedly an enzyme called pepsin and some cola nuts. The last two ingredients, as you may have guessed, supposedly gave Pepsi Cola its name.

Mountain Dew

The man behind Mountain Dew was a fruit-flavoring salesman named William "Bill" H. Jones, who bought his way into a drink company called Tip in the 1920s. Folklore has it that one of the company's investors handed him the rights to an inactive trademark for the name Mountain Dew—the drink had been made as a lemon-lime mixer for some time, but it never caught on. Jones decided to develop the product, however, and the Dew was reborn. Later, Jones, on the verge of bankruptcy, added orange flavoring to his soda, as well as more caffeine and sugar, and less carbonation.

A&W Root Beer

Ever wonder who the "A" and "W" in A&W were? Here's your answer: Roy Allen and Frank Wright. The business partners bought a root beer formula from (no surprise) a pharmacist in June 1919. They named the drink A&W in 1922.

Kool-Aid

Kool-Aid came out of some guy's kitchen. No really: A young man named Edwin Perkins experimented with mixes in his mother's home until he stumbled upon a combination that would become the fruity drink. Perkins first sold the drink under the name "Fruit Smack." After figuring out how to break the beverage down into powder form, he changed the name to Kool-Aid.

WORD HISTORIES

Turnpike: This word may bring to mind busy interstate highways filled with cars and tollbooths. But the term is way older than the automobile: In the 16th century, a turnpike was a large turnstile that blocked a road to traffic. Travelers couldn't pass until they paid a toll. Now that sounds familiar.

Vermicelli: Derives from the Latin *vermis,* or "worm." Literally translated from Italian, it means, "little worms."

Hogwash: This term has been around since the 15th century. Originally spelled "hoggyswasch," it first referred to pig swill. Eventually the word morphed into "hogwash," and its meaning changed, too. It began being used to describe any useless stuff around 1900.

Jumbo: In 1882, famed circus maven P. T. Barnum bought an elephant that he dubbed Jumbo. In the course of advertising, "jumbo" became the word to describe anything that, like the famous elephant, was huge.

Chop suey: This Chinese dish derives from two places: "Chop" is English for cut and "suey" comes from the Chinese *sui,* meaning bits. The meal is composed of chopped bits of meat and vegetables. Yum!

Auspicious: This word describes something marked by success or favorable circumstances. Appropriately, it comes from the Latin word *auspicium,* meaning someone who foretells the future by watching the flight of birds.

Madcap: Back in the 1500s, the word "cap" was often used to refer to a person's head, and "mad," of course, meant crazy. So madcap, then and as it is now, means someone (or something) who is a little bit silly or reckless.

Bandy: A game very similar to tennis resulted in this term for batting words back and forth.

Dandelion: The name of this weed comes from the French *dent de lion,* meaning "lion's tooth." The English spelled it with a d, making it *dend de lion* and eventually shortening it to dandelion. Surprisingly, however, the name doesn't apply to the well-known yellow flower of the plant, but to the saw-toothed leaf attached to the plant.

One Sheluva Guy

❖ ❖ ❖ ❖

Shel Silverstein may be most famous for his off-kilter children's poems, but his literary career ran the gamut from Playboy *cartoons and country hits to off-Broadway plays and even murder mysteries.*

Sketchy Existence

Truth is, Shel Silverstein disliked children's books, and he certainly never intended to write them. He was a satirist and a cartoonist, and that's how he hoped to make a living.

A native Chicagoan born at the start of the Great Depression, Silverstein got his first break while serving as a soldier in the Korean War, drawing cartoons that spoofed military life. Postwar success proved elusive, and Silverstein, a lifelong White Sox fan, split his time selling hot dogs at the stadium and pounding the pavement to peddle his cartoons. Fortunately, an upstart magazine called *Playboy* took a shine to Silverstein's work in 1956 and hired him as a freelancer— a role he played well into the late 1970s.

Chicks to Children

Books of his *Playboy* cartoons had already sold big time when Silverstein decided to write *Uncle Shelby's ABZ Book: A Primer for Adults Only*, published in 1961 by Simon & Schuster. The book was a send-up of contemporary children's books, which he felt played down to kids with fluffy "morals to the story."

Sarcastic as it was, his friend, children's author/illustrator Tomi Ungerer, convinced him to write an honest-to-goodness children's book. Reluctantly, Silverstein agreed, but he did it in his own way—without the predictable happy ending. *Lafcadio: The Lion Who Shot Back* was published in 1963 to rave reviews. *The Giving Tree* followed (1964), as well as *Where the Sidewalk Ends* (1974), *A Light in the Attic* (1981), and *Falling Up* (1996).

Far from being the stereotypical children's author, Silverstein was a true bohemian, not content to stay with one art form, one woman (he allegedly bedded thousands but pooh-poohed marriage), or one city (he shuttled between Sausalito, Chicago, New York, Martha's Vineyard, and Key West).

Renaissance Man

While writing stories and cartoons, Silverstein also hit the music scene. Though he could only play a few chords—and reportedly had an obnoxiously screechy voice—he proved a talented songwriter across multiple genres. Popular hits include Johnny Cash's "A Boy Named Sue" and "Cover of the *Rolling Stone*" for Dr. Hook and the Medicine Show. He also wrote scores for several films, including *Postcards from the Edge,* for which he won an Academy Award nomination in 1991.

Theatre also appealed to Silverstein. He staged his first off-Broadway play, *The Lady or the Tiger Show,* in 1981 and went on to write several more, even collaborating with playwright David Mamet to write the screenplay for the 1988 film *Things Change.*

In 1996, Silverstein took up murder-mystery writing and contributed to three different anthologies, the last of which, *Murder and Obsession,* debuted in March 1999. Two months later, Silverstein died of a heart attack in his Key West home. At age 68, he had still been working on a multitude of projects, leaving behind a trove of unfinished works the world will never see.

Shel-Shocking Facts

- *He suffered from extreme seasickness but loved being near water and even lived on a houseboat in Sausalito.*

- *In Chicago, Silverstein lived at the Playboy Mansion. He preferred the Red Room.*

- *Silverstein was perennially dressed in tattered secondhand clothes. At the height of his success, a bookstore clerk in Key West declined his credit card and reported that a bum had tried to pass himself off as Shel Silverstein.*

INSPIRATION STATION

He's the Boss

While the eponymous character of the *Austin Powers* movie series is popular, perhaps even more beloved is his archenemy, the wicked yet strangely adorable Dr. Evil. Mike Myers, the actor and comedian who created and portrayed both characters, has said that he drew inspiration from a number of sources while fleshing out the pale, bald Dr. Evil. Of course, the most obvious are the various villains who populated the *James Bond* series back in the 1960s and '70s, but anyone who has ever closely observed *Saturday Night Live* producer Lorne Michaels has to wonder. Michaels was Myers's boss from 1989 to 1995, and Dr. Evil's gestures and manner of speaking are sometimes a dead-on impression of Michaels. Perhaps the most telling clue is that although Dr. Evil claims to be Belgian, he often slips into a Canadian accent; Michaels was born and raised in Toronto and has the very same accent. Still, Michaels was a good sport about the character and even joked about it with Myers in a skit on *SNL*.

A Revolutionary Recovery

Andy Warhol revolutionized the idea of what "art" was when in 1964 he produced a painting of a can of Campbell's tomato soup. This seminal work may seem familiar and almost all-American to us today, but at the time it ignited a controversy that spread far beyond the art world and into the general public.

When asked what inspired his pop art, Warhol often referred to his childhood battle with the neurological disease Sydenham's chorea, commonly known as St. Vitus's Dance. A condition that causes jerking movements of the face and limbs, it kept young Warhol out of school and at home for months on end. While recovering from his sickness, he spent long hours alone in bed, with only a radio and a pile of magazines to entertain him. The colorful advertisements, whimsical illustrations, and portraits of glamorous Hollywood stars never left him, and they reemerged decades later as he reinvented the occupation of artist.

"Begin the unnecessarily slow-moving dipping mechanism!"
—*Austin Powers: International Man of Mystery*, Dr. Evil (Mike Myers)

Broadmoor's Most Famous Residents

❖ ❖ ❖ ❖

In Britain, the criminally insane wind up in Broadmoor mental hospital. Here one has a wide variety of neighbors, from artists and lexicographers to "rippers" and cannibals.

Welcome to Broadmoor

Completed in 1863, this imposing collection of brick structures stands on the Berkshire moors about 30 miles from London. The Broadmoor "criminal lunatic asylum" was the first institution dedicated specifically to the detained treatment of those deemed too mentally ill to be guilty but too dangerous to be free. Conceived as a hospital (not a prison), Broadmoor opened with a farm, 57 staff cottages, and a school. Its first patients were women, many of whom most likely suffered from what would now be identified as postpartum depression. Within a year, however, a block for men opened.

Patients of Note

Long the repository of some of England's most notorious individuals, over time Broadmoor has been identified with the violence committed by outwardly normal men whose minds compel them to perform horrific acts. Here are some of the Broadmoor's more notable inmates.

Richard Dadd (painter): On August 28, 1843, a young aspiring painter named Richard Dadd became possessed with the notion that his father was the devil, and so Dadd killed him with a razor. Committed to the Bethlehem Hospital (aka "Bedlam") asylum, Dadd was allowed to continue his painting and spent nine of his years there completing his most well-known work, *The Fairy Feller's Master-Stroke,* which now hangs in the Tate Gallery. In 1864, he was among the first male patients transferred to Broadmoor; there he prepared the stage scenery for the hospital's theater and painted murals and portraits for then-Superintendent Dr. William Orange. Dadd died in Broadmoor in 1886 of "an extensive disease of the lungs."

Thomas Hayne Cutbush (Jack the Ripper?): In 1888, young Thomas Cutbush began to act increasingly mentally unstable. His days were spent sleeping, and at night he could be found prowling the streets. Then Cutbush took to drawing anatomical portrayals of dissected women. Curious habits, particularly in light of the Jack the Ripper killings occurring in London at the time. When Cutbush's name appeared on a list of possible suspects, his uncle, a superintendent at Scotland Yard, had the name removed. Detained as a wandering lunatic, Thomas escaped, purchased a knife, and tried to kill two women before being apprehended. Deemed unfit for trial, he was sent to Broadmoor, where he spent the rest of his life. But was Cutbush Jack the Ripper? Consider the following:

- The Jack the Ripper killings, which targeted prostitutes, lasted from April 3, 1888 to February 13, 1891. Cutbush reportedly contracted syphilis in 1888 (indicating his involvement with prostitutes, as well as a possible explanation for his madness) and was arrested on March 5, 1891.

- When Cutbush's name later appeared in the papers in connection with the attempted stabbings, his uncle was devastated and committed suicide two years later.

- Recently released Broadmoor documents include a description of Cutbush's piercing blue eyes and limp, both physical characteristics noted by Jack the Ripper witnesses.

William Chester Minor (lexicographer): This American immigrated to England after suffering paranoid delusions brought on by his experiences as a surgeon during the Civil War. Minor's paranoia increased while living in London, and in 1871, he killed a man he believed meant to do him harm. Highly intellectual and artistic, Minor was allowed two cells, one of which he converted into an extensive personal library. In 1879, Minor noticed an advertisement calling for word citations for the enormous *Oxford English Dictionary* project recently taken over by Dr. James Murray. For decades after, Minor's work on the *OED* occupied his days as the demons of his severe mental illness occupied his nights. Submitting thousands of citations for the *OED* became the defining factor in Minor's life. When Murray finally visited his most prolific contributor, the two became close friends. In 1910, Minor was sent to an institution in America; he died there ten years later.

Robert Maudsley ("Hannibal the Cannibal"): Born in 1953, young Maudsley was subject to frequent and violent physical abuse at the hands of his parents. Cast in the streets, he turned to prostitution to survive. After strangling a man who showed him pictures of abused boys in 1974, Robert was sent to Broadmoor, where in 1977 he and another psychopathic inmate barricaded themselves in a cell with a pedophile. After torturing the man for nine hours, they strangled him and then allowed the staff to enter. It was observed that part of the victim's skull had been cracked open and a spoon inserted into the brain material. Maudsley admitted to consuming the brain matter. He was sent to Wakefield Prison, known as "Monster Mansion," where in 1978 he killed two inmates. Afterward, Maudsley was imprisoned in a two-room specially made cell of hard plastic featuring cardboard furniture.

Graham Young ("The Teacup Murderer"): In 1961, Graham Young began a lifelong fascination with poisons, which the 14 year old tested in small doses on his family. A year later, his stepmother died from these "experiments." Young confessed his hobby to a psychiatrist, who had him arrested. He served nine years of a 15-year sentence at Broadmoor, where he researched poisons in the library and tested his concoctions on fellow inmates.

After his release in 1971, Young went to work for a photographic supply store in Bovingdon where he prepared tea for clerks and customers. Over the course of several months, Young administered nonfatal doses of poison to more than 70 people. He kept a detailed journal of the poisons and their effects; he also noted which coworkers he ultimately planned to kill. When two employees at the shop died similarly agonizing deaths, the police launched an investigation into the so-called "Bovingdon Bug." Young helpfully suggested to the police that they should consider thallium poisoning as a possible cause. Not being stupid, the police searched Young's apartment, found his notebook and a small pharmacy of poisons. Young received a life sentence; he died of a heart attack in Parkhurst prison at age 42.

Fast Facts

- Charles Carroll was the only Catholic to sign the Declaration of Independence.

- Early in his career, a poor Pablo Picasso burned some of his drawings to keep warm.

- The fairy tales of Hans Christian Andersen initially received negative reviews and were deemed "quite unsuitable for children."

- Winston Churchill's mother invented the Manhattan cocktail.

- Florence Nightingale carried a pet owl in her pocket.

- In 1844, New York City policemen went on strike over the issue of wearing blue uniforms. They considered uniforms a sign of servitude.

- George Lucas, the creator of Star Wars, originally envisioned Obi-Wan Kenobi as being Asian. The studio convinced him otherwise.

- Recently, stinging jellyfish have become the scourge of ocean beaches throughout the world. One of them, the lion's mane jellyfish, has a body (or bell, as it's called) that is 7½ feet in diameter and has tentacles measuring 120 feet long, making it the world's longest animal. Luckily for swimmers, it lives in the Arctic region.

- In 1919, citizens of Enterprise, Alabama, erected a monument to boll weevils because the insect had destroyed their cotton crops and forced local farmers to diversify their agriculture, thus saving the local economy.

- In the ancient Mediterranean world, olive oil—not soap—was used for bathing.

Weird Science!

❖ ❖ ❖ ❖

Don't trust motion pictures to get their science straight.

If Indy Was a Weightlifter

At the beginning of *Raiders of the Lost Ark* (1981), Indiana Jones snatches an ancient gold idol off its pedestal by substituting a small bag of sand that he believes to be of equal weight. Then, with the idol tucked safely in one arm, our intrepid archeologist hightails it out of the booby-trapped temple.

It's a thrilling scene, but it had real scientists tearing out their hair, because the science was all wrong. Gold is twice as heavy as lead, so assuming that the idol was made entirely of the precious metal, it would weigh at least 60 pounds—too much for a man to carry in one hand.

Raiders of the Lost Ark is just one example of bad movie science. In fact, many movies—particularly sci-fi films and thrillers with stories based in science—get more science wrong than right. According to physicists, one of the most common errors in sci-fi movies is a scene of a rocket whooshing through space, or something loudly blowing up in space. As anyone who has taken even a basic science class knows, sound needs air to travel, and space is a vacuum. No air, no sound. So much for a big bang.

Not Fast Enough

The Keanu Reeves-Sandra Bullock action thriller *Speed* (1994) drew a laugh from scientists by ignoring one of the most basic laws of physics: gravity. If you've seen the movie, you'll remember the scene in which the bus must leap a level gap in a freeway bridge. There's no ramp to propel the bus over the abyss—it just flies over the gap at a speed of 70 miles per hour. In real life, gravity would cause the bus to plummet to the ground, regardless of how fast it was going.

Not-So-Superman

Superman (1978), starring Christopher Reeve, was a fun flick full of flawed science (and we're not talking about how, exactly, Superman is able to fly). In one scene, Superman saves Lois Lane after she falls from a tall building by flying up and snatching her in midair. It looks cool, but in reality Lois would be hurt or even killed because she falls into Superman's arms with the same force as if she had hit the ground. (You can test this concept by tossing a water balloon with a friend at greater and greater distances. The farther the distance, the more difficult it is to catch the balloon without breaking it.)

In another scene, Superman is able to travel back in time by reversing the Earth's rotation. Even ignoring the fact that time has nothing to do with a planet's rotation, the scene fails because Superman flies in the opposite direction from where he needs to go to make such a thing happen.

More So-Called Science

The Core (2003) is so rife with scientific inaccuracies as to be laughable. The movie is about a group of scientists who must burrow to the center of the Earth in order to save the planet. About 700 miles down, the group stops to stretch their legs. Oddly, the gravity is normal there, which doesn't make sense because a large percentage of the Earth's mass (which is key to gravity) is now above them. In other words, gravity toward the center of the Earth would be much less than on its surface.

Sadly, the science in *Armageddon* (1998) is even worse. One of its most egregious errors is the falling rain on the asteroid that Bruce Willis and his team are sent to destroy. A celestial body must have an atmosphere to produce rain, and asteroids have none.

Physics-Friendly Movies

Not all movies are rife with bad science. In fact, some actually get it right. One of the best examples is Stanley Kubrick's opus *2001: A Space Odyssey* (1968), which demonstrates the use of centrifugal force to generate artificial gravity, and craft flying silently through airless space. Equally laudable is *Apollo 13* (1995), which strives to adhere as closely as possible to the true story upon which it was based.

Call of the Wild

❖ ❖ ❖ ❖

*In Japan's Aokigahara Forest, the desperate take
their lives in the dark shadow of Mt. Fuji.*

Japan's suicide rate is one of the highest in the world, and, within the
country, Aokigahara Forest (nicknamed the Sea of Trees) is home
to the most self-inflicted deaths. Every year, scores of people, many
distraught over a wrecked economy, travel to the forest and take
their own lives, often by hanging themselves or exposing themselves
to the elements in the dead of winter.

So what attracts people to this dense forest? It could be the fact
that the forest sits at the foot of Mount Fuji, a naturally compelling
and spiritual place untouched by urban development. Perhaps it's
the promise of thick trees to hide their body, deed, and pain from
family and friends. Or maybe people find comfort in the idea that
the forest is full of the spirit of those who've gone before, or lore
that features the forest as a safe haven for suicide. In the 1960s, a
book called *The Pagoda of Waves* described a woman who kills herself in the forest; later, Seicho Matsumoto wrote a book called *Kuroi
Jukai (Black Sea of Trees)* that perhaps further romanticized the
notion. The story features two lovers who escape the consequences
of their affair by committing a double suicide within the Sea of Trees.

In 1994, a Japanese book called *The Complete Manual of Suicide*
named the Sea of Trees as "the perfect place to die." Police and
volunteers go into the forest once or more a year to collect the dead
bodies, but because of its dense nature, many bodies are never
found or are found only after many years.

The communities that surround the forest do their best to
prevent unnecessary deaths. Cameras look for suspicious hikers
(such as men in suits), and police regularly patrol the area. Words
of encouragement, such as, "Your life is a precious gift from your
parents," are scattered throughout the forest. There are also
counselors who work in the forest, looking for lost souls, and credit
consolidation companies post their phone numbers on trees as a
lifeline for the financially fallen.

Fast Facts

- The English were so ticked off over losing the American Revolution that they created the British Imperial Gallon to differentiate their measure from that of their upstart cousins across the pond. That'll show 'em!

- A giraffe's tongue is black and can extend 18 inches for food gathering.

- Whether it be boxers or briefs, major league baseball umpires are required to wear black underwear while working.

- Yellow houses sell faster than other color houses.

- Honey is the only food that, when sealed, doesn't spoil.

- The world's smartest dog breed is the border collie. Runners up include the poodle, German shepherd, and golden retriever.

- The first known North American bombing of a civilian aircraft in flight occurred in 1949 in Canada when Albert Guay decided to murder his wife for her life insurance. He didn't get the insurance—he got hanged.

- On the Canadian version of The Howdy Doody Show, *Buffalo Bob was replaced with Timber Tom, played by a young William Shatner. Interestingly, the role of Timber Tom was first offered to James Doohan, who went on to become Scotty on* Star Trek.

- The Avon Company started in 1886 as the California Perfume Company, after bookseller David McConnell realized the rose oil perfumes he handed out as samples were his most popular selling point. In 1939, the company was renamed Avon for Stratford-upon-Avon, the hometown of McConnell's favorite playwright, William Shakespeare.

- Before Lauryn Hill went on to make a huge splash in the music world both with the Fugees and with her debut solo album, The Miseducation of Lauryn Hill, *she played a troubled teen on the soap opera* As the World Turns.

A Boatload of Collective Nouns

❖ ❖ ❖ ❖

*When referring to a group of something, we often use a collective
noun. Some collective nouns are common, such as "a school of
fish." But you've probably never heard of a "smack of jellyfish,"
now have you? Mind you, collective nouns aren't just for
animals—if you're lucky, you can own "a cache of jewels."*

It's a bird! It's a plane! It's a...

mob of wallabies
wealth of information
ascension (or exaltation) of larks
passel (or parcel) of hogs
ostentation of peacocks
stud of mares
movement of moles
army of caterpillars
kindle of kittens
bed of oysters
patter of footsteps
congregation (or float) of crocodiles
pod (or herd, school) of whales
crèche of penguins
murder of crows
army of frogs
spring of seals
chorus of angels
clutch of chicks
charm of goldfinches
bevy of swans
ambush (or streak) of tigers
bloat (or herd, crash) of hippopotami
brow of scholars
team (or stable) of horses
aerie (convocation) of eagles
swarm of eels

Mao's War on Sparrows

❖ ❖ ❖ ❖

During 1958 and 1959, the Chinese people murdered at least eight million sparrows at the behest of their leader. Why?

In 1958, Chairman Mao Zedong introduced his "Great Leap Forward" program, stating, "It is possible to accomplish any task whatsoever." That one of those tasks would be the systematic elimination of the Chinese sparrow population proved not only disastrous for the birds, but for the Chinese people as well.

Why Sparrows?

Mao's Great Leap Forward divided the country into well-organized communes joined in a concerted effort to boost agricultural and industrial output to match that of the West. As part of the program, the Great Leader determined that the "four pests"—mosquitoes, rats, flies, and sparrows—must be eliminated. The first three were known to be carriers of disease; sparrows, on the other hand, were singled out simply because Mao, who knew nothing of birds, believed that they ate too much grain, thus depriving his workers of food.

At first, the Great Leap Forward program seemed to work wonders. Agricultural and industrial output soared, and the citizenry realized an unprecedented level of cooperation. As part of the directive  to eliminate the four pests, citizens wrote songs, created banners, and enthusiastically shot, netted, and poisoned as many sparrows as they could find. Many villages took to the fields en masse at designated times to bang pots and pans, causing the birds to endlessly fly around so much that they would die of exhaustion.

Great Success ... Sort Of

By 1959, Chinese factories were producing substandard equipment and farms were seeing progressively lower yields in the rush to meet unrealistic quotas. The program to kill the nation's sparrows, however, was very successful. On December 13, 1958, in Shanghai alone, the populace used primitive weapons to annihilate almost 200,000 sparrows. Children weren't exempt from the organized massacre—Mao stated that "the whole people, include five-year-old children" were to be mobilized in the effort. A 16-year-old boy named Yang She-mun was considered a national hero for personally killing 20,000 sparrows. His strategy: identify the bird's nests during the day and then strangle the avian families at night with his bare hands.

"Forget It"

In 1959, members of the Academy of Sciences brought a likely unwelcome finding to Mao's attention: The digestive systems of dissected sparrows contained three-quarters harmful insects and one-quarter human food. Armed with this knowledge, and the growing evidence that the Great Leap Forward was a failure, Mao is reported to have said *suanle* ["forget it"]. Bedbugs replaced sparrows on the list of the four pests.

Featherweight Ironies:

Birds Eat Bugs—The sparrows were killed because, in Mao's estimation, the grain they ate would be better used feeding people. However, the decimation of the bird population led to an increase in the locust population. This led to widespread destruction of crops, particularly grains, which contributed to a famine that killed as many as 30 million people.

Bested by a Nest—As the founding leader of Communist China, Mao Zedong's image appears on the ten yuan note, one of the country's most popular pieces of currency. In 2008, however, when the Chinese Central Bank issued commemorative Olympic editions of the ten yuan note, Mao's image was replaced with that of Beijing's newly completed Olympic Stadium, ironically nicknamed "The Bird's Nest."

Welcome Home Chairman Mao—The Chairman's famous retreat for his family and esteemed members of the Politburo is located on a picturesque bank on East Lake of Wuchang. Today, it is a popular stop for tourists who come to marvel at the size of Mao's indoor swimming pool, to view his ruby red slippers, and to stroll along the paths that cut through groves of trees filled with songbirds—including sparrows.

FROM THE VAULTS OF HISTORY

A Colorful Character

The English love their eccentrics, so much so that they are sometimes even willing to spend their hard-earned tax money keeping
eccentricities alive—even long after the oddballs themselves are
dead. Lord Berners, an avant-garde writer, composer, painter,
and choreographer, resided at the stately Faringdon House in
Oxfordshire, where he insisted on keeping a flock of doves dyed in
various bright colors. The doves were not harmed by this procedure; the dyes were vegetable-based and safe enough to be used
on children.

Berners passed away in 1950, and Britain's National Trust now
runs Faringdon House. Doves are still dyed and released there
every Easter, in loving remembrance of one of England's great
eccentrics.

The Perfect Gentlemen

Even before he became our nation's first president, George
Washington was known throughout the Colonies for his impec-
cable manners. The roots of his proper behavior can be found in
three notebooks, labeled "Rules of Civility & Decent Behavior in
Company and Conversation," which were handwritten by Washington as a teenager. Today they offer a peek into how children of
his time were educated on personal behavior and hygiene.

While most of the rules of courtesy he put to paper were just
plain common sense, it is still interesting (and a little odd) to think
of the future president writing things like "When in Company,
put not your Hands to any Part of the Body, not usualy [sic]
Discovered," "Rince not your Mouth in the Presence of Others,"
and "Put not off your Cloths in the presence of Others, nor go out
your Chamber half Drest."

Washington has become such a mythical figure in our minds
that to imagine him streaking through Philadelphia seems all but
blasphemous, but back then he was just another colonial kid,
copying down the same stuff as everyone else in class.

Motherly Matters

❖ ❖ ❖ ❖

You may not be able to quantify a mother's love, but
you can certainly appraise plenty of other things about
her. Here's a closer look at America's moms.

- There are about 83 million mothers living in the United States.

- The average American mom has 2.1 children. (Poor child number 0.1—he or she must always feel inadequate.)

- Utah tends to have the most fruitful moms, with a recent statewide average of 2.6 kids per mama. Vermont, the District of Columbia, and Rhode Island tie for the lowest at 1.7 tykes per mother.

- The average mom has her first kid at age 25.

- The most popular month for becoming a mom is July.

- The most popular day for baby-birthin' is Tuesday.

- Being an "octomom" isn't as unusual as it seems (at least, not when it occurs over several years instead of a single day): In 2006, 18,674 women gave birth to their eighth child.

- The woman with the honor of bearing the most kids lived in Russia during the 1700s. Legend has it she had 69 children over the span of 40 years.

- In 1961, a Turkish mom gave birth to a baby weighing 24 pounds 4 ounces. Kind of hurts to even think about it.

- Mothers gain about 30 pounds during an average pregnancy. Makes you wonder how much the Turkish mom ballooned.

- Most moms pull off an impressive 7,300 diaper changes by their kid's second birthday.

- According to industry estimates, each diaper change takes moms an average of 2 minutes and 5 seconds. That means in those first two years, a mommy's devoting a good 253 hours to poop patrol—a total of almost 11 full 24-hour days. (Dads, in contrast, take only about a minute and 36 seconds per change.)

- Some reports estimate that toddlers demand a mother's attention at least once every 4 minutes.

- About 5.3 million women are full-time stay-at-home moms. The majority of mothers, however, have jobs outside of the house: About 57 percent of women with infants consider themselves a part of the nation's workforce.

- Stay-at-home moms don't often stay at home for long. Eighty-three percent of women who leave work to tend to their newborns go back to the office within a year.

- Parenting groups estimate that an average mom spends 2.2 hours a day on chores—nearly double the time put in by dads. We're just sayin'.

- There are 9.8 million single moms with kids under age 18. That number has nearly tripled since 1970.

- In 2008, just over a third of mommies had their kids outside of marriage.

- Eighty percent of moms say they eat dinner with their young children. Fifty-eight percent do breakfast together.

- The first Mother's Day on record took place in May of 1908, after a woman named Anna Jarvis suggested a day celebrating moms. (And no, she didn't work for Hallmark.) The holiday became official just six years later when President Woodrow Wilson declared it a national event.

- Mother's Day is celebrated in a large number of other countries, too: Australia, Belgium, China, Denmark, Finland, Italy, Mexico, Turkey, and Thailand, to name a handful. Each nation doesn't celebrate it on the same day as the United States, though.

- Unofficial records suggest more than 122.5 million calls are made to moms across the country on Mother's Day. When she's not chatting, Mom may be found reading: 152 million Mother's Day cards are sent every year in the United States.

Odd Uses for Abandoned Structures

❖ ❖ ❖ ❖

After these sites and structures fulfilled their original purpose, they moved into their second act.

Piling It High in Old Virginny

In 1974, a 165-acre city park was opened in Virginia Beach, Virginia. Nothing out of the ordinary, right? But it's what the park was built upon that makes it so unusual: The aptly named Mount Trashmore was built on top of a sanitary landfill. The play space has the usual park features, such as swing-sets and basketball courts, but the developers didn't stop there. Two lakes were also added to the complex, Lake Windsor and Lake Trashmore. Ironically, Lake Trashmore is a freshwater pond that is regularly stocked for fishing. A staircase leads to the top of the former dump some 60 feet above the surrounding terrain. We hear the view is breathtaking—in more ways than one.

Subterranean Soiree

A unique nightclub once existed *under* the sidewalks of New York City. Known as "The Tunnel," the Chelsea-based operation, which opened in the late 1980s, took its name from its main dance floor, a subway tunnel in use until the early 1900s. Partiers were often packed like sardines into the elongated club. In addition to its namesake room, The Tunnel sported a darkened lounge replete with peeling paint and exposed pipes.

Dealing in dancing and debauchery, the ultra-hip hotspot often found Canadian owner Peter Gatien at odds with the law. Still, this didn't dampen the spirits of thousands of partiers on any given weekend. But, alas, all parties must come to an end, and with charges of tax evasion and the threat of deportation looming over Gatien's head, he was forced to close the club. The space sold in 2001.

High Life on the High Line

If you're in the machine-made canyons of New York City and suddenly hear the sounds of children playing, people jogging, and other forms of recreation, just look up—you're probably standing beneath the city's funkiest new park.

The High Line is an elevated rail line-turned-verdant patch that stands 30 feet above the streets of Manhattan and stretches for nearly a mile and a half. The rail line was constructed in the 1930s to lift freight trains off the streets. Within its seven-acre spread, overstressed city workers can escape the rat race, if only during their lunch break. Future additions may include a swimming pool, a sundeck, and a vegetal balcony. So, why build a park along an elevated railroad right-of-way? Why not? In New York City, where open space is at a premium, residents must work with what is available. The sky's the limit, as they say.

Bridge of Flowers

At one time, picturesque Shelburne Falls, Massachusetts, was an endpoint along the Shelburne Falls & Colrain Street Railway, a trolley line built to haul freight and passengers. But in 1928, a decision was made to abandon the line in favor of trucking, a cheaper and more modern shipping alternative. Did this mean that Shelburne Falls would lose a portion of its heritage? Certainly. But what replaced it was arguably better. In 1929, the good townspeople decided to turn the abandoned Deerfield River Bridge—a span leftover from the trolley days—into a "Bridge of Flowers."

These days a walking path forms the right-of-way over the 400-foot-long span, and wisteria, tulips, roses, mums, and other beautiful flowers bloom beside it. Gardeners and volunteers tend this aromatic space that has now become the defining feature of Shelburne Falls. Each year, more than 20,000 people take the time to stop and smell the roses and other wistful blooms as they cross this unusual bridge.

PALINDROMES

A palindrome is a phrase that reads the same in both directions. The word is derived from the Greek palíndromos, *which means running back again* (palín = *again;* drom-, dramêin = *to run*).

Step on no pets

Poor Dan is in a droop

Never odd or even

So many dynamos

Won't I panic in a pit now?

Too bad I hid a boot

A car, a man, a maraca

Was it Eliot's toilet I saw?

Wontons? Not now

We panic in a pew

Vanna, wanna V?

Was it a bat I saw?

Tons o' snot

"Naomi," I moan

No, it is open on one position

O, Geronimo—no minor ego

Senile felines

Sex-aware era waxes

Ten animals I slam in a net

A Santa lived as a devil at NASA

Yo! Banana boy!

Dennis sinned

Tooth Be Told

❖ ❖ ❖ ❖

In the United States, the Tooth Fairy usually trades cash for baby teeth. But how do other cultures handle this rite of passage?

Molar Mice

As it turns out, the Tooth Fairy isn't universal. In fact, she only visits kids in the United States, Canada, Australia, England, and Denmark (where she's called Tandfeen). But before you start feeling bad that the Tooth Fairy doesn't get around more often, know that in most parts of the world, it's a tooth *mouse* who reigns supreme.

Known as El Ratón in Mexico, El Ratoncito in Argentina, El Ratón Perez in Spain, and Le Petite Souris in France, this magical mouse has the same M.O. as the Tooth Fairy, taking baby teeth from under a pillow, or sometimes from a glass of water, in exchange for money or candy. But that's not the only place children put their baby teeth. In South Africa, mice swipe the tooth from a slipper, but in Uganda, the tooth is hidden behind a pot.

And not every culture trades teeth for trinkets. In Russia and Afghanistan, children drop their teeth down mouse holes in hopes that their teeth will grow in like mice's teeth: strong, sharp, and white. In Kazakhstan, teeth are dropped under bathtubs with similar wishes.

Tooth Tossers

Strange as it sounds, tossing a tooth on the roof is common in many cultures, although it's not always a mouse who makes the trade but another sharp-toothed rodent. In Sri Lanka, it's a squirrel; among the Cherokee, a beaver.

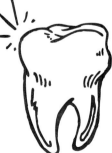

In the Dominican Republic and Haiti, the tooth is simply tossed on the roof. In China, Japan, and other Asian countries, only a lower tooth is tossed on the roof; an upper one is thrown straight to the ground, buried, or placed at the foot of the bed. The belief is that the new tooth will grow in the direction of the old one.

32.

It was 3:12 in the morning when Jesse pulled up in front of the Crowne estate on Paradise Neck. There was already a small generator in place and a couple of spotlights hooked to it. Two Paradise cruisers were there, and the Paradise Fire Rescue vehicle. Suit stood with Molly in the driveway. Peter Perkins squatted on his heels, taking pictures of a corpse. Jesse got out of the car.

"Mrs. Franklin," Molly said, as Jesse walked toward them. "Amber's mother."

Jesse nodded. He walked to the body and stood looking down. A lot of blood glistened darkly on the smooth, green lawn beneath her head. Perkins looked up when Jesse arrived and rested his camera on his thigh.

"Shot in the back of the head," he said from his crouched position. "Can't tell how many times. Small caliber, I think. No exit wounds."

"State ME been notified?"

"Yeah. On the way."

"Any idea how long?" Jesse said.

"That's the ME's line of work. Blood's dry. Body's kind of stiff."

Jesse nodded.

"Who found the body?" he said.

"Suit," Peter Perkins said.

Jesse turned and stared at Simpson, standing with Molly.

"Murder weapon?" Jesse said.

"Haven't searched yet," Perkins said. "It's not under the body."

Jesse nodded and walked over to Suit and Molly.

"How'd you find the body," Jesse said.

"I was just cruising by and I saw this form. So I stopped, investigated, and there she was."

"Cruising by at, what, two-thirty or so in the morning?" Jesse said. "You weren't on patrol tonight."

"Not tonight, no," Suit said. "I do that sometimes, though, just get up in the night and ride around, you know, see what I can see."

"Just sort of poking into things," Molly said.

Suit blushed a little. Jesse glanced at Molly. She seemed serene.

"Ever vigilant," Jesse said.

Neither Suit nor Molly said anything.

"Who was supposed to be sitting on Mrs. Franklin, Moll?" Jesse said.

"Buddy."

"He arrive yet?"

Molly pointed at the roadway behind Jesse's car.

"Right now," she said.

"Okay, whyn't you see if you can find a clue or something."

They both nodded. And as Jesse walked toward Buddy Hall's cruiser, parked behind Jesse's car, they both took out flashlights and began to walk the lawn, carefully.

"What happened," Jesse said to Buddy Hall.

"She must have snuck out the back," Buddy said. "I'm parked right outside her house all night until I hear the radio call about a body on Paradise Neck. So I call in, and Bobby Martin's working the desk, and he tells me Molly called it in to him, and that it's the Franklin broad. And I said, 'Jesus, she hasn't left the house.' And I call Moll on her cell phone and she says yes it is Franklin and she's been shot and I better get over there. So here I am."

"You check her house?" Jesse said.

"No, I come straight here. Should I have?"

"It's okay," Jesse said. "You help Molly and Suit on the crime scene. I'll go over there."

"Yeah, okay. Jesse, I'm sorry if I fucked up. I didn't think she'd sneak away."

"We'll play it as it lays, Buddy," Jesse said. "Go look for clues... and don't step on any."

Buddy Hall nodded his head very hard and hustled toward the wide lawn that led up to the now-empty school. Jesse followed, looking at the ground, walking carefully until he got to Molly.

"Moll," he said. "You run things here. Make sure everything

is gone and cleaned up and no trace before those little kids get here at eight a.m."

"Absolutely," Molly said.

A state car pulled up behind the other cars and parked, and a smallish man got out with a doctor's bag.

"Okay," Jesse said. "The state ME. I want a report as soon as he can get us one."

"I'll tell him," Molly said.

They watched as the ME trudged toward the body.

"Suit's got a girlfriend out here," Jesse said. "Doesn't he?"

Molly nodded.

"And she's, ah, inappropriate, probably married," Jesse said.

"Yes."

"And you discovered him, and he's made you promise not to tell."

"Yes. I gave him my word."

"But you can't resist busting his balls a little."

Molly smiled.

"Could you?" she said.

"Probably not," Jesse said. "One thing, though. If who he's banging becomes any kind of issue to a case, I need to know."

"I understand that, Jesse."

"Okay," Jesse said. "I'll trust your judgment."

"You can," Molly said.

"I know," Jesse said.

He walked back to his car and got in and headed back across the causeway toward Mrs. Franklin's house on Sewall Street.

33.

Now that he had to investigate her murder, Jesse decided to call her by her actual name, Fiona Francisco. In which case he could also think of the daughter as Amber Francisco, and stop messing around with the Franklin-slash-Francisco construct in his head.

He parked in front of her house. There were lights on in the front room. He tried the front door. It was locked. He walked around to the side where a tiny alley squeezed between two buildings. Jesse went down the alley. Behind the house was a tiny brick patio that was at a level lower than the front of the house and was accessed by a door in the basement. The door was open. Jesse looked around the patio. Looming behind it was the back end of another old house. To the left was a small set of stone steps that led up to a driveway at street level. The driveway opened onto a side street that ran perpendicular to Sewall. Jesse looked at it and nodded to himself.

He went in through the open door. He was in a cellar that had been converted, probably in the 1950s from the look of it, into a playroom. Pine-paneled walls, vinyl-tile floors, Celotex tile ceiling. The furnace and electrical panel and hot-water heater were in an alcove. Jesse went up the stairs on the far end and into the living room. It smelled like a tavern. There was a half-full bowl of bright orange cheese puffs on the coffee table in front of the shabby couch. There were four beer cans upright on the coffee table and one on its side. All of them were empty. A pink crocheted coverlet lay half turned back on the couch. Cheese puff detritus speckled the couch and the floor near the couch. The television was on, some sort of infomercial. The kitchen was empty, dirty dishes on the counter. A dirty frying pan on the stove. Jesse opened the refrigerator. Twelve cans of beer, some Velveeta, a loaf of white bread, some peanut butter, and three Diet Cokes. On the counter next to an unwashed coffee cup was a bottle of multivitamins.

That oughta balance everything out, Jesse thought.

He walked through the rest of the small house. The beds were unmade. Dirty laundry lay in piles in both bedrooms. There was a still-sodden towel on the bathroom floor. He went back to the living room and leaned against the front door. To his left was a fireplace that had been cold a long time. Over it was a small mantelpiece, and on the mantel was a school photograph of some-body who probably used to be Amber.

The cellar door had been unlocked. There was no sign of forced entry. It looked as if she had gone down to the cellar and out the back door and up the outside steps to the side street and was gone. *Did she walk? Was there a car? How did she end up out on Paradise Neck? More important, how did she end up dead?* It seemed an odd coincidence that she was found on the lawn of the Crowne estate. *Clearly, she had snuck out. There was no reason to go the way she went except to avoid Buddy Hall in the cruiser out front. Why would she sneak out? If she thought the bad ex-husband was after her, she'd have run to the cop, not away from him... Her daughter... If her daughter called... "Ma, it's Amber, can't talk now, sneak out so the cops don't see you and I'll meet you on Sea Street, behind the house."... Maybe love had failed and she was running from her boyfriend.*

Jesse walked to the fireplace and looked at Amber's picture on the mantel. It was in a cheap cardboard holder. The picture was garishly overcolored, as school pictures often are. The girl in it looked blankly sweet, with soft brown hair and a roundish, un-formed face. Jesse looked at it for a while. It told him nothing.

Maybe she wasn't looking for help. Maybe she lured her mother out to be killed... Maybe I been a cop too long... but maybe she did. If she did, who did the killing? Esteban? Why? And why take her to the Crowne estate. Did they kill her there? Kill her elsewhere and dump her there?

Jesse walked once more through the house, hoping it might tell him something. All it said to him was that it was an unpleas-ant place to live. He went out the front door and closed it behind him and got in his car. *'Course, Horn Street wasn't a week in Acapulco, either.*

He started the car and put it in gear and drove back toward the crime scene. The sky was starting to lighten. It was 4:58 on the dashboard clock. It would be daylight soon. Jesse knew it was too early to speculate. But he also knew it wasn't often that somebody got killed for no reason, or got killed by a perfect stranger. Now and then it happened. Like Son of Sam in New York, or the pair that Jesse had put away a few years ago. But they weren't common.

If a few more dumpy beer-drinking women with adolescent daughters get killed, Jesse thought, *I'll revise my position. But right now it's got something to do with Louis Francisco, and Amber, and maybe Esteban Carty. And maybe something about the Crowne estate.*

Or not.

34.

Amber was sitting cross-legged on the daybed, smoking a joint, while Esteban talked on his cell phone. They were alone in the garage with the huge television screen. The TV was on but silent. They both liked to smoke a joint and watch TV without sound.

"It'll be in the Boston papers, man, you want to go online and see," Esteban said.

He stood in the doorway with his back to Amber, looking down his alley.

"Yeah, I know you'll pay. I still got the other package to deliver."

Amber watched the shapes move on the silent screen. She

knew Esteban was talking to someone, and she could hear the words he said, but the words weren't real. What was real were the endlessly fascinating shapes.

"When I get the dough, I'll ship the package," Esteban said.

Amber took in some smoke and held it for a time before she eased it out. The colors on the huge television were very bright and had a kind of inviting density to them. She'd never realized quite how inviting they were.

"Sure it's a lot, man, but I can't just stick it on a plane, you know? I mean, it's gotta be driven down there. And somebody gotta go along with it, you know? I mean, it ain't gonna want to go at all, man. I gotta see to it that it does."

Amber took another toke. The movement and the colors tended to blend into something. She didn't know what. But it made her feel religious.

"Yeah, man," Esteban said. "You call me when you see the news about Momma. We'll arrange the other delivery."

He shut the cell phone off and came to the couch.

"You believe in God, Esteban?" Amber said.

She offered him her half-smoked joint.

"Sure, baby," Esteban said, "long as he believes in me."

"You believe in the devil?"

"Baby," Esteban said. "I am the devil."

Amber giggled. Esteban took a toke and passed the nearly burned-out roach to Amber. She finished it.

"I like to drink wine when we smoke a joint."

Amber was watching the colors. She didn't move. Esteban gave her a smart slap on the side of her butt.

"You gonna get us some wine?" he said.

Amber stood up.

"You don't have to hit so hard," Amber said.

"Told you, baby, I'm the devil."

She giggled happily and went to the refrigerator, and came back with a jug of white wine. She put out two unmatched water glasses and filled each one with the jug wine. There were four more joints rolled and lying beside a box of kitchen matches on the wooden crate that served as a side table. Esteban drank some wine and lit another joint.

"You talking to my daddy?" Amber said.

"Yeah, we was arranging the payoff for putting Momma down."

"Bye-bye, Momma," Amber said, and giggled.

"Bye-bye," Esteban murmured, and sucked in a big lungful of smoke. As it drifted slowly out of his lungs he murmured again, "Bye-bye."

35.

Jenn came into Jesse's office in the late afternoon.

"You look tired," Jenn said to him.

"Up most of the night," Jesse said. "I got a couple hours' sleep in one of the cells in the back."

Whenever he saw her, Jesse felt like jumping up and wagging his tail. He always wanted to tell Jenn how beautiful she was and how much he loved her and how nothing she could do or say would shake him on that. And the strain of not doing that, which both he and Dix had agreed was in his best interest, was very burdensome.

"So what can you tell me about this murder," she said.

"On the record?"

Jenn paused for a minute, then she sighed a little.

"I hate when you ask me that," she said.

"I hate that I have to ask it," Jesse said.

Jenn nodded.

"But you do," she said. "I'm in my professional reporter costume, so, yes, we're on the record."

Jesse nodded.

"The body was discovered by Officer Luther Simpson...." Jesse said.

"That's Suit's real name?" Jenn said.

"Yep," Jesse said, "on routine patrol at approximately two a.m. this morning, on the front lawn of the Crowne estate on Paradise Neck. The victim has been identified as Fiona Francisco, who was a resident of Eleven Sewall Street in Paradise. While she lived there she was using the name Frances Franklin."

"Why the alias?" Jenn said.

"We don't know yet."

"How long she live there?"

"We're checking that. I'm guessing two, three years."

"Cause of death?"

"ME says two twenty-two-caliber bullets in the back of the head at close range."

"Was she killed at the Crowne estate?"

"At or close," Jesse said. "She bled a lot on the grass where they put her."

"Do you see any connection to the Crown estate school project, which drew protesters when it began?" Jenn said.

"None so far," Jesse said.

"Next of kin?"

"She has a daughter, Amber Francisco," Jesse said, "who called herself Alice Franklin while she lived here."

"Where are they from?"

"Don't know yet," Jesse said.

"Any leads?"

"Not yet."

"Any suspects?" Jenn said.

"Not yet."

"Can we do a stand-up on camera?" Jenn said.

"Nope."

"Oh, poo, Jesse," Jenn said. "Why not?"

"I don't ever recall getting in trouble by not talking," Jesse said. "Especially on camera."

She smiled.

"What about my career," she said.

Jesse sucked in his cheeks a little and did a bad impression of Clark Gable.

"Frankly, my dear," Jesse said, "I don't give a damn."

"I know," Jenn said.

They were quiet. Jesse was always puzzled by the fact that despite all her talkative charm and bubble, Jenn never revealed much of what she was thinking. . . . *No,* Jesse thought, *of what she was* feeling.

"You know," Jesse said. "That's not true. I went for the easy joke. But it's not true."

"You do give a damn about my career?" she said.

"Yes," Jesse said. "There's self-interest in it. But if we are ever going to make it together, you have to be fully you."

"What did you say?"

"We can't..." He couldn't think exactly how to say it. "You can't care enough about me until you can care enough about you."

She stared at him in silence for what seemed to him a long time.

Finally she said, "I...I don't...I am very happy that you know that."

Jesse nodded.

"Give Dix the credit."

Jenn smiled.

"I already did," she said. "Is there anything off the record that you can tell me."

"Aha," Jesse said. "Putting it to the test already."

Jenn smiled again, and inclined her head.

"Well," she said. "Is there?"

"A lot," Jesse said.

Jenn took out a notebook, as Jesse started to talk.

When he was through she said, "So what's the connection between Crow and the Francisco family, and the Crowne estate?'

"I don't know," Jesse said.

"But you think there is one?"

"Give me something to investigate," Jesse said.

"What if it's a false lead?" Jenn said.

"Maybe I'll come across the real one in the process," Jesse said.

"Better than doing nothing?"

"The daughter, Amber, has a boyfriend who's a Hispanic gangster in Marshport," Jesse said. "The Crowne estate is a place where small Hispanic children are bused in from Marshport, despite local opposition. Amber's mother's body is found on the front lawn of the Crowne estate."

"Could be coincidence," Jenn said.

"Could be," Jesse said.

"But if I were on the story," Jenn said, "and I didn't follow up on the possible connection, they'd fire me."

Jesse nodded.

"What I don't get," Jenn said, "is Crow."

"Nobody entirely gets Crow," Jesse said.

"But if he doesn't want to kill the woman and return the girl, why doesn't he just go away?" Jenn said. "It's not like he hasn't done worse."

"Says he likes women."

Jenn nodded.

"You believe him?"

"He let those hostages off the boat ten years ago," Jesse said.

"And kept the money," Jenn said.

"Which he didn't have to split with anybody," Jesse said.

"So maybe it's just something he tells you," Jenn said. "That he likes women."

"Or tells himself," Jesse said.

"Or maybe it's true," Jenn said.

Jesse nodded.

"Or maybe it's true," he said.

36.

Crow had a bottle of champagne under his arm when he
knocked on Marcy Campbell's door at 5:45 in the evening. When
she answered the door, he held out the champagne.

"I thought we might want to drink this," Crow said, "and sort
of close the circle."

"The one that opened with me tied up on the couch in my office?" Marcy said. "Some years ago?"

"Yep."

"What if I decline?"

"You keep the champagne, I go my way," Crow said.

"Well," Marcy said. "I decline."

"Enjoy the champagne," Crow said, and turned and walked toward the street.

Marcy stood in the doorway watching him. He reached her front gate and opened it when she said, "No."

Crow turned.

"No?"

"Don't go," Marcy said.

Crow nodded and let the gate swing shut and walked back.

"I just got home," Marcy said. "I need to take a shower."

"Sure," Crow said.

While she was gone, Crow found the kitchen and improvised an ice bucket out of a mixing bowl. He popped the cork on the champagne, poured some into a wineglass, put the rest of the bottle on ice, and took it to the living room. He sat and sipped the champagne he'd poured and looked at the room. Colonial American antiques, braided rugs, pine paneling, pictures of sailboats. Very New England. He finished his champagne as Marcy appeared in the bedroom door wearing a white robe.

"Want some champagne first?" Crow said.

"No," Marcy said.

"Okay," Crow said.

He walked into the bedroom and took off his shirt. He was wearing a gun, which he took from the holster and placed on the bedside table. Then he took off the rest of his clothes. Marcy watched, standing by the bed.

"What's the scar from?" she said.

Crow shook his head. Marcy nodded and shrugged out of the robe. They looked at each other for a moment, then Marcy went to him and kissed him and half fell backward onto the bed. Crow went with her, ending up on the side near the nightstand, where his gun was.

Later they sat in the early-American living room, Crow with his clothes back on, Marcy in her white robe, and drank the champagne.

"How'd you know," Marcy said.

"We know things," Crow said.

"We?"

"Apache warriors," Crow said.

"Are you really an Apache?"

"Yes."

"And you knew I wanted this," she said.

"Yes," Crow said, and smiled. "And if I was wrong, what'd I lose?"

"A hundred-dollar bottle of champagne," Marcy said.

"Three hundred," Crow said.

Marcy smiled.

"So maybe all that Apache warrior stuff is crap," she said.

"Maybe," Crow said.

"But maybe not?" Marcy said.

"You'd like it to be real," Crow said. "Wouldn't you?"

"Yes," Marcy said. "I would."

"It's real to me," Crow said.

"I only ever wanted to do this once," Marcy said.

Crow nodded.

"I'd rather it not happen again," Marcy said.

"Okay," Crow said.

"Don't think it wasn't wonderful," Marcy said.

"I don't think that," Crow said.

"I had a fantasy and I fulfilled it."

"Sure," Crow said.

"You understand?" Marcy said.

"Sure."

The champagne was gone. Crow looked at the empty bottle and stood.

"Time to go," he said.

Marcy nodded. They walked to the door together. At the door Marcy put her arms around him and then kissed him hard.

"Good-bye," she said.

"Good-bye," Crow said, and walked out and closed the door.

37.

Miriam Fiedler invited Jesse for lunch at the Paradise Yacht Club. In honor of the occasion Jesse wore a blue blazer.

"Well," Miriam said when he joined her at a table on the veranda with a view across the harbor to the town. "You dressed up, I'm flattered."

"The blazer covers up my gun," Jesse said.

Miriam continued to smile brightly.

"I love this view of the town," she said, "don't you?"

"Yes," Jesse said.

A young waitress came to the table. Miriam ordered a Manhattan. Jesse had iced tea.

"You don't drink, Chief Stone?" Miriam said.

"I do," Jesse said. "But generally not at lunch."

"Oh, no one would even notice," Miriam said. "All of the members have a drink at lunch."

Jesse nodded.

"Well, I see that I have my work cut out for me," Miriam said.

"How so?" Jesse said.

"You're not much of a talker."

"As soon as I know the topic," Jesse said, "I'll jump right in."

"Why are you so sure there's a topic?"

"Last week you were rooting for my death," Jesse said. "Now lunch. There's a topic."

"Oh, Chief Stone," Miriam said. "Of course there is. I don't know why I pretended there wasn't. May I call you Jesse. Everyone seems to."

"You may," Jesse said.

"Please call me Miriam."

"Okay," Jesse said.

"Because I'm passionate about the issue," Miriam said. "I realize I've been far too strident in the matter of the Crowne estate, and I wish first to apologize."

"Good," Jesse said.

Miriam drank some of her Manhattan. Not like someone who needed it, Jesse noticed, merely like someone who liked it.

"And I wondered if we could find a way to join forces, as it were, to confront a problem which is now a mutual one."

She wasn't that bad-looking, Jesse thought. Probably fifty-something. Skin good. Slim, well-dressed, well-groomed, and her teeth were very white. She wore quite a bit of makeup and was quite artful with it. Jesse remembered how clever Jenn had been with makeup. He always paid attention to it in women.

"What would that problem be?" Jesse said.

"The murder," Miriam said, her voice full of surprise. "Murder on the very front lawn of that lovely estate."

Jesse waited.

"Well, surely you see the connection," Miriam said. "Once that element penetrates a town, then inevitably the crime rate soars, and the fundamental value of a beautiful residential town simply disappears."

"Obviously," Jesse said, "you're not claiming that one of those preschool kids shot Fiona Francisco."

"No, no, of course not. But once it starts, like the tiny trickle that overwhelms the dike...it's a tragedy," she said.

"Why do you think Fiona Francisco was killed by a Latino person?" Jesse said.

"Well, she was there on the front lawn, and obviously she wasn't killed by someone in Paradise."

"But you have no actual evidence," Jesse said.

"It's as plain as the nose on your face," she said.

Jesse nodded thoughtfully.

"That plain," he said. "What do you think I should do?"

"Well, first of all, close down that school. It will send them a message," Miriam said.

"I really have no right to close down a school," Jesse said.

"You have an obligation to protect us," Miriam said.

"I do," Jesse said.

He picked up the menu.

"What's good here," Jesse said.

Miriam stared at him.

"I'm not through talking," she said.

"I'm not surprised," Jesse said.

"Well, what are you going to do about this?"

Jesse put down the menu.

"I'll tell you what I'm not going to do," Jesse said. "I'm not going to sit here and talk ragtime with you. You have your reasons for wanting that school closed. But we both know they have little to do with the murder of Fiona Francisco."

"That's insulting," Miriam said.

"Yeah, I thought it might be," Jesse said. "Thanks for the iced tea."

He stood and walked through the open French doors, through the dining room, and out of the Yacht Club.

38.

Jesse stood with Jenn and Nina Pinero at the foot of the long, sloping lawn of the Crowne estate. At the top of the slope the children sat on the floor of the big front porch while one of the two teachers read them a book.

"Kids know about the murder?" Jesse said.

"Vaguely," Nina said.

"Press?" Jesse said.

"We've been able to keep them away pretty well." She looked at Jenn. "Until now."

"I'm Jenn Stone," Jenn said, "Channel Three News."

"Stone?" Nina said. "Any relation?"

"We used to be married," Jesse said.

"Does that give her special status?" Nina said.

"Yes," Jesse said. "It does."

"I won't bother the children," Jenn said. "I'm just gathering background for a larger story I'm working on."

"Didn't you used to do weather?" Nina said.

Jenn grinned at her.

"Sure did. Want some information on cold fronts and high-pressure systems?"

Nina smiled.

"No," she said. "I very much don't."

"No one seems to," Jenn said. "Except program directors and station managers."

"I would prefer you not talk to the children," Nina said.

"No need," Jenn said. "I have a lot of film from the first day they arrived."

"Nina," Jesse said. "Do I recall you saying that one of these Crowne estate kids had a brother in the Horn Street Boys?"

Nina looked at Jenn.

"This conversation is off the record," Nina said.

"Of course," Jenn said.

"Yes," Nina said to Jesse, "there's a brother."

"What's his name?"

"Why do you want to know?"

"The Horn Street Boys have a connection to the victim," Jesse said, "and a connection to the school. And the victim was found on school grounds."

"You think the Horn Street Boys are involved?"

"I only know what I told you," Jesse said. "I don't even have a theory yet."

"I won't give you a name," Nina said. "I shouldn't have even mentioned the brother."

"Why?" Jenn said.

"Improving life for these kids is so fragile a proposition," she said. "Anything can ruin us."

"Like having the head person in this program rat one of their brothers to the cops," Jesse said.

"Just like that," Nina said.

"But since you know of the relationship, the two boys must have some regular contact," Jesse said.

"Yes."

"So it's possible," Jesse said, "that the Horn Street Boys know abut the Crowne estate project and maybe even about the local opposition."

"Yes."

"You think they were making a statement?" Jenn said.

"I have no idea," Nina said.

"We're not the enemy," Jenn said. "We're just trying to help."

"That may be true," Nina said. "But what I said is also true. I don't know anything more about the Horn Street Boys than what I've told you."

Jesse said, "Thank you, Nina," and turned and walked toward his car. Jenn lingered a moment, and then said, "Thank you," and followed Jesse.

"That wasn't very productive," Jenn said, as they drove back across the causeway.

"I had to confirm what was a very passing remark, make sure I heard it right, so I'm not wasting time with a theory that isn't so."

"Meticulous," Jenn said.

"It's mostly what the work is about," Jesse said. "Keeping track of stuff."

"I wonder why people like Nina are so hostile to the media," Jenn said.

"You and Nina have different goals," Jesse said. "Even in the best case, you are trying to get at the truth. She is trying to salvage a few kids."

"Are the two incompatible?" Jenn said.

"Sometimes, yes," Jesse said. "Sometimes, no. People like Nina are intensely aware of the incompatible possibility."

"You said 'best case.' What's a worse case?"

"That your goal is not truth but advertising revenue," Jesse said.

Jenn smiled.

"Oh," she said. "That."

39.

They were sitting on a bench by the marina five blocks from Horn Street, looking at the boats, sharing a can of Pepsi and a joint.

"You know how to get to Florida?" Esteban said.

"Florida?" Amber said.

"I'm supposed to take you to Florida," Esteban said. "And I don't know where it is."

"What do you mean?" Amber said.

"Your old man's giving me ten thousand dollars to bring you down."

"I don't want to go to Florida."

"It's ten thousand dollars, baby," Esteban said.

"You gonna sell me to my father?" she said.

"No, no. I just bring you down, turn you over, he gives me the ten grand. I wait around a couple days. You run away and we come back up here. How long's it take to get to Florida?"

"I won't go," she said.

"Yeah, baby, you will," Esteban said. "Up front beside me, or in the trunk, either way you gonna go. Ten thousand dollars's a lot of money."

She looked at him in silence for a moment. Then she began to cry.

"Hey," Esteban said. "Hey, hey. This is for us, baby. You spend a couple fucking days with the old man, and we're outta there with the money."

Amber stood and ran. Esteban went after her, out along Marshport Way along the water. A hundred yards up from the marina was a red light. A half-painted, half-primed pickup truck that might once have been blue was stopped at the light. The back was full of loose copper pipe. Amber reached it as the light turned green and as the car started to move Amber stepped up onto the running board and hooked her arm through the window.

A big guy in a black tank top and a do-rag sat in the passenger seat. He had a thick gold chain around his neck.

"What the fuck are you doing," he said.

"Somebody's after me," she said. "Keep going."

The driver was a wiry kid with longish blond hair, tattoos on both forearms, and the scruffy beginnings of a beard.

"Keep going, hell," he said. "Whyn't we stop and clean his clock?"

"No, please, keep going," Amber said.

The driver looked in the rearview mirror.

"Hell," he said. "He's given up anyway. Lemme stop and you can get in."

She rode in the front seat between them, still crying.

"What's going on?" the big guy asked.

"I can't tell you," Amber said.

The big guy shrugged.

"Where you want to go?" the big guy said. "Want us to take you to the cops?"

"No," she said. "I . . . I want to go to Paradise."

"You want to take her to Paradise?" the big guy said to the driver.

"Sure," the driver said. "Better than running copper pipe all day."

40.

Crow came into the Paradise police station with Amber.

"Where the hell did you get her?" Molly said.

"She called me," Crow said. "From the shopping center."

"Paradise Mall?" Molly said.

Crow nodded.

"How'd she have your number?" Molly said.

"I gave it to her," Crow said. "When you cut her loose."

Molly looked at him for a moment and shook her head, and then looked at Amber.

Amber's eye makeup was ruined again by crying. She wore lace-up black boots, and black jeans that had been cut off very short, and a tank top with some kind of heavy-metal logo that Molly didn't recognize.

"How ya doing, Amber?"

Amber shook her head, looking down at the floor.

"He was going to make me go back to my father," she said.

"Who was?"

"My boyfriend," Amber said.

"And your boyfriend is?" Molly said.

Amber shook her head.

"Where is your father?" Molly said.

"Florida."

"Why was your boyfriend going to make you go back?" Molly said.

"My father paid him," Amber said.

"And what are you doing here?" Molly said.

"I ran away."

"And you called Crow," Molly said.

"He said he wouldn't make me go back," Amber said.

Molly looked at Crow again. Crow shrugged.

"So," Molly said to both of them, "what do you need from me?"

Amber continued to look at the floor. She shook her head and didn't speak.

"Stone around?" Crow said.

"He's not here at the moment," Molly said. "You're welcome to wait."

"Can I talk with you while I'm waiting?" Crow said.

"Sure."

"What about her?" Crow said.

"We can put her in a cell," Molly said.

"I don't want to be in jail," Amber said softly to the floor.

"Just a guest," Molly said. "Cell won't be locked. You can lie down, take a nap, if you wish."

Amber didn't say anything.

"You'll be safe there," Molly said. "Until we figure out a better arrangement."

Amber nodded faintly.

"We're going to keep you safe," Molly said. "I promise you."

"Take the cell," Crow said to Amber.

Amber said, "Okay."

Molly walked her back to the little cell block in the back of the station. There were four cells, all empty. The last one had a curtain made from a blanket that could be pulled across the door.

"This is where we usually put women," Molly said. "Give you a little privacy."

Amber went in and sat on the cot. There was a sink and a toilet.

"I'll leave the door open," Molly said, "and close the curtain. You need anything, come see me."

Amber nodded. Molly went back to the front desk.

"She jumps pretty quick when you speak," Molly said.

"She knows I mean it," Crow said.

Molly nodded. Crow was wearing a faded tan safari shirt with short sleeves. Molly was fascinated with the play of intricate muscles in his arms.

"So what do you think we're going to do with her?" Molly said.

"Her mother's dead," Crow said. "She doesn't want to go back to her father. She's on the run from her boyfriend."

"So you don't want to look out for her?"

"That's what I'm doing now," Crow said.

"We can't keep her here until she's like twenty-one," Molly said. "I mean, she can't live in the jail."

"Maybe we can figure something out," he said.

Molly nodded. They were quiet. Crow seemed comfortable with quiet. *He's all angles and planes,* Molly thought, *like some kind of really good machine, where everything works perfectly.* His eyes were black and seemed to penetrate everything. Molly felt as if he could see through her clothes. It was almost embarrassing.

"Why do you care?" Molly said to Crow.

"I feel like it," Crow said.

"You care because you feel like caring?"

"Yes."

"What if you didn't feel like it?"

"Then I wouldn't," Crow said.

He smiled at her.

"I know who you are," Molly said. "And I know what you do. Actually, you probably do worse than what I know."

"Much," Crow said.

"But there seems to be this streak of—What? Chivalry?— running through it."

"Maybe," Crow said.

"You like women."

"Yes."

"Why?"

Crow's eyes held on her. She felt herself blushing. Crow smiled.

"Besides that," Molly said.

"That's plenty," Crow said.

"But is that all?" Molly said.

"Trying to figure me out is a waste of time," he said.

"Have you figured you out?" Molly said.

"I know what I feel like doing," Crow said. "And what I don't."

"Is that enough?" Molly said.

"Yes," Crow said. "It is."

Again, Molly had the odd feeling that she was naked under his gaze. It was a puzzling feeling. *It's even more puzzling,* she thought, *that maybe I like it.*

41.

"Amber Francisco is here," Molly said when Jesse came into the station.

"Why?"

"Crow brought her in," Molly said.

"Where is he?"

"He left," Molly said. "Told me he'd check in with you later."

"Where is she?" Jesse said.

"In back," Molly said. "In the women's cell."

"Let's go see her," Jesse said.

"You want me to fill you in first?" Molly said.

"Nope. I'd rather start fresh. We'll talk with her and you can compare what she says to what you know."

Molly nodded and walked with Jesse back to the curtained cell. Molly pulled the curtain aside and looked in.

Amber was lying on her side with her legs bent and her eyes closed. She had washed her face and looked much younger.

"Amber?" Molly said. "You awake?"

Amber opened her eyes and didn't speak. Molly nodded and pulled the curtain aside and she and Jesse went in. Amber stared at them without moving.

"You remember me, Amber?" Jesse said.

She didn't say anything.

"If we're going to work this out, you'll need to talk. You may as well start now," Jesse said. "You remember me?"

"Yes."

"You know who I am?"

"Yes."

"How did you get here?"

"Guys in a pickup truck brought me from Marshport."

She remained lying on her side. Her face held no animation. Her voice was flat.

"How come?" Jesse said.

"My boyfriend was gonna sell me back to my father."

"Your boyfriend is Esteban Carty?"

She didn't answer.

"What's your boyfriend's name?" Jesse said.

She shook her head.

"Did he kill your mother?"

She didn't answer.

"Why won't you talk about him?" Jesse said.

"I won't," Amber said.

"Why not?"

"I don't know."

"Do you know who killed your mother?"

She didn't answer.

"Do you?" Jesse said.

"No."

"Why did you call Crow?" Jesse said.

She shrugged, which, Jesse thought, might not be easy lying on your side.

"You think he'd protect you from your boyfriend?"

"I had his phone number," she said.

"And you thought he'd protect you?"

"I thought Esteban would be afraid of him."

"Your boyfriend," Jesse said. "Esteban?"

"No. I didn't mean Esteban. My boyfriend is another man."

"But you said 'Esteban.'"

"No," she said.

Jesse nodded.

"You could have called us," he said.

"The police?"

"Uh-huh, nine-one-one would have done it."

"I was afraid you'd arrest me."

"Arrest you for what?" Jesse said.

"I don't know," she said. "For nothing...that's what cops do."

"Why don't you want to go back to your father?" Jesse said.

"He's creepy," Amber said. "He's got all these creepy guys around. And he'll make me go to school with the nuns. Nuns are creepy."

Jesse nodded.

"What's your father do for a living?" Jesse said.

"He does a lot of stuff. He makes a lot of money. But he's creepy."

"Any of the creepy guys around him bother you any?" Jesse said.

"Yeah."

"You ever tell him?"

"He told me to shut up and not talk dirty."

Jesse nodded.

"So you have a plan?"

"Plan?"

"Yeah," Jesse said. "Where you're going to live. What you're going to do for work."

She looked at him silently with her eyes wide and empty for a long time.

Then she said, "I don't have no plan."

"Well, you can bunk here for the moment until we work out something better," Jesse said. "You want something to eat?"

"I don't know."

Jesse nodded as if that made sense.

"Moll," he said. "Get whoever's on patrol to stop by Daisy's and pick up a couple sandwiches."

"Can I have ice cream?" Amber said.

"What kind?"

"Chocolate?"

"Sure," Jesse said.

He looked at Molly.

"Coming up," Molly said.

42.

The Paradise police firing range was outdoors, backing up to some wetlands and shielded by dirt bunkers that had been bulldozed. Jesse had a new Smith & Wesson .40-caliber semiautomatic handgun that he wanted to break in. He had his earmuffs off, reloading a magazine, when Crow parked on the street and walked through the short trail into the firing area.

"Officer Molly told me you were here," Crow said.

Jesse nodded.

"You want to shoot?" he said.

"Sure," Crow said. "Can I borrow a gun?"

Jesse smiled.

"You got a gun," Jesse said.

"It is illegal to carry a gun in this state without a permit," Crow said.

"You'd have a gun in the shower," Jesse said.

Crow smiled and spread his hands. Jesse nodded.

"In this town it is legal for someone to carry a gun to the firing range and shoot with the chief of police," Jesse said.

Crow looked steadily at Jesse for a moment. Then he nodded once, took a Glock nine-millimeter off his hip, crouched slightly, and, holding the Glock in both hands, put six rounds into the center of the target. Jesse finished loading the Smith & Wesson, turned sideways, and, firing with one hand, put six rounds into the center of the target.

"We're good," Crow said.

"We are."

"You fire like an old-time target shooter," Crow said.

"My father taught me that," Jesse said.

"Whatever works," Crow said.

Jesse put the Smith & Wesson down, and took his little .38 Chief's Special off his hip.

"You can hit the target with that thing?" Crow said.

"Sometimes," Jesse said. He began to crank the target toward them. "Especially if it's closer."

"Most shooting is close," Crow said.

"Yes," Jesse said, and put three rounds into the middle of the target.

"You didn't empty the weapon," Crow said.

"Neither did you," Jesse said.

"We're careful," Crow said.

"Got anything to tell me about Amber Francisco and friends?" Jesse said.

"Nothing I didn't tell Officer Molly," Crow said.

"And you got any thoughts on what we're gonna do with her?" Jesse said.

"You're the serve-and-protect guy," Crow said.

"You can't look out for her," Jesse said.

" 'Course not," Crow said.

"You got any thoughts on who killed her mother?" Jesse said.

"Probably Esteban," Crow said.

"Why?"

"Figure if he's talking to her daddy about bringing her to Florida, he may have talked to her daddy about killing her mother."

Jesse nodded.

"So why doesn't she say so?"

"Scared?" Crow said.

"Probably," Jesse said. "Loyal."

"Loyal?" Crow said. "He sold her out."

"She's got nothing else," Jesse said. "She can tell herself she loves him, and maybe convince herself that he loves her, she won't feel so alone."

"And this is better than going back to Daddy?" Crow said.

"Apparently."

"He must be fun," Crow said.

"So what're your plans," Jesse said.

"I'm considering my options," Crow said.

"Would one of those be to get out of town?" Jesse said.

"Not yet," Crow said.

"Why not," Jesse said.

"Unfinished business," Crow said.

"You want to see this through with the kid?"

"Something like that," Crow said.

"Let's not get in each other's way," Jesse said.

"Sure," Crow said

Jesse put the .38 back on his hip and the .40 in a small gym bag with two boxes of ammunition.

"You gonna pick up the brass?" Crow said.

"No," Jesse said.

"Great to be chief," Crow said.

43.

Molly and Jesse were in the squad room, drinking coffee.

"I'm sorry, Jesse," Molly said. "I can't take her."

"I know," Jesse said.

"I have a husband and four kids. I can't impose her on them."

"I know," Jesse said. "I guess I'll have to take her."

"Yourself?"

"Can't have her living here," Jesse said.

"You can't bring a fourteen-year-old girl home to live with you, Jesse, alone."

Jesse shrugged.

"I mean, what if she claims you molested her?" Molly said.

"I'll claim I didn't," Jesse said.

"But even if you can prove you didn't, that kind of thing will cling to you for life," Molly said. "It's not like this is a good kid. You can't tell what she'll do."

"I know."

"So, what about that female private detective you were dating?"

"Sunny Randall?"

"Yes. How about you get her to look after the kid."

Jesse shook his head.

"That book is closed," Jesse said. "Right now, I don't want to open it again."

"You cannot take her in alone," Molly said. "What if she's sick, what if . . . you just can't be parenting a fourteen-year-old girl that's not your daughter."

"Got any ideas?" Jesse said.

"How about Human Services?"

"This is not just a runaway kid," Jesse said. "Dangerous people are after her. You can't ask some social worker to fight it out with the Horn Street Boys . . . or whoever her old man sends."

"You think he'll send someone?"

"Crow thinks so," Jesse said.

"And you think he's right?" Molly said.

"Louis Francisco doesn't seem to be the kind of guy who would let Crow double-cross him, or allow his daughter to leave when he wanted her home."

"Maybe you should talk to that detective you met from Fort Lauderdale," Molly said. "Kelly something."

"Cruz," Jesse said. "Kelly Cruz. I already talked to her. She, too, says Francisco is the man in South Florida. Says she's going to talk to a Miami cop named Ray Ortiz about him, see what she can learn."

"So helpful," Molly said. "Did you sleep with her?"

"No," Jesse said.

"Wow," Molly said. "A rare exception."

"Doesn't mean I won't," Jesse said.

Molly grinned.

"I like your spirit," she said.

Jesse stood and got the coffeepot and poured some in Molly's cup and some in his own. Molly stirred some Splenda into hers.

"Jenn," Molly said.

Jesse put the coffeepot back and came and sat down. He poured some sugar from a yellow cardboard box and stirred it into his coffee.

"Jenn," he said.

"It would be her chance," Molly said, "to be personally involved in a real human-interest story, or a murder, or a gang war, or an arrest, or however it turns out.... *Here's Jenn Stone, Channel Three News, with the inside story.*"

"She might be in danger," Jesse said.

"Explain that to her, let her decide."

"I don't want her in danger," Jesse said.

"Jesse," Molly said, and paused, and then went on, "that would be for her to decide, I think."

Jesse didn't say anything. Molly and he each drank some coffee. The sun was hitting them both in the eyes through the east window of the room. Jesse got up and pulled the shade and came back and sat down and looked at Molly.

"I think you're probably right," he said.

44.

Four men wearing flowered shirts flew up from Miami on Delta. They picked up a Cadillac Escalade from a rental agency, drove to a motel on Marshport Road, and registered, two in a room. A half-hour after they arrived, an Asian man came to the door of one of the rooms with a big shopping bag that said Cathay Gardens on it.

One of the men from Miami opened the door. He was tall and straight and had salt-and-pepper hair.

"Mr. Romero?" said the man with the Cathay Gardens bag.

"Yes."

The delivery man held out the bag. Romero took it, gave him

a hundred-dollar bill, and closed the door. Romero's roommate was a squat bald man named Larson.

"What did we get?" Larson said.

Romero took the bag to the bed and opened it. He took out some cartons of Chinese food, four semiautomatic pistols, and four boxes of ammunition. Romero checked. All the guns were loaded. Larson opened one of the cartons.

"May as well eat the food," he said.

At 4:40 in the afternoon, the four men from Miami parked the Escalade at the head of Horn Street and got out. Parked a half-block away, on the corner of Nelson Boulevard, Crow watched them go down the alley. He smiled.

Didn't take long, he thought.

At 12A Horn Street, Romero knocked on the door. Esteban answered.

"You Carty?" Romero said.

"Yes."

"So where's the girl?" Romero said.

"You from Mr. Francisco?" Esteban said.

Romero nodded.

"He wants to know about the girl," Romero said.

Esteban jerked his head and stepped aside and the four men went in. There were half a dozen Horn Street Boys inside. The four men from Miami ignored them.

"I was just about to bring her over there," Esteban said.

"Over where?"

"To Florida," Esteban said. "And she run off."

"Where'd she go?"

"I don't know. Paradise, maybe," Esteban said. "That's where she lived with her old lady."

"Next town," Romero said.

"Yeah," Esteban said. "I didn't think she'd run off."

"But she did," Romero said.

"I did a good job on the old lady, didn't I?" Esteban said.

"And you got paid," Romero said. "Now we want the girl."

"I can take you over there," Esteban said. "Show you where she lived with her old lady."

Romero nodded.

"How about a guy named Cromartie, calls himself Crow?" Romero said.

"That sonovabitch," Esteban said.

"He in Paradise, too, you think?"

"Yeah, man," Esteban said. "He's there. Maybe got the girl, too. Okay with me you take the girl. But not Crow. I want him for myself."

Romero smiled.

"You think you can handle him?" Romero said.

"He killed one of us," Esteban said. "You kill a Horn Street Boy, you got to kill them all."

Romero shrugged.

"I don't care who kills him as long as somebody does. Mr. Francisco wants him dead."

"He pay somebody to do it?" Esteban said.

"You think we're up here for the hell of it?" Romero said.

"Maybe I get there first, I get the ten thousand."

"Ten thousand," Romero said.

"That's what I got for the old lady," Esteban said.

Romero nodded.

"That's what I was going to get for the girl," Esteban said. "Maybe still will, I get there first."

"Twenty grand," Romero said. "Set for life."

"You gotta problem with that?" Esteban said.

"I got a problem," Romero said, "you'll be the first to know."

"I got a right to that money," Esteban said.

Romero looked at him for a moment, then he shook his head and turned and went out. The other three men from Miami followed him.

45.

Jesse sat in his living room with Amber and Jenn. Jesse had scotch. Jenn had a glass of wine. Amber was drinking coffee. She was wearing the same clothes she'd come to the jail in, and the same tear-streaked eye makeup.

"I can drink booze," Amber said.

"Not with me," Jesse said.

Amber was looking around the condo.

"How long I gotta stay here?" she said.

"You don't have to stay here at all," Jesse said. "You can leave right now . . . but where you gonna go?"

"I could find someone to stay with," Amber said.

"You have someone to stay with," Jesse said.

"You?"

"Me."

"Why's she here," Amber said.

"Jenn and I used to be married," Jesse said. "She's come to help me with you."

"Why do you need help with me?" Amber said.

"Because you're a fourteen-year-old girl and there needs to be a woman here, too," Jesse said.

"Oh, man, are you drab."

"Drab," Jesse said.

"Who cares about who stays with who. Man, try being free, you know? Jesus."

"Jenn is a television reporter," Jesse said. "She's doing this in hopes of a story."

"Story about what," Amber said.

"About you," Jenn said. "And your parents. And the Horn Street Boys. And maybe the Crown estates project . . . like that."

"What the hell kind of story is that?" Amber said.

"We'll see," Jenn said. "I had some vacation time coming and the station gave me a couple weeks to see if there was a story."

"So am I gonna be on TV?" Amber said.

"We'll see," Jenn said.

"I don't want to go to my father," Amber said.

"Okay," Jesse said.

"And I don't want to go back to Esteban, the lying fuck."

"Okay there, too," Jesse said. "I've been talking to a friend who's a lawyer, and she's going to put me in touch with specialists in child custody and placement."

"Child custody? I'm not in fucking child custody," Amber said.

"Officer Molly Crane will be with you and Jenn much of the day," Jesse said to Amber. "I will be with you most of the rest of the time. Occasionally, one of the other cops may fill in. There will always be a police officer with you."

"So my old man won't get me," she said. "Or Esteban."

"Or anyone else," Jesse said.

"What about Crow?" Amber said.

"What about him?"

"Is he gonna be around?"

"Crow pretty much does what he wants to," Jesse said. "If I see him, I'll ask him."

"So what am I supposed to do all day while you're all watching me?"

"What would you like to do?" Jesse said.

"I don't know."

"There's a start," Jesse said. "How about taking a shower?"

"Here?"

"Yes."

"I got no clean clothes," Amber said.

"Tomorrow you and Jenn and Molly can go buy some. Meanwhile, you can wear one of my shirts for a nightie."

"What should I do with my other clothes?"

"We could burn them in the fireplace," Jesse said.

"Throw them out of the bathroom," Jenn said. "I'll put them through the washer."

"Another thing we have to consider," Jesse said. "Jenn will be in my bedroom. Amber will be in the guest room. I will be on the couch. There is one bathroom."

"So?" Amber said.

"So keep it in mind," Jesse said.

"How come you and her don't sleep together?" Amber said.

"Too drab," Jesse said.

46.

Suitcase Simpson came into Jesse's office and closed the door and sat down in a chair facing Jesse. His face was red, and he seemed to be looking steadily at the top of Jesse's desk.

Jesse waited.

Suit didn't say anything.

Jesse waited.

"I'm having sex with an older woman," Suit said.

"Miriam Fiedler," Jesse said.

Suit raised his eyes.

"How'd you know that?" he said.

Jesse shrugged.

"I'm the chief of police," Jesse said.

"Molly told you," Suit said.

"No," Jesse said. "She didn't."

Suit looked back at the desktop.

"Suit," Jesse said. "Mostly, I don't care what you do with your dick when you're off duty."

"I know," Suit said.

"So?"

"So she's asking me a bunch of questions," Suit said.

"About?"

"You, the department, the Crown estate deal," Suit said.

"Like what?"

"Were you a good cop," Suit said. "Did I think you'd ever take a bribe? Did you have a relationship with Nina Pinero? Was it true you were fired in L.A.? What's going on with you and Jenn? She wanted to know anything I knew about the murder. Did I think there was any Hispanic involvement?"

"Concerned citizen," Jesse said.

"I figured you should know."

Jesse nodded.

"She is very committed to this problem," he said.

"She is," Suit said.

"Why?" Jesse said.

"Real-estate values?"

Jesse shrugged.

"Maybe," he said. "Seems awful important to her."

"You think there might be something more?"

"Maybe," Jesse said. "How's she compare to Mrs. Hathaway?"

Suit reddened again.

"Come on, Jesse."

"No kiss-and-tell?" Jesse said.

"Or whatever," Suit said.

"Good boy," Jesse said.

"Miriam says so, too," Suit said. "Want me to break it off?"

Jesse shook his head.

"I'd like you to stay with it," Jesse said.

Suit grinned.

"Undercover, so to speak," he said.

"So to speak," Jesse said. "See what else you can learn."

Suit grinned again.

"Tough dirty work..." Suit said.

Jesse nodded.

"But somebody's got to do it," he said.

47.

Romero was driving. Esteban was beside him. Two men from Miami were in the backseat, and Larson was way back in the third seat.

"Cromartie lives someplace called Strawberry Cove," Romero said.

"In Paradise?" Esteban said.

"Yeah. You know where that is?"

Esteban shook his head. Romero shrugged and reached his hand back over the seat. One of the men from Miami opened a briefcase and took out a sheet of paper. Romero looked at it.

"Off Breaker Avenue," he said to Esteban. "You know where that is?"

"No," Esteban said. "How you guys know this?"

"We checked," Romero said. "You think we just jumped on a plane and come up here to mill around?"

"But how did you check?" Esteban said. "Ain't it a long way?"

"The town paper prints a summary of the week's real-estate transactions every Thursday."

"You can get the Paradise paper over there?" Esteban said.

"We got people to do it for us," Romero said.

He punched the navigation system that came with the car, and in a moment the directions came up. Esteban stared at it.

"How far you been from Horn Street, kid?" Romero asked.

"I ain't no kid," Esteban said. "I'm twenty years old, man."

"How far you been?"

"Got no reason to go far," Esteban said. "Got all I need right there. Got my boys. Got pussy, beer, wheeze. Nobody fucks with us. Got no reason to leave."

"Ever kill anybody, Esteban?" Romero said.

"Hey, man, I just scragged the old lady a little while ago, you know that."

"Ever kill anybody who could kill you?" Romero said.

"Shit, man, what are you saying? I kill anybody needs to be killed, man. I ain't scared."

"You recognize Cromartie if you see him?"

"I'll recognize the cocksucker."

"Good," Romero said. "You see him, you tell me."

"You gonna kill him?"

"Yes," Romero said. "We are."

"You don't know what he looks like?" Esteban said.

"I do," Romero said.

"I can show you where little hot pants lives, too," Esteban said.

"Name's Amber," Romero said. "I don't think Mr. Francisco would like it to have you call her 'hot pants.'"

"Fuck him," Esteban said. "I say what I want."

Romero nodded.

"I don't much like it, either," Romero said.

"So fuck you, too," Esteban said. "You think I'm scared of you?"

From the backseat one of the men from Miami caught Romero's eye in the rearview mirror and made a shooting gesture with his forefinger and thumb at Esteban. Romero shook his head.

"Well," Romero said to Esteban, "you probably know what you're talking about."

"You got that right, man," Esteban said. "*Hot...Pants!* You want to see where she lives?"

"Be easier to take her to Miami," Romero said, "if we kill Crow first."

"Sure," Romero said, and turned left onto Breaker Avenue.

The men in the Escalade had no expectation of being followed, so it was easy enough for Crow to keep them in sight. When they took the turn onto Breaker Avenue, Crow smiled. He knew where they were going. When the Escalade parked in front of his condo, Crow drove on past them and turned left, away from the water, onto a side street a hundred yards up the road, and parked.

It was a condo neighborhood. No kids. Everyone working. The stillness was palpable. Crow got out of the car, walked to the corner of the street, leaned on a tall blue mail-deposit box, and looked back down toward his condo. The five men from the Escalade had gotten out and were standing on the small lawn in front of the four-unit building. Crow's unit was first floor left. The men spread out as they walked toward the door. Each had a handgun out, holding it inconspicuously down. *Pros,* Crow thought. *Not scared of much. Don't care if somebody sees them. Nobody home in the neighborhood anyway.*

The squat man with the bald head rang Crow's doorbell. The men waited. The bald man rang again. Then he looked at the tall man with the graying hair. The tall man said something and the bald man stepped back and kicked the door. It gave but not enough. He kicked it again and they were in.

Crow went back to his car, opened the trunk, selected a bolt-action Ruger rifle, and left the trunk ajar. He didn't check the load. He knew it was loaded. His weapons were always loaded. Crow saw no point to empty guns. Carrying the Ruger, Crow went back to the mailbox and rested the rifle on top of it. There were a couple of late-summer butterflies drifting about. And a dragonfly. Nothing else moved. In perhaps three minutes, the men filed out of Crow's broken front door. Their handguns were no longer visible. They headed for the Escalade.

Carefully, Crow rested his front elbow on the mailbox and sighted the Ruger in on the bald man. *One's as good as another,* Crow thought. *Except Romero. Romero was the stud.* If he killed Romero the rest of them would go home. He took a breath, let it out, took up the trigger slack, and shot the bald man in the center of his chest. Then he went to his car, put the rifle into the trunk, latched the trunk, got in the front seat, and drove away. *Besides,* Crow said to himself, *he had the ugliest shirt.*

In front of the condo the men were crouched behind the Escalade. They had their guns out.

"Anyone see where it came from?" Romero said.

No one had. After a moment, Romero stood and walked to where Larson lay. He squatted and put his hand on Larson's neck. Then he stood and walked back to the Escalade.

"Let's go," he said.

They got in and drove away, leaving Larson quiet on the front lawn.

48.

They were all in the squad room, except Molly, who was with Amber, and Arthur, who was on the desk. There was coffee, and an open box of donuts. Jesse sat at the far end of the conference table.

"We're all on call now, all the time, until this thing shakes out," Jesse said. "I'll try to get you enough sleep. But if I can't, I can't."

No one spoke.

"Here's what we know," Jesse said. "The vic is a guy named Rico Larson. His driver's license says he lives in Miami. He was carrying a Glock nine when he was killed by one bullet from a .350 rifle. The shot probably came from about a hundred yards down the road and across the street. He was shot in front of a condominium town house rented by Wilson Cromartie."

Suitcase Simpson reached across the table for a donut.

"Crow," he said.

Jesse nodded.

"Everybody in that neighborhood works during the day," Jesse said. "No one saw anything. No one heard a shot."

"We got a theory of the crime?" Peter Perkins asked.

"Guy in Miami," Jesse said, "his wife ran away, took his daughter with her. Guy in Miami—name's Francisco—hired Crow to find them. So Crow found them . . . here. Daughter's got a boyfriend in Marshport, gang kid named Esteban Carty. Crow calls up Francisco, says, 'I found them, what do I do now?' Francisco says, 'Kill the mother, bring back the daughter.' Crow says, 'No.' This much I get from Crow, and it's probably true."

"You been talking to Crow?" Buddy Hall said.

"Yes."

"How come he didn't do what the Miami guy wanted?"

"Crow says he likes women," Jesse said. "And besides, he didn't feel like it."

"You believe that?" Cox said.

"I believe he didn't do it," Jesse said.

"So how about the mother," Cox said. "Did he kill her?"

"Crow? I don't think so. He says it was probably the gang kid, Esteban."

"That make any sense?" Peter Perkins said.

"Esteban made a deal to turn her over to her father," Jesse said. "Maybe he made a deal to kill the mother, too."

"Girl say that?"

"Nope."

"Wouldn't she rat out the guy that killed her mother?" Cox said.

"She didn't like her mother," Jesse said.

These were small-town guys, most of them not very old, Jesse knew, most of them very conventional. The idea that you wouldn't like your mother was hard for them. No one said anything.

"She doesn't like her father, either," Jesse said. "That's why she ran away when she found out Esteban was going to take her down there."

"She come here?" Peter Perkins said.

"Crow brought her in," Jesse said.

"Crow?" Cox said. "What is it with Crow?"

Jesse shook his head.

"What about this guy in Miami?" Paul Murphy said. "He a bad guy?"

"Big player in the South Florida rackets," Jesse said.

"So who's the dead guy?" Murphy said.

"Now, it's all theory," Jesse said. "I figure that Francisco sent him up to kill Crow, and bring the girl home."

"You think he came alone?"

"No one would send one guy after Crow," Jesse said. "Besides, there's no car. How did he get there?"

"You think Crow shot him?"

"Probably," Jesse said.

"And the other guys split," Murphy said.

"Yep."

"If Crow's as good as everybody thinks he is," Murphy said, "how come he didn't get more than one?"

Jesse was quiet for a moment, thinking about Crow.

Then he said, "Maybe he didn't want to."

"That's crazy," Peter Perkins said.

"Crow's not like other people," Jesse said. "Suit, you go down to my house and stay with Molly and the kid. I'll relieve you later. Everyone else, shotguns in every car, cleaned, loaded, no plastic daisies in the barrel. Extra ammo in every car, shotgun and handgun. Vests with you at all times."

"Jesus, Jesse," Suit said. "It sounds like you're expecting a war."

"Always possible," Jesse said.

49.

Jesse sat with Jenn on the balcony outside his living room and looked at the harbor as it got dark. Amber was standing in the doorway drinking coffee. She had on tan shorts and a powder-blue T-shirt and too much makeup, but she was, Jesse thought, beginning to look a little less like a punk cliché.

"Have you done any research on the Crowne estate?" Jesse said.

He was sipping scotch. Jenn had a glass of Riesling.

"You mean the estate itself?" Jenn said.

"Yeah."

"No, you think I should?"

"Yes."

"Because?"

"Because you can and I don't have the resources," Jesse said.

"Why do you think it needs to be researched?" Jenn said.

"I think Miriam Fiedler's interest in the issue is too large," Jesse said.

"Explain," Jenn said.

"Suit says she's asking questions about me, and the department, and the murder, and can I be bribed."

"Suit?" Amber said. "The guy that was here with me and Molly?"

"Yes," Jesse said.

"Why would Miriam Fiedler be asking Suit questions?" Jenn said.

Jesse smiled. Jenn looked at him.

"Why?" Jenn said.

"Remember what I told you about Cissy Hathaway?" Jesse said. "Suit likes older women."

"Suit and Miriam Fiedler?" Jenn said.

"Suit's fucking somebody?" Amber said from the doorway.

"Well put," Jesse said.

"So maybe this Miriam Fiddler or whatever is fucking him so he'll tell her stuff," Amber said.

"Maybe," Jesse said.

"So," Amber said, "big deal. It happens all the time."

"You think?" Jesse said.

"How else do you get anything?" Amber said.

"Sometimes women have sex with men because they like them," Jenn said. "Even sometimes because they love them."

"Yeah, you bet," Amber said. "You like him?"

She nodded at Jesse.

"Yes," Jenn said. "I probably love him."

"So how come you don't fuck him?"

"Right now it doesn't seem like a good idea," Jenn said.

"So you like him, but you won't fuck him. And you love him but you're divorced."

"That's about right," Jenn said.

"You ever fuck some guy to get what you want?" Amber said.

"Yes," Jenn said.

"See?" Amber said. "No big deal."

"It is a big deal," Jenn said. "Because every time you do it you feel weak and worthless."

"Maybe you do," Amber said. "Not me."

"You will," Jenn said. "It's cumulative."

"Huh?"

"The more of it you do," Jenn said, "the more you feel bad."

"I like it," Amber said. "When I'm balling a guy, I'm in charge, you know?"

"Like Esteban," Jesse said.

Amber didn't say anything for a moment. Then her eyes filled, and she turned and went through the living room to her bedroom.

"You hurt her feelings," Jenn said.

"Esteban hurt her feelings," Jesse said.

"And you reminded her of it."

"She can't be lying to herself," Jesse said. "How is that good for her?"

"Maybe she has so little else," Jenn said. "You ever see *The Ice Man Cometh?*"

"No."

Jenn shrugged.

"Doesn't matter," she said.

"My parenting skills are limited," Jesse said. "But I'm pretty sure the truth is good."

"Maybe it's not always," Jenn said.

"Maybe it isn't," Jesse said. "But I'm not too sure about lying, either."

"I know."

They were silent. Jesse sipped his scotch. Jenn stared out at the harbor, where the darkness had thickened enough so that the lights on some of the yachts were showing.

"I can check the legal stuff about the Crowne estate," Jenn said. "Deed, title, whatever. Hell, I can probably get an intern to do that."

"Might be useful," Jesse said.

"I'll see what I can find out," Jenn said. "Now I'm going in to the bedroom and pat Amber on the shoulder for a little bit."

"Maternal impulse?" Jesse said.

"Damned if I know," Jenn said, and went inside.

Jesse put his feet up on the railing and looked at the harbor. Across it the lights were going on in houses along Paradise Neck. Suppers were being cooked. Spouses were having a cocktail together while it cooked. Jesse looked at his moisture-beaded glass. He liked the look of it with the dark gold booze and the translucent silver ice. Still half-full. And he could have another if he wished. Two drinks was reasonable. And after the two drinks, he and Jenn and maybe Amber would have supper in a not distasteful caricature of the lives being lived across the harbor.

I wonder how much Crow drinks, Jesse thought.

50.

"It was Crow," Francisco said on the phone.

"I didn't see him," Romero said.

"It was Crow," Francisco said. "Forget about him. Get Amber and bring her home."

"He killed Larson," Romero said.

"There's a million other Larsons," Francisco said. "Bring the kid home."

"I don't like having some guy shoot one of my people and walk away," Romero said.

"I don't give a fuck what you like. Farm Crow out to the local gangbangers. Bring the kid home now."

"How much to the gangbangers?" Romero said.

"Ten, same as if they brought the kid home."

"Ten?" Romero said. "To kill Crow?"

"That's more money than they can even count," Francisco said. "How many are there?"

"Maybe a dozen," Romero said.

"So if Crow kills a few, no sweat," Francisco said. "Still plenty left to do the job."

"Ten grand," Romero said.

"And they'll be happy to get it," Francisco said. "Turn Crow over to them. Bring the kid home. We got a lot of business to do down here."

"Okay, Lou," Romero said.

The phone went dead. Romero folded his cell phone and slid it back in his pants pocket. He looked at the other two men, Bobby Chacon and a guy named Mongo Estella, for whom Bobby had to translate.

"We give the Crow hit to Esteban," Romero said to Bobby. "And bring the girl home."

"We know where the girl is?" Bobby said.

"No," Romero said.

Bobby nodded and spoke to Mongo in Spanish. Romero started the Escalade.

"First thing," Romero said, "we make the deal with Esteban and his people."

"You think they good enough?" Bobby said.

"No. But they are maybe crazy enough. Crazy might work better than good, with Crow."

Bobby nodded.

Stranger in Paradise

Driving carefully behind them, Crow was cautious. They would be looking for him now. But the Escalade was big and uncommon on the streets of Marshport, and Crow stayed with them easily enough. He was driving a grayish-beige Toyota, of which there were usually three or four in sight at all times. At Horn Street, the Escalade parked. Two of the men got out and walked down the alley. Crow turned right and then left and parked on a parallel street where he could see the Escalade through a parking lot. In ten minutes the two men came out onto Horn Street and got into the Escalade and drove east. Crow drove parallel for a couple of blocks and then swung up onto the same street several cars behind them. He followed them for a while and then turned off left, took the next right, followed them in a rough parallel course until he passed them and turned back to their street, coming out ahead of them. He drove ahead of them, watching them in the mirror until they turned off. Then he U-turned and fell in behind them on the road to Paradise.

The Escalade parked on Sewall Street, near the house where Fiona Francisco had lived. Crow parked up on Washington Street where he could see them. The same two men got out and went to the house. The front door was locked. There was a lot of foot traffic. After a moment the two men walked around the house and Crow couldn't see them. He waited. After about fifteen minutes the two men came back and got into the Escalade. The big car drove down Sewall Street and parked on the wharf outside the Gray Gull. All three men got out and went into the restaurant. Crow drove in and parked at the far end of the wharf.

Crow sat and looked at the restaurant, and in a short while the three men appeared on the outside deck and sat at a table. Crow sank a little lower in the front seat of his car so that he could just see through the steering wheel. They had a drink. They read the menus. Crow studied them. Why had they gone to the house? Were they looking for him? No. They wouldn't look for him there. They were looking for the girl. If they found her, they'd take her straight to Miami. So who was going to kill him? Francisco would not let it slide. It wasn't how he worked. No one was allowed to cross him.

Crow sat in his car and watched the men drink and eat on the deck. He could probably step out of the car and kill all three of them . . . too easy. Crow wanted the war to evolve a little. Such a good opportunity, though. He got out and walked between the parked cars to the near edge of the wharf. Across about ten feet of harbor water he fired one shot and hit Mongo in the back of the head. Mongo pitched forward onto the table. The tableware scattered. Romero and Bobby Chacon hit the floor behind the table, fumbling for weapons as they went down. By the time they got them out and squirmed into a position to see, Crow was gone.

51.

"Another guy from Miami," Suit said.

He handed Mongo's driver's license to Jesse.

"Carrying a forty-caliber semiautomatic," Suit said. "Full magazine. Got a room key, too. Marshport Lodge."

"Molly," Jesse said. "Get the Marshport cops. Give them the room-key info, see what they can find."

"Armed and dangerous?" Molly said.

"You might mention that," Jesse said.

Molly went to one of the cruisers.

"Witnesses?" Jesse said to Suit.

"Lot of them," Suit said. "Nobody knows what happened. Three guys came in, sat down, ordered lunch. They're eating lunch, there's a shot. Nobody knows from where. Nobody saw the shooter. The other two guys hit the floor, they have guns. After a minute they get up and run from the restaurant."

"Car?" Jesse said.

"Nobody dared look," Suit said.

Jesse stood looking down at Mongo's body sprawled across the table.

"Shot had to come from the wharf," Jesse said. "No place else a guy could stand and hit him in the back of the head."

"Unless it was another long rifle shot," Suit said.

"Most people on a long shot don't aim for the head," Jesse said.

"Unless it was a lousy shot that worked out," Suit said.

"ME will tell us what kind of bullet," Jesse said. "Meanwhile, I'm sticking with the wharf."

Suit nodded. Jesse went out the restaurant and across the little gangway to the wharf and walked over so he was standing where he figured the shooter had stood. Suit walked with him.

"You think it was Crow?" Suit said.

"Yes."

"Can we prove it?"

"Not yet," Jesse said.

Suit was silent. They both looked at the corpse on the deck. It was an easy shot.

"You told me Crow could really shoot," Suit said.

"He's as good as I am," Jesse said.

"Wow!" Suit said.

Jesse smiled slightly.

"Right answer," he said.

"So a good shot," Suit said. "Standing here. Probably using a semiautomatic with ten, fifteen rounds in it. Why didn't he kill them all?"

"I don't know," Jesse said.

They stood again in silence, looking at the crime scene. The ME's truck had arrived. Peter Perkins had finished taking his pictures and was packing up his equipment. Arthur Angstrom was keeping the sightseers at bay behind some yellow tape. Molly and Eddie Cox were still talking to a huddle of restaurant workers and patrons and learning nothing.

"It wouldn't be conscience," Suit said.

Jesse smiled.

"No," he said. "It wouldn't be conscience."

52.

Marshport police headquarters was in a nineteenth-century brick and brownstone building with an arched entrance-way that looked like it might be a library, or a school. Jesse sat in the basement in a blank interrogation room with yellow walls, with a Marshport detective named Concannon, and an Essex County assistant DA named Tremaine. Concannon was a big, hard-looking man with black curly hair and a handlebar mustache. There was a small white scar across the bridge of his nose. Tremaine had short, thick hair with blond highlights, and big, round tinted glasses. Jesse thought her legs were good.

With them was Bobby Chacon.

"We got him with an unlicensed handgun," Concannon said.

"And we called Florida," Tremaine said, "and, to our amazement, we find that Bobby has two previous convictions."

"So this would make strike three," Jesse said.

"If it were a violent felony," Chacon said.

Nobody said anything.

"It's a simple gun possession," Chacon said. "Throw the book at me, I get maybe a year."

"It could be more serious," Tremaine said.

"Yeah? How?"

"We might find a way to up the stakes a little," Concannon said.

"I heard he actually fired at you when you were attempting to place him under arrest," Jesse said.

Concannon nodded.

"That would crank everything up some," Tremaine said.

"That's a fucking lie," Chacon said. "Excuse my language, ma'am."

"And cursing in front of a ladylike ADA," Tremaine said. "That must be some kind of fucking crime. Right?"

"It don't help none," Concannon said.

"I didn't resist no arrest," Chacon said.

"You know a guy named Larson?" Jesse said.

"Nope."

"He's from Miami, too," Jesse said.

"Big city," Chacon said.

"And he was registered at the same motel you were, next room."

"Don't know him," Chacon said.

"How about Estella?" Concannon said.

"Nope."

"That's odd," Tremaine said. "He was registered to the same room you were."

"Must be a mistake at the front desk," Chacon said.

"Guy named Romero shared the room with Larson," Tremaine said. "Know him?"

Chacon leaned back and tried to look contemplative. Then he shook his head.

"Nope," he said. "Sorry. Don't recognize the name."

Tremaine stood.

"I'm tired of this," she said. "He says something worth hearing, let me know."

She left the room. Chacon watched her go.

"Nice ass," he said.

Concannon slapped him hard across the face.

"Respect," Concannon said.

As soon as the door closed behind Tremaine, it opened again and a tall, fat cop with a shaved head and a roll of fat over the back of his collar came in and stood against the wall behind Chacon.

"I want a lawyer," Chacon said.

"Sure thing," Concannon said. "Your constitutional right. Usually takes a while to arrange, though. Probably won't get here until after you try to make a break for it, and end up falling down a long flight of stairs."

"You don't scare me," Chacon said.

"Not yet," Concannon said.

He took a pair of black leather gloves out of his hip pocket and began to inch one of them onto his left hand.

"You want to go outside, Chief Stone," Concannon said. "Sometimes small-town cops get a little queasy."

Jesse stood up.

"Look, Bobby," he said. "You can help us out here and we can probably look the other way on the gun charge." Jesse looked at Concannon, who shrugged. "Otherwise we'll frame you for something that'll put you away for life."

Chacon stared at Jesse.

"You say it right out?"

"Yes," Jesse said, "that's how it's going to go. I stay here, you tell me what's been going on. Or I leave and you get framed and fall down a long flight of stairs. It's why the ADA went out. She knows how it's going to go. She doesn't mind the frame job, but she don't like the stairs much."

Chacon gave Jesse a dead-eyed stare. Jesse shrugged and started for the door. Concannon was wiggling his right hand into the second glove.

"Okay," Chacon said. "I'll tell you some things."

53.

Suit was outside Jesse's condo in a squad car. Molly was inside, reading *The New York Times*. Amber sat crosslegged on the floor in front of the television, watching an inside Hollywood show on E! Amber was bored. She shifted her position, fiddled with her hair, yawned loudly.

"You married?" she said to Molly.

"Yes."

"What's your old man do?"

"My husband builds boats," Molly said.

"Any money in that?" Amber said.

"Some."

"So how come you work?"

"I like to work," Molly said.

"As a cop?" Amber said.

"I like being a cop," Molly said.

Amber shook her head sadly.

"You got kids?"

"Four," Molly said.

"Any daughters?"

"One," Molly said.

"You ever fool around?"

"You mean like sex?" Molly said.

"Like, duh?" Amber said. "Of course sex."

"Might be none of your business," Molly said.

Amber shrugged.

"So did ya?" she said.

Molly thought for a moment about the way Crow seemed to look through her clothes. She felt her face flush slightly.

"You did, didn't you?" Amber said.

"No," Molly said. "I have never cheated on my husband."

"Why not?" Amber said. "Doesn't it get boring doing it with the same guy every day?"

Molly smiled.

"When you've been married fourteen years, and you both work, and you got four kids, it's not every day," Molly said.

"Man, you're as drab as Jesse," Amber said. "You have any fun before you got married?"

"I got married pretty early," Molly said.

"Jesus," Amber said. "Tell me you weren't a freaking virgin."

"No," Molly said. "I wasn't a virgin."

"Christ, I hope not," Amber said. "You think you might fool around sometime?"

"I have no long-range plan," Molly said. "I'm pretty sure I won't fool around today."

Amber looked at the big picture of Ozzie Smith behind the bar.

"Who's the black guy?" Amber said.

"That's Ozzie Smith," Molly said. "He's in the Baseball Hall of Fame."

"So why's his picture here?"

"I guess Jesse admires him," Molly said.

"How come?"

"Jesse used to be a ballplayer," Molly said. "He was a shortstop, like Ozzie."

"Jesse played baseball?"

"In the minor leagues," Molly said. "He hurt his shoulder and had to stop."

"Bummer," Amber said. "And he ends up a cop."

"I think he likes being a cop," Molly said.

"How come?"

"He's good at it," Molly said.

"That's all?"

"That's enough," Molly said.

"Is that why you like it?"

"Yeah," Molly said. "Yeah, it is."

They were quiet for a time. The gossip program gurgled on.

"Must be why I like screwing," Amber said.

"Because you're good at it?" Molly said.

"The best," Amber said.

"My husband always says the worst sex he ever had was great," Molly said.

"What's that mean?"

"Maybe everybody's good at it," Molly said.

Amber was silent for a time. Then she shrugged.

"What's the difference," she said.

54.

Crow came into Jesse's office and sat down.

"Things happening in town," he said.

"All of them since you arrived," Jesse said.

"Think of me as a catalyst for change," Crow said.

"Or the Grim Reaper," Jesse said.

Crow smiled.

"You're not living in your house," Jesse said.

"Apache warriors can live off the land," Crow said.

"What do you do for food?" Jesse said.

"Room service," Crow said.

"Hardscrabble," Jesse said.

Crow nodded.

"Some people in here from Miami," Crow said.

"Fewer than there were," Jesse said.

"They're from Francisco," Crow said. "They supposed to kill me and take the girl home. But I think they handed me off to the Horn Street Boys, so they can concentrate on the girl."

"That's right," Jesse said.

"You know something," Crow said.

"We arrested Bobby Chacon," Jesse said, "and he talked to us."

"So that leaves Romero," Crow said.

"You know him?"

"Yes," Crow said.

"Think he'll try for the girl himself?" Jesse said.

"He's good enough," Crow said.

"But?"

"But he knows I'm around," Crow said. "And he has to assume once you got Chacon that he'd blab sooner or later."

"So you think he won't," Jesse said.

"He's got the balls for it," Crow said. "But I think he's a smart guy. Like you and me. He knows what he's doing. And right now, he's trying to do a job, and I think he'll wait until the odds are better."

"We checked the Miami flights," Jesse said. "He was on one two hours after Marshport busted Bobby Chacon."

Crow nodded.

"You think he'll be back?" Jesse said.

Crow nodded.

"And I think Louis Francisco will come back with him and I think he'll bring a lot of troops," Crow said.

"Francisco gets what he wants," Jesse said.

"He does," Crow said. "And right now he wants his daughter."

"How about you?"

"After the daughter."

"We'll keep an eye on the inbound flights from Miami," Jesse said.

"He won't come commercial. He's got his own plane."

"What kind?"

"Big one," Crow said.

"Like a commercial jet?"

"Yeah."

"We'll check where he might land," Jesse said.

"Francisco has a lot of resources," Crow said. "He's the real deal. If you had a team of bad guys, Francisco would hit fourth."

Jesse nodded.

"He's got all the money he needs. He's got no fear, and no feelings," Crow said. "I think the daughter thing is mostly about ego."

"You don't think he loves her?" Jesse said.

"I don't think he can," Crow said.

"Well," Jesse said after a moment of silence, "you're right about the Horn Street Boys. Chacon says they picked up your contract."

Crow grinned.

"How much?" he said.

"Chacon says ten grand."

"Ten?" Crow said.

Jesse nodded.

"That what they got for bagging the kid's mother?" Crow said.

"I believe so."

"Lot of money to those kids," Crow said.

"And they're mad at you for shooting Puerco," Jesse said.

"It was nothing personal," Crow said.

Jesse nodded slowly.

"It never is," he said. "Is it?"

Crow shrugged.

"Just thought I'd give you a heads-up," he said.

"Public-spirited citizens," Jesse said, "are our best defense against crime."

"Exactly right," Crow said.

55.

It was 6:30 in the evening when Jesse got home. Suit saw him start up the stairs to the condo. He waved, Jesse waved back, Suit pulled the cruiser out of the parking slot and drove away.

Fast shift change, Jesse thought. *Probably headed for a tryst with Miriam Fiedler.* When he went into his apartment, Amber was lying on her stomach watching some kind of reality show where husbands and wives fought with each other. When she heard the door open, Molly appeared at the kitchen door. She had a dish towel tucked into her belt.

"Nice look," Jesse said. "Is that like an apron?"

"You and Jenn don't cook," Molly said. "And I got bored. So I made you a casserole."

"Is it any good?" Jesse said.

"I'm of Irish Catholic heritage," Molly said.

"Oh, well," Jesse said.

Without taking her eyes from the television battle, Amber said, "What kind of casserole?"

"American chop suey," Molly said.

"Ick," Amber said. "What's that made of."

"Macaroni and stuff," Jesse said. "If you don't like it we'll make you a sandwich."

"I want peanut butter," Amber said. "And a Coke."

"Sure," Jesse said.

When Jenn arrived, Molly left. Jesse and Jenn took their drinks out onto the balcony and sat together. Amber hung around sometimes with them, sometimes in the living room with the door open. Partly with them, partly not. Jesse thought they could probably chart Amber's feelings about them by her proximity to the balcony.

"I've found out some things," Jenn said.

Jesse nodded. It had become domestic, coming home from work, having a drink before dinner with Jenn. Kid lingering near them. Sleeping on the couch, on the other hand, was not so domestic.

"The title to the Crowne estate is a little complicated," Jenn said.

"Uh-huh."

"The estate was originally built by a man named Herschel Crowne," Jenn said. "When he died it was left to his son, Archibald Crowne. At his death, Archibald left it in trust for the benefit of some disadvantaged children from Marshport."

Jenn paused.

Always dramatic.

"Being the ones now using the facility," Jesse said.

Jenn nodded.

"However, in the event that there was no use to which it could be put on behalf of these disadvantaged children, it would pass on to his only heir, his daughter, Miriam Crowne...who is married to a man named Alex Fiedler."

"Aha," Jesse said. "Miriam Fiedler."

"So maybe her motives aren't so pure," Jenn said.

"The motives she admitted to aren't so pure," Jesse said. "Know anything about Mr. Fiedler?"

"He apparently travels much of the time," Jenn said.

"Works out good for Suit," Jesse said.

"What works out for Suit," Amber said from the living room. "What are you all talking about out there?"

"The woman who owns the Crowne estate," Jesse said. "She would benefit if the kids from Marshport didn't go there."

"What about Suit?"

"Private joke," Jesse said.

"How come you won't tell me?" Amber said. "I know Suit. He's one of the cops sits outside when you're not here."

"I don't want to tell you," Jesse said.

"Then don't," Amber said. "I don't care."

"You know how much the Crowne estate is worth?" Jesse said to Jenn.

"A real-estate appraiser says eight to ten million."

"How about the Fiedlers?" Jesse said. "You know how much they're worth?"

"No, you think it matters?"

"Might. If they're worth a hundred million, the estate would be a drop in the bucket. If they're worth a hundred and fifty thousand, it would be something else."

"I just assumed they were rich," Jenn said.

"They seem rich," Jesse said. "Why does Mr. Fiedler travel?"

In the living room, Amber focused deeply on the television set.

"Haven't found out yet," Jenn said.

"Maybe Suit can find out," Jesse said.

"The undercover man," Jenn said, and smiled.

In the living room sprawled on the floor in front of the television Amber was silent, showing in every way she could how little she cared about the conversation.

56.

Molly lived close enough that she could walk to her home from Jesse's condo. It was raining gently and darker than usual for the time of day in late summer. She had put a kerchief over her hair and wore a light yellow raincoat over her uniform. As she turned onto Munroe Street, Crow fell in beside her.

"Evening," he said.

"Hello."

"Who's minding the kids?" Crow said.

"My mother," Molly said. "My husband is in Newport."

Why did I say that?

"Why?" Crow said.

"A boat he built got damaged in a storm," Molly said. "The owner won't let anyone else work on it."

"Good at his work," Crow said.

"Yes."

Crow nodded. They passed the head of the wharf.

"Got time for a drink?" Crow said.

Molly paused. She felt it in her stomach and along her spine. She looked at her watch.

"Sure," she said, and they turned onto the wharf and walked down to the Gray Gull.

"Bar or table?" Crow said.

"Damn," Molly said. "I'm in uniform."

"Leave the raincoat on," Crow said. "Who will know."

Molly nodded.

"Table," she said.

Crow nodded and pointed at a table, and the young woman doing hostess duty led them to it. Molly ordered a vodka gimlet; Crow had Maker's Mark on the rocks.

"How many kids have you?" Crow said.

"Four."

"They okay?"

"Sometimes I think no kids are okay, but they're as okay as anyone else's kids."

"Husband?"

"It's a good marriage," Molly said.

So what am I doing here?

"How's the Francisco kid?"

"A mess," Molly said. "If she were mine, I wouldn't know where to start."

"If she were yours," Crow said, "she'd be different."

Molly nodded.

"Probably," Molly said. "You married?"

"I'm not here to talk about me," Crow said.

"Even if I want to?"

"I don't talk about me," Crow said.

"So . . ." Molly paused.

Do I want to go this way?

"So," Molly started again. "What are we here to talk about?"

Crow smiled.

"Sex," he said.

She felt herself clench for a moment and release.

This is crazy. The man is a stone killer.

"What aspect of sex did you have in mind?" Molly said.

"You and me, once, no strings," Crow said.

Molly met his gaze. They were silent for a moment.

Then Molly said, "Why?"

"We both want to," Crow said.

"You're so sure of me?" Molly said.

"Yes."

"How can you know?"

Crow grinned at her.

"It's an Apache thing," he said.

"And my husband?"

"You'll continue to love him, and the kids," Crow said.

Molly sipped her gimlet.

My God!

"You ever sleep with an Indian?" Crow said.

"No."

Crow grinned again.

"And I never slept with a cop," he said.

"And would we do this where?" Molly said. "Behind the lobster pots? In the car?"

"Sea Spray Inn," Crow said. "I have a suite."

Molly nodded.

"Would you like to have dinner and think about it?" Crow said.

Molly shook her head slowly. She was aware of her breathing. Aware of her pulse. Looking straight at Crow, she took a long, slow breath. She let it out slowly. Then she smiled.

"I prefer to eat afterwards," she said.

Crow nodded. He took a hundred-dollar bill from his pocket and put it on the table. Then they stood up and left.

57.

Jesse was drinking coffee at his desk at 7:30 in the morning when Healy came in.

"I thought when you made captain you didn't have to get up so early," Jesse said.

"By the time you make captain," Healy said, "you been getting up early for so long, you can't change the habit."

He poured himself some coffee and sat down across the desk from Jesse.

"Solve any homicides recently?" Healy said.

"No," Jesse said.

"Me either," Healy said. "I had one of our accounting guys look into the Fiedlers' financial situation for you."

"And?"

"They have a net worth of two hundred eighty-eight thousand dollars," Healy said.

"Including their house?" Jesse said. "Their house must be worth three million."

"Almost none of it equity," Healy said. "There's two mortgages on it."

"They are supposed to be one of the wealthiest families in town," Jesse said.

"I remembered you telling me that," Healy said. "So I told the accountant to poke around a little. According to what he got from the IRS and God knows where else, the accountant says that ten years ago they had a net worth in the area of fifty million."

"What happened to it?"

"Don't know," Healy said. "Don't know if they hid it, or spent it, or lost it. What I know is what the accountant told me. They got a net worth lower than mine."

"Low," Jesse said.

Healy nodded.

"How you doing with your crime wave," Healy said.

"Badly."

"Any other help you want from the Massachusetts State Police?"

"I'm doing so badly," Jesse said, "I don't even know what help to ask for."

"Your man Crow involved in any of this?" Healy said.

"When did he become my man?" Jesse said.

"He's not mine," Healy said.

"Lucky you," Jesse said. "Sure he's involved. But I can't prove it . . . yet."

"Where do the Fiedlers come in?" Healy said.

"I don't know," Jesse said.

"But you wanted to know their finances," Healy said.

"Mrs. Fiedler seems so committed to stalling that school project," Jesse said. "I kind of wondered why."

"And her finances tell you?"

"Her maiden name was Crowne," Jesse said. "The property belonged to her father. He left it to charity, but if the charity doesn't use it, it goes to her."

"And it's worth a lot of money," Healy said.

"Ten million," Jesse said.

Healy nodded.

"If you got fifty million, another ten is nice but not crucial," Healy said. "However, if you're down to your last three hundred thousand . . ."

"And you have two mortgages on your house," Jesse said, "ten million could save your ass."

"Nice to know it's not simple bigotry," Healy said.

58.

The man was wearing very good clothes when he walked into Jesse's office. White suit, black-and-white striped shirt, white tie. Everything fit him exactly. His black shoes gleamed with polish. He had a neat goatee and, disconcertingly amid all the grooming, a lot of long, black hair.

"My name is Louis Francisco," he said.

"Jesse Stone."

"I'm looking for my daughter."

Jesse nodded.

"Do you know where she is?" Francisco said.

"I do."

"Where?" Francisco said.

"I won't say."

"With you?" Francisco said.

"No."

"She is a fourteen-year-old girl," Francisco said.

Jesse could hear no accent of any kind in Francisco's speech, neither ethnic nor regional. It was as if he'd been taught to speak by a radio announcer.

"She is safe," Jesse said. "There's a female police officer with her."

"You've been kind to take her in," Francisco said. "But I am her father."

Jesse didn't say anything.

"I've come to take her home," Francisco said.

"She doesn't want to go with you," Jesse said.

"Many children defy their parents. It doesn't mean they should be allowed to run wild."

"You can't have her," Jesse said.

"You do not, I believe, have any legal authority to prevent me," Francisco said.

Jesse nodded.

"Bring suit," Jesse said. "We'll run it through the courts."

Francisco smiled pleasantly.

"Perhaps I will," he said. "Do you happen to know a man named Wilson Cromartie?"

"I do," Jesse said.

"Do you happen to know his whereabouts?"

"I don't," Jesse said.

"Or a young man named Esteban Carty?" Francisco said.

"We've never met," Jesse said.

"Too bad," Francisco said. "I can't say you've been terribly helpful."

"Gee," Jesse said.

"Still, I believe we can manage without your help."

"Is that the royal we?" Jesse said.

"I have a number of employees with me," Francisco said.

"If you attempt to retrieve your daughter, I will arrest you," Jesse said.

"My employees may protest," Francisco said.

"If necessary," Jesse said, "I'll arrest them."

"There are many ways to skin a cat," Francisco said.

He stood up and stared at Jesse. Something changed in his eyes. It was like gazing suddenly into the soul of a snake.

"And," Francisco said, "to skin you, motherfucker."

His voice rasped when he said it. They looked at each other for a still moment.

Then Jesse said, "Ah, there you are."

59.

As soon as Francisco left the office, Jesse called Molly.

"Kid's father just left here," he said. "Suit out front?"

"Yes."

"I'll call him," Jesse said.

"Does the father know she's here?"

"Not yet."

"But you think he'll find out."

"Sooner or later," Jesse said.

"Is he alone?"

"I doubt if he's ever alone," Jesse said.

"Should we move her?"

"Where will she be safer?" Jesse said.

"I don't know."

"Okay, so stay with her," Jesse said. "Keep Suit awake. Call me if anything looks funny."

"Yes, sir."

"You wouldn't know where Crow is," Jesse said.

"Why are you asking me?" Molly said.

"Because you're the one I'm talking to on the phone," Jesse said.

"Why do you want to know?" Molly said.

"Because I'm trying to keep track of as many loose cannons as I can. Any idea where he is?"

"No," Molly said. "Of course not."

"Okay," Jesse said. "Where's the kid?"

"She doesn't get up until afternoon," Molly said.

"Jenn left for work yet?"

"She's in the shower," Molly said.

"Stay close," Jesse said.

When Jesse hung up, Molly looked at the phone.

Well, wasn't I jumpy! Maybe I'm not cut out for adultery.

Jenn came from the bedroom wearing a white terry-cloth robe. Her hair was still wet, and she wore no makeup.

God, she looks like a schoolgirl.

"Your hair's wet," Molly said.

"I just took a shower," Jenn said.

"Naturally curly hair?" Molly said.

"Yes. God was kind."

"If mine gets wet it goes floop," Molly said.

"God was kind to you in other ways," Jenn said. "Is that coffee?"

"It is."

Jenn poured some coffee into a thick white mug, put in a sugar substitute, and sat at the kitchen table opposite Molly.

"Amber's father has arrived," Molly said. "Jesse won't give her up."

"Does the father know she's here?" Jenn said.

"Not so far," Molly said.

"You think Jesse has a legal leg to stand on, keeping the girl from her father?" Jenn said.

"I don't think Jesse expects it to go through the legal system," Molly said.

"Because the father is a gangster?"

"Yes."

"That's kind of scary," Jenn said.

"Yes, it is," Molly said.

"Does it scare you?"

"I have a lot of training, and some experience, and I have great respect for Jesse Stone."

Jenn nodded.

"But does it scare you?'

"Some," Molly said.

"Me, too," Jenn said.

"But you'll stick?"

"I am not going to get to the big leagues," Jenn said, "if I run away from a developing story because I'm scared."

"Any other reason?" Molly said.

Jenn smiled. It wasn't exactly a happy smile, Molly thought.

"I, too, have great respect for Jesse Stone," Jenn said.

"And he thinks he's such a mess," Molly said.

"He is," Jenn said. "In many ways. And I have helped him to be a mess. But he's a good cop. And he won't quit on us. And at the very center of himself, he's a very decent man."

"Why can't you be together?" Molly said.

Jenn shook her head.

"I don't know, really," she said. "We work on it all the time."

"When you were married did you ever cheat on him?" Molly said.

"Yes."

"Why?"

"To get ahead. I thought I was an actress."

"And you slept with a producer?" Molly said.

"Yes."

"How'd you feel about it?"

"Lousy," Jenn said.

"Because you'd cheated?"

Jenn sipped her coffee, holding the mug in both hands, her elbows resting on the table, the light reflecting off the harbor brightening the room.

"Not exactly," Jenn said. "I guess I felt lousy because the sex was a means to an end."

"The end being your career?"

"I guess."

"The career was important, though," Molly said.

"I know," Jenn said. "Jesse seemed so complete, except for drinking too much."

"Even then?"

231

"Yes. And I felt so incomplete...." She shrugged and made a small half-laugh. "Still do."

"And guilty?"

Jenn nodded.

"That, too," she said.

Molly poured them both more coffee. Jenn added the sugar substitute and stirred slowly.

"How come you're so interested?" Jenn said.

Molly colored a bit. Jenn squinted at her as if the room had suddenly become too bright.

"Molly?" Jenn said.

Molly was looking at the dark surface of the coffee in her cup. Jenn waited.

"I don't feel guilty," Molly said.

"You had an affair," Jenn said.

Molly half-shrugged.

"Last night my husband was out of town. My mother had the kids, and I had sex with a man."

Jenn smiled.

"Anyone I know," she said.

"Crow."

"Jesus Christ," Jenn said.

"Have you ever met Crow?" Molly said.

"No, but I've heard."

"And I don't feel guilty," Molly said.

"Except that you feel guilty," Jenn said, "about not feeling guilty."

Molly nodded slowly.

"I guess so," she said.

"So why'd you sleep with him?" Jenn said.

"I wanted to."

"Any trouble at home?"

"No," Molly said. "I am happy with my husband. I love him. I love my kids. I love being married. . . . Hell, I love being a cop."

"Lot of protect and serve there," Jenn said.

"Maybe. But mostly it feels like I just wanted to. He is a very, very exciting man. He seems completely contained. There was no crap about love or anything. Just he wanted to have sex with me, I was a little flattered I suppose, and I wanted to have sex with him."

"How was it?" Jenn said.

"It was fine. He's adroit. I'm okay. And, if you'll pardon the pun, it was a one-shot deal."

"No commitments," Jenn said. "No promises."

Molly nodded.

"No when can I see you again," Molly said. "There was something sort of honest about it."

"One time only?" Jenn said.

"Yes," Molly said. "He wanted to. I wanted to. We did."

Jenn drank some coffee. Usually she was trying to figure out her own situation. This was kind of fun.

"Well," Jenn said. "Here's what I think. I think you did something for yourself, because it felt good. You don't feel guilty about it, so you won't confess to your husband—thank God. You are right where you were before Crow. And nobody has gotten hurt."

"So how come I felt the need to confess to you?" Molly said.

"I think you were bragging," Jenn said.

Molly reddened slightly. She laughed.

"Maybe," she said.

"And maybe looking for a little advice from an experienced adulteress," Jenn said.

"Maybe," Molly said. "What's puzzling me is, I'm an Irish Catholic mother of four and I'm not sure I can find any sense of sin in here."

"Don't let it make you unhappy," Jenn said. "That would be the sin."

Molly smiled.

"I like your theology, Jenn. I've committed adultery, but if I'm happy about it, I can still avoid sin."

"Ruining a happy marriage is the sin," Jenn said.

Molly nodded.

"And I haven't done that yet," Molly said.

"Not yet."

60.

Miriam Fiedler lived on Sea Street a mile and a tenth past the Crowne Estate School in a shingle-style house with a large veranda. Jesse sat with her on the veranda and told her what he knew of her and the Crowne estate.

She looked at him as if he were speaking another language as he talked. When he was through she said nothing.

"What I want to know is where the money went," Jesse said. "You used to be rich."

She still looked blankly at him. And then, almost as if she were merely the conveyance for someone else's voice, she began to speak.

"That was before I married Alex," she said.

There was no affect in her voice. It sounded like a recording.

"I was forty-one," she said. "My first marriage..."

They were each sitting in a wicker rocking chair. Neither of them was rocking. Jesse waited. Miriam didn't say anything. It was as if she had forgotten what she was saying.

"And Alex?" Jesse said.

"He was a year younger," Miriam said, "forty. He, too, had never married. I soon realized why."

Again silence. Again Jesse prompted her.

"Why?" Jesse said.

"Alex is homosexual," she said.

"But he married you."

"For my money," Miriam said.

"Which he spent?" Jesse said.

"Generally on his boyfriends," Miriam said.

They sat quietly in their rocking chairs. Motionless. Looking at the slow unspooling of her story.

"He travels," Jesse said after a time.

"Yes."

"But he doesn't work," Jesse said.

"No."

"And you pay."

"He tries not to embarrass me," she said. "That's worth something."

"Why not divorce him?" Jesse said.

"Then he would embarrass me."

Jesse frowned.

"Embarrass?" he said.

"I cannot stand to be thought a dupe," Miriam said. "I cannot stand having it revealed that I have been married all these years to a man who would only have sex with young men."

"And spent all your money in the process," Jesse said.

"Yes," Miriam said.

It was the first word with a hint of feeling in it.

"If I will give him one million dollars," Miriam said, "he will go away and get a quiet divorce—Nevada, perhaps—and I will be free of him."

"If you had one million dollars," Jesse said.

"Yes."

Jesse nodded and was quiet. The wind off the ocean brought with it the smell of salt and distance and infinite possibility.

"There is a developer," Miriam said, "Austin assures me, who will pay ten million for the Crowne estate, in order to build a resort. Austin says the town will not prevent him."

"Austin Blake," Jesse said.

"Yes."

"The zoning board might have a problem," Jesse said.

"Austin assures me there will be no problem."

"He's your attorney?" Jesse said.

"Yes. Do I need him here now?"

"I have no plans to arrest you," Jesse said.

"Will you keep my secret?" she said.

"If I can," Jesse said. "You'll need to lay off the kids at the estate, though."

"I know," she said.

"I'll use whatever undue influence I have to keep Channel Three from using it."

She nodded. Jesse thought it might have been a grateful nod.

"What am I to do?" she said.

Jesse took it as a rhetorical question. But she repeated it.

"What am I to do?" she said.

"What if you got the divorce, without selling the Crowne estate?" Jesse said. "And it was still done quietly?"

"I would at least be free to live my life."

"What would that mean?" Jesse said.

"I..." She stopped, struggling to say what she was trying to say. "I have a relationship with Walter Carr."

"Which you would be free to pursue?" Jesse said.

"Overtly," Miriam said.

Jesse dropped his head so she wouldn't see him smile. *This does not bode well for Suit,* he thought.

"Does Walter know all of this?" Jesse said.

"No."

"Any?" Jesse said.

"No."

"Was his opposition to the Crowne estate project at your solicitation?"

"He was not hard to solicit," she said. "No one was. Out here we were uniformly opposed to a bunch of little slum kids coming into the neighborhood."

"Do you know anything about the Francisco woman's body being found on the Crowne estate lawn?" Jesse said.

"No."

Jesse looked at her. She looked back.

"I did not," she said, with a small tremor of feeling in her voice.

Jesse nodded. And then quite suddenly she began to cry. For a moment it seemed to surprise her, and she sat perfectly still with the tears falling. Then she bent forward and put her face in her hands and cried some more. Jesse stood and put a hand gently on her shoulder. She shrank from it, and he took it away. *I know the feeling,* he thought. *Sometimes you don't want to be comforted.*

"Maybe we can work something out," Jesse said.

He turned and walked down the veranda steps and across the driveway to his car.

Like what?

61.

Esteban was on the vinyl-covered chaise, watching *Jerry Springer*, when his cell phone rang. He muted the television and answered. Three of the Horn Street Boys were watching with him, passing a bottle of sweet white wine among them. Smoking grass.

"It's Amber," a voice said.

"Yeah?" Esteban said. "So what?"

"I'm bored."

"Yeah?" Esteban said.

He grinned at his friends and made a pumping movement with his free hand.

A skinny Horn Street Boy with tattoos up and down both

arms mouthed the word *Alice?* Esteban nodded and made the pumping gesture again.

"Don't you want to know where I am?" Amber said.

"I got no interest in you," Esteban said.

"I miss you," Amber said.

"Yeah?"

"I could see you if you promise not to send me back."

"Yeah? Where are you?"

She giggled.

"I'm at the police chief's house," she said. "In Paradise."

"No shit," Esteban said.

He was still watching the soundless television as he talked to her. The Horn Street Boys who were watching with him didn't like it when he muted the television. But Esteban was the man, and no one argued with him.

"What are you doing?" she said.

"I'm thinking about how to kill Crow," Esteban said.

"If I help you, can I come back and you won't send me to Florida?"

"You walked out on me, bitch. Nobody walks out on me."

"I got Crow's cell phone number," she said. "I could call him, ask him to meet me, tell him I needed help. He'd come."

"And when he got there..." Esteban said.

"You and the other guys..." Amber said.

"Ka-boom," Esteban said.

"If I do that, can I come back and not go to my father?"

Esteban paused, watching the soundless *Jerry Springer* show.

"It'll go a long way," Esteban said. "A long way."

"I miss you," she said.

"You banging the chief?" Esteban said, and grinned at the other Boys.

"God, no, there's a couple cops here all day, and the chief and his ex-wife are here at night," Amber said. "They don't even let me smoke in the house."

"Must be pretty horny by now," Esteban said.

"I'm dying to see you," Amber said.

"Set that thing up with Crow," Esteban said. "Let me know."

"Where should I meet him?" Amber said. "He knows I'm in Paradise."

"Okay, meet him on that bridge thing, or whatever they call it that leads out to where we dumped your old lady."

"The causeway," Amber said.

"Tell him you'll meet him there," Esteban said. "He's got no cover out there, so we can come at him from the other side, drive by, and waste him without even stopping."

"In the middle?"

"Right in the middle," Esteban said.

"That's what I'll say," Amber said. "I love you."

"Sure, baby, love ya, too," Esteban said. "Call me back."

He broke the connection and sat back on the chaise for a time with the television still muted. The others in the room watched him but didn't speak. Then he picked up his cell phone, punched up a number, pressed send, and waited.

"This is Esteban Carty," he said. "Let me speak to Louis Francisco. . . . He knows who I am. . . . Tell him he needs to call me.... That's right, he needs to....I can maybe give him Crow and his daughter, at ten each.... Anytime. The sooner he calls, the sooner he knows the deal."

He shut off the cell phone and looked around the room.

"How does ten thousand each sound?" he said.

62.

Crow strolled into Jesse's office and sat down.

"You know this town better than I do," Crow said. "Is there any place worse to meet someone secretly than the middle of the causeway?"

"The causeway to the Neck?"

"In the middle," Crow said.

"I can't think of any place worse," Jesse said.

Crow nodded thoughtfully. Jesse waited.

"Got a message on my cell," Crow said. "From Amber Francisco. Says she's run off from your place and is in trouble and needs my help."

Jesse nodded.

"Says she wants to meet me in the middle of the causeway as soon as possible," Crow said. "And I should call her back and let her know."

"You didn't talk to her live," Jesse said.

"Not yet," Crow said. "What's it sound like to you?"

"You're being set up," Jesse said.

He picked up the phone and called Molly.

"Where's Amber," he said.

"In the bedroom," Molly said.

"Can you see her?"

"No," Molly said. "The door's closed."

"Go open it," Jesse said.

"Something up?"

"Just go look, Moll."

There was no conversation for a moment, and then Molly came back on the line.

"She's in there," Molly said.

"Okay," Jesse said. "Don't let her out of your sight."

"She's currently bitching about privacy."

"Let her shut the bedroom door," Jesse said. "Have Suit move around so he can watch the windows of the bedroom and the bath. You stay where you can watch the bedroom door. Everywhere else, you keep her in sight."

"What's going on?" Molly said.

"I'm not sure," Jesse said. "Just don't nod off."

He broke the connection and buzzed Arthur at the front desk.

"Who's on patrol?" Jesse said.

"Maguire and Friedman," Arthur said.

"Send them to my condo," Jesse said. "And have them park where they can watch the front door. Molly's inside, Suit's out back. Nobody in. Nobody out."

"Okay, Jesse."

Jesse looked at Crow.

"She called Esteban," Jesse said.

Crow nodded.

"For whatever reason," Jesse said. "You know he's got a contract on you."

"He's an idiot," Crow said.

"To try to kill you for ten grand?"

"Ten grand," Crow said, "is for drunken middle-aged broads."

"We both know," Jesse said, "that anyone can kill anyone. It's a matter of how much they want to and what they're willing to do."

"Got something to do with how good the *anyone* is," Crow said.

"Something," Jesse said.

"I figure she gets me to meet her in the middle of the causeway," Crow said. "Except she doesn't show up, and Esteban and company drive by and shoot me full of holes."

"And they'll come from the Neck," Jesse said. "Toward town, so if we respond quickly we can't seal them in by blocking the causeway."

Crow nodded.

"Her father came to visit me," Jesse said.

"He's in town."

"Yep," Jesse said. "Wants his daughter."

"You tell Amber?" Crow said.

"No."

"So we don't know if Esteban knows he's in town or not," Crow said.

"We know that Esteban can get in touch with Francisco," Jesse said.

Crow's eyes brightened and he smiled.

"And if you were Esteban?" Crow said.

"I figure he knows where she is now," Jesse said.

"She would have told him," Crow said.

"And he knows how to get in touch with her father," Jesse said. "And if I were Esteban, I might call Dad up and say for another ten big ones, I'll deliver Crow and your daughter. One each, dead and alive."

The two men sat quietly for a time in Jesse's office, looking at nothing.

"Why would she call him?" Jesse said.

Crow grinned.

"Love?" he said.

Jesse shook his head. They sat some more.

Then Jesse said, "Are we thinking the same thing?"

Crow shrugged.

"What are you thinking," Crow said.

"That if we manipulate this right, we might roll the whole show up at one time," Jesse said.

"We, White Eyes?" Crow said.

Jesse nodded.

"I don't know much about you, Crow," Jesse said. "And most of what I know, I don't understand. But I know you wouldn't miss this for the world."

Crow smiled.

"Maybe that's all there is to know," he said.

63.

Crow sat on the seawall in the middle of the causeway, talking on his cell phone.

"Can you hang on a couple days?" he said. "I'm in Tucson."

"I'm okay right now," Amber said. "But I have to see you."

"Couple days," Crow said.

It was a bright day. The wind off the water was steady on his back. Across the causeway, the sailboats bobbed at their moorings.

"Can I meet you someplace?" Amber said.

"Sure," Crow said. "As soon as I get back."

"On the causeway?" she said. "Like in my message?"

"Sure. Sounds like a perfect place," Crow said. "Can't miss each other."

"You promise?" Amber said.

"Soon as I get back. I'll call your cell."

"I hope you hurry," Amber said. "You're the only person I can trust."

"Absolutely," Crow said. "Couple days."

"Okay."

Crow closed the cell phone and put it away. He sat and looked around. It was a two-lane road. Traffic was slow. At the mainland end the road curved right, away from the ocean, shortly after it left the causeway, and vanished among the middle-market homes of East Paradise. At the point where the road reached Paradise Neck, at the other end of the causeway, it turned left and disappeared among the trees and shingled estates. Crow looked behind him. The seawall at this point dropped about five feet to a strip of rocky beach, maybe two feet wide, which dwindled from the full-fledged beach on the mainland side to nothing, maybe a hundred feet beyond him toward the Neck. It was high tide. Crow had already checked the tides. Crow stood and walked across the roadway. On this side the water of the harbor lapped against the base of the causeway. He would check it again at low tide. But he was pretty sure that the ocean side was better for his purposes. He went back and sat on the wall again on the ocean side. He looked to his right, toward the Neck.

They'd come from there. This wasn't a smart group of people, but nobody was stupid enough to do a drive-by shooting and keep going into a dead end. So they'd linger up around the bend on Paradise Neck until he appeared and took his place, and then they would drive down along the causeway, presumably at a moderate pace, like everyone else on the causeway, and when they got opposite, someone would open up at him, probably from the back window, probably with at least a semiautomatic weapon. One issue, if there was any traffic, would be for him to distinguish which car was carrying the shooter.

Meanwhile, if they could pull this off, Francisco and friends would be coming from the mainland end. They would have scouted the location, and would know that going toward Paradise Neck was a road to nowhere. But they had no reason to worry about escape. They would simply drive out on the causeway from the mainland end, planning to pick up the daughter in the middle, and follow the circular road around the Neck and back.

The crucial moment would come when Francisco saw no daughter, and people shooting at Crow. If they could get the timing to come out right, it might work. But it seemed to Crow that it needed tweaking. It would work better if Francisco could see people shooting at his daughter. But that would be tricky. He knew Stone would never let the kid be used as a decoy. And since a lot of this was about protecting the kid, Stone was probably right. But it wasn't all about protecting the kid. For Stone there was a case to close, maybe even some justice thing he cared about. For Crow there was the fun of it. Cops and robbers. Cowboys and Indians. With real guns and real bullets . . . *Crow's excellent adventure.*

It would go better if there were a decoy. Dressed properly, from a moving car, over a short span, with a kid he hadn't seen in several years, maybe a stand-in would work with Francisco. He looked slowly along the causeway, first toward the mainland, then toward the Neck. It wasn't a long causeway. The reaction time would be pretty brief. This could get him killed. Or not. The uncertainty made the game.

Alone on the seawall, with the wind still steady on his back, Crow smiled happily. Hard to be a warrior if death wasn't one of the options.

64.

In the back of Daisy's Restaurant, there was a bedroom with a single bed, and a bathroom with a shower.

"I lived here when I first opened the restaurant," Daisy said. "I was still single."

"And how is the lovely Mrs. Dyke," Jesse said.

"She's great. And she's starting to sell her paintings."

"Good for her," Jesse said.

"Makes her happy," Daisy said. "Which makes me happy."

"I got a kid," Jesse said. "A runaway, fourteen, I think. Mother's dead. Father's a gangster. She doesn't want to live with him. At the moment we're taking care of her at my place."

"We?"

"Jenn and me."

"Congratulations," Daisy said.

"It's temporary," Jesse said. "Molly can't work twenty-four hours a day, and I can't keep her there myself."

"That would be your style," Daisy said. "Sex with fourteen-year-old girls."

"They're so fun to talk with after," Jesse said. "How about you?"

Daisy grinned. She was a big blonde woman with a round, red face and when she smiled like that it was as if a strong light went on.

"I'm an age-appropriate girl, myself," she said.

"And the wife?" I said.

"Angela likes me," Daisy said.

"Okay," Jesse said. "If I can make it work, I'm going to keep her from her father, and I'm looking for someplace to put her."

"To raise?" Daisy said.

"No, to give her an option."

"And you think Daisy Dyke is going to play Mother Courage?"

"She can work in the restaurant, sleep in the back. I'll be responsible for her. Get her registered for school, take her to the doctor, whatever."

Daisy stared at him.

"She old enough to get a work permit?"

"I think so," Jesse said.

"Is she a pain?" Daisy said.

"You bet," Jesse said.

"Might she run off anyway?"

"Absolutely," Jesse said.

"And you think the town will feel much better about her living with two lesbians than they would about her living with you?"

"I think so," Jesse said. "More important, though, I think it would be better for her."

"Because a fourteen-year-old girl living alone with an unrelated man will tie herself into some kind of Oedipal knot?" Daisy said.

"You're pretty smart for a queer cook," Jesse said.

"I used to see a shrink," Daisy said. "When I was trying to figure out if I should be a lesbian."

"Well, it must have worked," Jesse said.

"I don't seem ambivalent about it," Daisy said, "do I."

"I don't know if this will happen," Jesse said. "It won't happen until I am sure her father will not present a problem for anybody."

"This is a just-in-case," Daisy said.

Jesse nodded.

"You want to discuss it with Angela?"

"No," Daisy said. "I'll do it."

"Like that?"

"I'm not from here, Jesse, and neither are you," Daisy said. "Neither one of us exactly belongs. And probably neither one of us ever will."

Jesse shrugged.

"And I didn't improve my chance for membership by marrying Angela Carlson," Daisy said. "Of the Paradise Carlsons."

"I think most people don't give much of a damn one way or the other," Jesse said. "Unless they're running for office and their opponent is winning."

Now Daisy shrugged.

"Maybe," she said. "You may recall, I got some nasty feedback when I got married. But you've had problems of your own, and you do a tough job well, and ever since I've known you, you've been a decent and welcoming friend. I love it that you called me a queer cook."

Jesse grinned.

"Can I take that as a yes?" Jesse said.

"You may," Daisy said. "And to prove it I'll give you the secret lesbian sign."

She put her arms around Jesse and kissed him. Jesse hugged her for a moment and stepped back.

"You know," he said, "we heteros have a similar sign."

65.

Crow drove the length of the causeway and clocked the distance, and on the way back stopped to check the water level at low tide. There was a wide strip of sand and rocks on the ocean side, but still no footing on the harbor side. Okay. He'd be leaning on the ocean-side seawall. At the mainland end of the causeway, he pulled into the town parking lot by Paradise Beach and parked and flipped open his cell phone. He punched in a number and waited.

"It's Crow," he said when a voice answered. "Got a message for Francisco."

Crow waited a moment, then spoke again.

"You call him what you want, and I'll call him what I want.

Tell him I got his daughter, and I've changed my mind. He can have her if the price is right."

He listened to the phone again as he watched a young woman take her beach robe off near the edge of the water.

"He knows the cell phone number," Crow said. "Tell him to give me a ringy-dingy."

The young woman's bathing suit was white, and barely sufficient to its task, though it contrasted nicely with her tan skin. She looked to be about twenty-five.

"Sure thing," Crow said, and closed the phone.

Crow wasn't choosy about age, though at twenty-five most women didn't seem very interesting. Older women had more to talk about. But younger women usually had firmer thighs.

"It's all good," Crow said aloud.

Most of the people on the beach were women and children. The women generally the mothers of the children, or the nannies. Most of them were a little softer-looking than Crow liked, a little too thick in the thighs, a little too wide in the butt.

Probably not a lot of time to work out when you got kids.

Not that Crow would have turned them away. Crow liked to be with women. And the women didn't need to be perfect. He liked to look at women. He thought about them sexually. Just as he liked to be with them sexually. But he thought about them in many other ways as well. He liked the way they moved, the way they were always aware of their hair. He liked the way they were with the children. He liked the thought they gave to their clothes, even at the beach. He liked how most of them found a way to keep a towel or something around their waists when they were in bathing suits. In health clubs, he noticed they did the same thing in workout tights. It always amused him. They wore revealing clothes for a reason, and covered the clothes with towels for a reason. Crow had never been able to figure out the reasons.

Ambivalence?

He'd asked sometimes but had never gotten an answer that made sense to him. He didn't mind. Part of what he liked in women was the uncertainty that they created. There was always a sense of puzzlement, of tension. Tension was much better than boredom.

Crow's phone rang. He smiled and nodded his head.

"Bingo," he said.

66.

"I need to run this by you," Jesse said.

Dix nodded.

"I'm not sure I'm doing the right thing," Jesse said.

"And you think I'll know?" Dix said.

"I think you'll have an informed opinion," Jesse said. "I will value it."

Dix tilted his head very slightly, as if he was almost acknowledging a compliment.

"I am conspiring with a contract killer, a known felon, named Wilson Cromartie, to keep a fourteen-year-old female runaway from the custody of her father, her mother is dead, and establish a life for her here in Paradise."

"Fourteen," Dix said.

"Yes, and a mess. Her father is a major criminal figure in Florida. I believe he had her mother killed. My guess is that when she lived with him she was molested, though probably not by him."

"Others around him?" Dix said.

"I think so," Jesse said. "I have her a job and a place to stay at Daisy Dyke's restaurant once we have worked something out with the father."

"Can you do that?"

"Not in any conventional sense, but Crow and I have a plan."

"Crow?"

"Wilson Cromartie," Jesse said. "If it works she will be on her own."

"At fourteen," Dix said.

"With Daisy Dyke, and I'll be responsible for her—school, doctor, stuff like that."

"Money?"

"We're working on that," Jesse said.

"You and Crow."

"Yes."

"Have you thought of Youth Services," Dix said. "Other agencies?"

"Yes."

"And?"

"I turn her over to an agency," Jesse said, "and she'll be gone in an hour."

"She might be gone in an hour anyway."

"Be her choice," Jesse said. "I won't have delivered her into the hands of what she would see as the enemy."

Dix nodded.

"Ever have a dog?" Dix said.

"Yes."

"Was it spoiled?" Dix said.

"Yes."

Dix smiled.

"For as tough a cop as you are," he said, "you are a very big old softie."

"That's why I'm talking to you," Jesse said.

"There may be other reasons," Dix said. "But for now, fill me in on this."

"You want details?" Jesse said.

"That's where the devil is," Dix said.

67.

"Francisco will do the wire transfer today," Crow said.

"One million?"

"One million," Crow said. "Wired to your account. When it arrives, I'll call him. He gets his daughter."

The two men stood with their backs to the seawall at midpoint on the causeway.

"That's what you told him," Jesse said.

"That's what I told him."

"You are a lying bastard," Jesse said.

"Doesn't make me a bad person," Crow said.

"Something did," Jesse said. "What I don't get is, Francisco gives no sign that he loves her, but he's willing to pay a million to get her back."

"*A,*" Crow said, "a million dollars doesn't mean much to him. And *B,* he's Louis Francisco. No one is allowed to tell him no."

"Ego," Jesse said.

"Partly," Crow said.

"And business."

"Yep."

"Power is real," Jesse said. "But it's a lot less real if it's not perceived as power."

Crow nodded. He was looking down the causeway toward the mainland end.

"Something like that," he said. "Timing is going to be pretty much everything here."

"I can help you with the timing," Jesse said.

"I've timed it out half a dozen times," Crow said. "We gotta start Francisco's car about ten seconds after Esteban hits the causeway."

"We'll set up some construction, and have one of my guys directing traffic," Jesse said.

"How you gonna know it's Francisco?" Crow said.

"You told him he had to come himself."

"Yeah. And he will. He won't come alone. But he's annoyed. He'll want to kill me himself."

"After he gets the girl," Jesse said.

"Yep. He can't let me get away with holding him up like this," Crow said.

"I've seen him," Jesse said. "I'll recognize him."

"Even in the backseat?" Crow said.

Jesse smiled.

"When he came to visit me, I made his car. Lincoln Town Car. A rental. He rented two of them. Got his license plate number while he was driving away. Got the other number from the rental company."

"Wow," Crow said. "What a cop!"

"Ever alert," Jesse said.

"We need somebody at the other end to let us know when Esteban starts," Crow said. "He'll be around the bend."

"If he comes from there," Jesse said.

"He'll come from that end," Crow said.

"And Francisco from the other," Jesse said.

Crow nodded.

"Scorpions in a bottle," he said. "You got enough people to keep them penned on the causeway?"

"I can get some Staties for backup," Jesse said.

"They'll go along with this?" Crow said.

"I may not tell them exactly what's going down," Jesse said.

Crow grinned.

"You lying bastard," he said.

"Doesn't make me a bad person," Jesse said. "When you want to do it?"

"Day after the money shows up in your account," Crow said.

"Time of day?"

"Morning is good, late enough for everybody to get here, early enough for me to have the sun at my back and shining in their eyes."

"Say about ten-thirty?" Jesse said.

"You been doing a few practice runs yourself," Crow said.

"Plan ahead," Jesse said.

They were quiet then, looking at the length of the causeway.

"I need a day to walk my people through it," Jesse said.

"You got tomorrow," Crow said, "even if the money shows up tomorrow."

"Wednesday morning, ten-thirty," Jesse said. "Rain or shine."

"Rain might not be a bad thing," Crow said. "If it blurred things a little."

"Sixty percent chance of rain," Jesse said, "for Wednesday."

"Like they know," Crow said.

"They sound like they know," Jesse said.

Crow snorted.

"Either way," Crow said. "What are the odds of pulling this off?"

"Terrible odds," Jesse said.

Crow grinned.

"Worst case," Crow said, "we got his money, and we're no worse off than we were before."

"Except some people might be dead," Jesse said. "Including you."

"What's the fun in winning," Crow said, "you got no chance to lose?"

68.

The easy late-summer rain had emptied the beach. Jesse sat with Jenn on the bench in the small pavilion watching the raindrops pock the surface of the ocean.

"Can we walk on the beach?" Jenn said.

"Umbrella?" Jesse said.

"No. I'd like to walk in the rain and get wet."

"And your hair?" Jesse said.

"I'll fix it when we get home," Jenn said.

The phrase pinched in Jesse's solar plexus. *Home.*

They stood and began to walk down the empty beach. The rain was steady but not hard. There was no wind.

"So the gang from Marshport," Jenn said. "They think Crow

has been set up by Amber and is expecting to meet her on the causeway, where instead they will shoot him dead."

"Correct," Jesse said.

"God, I wish I could use some of this," Jenn said.

"Maybe someday," Jesse said.

"And Amber's father thinks Crow will deliver his daughter to him in the middle of the causeway," Jenn said.

"Correct."

"And you hope to provoke conflict between the two groups and arrest them all."

"Exactly," Jesse said.

"Is any of this plan legal?" Jenn said.

"I may be able to make it look so," Jesse said.

"But you know who most of the villains are already," Jenn said.

"Plus, I know Crow killed a guy in Marshport, and certainly a couple guys here," Jesse said. "Though I can't prove it."

"But you're not trying to catch Crow," Jenn said.

"No."

"Why not?"

"I'm not sure," Jesse said.

"Can you trust Crow in this?"

"Probably not," Jesse said. "And I know that Esteban Carty and the Horn Street gang killed Amber's mother. And I know they have a contract on Crow, but all I have is secondhand information from a known felon, who would probably say anything he thought would serve him."

"What do you suppose Crow is up to in all this?" Jenn said.

"He may be looking out for the girl," Jesse said. "He may have an issue I don't know about that he's resolving with Francisco. But to tell you the truth, I think he's just playing."

"God," Jenn said.

"Crow's unusual," Jesse said.

"And doesn't the father have a legal right to his daughter?" Jenn said.

"Probably," Jesse said. "I got somebody from Rita Fiore's firm working on that."

"And the million dollars Crow has extorted from the father?" Jenn said.

"Rita's people are setting up a trust for Amber," Jesse said. "She stays here and finishes school and gets it at age eighteen. Meanwhile, we support her on the income."

"And if she runs off?"

"I don't know," Jesse said.

"This could blow up in your face," Jenn said.

"I know."

"You could lose your job," Jenn said. "Everything."

"I know."

"For what?" Jenn said.

Jesse shrugged.

"What does Dix say?" Jenn asked.

"He thinks that Amber is probably too damaged to save," Jesse said. "Though, being a shrink, he doesn't exactly say that."

"So you're going to jump off the cliff," Jenn said, "for maybe nothing."

Jesse shrugged again.

"Why?" Jenn said.

"Seems like the right thing to do," Jesse said.

They walked in silence then, except for the murmur of the ocean, and the hushed sound of the rain and the wet crunch their feet made in the sand.

"Be a better chance of all of this working if I could actually put Amber out there with Crow."

"Which you can't."

"No," Jesse said. "Nor Molly dressed up as Amber."

"I could..." Jenn started.

"No," Jesse said.

Jenn smiled faintly.

"Thank God," she said. "I didn't really want to."

"I wouldn't let you," Jesse said. "Even if you did."

"But," Jenn said, "I have a thought."

They stopped and stood in the rain. Their clothes were wet through. Neither of them minded.

"During my breathtaking film career," Jenn said, "I encountered an occasional stunt dummy."

"And went out with him?" Jesse said.

"Not that kind of dummy," Jenn said. "It's a floppy replica, like a rag doll with a realistic look. You know, the guy falls off the building and you see him land on the roof of a car?... What's landing is the stunt dummy."

"Can you get one?"

"Sure, there's a couple theatrical supply houses in town that have them," Jenn said. "We dress it like Amber, put on a black wig with a maroon stripe, maybe, and voilà."

"Better than an inflate-a-mate," Jesse said.

"Most things are," Jenn said. "I'll get it this afternoon and bring it out."

"Thank you," Jesse said.

They walked on. It had gotten darker. The sky was lower. The rain was coming a little harder.

"I don't know," Jenn said. "It may be all wrong, what you're doing."

"I know."

"But it's for all the right motives," Jenn said.

"Story of my life," Jesse said.

Jenn stopped and turned to him and put her arms around him and pressed her face against his chest.

"Jesse," she said. "Jesse, Jesse, Jesse."

He patted her back slowly.

69.

"Suit," Jesse said. "You and Molly bring Amber here tomorrow morning. No later than nine."

"If she objects?" Suit said.

"Bring her," Jesse said. "Handcuff her if you have to. Arthur, you man the desk. If there's an emergency, and I mean a real one, not somebody's cat is missing, you cover it and Suit will take the desk. Otherwise, Suit, you and Molly are in a cell with Amber. Vests and shotguns."

Suit nodded. Jesse looked around the squad room.

"She'll want to know why," Molly said.

"Don't tell her," Jesse said. "Peter, you're on the Neck. Buddy, you're at the construction detour. Murph, you're on the backhoe. Eddie, you're in a car on the Neck with John. Peter will join you when the balloon goes up. Steve and Bobby, you're in a car at the other end. Buddy and Murph will join you. There will be some Staties in unmarked cars in the parking lot at the beach. Commander is a corporal named Jenks. They'll pitch in . . . at my request . . . if they're needed."

"And you're in the van," Paul Murphy said.

Jesse nodded.

"At the construction site," he said. "I'll be in radio contact with everybody, including Crow. When it goes down, you wait for me, and when I say so, we come in from both ends and arrest everybody in sight."

"And do what with them?" Peter Perkins said. "We don't have a paddy wagon, and even if we did, we probably don't have enough cell space."

"Healy promised me a State Police wagon, and we can use the Salem City jail."

"Crow?" Suit said.

"Except Crow," Jesse said.

"I still don't get what's in this for Crow," Peter Perkins said.

"Nobody does," Jesse said. "He seems to think it's fun."

"Hell," Peter Perkins said. "I'm not sure what we're getting out of this."

"We might close a couple of cases, and give Amber Francisco a life," Jesse said.

"Sounds like protect and serve to me," Suit said.

"Me, too," Jesse said.

"On the other hand," Suit said, "how you gonna explain the million bucks to the IRS?"

"That's why they make accountants, Suit," Jesse said.

"Oh," Suit said. "I knew there was a reason."

"Screw the IRS," Steve Friedman said. "How you gonna explain it to Healy?"

"First," Jesse said, "let's see if it works."

"You're gonna have to explain this to a lot of people whether it works or not," Peter Perkins said. "We're all just obeying orders. But you're in charge."

"Glad you noticed," Jesse said.

"Healy ain't gonna like it," Perkins said.

"Maybe I'll get lucky," Jesse said. "Maybe somebody will shoot me."

70.

It was 6:15 in the morning, still raining as it had yesterday. Not a downpour but steady. Drinking coffee, Crow was putting on a Kevlar vest in a van at the construction site at the start of the causeway. Peter Perkins had slipped the radio into his hip pocket and was running the microphone and earpiece wires. When that was done, Crow strapped on two .40-caliber semiautomatic handguns below the vest, and slipped into a hooded sweatshirt. The microphone was clipped inside the neck, and the hood concealed the earphone.

Paul Murphy came into the van wearing work clothes. He poured some coffee for himself.

"There's a crack in the seawall," he said, "on the ocean side. I put a tenpenny nail in there and hung the dummy on it, just below the top of the wall."

Crow nodded, and drank some coffee.

"The timing is everything here," Jesse said. "You can't have Amber up there with you too soon, or Esteban may not shoot. On the other hand, she's got to be up there in time for the old man to see her getting shot at."

Crow nodded. He was impassive as he always seemed, but Jesse thought there was a ripple of electricity beneath the surface.

"Esteban's got to pass this site to get out on the Neck. When he does we'll know it."

"State cops?" Crow said.

"Sitting tight in the parking lot of the post office," Jesse said. " 'Bout four blocks that way."

"People at the other end?"

"Yep."

Crow nodded, flexing his hands a little.

"You nervous?" Jesse said.

Crow shook his head.

"I like to go over it," Crow said. "Like foreplay, you know?"

"I've always thought about foreplay differently," Jesse said.

Crow shrugged.

"Romero will be with Francisco," Crow said. "He's the stud. If somebody needs to get shot down, shoot him first."

"You know him?"

Crow shrugged.

"We move in the same circles," he said. "Rest of them will just be routine gunnies."

The back door of the van was open. Crow looked out at the rain.

"Guess it doesn't make so much difference where the sun's coming from," he said.

"Rain'll take care of that," Jesse said.

Crow nodded. He took a deep breath of the wet, salt-tinged air.

"Rain's good," he said. "Rain, early morning, hot coffee, and a firefight coming."

He grinned and nodded his head.

"Only thing missing is sex," he said.

"We pull this off," Jesse said, "you get to keep the dummy."

71.

At seven minutes past ten a new Nissan Quest picked its way through the narrowed construction lane.

In the van, Crow said, "That's Esteban driving."

"Let the van through," Jesse said on the radio. And Buddy Hall waved it on. It drove on across the causeway and disappeared around the bend.

"Peter," Jesse said into the radio, "a maroon Nissan Quest."

"Got it," Peter Perkins said. "It just U-turned and parked near the causeway."

Into the radio Jesse said, "Corporal Jenks? You standing by?"

"We're here," Jenks said.

At 10:23 Steve Friedman said on the radio, "Two Lincoln Town Cars coming down Beach Street. Right plate numbers."

"Okay," Jesse said. "Buddy, you hold them at the barrier. First in line."

"Roger," Buddy said.

"Murph," Jesse said. "Pull the backhoe in front of the van."

"Okay," Paul Murphy's voice came over the radio.

The backhoe edged in front of the van. Jesse looked at Crow. Crow looked back. Jesse nodded once. Crow nodded back. Then, shielded from the street by the backhoe, Crow stepped out of the van and started out along the causeway with his hood up against the rain. It was 10:26. The first of the two Lincolns pulled to a stop at the barrier just out of sight of the causeway. The passenger-side window went down.

"What's the holdup, Officer?" Francisco said.

"Just a minute, sir," Buddy said. "Gotta clear the other end. You'll be on your way in a jiffy."

At 10:28 Crow was leaning on the seawall at the spot where the Amber dummy had been concealed on the other side. The rain made everything slightly murky.

"Jesse," a voice said on the radio, "Peter Perkins on the Neck. A guy got out of the Quest and walked down to the bend where he could see the causeway. He's coming back now, walking fast. . . . He's getting in the van. They've left the slider open on the driver's-side backseat."

"You hear this, Crow?" Jesse said.

Crow's voice was muffled a little because the mike was inside the sweatshirt.

"Got it," he said.

"Van's under way," Perkins said.

Jesse looked at his watch.

"Get ready, Buddy," he said into the mike. "Seven seconds, six, five, four, three, two, one, send the Lincoln."

Buddy Hall stepped aside and waved the two Lincolns onto the causeway. Jesse jumped from the van and sprinted to his car parked in the beach parking lot right at the causeway. He could make Crow out through the rain, leaning against the seawall. The Quest was almost there. Suddenly Crow rolled up and over the seawall and Jesse heard the boom of a shotgun. *Boom, boom, boom,* in rapid sequence. *Christ,* he thought, *a street sweeper. Boom, boom, boom.* No sign of Crow. Then there was a flash of color at the seawall, and what seemed to be the body of a young woman appeared above the seawall and fell forward onto the causeway. Jesse put the car in gear and headed toward the scene. In front of him the two Lincolns spun sideways in the road and men with guns were out of both cars, shooting. Jesse turned on his lights and siren. Steve and Bobby behind him did the same, and from the Neck end of the causeway came Eddie Cox and John Maguire and Peter Perkins with the lights flashing and the sirens wailing.

In Jesse's earphone Corporal Jenks said, "Jesse, you need us?"

"Block the causeway by the beach," Jesse said. "And hold there. Nobody on or off."

"Roger."

Jesse got to the shoot-out first. The patrol cars from both ends of the causeway arrived right after he did at the shooting scene and swerved sideways to block the causeway. Jesse got out of his car, shielded by the open door. He had a shotgun. Most of the shooting stopped when the police arrived. Except the man with the street sweeper. From the van, the street sweeper kept firing toward the seawall. A tall, straight-backed man with salt-and-pepper hair walked from behind the lead Lincoln to the Quest, as if he was taking a walk in the rain. He fired through the open side door of the Quest with a handgun. After a moment a shotgun with a big round drum came rattling out onto the street. Behind it came the shooter, who fell beside the gun onto the street and didn't move. The Paradise police ranged on both sides of the shoot-out, standing with shotguns, behind the cars. At the mainland end of the causeway, State Police cars blocked the road.

"Police," Jesse said. "Everybody freeze."

The tall, straight man looked at the scene, and without expression dropped his handgun. The other men followed his lead. Jesse walked to the tall man.

"You Romero?" Jesse said.

"Yeah."

"I'm Jesse Stone."

"I know who you are," Romero said.

"You know him?" Jesse said, looking down at the dead man in the street.

"Esteban Carty," Romero said to Jesse.

"No loss," Jesse said. "You are all under arrest. Please place your hands on top of the car nearest you and back away with your legs spread." Jesse smiled slightly. "I bet most of you know how it's done."

Louis Francisco got out of his car and walked unarmed to the motionless Amber dummy in the street. He knelt down in the rain and looked at it and turned it over. He looked at it for a while, then he stood and looked over the seawall, and finally turned and looked at Jesse. His face showed nothing.

"I wish to speak with my attorney," he said without inflection.

Jesse nodded. Everyone was quiet. The only sounds were the movement of the ocean, and the sound of the rain falling, under the low, gray sky.

There is no quiet quite like the one that follows gunfire.

72.

Jesse sat with Healy, late at night, in his office, with a bottle of scotch and some ice.

"Quest was stolen," Jesse said.

"'Course it was," Healy said.

"We don't have much on Francisco," Jesse said. "He didn't even have a gun."

"And he was just innocently riding along when a firefight broke out," Healy said.

"We got the others for carrying unlicensed firearms, and for firing them. The claim is that they fired in self-defense."

"And the Horn Street Boys?"

"They got a twenty-six-year-old public defender," Jesse said. "They'll be lucky to avoid lethal injection."

"Jenks tells me there was some sort of dummy involved," Healy said.

Jesse shrugged.

"And where is this guy Crow?"

Jesse shrugged again.

"Just curious," Healy said. "But you're right. It's probably better if I don't know too much about what went down over there."

"Probably," Jesse said.

"What about this guy Romero?" Healy said. "The one that shot Carty?"

"We got him on the unlicensed gun thing," Jesse said. "But Francisco's lawyer says he can make a self-defense case on the shooting. And I think he might."

"Anyone you can turn?"

"I don't think so. We got the most leverage with Romero," Jesse said. "But he's a pro. He'll take one for the team if he has to."

Healy nodded.

"Besides," Jesse said. "I kind of like the way he walked in there and took Esteban out. For all Romero seemed to care, the kid could have been throwing snowballs."

Healy leaned forward and put some more ice in his glass and poured another inch of scotch for himself.

"I'm sure he's swell," Healy said.

Jesse sipped his scotch, and rolled it a little in his mouth before he swallowed.

"He's not swell," Jesse said. "But he's got a lot of guts."

"How about the kid?" Healy said.

"Amber?"

Healy nodded. Jesse drank another swallow of scotch. The room was half-dark. The only light came from the crookneck lamp on Jesse's desk.

"Francisco says he'll leave her be," Jesse said. "We got enough legal pressure on him up here, so he might mean it . . . at least for now."

"She's moving in with Daisy Dyke?" Healy said.

"Yes. She'll work there. I'll supervise her, get her in school, stuff like that."

"Maybe I'll stop by to watch you at the first parent-teacher meeting," Healy said.

Jesse shook his head.

"You're a cruel man, Healy," he said.

"Who buys her school clothes?" Healy said. "Pays the doctor's bills, stuff like that?"

"We have an, ah, financial arrangement with her father," Jesse said.

"Which is no more kosher than this freaking shoot-out on the causeway," Healy said.

"Probably not," Jesse said.

"So I'm better off not knowing about that, too," Healy said.

"We all are," Jesse said.

"You think the old man will let her be?"

"I don't think he gives a rat's ass about her in any emotional way. I think we got a little legal pressure on him. I think it'll be in his best interest to give all this a good leaving alone, for the time being."

"But?"

"But we'll keep a car around Daisy Dyke's as much as we can," Jesse said. "And I'll take her places she needs to go."

"Think she'll stay?" Healy said.

"I don't know. If she stays, she's got financial security. If she runs away, she doesn't. Her mother's dead. Esteban's dead. So she hasn't got any place to run away to, that I know about."

"Talk to any shrinks about her?" Healy said.

"My own," Jesse said.

"And what does he say?"

"He's not optimistic," Jesse said.

Healy nodded. He drank some scotch and sat back in his chair.

"Gotta try," he said.

73.

It was the first snow of the winter. The snowfall was deeper inland than it was along the coast, but in Paradise there was enough to make watching it fall worth doing. Jenn stood with Jesse at the French doors. It was late afternoon but not quite yet dark. Over the harbor the snow whirled in the conflicting air currents and disappeared into the asphalt-colored water. Most of the moorings were empty for the winter, but a few fishing boats still stood in the harbor and the snow collected on their decks. The snowfall was thick enough so that Paradise Neck on the other side of the harbor was invisible.

"What's in the bag?" Jesse said.

"A care package from Daisy, for supper," Jenn said. "Amber brought it."

Behind them, disinterested in snowfall on the water, Amber sat sideways in an armchair with her legs dangling over an arm and watched MTV.

"What did you bring?" Jesse said to Amber.

"A bunch of stuff," Amber said. "I don't know."

"Gee," Jesse said. "That sounds delicious."

"Whatever," Amber said.

Jenn went to the bar and made two drinks and brought them back to the window. She handed one to Jesse.

"Oh, God," Amber said. "You two booze bags at it again?"

"We are," Jesse said.

Jenn went and sat on the footstool near Amber's chair.

"How is school, Amber?" Jenn said.

"Sucks," Amber said. "Don't you remember school, for crissake? It sucks."

"Gee," Jenn said. "I loved school."

"Sure," Amber said. "You probably did. You were probably the best-looking girl there, and popular as hell."

Jenn nodded a small nod.

"Well," she said. "There was that."

"You like school, Jesse?" Amber said.

"No," Jesse said. "To tell you the truth, I thought it sucked, too."

"See?" Amber said to Jenn.

Jenn nodded.

"You want a Coke?" she said to Amber.

"Yeah, sure, if I can't have the good stuff," Amber said.

Jenn got up and got Amber a Coke. Jesse continued to look out at the snow. Jenn came back to stand beside him. Amber refocused on MTV.

"So much for motherly small talk with the kid," Jenn said.

"Maybe it's a little soon," Jesse said, "for motherly."

"Too soon for me?" Jenn said. "Or too soon for her?"

"You," Jesse said. "You seem a little...avant-garde...for motherly."

"I don't know if that's a compliment or not," Jenn said.

"It's an observation," Jesse said.

"Wouldn't it be odd," Jenn said, "if we put this together someday, and we had children."

"Yes," Jesse said. "That would be odd."

"But not bad odd," Jenn said.

"No," Jesse said. "Not bad odd."

The early winter night had arrived. The only snow they could see now was that just past the French doors, illuminated by the light from the living room.

"I saw where Miriam Fiedler got divorced," Jenn said.

"Yep."

"I thought that was going to be troublesome."

"Guess it wasn't," Jesse said.

Jenn looked at him for a minute.

"You have something to do with that?" she said.

"I talked with her husband," Jesse said. "He was pleasant enough."

"What did you say?"

"He and his boyfriend are opening a high-end restaurant on the coast of Maine, south of Portland. I suggested negative publicity about him spending all his wife's money on boyfriends and this restaurant would not help business."

"God, Jesse," Jenn said. "Sometimes I wonder which side of the law you're on."

"Me, too," Jesse said.

"But it worked?"

"It worked," Jesse said.

"That the broad the cop, Suitcase, was fucking?" Amber said from the armchair.

"Yes," Jesse said.

"You think he's still fucking her?"

"Probably," Jesse said.

"And you don't care?" Amber said.

"No," Jesse said.

"I think it's disgusting," Amber said.

"What I do care about, though," Jesse said, "is that they are people, and that this matters to them in some way, and they probably shouldn't be talked about like a couple of barnyard animals."

Amber stared at him for a moment, and then shrugged and sank a little lower into the armchair.

"I was just asking," she said.

Jesse went to the bar and made himself another drink. He looked at Jenn. She held up her half-full glass and shook her head. The doorbell rang. It was Molly, in uniform, with a heavy, fur-collared jacket on. She had a folded newspaper in her hand.

"You seen the paper today?" she said when she came in.

"No delivery today," Jesse said. "Snow, I suppose."

Molly handed it to him. She looked at Amber.

"Section two," she said. "Below the fold."

Jesse turned to it.

FLA. CRIME FIGURE KILLED

Louis Francisco, the reputed boss of organized crime in South Florida, was found shot to death today in the parking lot of a Miami restaurant.

Jesse read the story through without comment. A driver and a bodyguard had also been killed. Neither was named Romero. No arrests had been made. So far police had no suspects. Jesse gave the paper to Jenn and looked at Amber. Then he looked at Molly. She shrugged. Jesse nodded. He put his drink on the bar and walked over to Amber and sat on the hassock where Jenn had sat.

"Your father's dead," he said.

She looked away from the television screen and stared for a time at Jesse. Then, finally, she shrugged.

"Sooner or later," she said.

Jesse nodded. MTV cavorted on behind him.

"Who killed him," Amber said.

"You're so sure he was killed," Jesse said.

"Yeah. How else's he gonna go? He ain't much older than you."

Jesse nodded.

"It bother you?" Jesse said.

"That somebody killed him? No. He was a rotten bastard," Amber said. "Both of them were rotten bastards."

"You're not alone," Jenn said. "We will see that you're okay."

Amber was annoyed.

"I know that," she said. "And I got money, too."

"Yes," Jesse said. "You do. And no one's going to come back and bother you now...."

Jesse grinned at her.

"Except maybe me," Jesse said, "if you don't behave."

"I'm not scared of you," Amber said.

"No, why would you be," Jesse said.

"So who shot him, it say?"

"It doesn't say."

Molly looked at Jesse, and then at Amber and then back at Jesse.

"I think we can talk about this in front of Amber," Jesse said. "She's certainly an interested party."

"For crissake," Amber said. "He was my old man, okay?"

Molly nodded.

"You have a thought?" Molly said to Jesse.

"Guy had a beef with Francisco," Jesse said. "Took out two bodyguards and the boss in a public parking lot in the middle of Miami and disappeared. We know anybody like that?"

"Crow?" Molly said.

"A sentimental favorite," Jenn said, and then looked like she shouldn't have said it.

Molly blushed. Jesse saw it. *Molly? And Crow?* He smiled to himself. *It's like being police chief in Peyton Place.*

"I'd guess Crow," Jesse said. "Solved a lot of problems that way. He'd double-crossed Francisco twice. That meant Francisco would try to arrange Crow's death. Also frees up Amber here from fear of custody or kidnapping."

"You think that's why he did it?" Amber said.

Jesse looked thoughtfully at her for a moment.

"Yeah," he said. "I think so."

She smiled for maybe the first time since Jesse had met her.

"Okay," Molly said. "Gotta go home. We're cooking supper in the fireplace. It's a family tradition. Every year, first snowfall, we cook supper in the fireplace."

"Hardy pioneers," Jesse said.

"You bet," Molly said, and turned up her collar and left.

The three of them were quiet. Jesse walked over and put his arm around Jenn.

"Molly and Crow?" he said.

Jenn looked up at him and winked. Jesse nodded. Jenn lifted her face toward him and Jesse kissed her.

"Jesus," Amber said. "Can you wait until I'm out of the room to start necking."

"Guess not," Jesse said. "You want supper?"

"Yeah," she said. "Okay, if you people don't start doing it on the kitchen table."

"Promise," Jenn said.

Jesse picked up his drink and they walked into the kitchen. Amber sat at the table while Jesse and Jenn put out the food that Daisy had packed.

"God," Amber said. "Crow is so cool."

Dental Diners

Some cultures prefer to feed a child's tooth to a specific animal in hopes that the animal will replace the tooth with one like its own. The native Yupik of Alaska feed lost teeth to dogs. However, in the 19th century, children from Cornwall, England, had their first teeth burnt so as to avoid having "dog's teeth" grow in (that is, crooked teeth).

Fangs of Fire

Ancient Egyptians believed the sun strengthened teeth, which may explain why in many North African and Middle Eastern countries, such as Egypt and Libya, teeth are tossed toward the sun.

Bicuspid Burial

But why toss teeth when you can bury them? In Turkey, a tooth is buried at a site that symbolizes the parents' hope for their child's success. For instance, if they wish their child to become a doctor, the tooth is buried on the grounds of a hospital; a scholar, on the grounds of a university. Malaysian tradition believes that, as part of the body, teeth must be returned to the earth, and in Tajikistan, teeth are planted in a field so they can grow into warriors.

The Navajo traditionally take a lost tooth to the southeast, away from the family home, and bury it on the east side of a young bush or tree. Other native cultures, such as the aboriginal Australians and the Yellowknife Dene of Canada's Northwest Territories, plant a tooth inside a tree in hopes that as the tree grows straight, so will the child's new tooth.

Ivory Accessories

Still, there are cultures that are loath to part with their children's pearly whites. Lithuanians hang on to them as keepsakes, and in certain Central American countries, such as Chile and Costa Rica, a baby tooth is dipped in gold or silver and made into jewelry for the child to wear—a custom that resembles the Viking tradition of wearing baby teeth as good luck charms.

Northern Justice: Canada's Weird Laws

❖ ❖ ❖ ❖

Canada is one of the world's most peaceful and underpopulated countries, so naturally one would think it would be easy to keep the citizens in line. So why are all these strange laws still on the books?

Scamming the Queen

Canada is still technically a constitutional monarchy, so when Her Royal Highness visits, you'd best show some respect! For instance, it's a severe offense to sell the queen shoddy or defective merchandise.

Slaying Sasquatch

Some folks outside of Canada call it Bigfoot, but no matter what the name, it's against the law to hunt or shoot the fabled man-beast, who is rumored to live in the forests of British Columbia. Since the creature is presumably a human ancestor, plugging the 'Squatch gets the hunter dangerously close to a murder rap. Sasquatch is reportedly quite timid, but if it charges, you'd better hope that your interspecies negotiation skills are in top order.

No Fake Witches

Canada has complete freedom of religion, so if you're claiming to be a witch, you better be the real thing. Genuine witches, or wiccans, are considered fine, but should you grab a broom and a pointy hat and pretend to be a witch, you are violating the Criminal Code of Canada. Those who "pretend to exercise or use any kind of witchcraft, sorcery, enchantment, or conjuration" can be punished. Makes you wonder whether the jails are filled to capacity on Halloween.

Penny Pummeling

When Canadian kids leave coins on the railway tracks to be flattened by trains, they could be facing a year in juvenile jail or a $250 (that is, a 25,000-penny) fine. This is because they are defacing the currency of the country and the law clearly states that it is illegal to "melt down" or "break up" money.

Real Names of the Rich and Famous

❖ ❖ ❖ ❖

Below are the real names of some famous faces—
see if you can match the real name to the alias.

1. Reginald Kenneth Dwight

2. Paul Hewson

3. Mark Vincent

4. David Robert Jones

5. Caryn Elaine Johnson

6. Nathan Birnbaum

7. Archibald Leach

8. Eleanor Gow

9. Samuel Langhorne Clemens

10. Tara Patrick

11. McKinley Morganfield

12. Farrokh Bulsara

13. Frances Gumm

14. Robert Allen Zimmerman

15. Demetria Gene Guynes

16. Marion Morrison

17. Allen Konigsberg

18. Georgios Panayiotou

19. Jay Scott Greenspan

a. John Wayne

b. Cary Grant

c. Woody Allen

d. Elton John

e. Mark Twain

f. Freddie Mercury

g. Bob Dylan

h. George Michael

i. Whoopi Goldberg

j. Bono

k. Jason Alexander

l. Demi Moore

m. Vin Diesel

n. George Burns

o. David Bowie

p. Muddy Waters

q. Judy Garland

r. Elle MacPherson

s. Carmen Electra

ANSWERS

1. d; 2. j; 3. m; 4. o; 5. i; 6. n; 7. b; 8. r; 9. e; 10. s; 11. p; 12. f;
13. q; 14. g; 15. l; 16. a; 17. c; 18. h; 19. k

The Red Special

❖ ❖ ❖ ❖

Queen guitarist Brian May was a legend, and so was his guitar, dubbed the Red Special. Even more impressive, May and his father built the entire guitar by hand using mostly household items.

Some of the most influential songs to come out of the 1970s belong to the bombastic rock band Queen. Part of the band's unique sound was certainly the incredible vocal prowess of late singer Freddie Mercury. But just as unique were the sounds coming out of guitarist Brian May's guitar.

May's family was rather poor. So when young May decided he wanted an electric guitar, he and his father, Harold, an electronics whiz, decided to build one. The pair began construction around 1963; it took more than two years to build the guitar. When it was completed, everyone marveled at the unique sounds May was able to coax out of the red guitar, often using a sixpence coin rather than a guitar pick. Here's what went into the making of legend.

Mantle from a 100-year-old fireplace: When one of his neighbors was getting ready to throw out his old mantle, May took it to use for the guitar's neck, hand-carving the entire piece.

Mother-of-pearl buttons: Once the neck was carved, May turned his attention to the fretboard. For this he raided his mother's sewing kit for mother-of-pearl buttons.

Oak table: The Mays needed something for the guitar's body. An old oak table was perfect, since the oak would be strong enough to support any pressure May used on the neck of the guitar.

Bicycle saddlebag holder and a knitting needle: Every guitarist knows you can't have a good guitar without a tremolo bar. So May took part of a metal saddlebag holder and bent it, creating the bar. He then used the plastic tip from one of his mother's knitting needles to cap the bar off.

A knife and some motorcycle springs: May and his father took an old, hardened steel knife-edge and bent it into a v-shape. They then took two valve springs from a motorcycle and connected them to the knife-edge to complete the tremolo system.

Fast Facts

- Twenty-three percent of all photocopier problems are a result of people sitting on them to copy their backsides. Try explaining that to your boss.

- A honeybee dies after it stings a human, but a female bumblebee can sting more than once. Male bumblebees do not have stingers.

- Mountain Dew is the fourth most popular soft drink in the United States after Coke, Pepsi, and Diet Coke.

- Tiger Woods appeared on TV to putt with Bob Hope at age 2. By age 3, he shot a 48 for 9 holes, and he joined the pro circuit at age 20.

- Little Orphan Annie was originally supposed to be a boy named Otto. However, Joseph Patterson, publisher of the New York Daily News, told creator Harold Gray, "the kid looks like a pansy. Just put a skirt on him and we'll call him Little Orphan Annie!"

- The longest baseball game in Major League history took place May 8, 1984, between the Chicago White Sox and the Milwaukee Brewers at Comiskey Park in Chicago. It took eight hours and six minutes over 25 innings for the White Sox to finally win it 7–6.

- Underground cartoonist Robert Crumb, best known for such popular counter-culture characters as Fritz the Cat and Mr. Natural, drew greeting cards for American Greeting Corporation in the early 1960s.

- Only four U.S. presidents have sported 'staches without beards: Theodore Roosevelt, Chester A. Arthur, William Taft, and Grover Cleveland.

- Do rats have nine lives? A rat can fall from a five-story building without getting hurt.

♣ Behind the Films of Our Time

- While many people consider *Singin' in the Rain* to be the best musical of all time, the Academy apparently didn't agree. The movie didn't even get a nomination in 1952; instead, the Best Picture award that year went to *The Greatest Show on Earth.*

- You might recognize the carpet design in *Toy Story.* It's the same pattern used in *The Shining.*

- Director Alfred Hitchcock never won an Oscar for his work, although he did get a Lifetime Achievement Award in his later years.

- Alfred Hitchcock was known for making cameo appearances in his movies—sort of an onscreen *Where's Waldo?*

- The 1979 war flick *Apocalypse Now* is said to have more mistakes than any other movie, including continuity problems, anachronisms, and plain ol' factual errors.

- The first character to speak in the movie *Star Wars* is the robot C-3PO.

- In the movie *White Christmas,* the comedy act "Sisters" was not in the original script. Actors Bing Crosby and Danny Kaye were goofing around on the set, and the director liked the skit so much he had it written in.

- Tom Selleck was tapped to star as Indiana Jones in *Raiders of the Lost Ark.* But he passed on the role because he was already committed to the TV show *Magnum, P.I.*

- *Reefer Madness* may not have been the hit it was intended to be in 1936 when it was made to deter the younger generation from doing drugs. High school students are shown involved in manslaughter, rape, and suicide—all induced by a toke of marijuana. In fact, the film was a dud until it was rediscovered during the 1970s free-love, free-everything movement. It became such a cult classic that it was even made into an off-Broadway musical.

Don't Get Hysterical!

❖ ❖ ❖ ❖

In Victorian times, female hysteria was a widespread,
catchall diagnosis—and a weird one at that.

Of all the strange medical diagnoses of yore, hysteria might be one
of the strangest. Used frequently in the Victorian era (1830s–1900),
it eventually became one of the most common diagnoses in the history of Western medicine.

Hysteria, particularly female hysteria, was a catchall for any kind
of "woman problems" ladies might experience and was indicated by
a long list of symptoms: fainting, anxiety, insomnia, muscle spasm,
mood swings, loss of appetite, heaviness in abdomen, shortness of
breath, retention of fluids, disinterest in sex, etc. In other words, if
you were a woman who felt at all ill or were thought to be "acting
up," you were probably just hysterical and needed to get a grip! How
did doctors arrive at this diagnosis and what were the treatments?
The history of hysteria will make you glad medicine has progressed
since Victorian times.

Ancient Origins and Initial "Cures"

The word *hysteria* comes from the Greek word *hysterikos,* meaning
"suffering of the womb." In fact, during ancient times, the uterus
was thought to move through the body, wreaking all kinds of havoc
(e.g., strangling the woman and causing disease). This phenomenon,
first suggested by Aretaeus of Cappodocia, was known as the "wandering womb." According to the *Encyclopedia of Gender and
Society,* wombs continued to wander throughout the classical, medieval, and renaissance periods.

The ancient Greeks believed that women were actually
"incomplete" males; thus, the uterus was not cooperative and
rebelled against the female body. So the cure for hysteria was to
resituate the uterus or "lure it back" via rocking in a chair, riding a
horse, or receiving a "pelvic massage." It was recommended that
married women have sexual intercourse with their husbands, while
single women were encouraged to get married—pronto!

Victorian–Era Hysteria

In Victorian times, sex as a form of pleasure, rather than strictly a form of reproduction, was particularly taboo. Society upheld the notion of the "sexless woman." Therefore, almost any woman who deviated from this ideal or experienced sexual frustration or emotional turmoil was deemed hysterical. In fact, by the mid-19th century, physicians diagnosed a quarter of all women as hysterical. Meanwhile, the number of symptoms for this "disease" kept growing. One physician catalogued 75 pages of possible symptoms—a list he described as incomplete.

Goodbye, Leech Cures!

How to treat the hysterical masses? Doctors prescribed bed rest, seclusion, sensory deprivation, tasteless food, and pelvic massages (which basically brought about an orgasm). The latter were to be performed by a skilled physician or midwife and were often accompanied by a steady flow of water, otherwise known as a hydrotherapy treatment. The massage treatment eventually gave rise to the first electromechanical vibrator. Doctors also recommended that hysterical women stay away from any tasks that were too mentally strenuous, such as reading and writing. Of course, this sort of deprivation just created more problems. In *The Yellow Wallpaper*, the short story written by Charlotte Perkins Gilman in 1899, a woman is driven mad after being prescribed a "rest cure" for hysteria. She is locked in an upstairs room and denied any real form of social, physical, or mental activity. For Gilman, this turn of events hit close to home: She, too, was labeled "hysterical" and prescribed such a cure.

Some alternative remedies for female hysteria included prescribing cod liver oil or applying leeches to the cervix. In the early 20th century, the studies of Austrian psychiatrist Sigmund Freud supported the idea of a female sexual drive, so society eventually retreated from the idea of the "sexless woman." By mid-century, there was a noticeable decline in the number of diagnoses, and eventually, the American Psychiatric Association omitted hysteria from the list of official medical conditions. Doctors favored more specific and accurate diagnoses, reclassifying patients as having post-partum depression, anxiety disorders, schizophrenia, or other forms of mental illness, rather than hysteria.

The Times They Are A-Changin'

1922

- Insulin saves the life of a young man in its first use as a treatment for diabetes.

- Johnny Weissmuller, best known for his later film roles as Tarzan, swims the 100-meter freestyle race in 58.6 seconds, setting a world record and breaking the one-minute mark.

- President Warren G. Harding brings the White House into the modern age by installing the first radio.

- The Union of Soviet Socialist Republics (USSR or Soviet Union) is established in Eurasia.

- The $3 million Lincoln Memorial is dedicated on the shores of the Potomac River in Washington, D.C.

- Joseph Stalin becomes general secretary of the Communist Party. In 1924, he becomes leader of the Soviet Union, succeeding Vladimir Lenin.

- Georgia politician Rebecca Latimer Felton is appointed to fill a Senate vacancy and is sworn into office as the first female U.S. Senator. The 87-year-old former suffragette holds the seat for one day before a newly elected male senator takes her place.

- Libya can get hot in September. The city of El Aziziyah reaches a world record high temperature of 136.4 degrees Fahrenheit in the shade.

- Archaeologist Howard Carter and his team make an exciting discovery in Egypt's Valley of the Kings when they find the entrance to King Tutankhamun's tomb.

- In response to a challenge to the 19th Amendment, a woman's right to vote is unanimously upheld and declared constitutional by the U.S. Supreme Court.

- Construction of Yankee Stadium begins in the Bronx.

The Real Legends of Hollywood

❖ ❖ ❖ ❖

*They say that truth is stranger than fiction. Nowhere is
that more obvious than in Tinseltown, where legends are
born... and some really great urban legends are, too!*

Suicide in *The Wizard of Oz*

In *The Wizard of Oz,* Dorothy, the Tin Man, and the Scarecrow
leave the Tin Man's cabin and go skipping down the Yellow Brick
Road. Everything's upbeat and in Technicolor, right? However,
according to a persistant Hollywood tale, allegedly there's a
Munchkin in the trees preparing to hang himself. Seconds later,
his lifeless body is supposedly seen dropping from the trees as the
skipping trio exit the scene. Those close to the movie claim that
what appears to be a Munchkin is nothing more than an exotic
bird, such as a crane or an emu, brought to the set from the Los
Angeles Zoo to make the scene more realistic. Nevertheless, the
legend still refuses to die.

Three Men and a Baby...and a Ghost

According to legend, the ghost of a young boy who accidentally
shot himself haunts the building where portions of *Three Men and
a Baby* were filmed. Also, in one scene viewers can see the outline
of a phantom shotgun in the window, then seconds later, the boy's
ghost appears in the frame standing in front of the same window.

   Those images do appear in the background of a scene, but
producers claim the shotgun is just an optical illusion caused by
light on the curtains. As for the ghostly boy, they say it's nothing
more than a cardboard cutout of actor Ted Danson that was left in
the scene by mistake. To further squash the ghost story, producers
point out that the scenes were shot on a soundstage and not in an
actual apartment building.

The Texas Chain Saw Massacre Is a True Story

When Tobe Hooper's *The Texas Chain Saw Massacre* first hit
theaters in 1974, it was touted as being based on a true story, even

using the line "It happened!" on movie posters. But the truth isn't so black and white. Hooper did base the character Leatherface on a real person—murderer and grave robber Ed Gein. But although Gein was a convicted killer who also fashioned human body parts into jewelry and furniture, there is no evidence that he offed anyone with a chain saw. And he lived in Wisconsin, not Texas. Apparently *The Wisconsin Rifle-Shootin' Massacre* wasn't as scintillating.

O. J. Simpson Was Considered for the Lead Role in *The Terminator*

Most people are familiar with the iconic image of Arnold Schwarzenegger as the murderous Terminator cyborg. What many people don't know, though, is that one of the actors considered for the lead role was none other than O. J. Simpson. Produers passed on Simpson because they felt he was too "nice" and wouldn't be believable playing the role of a killer. Although ironic, this tale appears to be true.

Disney's Snuff Film

In the 1958 Disney documentary *White Wilderness,* dozens of lemmings are shown jumping to their deaths off a cliff into the ocean as part of a bizarre suicide ritual. There was only one glitch: Lemmings don't commit suicide en masse. When principal photographer James R. Simon arrived in Alberta, Canada to film, he was informed of this. But rather than scrap the project, Simon had the lemmings herded up and forced off the cliff while the cameras rolled. As the creatures struggled to keep from drowning, the narrator delivered the disturbing and all-too-telling line: "It's not given to man to understand all of nature's mysteries."

Despite the film winning an Oscar for Best Documentary in 1959, once the truth about what happened on those cliffs was revealed, it quickly and quietly was locked away, becoming one of Disney's deep, dark secrets.

The Death of Actor Vic Morrow Can Be Seen in *Twilight Zone: The Movie*

In the early morning of July 23, 1982, actor Vic Morrow and two children were re-creating a Vietnam War battle scene—complete with helicopters and explosions—for *Twilight Zone: The Movie.*

The scene began fine, but then one of the helicopter pilots lost control and crashed, killing Morrow and the two child actors. Multiple cameras were rolling at the time and caught the carnage on film, but the footage was locked away. However, while the deaths don't appear in the *Twilight Zone* film, some of the tragic scenes appeared in the 1992 direct-to-video flick *Death Scenes 2.*

The *Poltergeist* Movies Are Cursed

A series of strange, unexpected deaths surrounding actors who worked on the popular *Poltergeist* films have led many to believe that the supernatural theme of the movies has conjured up curses over those associated with them. There have been several untimely deaths, including 22-year-old Dominique Dunne, who played older daughter Dana Freeling in the original *Poltergeist.* She died in November 1982 as a result of injuries sustained when she was attacked by her abusive boyfriend. Little blonde Heather O'Rourke, who starred in all three movies as the perpetually haunted Carol Anne, died of septic shock on February 1, 1988, at age 12. Today, her grave site is a stop on the popular "Haunted Hollywood" tour.

Other cast member deaths were more expected. When Julian Beck, who played Kane in *Poltergeist II: The Other Side,* passed away in September 1985, he was 60 years old and had been battling stomach cancer for nearly two years. Similarly, Will Sampson, the lovable Native American guide from *Poltergeist II,* died from complications after receiving a heart and lung transplant. It's not apparent there's a *Poltergeist* curse, but there sure has been a lot of real-life tragedy.

Talk to the Expert

CAKE DECORATOR

Q: Cake decorators have been around forever, but shows such as *Ace of Cakes* seem to have brought new attention to the industry.
A: I think that people have become more educated in what they can ask for because they've seen it on TV. Although they're sometimes overeducated, because they think that's always feasible and practical.

Q: What's the most outrageous cake you've been asked to make?
A: It wasn't that it was outrageously decorated or that the design was so funny. It was what it said and its size. It was a very, very large cake—a full sheet—and it had polka dots, which of course are very "holey," and it said "Dear John, Welcome to the team. Love, God."

Q: Any notable mishaps?
A: There have been times when the cakes have turned out less than geometrically correct, and there's some creative propping up. When I used to do more children's cakes, there was a lot of miscommunication between the people who took the orders and the kitchen in the back. Once, the cake form was from this woman for her daughter's birthday, and it said she wanted a "frog wearing a purple clown on its head." So we did it; then she was incensed, because it was supposed to be a *crown.*

Q: What would people be surprised to learn about cake decorating?
A: How much food touching is involved—it's very hands-on. When I was first learning, I was surprised at how aggressive you can be with cake. You can really throw it around and do a lot of moving and pushing and poking. It's a much more full-contact sport than people might imagine.

Q: What are some of the biggest mistakes people make when they order cake?
A: Trying to have too much. It's best to have some thoughtful editing in their design.

Q: In your expert opinion, what's the best accompaniment to cake: coffee, milk, or champagne?
A: Champagne. That's a no-brainer.

If You Don't Gnome Me By Now

❖ ❖ ❖ ❖

*Some people think they're tacky. Sometimes the little fellas
are stolen from yards, gardens, and porches. But at The
Gnome Reserve and Wildflower Garden, garden gnomes
and pixies are treated with reverence and respect.*

Tucked into the lush English countryside, covering
four acres of rolling meadows, beechwood trees, and
a little stream, lies the land of gnomes. And it exists
thanks to a collector who, for three decades, has acted
as an ambassador for those jolly little bearded men.

In 1978, Ann Fawssett Atkin founded The
Gnome Reserve and Wildflower Garden in Devon.
Atkin has said that gnomes are the guardians of the
environment, and she has taken great pains to collect
(and make) more than a thousand of them.

Before you can start looking for these friendly
sprites, you have to adapt to the culture of the area.
Visitors are immediately given a red gnome hat. That's
right: As the reserve's Web site points out, "Gnome hats are loaned
free of charge together with fishing rods, so you don't embarrass the
gnomes!"

After getting properly attired, visitors may wander through the
grounds of the reserve, where they try to spot at least a few of the
more than 1,000 little figures hidden in the grass and trees. Once
visitors have their fill of gnomes, they may take a stroll through the
wildflower gardens, which feature more than 250 different species
of wildflowers, grasses, herbs, and ferns.

In addition to the great gnome outdoors, there's more to see
in the Gnome Gallery, including many of Atkin's own paintings,
featuring flower, sea, and forest scenes—with gnomes and pixies, of
course. Resin and concrete gnomes and clay pixies are also available
for purchase. "There is room in everyone's garden for a gnome," says
Atkin. "They are timeless creatures who are as ancient as the hills
yet as young as a child."

Fast Facts

- Thomas Edison adored songbirds, and at one point, he kept an aviary of 5,000 birds.

- At one point, Alexander Hamilton wanted to do away with individual states and call the country "the United State of America."

- During the Civil War's Battle of Antietam, nurse Clara Barton tended to the wounded so close to the front lines that a bullet once passed through the sleeve of her blouse and killed the soldier she was treating.

- Besides being a silversmith, Paul Revere was also a dentist.

- Isaac Newton dropped out of school at the urging of his mother, who wanted him to become a farmer.

- Sigmund Freud could not read a railroad schedule. Somebody almost always went with him on trips. Try not to read into that.

- In the 1800s, King Ferdinand II of Naples was so grossed out by the fact that pasta was then made by kneading the dough with bare feet—that is, often dirty and smelly bare feet—that he hired an engineer to design a pasta-making machine.

- The first Cadillac cost less than the original Ford Model T— $750 as compared to $875.

- In 17th-century America, the average married woman gave birth to 13 children.

- The cigarette lighter was invented before the match.

- Frida Kahlo aside, women historically have hated their lip hair. The first depilatory (using arsenic) dates back to 4,000 B.C.

Classic Monster Quiz

Think you know everything about Dracula, Frankenstein, and the Mummy? Don't be scared to give this classic monster quiz a shot!

1. How many times did Bela Lugosi play Dracula in the movies?

2. Who was originally supposed to play Frankenstein's Monster?

3. Which film came out first: *Frankenstein, Dracula,* or *The Mummy?*

4. In which long-running television show did Frankenstein's Monster portrayer Glenn Strange star?

5. What was Lon Chaney Jr.'s real name?

6. What actor kills the Wolf Man in the first *Wolf Man* movie?

7. How long does actor Boris Karloff appear as the completely bandaged mummy in *The Mummy?*

8. When the Invisible Man begins to unwrap his bandages for the curious townspeople, what is the first object he throws at them?

9. What actor starred in the pre-*Wolf Man* film *Werewolf of London?*

10. What was the name of Universal Studio's legendary makeup man?

11. What actor starred in all three of Universal's first movies in the series: *Frankenstein, Dracula,* and *The Mummy?*

12. How many roles did Elsa Lancaster play in *Bride of Frankenstein?*

13. Who bites Lon Chaney Jr. in *The Wolf Man* to turn him into a werewolf?

14. What is the first name of Dr. Frankenstein in the novel *Frankenstein?* And what is his name in the film version?

15. What was Boris Karloff's real name?

16. What was the human name of the Mummy in the first movie from 1932? What is his name in the sequels?

17. According to legend, where did *Frankenstein* director James Whale first spot Boris Karloff?

18. In all the *Mummy* movies but the first one, what substance is needed by the creature to keep him alive?

19. At the height of his fame, how was Boris Karloff listed in film credits?

ANSWERS

1. Two; 2. Bela Lugosi; 3. Dracula, in 1931; 4. Gunsmoke; 5. Creighton Chaney; 6. Claude Rains as Sir John Talbot; 7. Only for the first few minutes; 8. His false nose; 9. Henry Hull; 10. Jack P. Pierce; 11. Edward Van Sloan; 12. Two—The Bride and Mary Shelley; 13. Bela Lugosi; 14. In the novel, it's Victor; in the film, it's Henry.; 15. William Henry Pratt; 16. Imhotep in the first movie, Kharis in the subsequent films; 17. In the Universal Studios commissary; 18. *Tana leaves;* 19. Karloff the Uncanny

Can-Do Spirit

In 1810, British merchant Peter Durand revolutionized food preservation with his invention of the steel can—literally a lifesaver for soldiers on the field. There was only one problem: He didn't consider how to open the cans. While soldiers could easily use a rifle or bayonet to get at the vittles inside, regular folks were left to use hammers and chisels or screwdrivers. Also, the cans were inordinately heavy, weighing as much as a pound, even when empty.

Lighter cans debuted in the 1850s, and in 1858, Ezra Warner of Connecticut introduced the first can opener (though some say it was invented by Robert Yeats in 1855). Described as a kind of "twisted bayonet," the sharp-ended tool took some serious muscle power to work around a can. Nevertheless, one was rationed to each Union soldier during the Civil War.

In 1870, William Lyman's much-improved version of Warner's model hit the market as the first opener with a wheel for cutting in a smooth, continuous manner. Fifty-five years later, the Star Can Company patented another iteration of the opener, this time featuring the more contemporary two-wheel design, with a serrated wheel to grip the can and another wheel to cut around the edges.

Hook and Eyes on the Prize

It was frustration with the practical but annoying high-button shoe that prompted the invention of the zipper in 1893. Chicagoan Whitcomb Judson patented a fastening device called the "clasp locker" and modeled it at the Chicago World's Fair. Wealthy financier Colonel Lewis Walker partnered with Judson to launch the Universal Fastener Company.

Unfortunately, while Judson's early model had potential, it was bulky and was plagued with issues of jamming and unreliability. Despite several efforts to perfect his vision, Judson died in 1909 without a solid working model. In his stead, Swedish engineer Otto Friedrick Gideon Sundback picked up the project. In 1913, he patented the "hookless fastener"—a godsend to U.S. soldiers during WWI for flight suits and life vests. After the war, the fasteners began to find footing with consumers, but they still didn't make their way onto clothing until the mid- to late 1930s.

The term "zipper" was the 1921 brainstorm of the B. F. Goodrich Company in Akron, Ohio, which manufactured galoshes featuring the fastening device. The company wanted a word to describe "the way the thing zips."

Crockefeller

❖ ❖ ❖ ❖

What began as a search to find a missing girl uncovered 30 years of fraud, fake identities, and possible foul play. Before Christian Karl Gerhartstreiter was a convict, he was a con artist.

It started as a case of parental kidnapping not uncommon in custody battles: In July 2008, Clark Rockefeller, a descendant of the moneyed oil family, absconded with his seven-year-old daughter during a court-supervised visitation in Boston.

But oddly, FBI databases showed no record of a Clark Rockefeller, and the Rockefeller family denied any connection. His ex-wife, millionaire consultant Sandra Boss, confessed he had no identification, no social security number, and no driver's license. *So who was this guy?* The FBI released his picture, hoping for information. And that's when the stories—and aliases—began pouring in.

Fake Foreign Exchange

His real identity is Christian Karl Gerhartstreiter, a German national who came to the United States in 1978 at age 17, claiming to be a foreign exchange student. In truth, he showed up unannounced on the doorstep of a Connecticut family he'd met on a train in Europe, who'd suggested he look them up if he ever visited the States.

After living with them briefly, he posted an ad describing himself as an exchange student in search of a host and was taken in by the Stavio family. They threw him out after it became clear he expected to be treated like royalty. During this time, Gerhartstreiter allegedly became enamored with the *Gilligan's Island* character Thurston Howell III, the ascot-wearing millionaire, and even adopted Howell's snobbish accent.

Bogus Brit

In 1980, "Chris Gerhart" enrolled at the University of Wisconsin–Milwaukee as a film major and persuaded another student to marry him so that he could get his green card (they divorced as soon as he got it). Shortly after the wedding, he left school and headed to Los Angeles to pursue a film career—this time posing as the dapper

British blue-blood Christopher Chichester (a name he borrowed from his former high school teacher).

He settled in the swanky town of San Marino, living in a building with newlyweds John and Linda Sohus. The couple went missing in 1985, around the same time Chichester moved away; allegedly, he went back to England following a death in the family.

Chichester resurfaced in Greenwich, Connecticut, as former Hollywood producer and business tycoon Christopher Crowe. It was under this name that, in 1988, he tried to sell a truck that had belonged to the Sohus. Police investigators traced the Sohus's missing truck to Connecticut, and they soon realized that Crowe and Chichester were the same person. But by then, he'd already vanished.

Mock Rock

Now he was Manhattan's Clark Rockefeller, the new darling of the elite. It was here that he met and married the Ivy League-educated business whiz Sandra Boss. For most of their 12-year marriage, Sandra believed his elaborate stories. She even believed he'd filed the paperwork for their marriage to be legal (it appears he hadn't).

Eventually, however, Sandra grew suspicious. She filed for divorce and won full custody of their seven-year-old daughter, Reigh, and the two moved to London. Clark was limited to three court-supervised visits per year. It was on the first of these visits that he kidnapped her.

Con-clusion

In August 2008, the con man was arrested in Baltimore, and Reigh was returned to her mother. In June 2009, a judge sentenced him to four to five years in prison.

Gerhartsreiter has yet to be arraigned in California for the Sohus case, which went cold until 1994, when new owners found skeletal remains in the backyard of the San Marino home. Neighbors remember Chichester borrowing a chainsaw shortly before the Sohuses disappeared and complaining of "plumbing problems" when asked why the backyard was dug up.

Gerhartsreiter says he has no recollection of his life before the 1990s. And he insists on being called Mr. Rockefeller because that's his name, thank you very much.

WORD HISTORIES

Yogalates: This may sound like a drink, but it's actually much better for you. It's a term that began in the 1990s to describe a fitness routine that combines Pilates exercises with the breathing techniques of yoga.

Shyster: Wherever it may have come from, you don't want to be called this word! The first official record of its use was in the *Dictionary of American English* in 1848. Deriving from the German *shicer*, it means a person or thing that is deemed worthless. It most likely gets its meaning from an even earlier German word, *Scheisse*, which means excrement. You get the idea.

Mushroom: This name doesn't describe the fungus but probably resulted from the mispronunciation of the French word, *mousseron*. Before the French word became popular, the mushroom was often known by its more descriptive name: toad's hat.

Spinster: Originally the word "spinster" simply described a woman who spins wool. But the meaning has done some spinning of its own, ~ntually coming to mean a woman with little else to do but spin, as in a dried-up old woman or unmarried old maid.

Choconiverous: This modern word refers to the tendency to bite off the head of a chocolate Easter Bunny before any other part.

Gerrymander: "Gerrymandering" refers to dividing a geographic area into voting districts so that one political party has an unfair advantage in elections. Elbridge Gerry, former governor of Massachusetts, is the man behind the practice: His supporters were responsible for creating a voting district that supposedly resembled the shape of a salamander. Gerrymandering was first used in April 1812, when Gerry was thought to have created this political monster for his own gain.

Kowtow: Strictly meaning "to bow and touch your forehead to the floor," this verb has come to mean showing deference to someone else. The origin is a bit harsher, deriving from the Chinese words *kou* (head) and *tou* (to knock). Ouch.

Dad Data

❖ ❖ ❖ ❖

Here, at a glance, are America's fathers by the figures.

- There are 64.3 million fathers living in America.

- Of those, 140,000 listed themselves as stay-at-home dads in 2008.

- When it comes to coupling, 25.8 million fathers of kids younger than 18 are married.

- Meanwhile, 1.8 million are single dads. They're far outnumbered by single moms, though: According to census data, women make up 84 percent of single parents.

- Fifty-one percent of fathers are divorced, while 25 percent have never been married.

- Two percent of all dads say they live in someone else's home.

- Fatherhood isn't limited only to biological kids: 11 percent of dads live with stepchildren.

- In 2005, separated fathers owed $34.7 billion in child support. They paid only $22.4 billion of it.

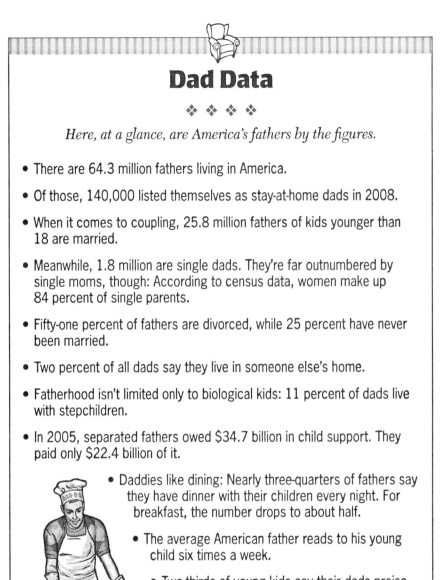

- Daddies like dining: Nearly three-quarters of fathers say they have dinner with their children every night. For breakfast, the number drops to about half.

- The average American father reads to his young child six times a week.

- Two-thirds of young kids say their dads praise them at least three times a day.

- The first Father's Day was celebrated in 1909. It wasn't until 1966 that President Lyndon B. Johnson declared that the third Sunday of every June would be known as Father's Day. Six years later, President Richard Nixon officially signed it into law.

Going to Hell (Michigan)

❖ ❖ ❖ ❖

When it comes to capitalizing on an interesting name, the
residents of Hell, Michigan, have a helluva talent.

Welcome to Hell

Some people claim to have gone through Hell; other people (approximately 266 of them) actually live there. The tiny unincorporated community in southeast Michigan attracts many visitors each year who are determined to have a "Hell of a time"—or at least leave with some memorable souvenirs. Fortunately, local residents (known as Hellions) have embraced their town's name and are happy to deliver the kitsch. Visitors can purchase a souvenir baseball bat, otherwise known as "A Bat Outta Hell," or an "Official Deed" to own one square inch of Hell. Among the town's hot attractions are Screams Ice Cream Parlor and Hell's Wedding Chapel. There's even a "fully non-accredited" school called Damnation University that provides souvenir diplomas.

Despite its name, the community of Hell is actually a serene place situated among hills and creeks. In the 1830s, a pioneer named George Reeves recognized its beauty and decided to settle there. He operated a dam and mill on what is now Hell Creek, and he also built a distillery, where he made whiskey out of excess wheat. Local farmers took a liking to the whiskey, and Reeves became a popular guy among other pioneers who came to Hell to "drink in the beauty."

To Hell and Back

There are different theories about the origin of the name. In one, a couple of German travelers arrived to the lovely landscape and said *"So schoene hell,"* which roughly translates to "So bright and beautiful." In another, state officials asked Reeves what the town should be named, and he supposedly responded, "You can name it Hell for all I care." Another theory is that the area, swampy and full of bugs, created a miserable experience for settlers, who deemed it Hell. Either way, thanks to some creative decision-maker, everyone with an interest in kitschy vacation destinations can now claim they've been "To Hell and back."

Fast Facts

- *The envelope came into use around 1839. Before that, people would fold their letters, seal them with wax, and write the address on the back.*

- *In Pacific Grove, California, it is a misdemeanor (punishable by a $1,000 fine) to kill or threaten a butterfly. No word on what happens if you're just rude to it.*

- *According to lore, the Greek playwright Aeschylus was killed by an errant tortoise. An eagle flying overhead had a tortoise in its claws, and it mistook Aeschylus's bald head for a rock and dropped the animal onto it.*

- *One reason that Benjamin Franklin was not considered to author the Declaration of Independence was the fear he would conceal a joke in it.*

- *Rudyard Kipling, author of* The Jungle Book, *was fired as a reporter by* The San Francisco Examiner *because "[he just didn't] know how to use the English language."*

- *Playwright George Bernard Shaw rejected receiving England's prestigious Order of Merit because, he said, "I have already conferred this order upon myself."*

- *In the 1830s, ketchup was sold in America as a patent medicine called Dr. Miles's Compound Extract of Tomato.*

- *British naval commander Viscount Horatio Nelson never got over his seasickness.*

- *Stainless steel was discovered by accident.*

- *Move over, Jumbo! The average American consumes six pounds of peanuts and peanut products every year.*

Before Basketball

❖ ❖ ❖ ❖

Meet James Naismith, the man behind basketball.

The Man Behind the Ball

Born in 1861, James Naismith was raised in the small Canadian village of Bennie's Corners, Ontario. Naismith grew up both morally and physically fit, performing heavy chores, walking five miles across frozen fields to school, and playing with his friends near the village blacksmith shop.

Later, at McGill University in Montreal, Naismith earned degrees in philosophy and Hebrew while playing hard-hitting sports such as rugby and lacrosse. Despite the prevailing Victorian opinion that sports were violent and vice-ridden, James was convinced that sports could be used to instill good values. He attended International Young Men's Christian Association Training School in Springfield, Massachusetts, where he worked toward his divinity degree while teaching physical education.

Playing Naismithball

In 1891, the school's superintendent challenged Naismith to develop an indoor sport that would keep the boys busy during the cold winter months and that would be "fair for all players, and free of rough play."

Naismith carefully planned this new sport. Games with larger balls were less violent, he noted, so he chose to use a soccer ball. Abuse between players occurred more frequently when the ball was near the goal. Naismith's new game would have goals placed above the player's heads. He also noticed that injuries occurred most often between players in motion. The players in his game would stop as soon as they had possession of the ball.

To solve the problem of how to get the ball into the goal, Naismith showed his students how to throw using a lobbing motion he and his friends developed while playing a game called "Duck on a Rock" in Bennie's Corners. Armed with their "Duck on a Rock" skills, Naismith's students played the first game of basketball in December 1891, using wooden peach baskets nailed to the walls of the gym. School members called for the game to be named "Naismithball" after its inventor, but he stuck to his guns and the game became known as "Basket Ball."

Spice It Up a Little

What would become the vast Marriott Corporation (which later included Marriott Hotels, Big Boy Coffee Shops, and Farrell's Ice Cream Parlors) began in 1927 as a tiny restaurant on a corner in Washington, D.C. John Marriott was only in his twenties when he opened the nine-seat Hot Shoppe diner, but before long he ran into trouble when business dipped along with the stock market. Desperate to lure customers, he begged the chef at the nearby Mexican Embassy to give him the recipes for chile con carne and hot tamales. The change in menu worked, and soon Marriott was on his way to building a fortune.

Statues of Limitations

Elizabeth Bonduel "Baby Doe" McCourt Tabor was the sensation of the rough-and-tumble American West. Arriving in the mining town of Central City, Colorado, in the late 1870s, she was married to a no-good lazy fella named Henry Doe Jr., and the couple had to move constantly because of lack of money. Elizabeth spent much of her time working in the mines to make ends meet. A woman working in the mines was rather unheard of at the time, but her fellow male miners admired her gumption, and dubbed her "Baby Doe."

But Baby Doe's ship came in when she ditched the loser and remarried Denver millionaire Horace Tabor (after a long struggle to get rid of his stubborn first wife). She was determined to impress the old biddies in Denver's high society but still maintain her sense of self. When they complained about the nude statues on the Tabors's lawn, she called in a seamstress to make dresses for the figures rather than simply moving them. Needless to say, Baby Doe's sense of humor did little to endear her to the city's snobbish matrons, and she was never admitted into Denver society.

The Vicious Circle

❖ ❖ ❖ ❖

*Sharp tongues and smooth martinis were standard fare in the
Rose Room of Manhattan's Algonquin Hotel circa 1920, where
some of the city's most prominent young literati—writers, critics,
humorists, and artists—gathered daily to drink, dine, and dish.
But visitors had to beware when this lunch bunch grabbed a bite.*

Joker's Wild

The whole thing started as a joke played on Alexander Woollcott, the
New York Times' sharp-witted theater critic. In June 1919, publicist
Murdock Pemberton organized a luncheon at the Algonquin Hotel
under the guise of welcoming the caustic critic back from his overseas service as a war correspondent. In reality, Pemberton planned
the event as a roast to poke fun at Woollcott and his tendency to
drone on with lengthy war stories. Invitations were sent to Woollcott's
friends, including well-known writers and critics such as *Vanity Fair's*
Dorothy Parker and Robert Benchley. Ultimately, Woollcott had such
a good time that he suggested the group meet at the hotel for lunch
every day.

A Rose by Any Other Name

In addition to Woollcott, Parker, Pemberton, and Benchley, the
group included a regular roster of up-and-comers on the Manhattan
art scene. Novelist Edna Ferber; comedian Harpo Marx; playwrights
Marc Connelly, George Kaufman, and Robert E. Sherwood; journalist Heywood Broun and his wife Ruth Hale; and *Times* columnist
Franklin Pierce Adams were among the core group. Other friends
and acquaintances made appearances as well, such as actress Tallulah
Bankhead and playwright Noël Coward.

For more than a decade, the group lunched at the hotel six days
a week (every day except Sunday). Initially they met in the Pergola
Room, today known as the Oak Room. Hotel manager Frank
Case served them complimentary celery, olives, and popovers and
gave them their own designated waiter to ensure repeat business.
Eventually, as more guests joined the party, Case designated a

large round table just for them in the Rose Room at the back of the restaurant.

At first the group called itself The Board and its lunchtime liaisons "Board Meetings." When the group got a new waiter named Luigi, this quickly became the Luigi Board—a play on the popular Ouija board craze of the day.

Pun-Upsmanship

Witticism was the pet pastime of the Algonquin group, who were famous for their one-liners. In one story, Benchley entered the Rose Room on a rainy day and announced, "I've got to get out of these wet clothes and into a dry martini."

In another favorite game, group members challenged one another to use obscure words in a sentence—the goal, of course, to one-up each other with clever puns, the more terrible the better. According to lore, it was during this game that Parker notably uttered, "You can lead a horticulture but you can't make her think" and "Hiawatha nice girl until I met you."

Sometimes the barbs were launched at each other. The group skewered Connelly's play *Honduras* as "the big Hondurance contest" and openly trashed Ferber's novel *Mother Knows Best.* Once, the effete playwright Noël Coward commented on the masculine cut of Ferber's suit, allegedly saying she "almost looked like a man."

"So do you," retorted Ferber.

Members of the group often collaborated; one of the most famous projects being the *New Yorker.* Editor and friend of the Round Table Harold Ross launched the magazine in 1925 with funds provided by the hotel, hiring Parker as the magazine's book reviewer and Benchley as the drama critic. (Today, guests of the Algonquin Hotel receive a complimentary copy of the magazine.)

For some visitors to the group, the constant verbal sparring proved too much, and they never came back. One guest claimed it was impossible to even ask for the salt without someone trying to make a "smartie" about it. The ruthless remarks inspired the group to call itself the Vicious Circle—although Ferber personally preferred Poison Squad. After a caricature of them appeared in the *Brooklyn Eagle* in 1920, the group publicly became cemented as the Algonquin Round Table.

The Bite Back

Naturally with so much success comes backlash, and artists outside the circle criticized the group deeply. Writer H. L. Mencken disparaged his contemporaries as "literati of the third, fourth, and fifth rate." Others complained group members were only interested in "self-promotion" and "back scratching." Still others accused the group of being too competitive and "forcing" its off-the-cuff humor, with some members even writing down one-liners in advance to casually toss out at the table.

Connelly once said that trying to remember the end of the Algonquin Round Table was like "remembering falling asleep"—it just sort of happened. But by the time the Great Depression of the 1930s hit, the Algonquin's boozy lunch bunch had all but disbanded. Some, such as Parker and Benchley, moved on to Hollywood to write for films.

Today, tourists can get a glimpse of the Algonquin Round Table's New York in a historic walking tour led by the president of the Dorothy Parker Society. Afterward, lunch is served at the hotel's restaurant, now named the Round Table after its legendary patrons.

They Said It

"Epitaph for a dead waiter: God finally caught his eye."

—George Kaufman

"I don't want you to think I'm not incoherent."

—Harold Ross

"Being an old maid is like death by drowning, a really delightful sensation after you cease to struggle."

—Edna Ferber

"Drawing on my fine command of the English language, I said nothing."

—Robert Benchley

"That woman speaks eighteen languages and can't say 'no' in any of them."

—Dorothy Parker

"Wit ought to be a glorious treat like caviar; never spread it about like marmalade."

—Noël Coward

Cleveland's Secret Cancer

❖ ❖ ❖ ❖

*Grover Cleveland, the only man elected president of the
United States to two nonconsecutive terms, was known
as "Grover the Good" for his honesty. However, there
was one time when Cleveland was not very honest.*

The Painful Truth

In 1893, Cleveland had only recently returned to the White House,
this time as the 24th president. America had just entered a national
economic depression, the Panic of 1893. To help the economy
recover, Cleveland wanted to repeal the Sherman Silver Purchase
Act and maintain the gold standard.

On June 13, 1893, Cleveland had some pain on the left—or
the "cigar-chewing"—side of the roof of his mouth. A few days
later, he noticed a rough spot in the area as well. Five days later,
he asked White House physician R. M. O'Reilly to take a look. The
doctor discovered a cauliflower-like area the size of a quarter in the
president's mouth. Samples were sent to several doctors for biopsy,
and the results came back as malignant. Cleveland's close friend
Dr. Joseph Bryant reportedly said to him, "Were it in my mouth,
I would have it removed at once."

We've Got a Secret

But having surgery wasn't that easy. With the economy on the skids,
the country jittery, and a pro-silver vice president (Adlai Stevenson),
Cleveland did not want to further upset the nation by announcing
that his health was at risk. So he ordered his condition be kept secret
from the public.

However, his medical team was racing against a deadline. It
was now late June. Congress would reconvene on August 7, and
Cleveland wanted to have recovered enough to personally campaign
to persuade wavering congressmen to vote for free silver repeal.
Meanwhile, the doctors were desperate to perform the surgery and
stop the cancer from spreading.

It was agreed the surgery was to be conducted on July 1. For maximum secrecy, the operation was to be held on the yacht *Oneida*, owned by the president's friend Commodore Elias Benedict. This was logical; Cleveland was often seen on Benedict's yacht, and with the July 4th holiday approaching it was an entirely plausible place for him to be.

Sink or Swim

The doctors had already slipped on board when Cleveland joined them on June 30. The yacht was floating in Bellevue Bay in New York City's East River—near Bellevue Hospital. Around noon on July 1, Cleveland went below deck and was propped up in a chair that was lashed to the mast. Fifty-six years old and corpulent, Cleveland was considered at high risk for a stroke if ether was used as an anesthetic. Dr. Bryant decided to use nitrous oxide instead and hope for the best. Bryant was so anxious about the operation and Cleveland's condition that he told the captain that if he hit a rock he should *really* hit it, so that they would all go to the bottom.

Over the next few hours, doctors removed Cleveland's entire left upper jaw, from the first bicuspid to past the last molar. Cleveland recovered in splendid isolation aboard the yacht for a few days, and then for a few weeks at his family's Cape Cod vacation home. A plug of vulcanized rubber was made to fill the huge hole in Cleveland's jaw. The press was told that Cleveland had been treated aboard the ship for two ulcerated teeth and rheumatism and was recovering nicely.

(Oh, and by the way, the free silver repeal did indeed pass Congress later that year, just as Cleveland had planned.)

Nixon Would Have Been Proud

That's where matters stayed for two decades. Even though a gabby doctor spilled the beans to the *Philadelphia Press* in late August 1898, in a wonderful pre-Watergate stonewalling effort, Cleveland's doctors and close friends managed to deny the story out of existence. Finally, in 1917—nine years after Cleveland's death—the full story was finally revealed in the *Saturday Evening Post*. Today, part of Cleveland's jaw can be seen at the Mütter Museum in Philadelphia.

Fast Facts

- Disney World, located in Florida, takes up 30,500 acres—about the same area as San Francisco.

- Ripon, Wisconsin, is known as the birthplace of the Republican Party.

- It's possible to make an estimated three to five baseball gloves from one cowhide.

- Necessity may be the mother of invention, but an 11-year-old created this treat: the Popsicle, invented back in 1905.

- Nearly 68 percent of a Hostess Twinkie is air.

- Sesame Street's Snuffleupagus wears a size 65 GGG shoe.

- A tiny drop of alcohol poured on a scorpion will cause it to go crazy and sting itself to death.

- Disney World in Florida manages to create about 120,000 pounds of garbage daily.

- Albert Einstein, Winston Churchill, William Shakespeare, and Leonardo daVinci all had learning disabilities.

- As many as 80 percent of all tall buildings are missing the 13th floor.

- The theme song of the popular TV show Frasier was sung by the show's star, Kelsey Grammer.

- "Mustache" comes from the Greek word mustax, meaning "upper lip."

'Toon Truths

❖ ❖ ❖ ❖

Animated cartoons have been around since the turn of the century, but in the past 40 years, the medium has become an integral part of popular culture. Read on for fascinating facts about a few of your favorite cartoons of yesteryear—and some contemporaries!

- During World War II, the Nazi propaganda newspaper *Das Schwarz* tried to discredit Superman by labeling the Man of Steel a Jew.

- *South Park* originated as a joke Christmas card video shared by Hollywood insiders. Among them was actor George Clooney, who distributed multiple copies of the short to friends. Later, Clooney showed his support for *South Park* creators Trey Parker and Matt Stone by voicing a gay dog named Sparky in an early episode of the series.

- The full names of the eponymous characters from the show *Ren & Stimpy* are Ren Höek and Stimpson J. Cat. By the way, Ren is a certified Asthma-Hound Chihuahua.

- *The Flintstones* was the first animated cartoon series to air in prime time, premiering on September 30, 1960. (Other series comprised of cartoon shorts had previously aired after 7 P.M., but *The Flintstones* was the first ongoing series with recurring characters.) The response was overwhelming. Critics praised the series, and both adults and children tuned in to enjoy the weekly antics of the "modern stone-age family." The initial series lasted six seasons and ran for several more years in syndication.

- *The Flintstones* was based in part on *The Honeymooners*, starring Jackie Gleason. The working title of the show was *The Flagstones*, but the name was changed after the producers received a letter from *Hi & Lois* creator Mort Walker, noting that his comic strip characters were named the Flagstones.

- The Reynolds Tobacco Company was an early sponsor of *The Flintstones*, so first-season episodes featured commercials in which Fred and Barney enjoy a smoke—something you would never see on a children's program today.

- Over the years, *The Flintstones* featured several real-life celebrities playing the stone-age version of themselves, including singer Ann-Margret (Ann-Margrock), songwriter Hoagy Carmichael (Stoney Carmichael), and actor Tony Curtis (Stoney Curtis).

- According to *Esquire* magazine, 58.2 percent of men surveyed found Betty Rubble more desirable than Wilma Flintstone.

- Jean Vander Pyl, who voiced Wilma, gave birth on February 22, 1963—the same day that Wilma gave birth to Pebbles on the show.

- It took *The Flintstones* producers two days of intensive meetings to decide whether the Flintstones would have a boy or a girl.

- *The Flintstones* proved so popular that a spin-off movie, a spy parody entitled *The Man Called Flintstone,* was released in 1966.

- On *The Jetsons,* George and Jane Jetson had an odd sleeping arrangement. In some episodes, their beds are apart. In others, their beds are pushed together. And in a few, they sleep in the same bed.

- On *Jonny Quest,* the character of Johnny's pal, Hadji, was based on the Indian actor Sabu.

- A young Tim Matheson, who later played Eric Stratton in *National Lampoon's Animal House,* provided the voice of Jonny Quest.

- Tweety Bird, the frequent foil of Sylvester the Cat, was originally pink. However, studio censors thought he looked a little too naked, so they demanded he be yellow instead.

- Actress Mae Questel, who voiced Olive Oyl in the early *Popeye* cartoons, also voiced Popeye in a handful of shorts while Popeye's regular voice actor, Jack Mercer, was overseas during World War II.

- Homer Simpson's e-mail address is Chunkylover53@aol.com.

- The Rio de Janeiro Tourist Board threatened to take legal action after an episode of *The Simpsons* portrayed the city as rife with crime and overrun by slums. (Executive producer James L. Brooks later apologized.) However, it wasn't the first time a municipality whined about its portrayal on the show. In season four, New Orleans city officials complained following an episode in which a musical production of *A Streetcar Named Desire* portrayed the city as "home of pirates, drunks and whores."

INSPIRATION STATION

Was *Utopia* a Utopia?

In 1516, Sir Thomas More wrote his most famous work: *Utopia*. Though the book portrayed the manners, religious habits, and political intrigues of the citizens of a fictional island called Utopia, More did not intend it to be read as some sort of far-flung fantasy. Indeed, he was inspired to write the story by events that were actually happening in England and Europe at the time.

Today, "utopia" is most often used to refer to a place of harmony and perfection, but More's story is anything but. In the book, slavery and euthanasia are both permitted by the Utopian government, and private property is forbidden. Modern readers often confuse More's interests and intellectual curiosity for advocacy, when in fact he was simply trying to spark debate on issues he felt would inevitably confront humans in the real world (for example, whether the church should include female priests). Indeed, it was one of these issues that brought about More's grisly end: After refusing to acknowledge the Church of England, Thomas More was beheaded by King Henry VIII in 1535.

Mother's Day

One of the greatest rap songs ever written, "Dear Mama" secured Tupac Shakur's legacy as a serious artist, but it came at the high price of heartbreak. The subject of the song, Shakur's mother Afeni Shakur, would never be confused with June Cleaver. A member of the radical Black Panther Party in the late '60s and early '70s, she later turned to welfare out of financial desperation and battled an addiction to crack cocaine. But in "Dear Mama," Shakur insists that even when zonked out on drugs, "you always was a black queen, Mama." The song goes on to describe how Afeni always managed to hold it together enough to keep Tupac and his younger sister relatively well cared for—until, that is, Tupac became a teen and was seduced by the easy money he could make selling crack with neighborhood thugs in Baltimore. Their love for one another ultimately triumphed, however, and when Shakur was killed in a drive-by shooting in 1996, he left her well cared for as executor of his estate.

Cross Country

❖ ❖ ❖ ❖

*Preacher Arthur Blessitt made history when he
set out on a four-decade-long pilgrimage.*

The "Minister of the Sunset Strip"

Arthur Blessitt was born in Mississippi in 1940, and at age 11 he converted to Christianity. By the time he was a young man in the 1960s, he had moved to California and was preaching the good word on Hollywood's infamous Sunset Strip. On Christmas Day in 1969, Blessitt claims he was called by Jesus to make a pilgrimage on foot to Capitol Hill in Washington, D.C. But he wouldn't make the journey alone: a 12-foot-tall, 45-pound wooden cross would accompany him. Blessitt put the cross on his back and began walking, with a mission to spread the word of Christ throughout the world.

These Shoes Were Made for Walkin'

Not long after he began, Blessitt realized his cross, which dragged on the ground, was losing about an inch of wood every day thanks to rough roads. He added a tricycle wheel to the base of his cross, which helped facilitate the trek.

Blessitt didn't stop his walk once he got to Capitol Hill. He didn't stop at the Atlantic Ocean, either. No, the preacher boarded a plane—he had to break the cross down to get it into a ski bag because it wouldn't fit on the aircraft—and flew overseas.

Over the next decade, Blessitt continued his journey. By 1984, he had walked across 60 countries on six continents. Of course, his quest wasn't easy, and sometimes it was downright dangerous. Still, he garnered quite a following and became an evangelical celebrity of sorts. He met with Yasser Arafat, Muammar al-Gaddafi, former UN Secretary Boutros Boutros-Ghali, and even Pope John Paul II.

Blessitt is credited with witnessing former president George W. Bush's conversion to born-again Christianity, and he proudly admits that over time, his cross-bearing shoulder built up an extra inch of bone. By the end of the pilgrimage, which ended in 2008, Blessitt had covered more than 38,000 miles on all seven continents.

MYTH CONCEPTIONS

Myth: Swallowing gum is dangerous because it will stay in your system for seven years.
Fact: Actually, gum doesn't just hang out in your guts. The gum will pass through your system and will likely come out the other end looking just like it did while you were chewing it. Ick.

Myth: Dried fruit isn't as good for you as fresh fruit.
Fact: Actually, ounce for ounce, dried fruit has the nutrients and vitamins that fresh fruit have, just less vitamin C. Stay away from dried fruit that has added sugar, but otherwise, eat all you want and rest easy knowing you got your fruit for the day.

Myth: If you don't dress warmly in the winter, you'll catch a cold.
Fact: Viruses, which cause the common cold, have no response to the temperature. People tend to get more colds in wintertime because they spend more time indoors with other people and viruses pass most easily between other humans.

Myth: Fingerprints are there to help you grip stuff.
Fact: Nope. Scientists in 2009 tested this age-old hypothesis and found that fingerprints don't improve a grip's friction. Why? Because fingerprints reduce our skin's contact with objects that we hold—and can actually loosen our grip in some circumstances. The actual reason for our fingerprints remains a bit of a mystery.

Myth: The trucks that collect recycling end up burning more energy and produce more pollution, making recycling pointless.
Fact: No way. It does take a lot of energy to recycle—in fact, it takes up about half of a recycling program's budget—but it's still worth it. It takes a lot less energy to convert something that already exists as, say, plastic, than to create plastic from raw materials. So keep recycling, kids.

Myth: Healthy folks poop once a day.
Fact: Though moving your bowels regularly helps keep away discomfort and constipation, studies show perfectly healthy people don't necessarily poop every day. You're not officially constipated until you've gone three days without a bowel movement.

That's Offal! 7 Dishes Made From Animal Guts

❖ ❖ ❖ ❖

For anyone raised on the standard American hamburger, the idea of eating the brains, guts, or feet of a cow may seem gross and totally out of the question. But in many parts of the world, those are the parts of the animal that are considered delicacies. The next time you make a trip to the butcher, ask for offal (the entrails and intestine) and rustle up something a little different for dinner.

1. Kokoretsi

In Greece, it's all about lamb. Skewered, baked, roasted—if it's lamb, the Grecians are cooking it. But these folks would never waste good meat: Kokoretsi is a traditional Balkan dish often served for Easter that includes lamb intestine, heart, lung, and kidneys, or a combination of any of the above. Chunks of these organs are speared onto a skewer and then wrapped up in the small intestine, which forms a kind of sausage casing. The spear is set over a fire and sprinkled with oregano and lemon juice. In a few hours, *opah!* Grilled guts for everyone!

2. Haggis

On paper, it just doesn't look appetizing: mix sheep's heart, liver, and lung meat with oatmeal and fat, and stuff the mixture into its own stomach; boil for three hours and enjoy. Still, that's exactly what haggis is, and the Scottish have been enjoying this dish for centuries. Traditionally served in a sauce with turnips and potatoes, this dish is used also in that popular national pastime, "haggis throwing."

3. Tripe

Is your stomach making those growly hungry noises? Try some stomach! Served in many countries across the globe, the stomach, known as tripe, is the main ingredient in many regional dishes. Beef tripe is the most commonly used stomach, but sheep, goat, and pig stomachs are often on the menu as well. Tripe is used often in soups and in French sausages, fried up in Filipino dishes, and used as a relish in

Zimbabwe. In Ireland and Northern England, tripe is simply served up with onions and a stiff drink.

4. Khash

If you're a cow, you'd better watch your step. Folks in Armenia are crazy about khash, a dish primarily made from cow's feet. First, the hooves are removed. Next, the feet are cleaned and cooked in plain boiling water overnight. By morning, the mixture is a thick broth and the meat has separated from the bone. Brain and stomach bits can be added for extra flavor. Armenians are careful about when they serve this favorite dish—it reportedly has strong healing properties—and it is usually served only on important holidays. Peppers, pickled veggies, and cheese go well with kash, but the favorite accompaniment is homemade vodka.

5. Yakitori

Who doesn't like a juicy grilled chicken skewer? Look closely if you purchase one from a Japanese street vendor, however. Yakitori are chicken skewers that contain more parts of the chicken than you may care to taste, including the heart, liver, gizzard, skin, tail, small intestine, tongue, and wing.

6. Rocky Mountain Oysters

There's not a lot on a farm animal you *can't* eat, as evidenced by Rocky Mountain Oysters, or bull testicles. Once the testicles of the bull (or lamb or buffalo) are removed, they're peeled, dipped in flour, and deep-fried to a golden crunch. This dish is commonly found in the American West, where bulls are prevalent, and also in bull-populated Spain.

7. White pudding

To make white pudding (and if you live in Scotland, Ireland, Nova Scotia, or Iceland, you might), you'll first need a big bowl of suet, or pork fat. It's the main ingredient in this dish, which also includes meat and oatmeal, and, in some earlier recipes, sheep brains. The pudding is similar to blood pudding, but without the blood. Sometimes formed into a sausage shape, white pudding can be cooked whole, fried, or battered and served in place of fish with chips.

The Science of Sleep

❖ ❖ ❖ ❖

*Insomnia is a serious issue in America—more than a third
of all adults suffer from sleepless nights (and not because of
active social lives, either). As anyone who's ever tossed and
turned till dawn can tell you, shutting down isn't always
simple. Here's a quick look at the science of sleep.*

The Faces of Insomnia

Insomnia comes in several variations. You can have
a tough time falling asleep, problems staying
asleep, or trouble sleeping late enough. You
can also just have problems getting the kind
of sleep that leaves you feeling refreshed. An
occasional bad night isn't necessarily a problem;
it's when the sandman stays away night after
night that insomnia comes into play.

Anyone can suffer from insomnia, although certain groups of
people are considered more susceptible: women, people over the age
of 60, and those who are depressed. Stress, noise, and an environment
that's too hot or too cold can make the condition worse, as well as the
overuse of caffeine and alcohol.

People who suffer from insomnia on a long-term basis may have
some physiological factor bringing those bags under their eyes every
morning. Sleep apnea, narcolepsy, and restless legs can all keep you
up, as can more serious conditions such as kidney disease or heart
failure.

Finding a Fix

Plenty of pills are available for sleep-starved zombies, both over-the-
counter and by prescription. The over-the-counter stuff won't usually
do much for true insomniacs, but medications such as Ambien and
Lunesta can provide relief (and perhaps unpleasant side effects). Some
doctors question whether pills are always needed and instead recommend working on learning to properly relax. Which, of course, would
be far less daunting after a good night's sleep.

⊡ Behind the TV Shows of Our Time

- Before he became a hugely famous movie star, Jim Carrey played a cartoonist on the 1984 flop sitcom *The Duck Factory.*

- The Chia Pet company once made a mohawked Mr. T Chia model.

- When Mary Tyler Moore named her production company MTM, she decided to spoof MGM's production slate of a lion roaring by using a tiny kitten meowing in her own production slate.

- Chuck Woolery, best known as the host of such game shows as *Wheel of Fortune* and *Love Connection,* once belonged to a psychedelic rock group named Avant Garde. The band had a minor hit with a song called "Naturally Stoned."

- Art Carney is best known for his role as dopey Ed Norton on *The Honeymooners,* but he went on to win an Academy Award in 1974 for his role in the film *Harry and Tonto.*

- One of the silliest attempts to capitalize on the 1970s women's movement was a very short-lived sitcom called *The Feminist and the Fuzz.* No, it wasn't about whether to shave one's armpits or not—it was just about a cop and a "women's libber."

- As an example of how prevalent the smoking habit once was, the 1971 TV movie *Cold Turkey* was about a town in which every adult citizen agrees to give up smoking at the same time.

- *Ferris Bueller,* an unsuccessful sitcom based on the movie *Ferris Bueller's Day Off,* costarred a very young Jennifer Aniston.

- When NBC aired the series finale of *Seinfeld* in 1998, the TV Land cable channel didn't even try to compete. Instead, they broadcast a sign that read, "WE'RE TV FANS; WE'RE WATCHING *SEINFELD.*"

- Football legend Joe Namath once wore Beauty Mist pantyhose in a commercial to show that Beauty Mist could "make any legs look like a million dollars." He quickly reassured viewers of his heterosexuality by adding with a wink, "...especially your legs."

- Before he was the voice of *Mister Ed,* actor Allan "Rocky" Lane starred in a number of B-movie westerns.

Solo Mission

❖ ❖ ❖ ❖

Thanks to paper cups, Dora Hall achieved her dreams of stardom.

Promotional Materials

Don't know who Dora Hall is? Don't fret—you're not alone. Hall was an obscure performer from the 1960s who was once called "the undisputed queen of vanity entertainment." She dreamed of making a career as a singer and actor but had very little performing experience—and well, she also came up a bit short in the talent department. Nevertheless, her utterly supportive husband, Leo Hulseman, was determined to make her show biz dreams come true.

Leo was founder of the Illinois-based Solo Cup Company, which made products such as disposable cups, bowls, and plates. Throughout the '60s, Leo paid for Dora to make a variety of record releases—featuring everything from country songs and show tunes to rock classics such as Elvis Presley's "I'm All Shook Up"—all of which were recorded on Solo subsidiary labels or affiliates, such as Calamo, Cozy, and Dot. Dora's albums were given away for free with Solo cups and plates as a "special promotion."

Dora Hits the Big Time

Leo then founded a TV production company in California called Premore Inc. Because Dora dreamed of being much more than a recording artist, Leo financed several elaborate TV specials (just one cost $400,000!), all of which were filmed at Premore. These quirky specials, such as *Rose on Broadway* and *Once Upon a Tour,* aired in the '70s and '80s, and they featured a now-elderly Dora as she sang and danced her way through various lighthearted story lines. She collaborated with the likes of Donald O'Connor, Rich Little, Ben Blue, Scatman Crothers, and Frank Sinatra Jr. What Dora lacked in sheer talent, she made up for in pizzazz and sparkly pantsuits.

Hall passed away in 1988, the grandmother of 16. Not much has been written about her career; thus, much about her remains a mystery. Even so, some people look back with fondness on her endearingly earnest performances.

Fast Facts

- The famous spy Mata Hari wore a new pair of white gloves and a specially tailored suit for her execution by a French firing squad.

- During the Middle Ages, it was believed that men had one rib fewer than women, because of the Biblical story that Eve had been created from Adam's rib.

- Until the 1850s, shoes could be worn on either foot.

- The famous Taj Mahal in India was nearly torn down in the 1830s.

- The Eiffel tower contains 2,500,000 rivets.

- Napoleon suffered from ailurophobia— the fear of cats.

- The middle initial in Harry S. Truman's name stood for nothing.

- Only one American president has been a bachelor: James Buchanan.

- After the telephone was invented, a phone booth in a hall in the White House served as the president's private phone.

- President James A. Garfield could simultaneously write Latin with one hand and Greek with the other.

- The Congress Avenue Bridge in Austin, Texas, is home to the largest urban bat colony in North America. From March to October—before the bats head south for the winter—tourists gather at dusk to watch nearly 1.5 million bats fly out to search for food.

Crater of Light

❖ ❖ ❖ ❖

James Turrell's Roden Crater is an epic earthwork-in-progress.

On the western edge of the Painted Desert northeast of Flagstaff, Arizona, a dormant volcano is the setting for an elaborate art project. Quaker artist James Turrell purchased the 400,000-year-old, two-mile crater in 1979, and since then he has been carving out tunnels, rooms, and circular openings that allow in light and a view of the sky. But when will Roden Crater be completed and visitors let in? That's a question Turrell fans—and others who "dig" land art installations—have been asking for years.

Digging a Hole

Throughout his artistic career, Turrell has played with space, light, and perspective. In fact, some people call him a "sculptor of light." He designed the Live Oak Meeting House in Houston, Texas, for the Society of Friends. It features what he calls a "skyspace," a square in the roof that opens to sky, creating (according to Turrell, speaking on a PBS program) "a light that inhabits space, so that you feel light to be physically present." Skyspaces pop up in other works by Turrell—such as a hotel and art gallery he codesigned on Japan's Benesse Island—and their particular shapes and angles allow light to enter in stunning ways.

Turrell spotted Roden Crater while he was working as an aerial cartographer. At the time, he was interested in land art, and he envisioned a series of tunnels and light-filled chambers inside the volcano. The entire place would function as a kind of naked-eye observatory in which visitors could observe the sun, moon, stars, clouds, and amazing celestial events. With its low light pollution and warm, clear climate, Arizona is perfectly suited to this kind of observation.

Time and Money

Using grants from the prestigious Guggenheim Foundation and the Dia Art Foundation, Turrell purchased the crater and got to work moving tons of earth to fulfill his artistic vision. This has been an architectural project as much as an artistic one. It turns out that moving tons of earth takes a lot of effort… and money. But the artist did not want to scale back his plans. When certain funding sources dried up, Turrell had to look elsewhere for help, such as the Macarthur Foundation and the Santa Fe–based Lannan Foundation.

Meanwhile, a project that was supposed to take a few years began to take decades. Now the crater is not slated to open to the public until 2011 or 2012. That's *if* Turrell can carve out the time: While Roden Crater is certainly his priority, the artist still lectures and exhibits his art elsewhere around the globe.

What's Inside?

Although Roden Crater is unfinished, there are certain completed features, including a long tunnel through the heart of the volcano and a pair of breathtaking skyspaces that frame the Arizona sky above. According to Turrell, the completed art piece will include more than 1,000 feet of tunnels and seven viewing rooms, as well as a feature called "The Eye of the Crater," situated 38 feet below the volcano's center.

Meanwhile, Turrell's admirers can't wait to see the finished product. Some people have snuck onto the site to see the work-in-progress and snap some pictures. A few art critics and VIPs have been invited inside the crater. Roden Crater was featured on a show in the UK called *Sculpture Diaries* and on the PBS program *Art: 21*. In 2007, it was the subject of a *New York Times* article in which the reporter, Jori Finkel, stressed just how highly anticipated it is: The crater, she said, "is one of the hottest tickets around. Writers have compared it to Stonehenge and the Mexican pyramids." Others have predicted that the cinder cone will be the "Sistine Chapel" of the United States or one of our newest "Wonders of the World."

Once open, no doubt Roden Crater will be recognized as something spectacular—a blend of art and architecture that, by placing light at the center, will seem effortless in its construction, even though it took years to complete.

Odd Ordinances

- Women wearing false teeth in Vermont are required to get their husband's permission before putting in the teeth.

- Kissing someone for more than five minutes is a crime in Iowa.

- Having sexual relations while unmarried is against the law in Virginia and Oklahoma.

- Flirting with a member of the opposite sex on the streets of Little Rock, Arkansas, can earn you a 30-day jail sentence.

- In the states of Kentucky and Tennessee, heckling public speakers is within the bounds of civility, but throwing eggs at them can draw a year in jail.

- If "cleanliness is close to godliness," Kentuckians are among the blessed, provided they abide a state law ordering that people must have a bath once a year.

- Training a seal to balance a ball on its nose is illegal in Sweden.

- It is illegal to own an armadillo in the state of Maine.

- Kissing a woman while she's asleep is a crime in Logan County, Colorado.

- Any man with a mustache is not allowed to kiss women in Eureka, Nevada.

- Michigan law states that a woman's hair is technically owned by her husband.

- It's illegal for kids under seven to attend college in Winston-Salem, North Carolina.

- Talking on the phone without a parent on the line is a crime in Blue Earth, Minnesota.

- Any man who comes face-to-face with a cow has to remove his hat in Fruithill, Kentucky.

To Pee or Not to Pee

❖ ❖ ❖ ❖

Some alternative medicine proponents claim urine therapy can cure a long list of ailments. Read on about this, uh, interesting cure.

Urine Business!

Urine is something even moderately healthy people see on a daily basis. A fluid carrying waste from the kidneys out of the body, urine has an ammonialike smell due to the nitrogenous wastes that make up a small percent of it (the remaining 95 percent being water.) The chief constituent of the nitrogenous wastes in urine is *urea,* a product of protein decomposition. When your body doesn't need urea or can't use it, it's processed through your system and comes out in your urine.

Pee as Medicine

In ancient Rome, there are accounts of people to the west that brushed their teeth with urine for a whitening effect. In India, a Sanskrit text promotes the benefits of "pure water," or urine, for treating afflictions of the skin. The prophet Muhammad is said to have advocated drinking camel urine when sick, and some point to a line in the Bible as proof urine is supposed to be used medicinally: "Drink waters from thy own cistern, flowing water from thy own well." (Proverbs 5:15)

Urine *is* sterile (though only fresh urine qualifies) and does contain various elements that are found in medicines, such as urea and whatever vitamins the body decided it wasn't going to absorb, but scientists and doctors have found that it doesn't contain enough of any of these to really be an effective medicinal tool. Many folks will tell you that urine can be used to treat athlete's foot, but there's no scientific evidence that this is true.

However, urine therapy *is* helpful on a battlefield, when water is unavailable to clean a wound. In those cases, using urine in place of water is better than nothing, but it's still a last resort. Research shows that while you're unlikely to die if you drink your own pee, there have been some cases where folks became ill after doing so. It's always a good idea to consult your doctor before experimenting with any home health remedies, including this one.

Say What?

"Somewhere on this earth, every ten seconds, there is a woman giving birth to a child. She must be found and stopped."

—Sam Levenson

"If it wasn't for pickpockets and frisking at airports, I wouldn't have any sex life at all."

—Rodney Dangerfield

"I blame my mother for my poor sex life. All she told me was, 'The man goes on top and the woman underneath.' For three years, my husband and I slept in bunk beds."

—Joan Rivers

"I'm dating a woman now who, evidently, is unaware of the fact."

—Garry Shandling

"The number-one fear in life is public speaking, and the number-two fear is death. This means that if you go to a funeral, you're better off in the casket than giving the eulogy."

—Jerry Seinfeld

"The best contraceptive for old people is nudity."

—Phyllis Diller

"It's a sobering thought: When Mozart was my age, he had been dead for two years."

—Tom Lehrer

"My husband and I are either going to buy a dog or have a child. We can't decide whether to ruin our carpet or ruin our lives."

—Rita Rudner

"A tourist is a fellow who drives thousands of miles so he can be photographed standing in front of his car."

—Émile Genest

"Hollywood is a place where people from Iowa mistake each other for movie stars."

—Fred Allen

"I hate the office; it cuts in on my social life."

—Dorothy Parker

Strange Plants

❖ ❖ ❖ ❖

*When the first Western explorers returned from the Congo, they told
tall tales of monstrous plants that demanded human flesh. Although
we now know that no such plants exist, there are plenty of weird
and scary plants in the world—enough for a little shop of horrors.*

Kudzu—Native to China and Japan, when this vine was brought to
the United States in 1876, its ability to grow a foot per day quickly
made it a nuisance. With 400-pound roots, 4-inch-diameter stems,
and a resistance to herbicides, it is nearly impossible to eliminate.
Kudzu currently covers more than two million acres of land in the
southern United States.

Cow's Udder—This shrub is known alternately as Nipple Fruit, Titty
Fruit, and Apple of Sodom. (Did a group of 4th graders name it?)
A relative of the tomato, it sports poisonous orange fruit that look like
inflated udders.

King Monkey Cup—The largest of carnivorous pitcher plants traps
its prey in pitchers up to 14 inches long and 6 inches wide. It then
digests them in a half gallon of enzymatic fluid. The plant has been
known to catch scorpions, mice, rats, and birds.

Titan Arum—Known in Indonesia as a "corpse
flower," this plant blooms in captivity only once every
three years. The six-foot-tall bloom weighs
more than 140 pounds and looks, as its Latin
name says, like a "giant shapeless penis."
Even less appealingly, it secretes cadaverene
and putrescine, odor compounds that are
responsible for its smell of rotting flesh.

Resurrection fern—This epiphyte (that is, air
plant) gets its nutrients and moisture from the air.
Although other plants die if they lose 8–12 percent
of their water content, the resurrection fern simply
dries up and appears dead. In fact, it can survive despite
losing 97 percent of its water content.

Wollemi pine—Previously known only through 90 million-year-old fossils, the Wollemi pine tree was rediscovered in Australia in 1994. Fewer than 100 adult trees exist today. Although propagated trees are being sold around the world, the original grove's location is a well-guarded secret, disclosed to only a few researchers.

Rafflesia arnoldii—Also known as a "meat flower," this parasitic plant has the largest single bloom of any plant, measuring three feet across. It can hold several gallons of nectar, and its smell has been compared to "buffalo carcass in an advanced stage of decomposition."

Hydnora africana—This parasitic plant is found in Namibia and South Africa growing on the roots of the Euphorbia succulent. Most of the plant is underground, but the upper part of the flower looks like a gaping, fang-filled mouth. And, because smelling like rotting flesh is de rigueur in the weird-plant world, it emits a putrid scent to attract dung or carrion beetles.

Aquatic duckweed—Also known as watermeal because it resembles cornmeal floating on the surface of water, this is the smallest flowering plant on earth. The plant is only .61 millimeter long, and the edible fruit, similar to a (very tiny) fig, is about the size of a grain of salt.

Spanish moss—Although it is a necessary prop in Southern Gothic horror tales, Spanish moss is neither moss nor Spanish. Also known as Florida moss, long moss, or graybeard, it is an air plant (epiphyte) that takes nutrients from the air. It's also related to the pineapple and has been used to stuff furniture, car seats, and mattresses.

Baobab tree—The baobab is the world's largest succulent, reaching heights of 75 feet. It can also live for several thousand years. Their strange, root-like branches gave rise to the legend that they grow upside down. Their enormous trunks are often hollowed out and used as shelter, including a storage barn, an Australian prison, a South African pub, bus stops, and in Zambia, a public toilet (with flushing water, no less).

Fumbling Felons

Wisconsin Women Get Revenge

They say they were the victims, but in this case of lover's revenge, four Wisconsin women may have gone a bit too far. Therese Ziemann, who met a Fond du Lac man online through Craigslist, says she fell in love with him and gave him $3,000 before finding out that he was married and had at least two other girlfriends. (And this info came from his wife!)

The four women devised a plan to embarrass the philanderer. They began by luring him to a motel. Hoping for a little action, the man agreed to be bound and blindfolded by Ziemann, who then texted the other women to join her. That's where the plot went awry: Instead of just chatting, Ziemann hit the fella in the face and glued his penis to his stomach with Krazy Glue. The women are now charged with varying degrees of felony false imprisonment, and Ziemann has the added charge of 4th degree sexual assault. Who's embarrassed now?

Apologetic Bank Robber Gets Caught

Donteh Smith, a Century College student and father, was very nice when he tried to rob the TCF Bank in St. Paul, Minnesota. He handed the teller a note apologizing and asking for money to feed his kids. Smith was also very helpful—he even wrapped the note around his college ID. The clerk smiled and passed the man his money, which contained a dye pack. When the dye exploded, Smith knew the jig was up. He flagged down a police car responding to the robbery and turned himself in.

Impersonating an Officer...Badly

An Oakland, California, man was arrested in July 2009 when he picked the wrong target. Antonio Fernando Martinez was impersonating a police officer and driving down the road in a Crown Victoria car complete with flashing lights and speakers. Unfortunately for Mr. Martinez, he pulled over a real policeman in an unmarked car. Already on probation for car theft, Martinez's probation was revoked, and he's now facing possible prison time.

"Capital punishment would be more effective as a preventive measure if it were administered prior to the crime."

—*Woody Allen*

Bird Is the Word

It continues to be a source of much debate: Was there a turkey at the first Thanksgiving in 1621? Early accounts from the event say four men went "fowling," so most likely turkeys were included, along with geese, ducks, and pigeons. So why has the turkey alone persevered as the primary bird we associate with Thanksgiving?

For one thing, the Pilgrims already had a taste for turkey. Spaniards brought turkeys back from Mexico in the 1500s, and the bird's popularity quickly spread throughout Europe. But historians say the real reason turkeys have become the centerpiece dates back to the post–Civil War era, when poultry producers launched a marketing campaign encouraging people to eat more turkey, particularly for Thanksgiving dinner. Deliberately or just by chance, the campaign coincided with artist renditions and newspaper illustrations of families sitting around a giant roast turkey on Thanksgiving Day. Since then, Turkey Tom has dominated Turkey Day.

Treed and True

For centuries, evergreen trees have held powerful meaning for many cultures, including the druids of northern Europe, who held the evergreen as a symbol of everlasting life.

But the contemporary Christmas tree originated in 16th-century Germany, when devout Christians put up triangular trees (possibly to represent the holy trinity). Observing how beautiful the stars looked twinkling through the branches of an evergreen tree, Protestant reformer Martin Luther came up with lighting the tree using candles to create a similar effect. That remained the tradition until the late 19th century, when Thomas Edison developed miniature electric lights to string on trees.

The tree custom arrived in America in the 18th century with the German immigrants. Americans viewed the tree with skepticism as a pagan symbol, until a British paper showed royal "It" girl, Queen Victoria, posing around a decorated Christmas tree in 1846. Suddenly, the English as well as fashionable East Coast Americans simply had to have a Christmas tree.

The first Christmas tree lot opened in Manhattan in 1851. Today 30 million Christmas trees are sold in the United States every year—fake trees not included.

Sounds for Space

❖❖❖❖

This gold record doesn't climb the charts—it sails through deep space.

Voyagers Abroad

Somewhere in space, two unmanned scientific probes—Voyagers 1 and 2—move through previously unexplored areas of our solar system. NASA launched the twin probes in 1977, hoping they would uncover valuable information about Jupiter, Saturn, and the outer planets. And indeed they have: The spacecraft found active volcanoes on Jupiter's moon and a surprising amount of structure in Saturn's rings. *Voyager 2* launched first and is the only spacecraft to have visited Uranus and Neptune. But *Voyager 1*, moving at a brisk 38,000 miles per hour, has probed the farthest.

Hit Record

Aboard each *Voyager* is a 12-inch, gold-plated copper disc called The Golden Record. This disc is a time capsule of sorts, containing a hodgepodge of sounds and images intended to convey to extraterrestrials what life on our planet is like. That's right: It's an LP designed for aliens—on the infinitesimally small chance that they exist and that The Golden Record will reach them in the distant future.

Astronomer Carl Sagan curated the project along with his future wife, Ann Druyan, and a committee of scientists. The group selected 115 images to depict human life, as well as sounds from nature, including birdsongs, crickets, wild dogs, and wind. They also included music from various cultures, including Peruvian panpipes, an Indian raga, the song "Johnny B. Goode" by Chuck Berry, greetings in 55 languages, and printed messages from U.S. President Jimmy Carter and UN Secretary-General Kurt Waldheim.

As Sagan noted, the likelihood of an advanced civilization encountering the record is so rare as to be nearly impossible, yet "the launching of this 'bottle' into the cosmic 'ocean' says something very hopeful about life on this planet." In 2008, the *Voyager 1* slipped out and away from our solar system—who knows who (or what) will find its cargo?

Fast Facts

- Silent movie legend Lon Chaney, best known for his portrayals of the Hunchback of Notre Dame and the Phantom of the Opera, made only one "talkie" during his career—The Unholy Three (1930). It was also his last film.

- The giant squid can grow up to 60 feet long, including tentacles, and weigh up to one ton. In comparison, one species of sepiolid squid reaches a maximum length of only 0.7 inches.

- Donald Duck made his movie debut in the 1934 animated short "The Wise Little Hen." He was voiced by Clarence Nash, who provided Donald's voice in more than 180 cartoons and movies during a career that spanned nearly 50 years.

- Donald Duck's nephews, Huey, Dewey and Louie, were named after politicians Thomas Dewey and Huey Long—and a Disney employee named Louie Schmitt.

- Talk about bad timing! Actor Mark Lindsay Chapman nearly played John Lennon in the 1985 telefilm, John and Yoko: A Love Story, but he was turned down because of the similarity in name to Mark Chapman—Lennon's assassin.

- With more than 170 films under his cape, Dracula has been the subject of more horror films than any other character.

- The New York Times dismissed David Lean's epic film Lawrence of Arabia (1962) as "just a huge thundering camel-opera." The movie went on to earn seven Academy Awards, including Best Picture and Best Director.

- The smallest set used for the entire action of a motion picture was a lifeboat that held the nine protagonists in the 1944 Alfred Hitchcock thriller called, appropriately, Lifeboat.

Top-Secret Locations You Can Visit

❖ ❖ ❖ ❖

There are plenty of stories of secret government facilities hidden in plain sight. Places where all sorts of strange tests take place, far away from the general public. Many of the North American top-secret government places have been (at least partially) declassified, allowing average Joes to visit. We've listed some locations where you can play Men in Black.

Titan Missile Silo

Just a little south of Tucson, Arizona, lies the Sonoran Desert, a barren, desolate area where nothing seems to be happening. That's exactly why, during the Cold War, the U.S. government hid an underground Titan Missile silo there.

Inside the missile silo, one of dozens that once littered the area, a Titan 2 Missile could be armed and launched in just under 90 seconds. Until it was finally abandoned in the 1990s, the government manned the silo 24 hours a day, with every member being trained to "turn the key" and launch the missile at a moment's notice. Today, the silo is open to the public as the Titan Missile Museum. Visitors can take a look at one of the few remaining Titan 2 missiles in existence, still sitting on the launch pad (relax, it's been disarmed). Folks with extra dough can also spend the night inside the silo and play the role of one of the crew members assigned to prepare to launch the missile at a moment's notice.

Peanut Island

You wouldn't think a sunny place called Peanut Island, located near Palm Beach, Florida, could hold many secrets. Yet in December 1961, the U.S. Navy came to the island on a secret mission to create a fallout shelter for then-President John F. Kennedy and his family. The shelter was completed, but it was never used and was all but forgotten when the Cold War ended. Today, the shelter is maintained by the Palm Beach Maritime Museum, which conducts weekend tours of the space.

Wright-Patterson Air Force Base

If you believe that aliens crash-landed in Roswell, New Mexico, in the summer of 1947, then you need to make a trip out to Ohio's Wright-Patterson Air Force Base. That's because, according to legend, the UFO crash debris and possibly the aliens (both alive and dead) were shipped to the base as part of a government cover-up. Some say all that debris is still there, hidden away in an underground bunker beneath the mysterious Hanger 18.

While most of the Air Force Base is off-limits to the general public, you can go on a portion of the base to visit the National Museum of the U.S. Air Force, filled with amazing artifacts tracing the history of flight. But don't bother to ask any of the museum personnel how to get to Hanger 18—the official word is that the hanger does not exist.

Area 51

Located in the middle of the desert in southern Nevada lies possibly the world's best-known top-secret location: Area 51. If you've read a story about high-tech flying machines—either ours or extraterrestrial—chances are Area 51 was mentioned. That's because the government has spent years denying the base's existence, despite satellite photos showing otherwise. In fact, it was not until a lawsuit filed by government employees against the base that the government finally admitted the base did in fact exist.

If you want to find out what's going on inside Area 51, you're out of luck. While the dirt roads leading up to the base are technically public property, the base itself is very firmly not open for tours—if an unauthorized visitor so much as sets one toe over the boundary line, he or she is subject to arrest or worse. Let's just say that the sign stating the "use of deadly force is authorized" is not to be taken lightly.

Los Alamos National Laboratory

Until recently, the U.S. government refused to acknowledge the Los Alamos National Laboratory's existence. But in the early 1940s, the lab was created near Los Alamos, New Mexico, to develop the first nuclear weapons in what would become known as the Manhattan Project. Back then, the facility was so top secret it didn't even have a name. It was simply referred to as Site Y. No matter what it was called, the lab produced two nuclear bombs, nicknamed Little Boy and Fat Man—bombs that would be dropped on Hiroshima and Nagasaki, effectively ending World War II. Today, tours of portions of the facility can be arranged through the Lab's Public Affairs Department.

Fort Knox

It is the stuff that legends are made of: A mythical building filled with over 4,700 tons of gold, stacked up and piled high to the ceiling. But this is no fairytale—the gold really does exist, and it resides inside Fort Knox.

Since 1937, the U.S. Department of the Treasury's Bullion Depository has been storing the gold inside Fort Knox on a massive military campus that stretches across three counties in north-central Kentucky. Parts of the campus are open for tours, including the General George Patton Museum. But don't think you're going to catch a glimpse of that shiny stuff—visitors are not permitted to go through the gate or enter the building.

Nevada Test Site

If you've ever seen one of those old black-and-white educational films of nuclear bombs being tested, chances are it was filmed at the Nevada Test Site, often referred to as the Most Bombed Place in the World.

Located about an hour north of Las Vegas, the Nevada Test Site was created in 1951 as a secret place for the government to conduct nuclear experiments and tests in an outdoor laboratory that is actually larger than Rhode Island. Out there, scientists blew everything up from mannequins to entire buildings. Those curious to take a peek inside the facility can sign up for a daylong tour. Of course, before they let you set foot on the base, visitors must submit to a background check and sign paperwork promising not to attempt to photograph, videotape, or take soil samples from the site.

Lifestyles of the Eccentric

❖ ❖ ❖ ❖

William Lyon Mackenzie King (1874–1950)

As Canada's longest-serving prime minister, William Lyon Mackenzie King kept unusual political advisors—particularly, the spirits he summoned through his Ouija board and crystal ball. Canadian voters considered King to be rather dull, but postmortem details from his journals revealed frequent chats with his deceased mother, Leonardo da Vinci, and several generations of dead pet terriers (all named Pat).

Sir George Sitwell (1860–1943)

A delightfully eccentric nobleman, Sir George wrote countless unpublished books, including *The History of the Fork, Lepers' Squints,* and *Acorns as an Article of Medieval Diet.* He was also the inventor of a musical toothbrush, a gun for shooting wasps, and an egg made out of meat. A sign posted at Sitwell's estate stated: "I must ask anyone entering the house never to contradict me in any way, as it interferes with the functioning of the gastric juices and prevents my sleeping at night."

Benjamin O'Neill-Stratford (1808–c. 1870)

This Irish eccentric worked for more than 20 years designing and building the world's largest hot air balloon. He kept only one servant, had his meals delivered so he didn't have to employ a cook, and even bought a landing strip by the Seine River in preparation for his maiden voyage. Unfortunately, a fire destroyed both the balloon and O'Neill-Stratford's dreams. He ended up a broken man, hoarding dirty dishes in hotel rooms in Spain, only moving out after the dishes filled the room.

Richard Feynman (1918–1988)

A true genius who won the Nobel Prize for physics and participated in the development of the atomic bomb, Feynman found time to pursue a variety of hobbies: juggling, lock picking, and samba bongo drumming. Feynman once proclaimed strip clubs to be a "public need," and indeed, much of his research was done in adult entertainment joints. The title of one of his popular books says it all: *What Do You Care What Other People Think?*

The Times They Are A-Changin'

1932

- Ten years after a woman was appointed to the U.S. Senate (and served for one day), Hattie W. Caraway becomes the first woman to be elected to the office.

- Radio City Music Hall opens in New York City. Over the next 75 years, 300 million visitors will attend shows at this spectacular "palace for the people."

- The Dow Jones Industrial Average bottoms out at 41.22, the lowest level of the Great Depression.

- Aviator Charles Lindbergh makes headlines when his son, Charles Lindbergh III, is kidnapped. The boy is found dead 11 days later in Hopewell, New Jersey, about four and a half miles from the Lindbergh home.

- Residents of Archie, Missouri, are surprised when an 11.2-pound chondrite type meteorite crashes into their community, breaking into at least seven pieces.

- Comedian Jack Benny launches his first radio show, *The Jack Benny Program.* The wildly successful show airs until 1955.

- Amelia Earhart makes history twice this year. She is the first female pilot to make a non-stop solo flight across the Atlantic Ocean, flying from Newfoundland to Ireland. Three months later, she becomes the first woman to fly non-stop across the United States from Los Angeles to Newark.

- The Federal Bureau of Investigation (FBI) opens its first Crime Lab in Washington, D.C., with a single employee, agent Charles Appel.

- President Franklin Delano Roosevelt defeats opponent Herbert Hoover in a landslide victory. It will be the first of his four historic terms.

Beyond the Blast: Hiroshima's Trees

❖ ❖ ❖ ❖

On August 6, 1945, American forces dropped an atomic bomb on the Japanese city of Hiroshima. Buildings were decimated, and between 70,000 and 100,000 people died from the bombing. But throughout the city, there are trees that somehow survived the blast and now rank among the most sacred and beloved of Japan's treasures.

"Nothing Will Grow"

The atomic bomb was the outcome of an undertaking known as the Manhattan Project. Two days after the blast, one of its scientists, Dr. Harold Jacobsen, deemed Hiroshima contaminated with radiation and barren of life. Manhattan Project leader Dr. Robert Oppenheimer, however, contradicted Jacobsen's claim. Nevertheless, American armed forces in Japan issued the following statement: "Hiroshima will be barren of human and animal life for 75 years. Any scientists who go there to survey the damage will be committing suicide."

Professor Masao Tsuzuki, leader of the Hiroshima Disaster Survey Team, also disagreed with Jacobsen. Beginning on August 30, he conducted a survey of the city. "The rumor about 75 years is completely mistaken," Tsuzuki wrote. "In the ruins of Hiroshima's Gokoku Shrine, sprouts have already grown to 15 centimeters." Today Gokoku Shrine is one of the city's most treasured places.

Rising from the Ashes

Many of the trees that survived the atomic blast were sheltered by buildings or natural declivities. However, a surviving cluster of Chinese parasol trees (or phoenix trees) grouped nearly one mile from the blast center stood exposed. That anything of them remained at all following the explosion was unbelievable; that they should continue to grow is something of a miracle. Yet, stripped of their branches, their trunks hollowed out and badly burned, the Chinese parasols sprouted new leaves the following spring. Today, they serve as symbols of the city's rebirth.

Prehistory vs. the Atomic Age

Having survived for about 200 million years, ginkgo trees are among the oldest living seed plants. They are exceptionally hardy—individual trees can live for thousands of years. The resilience of these prehistoric trees was demonstrated by the six ginkgos that stood within 1.24 miles of the Hiroshima atomic blast hypocenter. They include four trees shielded by temples (that were later rebuilt around the surviving trees), a tree in the Shukkeien Sunken Garden whose trunk collapsed but now flourishes, and a tree next to the Senda Elementary School that was stripped of limbs and foliage but began to bud soon after a school was re-established on the site. Today the ginkgo tree is regarded as the "bearer of hope" throughout Japan.

Instead, Let's Blow Up Some Trees

If Special Assistant to the Secretary of the Navy Lewis Strauss had his way, many more Japanese trees would be dead (although perhaps many less civilians). Strauss recommended that the United States demonstrate the power of its awesome new weapon by dropping the first bomb over an easily observed area where Japanese officials could fully appreciate its destructive power. To this end, he suggested a forest of cryptomeria trees (a type of conifer) near Tokyo, reasoning that a high-altitude blast would splay the trees in a radial pattern and create a firestorm at the center. Such a sight, he felt, would convince the Japanese government to surrender immediately. As history shows, the U.S. government didn't use Strauss's idea.

A Different Sort of Tree

In December 1945, a woman living in Hiroshima erected a small metal-and-plastic Christmas tree in her family's ruined home. There wasn't much to celebrate: She lost one of her young sons to the atomic blast, and the city was a smoldering wasteland. But she kept the Christmas tree tradition alive as she had every year since 1937 when her husband had purchased the tree in Hawaii. Even during the war, when possession of a Christmas tree was grounds for arrest, the Iwatake family displayed the small tree in a back room away from windows. The same tiny tree remains an Iwatake family tradition, displayed in their home as a remembrance of those who died during the war.

Fast Facts

- French actress Sarah Bernhardt was obsessed with death, and she sometimes slept in a coffin.

- Cats cannot taste sweet things.

- A sea lion can get sunburned.

- The first moving picture copyrighted in America showed a man sneezing.

- Mary Pickford's movie sets were often enlarged to enhance her diminutive appearance. Furniture and props were scaled one-third larger than life size, and doors and windows were made larger than normal.

- The U.S. Automobile Association was formed in 1905 so that its scouts could warn drivers of police "traps."

- Southerner Edmund Ruffin, believed by many to have fired the first shot in the Civil War, committed suicide after General Robert E. Lee surrendered.

- Benjamin Franklin once chased a small tornado while on horseback. He tried to dissipate the storm by striking it with his whip.

- In 1910 or 1911 (sources vary), Bobby Leach became the first male to go over Niagara Falls in a barrel. He suffered numerous broken bones but survived. In 1926, he slipped on an orange or banana peel and died from complications from that injury.

- Genetics play a role in freckles; some studies have shown that if your dad or mom had freckles, you'll have them too, sometimes even the exact number of one of your parents.

17 Films of Linnea Quigley

❖ ❖ ❖ ❖

Curvy, blonde, and petite (5' 2", 98 pounds), Linnea Quigley has made 90 feature films since she moved to Hollywood in 1975. She landed her first acting gig while still in her teens, and quickly became a "scream queen"—a beauty performing mainly in R-rated horror flicks. While these films aren't necessarily highbrow, the piquant titles on Quigley's resume are totally worth it.

1. *Psycho from Texas* (1975): A drifter is hired to kidnap and kill a Texas oil millionaire; Quigley plays a barmaid in this, her first feature film.

2. *The Return of the Living Dead* (1985): Flesh-eating zombies assault teens trapped in a warehouse. This was Quigley's breakthrough movie. She plays Trash, a punk rocker who performs an exotic dance atop a tombstone.

3. *Creepozoids* (1987): Ragged survivors of World War III straggle into an abandoned laboratory that is crawling with cannibalistic humanoids created following a botched government experiment in food research. Quigley fights monsters and takes a shower.

4. *Nightmare Sisters* (1987): Three geeky college girls are possessed by an evil spirit and become ravenous sex bombs. Can the boy geeks save them? Top-billed Quigley is joined by fellow scream queens Brinke Stevens and Michelle Bauer.

5. *Sorority Babes in the Slimeball Bowl-O-Rama* (1988): Skimpily attired sorority gals are trapped in a bowling alley with an evil imp who has been released from a shattered bowling trophy. Quigley battles the imp and bowls.

6. *Hollywood Chainsaw Hookers* (1988): A private detective runs up against prostitutes who carve up their johns in cultish blood rites. The movie's tagline: "They charge an arm and a leg!"

7. *Blood Nasty* (1989): An ordinary fellow dies and is reanimated with the soul of a serial killer. Problem: The innocent guy's mom would rather he stay dead (life insurance, you see). Meanwhile, the serial killer is determined to continue his mischief.

8. *Assault of the Party Nerds* (1989): A four-member fraternity tries to enlist more members in the days before graduation. Quigley plays Bambi, a cutie enlisted to help swell the rolls.

9. *Robot Ninja* (1990): A lonely comic book artist transforms himself into Robot Ninja, a violent crime fighter. Besides Linnea, this one features Burt Ward, who enjoyed fame in the '60s as Robin on TV's *Batman.*

10. *Beach Babes from Beyond* (1993): Interstellar beach girls land on Earth and enter a bikini contest to help an old fella hang on to his beach house. Burt Ward makes an appearance along with Jackie Stallone (Sly's mom) and Joey Travolta (John's brother).

11. *Sick-o-Pathics* (1996): Art imitates life in this horror/comedy: Quigley plays a scream queen in a bit called "Commercial: Dr. Riker's Hair Lotion."

12. *Mari-Cookie and the Killer Tarantula* (1998): Spider queen Mari-Cookie (played by vintage cult actress Lina Romay) kidnaps men and strings them up in gigantic gooey webs. Quigley, in a costarring role, wears a teeny bikini.

13. *Kannibal* (2001): Quigley plays crime boss Georgina Thereshkova, who finds herself in the crosshairs of the police and a male mob chief.

14. *Corpses Are Forever* (2003): When the gates of hell open, the world is overrun with zombies. Humankind's only hope is an amnesiac spy and his odd assortment of allies. Third-billed Quigley takes a back seat to scream queens Brinke Stevens and Debbie Rochon.

15. *Zombiegeddon* (2003): It's a zombie apocalypse as the walking dead take over the world. At age 45, Quigley plays a school principal.

16. *Hoodoo for Voodoo* (2006): College students at Mardi Gras pick up a dose of real voodoo and drop dead. Quigley plays a more mature character named Queen Marie.

17. *Spring Break Massacre* (2007): Six sorority girls on a sleepover are stalked by an escaped serial killer. No bikini for our gal Quigley in this one—she's the deputy sheriff.

WORD HISTORIES

Plagiarize: To use the writings or ideas of someone else as your own. "Plagiarize" comes from the Latin word *plagiarius,* meaning kidnapper.

Carrotmob: In our environmentally conscious world, "carrotmob" means swamping a "green" store with business, instead of boycotting one that is not so environmentally friendly.

Sanguine: Here's a weird one. The word derives from the Middle English word, *sanguine,* which means blood. In this case, "blood" is a happy word, meaning cheerful confidence and optimism. In those days, people thought the body was made up of four humors, or bodily fluids. If your predominant humor was blood, you'd have a ruddy face and cheerful personality.

Sanguinary: If you think this one must be a happy word, too, think again; it actually means bloodthirsty. It comes from a similar root, but this one is the Latin *sanguineus,* meaning blood or bloody—but not humorous in the least.

Derrick: This word is in common usage today as a lifting device fashioned with a mast that resembles an old-fashioned gallows. The device gets its name from Godfrey Derrick, who was a London hangman around the year 1600. He was thought to have carried out more than 3,000 executions.

Rookie: A large annoying black bird found in rural medieval England was known as a rook. When young farmers went to the local fairs and were taken by the swindlers there, they compared the thieves to the rooks; ultimately, those conned in the swindle became known as rookies. The word came to be used in modern language to describe anyone young, naïve, or new at something.

Alcatraz: The famous prison in San Francisco Bay actually got its name from the pelicans that live in the area. The word derives from the Spanish *Alcatraces;* which means something akin to "pelican" or "strange bird." Sailors picked up the name and when they saw the California island filled with these birds, promptly named it Alcatraz.

Goad: Originally used to prod oxen, a goad was a stick with spikes at one end. Now we use the same word to get another human to do something a little faster.

Canada's Cryptic Castaway

❖ ❖ ❖ ❖

This mute amputee has a foothold in Nova Scotian
folklore—nearly a century after his death.

Who Is This Man?

On September 8, 1863, two fishermen in Sandy Cove, Nova Scotia, discovered an unusual treasure washed ashore: a lone man in his twenties with newly amputated legs, left with just a loaf of bread and jug of water.

There were a few clues, such as his manner of dress, that led the townspeople to speculate on whether the fellow was a gentleman, an aristocrat. But there was no point in asking him— he didn't speak. In fact, he was said to have uttered only three words after being found: "Jerome" (which the villagers came to call him), "Columbo" (perhaps the name of his ship), and "Trieste," an Italian village.

Based on these three words, the villagers theorized he was Italian and concocted various romantic stories about his fate: that he was an Italian nobleman captured and mutilated by pirates (or perhaps a pirate himself), a seaman punished for threatening mutiny, or maybe he was an heir to a fortune who had been crippled and cast away by a jealous rival.

Charity Case

Jerome was taken to the home of Jean and Juliette Nicholas, a French family who lived across the bay in Meteghan. There was still a chance Jerome could be French and Jean was fluent in five languages. (Although none of which proved successful in communicating with Jerome.)

In 1870, the Nicholases moved away. The town, enthralled with their mysterious nobleman, rallied together and paid the Comeau family $140 a year to take him in. On Sundays after mass, locals would stop by and pay a few cents for a look at the maimed mute. Jerome lived with the Comeaus for the next 52 years until his death on April 19, 1912.

Records suggest Jerome was no cool-headed castaway. Though he never spoke intelligibly, hearing certain words (specifically "pirate") would send him into a rage. It's also been said that he was particularly anxious about the cold, spending winters with his leg stumps shoved under the stove for warmth. Though in his younger days he enjoyed sitting in the sun, he allegedly spent the last 20 years of his life as a complete shut-in, huddled by the stove.

Mystery Revealed

Jerome's panic about the cold makes sense—if the latest hypotheses about him are true. Modern historians have posited a couple of different theories, both of which trace Jerome to New Brunswick.

One group of scholars uncovered a story in New Brunswick about a man who was behaving erratically and couldn't (or wouldn't) speak. To rid themselves of the weirdo, members of his community put him on a boat to New England—but not without first chopping off his legs. The man never made it to New England but instead wound up on the beach at Sandy Cove.

Another theory links Jerome to a man—believed to be European—who was found in 1861, pinned under a fallen tree in Chipman, New Brunswick, with frozen legs that had to be amputated. Without a doctor nearby, the man was sent down the St. John River to Gagetown and then shipped back to Chipman, where he was supported for two years by the parish and nicknamed "Gamby" by the locals (which means "legs" in Italian). At that point, the parish got tired of taking care of him and paid a captain to drop him across the bay in Nova Scotia. Another account suggests that after the surgery, the man wasn't returned to Gagetown but put directly on a boat.

Regardless of which theory is more accurate, all suggest that the reason for Jerome's arrival in Nova Scotia is that an entire town disowned him.

But New Brunswick's loss has been Nova Scotia's gain. There, Jerome is a local legend. He has been the subject of a movie (1994's *Le secret de Jérôme*), and a home for the handicapped bears his name. Tourists can even stop by his grave for a quick snapshot of the headstone, which reads, quite simply, "Jerome."

HOW IT ALL BEGAN

Alarmed and Dangerous

Historians say the Greeks devised an alarm clock as early as 250 B.C. that used rising water to trigger a mechanical whistle; the Germans had a large iron wall piece rigged with bronze bells in the 15th century. And chimes have sounded on clocks since the Middle Ages; the word "clock" even comes from the French word *cloche,* meaning "bell."

But the modern alarm clock we all know and love (or hate) got its start in Concord, New Hampshire, in 1787, courtesy of 26-year-old clockmaker and staunch early riser, Levi Hutchins. Yet without the sun to wake him in the wee hours, Hutchins tended to oversleep. So he gutted a large brass clock, placed the innards inside a pine cabinet, and inserted a gear tripped to sound at 4 A.M. (However, it couldn't be set for any other time.)

Hutchins's idea worked, but he never patented it. That credit goes to the Seth Thomas Company, which in 1876 patented a bedside windup alarm clock that could be set for any hour. Eighty years later, General Electric-Telechron introduced the snooze alarm (thank goodness).

Wrist Assured

At the turn of the 20th century, manly men carried pocket watches. Only women wore the more-jewelry-than-timepiece "wristlet," popularized by Parisian ladies in the early 1900s.

But wartime changed this. Pocket watches were clumsy and awkward in combat, so soldiers began fitting them into leather straps to wear on their wrists. This wasn't entirely new: In the 1880s, Swiss watchmaker Girard-Perregaux "armed" the German Imperial Navy with watches on leather straps, which proved essential for synchronizing attacks. British soldiers even credited the watches for their victory in the Anglo-Boer War in South Africa. American troops didn't discover the wristwatch until they joined the British in World War I. As U.S. soldiers returned home sporting souvenir watches on their wrists, the gadget quickly went from a frou-frou fashion piece to a badge of bravery that civilians wanted, too.

Becoming *Black Like Me*

❖ ❖ ❖ ❖

*Journalist and writer John Howard Griffin used deception
to force America to take a closer look at racism.*

In 1959, John Howard Griffin, a white Mansfield, Texas, native, pondered the issues of race in the United States. The Civil Rights Movement had started only four years prior, and Griffin decided the best way to find out how a black man lived was to transform himself into one and travel through the segregated Deep South. Griffin detailed his odyssey in a series of articles for *Sepia* magazine, a monthly black publication.

Before Griffin assumed his new persona, he visited Georgia, Alabama, Louisiana, and Mississippi as a white man. He reported meeting many friendly, hospitable people along his route. Next, with the aid of a dermatologist, Griffin ingested oral pigmentation medication followed by ultraviolet ray treatments, which greatly darkened his skin. He shaved the hair on his head and hands, lest they provide clues to his real identity.

When he returned to the same towns he had previously visited, now as a black man, he received a completely different (and very negative) reaction. He traveled for six weeks, later reporting that the daily difficulties of living as a black man outweighed even those moments of overt racism. Seemingly small tasks white people took for granted—getting a bite to eat, requesting a glass of water, using a restroom—took up a large amount of his time. Often he would be turned away from establishments and directed toward black-only diners and shops, and those would usually be located far away.

Griffin's story spread like wildfire. In 1961, he wrote a best-selling book, *Black Like Me*, which told of his journeys. Television interviews and magazine features followed. White Americans finally were able to realize what life was really like for a black man in the Deep South.

For his troubles, Griffin received criticism and protests. After he was hanged in effigy and confronted with death threats, Griffin moved his family to Mexico. He had peeled back the veneer of Southern society and provided an eye-opening look under its surface, but he paid a steep price for the revelation.

Fast Facts

- *Before the federal government began paying pensions to the widows of former presidents, steel magnate Andrew Carnegie donated the money.*

- *In medieval times, thunderstorms were thought to be the work of demons. Church bells would be rung in an attempt to stop the storms.*

- *The original name of the "Star-Spangled Banner" was "The Defense of Fort McHenry."*

- *Abner Doubleday is thought by many to have invented baseball—despite no supporting evidence.*

- *Wilt Chamberlain never fouled out of a basketball game.*

- *The* Chicago Times *newspaper gave Lincoln's Gettysburg Address a poor review, saying it contained "dish-watery utterances."*

- *Samuel Clemens, aka Mark Twain, was born in 1835, the year that Halley's Comet appeared. He predicted that he would die on its next appearance in 1910. He was right.*

- *In the 1970s, the Rhode Island legislature proposed that every act of sexual intercourse be taxed $2.*

- *When men in ancient Rome swore to tell the truth, they placed their right hand on their testicles.*

- *Amos 'n' Andy was such a popular radio program in the 1930s that movie theaters had to change their curtain time from 7:00 P.M. to 7:15 to accomodate it.*

- *T. E. Lawrence, aka Lawrence of Arabia, stood at 5'5".*

Ghosts of the Gold Rush

❖ ❖ ❖ ❖

The California Gold Rush of 1848—its frenzy of ambition and greed is what made the Wild West truly wild. So it's little wonder that some folks would find it difficult to leave, even after they've supposedly passed on to the great gold mine in the sky. Check out these haunted locales next time you wander through California's Gold Rush territory.

Jamestown Hotel

Over the years since opening in 1858, the Jamestown Hotel in Jamestown has served as a boarding house, bordello, bus depot, and hospital. The resident ghost story is every bit as dramatic as the building's history. In 1938, Mary Rose, the granddaughter of a wealthy and influential prospector, fell in love with a handsome British soldier. Her grandfather was not pleased. The soldier was promptly shipped off to India, where he met a violent death. Mary Rose, desolate, pregnant, and unmarried, checked into what was then the Mother Lode Hospital to await the birth of her child. Unfortunately, neither mother nor child survived childbirth, but guests at the hotel say they've seen misty apparitions of the spirits of Mary Rose and her soldier.

1859 Historic National Hotel

With doors slamming, lights flickering on and off, clothes being tossed from suitcases by unseen hands, and an invisible woman sobbing in the hallway in the middle of the night, how does anyone get any sleep in this place? Also located in Jamestown, the 1859 Historic National Hotel's resident ghost, affectionately named Flo, usually remains upstairs, favoring the rooms toward the front of the building. She has occasionally been spotted floating through the downstairs dining room, but only in the early morning.

Current hotel owner Stephen Willey says that, although he's never personally encountered Flo, he has come across many a hotel guest who arrived a skeptic and left a believer.

Willow Steakhouse & Saloon

A mine once ran underneath what is now the Willow Steakhouse (located in, you guessed it, Jamestown), and it plays a part in the restaurant's violent history. There, a mine collapse killed 23 miners; there were violent deaths at the Willow's bar; and a man was lynched in his own room. From the time the building was first built in 1862, a series of mysterious fires have plagued the property, the most recent in 1985. Some blame restless spirits, saying that the place is crowded with ghosts, including a short man who roams the upstairs halls, a dapper gambler who favors the bar, and a redheaded woman who was shot by her husband in the bar during the Gold Rush years.

City Hotel

Located within the Columbia State Historic Park, this Gold Rush-era hotel still welcomes guests, although visitors may share their lodgings with an unexpected roommate. When the hotel was restored for its current use, authentic period antiques reflecting Columbia's heyday (1850–1870) were brought in from nearby San Francisco. Among them was an especially ornate and finely carved wooden bed, originally imported from Europe more than a century before it found its way to the City Hotel. With the bed came the hotel's resident ghost, Elizabeth, a woman who reportedly died in it during childbirth. Since the arrival of the bed (and Elizabeth), doors now open and close at random in Room 1; a sweet perfume often wafts through the air; and guests, especially children, have reported seeing a woman in a white dress standing at the foot of the bed.

The Groveland Hotel

This historic hotel in Groveland is actually two buildings: One was built in 1849 and served as lodging for miners and prospectors working at the now defunct gold mine behind the building. The other was built in 1919 for workers doing construction on the Hetch Hetchy Dam. According to lore, a prospector named Lyle remains. A recluse, Lyle was dead for several days before anyone thought to check his room to see if he was all right. As a ghost, Lyle is quirky. He can't stand to see women's cosmetics on the dresser, and he's not shy about moving them. When people talk about him, Lyle tends to respond by flickering the lights or rushing by as a cold breeze. Once Lyle even helped current owner Peggy Mosley with her baking by flinging open the oven door at the precise moment the bread was finished. Sometimes Lyle disappears for weeks—perhaps to go prospecting—but he always returns to The Groveland Hotel.

Vineyard House

Modern visitors to this beautiful bed-and-breakfast in Coloma would never guess its troubled and violent past. Construction on the house finished in 1878, and a year later, its first owner reportedly went insane and had to be chained in the home's cellar "for his own protection." He went on a hunger strike, starving himself to death and leaving his wife in dire financial straights. The family's grapevines dried up and its wine business went under. The widow was forced to take in boarders to make ends meet and for a time even resorted to renting the house as a jail, a period when two hangings took place in the front yard. Misty apparitions roam the hotel, accompanied by the sound of rattling chains.

Bodie, California

Sure, it's not a hotel, but in its heyday, Bodie personified the Wild West. A Gold Rush town that seemingly sprang up overnight, more than 10,000 people called Bodie home in the late 1870s. No fewer than 70 saloons served up suds to the men who worked the area's 30 mines. Numerous bordellos, gambling halls, and opium dens provided further "amusement," and gunfights were common. During this period, at least one man was killed every day in Bodie. When the gold veins depleted, the town withered; by the time the last mine closed during World War II, only six people remained. Today about 160 buildings still stand, left just as they were when their inhabitants departed. However, some Bodie residents remain eternally. The sound of a nonexistent piano often floats through the streets, and a spectral white mule haunts the Standard Mine on the outskirts of town.

PALINDROMES

A palindrome is a phrase that reads the same in both directions. The word is derived from the Greek palíndromos, *which means running back again* (palín = again; drom-, drameîn = to run).

Stop! Murder us not, tonsured rumpots

Stab nail at ill Italian bats

A man, a plan, a canal: Panama

Sums are not set as a test on Erasmus

Doc, note I dissent. A fast never prevents a fatness. I diet on cod

Eros? Sidney, my end is sore

Sit on a potato pan, Otis

Madam, I'm Adam

I roamed under it as a tired, nude Maori

Lager, sir, is regal

Dennis and Edna sinned

Cigar? Toss it in a can. It is so tragic

Straw? No, too stupid a fad. I put soot on warts

Campus motto: Bottoms up, Mac

Dammit, I'm mad

Dee saw a seed

Was raw tap ale not a reviver at one lap at Warsaw?

Too hot to hoot

Tangy gnat

So, Ida, adios

I'm, alas, a salami

Kodak ad, OK

Ah, Satan sees Natasha

Fast Facts

- The 102nd floor of the Empire State Building was supposed to be a landing point for dirigibles.

- For years after the Battle of Waterloo in 1815, so-called "Waterloo teeth" were popular in Europe. These were dentures made from teeth that had been pulled from the many young soldiers who had died in the battle.

- Because cemetery land was not taxable in ancient Rome, the poet Virgil held a funeral for a fly and buried it on the land surrounding his villa.

- The element einsteinium, discovered in 1952, is named after Albert Einstein.

- The remains of Alexander the Great were preserved in a crock of honey.

- An estimated 300 women disguised themselves as men in order to fight during the Civil War.

- People executed by having their head cut off in medieval England had to tip the executioner to assure that he did the job with one swift blow, rather than several botched ones.

- In 18th century England, eyeglasses were often worn strictly as a fashion accessory, even to the point of using only the frames with no glass in them. Of course, this trend has reemerged in today's hipster community.

- The first novel submitted to a publisher that was written on a typewriter was The Adventures of Tom Sawyer by Mark Twain.

Labor of Love: The Taj Mahal

❖ ❖ ❖ ❖

Known as one of the Wonders of the World, the Taj Mahal was a shrine to love and one man's obsession. Today an average of three million tourists a year travel to see what the United Nations has declared a World Heritage site.

Taj Mahal: Foundations

The Mughal (or "Mogul") Empire occupied India from the mid-1500s to the early 1800s. At the height of its success, this imperial power controlled most of the Indian subcontinent and much of what is now Afghanistan, containing a population of around 150 million people.

During this era, a young prince named Khurram took the throne in 1628, succeeding his father. Six years prior, after a military victory Khurram was given the title Shah Jahan by his emperor father. Now, with much of the subcontinent at his feet, the title was apt: *Shah Jahan* is Persian for "King of the World." (17th-century emperors were nothing if not modest.)

When Khurram Met Arjumand

Being shah had a lot of fringe benefits—banquets, treasures, and multiple wives, among other things. Shah Jahan did have several wives, but one woman stood out from the rest. When he was age 15, he was betrothed to 14-year-old Arjumand Banu Begam. Her beauty and compassion knocked the emperor-to-be off his feet; five years later, they were married. The bride took the title of *Mumtaz Mahal,* which means, according to various translations, "Chosen One of the Palace," "Exalted One of the Palace," or "Beloved Ornament of the Palace." You get the point.

Court historians have recorded the couple's close friendship, companionship, and intimate relationship. The couple traveled extensively together, Mumtaz often accompanying her husband on his military jaunts. But tragedy struck in 1631, when on one of these trips, Mumtaz died giving birth to what would have been their 14th child.

Breaking Ground

Devastated, Shah Jahan began work that year on what would become the Taj Mahal, a palatial monument to his dead wife and their everlasting love. While there were surely many hands on deck for the planning of the Taj, the architect who is most often credited is Ustad Ahmad Lahori. The project took until 1648 to complete and enlisted the labor of 20,000 workers and 1,000 elephants. This structure and its surrounding grounds covers 42 acres. The following are the basic parts of Mumtaz's giant mausoleum.

The Gardens: To get to the structural parts of the Taj Mahal, one must cross the enormous gardens surrounding it. Following classic Persian garden design, the grounds to the south of the buildings are made up of four sections divided by marble canals (reflecting pools) with adjacent pathways. The gardens stretch from the main gateway to the foot of the Taj.

The Main Gateway: Made of red sandstone and standing approximately 100 feet high and 150 feet wide, the main gateway is composed of a central arch with towers attached to each of its corners. The walls are richly adorned with calligraphy and floral arabesques inlaid with gemstones.

The Tomb: Unlike most Mughal mausoleums, Mumtaz's tomb is placed at the north end of the Taj Mahal, above the river and in between the mosque and the guesthouse. The tomb is entirely sheathed in white marble with an exterior dome that is almost 250 feet above ground level. The effect is impressive: Depending on the light at various times of the day, the tomb can appear pink, white, or brilliant gold.

The Mosque and the Jawab: On either side of the great tomb lie two smaller buildings. One is a mosque, and the other is called the *jawab,* or "answer." The mosque was used, of course, as a place of worship; the jawab was often used as a guesthouse. Both buildings are made of red sandstone so as not to take away too much from the grandeur of the tomb. The shah's monument to the love of his life still stands, and still awes, more than 360 years later.

📺 Behind the TV Shows of Our Time

- Morton Downey Jr. became famous—or infamous—as the host of an eponymous talk show. His father was a popular singer best known for Irish ballads, and his mother was the actress Barbara Bennett, sister of Constance and Joan.

- Werner Klemperer, who played the Nazi Colonel Klink on *Hogan's Heroes*, was the son of Otto Klemperer, widely considered one of the greatest musical conductors of the 20th century. Ironically, the family was forced to flee Germany in 1933 because they were Jewish.

- In a class reunion episode, it was revealed that *The Andy Griffith Show's* Barney Fife's full name was Bernard Milton Fife and that (unsurprisingly) he had been a hall monitor in high school.

- In an episode of *The Jeffersons* called "George and the President," George Jefferson claims to be the descendant of Thomas Jefferson and flounces around in a powdered wig and tights. George was made to look the fool at the time, but given the president's relationship with his slave, Sally Hennings, maybe he was right after all.

- Richard Pryor guest-starred on a 1971 episode of *The Partridge Family* called "Soul Club."

- Though *The Adventures of Ozzie & Harriet* is now thought of as the epitome of all-American blandness and prudery, Ozzie and Harriet were actually the first married TV couple to be shown sharing a king-sized bed. Previously, couples were shown sleeping in separate twin beds.

- In the wedding episode of *Rhoda,* a wedding dress-clad Rhoda Morgenstern dashed through Manhattan and the Bronx, passing show creator James L. Brooks, who made a cameo as a man who gives her a sympathetic glance on a subway platform.

- Sammy Davis Jr. made guest appearances on many sitcoms, but his most famous sitcom appearance was in an episode of *All in the Family*, in which he surprised the bigoted Archie by kissing him on the cheek as a camera snapped their photo.

- Ted Cassidy, who portrayed Lurch on *The Addams Family*, usually played Thing, the disembodied hand.

Bye-Bye Brewskis

❖ ❖ ❖ ❖

As the largest 100-percent Canadian-owned brewery, Moosehead is one of the country's most beloved brand. In fact, a few Canadians have taken the opportunity to steal large quantities of the brew.

Wanted: Beer and Bear

In August 2004, a truck driver named Wade Haines was transporting 54,000 cans of Moosehead beer to Mexico, when suddenly the delivery went missing. Police found Haines's empty rig idling in a parking lot on the outskirts of Fredericton, New Brunswick. Soon afterward about 8,000 cans were found in a makeshift trailer that had overturned off the road in a wooded region near Woodstock, New Brunswick. But what happened to the rest of the brew?

The local population, the police, and the national media embarked on a frenzied search for the missing beer. Thousands of cans were recovered from the surrounding area, including in the woods and by a cemetery. In October, police discovered a marijuana farm that had 200 of the stolen cans, six of which showed clear signs of having been bitten by a bear. Neither the bear nor the farmers, however, could be located for questioning.

In another daring move, in September 2007, thieves used stolen tractors to heist two trailers holding 70,000 cans and 44,000 bottles of Moosehead, adding up to a loss of more than $200,000. Never fear, beer drinkers: Ontario was restocked with Moosehead a week later, a testament to the brewery's dedication to its fans.

Not Just for Canucks

In March 2008, Americans in Daytona Beach, Florida, apparently were willing to steal Moosehead as well. But unlike their Candian counterparts, the American thieves failed to steal actual beer; instead, the thieves made off with the company's 30-foot-tall inflatable bottle of Moosehead Light. To show it could take a joke, or perhaps to compensate the thieves for the blow-up bottle's lack of liquid, Moosehead offered a year's supply of beer for the return of the $5,000 display.

FROM THE VAULTS OF HISTORY

- The chronicler of the ballet and racetrack, painter Edgar Degas wasn't like many of his starving artists friends—he came from a family of prominent and wealthy bankers.

- Charles Osborne started hiccupping in 1922 and didn't stop till 1990. That's 68 years of hiccupping—and a world record.

- On a cold winter day in 1626, while traveling from London, Francis Bacon decided to find out if freezing would help preserve food. He stopped his carriage, bought a chicken, and stuffed it full of snow. Bacon died of pneumonia soon after his experiment, prompting claims that he died as a result of a frozen dinner.

- In 1888, American undertaker Almon Strowger invented the dial telephone. Convinced that his calls were being diverted by the town telephone operator to another undertaker in town (the operator was the rival's wife), Strowger invented the first dial system enabling callers to make the calls themselves.

- The famous phrase, *cognito ergo sum* (or, "I think, therefore I am") is traditionally credited to philosopher René Descartes. But 1,200 years earlier, St. Augustine uttered a very similar phrase: "Of this last doubt, I cannot doubt: that I doubt." Trust us, it means pretty much the same thing.

- Influential psychoanalyst Sigmund Freud once analyzed a childhood reminiscence of Leonardo da Vinci's. Unfortunately, Freud misinterpreted the Italian word for "kite" as "vulture," so his analysis was a little off.

- During the late-16th-century reign of Queen Elizabeth I, when far less was known about health and grooming, bathing was regarded with some trepidation. Elizabeth herself claimed that she bathed once every three months, whether she needed it or not.

Breaking the Bonds: Divorce Around the World

❖ ❖ ❖ ❖

Scholars and experts have long studied the different ways cultures around the world say, "I do." But how do they say, "I don't anymore"? Divorce laws date back as early as 2000 B.C., which means that almost as long as couples have been binding together, they've been looking to cut the ties.

I'd Like to Return This Faulty Wife, Please

Who knew brides had a warranty? In ancient Greece, a man simply had to send his wife back to her father—dowry in tow—to end their happily-ever-after. In ancient China, divorce was seen as a big no-no. One old proverb passed down to newlyweds was "You're married until your hair turns white." Of course, that didn't mean a man couldn't divorce his wife—all he had to do was send an emissary to his wife's father, declaring that he "cannot worship at the ancestral shrine with your daughter any longer."

Hit the Road, Jack

Other cultures like to keep the separation simple: If an Eskimo couple wishes to separate, they just start living apart from one another. Among certain Native Americans, a woman could initiate divorce by placing her husband's moccasins outside the dwelling, indicating he should walk away and not come back (an early form of throwing his stuff on the lawn?). An Australian Aborigine woman has a tougher time dissolving her marriage: If she can't convince her husband to leave her, she has only one option: elope with someone else.

High-Speed Separation

If a quick separation is what you're after, check out the laws in Japan, Russia, and Sweden. In Japan, if both husband and wife are in agreement that the marriage is kaput, they need only sign a document saying so and drop it off at city hall. In Russia, a couple has to go to court only if children are involved or if one person doesn't want the divorce. It's a similar story in Sweden: divorces are granted instantly upon application to couples who are on the same page about ending their marriage; if kids are involved or one party is anti-divorce, a "reconsideration period" of six months is required.

Under Islamic law, a man can divorce his wife by simply gathering two witnesses and announcing "I divorce thee" once. (Saying it three times is considered a sin.) But recent technology has made the process even easier: Men can now deliver the decree via text message, leaving women to find out they're single via cell phone. (Worth noting: Arab women can, and do, divorce their husbands in court, but the process tends to be longer and more complicated.)

Technically Divorced

Technology hasn't just sped up the divorce process—in some cases, it's driving couples to split. In 2008, a UK couple divorced after a wife found her husband on the couch with another woman—well, a "virtual" woman on a "virtual" couch; after all, he was playing the online simulation game *Second Life*. In another case, two Jordanians trapped in an unhappy marriage found their real soul mates in an online chatroom . . . only to meet in person and discover their soul mates were actually each other. The couple soon divorced, and each accused the other of cheating.

Look Before You Leave

Dissolving a marriage isn't quite so easy in Canada and Italy. Canadian couples can't divorce without going through a one-year trial separation (extreme situations notwithstanding), and the law requires divorce attorneys to encourage reconciliation or couples' counseling.

In Italy, couples must undergo a three-year trial separation, after which would-be divorcees face a lengthy legal process and low child-support benefits. (No wonder so many Italian couples reconcile!)

Pay As You Go

For some couples, however, the cost of separating is no match for the price of freedom:

• In 1999, media mogul Rupert Murdoch paid his wife of 31 years $1.7 billion in assets, making it the most expensive divorce ever.

- In 2006, Sir Paul McCartney paid a rumored $38.5–$50 million to walk away from his four-year marriage to Heather Mills. The settlement was topped by director James Cameron's $50 million payout to his wife of 17 months, actress Linda Hamilton, in 1999.

- Their cheatin' ways cost Ted Danson, Michael Douglas, Kevin Costner, and Neil Diamond big money. Danson's dalliances cost him $30 million in settlement with his first wife in 1992; Diandra Douglas left her husband with $45 million in her pocket in 1997; Costner shelled out $80 million to his first wife in 1994. Also that year, Diamond coughed up $150 million in cash to his wife of 25 years in the most expensive celebrity divorce on record. That is, until 2007, when basketball legend Michael Jordan paid his ex-wife $168 million. Slam-dunk!

- When Madonna and her ex, filmmaker Guy Ritchie, divorced in 2008, she was ordered to pay him $76 million.

Divorce Rates Worldwide
Ironically, cultures where marriage is based on personal choice (that is, love and happiness) tend to have the highest divorce rates, whereas countries where the Catholic Church and arranged marriages dominate tend to have the lowest. In a 2008 study, 44 states and D.C. reported 2,162,000 marriages. The marriage rate in the study was 7.1 per 1,000 people (total population), and the divorce rate was 3.5 per 1,000 people.

Top 10 Highest Countries (divorces per 1,000 people, 2002)
1. Maldives (10.97)
2. Guam (4.34)
3. Russia and Belarus (4.3)
4. United States (4.1)
5. Ukraine (4)
6. Puerto Rico (3.82)
7. Cuba (3.54)
8. Estonia (3.1)
9. Czech Republic and Lithuania (2.9)
10. Switzerland (2.8)

Fumbling Felons

Just Change the Oil
Not knowing anything about cars proved to be the downfall of a woman from San Antonio, Texas. After hiding 18 bags of marijuana under her hood, she went in for an oil change. The mechanic discovered the stash and called police who promptly arrested the woman on drug charges. She said she didn't realize they'd have to open the hood in order to change her oil.

Don't Move!
In Detroit, Michigan, two would-be robbers charged in to a store, waving guns in the air. One of them shouted, "Nobody move!" Just then the second robber made a sudden movement, surprising his buddy—who shot him.

Paying with Pot
When a customer at a McDonald's restaurant in Vero Beach, Florida, realized he didn't have enough cash to pay for his order, he offered to trade the clerk some marijuana for the food. The cashier declined the offer and called the police instead, describing the car in question. Police stopped the vehicle soon after and found—surprise, surprise—a baggie of weed. Now he'll be eating his Big Mac in the Big House.

Don't Ask and Certainly Don't Tell
On trial for a convenience store robbery in Oklahoma City, Dennis Newton fired his attorney and decided to represent himself in court. The alleged robber actually was handling the defense pretty well until the store manager took the stand. She identified him as the robber, and Newton blew up, shouting, "You're lying! I should have blown your head off!" Realizing his gaffe, he quickly added, "If I'd been the one who was there." But it was too late—the jury found him guilty within 20 minutes and recommended 30 years in jail.

Call It Multitasking
Apparently no one told Efe Osenwegie of Ontario, Canada, that he should keep his eyes on the road. When he was pulled over for speeding on Highway 401, police discovered he was watching a porn movie on a portable DVD player in the front seat. Osenwegie was charged with speeding and operating a motor vehicle with a television visible to the driver.

LEGO Love

❖ ❖ ❖ ❖

For decades, kids—and more than a few adults—have delighted in the mighty LEGO. In fact, video games, high art, amusement parks, and fan clubs have evolved from this humble little brick.

- British inventor Hilary Fisher Page actually patented the interlocking brick years before LEGO came into the picture. Called the "Kiddicraft Self-Locking Building Brick," the idea was copied, more or less, by LEGO founder Ole Kirk Christiansen. The LEGO brick arrived in 1958.

- The acronym "LEGO" comes from the Danish words *leg godt,* which means "play well." *Lego* also means "I put together" in Latin.

- There are 62 LEGO bricks for every one of the world's 6 billion inhabitants.

- Little LEGO people are called "minifigures" or "minifigs" for short. They came on the LEGO scene in 1974 and, at that time, had no arms.

- LEGO also makes small tires for building cars, trucks, and moon buggies. The LEGO factory manufactures around 306 million tiny rubber tires every year—more than any other tire manufacturer in the world.

- Six LEGO bricks can be arranged in 915,103,765 different ways.

- Seven LEGO sets are sold around the world every second.

- In 2003, the longest LEGO chain was built by 700 children in Switzerland. It was 1,854 feet long, had 2,211 chain links, and was made from 424,512 LEGO bricks.

- Minifigs are traditionally yellow, but when LEGO debuted its basketball series in 2003, a variety of realistic skin tones were introduced.

- More than 400 billion LEGO bricks have been produced since their inception. Stacked on top of each other, this is enough to connect the Earth to the Moon ten times over.

Fast Facts

- During World War II, the Oscar statuettes presented at the Academy Awards were made of plaster due to a scarcity of metal.

- Talk about unbeatable! Walt Disney won the first eight Academy Awards given for Best Animated Short Subject.

- Sneezes can reach 100 miles per hour.

- The average person drinks 16,000 gallons of water in their lifetime.

- Grover Cleveland was the only U.S. president to serve two nonconsecutive terms.

- "Silent Night" was first performed on Christmas Eve in 1818 at the small village St. Nicholas church in Oberndorf, Austria. It was composed for the guitar and sung by the assistant priest and the composer, choir director, Franz Gruber.

- You can make change for a dollar in 293 different ways.

- Let there be light: The streetlights in Hershey, Pennsylvania, are shaped like Hershey Kisses.

- On a circus train, the animals ride in the stock cars that are positioned directly behind the locomotive, because this spot gives them the smoothest ride.

- To get the smell of onions off your hands, wet your fingers and rub them on stainless steel.

- It's possible for snakes to see through their eyelids.

- It doesn't matter if it's low fat, low carb, or something else— the chance of keeping weight off for two years after a diet is only 15 percent.

Cher Ami: Heroic Pigeon

❖ ❖ ❖ ❖

*A carrier pigeon named Cher Ami braved brutal enemy
fire to save nearly 200 trapped American servicemen!*

During World War I, the U.S. Army Signal Corps put nearly 600 carrier pigeons into service in France. Among the best known is Cher Ami, a genuine hero among heroes.

During the Meuse-Argonne offensive in October 1918, more than 500 members of the 77th Infantry Division, led by Major Charles Whittlesey, found themselves surrounded behind enemy lines. Worse, their location began taking artillery fire from fellow American forces unaware of their predicament. By the second day, little more than 200 members of the 77th were still alive.

Desperate, Whittlesey dispatched messages to division headquarters via carrier pigeon. The first birds were quickly shot down, leaving only a pigeon named Cher Ami to finish the mission. A barrage of bullets whizzed past the little bird as he rose from the bushes; for a moment it seemed he would suffer the same fate as his comrades. Cher Ami took a bullet in the chest, and another bullet nearly severed the leg holding his message canister, but he stayed aloft, flying directly to his roost at division headquarters. Within hours the surviving members of Whittlesey's "Lost Battalion" were safely back behind American lines.

Cher Ami was hailed a hero. Army medics worked hard to save his life, going so far as to carve a tiny wooden leg to replace the one that had been injured by enemy fire. The pigeon was awarded the French Croix de Guerre with Palm medal for his service and later became the mascot of the Department of Service.

Cher Ami died June 13, 1919. He was inducted into the Racing Pigeon Hall of Fame in 1931 and received a gold medal from the Organized Bodies of American Racing Pigeon Fanciers in recognition of his service. He is now on display at the National Museum of American History in Washington, D.C, in an exhibition titled, "The Price of Freedom: Americans at War."

Safe War?

Here's something they didn't teach you in high school history class: Condoms were incredibly important during the invasion of Normandy by Allied troops in World War II in 1944. Sure, condoms kept soldiers free of sexually transmitted diseases, and they no doubt helped to prevent a lot of out-of-wedlock pregnancies. But condoms were also used for more heavy-duty purposes. Soil samples collected on Omaha Beach were stored in the durable rubber receptacles. And when our boys bravely charged out of the flat-bottomed landing boats, their guns were protected from water damage by the condoms that covered their barrels. (Perhaps the director edited out that detail in *Saving Private Ryan*.)

Things Unspoken

Queen of France Marie Antoinette may not have been a very nice person, and she may have made many foolish or unkind statements, but she almost surely never said the sentence that most people associate with her: "Let them eat cake." We know this because the phrase appears in Jean-Jacques Rousseau's *Confessions,* which was completed in 1769. Rousseau attributed the unsympathetic remark—supposedly said in response to the French people starving—to a "young princess," but the phrase had been ascribed to various other sovereigns for decades before Marie arrived in France in 1770.

While it is possible that Marie was familiar with *Confessions,* as it was published 20 years before the French Revolution began, it is highly doubtful that she actually read it—she wasn't exactly known as an intellectual. A more likely scenario is that someone on the side of the Revolution read Rousseau's work, decided the arrogant remark sounded like something the queen would say, and simply started spreading the rumor.

City of Darkness: Kowloon Walled City

❖ ❖ ❖ ❖

Today, it's a gem of a tourist attraction: a traditional Chinese garden in the heart of Hong Kong, filled with historic relics. But just 25 years ago, this lush expanse was home to what locals called Hak Nam—the City of Darkness, one of the world's most dangerous slums.

Wonder Wall

Located on the Kowloon Peninsula, the Walled City originated as a simple fort. Chinese soldiers built it after the British takeover of Hong Kong Island (right across the bay) in 1841 to protect mainland China from possible attack. Then, to further ensure China was safe from British invasion, they built a 6.5-acre stone wall around the fort, with six watchtowers and four guard gates. Behind the walls, a city began to emerge as more military men moved with their families to the area.

In 1860, the British took control of the southernmost tip of the Kowloon Peninsula, and the Walled City became an even better spot for the Chinese to observe the actions of the British. Over the next few decades, the city's population rapidly grew with an influx of not only Chinese soldiers but also civilian business owners and their employees. In most cases, these "businesses" were opium dens, gambling houses, and brothels. With a prime location between British territory and mainland China, the Walled City became a popular stop for folks to get a quick fix before heading on their way.

Exception to the (British) Rule

The year 1898 marked the infamous signing over of Hong Kong, the Kowloon Peninsula, and all of the surrounding territories to the British under a 99-year lease—with one exception: Kowloon Walled City would remain a Chinese territory and the Chinese military could stay there so long as its actions supported colonial efforts.

Within a year, the agreement was void: In 1899, Chinese troops helped peasants revolt against the new British rule, and, as could be expected, the colonial government changed its mind about letting the Walled City remain under Chinese jurisdiction. By the end of the year, the last of China's administrators had been kicked out of town. Still, the British couldn't get a foothold in the Walled City. On a good day, the stubborn citizens ignored the colonial laws outright; on a bad day, they rebelled violently.

Caught in a kind of limbo—*within* British territory but *without* British authority—the "city within a city" quickly spiraled into anarchy and squalor.

Boom Town

During World War II, Japanese troops tried to destroy the city by removing the wall around it—but they couldn't remove the people. In fact, just the opposite happened. The population of the now wall-less Walled City exploded after the war, with thousands of refugees flocking to the tiny area (which measured only 656 by 492 feet) in search of asylum from poverty, political persecution, and famine.

The burgeoning community was a blight on the British, who sought to demolish the Walled City in favor of a park. In 1948, the colonial government tried to take a stand by evicting 2,000 settlers from the area; local residents promptly set fire to the British consulate in protest.

The colonial government's last attempt to interfere came after the Chinese Cultural Revolution in 1966, when residents flew a Communist flag over the city. British officials attempted to remove the flag, but violent revolts led them to drop the issue—leaving the Walled City to fend for itself.

Vice City

Over the next 20 years, ramshackle tenements sprang up throughout the city, reaching as high as 10 to 12 stories. The buildings were packed so tightly that no four-wheeled vehicle could fit on the streets, and barely a shred of sunlight could pass through, even at high noon.

Without any official government in place, power fell to the Chinese street gangs, who ruled over the Walled City's dank, dark, alleyways, which teemed with drugs, prostitution, and unlicensed medical and dental practices. (Chinese doctors and dentists who lacked the proper license to practice under British rule often set up illegal shops in the Walled City, offering services at a deep discount.)

Nevertheless, with water and electricity illegally siphoned from Hong Kong, the city had become a fully functioning town in its own right.

Garden Walk

Meanwhile, tensions continued to mount between the Chinese and British governments about what to do with this enclave of anarchy. While the British clearly wanted it gone, the Chinese resisted. Finally, in 1987, the two parties reached an agreement to raze the city and build a park on its grounds by 1997, the year Hong Kong would officially return to Chinese rule.

Between 1988 and 1992, more than 35,000 people were ousted from the Walled City's cramped slums, and by April 1994, demolition was complete. The Kowloon City Walled Park officially opened on December 22, 1995, featuring relics from the city's original stone wall and military fortress.

- *The Kowloon Peninsula is named for the string of mountains that forms its northern border:* Gau Lung, *which means "nine dragons." Legend has it that 800 years ago, the boy emperor Ping was planning to name the mountain chain "Eight Dragons," based on the belief that dragons live in mountains. Then a courtier pointed out that, since emperors are also considered dragons, the mountain range should be called "Nine Dragons," with Ping, of course, being the ninth.*

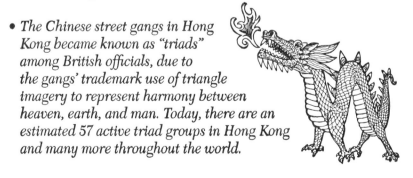

- *The Chinese street gangs in Hong Kong became known as "triads" among British officials, due to the gangs' trademark use of triangle imagery to represent harmony between heaven, earth, and man. Today, there are an estimated 57 active triad groups in Hong Kong and many more throughout the world.*

- Peanuts are a multipurpose nut: Sure they're tasty, but they're also one of the components of dynamite.

- The first CT (computed tomography) imaging machine was developed by EMI, a company known for its work in the recording world. Some historians say it was because of The Beatles' success that EMI was able to fund the research into the machine.

- London was the first city with a subway system. Affectionately called the Tube, it was finished in 1863.

- According to a 2007 poll, 43 percent of dog owners give their pooches a birthday present.

- Whoopi Goldberg was born Caryn Elaine Johnson.

- Early 20th-century railroad crossing signals were known as "wigwags" for the swinging, pendulumlike motion they made when signaling an oncoming train.

- A bowling pin needs to tilt at least 7.5 degrees to fall over.

- Rudolph the Red-Nosed Reindeer was the brainchild of Mongomery Ward for their 1939 Christmas promotion.

- Only 3–5 percent of mammals are monogamous.

- Vultures take their mating seriously and will attack any vultures caught philandering.

- The odds of being struck by lightning in the United States in any given year: 1 in 700,000. The odds of being struck by lightning in your lifetime: 1 in 3,000.

🎥 Behind the Films of Our Time

- In the 2009 movie *GI Joe: The Rise of Cobra,* the film shows scenes outside the base where mountains are visible in the background. Since the base is near the North Pole, however, there shouldn't be any mountains around—only ice.

- How could three acclaimed actors make such a bad movie? In 1987, *Ishtar* hit theaters, starring Warren Beatty, Dustin Hoffman, and Isabella Adjani. It was an attempt to reproduce the old road movies of Bob Hope and Bing Crosby, but it didn't quite hit the mark. Gary Larson later based one of his *Far Side* comics on the movie, depicting Hell's Video Store, where all the movies on the shelves were copies of *Ishtar.* Larson said he hadn't actually seen the movie at the time. He later apologized, saying it wasn't really all that bad.

- Some say that Bert and Ernie of *Sesame Street* fame were named after the policeman and the taxi driver in *It's a Wonderful Life.*

- The sorcerer in Disney's *Fantasia* is called Yen Sid—that's Disney spelled backward.

- It's hard to imagine Adolf Hitler at the movies. Even so, der Führer's favorite was *King Kong.*

- Here's a mistake for '70s trivia buffs. In *The Rocky Horror Picture Show,* the criminologist says the action takes place on an evening in late November. On the car radio, however, President Nixon's resignation speech is heard. Nixon resigned in August of that year.

- Did anyone see the cameraman in the dueling scene of *Harry Potter and the Chamber of Secrets?* Right after Snape helps Malfoy back onto his feet, you can see the crewman on the far left of the screen.

- Buddy Ebsen (famous for his Jed Clampett role on TV's *Beverly Hillbillies*) was originally cast as the Tin Man in 1939's *Wizard of Oz,* but he had to drop the role due to an allergic reaction to the silver dust make-up.

Blonde Ambition

❖ ❖ ❖ ❖

Estimates vary, but only an estimated 2–15 percent of blondes are au naturale; *most get their light locks from a bottle of peroxide or by bleaching it at the salon. Read on for some of history's most famous flaxen-haired women.*

Madonna

Throughout her career, queen of pop Madonna has obsessively changed her look. But ask anyone what color Madonna's hair is, and they'll probably say blonde. She dyes her hair constantly, but whether it's platinum or dishwater, golden or nearly white, this (naturally brunette) superstar always returns to her signature shade.

Jean Harlow

The original "Blonde Bombshell" movie star goddess, sassy and sexy Jean Harlow turned heads and made history when she appeared in early Hollywood pictures such as *Hell's Angels.* MGM Studios managed to stay afloat throughout the Great Depression, and many credit Harlow's overwhelming popularity. Her bleached tresses sent many women across the country to the hairdresser, demanding a similarly peroxide look.

Aphrodite

In 360 B.C., sculptor Praxiteles is said to have used his blonde mistress as a model for a statue of goddess of love Aphrodite. Homer describes this Greek goddess as emerging from the water with only her blonde tresses to cover her nakedness. The statue was reproduced countless times, inspiring women for centuries to lighten their hair with the tried-and-true lemon juice and sun exposure combo.

Mary Magdalene

Was Mary Magdalene a blonde? It's possible. In his 1426 painting *Crucifixion,* Masaccio portrays Magdalene at the foot of Christ's cross, her flaxen tresses shining. This portrayal may have been a result of the continuing stereotype of blonde women as temptresses.

Doris Day

Her era has since ended, but actress and singer Doris Day remains the number-one female box-office star of all time. This is due to Day's mammoth popularity throughout the 1940s and '50s, when her squeaky-clean, approachable blondeness attracted housewives, servicemen, and entertainment lovers across the globe.

Supergirl

The female counterpart to DC Comics hero Superman, Supergirl was drawn to be as blonde as possible. The first recurring appearance of Supergirl debuted in 1959, in which the teenage hero's secret identity was painted as Linda Lee, an orphan forced to conceal her blonde hair under a brown wig.

Mae West

Actress, comedienne, writer, sex symbol, and musician, Mae West was a multitalented blonde who held the nation's attention in the early part of the 20th century with her presence in various forms of media and her cavalier attitude. One of her more famous quips: "Is that a pistol in your pocket or are you just happy to see me?"

Barbie

First produced by Mattel in 1959, the Barbie doll is, for better or worse, an all-American icon. Though the first Barbie came with either blonde or brunette hair, the prevailing look of Barbara Millicent Roberts (her full name) was blonde. More than 1 billion Barbies have sold in more than 150 countries—that's a lot of blonde ambition!

Marilyn Monroe

What list of famous blondes would be complete without Marilyn? Although she was born a brunette, thanks to hair dyes, it's safe to say that this actress, model, and ultimate American icon is single-handedly responsible for decades of men and women who equate blonde with beautiful.

If You See Only Five...

Amazing Animation

❖ ❖ ❖ ❖

Animation is almost as old as cinema itself. Here are five outstanding features that illustrate all that the genre has to offer.

1. *Snow White and the Seven Dwarfs* **(1937)**—An undisputed classic, this take on the Grimm fairy tale is historic for being one of the world's first full-length animated features, as well as the first to be produced by Walt Disney. In 1939, Disney was given an honorary Academy Award for *Snow White*—an award made especially for him, consisting of one statuette and seven miniature statuettes.

2. *Fantasia* **(1940)**—A commercial failure at the time of its release (film critic Roger Ebert blames a World War II–era lack of whimsical spirit), this wondrous ode to classical music is now an acknowledged masterpiece that was well ahead of its time in both theme and execution.

3. *Shrek* **(2001)**—Based on the children's picture book by William Steig, the computer-animated *Shrek* stars Mike Myers as the titular green ogre, Eddie Murphy as a wise-cracking donkey, and Cameron Diaz as Princess Fiona. This was the film that put DreamWorks on the map, as it pokes hilarious fun at popular culture (and all things Disney), with plenty of guffaws for children and adults alike.

4. *Spirited Away* **(2001)**—The Japanese consider animation a genuine art form, and Hayao Miyazaki, who wrote and directed this anime classic, is revered as one of the genre's masters. The story concerns Chihiro, a young girl who wanders into a bizarre world of spirits and monsters. *Spirited Away* (real name: *Sen to Chihiro no kamikakushi*) won the Academy Award for Best Animated Feature in 2003. If you've never experienced Japanese animation, this is a great place to start.

5. *WALL-E* **(2008)**—The delightful story of an endearing (and industrious) little robot who falls in love, travels into space, and ultimately saves the world, *WALL-E* deservedly won the 2009 Academy Award for Best Animated Feature. It's the perfect blend of story, character, and eye-popping computer animation in one neat package. It might also make you shed a tear or two.

D'oh! I Know That Voice!

❖ ❖ ❖ ❖

Since its TV premiere in 1989, The Simpsons *has become a genuine cultural phenomenon. Being invited to appear (well, vocally, anyway) in an episode is a high honor. Here are some celebrities who have stepped up to the mic.*

Going Incognito

Not every celeb wants their name on the credits. Take "John Jay Smith," for example. He voiced the character of Leon Kompowsky, a burly white guy institutionalized because he thought he was singer Michael Jackson, right down to the high-pitched voice and dance moves. But John Jay Smith was actually a pseudonym for the real Michael Jackson, a longtime *Simpsons* fan. Interestingly, the character's singing was done by Jackson impersonator Kipp Lemon.

Jackson wasn't the first big name to appear on the show incognito. Oscar-winning actor Dustin Hoffman, listed as "Sam Etic" in the credits, voiced Mr. Bergstrom, a sympathetic substitute teacher who inspires Lisa Simpson.

More Stars Than Homerpalooza

Most of the Fab Four have appeared on *The Simpsons* (minus John Lennon, of course). Paul McCartney and his late wife, Linda, were in a memorable episode called "Lisa the Vegetarian." A song plays during the closing credits that, when played backward, is really a lentil soup recipe read by Paul. Other celebrities who have appeared on the show include:

- Meryl Streep
- James Earl Jones
- The Ramones
- Elizabeth Taylor
- Johnny Cash
- Buzz Aldrin

- Hugh Hefner
- Stephen Hawking
- Stephen King
- Gore Vidal
- Tom Wolfe
- Roger Clemens

- Ken Griffey Jr.
- Johnny Carson
- Mick Jagger
- Aerosmith
- Sting
- Barry White

Fast Facts

- *Have a fear of going to the dentist? It may not help to know that a dentist named Dr. Alfred P. Southwick was the inventor of the electric chair.*

- *Would the hit TV show* Friends *have been as popular with one of the other titles considered:* Insomnia Café?

- *Kleenex was first produced in 1914 during WWI for use as a bandage and mask filter. After the war, the Kleenex tissue was promoted as a make-up remover. Finally, consumers began using the tissue as a disposable handkerchief.*

- *The first computer mouse, used in 1964, was made from wood.*

- *The original name for Cheerios was Cheerioats.*

- *The DePaul University Blue Demons are not into the occult: The first DePaul athletes in 1900 were given varsity letters, which earned them the name D-men. That eventually evolved into Demons. The "Blue" was added after school colors were chosen.*

- *Pistachios and almonds are the only nuts found in the Bible.*

- *There was a widespread rumor that the last word of the final Harry Potter book,* Harry Potter and the Deathly Hallows, *would be "scar." Author J. K. Rowling agreed with this rumor for a long time, but she decided to change the final word when she finished writing the book.*

- *Lightning isn't associated only with thunderstorms. It is also commonly seen in volcanic eruptions, and even hurricanes.*

Exotic Fruit Explosion

❖ ❖ ❖ ❖

*As U.S. consumers grow increasingly fond of "superfruits,"
the time is ripe for some exotic new flavors.*

Prior to about 2005, few U.S. consumers had heard of "super-fruit." Coined by marketers to describe fruit that is nutrient- and antioxidant-rich (as well as somewhat of a novelty), the term quickly gained widespread (perhaps even *super*) usage. Some of the first fruits marketed as ultra-healthy superfruits included blueberry, mango, and pomegranate, followed by açaí, mangosteen, and goji berry. Using these flavors, food and beverage companies have launched a variety of health products and trendy treats.

So what other flavors are likely to achieve superfruit status? Some of the following exotic fruits have already been showing up in energy drinks, beauty products, and fancy fortified water.

Camu-camu: This fun-to-say fruit is native to Peru and is very acidic in taste. Organically prepared camu-camu is said to contain more vitamin C than any other fruit on the planet. It is popular in Japan as a food and as an ingredient in beauty products. Camu-camu also is in energy drinks, juice, and dietary supplements.

Cherimoya: This heart-shape fruit from South America tastes like a tropical blend of pineapple, banana, and strawberry. Its healthy properties include vitamin C, calcium, and fiber, and it is particularly used in beverages, smoothies, or ice cream.

Lulo: Also known as "naranjilla," or "little orange," this is a small, tangy fruit hailing from Columbia, Ecuador, and Peru. Some say the green juice of lulo tastes like a combination of lime and rhubarb. The fruit contains vitamins B and C, calcium, and iron, and is popular in beverages and purees.

Rambutan: This distinctive-looking fruit comes from Southeast Asia. *Rambutan* translates to "hairy" in some Asian languages, and indeed, the fruit has a hairy exterior. Often used in desserts, the rambutan's sweet taste is similar to that of a litchi, and the fruit is a reliable source of vitamin C and calcium.

The Dyatlov Pass Incident

❖ ❖ ❖ ❖

Nine experienced hikers and skiers trek into the Russian wilderness and promptly disappear. Weeks later, their mangled bodies are found among the ruins of the campsite, with no trace of evidence as to how they died. Read on for a closer look at one of the greatest (and creepiest) unsolved mysteries of modern times.

Off to the Otorten Mountain

In early 1959, a group of outdoor enthusiasts formed a skiing and hiking expedition to Otorten Mountain, which is part of the northern Ural Mountain range in Russia. The group, led by Igor Dyatlov, consisted of seven other men and two women: Yury Doroshenko, Georgy Krivonischenko, Alexander Kolevatov, Rustem Slobodin, Nicolas Thibeaux-Brignolle, Yuri Yudin, Alexander Zolotaryov, Lyudmila Dubinina, and Zinaida Kolmogorova.

The group's journey began on January 27. The following day, Yudin became ill and had to return home. It would be the last time he would see his friends alive. Using personal photographs and journals belonging to the members of the ski trip to piece together the chain of events, it appeared as though on February 1, the group got disoriented making their way to Otorten Mountain and ended up heading too far to the west. Once they realized they were heading in the wrong direction, the decision was made to simply set up camp for the night. What happened next is a mystery to this day.

Mountain of the Dead

When no word had been heard from the group by February 20, eight days after their planned return, a group of volunteers organized a search. On February 26, they found the group's abandoned campsite on the east side of the mountain Kholat Syakhl. (As if the story were written by a horror novelist, *Kholat Syakhl* happens to mean "Mountain of the Dead" in the Mansi language.) The search team found a badly damaged tent that appeared to have been ripped open from the inside. They also found several sets of footprints. Following the trail of footprints, searchers discovered the bodies of Krivonischenko and Doroshenko, shoeless and dressed only in their underwear. Three more bodies—those belonging to Dyatlov, Kolmogorova and Slobodin—were found nearby. It was later determined that all five had died from hypothermia.

On May 4, the bodies of the four other hikers were recovered in the woods near where the bodies of Krivonischenko and Doroshenko had been found. The discovery of these four raised even more questions. To begin with, Thibeaux-Brignolle's skull had been crushed and both Dubunina and Zolotaryov had major chest fractures. The force needed to cause these wounds was compared to that of a high-speed car crash. Oddly, Dubinina's tongue appeared to have been ripped out.

Looking at the evidence, it appeared as though all nine members had bedded down for the night, only to be woken up by something so frightening that they all quickly left the tent and ran into the freezing cold night. One by one, they either froze to death or else succumbed to their injuries, the cause of which was never determined.

Remains a Mystery

Things got even stranger at the funerals for the nine individuals. Family members would later remark that some of the deceased's skin had become orange and their hair had turned grey. Medical tests and a Geiger counter brought to the site showed some of the bodies had high levels of radiation.

So what happened to the hikers? Authorities eventually concluded that "an unknown compelling force" caused the deaths. The case would be officially closed in the spring of 1959 due to the "absence of a guilty party." Stories and theories still abound, pointing to everything from the Russian government covering up secret military exercises in the area to violent UFO encounters. Today, the area where the nine hikers met their untimely demise is known as Dyatlov Pass, after the leader of the ill-fated group.

Say What?

"They say hot dogs can kill you. How do you know it's not the bun?"
—*Jay Leno*

"Cleaning your house while your children are still growing is like shoveling the walk before it stops snowing."
—*Phyllis Diller*

"One out of four people in this country is mentally imbalanced. Think of your three closest friends, and if they seem okay, then you're the one."
—*Ann Landers*

"A word of advice: Don't give it."
—*A. J. Volicos*

"God heals and the doctor takes the fee."
—*Ben Franklin*

"Diets are for people who are thick and tired of it."
—*Jacob Braude*

"Whenever I feel like exercise, I lie down until the feeling passes."
—*Robert M. Hutchins*

"A preposition is something never to end a sentence with."
—*William Safire*

"If anything happens to me, tell every woman I've ever gone with I was talking about her at the end. That way, they'll have to reevaluate me."
—*Albert Brooks*

"If life was fair, Elvis would be alive and all the impersonators would be dead."
—*Johnny Carson*

"His toupee makes him look 20 years sillier."
—*Bill Dana*

"If all the young ladies who attended the Yale prom were laid end to end, no one would be the least bit surprised."
—*Dorothy Parker*

"A lie can travel half way around the world while the truth is putting on its shoes."
—*Mark Twain*

Mutiny or Mistake?

❖ ❖ ❖ ❖

Military casualties aren't always the result of combat.
A commander's own men can turn against him,
too—whether by accident or by design.

Being a military commander sometimes means becoming a target, whether by the enemy or their own troops. Here are nine commanders who found themselves dead at the hands of the men serving directly beneath them.

Nadir Shah
Cause of death: mutiny
Persian leader Nadir Shah ruled his empire during the 1700s, leading his army to victory over the Mongols, Turks, and other rivals. His career came to a sudden stop, however, when his military-appointed bodyguard murdered him. Since Shah was said to be cruel, the other troops weren't too torn up about his death.

Colonel David Marcus
Cause of death: mistake
In the late 1940s, U.S. Army Colonel David Marcus decided to join Israel's army, as the nation was in the midst of a tense war. Marcus was helping build a road from Tel Aviv to Jerusalem. One night, he couldn't sleep. He got up to go for a walk and an Israeli Army guard opened fire and killed him. Apparently, the guard saw a bed sheet wrapped around Marcus and thought he was an Arab fighter. His story was made into the 1966 film, *Cast a Giant Shadow,* starring Kirk Douglas.

Colonel John Finnis
Cause of death: mutiny
This one may not be a shock: Colonel John Finnis was slaughtered while lecturing his troops about insubordination. In 1857, the British Indian Army commander went to address his men after learning they were moving toward mutiny. Unfortunately, his message didn't carry much weight—the troops killed him midspeech. The incident became known as the Sepoy Mutiny.

General Thomas "Stonewall" Jackson
Cause of death: mistake
On May 2, 1863, famed Civil War Confederate General "Stonewall" Jackson went out with a small crew to scout out his team's upcoming path. When he came back to camp, a group of Confederate fighters thought he was a Yankee and shot him. He died eight days later.

Captain Pedro de Urzúa
Cause of death: mutiny
In the mid-1500s, Spanish Captain Pedro de Urzúa found himself on the wrong side of his troops while leading soldiers on a mission across the Andes. De Urzúa's men rallied together and decided to take their leader's life, pledging their allegiance instead to another uniting figure. The story was later told in the 1972 movie, *Aguirre, the Wrath of God.*

Corporal Pat Tillman
Cause of death: mistake
Corporal Pat Tillman, famous for his time playing football with the Arizona Cardinals, died in April 2004 while serving in the U.S. Army. According to a military investigation, Tillman was killed by friendly fire while serving in Afghanistan. Tillman's family accused the army of withholding that information for a month so that it could benefit from media coverage surrounding Tillman's memorial.

Captain Yevgeny Golikov
Cause of death: mutiny
In 1905, Captain Yevgeny Golikov died over a dispute about meat. His crew, apparently upset over the low quality of meat available onboard, grabbed Golikov and tossed him into the sea. The story was the inspiration for the 1925 film, *Battleship Potemkin.*

Lieutenants Richard Harlan and Thomas Dellwo
Cause of death: suspected mutiny
The March 1971 deaths of U.S. Army lieutenants Richard Harlan and Thomas Dellwo are still a mystery. The men were at a military base in Vietnam when someone believed to be a soldier tore open the window screen and threw in an explosive. An army private was arrested but later acquitted; the actual killer was never determined.

Odd Ordinances

- It's illegal to buy meat or mattresses on Sunday in Washington State.

- In Seattle, conceal laws prohibit carrying a weapon more than six feet long.

- It's illegal to eat chicken with a fork in Gainesville, Georgia.

- You could go to jail for making an ugly face at a dog in the state of Oklahoma.

- A frog—yes, a frog—can be arrested for keeping a person awake with its "ribbit" noises in Memphis, Tennessee.

- Don't get too friendly at happy hour in Nyala, Nevada—buying drinks for more than three people in a single round is against the law.

- If Alaska's your haunt, don't invite a moose out on the town; serving alcohol to the animal is strictly prohibited.

- North Dakota has outlawed the serving of beer with pretzels at public restaurants and bars.

- Riding a tricycle on the sidewalk of Spring Valley, New York, is not allowed.

- It is illegal to go "underneath a sidewalk" while in the state of Florida.

- Exporting bullfrogs out of the state of Arkansas is a crime.

- Driving livestock on a school bus is illegal in Florida.

- Sex toys are not legally allowed in Georgia.

- Drivers in Pennsylvania who encounter multiple horses coming toward them are required to pull off the road and cover their cars with blankets until the animals pass.

- Owning six artificial penises is considered a felony in Texas.

Sitting on Top of the World

❖ ❖ ❖ ❖

Who were the first two men to reach the North Pole?
Many people can identify Robert E. Peary, but the
other explorer is not nearly as well known.

"I Can't Get Along Without Him"

Matthew Henson was born in Maryland on August 6, 1866, one year
after the Civil War ended. At the age of 13, the young African American began working aboard a ship, and it was there that he learned to
read, write, and navigate.

In 1887, Henson met explorer Robert Peary. Peary hired Henson
as a valet, but quickly found him indispensible. "I can't get along
without him," Peary said.

Henson joined Peary in 1890 to help the explorer reach his dream
of being the first to reach the North Pole. Over the next 18 years
the two men repeatedly tried to reach the pole, only to be thwarted
every time. Henson's worth and value to the expeditions grew, and
Peary gave him more and more responsibility. In 1910, Peary wrote,
"Matthew A. Henson, my Negro assistant, has been with me in one
capacity or another...on each and all of my northern expeditions
except the first. He has shared all the physical hardships of my Arctic
work. [He] can handle a sled better, and is probably a better dog
driver than any other man living... except some Eskimo hunters... "

On Top of the World

In August 1908, Peary and Henson set out once again for the North
Pole. By the following April, they were closing in at last on their
elusive goal. On April 6, 1909, the group—Henson, Peary, and four
native Inuits—drove farther than they had ever gone before. Henson arrived at camp 45 minutes before Peary. By dead reckoning, he
figured that the Pole had been reached. When Peary arrived, Henson
greeted him by saying, "I think I'm the first man to sit on top of the
world."

As Henson recalled, Peary was furious. Peary soon determined
that the Pole was still three miles away, but he left to cover the final

distance on his own (without longitudinal coordinates, so knowing which direction to go was problematic), without waking the sleeping Henson. "It nearly broke my heart," Henson recalled of Peary's actions.

"From the moment I declared to Commander Peary that I believed we stood upon the Pole he apparently ceased to be my friend," Henson wrote in 1910.

Upon his return, Peary was widely hailed as the first one to reach the North Pole. (Today his claim is hotly disputed.) He received awards and honors galore for this achievement. But for Henson, the disappointment had just begun.

Was Race a Factor?

Peary spent the rest of his life being feted as the first man to reach the North Pole. He died in 1920, but not before some waves of controversy emerged. At first, Henson's contributions were not only overlooked, but ignored, and he settled into a desk job working as a clerk in a customs house in New York City.

But in 1912, Henson wrote a book about his experiences, which enraged Peary. A debate exploded, with some people speculating that a large reason Peary had chosen Henson to join him on the expeditions was due to his race—that he figured because Henson was African American, that he would not dare contradict Peary's claims, and if he did, people would not believe him.

In a 1939 magazine interview, Henson was stoic, even philosophical. "Mr. Peary was a noble man," he said. "He was always my friend. I have not expected much, and I have not been disappointed."

Gradually, because it was clear Henson's contributions had been so vital, public opinion began to turn around. In 1944, Congress awarded Henson a duplicate of the silver medal Peary had received. Presidents Truman and Eisenhower both honored him. Henson died in 1955, and in 1988 his coffin was reinterred in Arlington National Cemetery.

Finally, in 2000, the National Geographic Society posthumously awarded Henson its highest honor: the Hubbard Medal—the same award Peary had received in 1906.

Proust's Weird and Wordy Life

❖ ❖ ❖ ❖

*Some people just don't know when to stop. French writer
Marcel Proust spent the last 13 years of his life penning a
novel that topped out at more than one million words.*

Marcel Proust (pronounced "Proost") was born to well-to-do parents
in France in 1871. A known eccentric, at one point he helped bankroll
a house of male prostitution. He wore a fur coat year-round, was a
bisexual bachelor, and traveled in the highest circles of Parisian society. Proust became a keen observer of the ways of the wealthy, and he
scribbled notes on the white cuffs of his dress shirts while at parties.

After the death of his mother in 1905, Proust dramatically
changed his lifestyle. His busy nightlife was abandoned, and he
lined his apartment with cork to keep out noise. He wrote all night,
propped on his bed with a pile of pens, so that he would have a fresh
pen handy should it drop. Once one hit the floor, Proust considered it
too germ-laden to reuse.

Proust had already published many short essays and stories
when he started his final work in 1908. The title, *À la recherche
du temps perdu,* has translated as both *In Search of Lost Time* and
Remembrance of Things Past. Based on the social intrigue he had
observed in upper-class Parisian parlors and nightclubs, the book
ultimately filled seven volumes. The final installments of the book
appeared after the Proust's death in 1922. His massive masterpiece
is now considered one of the world's major literary achievements.

From Proust's Pen

- *"Happiness is beneficial for the body, but it is grief that develops
  the powers of the mind."*

- *"If a little dreaming is dangerous, the cure for it is not to dream
  less but to dream more, to dream all the time."*

- *"Like many intellectuals, he was incapable of saying a simple thing
  in a simple way."*

The Times They Are A-Changin'

1942

- Here comes the sun! Daylight Saving Time is reintroduced in the United States.

- President Franklin D. Roosevelt invokes Executive Order 9066, which calls for the internment of more than 120,000 Japanese Americans to "relocation centers" until the end of World War II.

- A mine explosion in Honkeiko Colliery, Manchuria, kills 1,549 miners.

- On June 12, Anne Frank receives a diary for her 13th birthday. A month later, her family is forced into hiding in an attic above her father's Amsterdam warehouse office.

- Glenn Miller and his orchestra have 11 Top Ten hits in 1942; they play together for the last time in September before Miller enters the U.S. Army.

- Pan American Airlines becomes the first commercial airline to offer a flight that goes around the world.

- In WWII news, the United States' first aircraft carrier, the USS *Langley*, is sunk by Japanese warplanes.

- Barbra Streisand, Jimi Hendrix, and Harrison Ford are born.

- The average cost of new house is $3,770. The average annual income is $1,880.

- The Battle of Midway begins when the Imperial Japanese Navy attacks Midway Island upon the orders of Japanese Admiral Chuichi Nagumo.

- Albert Camus writes his existential classic, *L'Etranger* (*The Stranger*).

- Physicist Enrico Fermi successfully produces a controlled nuclear reaction at the University of Chicago. The experiment is part of the Manhattan Project, the U.S. government's top-secret effort to create a nuclear bomb.

- Movies are a popular release; top films this year include *Casablanca*, *Road to Morocco*, and *Bambi*.

Amulet Live and Let Die

❖ ❖ ❖ ❖

Ever wonder why casinos are often named "Horseshoe" and black cats frequent Halloween? Toss some salt over your shoulder, grab a four-leaf clover, and find out more about the history of these popular symbols of luck and lucklessness.

Lucky Charms

Horseshoe: Not only is the horseshoe forged from iron—which the ancient Egyptians believed was the sacred metal of the sky—but it's also in the shape of the crescent moon, another sacred sign. The horseshoe's reputation as a symbol of good luck could also come from its two-pronged, animal-horn shape, which some ancient peoples thought repelled the evil eye. Though most cultures believe tacking a horseshoe over a doorway brings good fortune, there's disagreement if the prongs should point up, to keep luck from running out, or down, so luck endlessly diffuses.

Four-leaf clover: Four-leaf clovers have been considered lucky for so long, no one quite knows when it began. Doubtlessly it has something to do with their rarity, but the oldest accounts suggest that Eve (before her eviction from the Garden of Eden) picked a four-leaf clover, which served as a reminder of her days in paradise.

Knocking on wood: This custom likely comes from the Christian practice of touching wood on happy occasions to show gratitude to Jesus Christ, who died on a wooden cross. Other experts say the tradition is pagan in origin, stemming from the ancient Druids, who believed deities lived in trees. Knocking (respectfully) on trees also ensured good fortune.

Rabbit's foot: Legend has it that if you rub a lucky rabbit's foot, the characteristics of the animal will rub off on you. It was believed that rabbits were born with their eyes open, so they could recognize (and flee!) the devil from their earliest moments. Others thought the bunny's famous fertility brought prosperity.

Bad Omens

Black cat: This icon of evil dates back to the Middle Ages, when black cats were believed to be the companion of witches. A book called *Beware the Cat* (1584) warned that black cats are witches in disguise—and don't bother killing a cat, because witches can inhabit them up to nine times (a belief that dates back to the Egyptian cat-headed goddess, Bast, who was said to have nine lives). Interestingly, in England, it's the white cat that's considered bad luck and the black cat that's good.

Walking under a ladder: The underside of a ladder is a resting spot for spirits. Don't buy that? Try this: In cultures where the triangle is sacred, the natural triangle formed by a ladder leaning against a wall is considered a holy space to be revered and thus avoided. The ladder also recalls early gallows, when victims climbed a ladder to be hanged to death.

Spilling salt: The lucklessness of spilling salt likely comes from the vital role it played in ancient cultures, which valued the seasoning as much as gold; in fact, Greek and Roman soldiers received part of their pay in salt. Others say the stigma of spilled salt comes from the belief that Judas knocked over the saltshaker at the Last Supper (as depicted in the Leonardo da Vinci painting). In any case, the tradition of throwing spilled salt over the left shoulder comes from the ancient belief that evil spirits are perched there, waiting to attack. Salt thrown over the shoulder—and presumably into their eyes— acted as a kind of pepper spray, putting them out of commission.

Breaking a mirror: Ancient Greeks considered mirrors the gods' porthole into the future: If a mirror broke, it meant the future held ugly things the gods didn't want to show. The penalty of "seven years bad luck" dates back to the ancient Roman belief that a person's health changed every seven years. Since mirrors reflected a person's appearance and health, to break one was to shatter your health for the next seven years.

Fast Facts

- The first true movie stuntman was an ex-cavalryman named Frank Hanaway, who was given a part in The Great Train Robbery (1903) because of his ability to fall off a horse without getting hurt.

- Though it's long been referred to as the Red Planet, Mars is actually more of a butterscotch color.

- Mars is home to the largest volcano in the solar system, Olympus Mons. It's roughly three times the height of Mount Everest and covers an area nearly the size of Arizona.

- Actor Paul Robeson attended Rutgers University in 1915 and was the first African American football player to play on the All American football team.

- Myrna Loy was the first leading lady to wear women's trousers on screen, donning said duds in What Price Beauty? (1925).

- The first movie review appeared in the June 15, 1896, issue of The Chap Book. The movie was The Widow Jones (also known as The Kiss), which also contained the first on-screen kiss. The critic's comment: "Absolutely disgusting."

- Kangaroos have a difficult time moving backward.

- The only bone in the human body not connected to another bone is the hyoid, a u-shape bone located at the base of the tongue between the mandible and the larynx. Its job is to support the tongue and its many muscles.

- There's only one common seven-letter word in the English language that contains all five vowels. Can you name it? (Answer: sequoia)

- Jimmy Carter was the first American president born in a hospital.

Bestsellers from Beyond the Grave

❖ ❖ ❖ ❖

V. C. Andrews has sold more than 100 million copies of her novels. And the books keep rolling out—even after her death.

Portrait of the Novelist as a Young Woman

Born Cleo Virginia Andrews in 1923, our heroine didn't endure the sort of over-the-top evil she later wrote about. But her childhood wasn't easy: A bad fall resulted in a lifetime of back pain, botched surgeries, and limited mobility.

Andrews worked as a fashion illustrator and commercial artist, and she also began to write stories. During the 1970s, she penned nine novels and more than 20 short stories. The tales tended to be on the lurid side, as evidenced by her first published short story (under a pseudonym), called, "I Slept With My Uncle on My Wedding Night."

Success in Hand

In 1978, Andrews submitted what was to become the title that put her on the map: *Flowers in the Attic.* The original manuscript had promise, she was told, but it needed another draft. Andrews said that after she added "unspeakable things my mother didn't want me to write about," the story was purchased by Pocket Books for $7,500. Within weeks, it was a mammoth hit. *Flowers* tells the story of the ill-fated Dollanganger children, who are whisked away to secretly live in an attic by their evil grandmother. A tawdry tale of incest, abuse, obsession, and intrigue, both the book and the author were suddenly on everyone's lips.

A sequel, *Petals on the Wind,* was released the following year and spent 19 weeks on the *New York Times* bestseller list. Other novels and series followed over the years, and a movie version of *Flowers* was released in 1987, featuring a cameo by the author as a window washer.

Breast cancer claimed Andrews's life in 1986, but that hardly stopped her books from appearing. Since her death, V. C. Andrews (as ghostwritten by Andrew Neiderman) has published dozens of novels. With fan clubs and Web sites that extensively outline and interpret Andrews's body of work (whether or not she actually wrote them), the enormous demand for these modern gothic tales means there will be more for fans to enjoy in the years to come.

WORD HISTORIES

Hypocrite: Ancient Greeks called their actors *hypokrites*, from a verb meaning "to pretend." The word came to describe a pretender or liar; it showed up again in the 14th century in a Biblical reference to a spiritual pretender or someone who hides their true self in a role.

Awful: This one started out meaning just the opposite. In the ninth century, *awefull* meant just that—full of reverent awe, often in reference to God. Eventually, the word came to be used to describe anything causing fear or awe, and it slowly took on the more negative meaning it has today.

Dude: Originally from a German word meaning fool, this term eventually came to mean a city slicker vacationing in the Wild West. It has since evolved into a general term for a guy, or in some cases, it's an affectionate word for a member of someone's own group. Basically, "dude" has come full circle from outsider to insider.

Hock: This was a Middle English word meaning the tarsal joint of the hind leg, as in "ham hock." However, someone "in hock" is usually in debt. But the word actually comes from a Dutch word meaning prison or jail. A person in hock, then, spent time in prison to repay their debts. Yikes.

Galvanize: Named for 18th-century scientist Luigi Galvani, this word represents his major discovery: that electricity can be produced by a chemical reaction. If someone is galvanized, they do just that: jump as though they'd been prodded with by an electric shock.

Afraid: This word comes from the less-used verb *affray*, which means to startle. Someone who is afraid has been startled or frightened.

Calico: Although in America, we usually think of calico to describe a printed cloth or a patterned cat, it began in the 16th century to describe any cloth that came from Calicut, India.

Ramshackle: From the Icelandic *ramskakkr*, we get this very twisted word that we use to describe something that is falling down or crumbling. *Ramr* means "very" and *skakkr* is Icelandic for "distorted."

Stigma: In Greek and Roman times, slaves that escaped and were recaptured were branded on the forehead. The Greek word for the brand was *stigma*. Today it's used to refer to someone who is marked with disgrace.

HOW IT ALL BEGAN

Air Flair

Necessity, they say, is the mother of invention. In the case of Doc Marten work boots (aka DMs), it's also the doctor.

In 1945, Dr. Klaus Maertens hurt his foot skiing in Bavaria and needed a shoe with some cushioning. Inspired by the auto industry's use of compressed air, he cut up some old tires and sewed them to his shoes. It didn't quite work.

Maertens tapped his electrical-engineer friend, Dr. Herbert Funck, to figure out how to trap air inside a shoe sole. Instead of tires, Funck molded raw PVC rubber to form air pockets, and DM's trademark "air-cushioned sole" was born. The shoes were initially marketed only to soldiers, but eventually mine and factory workers caught on as well.

To expedite production of DMs—and hopefully popularize them beyond Germany—Maertens and Funck began searching for an industrial partner. They teamed up with British manufacturer R. Griggs in 1959. Griggs, who was already known for producing quality work boots, purchased the patent for Doc Maertens and changed the spelling to "Martens" for broader audience appeal. On April 1, 1960, Griggs distributed the first pair of cherry-red, eight-eyelet, air-cushioned work boots, named 1460 in honor of the date. Today, the 1460 model remains the company's top seller.

Star Power

One of the best-selling shoes of all time is the Converse All Star, the brainchild of Marquis M. Converse. In 1908, he launched the Converse Rubber Shoe Company in Malden, Massachusetts, specializing in winter boots. He soon realized he could make more money if he produced shoes for all seasons, so in 1912 or 1915 (sources vary), Converse introduced a canvas sneaker. This was followed in 1917 by the high-top Converse All Star, a sneaker specifically designed for the new sport of basketball.

From there, much of the shoe's success goes to pro player Chuck Taylor, who began wearing the shoes in 1918. He became such a fan that he joined the Converse sales force in 1921, promoting both his sport and his shoe. When basketball debuted in the 1936 Olympics, so did the Converse All Star; by World War II, the All Star was the official shoe of U.S. soldiers, who wore them during training exercises. Today, the iconic shoe has managed to keep its footing and remains on the market.

The Big Shakedown

❖ ❖ ❖ ❖

*In 1811 and 1812, Missouri and its surrounding
states were rocked by devastating earthquakes.*

In late September 1811, Shawnee Chief Tecumseh did more than
make an appeal for tribal unity against the whites—he vaunted
himself a force of the highest order. "You do not believe the Great
Spirit has sent me. You shall know," he reportedly said, "I . . . shall go
straight to Detroit. When I arrive there, I will stamp on the ground
with my foot and shake down every house in Tuckhabatchee."

On December 16, the day Tecumseh was thought to have arrived
in Detroit, the first of a series of earthquakes—the most powerful
ever to hit the United States—occurred in New Madrid, Missouri,
and destroyed the small town of Tuckhabatchee.

In 1811, New Madrid was a popular destination for boatmen
traveling the Mississippi River. New Madrid also sat directly on an
active seismic fault zone three miles below the Earth's surface. By
December, pressure that had been building up for centuries reached
the breaking point.

December Jolt

The first quake happened on December 16 around 2:15 A.M. Suddenly, there was a sound like distant thunder. All at once the earth
began to shake violently; people were thrown from their beds, furniture went flying across rooms, and trees snapped like twigs.

There was a "complete saturation of the atmosphere, with
sulphurious vapor, causing total darkness," recalled an eyewitness.
Lightning bathed the scene in eerie light. Ducks, geese, and other
birds flew overhead, screeching loudly. Cattle stampeded. Panicked
birds landed on human heads and shoulders. Chimneys crashed to
the ground. "Confusion, terror and uproar presided," said one man.

New Madrid was not the only area hit hard. The town of Little
Prairie, 30 miles downriver, was completely destroyed by the quake
and its numerous aftershocks. One eyewitness saw the ground
"rolling in waves of a few feet in height, with a visible depression

between. By and by those swells burst, throwing up large volumes of water, sand and a species of charcoal."

On the water it was even worse. Boats were tossed around and swamped by the tremors. One boat was lifted 30 feet and propelled upriver for more than a mile—the Mississippi was running backward. "...All Nature was in a state of dissolution," one spectator later commented.

"The Devil Has Come Here"

For the next month, the earth continued its restless movement. On January 23, 1812, another quake struck. Eyewitness George Henrich Crist, who lived in north-central Kentucky, remembered:

"The earth quake or what ever it is come again today. It was as bad or worse than the one in December. We lost our Amandy Jane in this one—a log fell on her. A lot of people thinks that the devil has come here. Some thinks that this is the beginning of the world coming to a end."

Final Shot...?

Like a seasoned stage performer, Nature saved its biggest bang for the finale. The quake on February 7, which struck around 3:15 A.M., was as big or worse than the ones before it. It completely destroyed New Madrid. A boatman anchored off New Madrid wrote of "The agitated water all around us, full of trees and branches." He decided to keep his craft where it was as nearly two-dozen other boaters frantically cut their mooring lines and headed for open water. They were never heard from again. A trapper hunting in Tennessee saw the ground "sink, sink, sink, carrying down a great park of trees."

"If we do not get away from here the ground is going to eat us alive," said Crist in Kentucky.

The New Madrid earthquakes were felt as far east as New York City (over 1,000 miles away) and as far south as Milledgeville, Georgia (575 miles). Only the area's scarce population prevented a greater loss of life.

Today the population of the area has grown enormously. And underneath them lies the New Madrid fault, like a ticking time bomb waiting to go off.

Frankly Freakish: The Crazed Genius of Frank Zappa

❖ ❖ ❖ ❖

This Mother of Invention lived his rock 'n' roll life to the fullest.

Chemical Kid

Frank Zappa was born feet-first with his umbilical cord snagged around his neck on December 21, 1940. Such a wild beginning belied his music career based on unrelenting contrariness.

The fertile seeds of Zappa's creativity and rebellious nature were sown in his unusual childhood. He was the oldest of four children born to an Italian mother and a Greek-Arab, Italian-born father. Growing up, Zappa suffered many ailments that may have been related to his father Francis's job as a chemist for the defense industry in Baltimore. Safety standards were rather lax at the time, and Francis often came home swathed in bandages where he had allowed dangerous substances to be tested on his body for bonus pay. The family also once lived close to a mustard gas facility, and Francis kept a large sack of the insecticide DDT, a potent carcinogen, in the hall closet because he believed that it was harmless enough for a person to eat.

Shuffled from school to school, Zappa never quite fit in. The tall, sickly boy was also tormented by sinus problems, which were probably only exacerbated when radium pellets were shoved up his nostrils as a supposed cutting-edge treatment. Left to his own devices, Zappa began playing guitar as a teenager, an instrument he mastered in an amazingly short time. His influences were wildly varied: Soul, jazz, doo-wop, and avant-garde composers such as Igor Stravinsky and Varèse all played a part in his musical coming-of-age.

Jailhouse Shock

After high school, Zappa fell in with a succession of small local bands until he eventually bought his own recording studio in Cucamonga, California. By the mid-'60s, Zappa was in a band called the Mothers (short for a vulgar phrase); with this band he threw himself into creating music that exposed what he considered the world's hypocrisy. The group changed its name to the Mothers of Invention after their nervous record company insisted on a more benign moniker. The group's first album, *Freak Out!* blew up the 1966 charts.

Home, Home on the Strange

Married twice but well-known for dalliances with other women, Zappa had a chaotic personal life. In early 1968, he and his second wife, Gail, moved into a Los Angeles log cabin-style mansion built by cowboy movie legend Tom Mix. The rambling estate soon attracted a growing gaggle of musicians, staff, and hangers-on. The couple felt it was too crowded, so they bought a second home in Laurel Canyon and redecorated it Zappa-style: The reception area was done entirely in purple, a mural of fire-breathing dragons enlivened the living room, and in the basement lurked a ten-foot-long plastic shark.

And then there's the matter of their children. Apparently the Zappas didn't own a traditional baby name book, as their four children are named Moon Unit, Dweezil, Ahmet, and Diva Muffin.

Legend Low-Down

Although Zappa maintained a no-holds-barred attitude toward subject matter for his music and films, not all popular beliefs about Zappa's depravity are true. Unlike most rock stars of the day, Zappa seldom used drugs. Probably the most persistent (and disgusting) Zappa myth is that he once ate human excrement on stage. The rumor spread rapidly among his groupies; after concerts, girls would wait in line to present him with their own carefully collected stool samples. (Uh, thanks.)

Zappa died of prostate cancer in 1993 at age 52, with an astonishing 64 albums under his belt. And his legacy lives on in a variety of ways. Many of Zappa's orchestral compositions are still played by classical music ensembles. Also, a gene and several species of invertebrates, such as the *Pachygnatha zappa* spider, have been named after him. And outer space aficionados can look to the starry heavens and know that somewhere in the night sky flies an asteroid that will forever be known as Zappafrank.

Learn to Talk Trucker

❖ ❖ ❖ ❖

*Learn these trucker terms, and you'll be
the king (or queen) of the road!*

- **Bear:** term for a cop; also "smokey" or "smokey bear"
  —Full-grown bear: state trooper
  —Bear in the air: cop in a helicopter

- **Motion lotion:** fuel

- **Bumper sticker:** car following too close behind

- **Cash register:** toll booth

- **Chicken coop:** weigh station

- **Double nickel:** 55 mph speed limit

- **Flip-flop:** U-turn; also refers to the return trip ("Catch ya on the flip-flop")

- **Gator:** tire tread lying in the road

- **Good neighbor:** also known as "bubba," a friendly term between drivers. This has replaced "good buddy," which is now considered an insult and used only sarcastically.

- **Granny lane:** the right, or slow, lane

- **Hammer lane:** the left, or passing, lane; to "hammer down" means to drive fast

- **Gumball machine:** lights on top of a police car

- **Takin' pictures:** police using a radar gun to catch speeders (gear jammers). These cops are also called "Kojak with a Kodak."

- **Ten-four/Forty-two:** two ways of expressing agreement. Ten-four means "I heard what you said." Forty-two means "right on" (another driver says, "I love me some Waffle House," and you say, "Forty-two").

Fumbling Felons

Old Enough to Drink
A man walked into the corner store intending to rob it, and he started by asking for all the money in the register. It doesn't sound particularly strenuous, but the effort must have made him thirsty, because he added a bottle of scotch to his order. The clerk refused, saying she didn't think he was over 21, the legal drinking age. The robber swore that he was and pulled out his driver's license to prove it. She looked it over thoroughly and gave the man a bag filled with the cash and the liquor. As soon as he left the store, the clerk called the police with the robber's name and address. He was arrested two hours later.

Two Times—No Charm
John Millison, of Drexel Hill, Pennsylvania, is very loyal to the PNC Bank in Marmora, New Jersey. He was convicted of robbing the bank in August 2003 and served six years in jail for the crime. Just nine months after his release, Millison chose the same bank for a repeat robbery. A surveillance tape showed some similarities in the crimes, and authorities quickly deduced it was the same man. See, although Millison wore pantyhose over his face, and what many criminals don't realize is that face (albeit mashed looking) is still identifiable under nylons.

The Wrong Bar
An 18-year-old Janesville, Wisconsin, man got into trouble at a local bar—but it wasn't for underage drinking. In August 2009 at 11:00 P.M., he burst into Quotes Bar and Grill with a bandana covering his face. Although he didn't actually have a weapon, he had his hand placed in his pants pocket as though he was armed. But the teen picked the wrong night and the wrong bar: The Wisconsin Professional Police Officers Association was in town for their annual golf outing, and Quotes was full of cops from around the state. On the bright side, police responded so quickly to the robbery that the man didn't have time to demand money. He claimed he wasn't planning to rob the bar, but that he sported the mask so no one would recognize him. He was charged with disorderly conduct.

"It's a proven fact that capital punishment is a detergent for crime."
—Carroll O'Conner as Archie Bunker in *All in the Family*

Battle of Gettysburg Quiz

Roll up your sleeves for this Civil War challenge!

1. What was the large battle that the Confederates won in May 1863, prior to Gettysburg?

Chancellorsville

2. How long did the Battle of Gettysburg last?

Three days

3. Who were the commanding generals for each side?

Robert E. Lee for the Confederacy; George G. Meade for the Union

4. What role did Stonewall Jackson play in the battle?

None—he was dead

5. What Union general first made contact with the Confederates?

Major General John Buford

6. What Union general was killed by a Confederate sniper just as the Battle of Gettysburgh was unfolding on July 1?

Major General John Reynolds

7. What was the nickname of Union general Winfield S. Hancock?

Hancock the Superb

8. Which Confederate general failed to attack the disorganized Union troops on Cemetery Hill on July 1?

Lieutenant General Richard Ewell

9. What battle plan did Confederate general James Longstreet propose to Robert E. Lee on the second morning of the battle?

To attack the Union army from the rear

10. What Union general asked for permission to move his troops on July 2, was denied it, but did so anyway?

General Dan Sickles

11. **What Union general discovered that Little Round Top had been abandoned and rushed to find reinforcements just as the Confederates advanced on it?**

Gouverneur K. Warren

12. **Who was killed at Gettysburg within a few yards of the home in which he grew up?**

Wesley Culp

13. **What was the name of the crazy jumble of large boulders that both sides fought over?**

Devil's Den

14. **At which part of the Union line—left, center, or front—was Pickett's Charge aimed?**

The Center

15. **How long was the distance covered by Pickett's Charge?**

This one's tricky: Historians disagree whether it's three-quarters or one mile.

16. **What order did Confederate general James Longstreet give to begin Pickett's Charge?**

None—he only bowed his head.

17. **What Confederate general led his men forward with his hat poised on his sword?**

Lewis Armistead

18. **How many casualties occurred at Gettysburg?**

51,000

19. **What is known as the High Water Mark of the Confederacy?**

A grove of trees on the Gettysburg battlefield that was the objective of Pickett's Charge

20. **How long did it take President Lincoln to deliver the Gettysburg Address?**

Just over two minutes

Fast Facts

- What do the letters M, O, V, W, and Z have in common? They're all single-letter titles of motion pictures.

- In 1965, Star Trek's William Shatner starred in the horror movie Incubus, *the only motion picture ever made in which the entire dialog is spoken in the "universal" language of Esperanto.*

- The Terror of Tiny Town (1938) is the world's only musical western cast entirely by people of short stature.

- The ant farm was introduced in 1956 by Uncle Milton Industries, which still manufactures them to this day.

- Hugh Hefner paid just $500 for the rights to the nude photograph of Marilyn Monroe that became the centerfold in the first issue of Playboy *magazine in 1953. Thanks to Monroe, it sold more than 50,000 copies.*

- Just like human fingerprints, the ridged pattern on every cat's nose is unique. The same is true of dogs.

- Calico cats are almost always female.

- At 110–140 beats per minute, a cat's heart beats twice as fast as a human heart.

- The largest breed of domesticated cat is the ragdoll. Males can weigh up to 20 pounds, and females up to 15 pounds.

- The Hula Hoop was once banned in Indonesia because officials feared it would "stimulate passion."

- Officials at Wham-O considered several names for the toy that eventually became the Hula Hoop, including "Swing-A-Hoop" and "Twirl-A-Hoop."

High-Flying Adventurer

❖ ❖ ❖ ❖

Whether training horses or flying solo across the
Atlantic, Beryl Markham navigated new terrain.

A Wild Life

The life of pioneering aviator Beryl Markham was marked by adventure. In her various daring pursuits, she often went where no woman had gone before. And yet, unless you have read her 1942 memoir, *West with the Night,* you've probably "beryl-y" heard of her.

Born in England in 1902, Beryl Markham (née Beryl Clutterbuck) moved with her parents to British East Africa (modern-day Kenya) when she was four years old. Markham grew up on the family's farm in the town of Njoro. Here she lived a carefree life—one that was, in her words, "happily provincial." She hunted wild game, survived a lion attack, speared a deadly black mamba snake, and generally "lived it up." Her father began to breed and train horses, and as an adult, Markham followed suit and soon became the first licensed female horse trainer in Kenya. She also entertained a number of lovers, including the Duke of Gloucester, writer Antoine de St. Exupéry, and hunter Denys Finch Hatton.

Daring-Do

What Markham is most remembered for, however, is her career as a pilot. She was the first woman to receive a commercial pilot's license in Kenya and spent many years transporting mail, supplies, and passengers to remote African villages. In 1936, she flew solo across the Atlantic, departing from England and crash-landing in Nova Scotia. She was not the first person to fly solo on a transatlantic east-to-west flight—though many credit her as such (Jim Mollison accomplished this record a few years prior)—but she was the first female pilot to accomplish this feat.

Her memoir, *West with the Night,* was published in 1942 after Markham's move to the United States. Ernest Hemingway called it a "bloody wonderful book," and when it was republished in 1983, its popularity soared. Markham later returned to Kenya, where she passed away in 1986 at age 84.

Jester? I Don't Even Know Her!

The earliest recorded appearance of court jesters in the royal courts of Europe was in 1202. Also known as fools, wit-crackers, buffoons, or jokers, these multi-talented men were more than just entertainers: They were often the only people who could speak the truth to all-powerful kings and queens who were otherwise sur-rounded by nothing but yes-men. By couching political arguments in lighthearted jokes and silly stories, jesters often had a great deal of practical "pull" with their royal masters. While no English or European ruler would simply come right out and ask a jester what should be done about this war or that rebellion, the jester's opinions had a subliminal effect that sometimes translated into action. The fact that English jesters were known as "licensed fools" tells us that their comedy was a serious business.

A Lasting Change

A tremendously popular health craze swept over the United States in the 1890s. Behind it was a physician named John Harvey Kellogg, who was determined to save Americans from themselves by chang-ing their everyday habits. Kellogg warned that their meat-heavy, fat-laden diets and lack of exercise would take years off their lives, and many Americans listened. So many, in fact, that he opened what we would now call a "spa" but was then called a "sanitarium"—Battle Creek Sanitarium, aka The San. Thousands of Kellogg's followers—known as "Battle Freaks"—flocked to The San to follow his regimen, but they worried about how they would continue to eat healthy after they left. For this reason, Kellogg invented his famous Toasted Corn Flakes, still a popular breakfast cereal today. Kellogg's routine sure seemed to work for him—he lived to be a ripe old 91—and his ideas about health and wellness continue to affect our lives.

Curse of the Little Rascals

❖ ❖ ❖ ❖

Beginning in 1922, the mostly kid cast of the Our Gang *comedies, more commonly referred to as* The Little Rascals, *filmed a staggering 221 episodes over the course of several decades. After the series ended, many of the cast members met strange or untimely deaths.*

Alfalfa

After leaving the Little Rascals gang, Carl "Alfalfa" Switzer was never able to find steady acting work, but he did seem to find a lot of trouble. In late 1958, Switzer was shot and wounded while getting into his car, by an unknown assailant. On January 21, 1959, 32-year-old Switzer was shot and killed during an argument with another man over a $50 debt. The shooter was acquitted when it was ruled he acted in self-defense.

Chubby

His unnatural girth may have brought lots of belly laughs, but off-camera, Norman "Chubby" Chaney's weight was the cause of some concern. When he first joined the series in 1929, he was an 11-year-old who wasn't quite 4 feet tall and weighed more than 110 pounds. In 1935, in bad health and with his weight at around 300 pounds, Chaney underwent an operation to correct a glandular problem. After the operation, Chaney quickly lost more than 135 pounds, but his health continued to deteriorate. Chaney passed away on May 29, 1936, at age 18.

Froggy

Forever known for his bizarre, croaking voice, Billy "Froggy" Laughlin will also be remembered as the youngest Rascal to die. On August 31, 1948, the 16 year old was riding a scooter in La Puente, California, when a bus or truck struck him. He died instantly.

Mickey

Mickey Daniels had the unique opportunity of having been a child on the series and then returning as an adult, playing a truant officer and even providing the laugh of the gang's donkey, Algebra. After the series ended, however, Daniels sank into alcohol-induced obscurity. On August 20, 1970, Daniels's body was discovered in a San Diego hotel room. The official cause of death was complications from cirrhosis of the liver.

Jay

Freckly Jay R. Smith replaced Mickey in 1925. Although he lived to age 87, far longer than many of the other Rascals, Smith still suffered one of the most violent deaths. After he was reported missing from his Las Vegas home in October 2002, a massive search was launched. Several days later, Smith's body, riddled with stab wounds, was found dumped in the desert. An investigation found that Smith had been murdered by a homeless man that he had recently tried to befriend and help.

Scotty

Forever by Spanky's side, Scott "Scotty" Beckett was one of the most-loved members of the Little Rascals. After leaving the series, Beckett enjoyed a successful acting career that was suddenly cut short by a series of run-ins with the police, including a shootout. On May 8, 1968, Beckett checked himself into a Hollywood nursing home, needing medical attention for what appeared to be wounds from a fistfight. Two days later, the 38 year old was found dead in his bed. Despite the fact that a suicide note and a bottle of pills were said to have been found on his nightstand, the coroner claimed he was unable to determine the cause of death.

Wheezer

Born March 29, 1925, Robert "Wheezer" Hutchins was only two years old when he appeared in his first *Our Gang* episode. Over the next six years, Hutchins would star in nearly 60 shorts. After graduating high school, Hutchins joined the Army Air Corps during World War II (though he didn't see overseas combat). After the war, Hutchins decided to become an air cadet. On May 17, 1945, Hutchins was killed when his plane collided with another aircraft during training exercises at Merced Army Air Corps Field in California. He was only 20 years old.

MYTH CONCEPTIONS

Myth: The "10 second rule" applies.
Fact: Many people believe that if food drops on the ground and is picked up quickly, it's perfectly fine to eat. Not so fast. Scientists discovered food that has touched the ground does pick up large amounts of bacteria. So just get a new potato chip, okay?

Myth: Single people have more active sex lives than married people.
Fact: Actually, in one recent survey, 43 percent of married men reported having sex two to three times per week, compared to only 26 percent of single men.

Myth: Halloween is a major holiday.
Fact: The National Retail Foundation actually lists Halloween as sixth on its list of holidays that count as "major," spending-wise. Halloween candy is a big seller, but it lags far behind Christmas shopping and Easter or Valentine's Day sweets purchases.

Myth: If you swim on a full stomach, you'll get a cramp and drown.
Fact: Nah. It's true that when you eat a big meal, your body has to work harder to digest it. You might be uncomfortable if you swim with a belly full of food, but you'll probably not get a cramp and drown at your cousin's barbeque this summer—even if you ate six bratwursts.

Myth: My dog humps my leg. It's a sex thing.
Fact: Actually, it's a domination thing. Both male and female dogs do it, and it's much more of an act of aggression or dominance than it is a sexual behavior.

Myth: Your hair and nails keep growing after you die.
Fact: What actually happens is the retraction of skin as it dehydrates during the breakdown of the body. The shrinking skin on a cadaver makes it appear as though hair and nails are still growing, but they're not.

Presidential Pets

❖ ❖ ❖ ❖

Nearly all of the American presidents have had pets—but don't assume that all of these presidential pals were pooches!

Early First Pets

As the first president of the United States, George Washington had to set the example for future leaders to follow. So perhaps it's not surprising that Washington started the presidential cavalcade of critters. According to the Web site for the Presidential Pets Museum in  Williamsburg, Virginia, Washington had numerous hounds with names such as Drunkard, Tipsy, and Sweetlips; horses named Nelson and Blueskin; and a parrot (that belonged to his wife).

Sometimes pets arrived as gifts. Thomas Jefferson had two bear cubs that adventurers Lewis and Clark brought back from their journeys. The Marquis de Lafayette gave John Quincy Adams an alligator, and the Sultan of Oman gave Martin Van Buren two tiger cubs. Even James Buchanan found himself with a herd of elephants, courtesy of the King of Siam.

Hail to the Chief Zoo Keepers

The two presidents who had so many animals that they could have hosted *Wild Kingdom* were Theodore Roosevelt and Calvin Coolidge. Roosevelt's extensive menagerie included snakes, guinea pigs, bears, kangaroo rats, roosters, owls, a flying squirrel, a lion, a hyena, and a zebra. Coolidge matched him with various breeds of dogs and cats, raccoons, canaries, a donkey, a bobcat, a goose, a bear, a wallaby, and lion cubs. For good measure, he added a pygmy hippo.

Vote-getters

Some pets are credited with helping turn political fortunes. When Franklin Roosevelt thundered that critics couldn't pick on "his little dog" (named Fala), it reportedly helped him win the 1944 election. And even though he wasn't president at the time, Richard Nixon's "Checkers speech" is credited with saving his spot on the Eisenhower ticket.

Fast Facts

- The Hoover Dam was completed in 1935, two years ahead of schedule.

- The workers who constructed Hoover Dam didn't get rich. The highest wage was $1.25 an hour; the lowest, 50 cents.

- Boulder City, which was constructed as a place for those working on the Hoover Dam to live, is one of two towns in Nevada that still prohibit gambling.

- Randy Quaid is the only cast member of Saturday Night Live to be nominated for an acting Academy Award before joining the show. He received a Best Supporting Actor nomination for The Last Detail in 1973.

- "SHAZAM!" is the exclamation that transforms teenage Billy Batson into comic-book superhero Captain Marvel. The word is an acronym for Solomon (wisdom), Hercules (strength), Atlas (stamina), Zeus (power), Achilles (courage), and Mercury (speed).

- As an alligator's teeth wear down, they are replaced with new ones. As a result, the average alligator can go through 2,000 to 3,000 teeth over its lifetime.

- Albert Einstein was offered the presidency of Israel in 1952. (He declined.)

- Despite its tremendous scientific importance, Albert Einstein never received a Nobel Prize for his theory of relativity. However, he did win the 1921 Nobel Prize in physics for his work on the photoelectric effect.

- Pluto is so far away from the Sun that it takes sunlight 5½ hours to reach it. By comparison, it takes approximately eight minutes for sunlight to reach Earth.

Snow On and Snow Forth

❖ ❖ ❖ ❖

Canadians are known as good communicators on the world stage: polite and articulate. We'll let you be the judge based on the following quotes and quips. If you don't like them, then "Fuddle-duddle" to you!

- "If some countries have too much history, we have too much geography." —*Eccentric Canadian Prime Minister William Lyon Mackenzie King, remarking on the country's immense size in 1936*

- "Fuddle-duddle" —*Prime Minister Pierre Eliot Trudeau, said on the floor of the House of Commons in 1971. Others reportedly heard the F-bomb.*

- "If the national mental illness of the United States is megalomania, that of Canada is paranoid schizophrenia." —*Canadian writer Margaret Atwood*

- "A Canadian is someone who knows how to make love in a canoe."
  —*Canadian writer Pierre Berton*

- "Patriotism is not dying for one's country, it is living for one's country. And for humanity. Perhaps that is not as romantic, but it's better."
  —*Agnes Macphail, first female member of Parliament*

- "The Americans are our best friends whether we like it or not." —*Robert Thompson, leader of the Social Credit Party of Canada*

- "Living next to [the United States] is in some ways like sleeping with an elephant. No matter how friendly or even-tempered is the beast, if I can call it that, one is affected by every twitch and grunt." —*Prime Minister Pierre Eliot Trudeau*

- "They told me I was going to have the tallest, darkest leading man in Hollywood." —*Canadian-born actress Fay Wray, referring to her giant costar in the 1933 movie* King Kong

- "I am so excited about Canadians ruling the world." —*Prime Minister John Diefenbaker*

- "Behind every great man is a woman rolling her eyes." —*Canadian comedian Jim Carrey, in the 2003 movie* Bruce Almighty

- "When fortune empties her chamber pot on your head, smile and say 'We are going to have a summer shower.'" —*John A. Macdonald, Canada's first Prime Minister, in 1875*

- "Ladies and gentlemen, please forgive me, but that man [pointing to a political opponent] makes me sick." —*Prime Minister John A. Macdonald, whose chronic alcoholism caused him to vomit in the Canadian House of Commons on more than one occasion*

- "No longer can a hero of a romantic novel be described as standing 'six foot in his stocking feet' and 'without an ounce of superfluous fat on him.' Nor will he be able to thrash a villain 'within an inch of his life'— although the villain will no doubt try for his 0.45359 kilograms of flesh. Naturally, a miss will be as good as 1.609 kilometres." —*Maurice de Soissons, commenting on Canada's adoption of the metric system in a 1970 issue of* Chatelaine *magazine*

- "I am rather inclined to believe that this is the land God gave to Cain." —*Jacques Cartier's first description of the Canadian East Coast, in 1534*

- "Character, like a photograph, develops in darkness." —*Turkish-born Canadian photographer Yousuf Karsh*

- "You know that these two nations have been at war over a few acres of snow." —*French satirist Voltaire, describing the spoils of battle in the French/British conflict over Canada in 1759*

- "I took possession of Baffin Island for Canada in the presence of several Eskimo, and after firing 19 shots, I instructed an Eskimo to fire the 20th, telling him that he was now a Canadian." —*Captain J. E. Bernier, upon claiming the Arctic Circle on July 1, 1909*

- "Whatever women do, they must do twice as well as men to be thought half as good. Luckily, this is not difficult." —*Charlotte Whitton, mayor of Ottawa and Canada's first female mayor, in 1963*

- "Never retract, never explain, never apologize. Get the thing done and let them howl." —*Nellie McClung, early Canadian feminist, in 1915.*

What Goes Up...

❖ ❖ ❖ ❖

Popular in the 17th and 18th century in Europe, fox tossing (or Fuchsprellen *in German) was a competitive sport that is akin to hunting. Today, of course, such a game simply wouldn't fly.*

Go Long!

In this "sport" of yore, men and women (hunters, servants, and people of the court) would hold a blanket or net and put a fox (or other animal of choice) in the middle. The group (or a particularly strong solo person) would then toss the animal into the air. The ground was covered with sand or sawdust to provide a softer landing for the animal and prolong the play for the participants—after all, they didn't want the animal to die on the first toss! The higher the toss, the better. Skilled tossers could reach heights of 24 feet.

It was a popular spectator sport, and it often took place in a courtyard with fans looking on (and presumably cheering) from the palace windows. And the sport wasn't just for strapping young lads looking to offload a little testosterone—it was common for couples to play against each other, and for the event to be turned into a sort of party featuring masks and costumes for players and animals alike. The players would dress up as sprites, nymphs, sphinxes, and other mythological creatures, and the animals would play the part of unpopular enemies and political figures.

Beware of Falling Animals

Today, PETA would undoubtedly cry foul on the sport, since it was nearly always fatal to the participating animal. In fact (animal lovers, close your eyes), in a 1648 match that took place in Dresden, Germany, an outstanding number of animals were thrown and killed, including 647 foxes, 533 hares, 31 badgers, and 21 wildcats. And the sport wasn't only dangerous for the critters. A tossed animal isn't a particularly happy or friendly animal, and it wasn't unusual for them (especially the wildcats) to turn on the players and attack.

Frankly, we can't say we blame 'em.

Say What?

"I'm tired of all this nonsense about beauty being only skin deep. That's deep enough. What do you want, an adorable pancreas?

—*Jean Kerr*

"I look just like the girl next door—if you happen to live next door to an amusement park."

—*Dolly Parton*

"When I married Mr. Right, I didn't know his first name was Always."

—*Anne Gilchrist*

"I was the best man at the wedding. So why is she marrying him?"

—*Jerry Seinfeld*

"My wife thinks I'm too nosy. At least, that's what she writes in her diary."

—*Drake Sather*

"I'd like to go to assertiveness training class. First I need to check with my wife."

—*Adam Christing*

"The clearest explanation for the failure of any marriage is that two people are incompatible; that is, one is male and the other female."

—*Anna Quindlen*

"If women knew what we were thinking, they'd never stop slapping us."

—*Larry Miller*

"The only time a woman really succeeds in changing a male is when he's a baby."

—*Jacob Braude*

"You know who must be very secure in their masculinity? Male ladybugs."

—*Jay Leno*

"I want to know why, if men rule the world, they don't stop wearing neckties."

—*Linda Ellerbee*

"They say he rides as if he's part of the horse, but they don't say which part."

—*Robert Sherwood, reviewing cowboy hero Tom Mix*

Toxic Times Beach

❖ ❖ ❖ ❖

*Nestled in the flood plains of the Meramec River just outside St.
Louis is the tiny town of Times Beach, Missouri. In 1972, it became
the site of one of the nation's worst chemical disasters when it was
discovered that the oil sprayed onto the town's dirt roads to solve a
dust problem was actually Agent Orange. How could this happen?*

A Deadly Solution

In the early 1970s, the small 480-acre town of Times Beach and its
approximately 1,200 residents hit on a cost-effective solution to the
town's growing dust problem: Instead of paving the roads, which was
too expensive for the lower-middle-class community to afford, why
not have the roads sprayed with oil? This was hardly considered a
crazy idea; many dirt-road towns followed the same practice, since
oil was deemed much more effective than water.

Professional waste-hauler Russell Bliss was hired to do the deed
and sprayed the roads with oil at regular intervals from 1972 to
1976, at a cost of six cents per gallon. Former residents remember
local children following Bliss's truck as he drove through town,
playing and sliding in the thick oil slick it left behind. But for some
reason, the streets turned purple after Bliss drove through; birds
dropped dead in ditches; puppies and kittens were stillborn. No one
suspected Bliss was dredging "The Beach" with poison.

Bliss-fully Ignorant

What the town didn't know was that Bliss was mixing the oil with
waste he'd been subcontracted to haul for a company down-state,
the Northeastern Pharmaceutical and Chemical Company
(NEPACCO).

During the Vietnam War, NEPACCO manufactured the highly
toxic Agent Orange; the waste clay and water Bliss removed from
the plant contained levels of dioxin 2,000 times higher than the
dioxin content in Agent Orange. Bliss, who later professed ignorance
of the dioxin-laced oil, used his deadly blend not only on the town of
Times Beach but on several local horse stables as well.

In 1971, after a routine stable spray left 62 horses dead, stable owners became suspicious of Bliss, who claimed his spray was simply old engine oil. Nevertheless, the owners began tracking Bliss's actions, and after other stables reported similar problems, the Centers for Disease Control and Prevention (CDC) launched an investigation. In late 1979, a NEPACCO employee admitted to the company's use of dioxin—a poison so toxic that it is considered the deadliest chemical made by man.

Back to the Beach

Amazingly, the citizens of Times Beach remained in the dark about dioxin until some three years later when, on November 10, 1982, a local reporter called city hall with news that the town may have been among the sites contaminated by Russell Bliss. The Environmental Protection Agency (EPA) called shortly after to verify the news, and on December 4, official testing confirmed the town's dioxin contamination level was 33,000 times more toxic than what the EPA deemed safe.

Days later came the death knell for tiny Times Beach: The Meramec River crested at 43 feet, flooding the town and spreading dioxin-contaminated soil even further throughout the community and its surrounding areas. On December 23, the town's officials issued a horrifying holiday message: If you're here, leave; if you're gone, don't come back.

By 1985, not only had the entire area been evacuated (with the exception of an elderly couple who refused to leave), but also the governor had issued an executive order dissolving the town. The site was officially quarantined. Security checkpoints reminiscent of international border controls were set up along the perimeter to keep visitors and former residents from trespassing.

Route 66 State Park

Following its evacuation, the area once known as Times Beach sat empty for more than a decade—a modern-day ghost town—before the federal government began its clean-up efforts in March 1996. By June 1997, more than 265,000 tons of contaminated soil had been removed from the area and destroyed (using an incinerator made by Syntex, the parent company of NEPACCO).

In October 1999, the state of Missouri opened Route 66 State Park on the grounds of what was once Times Beach. Now verified as clean and toxin-free, the site features hiking trails, picnic tables, and a multitude of flora and fauna. The only original building still standing is the park's visitor center: formerly the Times Beach Steiny's Inn, formerly the headquarters of the EPA's clean-up efforts, and today, a testament to the area's checkered past.

Other Contaminated U.S. Communities

The Love Canal: In the late 1800s, William T. Love planned to build a model community at this site near Niagara Falls. By 1920, the canal had been abandoned due to a lack of funding, and it became a dumping site for the Niagara Falls township. In the 1940s, Hooker Chemical was permitted to dump 21,000 tons of waste in the abandoned canal; a decade later, a school was constructed on top of it and a housing development built nearby. Though no one suspected contamination at the time, in the late 1970s, health issues began surfacing among residents, who were ultimately relocated and paid $129 million in retribution by Hooker.

Picher, Oklahoma: The same zinc and lead mines that put Picher on the map are wiping it out. Following the mine closures in the 1970s, officials discovered that contaminated mine waste was spread across 25,000 acres and poisoning residents. Still, many people refused to leave until 2007, when federal buyouts made it worth their while.

Centralia, Pennsylvania: When workers set a routine fire to burn trash in this tiny mining town in 1962, they unwittingly ignited an exposed vein of highly flammable anthracite (hard) coal. Though firefighters quickly extinguished flames on the surface, the fire continued to rage below the earth, rapidly spreading beneath the town and releasing harmful carbon monoxide into homes. After 20 years and $7 million spent (unsuccessfully) fighting the fire, the state government decided to call it quits and demolish the town, though as of 2010, less than a dozen people remain. The fire continues to burn today.

Fast Facts

- *Harpo Marx, the silent member of the Marx Brothers, was offered $50,000 by United Artists if he would utter just one word in the 1946 film* A Night in Casablanca. *He refused.*

- *The Three Stooges hold the unique distinction of appearing in more films than any other comedy team.*

- *Tupperware is named after its developer, Earl S. Tupper, a DuPont employee who began exploring the wonderful world of plastics in the 1930s.*

- *Cowboys were often called "cowpokes" because they poked cows with sticks to drive them onto loading ramps.*

- *Most hair stays with you between three and seven years.*

- *A breed of dog known as the Lundehune has six toes and can close its ears.*

- *Down, boy! An average-size dog's mouth can exert up to 200 pounds of pressure per square inch. Larger breeds can exert up to 400 pounds per square inch.*

- *Basset hounds cannot swim well. They are, however, quite adorable.*

- *Three dogs survived the sinking of the RMS* Titanic: *a Newfoundland, a Pomeranian, and a Pekingese.*

- *The Great Pyramid of Giza was originally 481 feet high. Today, it stands 455 feet high. It is estimated to weigh approximately 6.5 million tons.*

Visualizing a Better Life

❖ ❖ ❖ ❖

In advocating for animal welfare and individuals with autism, Temple Grandin pictures a better world.

"I think in pictures," writes Dr. Temple Grandin, in the opening chapter of her book, *Thinking in Pictures.* "Words are like a second language to me. I translate both spoken and written words into full-color movies, complete with sound, which run like a VCR tape in my head." Throughout her life, this visual thinker has sought to explain what it is like to live with autism. Born in 1947, she was diagnosed with the developmental disorder in 1950. By sharing her perspective and experiences, she hopes that she will enlighten and empower others.

Grandin is also a Professor of Animal Science, a world-renowned advocate for animal welfare, and a prolific author. She also has had considerable influence in the livestock industry, where she has helped design more humane facilities, served as a consultant for firms such as McDonald's and Burger King, and educated people about proper animal handling. These accomplishments earned her such nicknames as "The Woman Who Thinks Like a Cow." She has said that "using animals for food is an ethical thing to do," but that it requires respect: "We've got to do it right. We've got to give those animals a decent life and we've got to give them a painless death."

The Squeeze Machine

As is common with autistic children, Grandin did not speak until age three and a half. Instead, she would communicate via screaming or humming. She was also highly sensitive to touch and sound. Doctors told her parents that she should be placed in an institution, but Grandin remained in school. Although she often endured ridicule from classmates, she was an imaginative thinker and developed her own strategies for coping with stress and anxiety. In one of her more profound instances of "thinking like a cow," in 1992, Grandin developed something called the "squeeze machine" or "hug box" for those with autism. Modeled after the squeeze chutes used to restrain cattle while they're being given veterinary treatment, this machine applies deep pressure stimulation (similar to a firm and long-lasting hug) to the person using it. "As a little kid, I wanted to experience the nice feeling of being held, but it was just too much overwhelming stimulation," Grandin said in a BBC documentary about her life, *The Woman Who Thinks Like a Cow.* Using the machine gives her more control of the situation, which allows her to relax and enjoy the feeling.

Other Innovations

Another one of Grandin's groundbreaking inventions is a curved chute or race system for corralling cattle. Designed to lower stress and fear in the animals, the curved chutes are more efficient than straight chutes, because, Grandin explains, "they take advantage of the natural behavior of cattle." (Cows have a natural tendency to return to where they came from.) Now processing plants throughout the world—businesses that slaughter millions of cattle and pigs for human consumption—use this type of corralling method. Grandin also developed an objective scoring system to assess how well cattle and pigs are handled at these plants. In addition, she has studied bull fertility, stunning methods for cattle and pigs, and cattle temperament. Grandin credits her strong visual thinking skills for her sensitivity to animals' experiences and ability to come up with humane treatment solutions.

Telling Her Story

In addition to working as a consultant to the livestock industry and teaching courses on livestock behavior and facility design, Grandin is the author of a number of bestselling books, including, *Emergence: Labeled Autistic, Animals in Translation: Using the Mysteries of Autism to Decode Animal Behavior,* and *Animals Make Us Human: Creating the Best Life for Animals.* She has also written articles for numerous magazines and is a go-to expert on most things cow-related. The neurologist Oliver Sacks wrote about her in his book, *An Anthropologist on Mars.* In sharing her experiences, Grandin aims to provide hope and insight to individuals on the autism spectrum.

If You See Only Five...

Classic Sci-Fi Flicks

❖ ❖ ❖ ❖

Science fiction has been a popular and successful movie genre ever since French filmmaker Georges Méliès wowed audiences with his groundbreaking short A Trip to the Moon *in 1902. Since then, hundreds of futuristic films have graced the silver screen. Here are five visionary sci-fi films to satisfy your inner geek.*

1. *Metropolis* (1927)—Directed and cowritten by Fritz Lang, a student of the German impressionist movement, *Metropolis* reveals a bleak future in which society has been divided into two castes: privileged thinkers and the underground-dwelling workers who struggle to keep the technology running. Stunningly filmed, many later sci-fi hits were influenced by *Metropolis*, including *Star Wars*, *Blade Runner*, and Tim Burton's *Batman*.

2. *The Day the Earth Stood Still* (1951)—Based on the short story "Farewell to the Master" by Harry Bates, *The Day the Earth Stood Still* concerns an alien being named Klaatu (Michael Rennie) who, with his robot guardian Gort, drops by with a little warning for the people of Earth: Stop your violent ways or risk global annihilation. A genuine classic.

3. *Forbidden Planet* (1956)—With a nod to William Shakespeare's *The Tempest*, the movie *Forbidden Planet* successfully combines an intriguing love story with the best elements of science fiction, including flying saucers, a deadly monster, a robot named Robbie, and a long-dead alien race called the Krell. A treat for all ages.

4. *Star Wars* (1977)—There have been six "chapters" in this saga, but it was the first in the series (*Episode IV: A New Hope*) that set the world on fire and made science fiction fun again. One of the most successful movie franchises in history, it even inspired a new religion: The Jedi Church.

5. *Alien* (1979)—The story is simple enough: A deadly alien creature is accidentally let loose aboard an intergalactic mining ship. The result is one of the most terrifying science-fiction films ever made.

Houdini Unbound

❖ ❖ ❖ ❖

Magic still thrives, thanks to the mystifying antics of entertainers such as David Blaine and Criss Angel. But none hold a candle to the great Harry Houdini, master magician and escape artist extraordinaire.

The Early Years

Houdini was born Ehrich Weisz on March 24, 1874, in Budapest, Hungary. His family immigrated to the United States when Ehrich was about four years old, settling in Appleton, Wisconsin. A precocious youngster, Ehrich started performing magic at age 12, billing himself as Eric the Great. He ran away from home to entertain at fairs and circuses, but he rejoined his family at their new home in New York City a year later.

When he was 15, Ehrich read a biography of famed French magician Jean Robert-Houdin. The book changed his life. In honor of his hero, he took the stage name Harry Houdini. He performed solo for a while, and then, in 1892, teamed up with his brother Theo. As the Houdini Brothers, the duo performed at a variety of venues, including Coney Island and the 1893 Chicago World's Fair. In 1894, Houdini married Wilhelmina Rahner, who replaced Theo in the act.

The Escape Artist

Houdini was skilled at magic, card tricks, and escape artistry, but widespread fame eluded him until he took the advice of renowned vaudeville booking agent Martin Beck, who encouraged him to eschew the small stuff and concentrate on illusions and escapes. Beck put Houdini on the vaudeville Orpheum circuit, which took him throughout the country. To generate publicity in each town he visited, Houdini would ask the local police department to lock him in their sturdiest cell—from which he would promptly escape.

Houdini traveled to Europe in 1900, and it was there that he really made his reputation, routinely escaping from the seemingly inescapable. Soon he was the highest-paid entertainer on the continent, raking in $2,000 a week. When he returned to the United States, the master magician set out to prove that there was virtually nothing from which he could not escape, including padded cells; burglar-proof safes; a diving suit; a water-filled, padlocked milk pail; and the Washington, D.C., jail cell that had once held Charles Guiteau, assassin of President James Garfield. Several of Houdini's stunts were literally death-defying: One time he came frighteningly close to suffocating while escaping from a buried coffin.

In 1918, Houdini created a magic act that would become a staple for later magicians such as David Copperfield—he made a live elephant disappear at the famed Hippodrome in New York City. He also introduced another fan favorite, swallowing several needles and a piece of string, then pulling the string from his throat with the needles threaded. "My professional life has been a constant record of disillusion," said Houdini, "and many things that seem wonderful to most men are the every-day commonplaces of my business."

More than a Magician

Houdini became the planet's premier magician and escape artist, but he was also much more. In 1910, he became the first person ever to make a sustained plane flight on the continent of Australia, and in 1919 he appeared in several motion picture thrillers. (He later produced two movies in which he was the star.) Houdini also was a prolific writer and lecturer.

In the 1920s, Houdini established himself as a debunker of fake spiritualists, testifying before a congressional committee on the subject in 1926. As a magician, he knew the tricks of the trade, and would often don a disguise to visit "spiritualists" who claimed to be able to talk to the dead. Once they'd gone through their act, Houdini would reveal how the tricks were done. It was Houdini's way of giving back—he hated charlatans who preyed on grieving families.

Houdini died on October 31, 1926—not in a failed escape attempt, as some legends have it—but from complications from a ruptured appendix. There is some debate regarding the details leading up to his death, which almost certainly involved an incident in which he was punched in the stomach by a student at McGill University in Montreal. Houdini's funeral was held on November 4th in New York, attended by more than 2,000 mourners.

MATCHMAKER

Q: Before you started your career as a matchmaker, were you always the person who was trying to set up your friends?
A: I did it a handful of times prior to starting this career, and it resulted in marriages. So yeah, I just kind of have a knack for doing that. Part of the reason I'm a good matchmaker is that prior to this, I was a headhunter and executive recruiter. And I was really good at doing that. So I've always had sort of a keen eye for people's personalities and making good matches.

Q: A lot of people like to play matchmaker, but what makes a *good* matchmaker?
A: The average person will introduce someone to their friend based on the fact that the two people are single. But they're not taking a look at the person's interests, their religious background, their desire for children, what they like to do for fun, their reasoning, what they really desire in a mate, what's worked in the past, what has not worked. Left to their own devices, people tend to date the same type of person over and over again, which is why the relationships don't work out. A matchmaker can figure out what you're doing wrong and try to explain why you're not having success.

Q: What are some common mistakes singles make?
A: Dating the same type of person and expecting a different outcome. Dating people based on looks or socioeconomic status. I mean, we want people we are attracted to, but if *you're* not a supermodel, what makes you think you're entitled to date a supermodel? And if you're not a millionaire, why are you looking for someone to take care of you at that level? If people would focus more on the internal qualities, they're much more a measure of a person. The external things are really bonus points.

Q: Do you think there's someone out there for everyone?
A: No. I think some people shouldn't be married.

The Great Cheese Chase

❖ ❖ ❖ ❖

Would you risk life and limb for a piece of cheese? For competitors in the annual Cooper's Hill Cheese-Rolling and Wake, the answer is a resounding yes, indeed.

It's just before noon on the last Monday in May in western England's Brockworth, Gloucestershire, and the hills are alive with the sound of voices chanting, "Roll the cheese!"

Welcome to Cooper's Hill, which is actually more like a cliff: a 215-yard-long, almost completely vertical incline averaging a 1:2 and sometimes even 1:1 ratio in some places—a 70-degree angle nearly perpendicular to the sky. It's so steep, say locals, that the sun's rays never fall directly on the slope. So steep that it's impossible to run down and maintain balance. So steep that more than 100 people show up every year to race, tumble, and/or fall down the hill, chasing after an eight pound wheel of cheese the size of a dinner plate.

Welcome to the annual Cooper's Hill Cheese-Rolling and Wake. No one is quite sure when the tradition began, but the earliest written record of the event is from 1826—but even then it was considered an old favorite.

Going Downhill Fast

Runners come from all over the globe to compete in one of five races, held at 20-minute intervals.

After an arduous climb to the top, the runners—around 20 per race—sit in a line and wait for the Master of Ceremonies to escort the guest cheese-roller to his or her position. After the emcee gives the starting command, the runners scramble after the cheese, encased in corrugated paper and decorated with blue and red ribbons, which can reach speeds up to 70 mph. In rainy years, the hill is a muddy mess but easier for competitors to slide down; in dry years, the ground is a hard, unforgiving course ripe for scraping skin. To win, a runner must finish in about 12 seconds.

The grand prize, of course, is the cheese. Second and third place winners receive a small cash prize of ten and five pounds (about $15 and $7 respectively).

Extreme Cheese

If it sounds ridiculously dangerous, it is. There are an average of 30 injuries each year—mostly bumps and bruises, though the occasional broken bone and concussion is not unheard of. Spectators are also at risk: Those leaning too close to the edge may fall over. Others may get hit by a runner, or by the rampant cheese.

To minimize injuries, bales of hay are perched at the bottom of the hill to catch the runners, as is a local rugby team. Also onsite is a cave rescue team, ready to climb up after fallen contestants and carry them to nearby ambulances.

Big Wheel Keep on Turning

Nothing has ever stood in the way of Gloucestershire and its cheese roll. Even when rationing during both World Wars limited the nation's cheese supply, a wooden wheel was constructed instead, with a token nugget of cheese tucked inside for authenticity. Recent events have also canceled the public festivities. In 1997, there was a record-breaking number of injuries (33), which led to the cancellation of the event in 1998 due to safety concerns. The roll has also been canceled because of the foot-and-mouth disease outbreak of 2001, and the unavailability of the local search-and-rescue team in 2003. But even so, the Gloucestershire cheese-rolling committee gathered together to roll a single cheese down the hill. After all, the cheese must go on.

- *Since 1988, the cheese used is a handmade wheel of double Gloucestershire, produced by local cheesemaker Diana Smart.*

- *The largest cheese ever used was a 40-pound wheel from New Zealand in 1958.*

- *The oldest winner is 43-year-old local runner Stephen Gyde, who has also won the most races (21).*

Fast Facts

- *It is believed that more than 4,000 skilled stone masons were involved in the construction of the Great Pyramid. Whether it was a union job remains unknown.*

- *Spider silk is more flexible than nylon, and has been noted in some cases to be stronger than steel and kevlar.*

- *Most spiders are nearsighted. To compensate, they rely on their body hair to feel their way around and to detect when other animals are near.*

- *With a length that can exceed 100 feet, the blue whale is the largest animal ever to live on Earth.*

- *At 6'4", Abraham Lincoln was the tallest U.S. president. He was also the first president to have a beard.*

- *George Washington was the only president to be unanimously elected, running unopposed for both of his terms. He declined to run for a third term, setting a precedent that held until Franklin Roosevelt was elected to a third term in 1940.*

- *There are 920 different breeds of cows in the world.*

- *Cows can live up to 25 years. Like the rings on a tree, you can get an accurate estimate of a cow's age by counting the number of rings on its horns.*

- *Don't try to sneak up on a cow. They can smell odors up to five miles away.*

- *God is the only character on* The Simpsons *to have five fingers.*

- *President John Adams was so short and chubby that he was called "His Rotundity."*

You Big Fakers!

❖ ❖ ❖ ❖

*Celebrities are known to do weird things—bark crazy demands,
shave their head (hello, Britney!), throw objects at their
employees, or—in extreme cases—fake his (or her) own death.
Granted, sometimes it's not the celeb's fault—enduring fans
often simply refuse to let their heroes die. Here are some stories
of celebrities whose obituaries may or may not be false.*

Elvis Presley

Elvis might have left the building, but
many of his devoted fans believe he is still
among the living. Despite reports of his
death at Graceland on August 16, 1977,
some believe Presley had grown weary of
the star lifestyle and just wanted out.

However, death doesn't mean The King hasn't been making the
rounds. Presley is one of the most impersonated singers in the world,
which makes it hard to determine whether sightings of the singer are
indeed real. The first sighting reportedly occurred just hours after
Presley's death was announced, when a man by the name of John
Burrows paid cash for a one-way ticket to Buenos Aires—and the
name John Burrows was one of the aliases that Presley often used.
Today, more than 30 years after his death, there are still regularly
reported Presley sightings.

Jim Morrison

Starting as early as 1967, The Doors' snakelike singer, Jim Morrison,
was talking about possibly faking his own death and starting anew
in Africa. He even invented an alter ego, Mr. Mojo Risin' (an anagram of his name). So when he was found dead in a bathtub in Paris,
France, on July 3, 1971, some people had their doubts. Rumors
were fueled by the fact that in the time it took his parents, family,
and friends to get to Paris, Morrison's body was already sealed inside
a coffin. Upon seeing Morrison's gravesite, Doors drummer John
Densmore is said to have remarked that the grave was too short.

The first two years after Morrison's death were when he was most often spotted. In 1973, he was even reportedly spotted inside the Bank of America in San Francisco conducting business. But as time went on, the sightings eventually stopped, leaving all of us to scratch our heads and wonder if and when Morrison finally decided to break on through to the other side.

Weldon Kees

Even as tourists are snapping away taking photographs of the iconic Golden Gate Bridge in San Francisco, few are aware of its dark side. Since 1937, more than 1,280 individuals are known to have committed suicide by jumping from the bridge—a number that more than likely is higher because some bodies are never recovered. So on July 19, 1955, when the car belonging to author Weldon Kees was found on the north end of the Golden Gate Bridge, keys still in the ignition, most believed he had become another sad statistic. Friends reported that Kees had been depressed; he had even telephoned his friend Janet Richards to tell her, "things are pretty bad here."

Yet there seemed to be something staged about the whole scene at the Golden Gate Bridge. It seemed too perfect. After friends searched his apartment and discovered that items such as his wallet, savings account book, and sleeping bag were missing, it was thought that Kees might have faked his own death. Perhaps he was depressed with the way his life had turned out and was looking to reinvent himself. A possible clue lies in one of the things Kees said to Richards the day before he disappeared: "I may go to Mexico. To stay."

Alan Abel

On January 2, 1980, both *The New York Times* and *The New York Daily News* published an obituary for author and satirist Alan Abel, stating that he had died of a heart attack while skiing at a Utah resort.

There was only one problem—Abel was still alive. The following day, Abel held a press conference to declare the whole thing an elaborate hoax. Abel said he had spent more than six months plotting out the specifics of the clever ruse, including having an actor stop by the ski resort claiming to be a funeral director who needed to collect Abel's belongings. Abel also had a woman pretend to be his widow and contact the newspapers to verify his death. Years later, a mutual friend introduced Abel to an aspiring actor and comedian that was fascinated with Abel's death hoax: Andy Kaufman.

Andy Kaufman

Whether it was proclaiming himself the holder of a nonexistent wrestling title or staging fistfights on live national television, Kaufman loved nothing better than to pull a fast one. So when it was announced on May 16, 1984, that Kaufman, a nonsmoker, had passed away at age 35, a mere five months after being diagnosed with a rare form of lung cancer, people couldn't help but think it was his latest stunt. Even Kaufman's close friend and sometime co-conspirator Bob Zmuda had his doubts, especially since Kaufman had previously said that he was considering faking his own death. In the years following his death, there were several reports of Kaufman making appearances in nightclubs disguised as one of his alter egos, Tony Clifton.

On May 16, 2004, the 20th anniversary of Kaufman's death, Zmuda and some of Andy's closest friends threw a "Welcome Home" party and patiently waited for Andy to crash it. Unfortunately, he never showed.

Gone Before Their Time

- **Sister Janelle Cahoon:** In 2005, *The Duluth News-Tribune* mistakenly wrote that the Benedictine nun had passed away. Cahoon was reportedly very amused when they resurrected her in a correction days later.

- CNN.com screwed up big time when they reported Cuban leader **Fidel Castro** as dead in April 2003. Apparently, draft versions of several famous figures' deaths were mistakenly put online. Castro's obituary was based on the template used for Ronald Reagan's, and it called Castro a "'lifeguard, athlete, movie star." **Dick Cheney** suffered the same fate: His obit was based on the Queen Mother's, and it called the ex-vice president "Queen Consort" and the "UK's favorite grandmother."

🎼 Behind the Music of Our Time

- Minnie Riperton, who had a No. 1 hit in 1975 with "Lovin' You," is the late mother of former *Saturday Night Live* star Maya Rudolph.

- Though he'd had more than 70 Top 40 hits in England, Cliff Richard just couldn't get a hit in America. Cheekily, he named his 1976 album *I'm Nearly Famous;* sure enough, the song "Devil Woman" went to No. 6 on the U.S. charts.

- Paul Simon's first solo hit, "Mother and Child Reunion," was inspired by an egg-and-chicken dish served at a Chinese restaurant he frequented.

- In 1984, the Nitty Gritty Dirt Band, whose hits include "Mr. Bojangles," became the first American band to tour the Soviet Union.

- Blood, Sweat and Tears reached No. 2 with their first three singles ("You've Made Me So Very Happy," "Spinning Wheel," and "And When I Die"), but they never seemed able to top the charts.

- John Winston Lennon was named for Winston Churchill, but he later legally changed his middle name to "Ono," after his wife, Yoko Ono.

- When producer Calvin Carter of Vee-Jay Records felt Betty Everett's song "You're No Good" needed a little more *oomph,* he asked the group the Dells, who were observing the recording session, to stomp their feet to the beat.

- Though The Ronettes have had a huge influence on other musicians and are remembered fondly by the public, they only had one Top 10 hit: "Be My Baby" in 1963.

- The Tokens based their hit "The Lion Sleeps Tonight" on an African folk song called "Mbude." Translated, the word is Zulu for "lion." The Tokens chant this word throughout their song.

- The Ray Stevens novelty song "Jeremiah Peabody's Poly Unsaturated Quick Dissolving Fast Acting Pleasant Tasting Green & Purple Pills" had the longest title of any song to ever make *Billboard*'s Top 100 (at No. 35).

- In 1992, child rappers Kriss Kross wore their clothes backward to get attention for their single, "Jump." It must have worked, because the song went to No. 1.

The Relished Relic

❖ ❖ ❖ ❖

Relics are an important element in several of the world's major religions. These ancient holy artifacts—thought to be pieces of a saint's or a significant leader's body or one of their personal belongings—are said to be imbued with spiritual power and are highly protected. But are they real or not? As some believers would say, you just have to have faith.

Many people dispute the authenticity of these holy objects. For example, it's impossible to be 100 percent sure that an old sword actually belonged to the real Saint Peter. Even so, people come from all over the world just to bask in the presence of these (often odd) artifacts.

The Holy Prepuce

According to New Testament apocrypha (writings by early Christians about Jesus and his teachings that were not accepted into the holy canon), after baby Jesus was circumcised, an old Jewish woman saved his foreskin. But by the Middle Ages, several different foreskins were touted as the original and were worshipped as holy relics by various churches. Stories abound of various prepuces gifted to monks, stolen by thieves, dismissed by Popes, and marched in parades, all adding to the mystery of this particular (and particularly weird) relic.

The Tooth of Buddha

After the Buddha died (approximately 500 B.C.), it's said that his body was cremated. As the story goes, after the cremation, a follower retrieved the Buddha's left canine tooth from the funeral pyre. The tooth was given to the king and quickly became legendary: Whoever claimed the tooth would rule the land. Wars were fought over possession of the tooth for centuries, and now the tooth—or what's left of it 2,500 years later—rests in a temple in Sri Lanka.

The Sacred Relics

From the 16th to 19th centuries, sultans of the Ottoman Empire collected religious items of the Islamic faith. Most were said to be relics of various Islamic prophets, though many of the pieces are of questionable origin. Included in the collection, now held in Istanbul, are Moses's staff, a pot belonging to Abraham, and a piece of the prophet Muhammad's tooth. Perhaps the most important of the relics is the Blessed Mantle, the black wool shawl said to have been placed on a poet's shoulders by Muhammad himself.

Relics of Sainte-Chapelle

If you find yourself in Paris, visit Notre Dame to behold the collection of Sainte-Chapelle relics, including shards of the True Cross (believed to be actual wood from Christ's cross), relics of the Virgin Mary, the Mandylion (a piece of fabric similar to the Shroud of Turin on which Christ's face is said to appear), and something called the Holy Sponge, a blood-stained sponge that was said to be offered to Christ to drink from when he was languishing on the cross. The authenticity of these objects is as contested as any on this list, but the items are impressive if nothing else for surviving the French Revolution, when many relics were destroyed or lost.

Veronica's Veil

According to tradition, a woman named Veronica (she's not mentioned by name in the Bible) wiped the face of Jesus on his way toward Calvary. The fabric she used was said to have taken the imprint of Jesus' face. The veil can now be found in St. Peter's Basilica in Rome. Or maybe it's held in a friary outside of Rome—there's another version of the veil there. Regardless, plenty of people claim to have seen the bloodstained face of Jesus in the fabric of Veronica's veil and continue to make pilgrimages to worship it.

The Shroud of Turin

Of all the relics on this list, the Shroud of Turin is the one whose authenticity remains the most hotly debated, even more than 100 years after its discovery. Carbon dating originally proved the material, purportedly the shroud laid over Christ at the time of his burial, was produced in the Middle Ages, but it has since been proven incorrect—the garment is in fact older. Perhaps most fascinating about the Shroud is that the image itself is a negative; photographic methods were hardly known at the time of Christ's death, so how could anyone have faked such an image?

Odd Ordinances

- In Chico, California, you'll be fined $500 if you set off a nuclear device within city limits.

- If you have the itch to rip those tags off your pillows and mattresses (that clearly say "Do Not Remove"), Colorado is the place for you. It's legal there to do so.

- It's illegal to offer to loan your neighbor your vacuum cleaner in Denver.

- Here's a law that might be easier said than done: In Sterling, Colorado, cats that run free must be fitted with a taillight.

- For a good evening view in Devon, Connecticut, you'd better walk west—it's illegal to walk backward after sunset.

- Moms might rejoice at this law: Silly string is prohibited in Southington, Connecticut.

- Keep the speed down when biking in Connecticut. You aren't allowed to exceed 65 mph.

- It's against the law to whisper in church in Rehoboth Beach, Delaware.

- Laws in Delaware prohibit you from flying over a body of water unless you are carrying ample supplies of food and drink.

- In case you wondered: It's not legal to sell your children in Florida.

- Floridians must have very clean clothes—it's illegal to shower naked there.

- If you don't want to end up in jail, don't have sex with a porcupine in Florida.

- In Georgia, watch your tongue around dead people. It's unlawful to swear in front of a dead body in a funeral home or coroner's office.

- Happy Hour is not quite as happy in Athens-Clarke County, Georgia. Selling two beers for the price of one is outlawed.

Totally Tintin

❖ ❖ ❖ ❖

Anyone serious about graphic novels and comics should get to know Tintin, whose stories broke the genre's mold worldwide.

In his native Europe he is more popular than Mickey Mouse. In Canada he is as familiar as Superman. Since his first appearance in 1929, his fans have included luminaries such as Madame Chiang Kai-shek and Andy Warhol. French President Charles DeGaulle cited him as his only international rival. More importantly, millions of children throughout the world have grown up avidly following the adventures of Tintin, the 14-year-old reporter; his faithful dog, Snowy (Milou in French); the coarse, hard-drinking, but eminently lovable Captain Haddock; and their colorful collection of enemies and friends.

A Tintin Primer

• Tintin, who sports a distinctive slightly-curled spike of blonde hair atop his head and a pair of knickers, was the creation of Belgian artist Hergé (the nom de plume of Georges Prosper Remi), who pioneered the art deco-derived *ligne claire* (clear line) style of drawing that has since influenced several generations of artists.

• The Tintin comic series draws its inspiration from the spirit of Jules Verne's fantastical stories as well as *National Geographic*'s detail-oriented imagery.

• Readers enjoy a cavalcade of exotic locales, subtle humor, captivating technology, political intrigue, plot twists, and plenty of cliff-hanging action. Titles included such tantalizing fare as *The Crab with the Golden Claws, Explorers on the Moon,* and, considered by many to be Hergé's masterpiece work, *Tintin in Tibet.*

So, Who Likes Tintin?

Aside from hundreds of millions of fans around the world and a growing number in America, Tintin's friends include director and producer Steven Spielberg, who is directing the film, *The Adventures of Tintin:*

Secret of the Unicorn, slated for release in 2011. Before Spielberg, however, other directors, including Walt Disney and Roman Polanski were interested in filming the boy reporter's exploits. Spielberg's enormously popular Indiana Jones series of films also drew inspiration from Tintin's tales.

Who Didn't Like Tintin?

Villains: In the course of his adventures, Tintin meets up with plenty of bad guys, including several American capitalists and a character named Musstler, who, as a thinly disguised amalgam of Hitler and Mussolini, led the evil nation of Borduria (an obvious stand-in for Nazi Germany) in 1938's *King Ottokar's Scepter.*

Anti-fascists: At the start of World War II, Hergé, on leave from the Belgian army, fled to Paris ahead of the Nazis but returned to Belgium after King Léopold III appealed to his subjects to return to work. During the occupation, Hergé abandoned political issues in his Tintin books and concentrated entirely upon exotic scenarios intended to entertain a downtrodden populace. After the war, Hergé was briefly imprisoned for working under the occupation. Though quickly released, he was blacklisted for many years.

The American consumer: The 1950s were a tumultuous time for the American comic book industry. Despite being wildly popular with children (or perhaps because of it), comics were viewed by educators as anathema to learning and morally debased. In 1955, comics were banned by the New York Senate panel. Tintin's American debut was carefully orchestrated to present comics in a different light. Even London's *The Times Literary Supplement* had high praise for the books, celebrating the comics as "works of high quality and even beauty... brimming over with intelligence and life." Figuring people would believe a work of beauty would cost more than a lowly comic, the American publisher produced high-quality issues of Tintin at $1.95 each (whereas most comics cost 20 cents). Unaccustomed to the concept of comics as serious literature and deterred by the high price tag, American consumers balked. The first four titles sold a combined 32,000 copies over the 1959 holidays. Meanwhile, Europeans were purchasing about 250,000 Tintin books every week.

Cheers!

❖ ❖ ❖ ❖

*Raising glasses to one another is a custom that
occurs in dozens of countries around the world.
Here are some of the many ways to toast.*

Cheers—English, North
America

Živjeli—Croatian

Fisehatak—Arabic

Prost—German

Salud—used in many Latin
countries, including Spain,
Mexico, and Argentina

Na zdorov´ya—Bulgarian

Gan bei—Mandarin

Pura vida—Costa Rican

Kippis—Finnish

À votre santé—French

Sláinte—Irish (Gaelic)

Yamas—Grecian

Okole maluna—Hawaiian

L´Chaim—Hebrew

Egészségedre—Hungarian

Pro—Indonesian

Kampai—Japanese

Chukbae—Korean

Saha wa´afiab—Moroccan

Skål—Norwegian

Sanda bashi—Pakistani

Na zdrowie—Polish

A sia saide—Portugese

Noroc—Romanian

Chtob vse byli zdorovy—Russian

Seiradewa—Sri Lankan

Afya—Swahili

Choc-tee—Thai

Budmo—Ukranian

The Times They Are A-Changin'

1952

- *The Today Show* debuts on NBC as TV's first morning news show.

- Prime Minister Winston Churchill announces that the United Kingdom has an atomic bomb. The nuclear weapon is successfully tested later that year.

- Hussein bin Talal succeeds his father as King of Jordan.

- The first broadcast of *Bandstand* is launched in Philadelphia, hosted by Bob Horn. The popular live dance program becomes a hit with the nation's teens. The show becomes legendary as *American Bandstand* with Dick Clark as host.

- The U.S. occupation of Japan comes to an end.

- Puerto Rico becomes a commonwealth of the United States, and the U.S. Congress approves its Constitution.

- The card industry gets a boost when Secretary's Day is celebrated for the first time. (It is now known as Administrative Professional's Day.)

- A new world record for rainfall in one day is set in Cilaos, located on the French island of Réunion in the Indian Ocean, when the village receives about 73 inches of rain in 24 hours.

- The United States successfully detonates "Mike," the first hydrogen bomb, in the Pacific Ocean's Bikini Atoll.

- Ernest Hemingway writes *The Old Man and the Sea*.

- Former G.I. George Jorgensen Jr. becomes Christine Jorgensen after undergoing the first successful sex-change operation.

- Mystery writer Agatha Christie's new play, *The Mousetrap*, opens in London at the Ambassadors Theatre. It continues to be the longest continuously running play in history.

Eat Worms, Lose Weight!

❖ ❖ ❖ ❖

*No matter what anyone tells you, the only way to
successfully lose weight is to eat less and exercise more.
Yet this common-sense knowledge hasn't stopped millions
from trying anything to make the road to weight loss
smoother—including purposely ingesting parasites. Wouldn't
it be easier to just go on a walk and skip dessert?*

Those Wacky Early 1900s

There was a time when cocaine was the cure for a
sore throat and smoking was considered a healthy
habit. So not many feathers were ruffled when
ads showed up advertising a tapeworm pill for
ladies looking to slim down. The ads, which first
appeared between 1900 and 1920, claimed that
by ingesting a pill containing tapeworm larvae,
you could give a hungry worm a happy home and lose that pesky
weight. You could eat all you wanted, content in the knowledge
that your new friend would be eating up most of the calories you
consumed, thus allowing you to lose weight without thinking twice
about it.

No one can prove that the pills advertised back then actually
contained worm larvae. The pills could've been placebos, and for
the foolish folks who tried the diet fad, we can only hope that's what
they were.

The Worm Is Back!

The weight loss via tapeworm idea died down for many years
(obesity was not as much of an issue during the Great Depression
and both World Wars), but talk of it resurfaced in the 1960s.
Rumors that the new appetite suppressant candy introduced to
the market contained worm eggs started getting around, though of
course this was entirely false.

After a remarkable weight loss of an estimated 65 pounds,
acclaimed opera star Maria Callas endured heavy gossip that she

had purposely acquired a tapeworm to do it. Though the singer indeed was diagnosed with a tapeworm, her doctor suggested it was due to her fondness for eating beef tartare. Other celebrities are rumored to have swallowed tapeworm pills to whittle down their figures, including model Claudia Schiffer, though this was never confirmed.

An Internet search these days reveals companies that advertise "sterile tapeworms" for a variety of medicinal uses (whether they're selling a real product or scamming the public is another article). The fine print is lengthy, however, as using tapeworms to treat any condition has not been approved by the USDA. To get your worms, you'll likely have to go to Mexico. These stowaways will get you in big trouble if you try to bring them back across the border.

Tapeworms: Not a Good Pet

A lot of time and attention is spent around the world trying to keep worms from getting into the human body via water, food, or skin. Simply put: Having a tapeworm is not a good thing. In the case of the fish tapeworm, especially, the essential vitamin B12 is sucked out of the host's body and depletes the vital ingredient for making red blood cells.

Adult tapeworms can grow up to 50 feet long and live up to 20 years. Depending on the worm, a host's symptoms range from epileptic seizures, diarrhea, nausea, fatigue, a swollen belly (oh, the irony), and even death. While it's likely a person with a worm will lose weight, they'll also suffer from malnutrition—B12 isn't the only nutrient eaten by the parasite. And tapeworm eggs are an inevitable byproduct of a tapeworm. The fish tapeworm can produce a million eggs in a single day, and the larvae tend to burrow out of the intestines and find homes elsewhere in the body, like the brain, for example. Worms also have the habit of popping out of various orifices without warning, too.

Still interested in tapeworms as a form of weight loss? Then perhaps it's your head, and not your pants size, that's the issue!

"Which came first, the intestine or the tapeworm?"

—*William S. Burroughs*

The Last Shot

❖ ❖ ❖ ❖

The last shot of the American Civil War
was fired—surprise!—in Alaska.

It all began with the *Sea King,* a steamer ship built as a British troop transport in the summer of 1863. A Confederate agent working in Britain noticed the vessel and went about purchasing it for the Confederacy. In early October 1864, the *Sea King* went on a "trading voyage," ostensibly to India. However, the ship rendezvoused at Funchal, Madeira, with another ship. Guns, officers, and other military items were brought aboard the *Sea King,* transforming it into the Confederate warship *Shenandoah.* Lieutenant James I. Waddell was placed in command and given the mission of finding and destroying the Union's water-borne shipping and commerce.

Waddell continued south, intending to prey on ships in the area between the Cape of Good Hope and Australia. He captured six prizes (enemy ships) before arriving at Melbourne, Australia, on January 25, 1865, for repairs and fresh supplies.

By now the Confederacy was on life support, but Waddell was aboard his ship and unaware, and he continued to terrorize American whalers in the North Pacific. Finally, on June 23, while in the Bering Sea, Waddell was shown a San Franciscan newspaper that reported on Lee's surrender at Appomattox. But also in the paper, Confederate President Jefferson Davis stated that, "the war would be carried on with re-newed vigor." Waddell took that as a sign that the war was still on, and he continued attacking whaling ships, taking 21 more prizes. Finally, on August 2, the *Shenandoah* encountered a British ship and Waddell learned that the war had indeed ended in April. The prizes he had taken in June were the last shots fired in anger of the Civil War.

Waddell surrendered to British authorities, since traveling to America meant surrendering as a pirate (and thus facing its punishment: death by hanging). After traveling approximately 44,000 miles, its far-reaching voyages made the *Shenandoah* the only Confederate warship to circumnavigate the globe.

Fast Facts

- The following are all classified as fruits, not vegetables: cucumber, eggplant, pumpkin, tomato, and okra.

- English gambling dens in the 18th century had an employee whose sole job was to swallow the dice in the event of a raid by police.

- In 1875, the director of the Patent Office of the United States asked that his office be closed because there was nothing left to invent.

- A "monkey wrench" gets its name from its inventor, Englishman Charles Moncke.

- The Miami Dolphins is the only team to play in the Super Bowl and not score a single touchdown. During Super Bowl VI in 1972, Garo Yepremian managed to kick a field goal, but the Dolphins still lost 24–3 to the Dallas Cowboys.

- If you were caught drinking coffee in Turkey in the 16th and 17th centuries, you could be put to death.

- All but one of the 12 apostles of Christ died violently. St. John, the only apostle to witness Christ's crucifixion, was persecuted for his beliefs but lived a long life, dying peacefully in bed around A.D. 100.

- Voltaire did not like Shakespeare's writing, calling him "that drunken fool."

- Jonathan Swift accurately described the size of the two moons of Mars, Phobos and Deimos, a century before they were discovered.

- Samuel Taylor Coleridge's epic poem, "Kubla Khan," came directly from a dream he had. As he was writing down his recollections, a knock on the door interrupted him. When he resumed writing, his dream recollections were gone, which is why "Kubla Khan" is unfinished.

The Bordentown Bonaparte

❖ ❖ ❖ ❖

Not many people know that after the Battle of Waterloo in June 1815, Napoleon Bonaparte had the chance to flee to America. Though he didn't flee—at least not then—his older brother Joseph did, and wound up in ... New Jersey.

Born to Run?

As all of Napoleon's dreams and ambitions were crashing down around him, in July 1815, the general and his brother Joseph met at Rochefort on the Atlantic coast of France. The men needed to make a big decision. Joseph urged his brother to flee to the United States, but Napoleon was unwilling to run like a common criminal. He remained behind, while Joseph set sail for America.

Joseph tried living in New York City and then Philadelphia, but found that he could not blend into the crowded city background without meeting someone who knew him. What he needed was an isolated country estate. What he found was Point Breeze in Bordentown, New Jersey.

Peace and Quiet

Situated between Crosswicks Creek and the Delaware River, Point Breeze was a 211-acre estate that gave Joseph ample opportunity to indulge his passion for landscaping, gardening, and building. Joseph closed on the property in either 1816 or 1817 (sources differ), paying $17,500. The total property eventually included 1,000–1,800 acres.

Having ruled as both King of Naples and Sicily (1806–1808) and King of Spain (1808–1813), Joseph had developed a love of finery, and so he began building a house to be second only to the White House. He had hated the politics thrust upon him in Europe, and so he reveled in the peace of Point Breeze. "This country in which I live is very beautiful," he wrote. "Here one can enjoy perfect peace... the people's way of life is perfect."

Joseph spent hours roaming his estate and beautifying the grounds. He created artificial lakes and planted many trees and a great lawn in front of his house bordered with rhododendrons and magnolia bushes. He covered the grounds with miles of winding carriage lanes, placed sculpture, and built pastoral cabins.

He didn't neglect the magnificent house he was building either. He filled it with valuable furniture, fine works of art and sculpture, and thousands of books. When all was done, Joseph had a house that rivaled the finest in America.

Then, on January 4, 1820, the house burned to the ground.

Joseph, in New York at the time, hurried home to find that many of his treasures had been saved by the townspeople. Not used to this sort of kindness and honesty in his previous life of war and intrigue, he wrote a letter gratefully thanking the residents of Bordentown.

Joseph built an even more fabulous home, with great fireplaces, marble mantels, and winding staircases. He employed many locals, which endeared him to the residents. He filled the grounds on his property with pheasants, hares, and swans. Local children played on the deer and lion statues in the park and went ice-skating on his lakes in winter.

Mystery Man

But much like Joseph, his estate was more than met the eye. He had also built a network of tunnels underneath the house. Ostensibly built to bring supplies into the house, and for the convenience of females to move between buildings in foul weather, later the tunnels gave rise to speculation that they were built so Joseph could escape capture by anti-Bonaparte forces.

In 1914, *The World Magazine* had a better theory: Perhaps Napoleon did not die at St. Helena in 1821, but escaped to America—and to Joseph.

"He could have been rowed from the Delaware River directly into his brother's house," postulated the writer. "And during the years that he was watching for a chance to return to power, he could have had the freedom, through a labyrinth of secret underground passages, of one of the most beautiful estates in America."

Eventually Joseph abandoned Point Breeze and returned to Europe, where he died in 1844. Did his brother live with him in New Jersey? Unfortunately, we may never know—though the idea of Napoleon prowling the streets of tiny Bordentown late at night is too intriguing to completely dismiss.

Where the Wired Things Are

Pretty much as soon as paper-use became widespread (around the 13th century), people started looking for ways to attach more than one piece together. Sure, you could bind pages together in book fashion, but that was unnecessarily formal (and permanent) for things such as letters and reports. For a while, people used ribbons to tie pages together. Then, in 1832, the mechanization of the straight pin popularized the "desk pin"; alas, this too proved problematic: The pins rusted over time, caught on other papers, left unsightly holes, and presented a stabbing hazard.

Around this time, a bendable substance called steel wire hit the market, and creative types began experimenting with new ways to fold it as a paper fastener. Beginning in the 1860s, patent after patent was issued for variations on the "paper clip."

Finally, a solution appeared, and it's the classic model still used today. No one knows who, exactly, first developed the oval "loop within a loop" paper clip, but it was William D. Middlebrook of Waterbury, Connecticut, who revolutionized its production. In 1899, he patented the paper clip-making machine and sold it to manufacturers Cushman and Denison, who named their new paper clip the Gem.

Some say Middlebrook also patented the modern design of the paper clip. Others say the paper clip was designed years before and Middlebrook just mechanized it, while still others claim the paper clip is of British origin.

A Clip on Their Shoulder?

Interestingly, Norway proudly takes credit for the modern shape of the paper clip. They claim countryman Johan Vaaler patented the design in 1899. Despite this discrepancy, Norway's pride continues unabated. A statue has been erected for Vaaler, and during World War II, patriotic Norwegians wore a paper clip on their lapels as a symbol of national unity.

Today, an estimated 20 billion paper clips are sold every year. And though many varieties of paper clips have flooded the market over the years, the most common ones found in office supply rooms and on desks around the world is still the original Gem.

Odd Ordinances

It's illegal to put pennies in your ear in Hawaii.

Residents of Hawaii can receive a fine for not owning a boat.

Adultery is subject to a $20 fine in West Virginia.

Best idea ever or worst? In Idaho, it's illegal for a man to give a woman a box of candy that weighs less than 50 pounds.

In Boise, Idaho, you cannot fish from a giraffe's back.

Grin and bear it: By law, anyone out in public in Pocatello, Idaho, must have a smile on their face.

If you can't finish your whiskey sour in Illinois, don't give it to your dog—it's illegal to give a dog whiskey.

In Kenilworth, Illinois, a rooster must be 300 feet from a residence in order to crow.

Winter must get long in Indiana. Bathing is prohibited from October through March.

Liquor stores cannot sell milk in Indiana.

Not wanting to deal with decimals, Indiana law declared that Pi would be equal to 4 rather than 3.1415. However, due to mathematical confusion, this law was repealed.

Firefighters in Fort Madison, Iowa, will be well prepared to fight fires—that is, if the building doesn't burn down first. They are required to practice fire fighting for 15 minutes before answering a fire call.

No atheists allowed in Vermont—it is illegal to deny that God exists.

Whistling underwater is not legal in Vermont. It's also just plain difficult to do.

In Virginia, children may not trick-or-treat on Halloween.

Having a dirty car is forbidden in Russia.

It is illegal to eat a snake on Sunday in Iran.

Mabel Stark: The Ultimate Cat Lady

❖ ❖ ❖ ❖

*Barely five feet tall in her signature white leather suit and
knee-high boots, Mabel Stark didn't look fierce enough to train
tigers. But some girls won't back down from a catfight.*

Talk about a caveat: The young woman who'd previously held Mabel
Stark's position as an assistant to the tiger trainer for the Barnes Circus
met a grizzly fate: attacked and eaten by a tiger in the ring. But Stark
couldn't sign up for the gig fast enough. Training tigers is what she'd
wanted to do her whole life.

Born Mary Haynie sometime between 1889 and 1904—she was
cagey about her real age, and dubious about many facts of her life—
to Kentucky tobacco farmers who died when
she was 13, the orphaned girl was shipped off
to Louisville to live with an aunt and uncle
who never wanted her around. Stark took to
spending her afternoons at the zoo, dreaming
about becoming a wild animal trainer. But
societal conventions held sway, and the petite
blonde headed to nursing school when she was
(supposedly) 18 years old.

What happens next is subject to some
debate, but both stories end with Mabel in the
ring with tigers.

The Lady or the Tiger?

By her own account, Stark headed to Los Angeles in 1911 on a post-
graduation trip, where, on her first night, she ran into Barnes Circus
owner A. G. Barnes. Stark was hired on the spot and the next day
reported to work as an animal trainer—but she was disappointed to
find that she'd been assigned to train a horse. When her contract came
up for another year, Stark demanded she work with tiger trainer, Louis
Roth, to learn his trade.

In another version, historians say Mabel left nursing school in 1911
to become a stripper in the Great Parker Carnival, working under the
name Mabel Aganosticus. (This was possibly the last name of her first

ex-husband; she would go on to collect four or five more.) A year later, she left to marry a "rich Texan," but the relationship quickly went kaput.

In keeping with the second story, now using the surname "Stark," Mabel returned to the carnival where she hung around the animals and befriended their trainer, Al Barnes. A year later, Barnes left to start his own circus and took Mabel with him as an animal trainer—but she was disappointed to find that she'd been assigned to train goats. To convince tiger trainer Roth to hire her as a replacement for his assistant who'd been devoured, she married him.

In the early 1900s, Ivan Pavlov hadn't yet done his experiment with dogs and bells, so no one knew for sure how to train an animal to do something. But Roth had a hunch. While most animal trainers at the time beat their subjects into submission, Roth used a method called "gentling," rewarding tigers for good behavior with fresh horse meat.

Roth devolved into alcoholism, and the two divorced. Stark took the gentling method into the ring, though she also packed a whip and a pistol that fired blanks, noisy enough to frighten the tigers.

Maim Attraction
Over the decades, Stark made a name for herself, performing her "cat act" with Barnes, Ringling Brother's Barnum and Bailey, and several small circuses before landing with the JungleLand theme park in Thousand Oaks, California.

Stark firmly believed that tigers could never be tamed, only subdued, and only when they felt like it. Eighteen times Stark was mauled, yet she never blamed the cats for acting out—only herself for not paying attention. And though nearly every inch of her body was eventually covered with scars, she continued working well into old age.

Stark Says Goodbye
Stark once said she couldn't live without her tigers, and that would prove true. Stark's demise was shrouded in rumor, much like her beginnings. In 1968, JungleLand closed its doors. Also, some say Stark's favorite tiger, Rajah, whom Barnes had given to her as a cub and whom she'd brought home and walked like a dog around her neighborhood, had died. Three months after the park closed, Stark was found dead in her home of an apparent barbiturate overdose—an unfortunate end to an exciting life.

Fast Facts

- Towns in ancient Japan held contests to see which person could break wind the loudest.

- In medieval Japan, any woman found alone in a room with a man other than her husband was immediately put to death, no questions asked.

- At one time, natives of the Solomon Islands used dog teeth as money.

- When inflation was running rampant in Germany's Weimar Republic in the early 1920s, one American dollar was equal to one trillion German marks.

- Flounders are one flatfish that's learned to adapt. They spend much of their lives lying on their side on sea beds, which should mean that one eye is always in the sand, right? Well, not quite. The eye in the sand moves to the topside of the flounder's head so that both eyes are facing up.

- BVD stands for Bradley, Voorhees and Day—the New York City company that initially made the brand of underwear.

- When the volcano Krakatau erupted in 1883, people in Bangkok, China—3,000 miles away—heard the sound.

- Famed adventurer and lover Casanova ended his life as a librarian.

- Lord Byron kept four geese as pets and brought them everywhere.

- Your hair doesn't all grow at the same time; each hair is on a separate and slightly staggered schedule.

Art by the Numbers:
The Vogel Collection

❖❖❖❖❖

So you like art, but you're operating on a shoestring budget, huh? Take a few pointers from this New York couple, who managed to amass an outstanding collection in an unlikely way.

You don't have to be a mega-millionaire to collect great works of art. Take it from Herb and Dorothy Vogel, two New Yorkers who, back in the mid-1960s, began collecting art that they liked, could afford, and could fit into their modest apartment. And they liked a lot, could afford more than they thought, and managed to fit more than 2,000 works into their modest one-bedroom apartment.

In the Beginning, There Was Art

In 1962, Herb, a postal clerk, married Dorothy, a librarian. It was their mutual love of art that initially brought them together. Dorothy was once quoted as saying that when it came to their relationship, "It was art or nothing"—clearly a serious commitment to both one another and their shared interest. However, the Vogels were about as well off as the starving artists they patronized. But the couple made do: By living off Herb's salary and buying art with Dorothy's, they embarked on their art odyssey.

Although the art the Vogels could afford wasn't the sort sold at Sotheby's, that didn't stop them. This was the second half of the 20th century, and New York was bursting at the seams with an influx of minimalists, conceptualists, painters, sculptors, and artists of every kind, many at the beginning of their soon-to-be-lauded careers. Herb and Dorothy, aside from just loving art in general, happened to have a keen eye for the truly talented. Around 1967, the two met conceptual artist Sol LeWitt and were the first people to buy his work. This kicked off their collection, and they subsequently bought many more pieces from LeWitt, who eventually made quite a mark on the American art world.

Their collection grew. Among the artists represented by the Vogels's collection were early works by the likes of Christo, Andy

Warhol, Chuck Close, Carl Andre, and hundreds of others. They bought often and cheaply, and never, ever sold anything.

Not So User Friendly

Sure, the couple had an exceptional eye for artwork, but where to store it all? The Vogels were unfazed by their typically cramped New York headquarters and refused to move or rent additional space to house their collection. While almost every inch of their walls was covered in the pieces they had bought, most of the art Herb and Dorothy collected was hoarded away in closets or piled on top of shelves and boxes. As art lovers, the Vogels painstakingly maintained the upkeep of their collection, but some accidents were inevitable: Once, water from a fish tank splashed onto a Warhol canvas, and it had to be restored.

Bursting at the Seams

The Vogels might have been a bit preoccupied with art purchases, but they weren't hermits or recluses. In fact, they were often seen out and about with the artists they collected. For Herb and Dorothy, forging a connection with the artists who produced the art was a natural part of the art-buying process.

Finally, aware that they were running out of space, in 1992 the Vogels pledged their collection, comprised of a whopping 2,000 pieces, in installments to the National Gallery of Art in Washington, D.C.—where they spent part of their honeymoon decades ago. No longer stored in a coat closet, these incredible works of art could be enjoyed by all.

The public and art elite alike lauded the Vogels, embracing the couple and their collection for its scope, intensity, and foresight. In 2009, a documentary called *Herb and Dorothy* debuted about the couple and their lifelong ambition. The director, Megumi Sasaki, remarked, "I thought I was going to make a small film about beautiful, small people. But I learned… they are giants of the art world."

More Collective Nouns

❖ ❖ ❖ ❖

Here are more ways to describe a group of animals, birds, or general, well, things.

It's a bird! It's a plane! It's a...

blessing of unicorns
generation (or nest) of vipers
shrewdness of apes
pod of dolphins
trip (or tribe, herd, drove) of goats
charm of hummingbirds
pride of lions
zeal (or herd) of zebras
flock of camels
company of parrots
herd of llamas
sleuth (or sloth) of bears
leap (or leep) of leopards
phalanx of umbrellas
babble of barbers
husk of jackrabbits
erudition of editors
swarm of eels
quarrel (or host, ubiquity) of sparrows
string of ponies
passel of possum
soufflé of clouds
dray (or scurry) of squirrels
streak of tigers
hover of trout
cast (or business) of ferrets
fold (or flock, trip) of sheep
bale of turtles

FROM THE VAULTS OF HISTORY

- Peter Mark Roget, creator of *Roget's Thesaurus*, was 73 when his reference work was finally realized. The first printed edition in 1852 was called *Thesaurus of English Words and Phrases Classified and Arranged so as to Facilitate the Expression of Ideas and Assist in Literary Composition.*

- The writer Honoré de Balzac was seriously addicted to caffeine. It wasn't uncommon for him to write for 16–20 hours nonstop, aided by massive quantities of coffee. He drank so much of the stuff that it enlarged his left heart ventricle, which probably contributed to his death.

- The artist Caravaggio had quite the temper. While playing a game of tennis in 1606, he and his young opponent got into an argument. Caravaggio stabbed and killed him and immediately had to flee Rome.

- The three best-known Western names in China reportedly are Jesus Christ, Richard Nixon, and Elvis Presley.

- Julius Caesar was epileptic.

- The age-old story of Cinderella isn't just a Western fairy tale. The heroine of the story is known as Rashin Coatie in Scotland, Zezolla in Italy, and Yeh-hsien in China.

- Colgate ad execs faced a major obstacle marketing their toothpaste (created by Samuel Colgate in 1873) in some Spanish-speaking countries. When using the voseo form of the language, where the second person singular pronoun is *vos* instead of *tú, colgate* translates into the command "go hang yourself."

- Pitcher Darold Knowles pitched all seven games of the 1973 World Series.

- Herbert Hoover, the 31st president of the United States, turned over to charity all the federal salary checks he received during the 47 years he served in government offices.

- In 1909, the 27th president of the United States, William Taft, converted the White House stable into a four-car garage.

15 Fast Food Facts

❖ ❖ ❖ ❖

For better or for worse, Americans love fast food. Here are some bite-size facts on the supersize industry.

1. McDonald's started in 1940 when Dick and Mac McDonald (yes, there was really a Mac McDonald) opened a restaurant called McDonald's Bar-B-Que in San Bernardino, California. The early McD's even offered carhop service.

2. French fries weren't introduced at Mickey D's until 1949. Until then, potato chips had been offered instead.

3. Burger King says there are 221,184 possible ways you could order its Whopper hamburger.

4. Taco Bell comes from a family name: Glen Bell started working on the chain in the late 1940s in San Bernardino—the same place where McDonald's was born. His first venture was a hot dog stand called Bell's Drive-In. By the early '50s, he started adding Mexican items onto the menu, eventually opening a secondary restaurant called Taco Tia.

5. The first actual Taco Bell didn't open until 1962. Glen Bell stepped down as chairman in 1975, and PepsiCo, Inc., bought the chain three years later.

6. Perhaps the most recognizable fast food icon, Ronald McDonald first appeared in 1966 when Mickey D's aired its first television commercial. The Hamburglar, Grimace, and Mayor McCheese joined him five years later.

7. Wendy's joined the fast food mix in 1969 when founder Dave Thomas opened his first restaurant in Columbus, Ohio. By 1976, 500 of the restaurants were sprinkled across the country. The number doubled to 1,000 locations by 1978.

8. Wendy's was named for Dave Thomas's daughter, Melinda Lou "Wendy" Thomas.

9. Arby's entered the restaurant world in 1964. The first location opened in Boardman, Ohio, featuring the roast beef sandwiches that are still the chain's signature item today.

10. The name Arby's actually represents the initials "R" and "B." The letters stand for "Raffel Brothers," in homage to founders Leroy and Forrest Raffel, although the company says many suspect it also stood for "roast beef."

11. McDonald's has its own university (of sorts). Hamburger University opened in 1961. There graduates receive "Bachelor of Hamburgerology" degrees, which we're sure are incredibly impressive on any résumé. More than 5,000 employees attend the school each year.

12. KFC's iconic founder, Colonel Sanders, was never in the military. Kentucky Governor Ruby Laffoon named Harland Sanders an honorary colonel "in recognition of his contributions to the state's cuisine," the company claims.

13. The Double Six Dollar Burger at Carl's Jr. is the unhealthiest hamburger option in America, according to an analysis by *Men's Health* magazine. The burger packs a whopping 1,520 calories and 111 grams of fat.

14. Chipotle's Mexican Grilled Chicken Burrito takes the prize for unhealthiest Mexican entrée, *Men's Health* says. One burrito will put 1,179 calories into your body.

15. According to the book *Eat This, Not That,* Chick-fil-A is the healthiest overall fast food chain. Subway, Jamba Juice, and Au Bon Pain also rank well.

FLUBBED HEADLINES

"One-Armed Man Applauds the Kindness of Strangers"
That action, without doubt, deserves an ovation.

"Tiger Woods Plays with Own Balls, Nike Says"
Hey, even world-famous golfers like to use their own equipment
sometime.

"Safety Experts Say School Bus Passengers Should Be Belted"
Don't make the safety experts stop the car!

"Amazon Goes Down"
That is, the Web site, not the American Gladiator.

"Finale Climaxes in Explosive End"
Sometimes the media covers the darndest things.

"Local High School Dropouts Cut in Half"
Never ask a magician how the trick works.

"Joint Committee Investigates Marijuana Use"
At least the committee is up-front about its job.

"Sorority Gets Wet; Frat Gets Hammered"
Quiz time: Is it (a) a headline about the University of Central Florida during
Hurricane Frances, or (b) a headline from a college's school newspaper on
an average week?

Chick Accuses Some of Her Male Colleagues of Sexism
To be fair, the story was about a Los Angeles councilwoman named Laura
Chick.

"Nicaragua Sets Goal to Wipe Out Literacy"
Well, it's good to have goals...right?

Pardon Me? Foreign Slang Terms

❖ ❖ ❖ ❖

English borrows freely from nearly every language it comes into contact with. However, there are still many concepts and situations for which Anglophones still lack le mot juste. Here are some suggested foreign words to add to the English dictionary.

Backpfeifengesicht (German): a face that's just begging for someone to slap it—a familiar concept to anyone fond of daytime TV.

Bakku-shan (Japanese): a girl who looks pretty from the back but not the front. This loanword would in fact be a loanword regifted, since it's already a combination of the English word "back" with the German word *schoen,* meaning "beautiful."

Kummerspeck (German): literally this means "grief bacon": excess weight gained from overeating during emotionally trying times.

Ølfrygt (Viking Danish): the fear of a lack of beer. Often sets in during trips away from one's hometown, with its familiar watering holes.

Drachenfutter (German): literally "dragon fodder": a makeup gift bought in advance. Traditionally used to denote offerings made by a man to his wife when he knows he's guilty of something.

Bol (Mayan): For the Mayans of South Mexico and Honduras, the word *bol* pulls double duty, meaning both "in-laws" as well as "stupidity."

Uitwaaien (Dutch): walking in windy weather for the sheer fun of it.

Blechlawine (German): literally "sheet metal avalanche": the endless lineup of cars stuck in a traffic jam on the highway.

Karelu (Tulu, south of India): the mark left on the skin by wearing anything tight.

Fumbling Felons

If Only He Could Have Stayed Awake

After a Campbelltown, Australia, man allegedly stole a car, he drove it to a local car wash. Maybe he wanted to wash off any evidence, or perhaps he was hiding out. Heck, maybe the guy just needed a nap. After an hour passed with him sleeping inside the stolen vehicle, the attendant called the police. The sleepy fella was charged with car theft and illegal use of a motor vehicle.

Where Are Those Keys?

When a Texas man robbed a pharmacy of hydrocodone and Xanax, he left his car running for a faster getaway. There was just one problem: He discovered that he had locked the keys inside the car. To add insult to injury (or vice versa in this case), when the man tried to flee the scene on foot, the police, who thought he was armed, shot him in the shoulder. Now he's really going to need those painkillers.

It Doesn't Pay to Lie

Sandy Hamilton of Lincoln, Nebraska, presumably left his house with no criminal intent whatsoever but managed to wander into trouble along the way. The 19-year-old was arrested after he was spotted walking around an area park with no clothes on. When the police stopped him, Hamilton claimed that a man had tried to rob him at gunpoint; when he said he had no money, the robber took his clothes instead. Police eventually concluded that Hamilton took off the clothes because he was hot. Unfortunately, after walking around naked for a while, he forgot where he left his clothes and concocted the story about the robbery. As a result of the lie, Hamilton was charged not only with indecent exposure, but also with suspicion of making a false statement to police.

Look Before You Leap

Jermaine Washington was so focused on his goal—robbing someone in New York City's Riverside Park—that he didn't even register what his victims looked like. If he'd taken a closer look, he would have realized that they were two of New York's finest, in uniform, no less. Washington pulled a fake gun; the officers pulled real guns, and Washington was promptly taken into custody.

Senior Stats

❖ ❖ ❖ ❖

Nearly 38 million Americans are 65 or older. Here are some standout stats about the senior citizens of our nation.

- Senior citizens account for approximately 13 percent of the U.S. population.

- The number of people 65 or older is expected to more than double by 2050, with projections putting the grand total of granny-aged geezers at 88.5 million.

- There are more older women than older men—in fact, for every 100 women over the age of 85, there are only 48 men.

- Nearly 100,000 Americans are 100 years or older.

- By 2050, more than 600,000 Americans are expected to be still kickin' it as centenarians.

- Florida may have the reputation of being Retirement Central, but California actually has the most seniors of any state: The Golden State is home to 4 million people ages 65 or older, while Florida has 3.1 million.

- Relatively speaking, Florida does have the highest percentage of seniors in a state: Seventeen percent of the state's residents are over 65.

- Grandma and Grandpa may not be as technologically illiterate as you think. More than a third of senior citizens are active on the Internet, researchers estimate. The majority of surfin' seniors use the Internet for keeping in touch with family and friends or searching for information.

- Nine million senior citizens are U.S. military veterans.

- Approximately three-quarters of the senior-citizen population have a high school diploma. Only 19 percent have a bachelor's degree.

- A little more than half of the older generation is still married. A third is widowed.

- About 15 percent of American seniors are still working. That number is expected to nearly double by 2016.

Sunken Civilizations

❖ ❖ ❖ ❖

*Researchers have discovered the tantalizing remains of
what appears to be advanced Mesolithic and Neolithic
civilizations hidden for millennia under water or sand. But
are the ancient cities real, or is it just wishful thinking?*

La Marmotta: Stone Age Lakefront

What is now the bottom of Italy's six-mile-wide Lake Bracciano was
once a lovely and fertile river floodplain. In 1989, scientists discovered
a lost city, which they renamed La Marmotta. Dive teams have recovered artifacts ranging from ancient timbers to uneaten pots of stew, all
preserved under ten feet of mud.

The site dates back to about 5700 B.C. around the late Stone Age
or Neolithic era. Though not much is known about the people who
lived there, scientists do know that the city's residents migrated from
the Near East or Greece in 35-foot-long, wooden dugout boats with
their families. They had domesticated animals, pottery, religious
statues, and even two species of dogs. They laid out their village with
large wooden houses. Items such as obsidian knives and greenstone
ax blades show that La Marmotta was a busy Mediterranean trade
center. But after 400 years of occupation, it seems the village was
hastily abandoned. Why they fled still puzzles researchers.

Atlantis Beneath the Black Sea

Ever since the Greek writer Plato described the lost island of
Atlantis in the fourth century B.C., scholars have searched for the its
location. One oft-suggested candidate is a grouping of underwater
settlements northwest of the Black Sea. Researchers claim this
advanced Neolithic population center was once situated on shore
along a freshwater lake that was engulfed by seawater by 5510 B.C.
Ancient landforms in the area seem to have centered around an island
that roughly fits the description of Atlantis. Similarities between the
lore of Atlantis and this settlement include the use of a form of early
writing, the existence of elephants (from eastern trade routes), obsidian used as money, and circular observatory structures.

Japan, Gateway to Mu

According to Japanese geologist Masaaki Kimura, a legendary lost continent called Mu may have been discovered off the coast of Japan. Kimura says underwater formations that were found in 1985 at Yonaguni Island indicate that they were handmade and that they possibly once resembled a Roman city complete with a coliseum, a castle, statues, paved streets, and plazas. Although photos show sharp, step-like angles and flat surfaces, skeptics still argue these "roads" were actually created by forces such as tides or volcanoes. Nevertheless, Kimura maintains his belief that the ruins are the proof of a 5,000-year-old city.

Ancient Alpine Lake Towns

Today, most people would associate the Alps, the mountain region that borders Germany, Switzerland, and Italy, with skiing. But in late Stone Age or Neolithic period (6000–2000 B.C.), the region's lakes dominated the action. A dry spell in the mid-1800s lowered water levels and allowed evidence of ancient villages to surface within many lakes in the region. One site at the Swiss town of Obermeilen yielded exciting finds such as wooden posts, artifacts made from antlers, Neolithic clay objects, and wooden utensils. It is now believed that the posts supported large wooden platforms that sat over the water, serving as docklike foundations for houses and other village structures.

Hamoukar: City of Commerce

Until the mid-1970s, when the ancient settlement of Hamoukar was discovered in Syria, archaeologists believed the world's oldest cities—dating back to 4000 B.C.—were in present-day Iraq. But the massive, 750-acre Hamoukar, surrounded by a 13-inch-thick wall and home to an estimated 25,000 people, was already a prosperous and advanced city by 4000 B.C.

Situated in the land between the Tigris and Euphrates rivers, Hamoukar was sophisticated enough to support commercial bakeries and large-scale beer breweries. People used clay seals as "brands" for mass-produced goods, including delicate pottery, jewelry, and stone goods. The city was also a processing area for obsidian and later, copper. The settlement was destroyed in a fierce battle around 3500 B.C., leaving more than 1,000 slingshot bullets in the city's ruins.

The Great Danes

They sure ate a lot of shellfish—that much is known about the Mesolithic European culture that lived along the coast of what is now Denmark between 5600 and 4000 B.C. The now-underwater cities were investigated in the 1970s; the first is known as Tybrind Vig and its people are called the Ertebölle. The Ertebölle skeletons resemble those of modern Danes, but some also show Cro-Magnon facial features such as protruding jaws and prominent brow ridges. Archaeologists have found implements made of antler, bone, and stone sticking out of the Danish sea floor. They also found large piles of shellfish at the oldest sites, indicating that the inhabitants loved seafood. Preserved remains of acorns, hazelnuts, and other plants showed their diet was well rounded.

The Ertebölle made clever use of local materials. They lived in wattle or brush huts; "knitted" clothing from plant fibers; made ceramic pots decorated with impressions of grains, cord, and bones; and created art from polished bone and amber. Eventually, it is assumed, the Ertebölle hunter-gatherers either evolved into or were replaced by people with farming skills.

Mystery of the Bimini Blocks

The reason adventurers Robert Ferro and Michael Grumley traveled to the Bahamas was that they had read psychic Edgar Cayce's 1936 prediction that Atlantis would be found in the late 1960s off Bimini Island in the Bahamas. Needless to say, their discovery in the late '60s of giant rows of flat, rectangular blocks resembling a road off northern Bimini was a tad controversial.

The sunken, geometrically arranged rocks stretched for an estimated 700 to 1,000 feet. Several investigators estimated the "structure" dated back to 10,000 B.C. Since then, other explorers have claimed to find additional stones that may have once formed part of an encircling wall around the entire island. Author Charles Berlitz observed that the stones resembled work by pre-Incan Peruvians.

However, geologists have noted that island shore rocks may split into regular planes due to a combination of solar exposure and shifting subsoil—formations resembling the Bimini Blocks also exist off the coast of Australia.

Fast Facts

- Rudyard Kipling could only write when his pen was filled with black ink.

- Beethoven liked to stimulate his brain by pouring ice water over his head.

- The French hero of the American Revolution's full name was Marie Joseph Paul Yves Roch Gilbert du Motier Marquis de Lafayette.

- Éleuthère Irénée DuPont, president of the DuPont Company, had pet iguanas that he taught to stand at attention and come when called.

- Tycho Brahe, the famous Danish astronomer, wore a metal nose as a replacement for one he lost in a drunken duel.

- Robert Todd Lincoln saw three presidents assassinated: his father, Abraham Lincoln; James Garfield; and William McKinley.

- Clinophobia is the fear of going to bed.

- French monarch Louis XIV obviously didn't have clinophobia—he owned 413 beds.

- Anne Boleyn, the second wife of Henry VIII, had six fingers on one hand. She wore special gloves to hide the condition.

- England's Queen Elizabeth I owned 3,000 gowns.

- Volleyball was originally called mintonette.

- American babies tend to like applesauce and sweet foods, but the best-selling Gerber's Baby Food in Japan is sardines.

ANAGRAMS

An anagram is a word or phrase that exactly reproduces the letters in another word or phrases. The most interesting of them comment on the subject of the first.

Eleven plus two—Twelve plus one

Elvis—Lives

Smoking Hot—Gosh, I'm knot

Bill Gates—Big at sell

California—A frail icon

National debt—I bad, lent a ton

Yasmin Le Bon—Mainly bones

Romance Novel—Crone love man

Basketball—Be tall, bask

Airplane—Real pain

Imelda Marcos—I'm scam ordeal

Alarm clock—AM rock call

Insurance—I can nurse

Deep Throat—Red-hot tape

Cable news—Bawl scene

Football season—Foe no toss a ball

Paris Hilton—Ha! Prison 'til...

Clint Eastwood—Old West action.

Vietnam War—Met vain war

Pitt–Aniston—It not in past

Hospital gown—Hang low, I spot

Astronomer—Moon starer

Tales from the Spinning Rack

❖ ❖ ❖ ❖

*Nine comic books that helped to make the art
form what it is today.*

Comic books are an integral part of popular culture, and even those
who don't read them (or won't admit to it) are familiar with the
medium's most famous characters. Hundreds of titles and thousands
of stories have been published since the very first comic books were
created in the 1930s, but only a handful have actually advanced the
art form. We've listed some of the most influential comics here.

1. *Funnies on Parade* (1933): Most historians consider this
Procter & Gamble promotional giveaway the progenitor of comic
books as we know them today. Inside were reprints of popular Sunday comics, including Mutt & Jeff and Joe Palooka. The first commercial comics soon followed, selling for ten cents a copy.

2. *Action Comics #1* (1938): This comic's cover image has
become a national icon. This issue heralded the debut of Superman,
one of the best-known fictional characters in the world and the first
popular costumed superhero (there are those who would argue that
either Mandrake the Magician [1934] or The Clock [1936] is the
actual *first* costumed superhero). Extremely rare and quite collect-
able, a mint copy sold at auction in March 2010 for $1 million.

3. *Detective Comics #27* (1939): It's here that The Batman
made his debut, beginning a franchise that would almost equal
that of Superman. Though he possessed no superpowers, the Dark
Knight caught readers' attention from the start and never let go.

4. *Sensation Comics #1* (1942): Wonder Woman, one of the
comics' first female superheroes, was introduced in *All-Star Comics
#8,* but she found a permanent home in *Sensation Comics.* Created
by psychologist William Moulton Marston and first illustrated by
Harry G. Peters, the Amazon Princess would evolve into a feminist
icon.

5. *MAD #1* (1952): The brainchild of satirist Harvey Kurtzman,
MAD was the first comic book to poke serious fun at popular culture. It became a huge hit and spawned a host of imitators, few of

which lasted more than a couple of issues. *MAD* soon converted to a magazine format to avoid censorship by the newly formed Comics Code Authority.

6. *Amazing Fantasy #15* (1962): This This Marvel comic book featured the first appearance of Spider-Man and introduced the concept of the troubled superhero. Though Spider-Man possessed an array of remarkable superpowers, his teenage alter ego, Peter Parker, was beset by the same problems that afflicted most young people, including girl trouble and difficulties in school.

7. *Zap Comics #1* (1967): Robert Crumb's *Zap Comics* wasn't the first underground comic book, but most historians consider it the official vanguard of the underground "comix" movement. In later issues, Crumb gave space to some of underground comics's most influential artists, including S. Clay Wilson, Rick Griffin, Spain Rodriguez, and Gilbert Shelton. Crumb, creator of the characters Fritz the Cat and Mr. Natural, among other characters, is still revered as a counter-culture icon.

8. *Raw Magazine #2* (1980): Though not a comic book in the traditional sense, *Raw Magazine* #2 is historically significant for presenting the first installment of *Maus,* Art Spiegelman's graphic adaptation of his father's life, particularly his time as a prisoner in a Nazi concentration camp. Rather than tell the story with people, Spiegelman depicted the Jews as mice and the Nazis as cats. The saga was later published as a graphic novel and went on to win a Pulitzer Prize Special Award in 1992.

9. *Watchmen* (1986): No comic series in the past 30 years has so dramatically affected both the medium and popular culture like *Watchmen.* With penetrating character psychology and layers of metaphoric imagery, Alan Moore and Dave Gibbons didn't reinvent the superhero genre—they made it seem as if it hadn't existed until that point.

INSPIRATION STATION

A Glamorous Homage

In the early years of MTV, music videos were often cheap and uninspired, even when used to market acts with terrific songs (the oeuvre of Hall & Oates being perhaps the most egregious example). All that changed in the late 1980s, when musicians such as Peter Gabriel and Tom Petty began using their videos to make visual, as well as musical, artistic statements.

Still, no one was prepared for Madonna's $5 million video for her hit song "Express Yourself," which made its MTV debut on May 17, 1989. Inspired by German filmmaker Fritz Lang's classic sci-fi silent movie *Metropolis* (1927), the dark and moody video set a standard for quality and creativity that is rarely met even two decades later. "Express Yourself" built on Lang's theme of holding onto one's humanity in the face of relentless, harsh industrialism by adding a distinctly feminist (or, some would argue, post-feminist) twist.

Before Britney…

Though its subject matter is controversial, Vladimir Nabokov's *Lolita* is considered by many to be the greatest novel ever written. The story of a middle-age man who becomes obsessed with a 12-year-old girl, *Lolita* combines a taboo topic with rapturously beautiful prose. The musician Sting of the British rock band The Police was inspired by the book to write one of his biggest hits, "Don't Stand So Close to Me," which became the top-selling single of the year in the United Kingdom in 1980. The author of *Lolita* is even namechecked in the song when Sting sings, "Just like the old man in that book by Nabokov." In the video used to promote "Don't Stand So Close to Me," Sting plays a teacher who is distracted by a young female student in his class. There are no skimpy schoolgirl uniforms, which Britney Spears would use so effectively decades later in her own *Lolita*-esque videos, but Sting does remove his shirt for no apparent reason whatsoever.

Take a Walk on the Other Side

❖ ❖ ❖ ❖

At England's Falstaff's Experience, ghosts—and the ghostly possession of visitors—are routine occurrences.

By day, the Falstaff's Experience in England's Stratford-upon-Avon is an amusing historical and ghost-themed attraction. Costumed mannequins, coffins dripping fake blood, and a re-creation of a "plague cottage" are among the displays that provide chills and thrills to visitors. At night, however, the atmosphere can turn sinister. In total darkness, dozens of spirits freely roam both floors of the building and appear on the staircases between them. Only ghost hunters with nerves of steel should join one of the nightly "midnight vigils" at the Falstaff's Experience.

A Beastly Barn

The land under the Falstaff's Experience was probably a Saxon cemetery in the sixth century. As Christianity became popular in Britain, early burial grounds such as this were typically dismissed as pagan and built over. By the 12th century, the site included a home and a barn used for trading sheep and wool (hence it's name: Sheep Street). However, that wool became infamous in the 14th century when it carried fleas infested with bubonic plague to the area. Thousands of people died; their homes became known as plague cottages.

Later, the barn and house belonged to one of King Henry VIII's archers, William Shrieve. Even today, many people refer to the site as "Shrieve's House," particularly because his ghost has been seen there.

During the English Civil War in the 17th century, the barn was used as a hospital, and some people think the spirits of many wounded soldiers have never left the building. The soldiers died slow, bloody, and feverish deaths in an era when painkillers barely existed. When the TV show *Most Haunted Live* filmed at the Falstaff's Experience in 2004, medium Derek Acorah was possessed by a soldier whose arm was being amputated. From Acorah's slurred speech and drunken singing, it appeared that the soldier's only anesthetic was liquor. Today the barn is known as one of the most haunted places in Britain.

Midnight Vigils

During nightly midnight vigils at the Falstaff's Experience, visitors explore several ground-floor rooms of the old barn before they're led up the stairs. People often report feeling a sense of dread as they climb these steps—some even leave the tour before reaching the upper floor. Many visitors describe invisible hands grabbing them around the ankles; others have seen bloody soldiers who prevent them from continuing. Other people talk about a sense of imminent danger or even death. For those who make it up the stairs, even more haunting experiences await.

Visitors have been known to see streetlights shining through an open window several feet above the haunted staircase. This seems normal enough, until the tour guide turns on the building's interior lights to reveal that there is no window and nothing to explain the lights. Some believe the image is from an earlier time when a window was there; others feel it may be a portal to another, ghostly dimension. Women are especially vulnerable near the staircase, where they may encounter the malicious spirit of John Davies.

Sharpened Senses

In the Middle Ages, John Davies traveled the countryside sharpening knives and axes. The weapons came in handy, for Davies is known as one of England's earliest serial killers. Several of his victims, usually women, were killed on Sheep Street, where he often conducted business.

When Davies's ghost appears at the Falstaff's Experience, it's been said that he's an average-looking man wearing a white shirt and brown breeches. Of particular note are the bloody knife he appears to be carrying and the stench of his breath. His ghost has been known to frighten women by breathing on them—usually on the cheek or neck—in the upper floor of the barn.

Playful Lucy

As visitors move past the staircase and onto the upper level, they'll come to Lucy's room. Little Lucy is a mischievous ghost-child whose mother was accused of witchcraft in the 1700s. The young girl was questioned, tortured, and killed, but she never betrayed her mother.

Today, Lucy allegedly pats visitors' hair, tugs at jewelry, and moves small items around her room. People have taken off their necklaces and held them out, only to find ghostly hands pulling at the jewelry. It's as if she never gets tired of playing. Lucy's innocence is in sharp contrast to other areas of the Falstaff's Experience.

Ghostly Slideshow

Visitors courageous enough to stand directly beneath the upstairs smoke alarm may see something startling. In the eerie green light from the alarm, a visitor's appearance is often transformed to resemble a ghost. A few seconds later another ghost manifests, and so on. People have seen as many as half a dozen different apparitions of varying ages, genders, and hairstyles. Some wear jewelry, and even their clothing may be visible.

Those who volunteer are not permanently possessed. Apparently, the ghosts are simply using the person as a backdrop to project their images—think of it as Possession Lite. Mostly, volunteers have described a sense of imbalance, saying the experience is not scary, just very strange.

Don't Look Back

History has shown that after leaving one room in the Falstaff's Experience, it's best not to go back into it. Visitors who have returned to an earlier room have described feeling disoriented, as if they've stepped into a portal or fallen down the rabbit hole in *Alice's Adventures in Wonderland*.

Some ghost hunters have seen an unidentified hooded figure when they returned to Lucy's room. Others felt as if the furniture was floating around them or they were sinking into another dimension. Videos taken by visitors have shown unexplained figures moving in front of the camera. It's as if the ghosts are willing to let people pass through their home, but they want them to keep moving. The one exception is Davies, the knife sharpener. He often follows guests from room to room until they leave the building.

No matter the experience, it's pretty safe to say that the Falstaff's Experience offers one of the few places in the world where you can safely get a sense of what it's like on "the other side."

Testing the Waters

❖ ❖ ❖ ❖

*Future visitors to Poseidon Resorts will dive
into a whole new vacation experience.*

Living Underwater

Whether walking on the moon or summiting Himalayan peaks,
humans have a history of wanting to visit places largely inaccessible
to them. Now there's a wave of interest in underwater living.

In the 1960s, Jacques Cousteau conducted research into this sort
of living by building various Conshelf (Continental Shelf Station)
habitats under the sea. Conshelf II was the first habitat on the sea
floor, inhabited for 30 days by a group of "oceanauts." They breathed
a combination of oxygen and helium, and their research provided
useful information about human physiology underwater.

A Bubble with a View

So where do people go if they just want to eat fine meals and admire
undersea coral gardens? Well, in the 21st century, they take a trip to
Poseidon Resorts, the world's first seafloor resort off Poseidon
Mystery Island, a private island in Fiji. Accessible by yacht or the
resort's twin-engine aircraft, the projected getaway is located within
a coral atoll (a ring-shape coral reef) 40 feet underwater.

Visitors will take an elevator down to the futuristic-looking hotel.
The resort will feature the world's largest undersea restaurant and
lounge and a series of undersea suites. Besides the usual hotel
features—bed, bath, TV—each suite will be surrounded in thick
transparent acrylic plastic, so as to provide stunning views of the
ocean life surrounding them. The hotel is situated near a reef
teeming with life because, according to the resort's official Web site,
"No one wants to look out on open ocean and peer into water with
poor visibility." (So true.) Poseidon Resorts even advertises that
guests will be able to push a button from their "control console" to
feed the fish outside.

Sound fishy? Only time will tell if Poseidon Resorts will make a
splash as a new sort of luxury destination.

WORD HISTORIES

Coconut: Of course, the coconut is not a nut at all, but it looked like one to the early Portuguese explorers as they sailed around Africa. They saw the fruit hanging from trees and thought it looked like small heads, grinning. *Coconut* resulted from a combination of *nut* and the Portuguese word *coco*, which means "a grinning face."

Escape: This one is pretty literal: It's from the Latin words *ex* for out and *cappa* for cape. Thus, someone who slipped out of his or her cape to get away would have escaped.

Daredevil: This one stems from the two English words it contains: dare and devil. The term describes a person who is so reckless or foolhardy that he or she would be willing to dare the devil.

Magenta: A town in Italy named Magenta was the site of a great French victory in an 1859 battle. The name of the color refers to the bloodshed at the battle.

Gossip: Once an approved manner of discussing someone's business, this word came from the religious rite of baptism. Those adults who stand up for a baby during the ceremony are known as godparents. The godparents of one child were considered "related" to the godparents of another child in that family and became known to each other as "godsibb." These insiders were given the right to discuss family business among themselves. A little too much discussion might have made way for a broader definition of "godsibb," or "gossip" to mean people who tell tales, spreading both truth and rumor.

Guy: Today the word *guy* is an accepted substitute for man or boy, but it came about in a less than positive manner. In the early 17th century, Guy Fawkes was instrumental in a plan to blow up England's Parliament. He was captured and hanged, but people celebrated the day by carrying effigies of Guy throughout the streets. Anyone resembling Guy or his manner of dress became known as a guy.

The Watermelon War

❖ ❖ ❖ ❖

This riot erupted due to some seedy behavior.

To say that American-Panamanian relations were extremely tense during the second half of the 19th century would be a bit of an understatement. Much of the tension was due to labor conflict: After completing the trans-Panama railroad, the United States did away  with jobs occupied by native-born residents and placed Americans in managerial roles. Race riots became commonplace, but one notable revolt began over a watermelon.

On April 15, 1856, the *John L. Stephens,* a steamer carrying 1,000 passengers to Panama City, docked on Taboga Island. Many of those onboard had been guzzling booze; when they disembarked to stroll around a local market, an inebriated white American passenger named Jack Oliver grabbed a watermelon slice from a black vendor.

When Oliver refused to pay for it, the vendor pulled out a knife. While one of the men in Oliver's party attempted to pay for the melon, Oliver drew a gun. The gun went off accidentally, injuring a bystander. A riot broke out, and a mob of angry Panamanians rushed in and began beating the Americans, looting hotel rooms, and destroying property. When authorities tried to break up the fight, one of them was shot, thus inciting the police to join the melee. Some Americans took refuge in the railroad station; outside, Panamanians were attempting to ram their way in using a broken telephone pole. In the end, 15 Americans and 2 Panamanians were killed and dozens were wounded.

In response to the Watermelon War, and in an attempt to protect American economic interests in Panama, the U.S. military unlawfully occupied the isthmus and railroad station. Eventually, the occupation was abandoned, but the United States still pursued payment for the damage caused by the riot. The Republic of New Granada, which encompassed present-day Panama and Columbia, begrudgingly paid approximately $400,000 in damages. For years, relations remained sticky. The Watermelon War was a devastating conflict any way you slice it.

Where Madness Meets Medicine

❖ ❖ ❖ ❖

*There's a place where visitors can view a Lunatic Box,
a Bath of Surprises, and a human-size gerbil wheel.
Welcome to the Glore Psychiatric Museum.*

Interested in the history of mental health care? Curious about what goes on in the mind of the clinically insane? A visit to the Glore Psychiatric Museum in St. Joseph, Missouri, provides a shocking look at the profession's past. In many cases, what today appears to be a medieval torture device was not too long ago employed in the "treatment" of the mentally ill. Frankly, it's a wonder how anyone ever recovered.

Foreign Objects

As far as medical museums go, a curator is fairly certain to strike gold when his or her featured attraction is a case of rusty nails retrieved from a madwoman's stomach. Nearly 1,500 objects, including safety pins and saltshaker tops, all neatly arranged in a flower pattern, comprise the former intestinal contents of a mental patient who suffered from a form of allotriophagy, a bizarre desire to eat foreign objects.

The display is just a taste of what you'll find at the Glore Psychiatric Museum. The collection was housed in what was once known as State Lunatic Asylum No. 2, which opened in 1874. George Glore, a longtime state mental health employee, founded the museum in 1968; today it features replicas of a multitude of 16th-, 17th-, and 18th-century treatment devices. (Many of the replicas were made with help from asylum inmates.) The exhibit proved so perversely successful that it became a permanent fixture.

This Will Only Hurt a Bit

Some items in the museum's collection date back to a time when the mentally ill were treated more like prisoners than patients. Devices that originated with the hospital's late 19th-century beginnings represent a dark age of psychiatric medicine, a time when doctors held the belief that mental illness could be driven out of a person purely by physical torment.

A prime example is the Fever Cabinet, which is basically a light bulb-filled box designed to enclose a patient's body and drive up his or her body temperature. Conversely, there was the Dousing Tub, in which difficult inmates were bound and blasted with water, and the "Bath of Surprise," a gallows device that dropped patients suddenly into a pool of shockingly cold water "to break the chain of delusional ideas and perhaps create conditions favoring sane thinking."

Other contraptions include the Lunatic Box, a narrow enclosure that forced patients to remain confined indefinitely in a standing position; the Tranquilizer Chair, a seat with a built-in toilet, leg irons, and a box to cover the head; and O'Halloran's Swing, which spun its victims at up to 100 revolutions per minute. Patients who needed some exercise could also walk in the giant wooden enclosed treadmill—a human-size hamster wheel.

While some visitors find the museum experience disturbing, Glore clearly believes the collection serves an important purpose. "We really can't have a good appreciation of the strides we've made if we don't look at the atrocities of the past," he said in a 1995 interview with the *Los Angeles Times*.

Let the Healing Begin

In another part of the museum, visitors are treated to a peek at the artistic and compulsive sides of the mentally disturbed. In one area are cars that were customized by patients. A wall features a selection of more than 500 handwritten notes that had been stuffed into a mental ward television set. Though the author's intention was never fully explained, he had stuffed the slips of paper one by one through a slot in the back, possibly as some imagined method of transmitting his thoughts to the outside world. Nearby, a cage holds 100,000 cigarette packs amassed by another patient, who was working toward an imagined redemption scheme to win a new wheelchair.

Glore served as the museum's curator for three decades and retired in the mid-'90s. Due to its popularity, the collection eventually moved out of the asylum and found an even bigger home. If you're ever in St. Joseph, be sure to stop by. You'd be crazy not to!

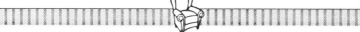

Talk to the Expert

PUPPETEER

Q: So you are a "master puppeteer." Is that like having a black belt in puppetry?
A: Well, I do like to think of myself as a ninja sometimes, and one of the skills a puppeteer needs is the ability to disappear. So, yeah, I guess it's kind of like having a black belt.

Q: Puppetry is one of the world's oldest art forms. What do you think continues to be the draw?
A: Why puppetry works specifically for kids is that it's a simple convention, and a convention is just an agreement between the audience and performer. The convention of puppetry is that this piece of fabric or this chunk of wood will represent a particular character, and the audience hopefully enters that agreement. They'll accept that the piece of fabric is Little Red Riding Hood. Obviously kids aren't so stupid that they'll think it's real. It's just their imagination will say, "OK, yeah, for this time, that piece of red fabric is Little Red Riding Hood. Let's play."

Q: How are puppets received differently by kids and adults?
A: There's a lot more doubt in an adult imagination. A lot more acceptance of what's real and a lot more denial of what's impossible. [After an adult show I directed], the comments I got back from the audience were that they were really surprised they had an emotional attachment to the characters, even though they were just puppets. It's interesting to me that it's more natural for them to gain an emotional attachment to an actor that's clearly playing a role just as much as the puppet is playing a role.

Q: So what's your favorite part of your job?
A: Performing for a really good audience. I've done thousands of puppet shows over my career, and it's such a magical moment to think, "They're with me and we're in this together."

Q: Most difficult part?
A: I want to say keeping your arm straight for long periods of time. Yeah, I'm sticking with that.

A Daring Young Man

On November 12, 1859, the audience at the Cirque Napoleon in Paris was delighted and amazed to witness the world's first flying trapeze act. Jules Léotard thrilled the crowd by sailing between three trapezes and turning a somersault in midair, with only a few mattresses and carpets to protect him from a hard fall. The young daredevil's act only lasted 12 minutes, but it left a huge impression on French (and indeed all of Western) culture that lasts to this day. He called the very tight one-piece garment he wore a *maillot,* but since that time, the tights that circus performers and dancers wear have been renamed leotards. Interestingly, *maillot* now refers to a swimsuit.

A Woman Scorned

You had to be careful whom you dumped in the 12th century. King Louis VI of France wasn't too happy when his wife, Eleanor of Aquitaine, bore him only two daughters and no sons. The marriage was annulled, but Eleanor had no intention of going quietly and leading a dull, lonely life. She made sure that she retained every acre of land in southwest France that she had brought into the marriage. She also promptly remarried Henry II, who became king of England and made her queen. A victim of the adage, "You made your bed, now lie in it," Louis wasn't too thrilled when he realized that an English king now owned more property in France than he did.

History Quickies

- Virginia Woolf wrote all her books while standing up.
- The first American to have indoor plumbing was Henry Wadsworth Longfellow in 1840.
- Maurice Grey was the inventor of a machine that mass-produced fine textured mustard. Auguste Poupon was also an established mustard maker. In 1886, the two mustard manufacturers joined forces and Grey Poupon was born.

You're Suing Me For *What?*

❖ ❖ ❖ ❖

The law can protect us, but it can also subject us to strange lawsuits that seem custom-written for late-night monologues. Here are eight of the oddest and most amusing lawsuits.

1. Thongs of Pain

They may not be the most comfortable things, but it turns out thongs can also injure you—at least, according to a 2008 lawsuit filed against Victoria's Secret. A woman claimed her thong snapped while she was putting it on and ended up hitting her in the eye. The underwear apparently had metal links holding a jewel in place on its waistband, which, upon contact caused her "excruciating pain."

2. Bathroom Explosion

A bank president sued a construction company after the toilet in his executive bathroom flooded. The water "came blasting up out of the toilet with such force it stood him right up," the man claimed, and the resulting media coverage wiped away his good reputation. A judge didn't buy it.

3. Reality Show Regurgitation

Sure, bad reality TV is painful to watch, but is it bad enough to warrant a $2.5 million lawsuit? In 2005, Austin Aitken sued NBC over its *Fear Factor* program. The man said the show's disgusting displays caused him to become lightheaded, then vomit and run into a doorway. The courtroom tribunal voted him off the stand, and he didn't get a dime of NBC's dough.

4. Beer Disappointment

Getting a buzz wasn't enough for one Michigan beer drinker. In 1991, he decided to sue Anheuser-Busch for $10,000, saying the company's Bud Light commercials provided false and misleading advertising. His beef? The ads depicted regular guys having a grand time with beautiful women while drinking the beer, and no matter how many cold ones he pounded back, this kind of "unrestricted

merriment" just wasn't occurring. It's probably no surprise that this lawsuit fell flat.

5. Killer Whale Confusion
The killer whale really needs to make its intentions more clear. In 1999, a man snuck past security guards at SeaWorld Orlando to take a late-night swim. He was later found naked and dead in a killer whale's tank. His parents sued the park, saying there was no kind of "public warning" that the killer whale might be inclined to, well, kill someone. SeaWorld described the lawsuit as being "as crazy as they come."

6. I'm Suing Myself
Can't find anyone good to sue? You can always sue yourself. In 1995, a prisoner from Virginia filed a lawsuit against himself for $5 million, claiming he had violated his own civil rights by consuming alcohol and committing the crimes that got him locked up. Evidently, the man thought the state would have to pay the damages, since he was incarcerated and had no income. But the court wasn't so amused: The case was tossed and the inmate headed back to jail.

7. Mistaken Celebrity
Most people would love to be mistaken for a successful celebrity. But in 2006, Allen Heckard from Oregon found the fact that he looked like Michael Jordan insulting—so much so that he sued both Jordan and Nike, the shoe company he blamed for making Jordan a household name. Heckard said he'd experienced emotional pain and suffering from people noticing his resemblance to the NBA star. He asked for $832 million, leading one news agency to say the case was "so outrageous that it actually [gave] frivolous lawsuits a bad name."

8. Bathroom Bother
What does a guy have to do to use the bathroom in peace? A man attending a 1995 Billy Joel and Elton John concert in San Diego claimed to have seen women in every restroom he tried to use at the stadium. The fellow said the sightings caused him emotional distress, and he sued the stadium and city for $5.4 million. Probably even more distressful to him: He lost.

📺 Behind the TV Shows of Our Time

- The sitcom *The Flying Nun* was based on a novel by Tere Rios called *The Fifteenth Pelican*.

- The critically acclaimed drama *St. Elsewhere*, which ran on NBC from 1982 to 1988, was co-produced by the late Bruce Paltrow (Gwyneth's dad).

- The character of Jethro Bodine of *The Beverly Hillbillies* was born with a full set of teeth.

- In an episode of *Gomer Pyle, U.S.M.C.* titled "Flower Power," Gomer sings Bob Dylan's "Blowin' in the Wind" with a group of hippies.

- Vince Van Patten appeared on the mid-'70s action show *The Six Million Dollar Man* as a bionic boy whose paralyzed legs were replaced with techno-legs.

- Sonny Crockett, the *Miami Vice* detective portrayed by Don Johnson, lived on a sailboat named *St. Vitus' Dance* with a pet alligator named Elvis. We can believe that, but his owning a Ferrari Spider? Come on.

- The late McLean Stevenson will always be remembered for making one of the worst show business decisions in history: Leaving the role of Henry Blake on *M*A*S*H* in the show's third season. The four sitcoms in which he starred over the next decade were bombs.

- The first sitcom to feature an openly gay lead character was *Love, Sidney*, which starred Tony Randall as Sidney and aired from 1981 to 1983.

- The hour-long 1970s show, *The Love Boat,* was based on a book called *The Love Boats* by Jeraldine Saunders, who had once worked as a "cruise hostess."

- In 1982, actor Ed Asner accused CBS of canceling his show *Lou Grant* because he criticized the Reagan administration and its involvement in Central American politics. CBS said the cancellation was due to declining ratings.

Charles Waterton: Britain's Monkey Man

❖ ❖ ❖ ❖

Charles Waterton once referred to himself as "the most commonplace of men." He couldn't have been more off the mark. With monkeylike agility and a rude habit of biting friends in the leg, Squire Waterton was not your ordinary British nobleman.

Get Down From There!

Charles Waterton, born in 1782 in Wakefield, Yorkshire, had an interesting motto: "He falls not from the bridge who walks with prudence." It was a maxim he fulfilled. In 1817, the Englishman shocked Rome when he scaled a statue of an angel mounted upon the Castel Sant'Angelo, and then assumed the one-legged stance of a stork atop the angel's head. While in the city, he also climbed to the top of St. Peter's Basilica and left a glove behind on the building's lightning rod. Pope Pius VII asked him to remove it, for fear that the rod would no longer work. (Waterton complied.)

A naturalist, Waterton was also obsessed with the thought of flying, and after much study of bird wings, constructed his own flying contraption and dragged it to the top of an outhouse for a test. Friends could barely restrain him from jumping.

The Frankenstein of Taxidermy

Waterton was also passionate about all forms of wildlife, and he began the world's first nature preserve on his family's estate. He traveled to South America to study and collect birds but became famous for catching an alligator by riding it bareback and wrestling it to shore. He invented his own form of "hollow" taxidermy, using mercuric chloride to harden animal skins. In one formal portrait, Waterton is shown with his hair closely shorn in

an unfashionable crew cut, with a taxidermied bird on his finger and the head of a cat resting on a book.

But he took his art a step further by sewing parts from different animals together to create weird, Frankenstein-like conglomerations. Waterton's most famous invented creature was called "the Nondescript," rearranging the rear end of a howler monkey to make it resemble a weird monkey/man hybrid. He enjoyed making up stories about its origins, often claiming that it was a new species he'd found on his travels. He was also known to insist it was the head of a British customs agent against whom Waterton held a long-time grudge.

A devout Catholic, Waterton sometimes used his odd creations to make religious statements. He put together an owl and a bittern, for instance, and dubbed it a "Noctifer," explaining to people that it symbolized a new Dark Age brought to England by the Protestants.

Mad Dogs and Englishmen

Waterton's personal life was also, well, *interesting*. He was married at age 47 to a friend's 17-year-old daughter. After his beloved wife died of a fever after childbirth, he refused to sleep in a bed. Instead, he snoozed on wooden planks with an oaken block under his head. Waterton also allegedly kept a tree sloth in his room as a pet. His good friend Dr. Richard Hobson learned to avoid the entrance hall table when invited to Waterton's Yorkshire home, as the squire was often waiting underneath, ready to leap out and bite the good doctor on the leg.

Hobson also witnessed Waterton scratching himself behind the ear with his foot when the squire was well into his 70s. Another time, Hobson saw him hop on one leg across the edge of a rock that leaned over a great chasm. Unfortunately, Waterton's motto failed him in 1865 when he took a bad tumble on his estate. He died a few days later at age 82. His vast collection of artifacts and preserved animal oddities can still be seen at the Wakefield Museum in Yorkshire, England.

Fast Facts

- *In the early days of baseball, a runner was out if he was "soaked"—that is, he was hit by the ball thrown by a fielder.*

- *Also in early baseball, umpires sat in padded rocking chairs behind the plate.*

- *The Battle of Bunker Hill during the American Revolutionary War actually took place on Breed's Hill.*

- *The yo-yo was originally used as a weapon by natives in the Philippine Islands.*

- *After surgeon Joseph Lister published a report in 1867 regarding the value of hygienic methods in hospitals, deaths following surgery dropped from 40 to 50 percent to just 5 percent.*

- *Some snails are hermaphrodites and are able to fertilize one another. Other species of snail are asexual and don't need a partner at all.*

- *Washington Irving is responsible for the story that Christopher Columbus wanted to prove that the world was round.*

- *It is said that when asked what color his Model T automobiles should be, Henry Ford replied, "You can paint it any color, as long as it's black."*

- *Charles Lindbergh was not the first man to fly non-stop across the Atlantic Ocean. He was the first to do it solo.*

- *Paul Revere was an obscure and forgotten figure until Henry Wadsworth Longfellow wrote his famous poem about him.*

You. It's What's for Dinner.

❖ ❖ ❖ ❖

Anthropologists debate whether cannibalism is actually a common practice in tribal cultures, or whether it happens only occasionally and under duress, as it does in so-called "civilized" society. Over the years, many people have had a taste for—and tasted—human flesh. Ready for some grisly tales? Here are ten folks who have (or are rumored to have) taken a bite.

1. Sawney Bean—Sawney Bean lived circa the 1400s in a cave near Ballantrae, in Aynshire, Scotland with his wife and their numerous children and grandchildren. According to lore, from their hideout, they robbed, killed, pickled, dried, and devoured hundreds of passersby for more than 20 years. However, some scholars argue that Bean was merely a figment of English propaganda, designed to emphasize Scottish barbarism.

2. Diego Rivera—For a period in 1904, it is said that legendary Mexican painter Diego Rivera and his friends purchased female corpses from a morgue, preferring their flavor and texture to male flesh. He believed that cannibalism would become acceptable in the future, when "man will have thrown off all of his superstitions and irrational taboos." According to one biography, he made no bones about favoring "women's brains in vinaigrette."

3. Karl Denke—"Papa Denke," as his neighbors and fellow churchgoers in Munsterberg, Germany, knew him was the organist at his church and ran a popular boarding house. Upon his arrest in 1924, police found the remains of at least 30 former lodgers pickled in barrels in his basement. According to reports, he told police that he had eaten only human flesh for the past three years.

4. Albert Fish—Dubbed the "Gray Man" by witnesses, Albert Fish appeared to be a harmless old man, but in truth he tortured hundreds of children and reportedly killed more than a dozen throughout the East Coast. He was caught, convicted, and executed for the 1928 murder of ten-year-old Grace Budd, after he wrote to her mother and described how he killed, roasted, and ate her daughter.

5. Edward Gein—When police entered Edward Gein's Plainfield, Wisconsin, farmhouse in November 1957, they found a scene right out of a horror movie—a scene that was in fact the inspiration for the films *Psycho* and *Silence of the Lambs.* A woman's body was strung up and splayed, her heart was in a pot on the stove, and her head was in a paper bag. Human skulls were in use as bowls and decorating the bed frame, and there was a chair, lamp shade, and a wastebasket made of human skin. Despite the number of corpses that must have gone into such an endeavor, Gein was only prosecuted for the murder of two local women.

6. Joachim Kroll—This German killer lost count of how many people he had killed during his grisly career that spanned two decades, though he was sure that there had been at least 14. Kroll's activities were finally discovered in 1976 when a plumber was called to unblock the communal toilet in his apartment building, which Kroll said was clogged "with guts." The plumber pulled out a child's lungs and entrails; police found several bags full of human meat and a pot on the stove simmering with carrots, potatoes, and the hand of a four-year-old girl.

7. Nathaniel Bar-Jonah—Born David Paul Brown in 1957 in Massachusetts, Bar-Jonah was a convicted child molester and kidnapper with a history of sadistic violence toward young boys. In 1991, he was released from the Bridgewater State Hospital and moved to Great Falls, Montana, during which time he also changed his name. After he was arrested in 1999 for lurking near an elementary school, carrying a stun gun, he became a suspect in the death of a local ten-year-old boy. A police search of his apartment yielded encrypted recipes for dishes such as "Little Boy Pot Pie." Bar-Jonah's neighbors testified that he would frequently bring them casseroles or invite them to cookouts featuring funny-tasting meat he claimed to have hunted and dressed himself.

8. Katherine Mary Knight—On February 29, 2000, an Australian woman named Katherine Mary Knight stabbed her common-law husband 37 times, skinned him, and, using the skills she learned while working in a slaughterhouse, decapitated him. She then boiled his head, roasted pieces of his corpse, and served it with vegetables to his adult children. Knight was sentenced to life in prison without parole.

9. Armin Meiwes—In 2001, a German computer technician named Armin Meiwes went online for an odd purpose. No, he didn't scan the Web in search of a paramour; instead, he posted an advertisement for a well-built fellow who would be willing to be slaughtered and eaten. While it's hard to imagine anyone agreeing to this, a man named Bernd-Jürgen Brandes answered the ad. Brandes willingly came to Meiwes' house, where Meiwes sliced off Brandes' penis. The pair attempted to eat it but found it inedible. After Brandes passed out from alcohol, sleeping pills, and loss of blood, Meiwes stabbed and dissected him. He ate Brandes's body over a ten-month period, garnished with potatoes and pepper sauce. Shockingly, Meiwes also filmed the event. In jail, an unrepentant Meiwes became a vegetarian.

10. Marc Sappington—Also known in the press as the "Kansas City Vampire," Marc Sappington killed four people over his grisly career. In March 2001, what started as a run-of-the-mill armed robbery appears to have unleashed killer voices in Sappington's head. He finally succumbed to the voices in April, when he murdered a friend with a knife, and then drank his blood. Three days later, he stabbed another friend, intending to drink his blood, but lost his nerve. Later that day, he lured a 16-year-old boy to his house, shot him, hacked his body to pieces, and ate him. After his arrest, he didn't lose his appetite—in fact, Sappington asked if he could eat the investigator's leg.

Doin' the Dunk

❖ ❖ ❖ ❖

The slam dunk is one of the moves in basketball that never fails to elicit gasps and groans. Here's how it all began.

Whether it's called a dip, slam, jam, punch, stuff, flush, or dunk, the act of rising above the basketball rim with a single agile, athletic leap and propelling the ball down the barrel has become something of an art. But the dunk itself wasn't exactly invented; rather, it evolved as players grew in height and athletic ability.

George Mikan, a pioneer in pro basketball, who played for the Chicago American Gears and the Minneapolis Lakers through the 1940s and '50s, was probably the first man to use the dunk as an offensive weapon. Mikan would plant himself under the basket and use his 6'10" frame to his advantage. Back then, there was no rim hangs or wham-slam jams. Instead, Mikan would gently guide the globe, dropping the disc through the hoop. Purists pleaded for the NBA to ditch the dunk, but the league declined. However, college basketball officials weren't so reticent. In 1967, they introduced legislation forbidding the flush that became known as the Lew Alcindor Rule. Alcindor, the 7'2" star of the UCLA Bruins, went on to NBA fame as Kareem Abul-Jabbar. The rule was dropped in 1976.

The dunk as an art form was perfected by Julius "Dr. J" Erving, who used flamboyant moves and powerful slams to become the NBA's most electrifying entertainer in the 1970s. Gus Johnson (Baltimore Bullets, Phoenix Suns) and Darryl "Chocolate Thunder" Dawkins (Philadelphia 76ers, New Jersey Nets), added new panache to the plunge by ripping the rim from the backboard and shattering the glass. Dawkins memorably named one move "The Chocolate-Thunder-Flying, Robinzine-Crying, Teeth-Shaking, Glass-Breaking, Rump-Roasting, Bun-Toasting, Wham-Bam, Glass-Breaker-I-Am-Jam."

And new breakthroughs in dunking continue. Candace Parker became the first female to flush, dipping the ball in a NCAA tournament game, while in 2002, her 6'5" teammate on the Los Angeles Sparks, Lisa Leslie, became the first woman in the WNBA to do the dunk.

The Times They Are A-Changin'

1962

- Sam Walton takes discount retailing to a new level when he opens the first Wal-Mart store in Rogers, Arkansas.

- The United States launches the *Ranger 3* space probe to study the moon. Unfortunately, it misses the moon by 22,000 miles. A few months later, *Ranger 4* crashes into the moon.

- The first nuclear-powered passenger cargo ship, the NS *Savannah*, is launched to showcase Dwight D. Eisenhower's Atoms for Peace project.

- *The Tonight Show* on NBC changes hands after Jack Paar hosts his last episode in March. A young comedian named Johnny Carson takes over.

- The U.S. government bans Cuban imports and exports.

- President John F. Kennedy is honored at a birthday celebration at Madison Square Garden in New York on May 19. Marilyn Monroe sings her infamous rendition of "Happy Birthday."

- Bombs explode aboard Continental Airlines Flight 11, causing it to crash.

- African American James H. Meredith is barred from the University of Mississippi. He is later allowed to register, albeit escorted by federal marshals.

- The Beatles fire their first drummer, Pete Best, and replace him with Ringo Starr.

- Anxious to win the "Space Race," President Kennedy says the United States will send a man to the moon (and bring him home) by the end of the decade.

- *Mercury 6* astronaut John Glenn Jr. becomes the first American to orbit the Earth.

- Golfer Jack Nicklaus wins the U.S. Open at age 22.

Food Fight!

❖ ❖ ❖ ❖

Sure, parties are fun, but add in massive amounts of food and a reason to throw it around, and you've got yourself an international festival! The following are some of the world's craziest food-related events.

Hunterville Huntaway Festival, Hunterville, New Zealand: The highlight of this annual October event is the Shepherd's Shemozzle, a grueling endurance and obstacle race, in which shepherds and their dogs run through a course that includes a variety of culinary challenges, such as swallowing raw eggs or downing a delicious bowl of sheep's eye mixed with cream. The winnings include a monetary prize and a supply of dog food.

La Tomatina, Buñol, Spain: On the last Wednesday in August, thousands of people descend on this sleepy little village for the world's most impressive tomato fight. Nearly 140 tons of juicy red tomatoes are trucked in from the countryside. The trucks dump off the tomatoes, the people fasten their goggles, and then the fun begins. A word of advice: Don't wear your best clothes for this one.

Ivrea Carnival and Orange Battle, Ivrea, Italy: This is just like Spain's La Tomatina, only with oranges instead of tomatoes. It occurs 40 days before Lent, and it typically involves thousands of orange-hurling celebrants. Don't forget to duck—oranges can hurt!

West Virginia RoadKill Cook-Off, Marlinton, West Virginia: This festival, which typically occurs in September, is exactly as its name suggests. One can try delicious dishes such as Thumper Meets Bumper, Asleep at the Wheel Squeal, and Tire Tread Tortillas. Bottom line: If a critter's been smacked by a vehicle, it's as good as covered with gravy. Bon appétit!

Festival Gastronomico del Gato, La Quebrada, Peru:
In this small Peruvian village, every September 21 cats go from favorite pets to delicious main dishes as part of this bizarre celebration (the name translates to "Gastronomic Festival of the Cat"). Celebrants sauté Mr. Whiskers to commemorate the village's original settlers, slaves who at one time were forced to live on cat meat.

Olive Oil Wrestling Competition, Edirne, Turkey: For centuries, hundreds of burly Turks have donned trousers made of water buffalo hide, slathered themselves with slippery olive oil, and wrestled each other. These contests occur throughout the country, but the most famous tournament takes place in the town of Edirne. The winner receives a cash prize and the right to call himself "Champion of Turkey."

Night of the Radishes, Oaxaca, Mexico: This event, which takes place every December 23, is more of an art show than anything else as participants carve huge, gnarly radishes into elaborate scenes and figures. Ever wonder what the Virgin Mary would look like if carved into a radish? Here's your chance to find out.

Lopburi Monkey Festival, Lopburi, Thailand: This place is literally overrun with macaques, which in turn attract a lot of tourists. To show their appreciation, the locals host a party for the monkeys in November at the Prang Sam Yot temple. Thousands of pounds of food are presented to the pampered primates, including fruit, boiled eggs, cucumbers, and even soft drinks to wash it all down. Entrance to the festival costs 30 baht (approximately 90 cents). The ticket price includes a bamboo stick to ward off the more aggressive simians.

Demon-Chasing Ritual, Japan: Some Japanese are a bit superstitious, so every February 3, as winter gives way to spring, they chase away the evil from the previous year through a ritual known as *setsubun*. The ceremony involves shouting "Out with the demons, in with good luck!" while tossing roasted soybeans out the front door or at a family member wearing an Oni demon mask. Participants are also supposed to eat a soybean for every year they've been alive, plus one extra for the coming year.

Fast Facts

- *Pluto is approximately one-third the size of our Moon. After much debate, in 2006, the International Astronomical Union downgraded Pluto from planet to dwarf planet.*

- *Helen Keller was the first blind and deaf person to receive a college degree. She graduated from Radcliffe College with honors in 1904.*

- *Hot dogs were one of Helen Keller's favorite foods.*

- *Most penguins mate for life. So do bald eagles.*

- *Don't freak out, but there are an estimated 1,510 active volcanoes around the world. Nearly 80 are located under the Earth's oceans.*

- *Molten rock goes by two names: magma and lava. It's magma when still under the earth, and lava when it comes spewing out of a volcano. Either way, don't touch it.*

- *Adolf Hitler was a passionate nonsmoker who instituted numerous smoking cessation campaigns during his years as Germany's leader.*

- *Sharks don't have a mean bone in their bodies. That's because their skeletons are made up entirely of cartilage.*

- *The swell shark, a native of New Zealand, barks like a dog. It's unknown if it chases catfish.*

- *Over the years, a variety of bizarre items have been found inside sharks, including a bottle of wine, a suit of armor, and a torpedo.*

The Road of Death

❖ ❖ ❖ ❖

You're packed on an ancient bus, fog obscuring the mountainous road. The hairpin turns and the bus fishtailing on the muddy road make you queasy. Through the windshield, you see a coffee truck coming toward you. As the vehicles inch past each other, the bus's tires slip in the mud, and it goes careening down the mountain. Not exactly how you imagined your summer vacation.

A Dangerous Drive

Each year, hundreds of people die on Bolivia's Yungas road, earning it the title of "most dangerous highway in the world." Built in the 1930s, it runs between La Paz and Coroico, and is the main connection between coffee plantations in the highlands and a third of the country. It starts in La Paz, at an altitude of 11,900 feet. The road winds its way through the Andes mountains where it reaches a peak of 16,500 feet, then drops 15,000 feet to the tropical rainforest lowlands.

If It Ain't Broke, Don't Pave It

The 43-mile drive takes 4 hours, on average; that is, if there are no heavy rains and mist or mudslides and accidents blocking the road. With soaring cliffs on one side, steep drops on the other, blind turns, and no guardrails to speak of, this road is not for the faint of heart. For most of its length, the one-lane, two-way road is only ten feet across. Alongside the road are makeshift memorials of crosses and flowers.

In 2006, a Yungas bypass was opened. The Bolivian government and foreign investors financed this wide, paved highway for the purpose of opening up trade in the region. The $500 million, 20-year project was touted as a life-saving alternative for commercial trucks and tourist buses. However, Bolivian drivers have rejected it so far because the new route is considerably longer.

The deadly Yungas road is now one of Bolivia's most popular tourist attractions. It is especially popular with mountain bikers who enjoy the nearly 40-mile-long stretch of continuous downhill riding and challenge each other to see how fast they can go. Meanwhile, locals report hearing the tourists' screams as they plunge over the cliff.

The Guy Who Killed the Guy Who Killed Abraham Lincoln

❖ ❖ ❖ ❖

What's it take to bring down an assassin? Sharp-shooting skills and a story of your own.

The Mad Hatter

You might figure that a guy who takes down a presidential assassin is a stand-up sort of fellow. But according to legend, Thomas "Boston" Corbett, the man who shot Lincoln's assassin, John Wilkes Booth, was a few bullets shy of a full round.

Born in London in 1832, Thomas Corbett moved with his parents to Troy, New York, in 1839. As a young man, he became a hat maker and was exposed to the dangerous chemicals involved, included mercurious nitrate, which was used in curing felt. Long-term exposure would more than likely turn him into a certified "mad" hatter. After losing his first wife and child during childbirth, Corbett turned to the bottle. Later, however, he turned to Jesus Christ and moved to Boston. It was here that he rechristened himself as "Boston."

Described as a religious fanatic, an account from a Massachusetts hospital states that Corbett cut off his own testes after reading from the Bible the book of Matthew chapters 18 and 19 (which discuss removing offending body parts) and being approached by prostitutes on the city streets. After removing his offending body part, he apparently attended church and ate dinner at home before calling the doctor.

A Bullet for Booth

In 1861, Corbett enlisted as a private in Company I, 12th New York Militia. After several years in service, he found himself with a group on the hunt for the infamous assassin John Wilkes Booth. And though the cavalry was instructed to bring Booth in alive, it's generally accepted that Corbett shot him while Booth was surrounded in a burning barn. Given the chaos, the distance, and the smoke, it's surprising that the bullet even hit Booth.

Fifteen Minutes of Fame

Corbett wasn't punished for shooting Booth. In fact, he received a share of the reward money, totaling $1,653.85. For a short period of time, Corbett was considered a hero and even signed autographs for his fans.

Afterward, Corbett moved around for a few years and eventually settled in Concordia, Kansas, where, in 1887, he was elected as the assistant doorkeeper to the Kansas House of Representatives. He lived as a bit of a hermit, but he preached at the Methodist Episcopal Church and became known as something of a loudmouth evangelist. People still came from other towns to see the famed gunman who took down Booth. Then one day in the winter of 1887, Corbett threatened to shoot people over an argument on the floor of the House of Representatives. He was quickly arrested, determined to be unstable, and booked for a permanent vacation to a psych hospital.

Loose Ends

That wasn't the last America would hear from Boston Corbett. He escaped from the hospital on his second attempt in May 1888, stole a pony that was tied up in front of the hospital, and high-tailed it out of there. He reappeared one week later in Neodesha, Kansas, and was said to have later headed to Mexico.

Corbett seemed to have disappeared, though sightings were reported far and wide. As with everything surrounding the Lincoln assassination, there are plenty of conspiracy theories regarding Corbett: There are some who say that Corbett wasn't the one who shot Booth. Others say that it was not actually Booth who Corbett shot, and that Corbett later traveled to Enid, Kansas, to meet a man claiming to be Booth.

What is known about Corbett is that before he disappeared, he made a dugout home near Concordia, Kansas. Today, a stone marker between two trees in the middle of a pasture stands as a monument to the guy who killed the guy who killed the 16th president of the United States.

FROM THE VAULTS OF HISTORY

All in the Family

The Karni Mata temple in Deshnok, India is a place where rats are
worshiped, fed sumptuous meals, and pampered in every possible way.
Why would the humans in this place devote themselves to an animal
that is despised in nearly every other place in the world? It all began
with a woman named Karni Mata, who in the 14th century was known
for her good works and devotion to the poor. When Karni Mata's son
drowned, she used her powers as the incarnation of a goddess to bring
him back to life. She also decreed that no other members of her family
would ever die; instead, her loved ones would return in the form of
rats. That is why the human descendants of Karni Mata (now called
the Goddess Karni) take such good care of their rodent "relatives" at
the temple.

Medical Mystery as Myth

Sudden Unexplained Nocturnal Death Syndrome (SUNDS) is a disease that seems to target young, healthy people of Japanese and Southeast Asian descent. What scientists can't figure out is why 99 percent
of those people are men and 80 percent of them are between the ages
of 22 and 45. SUNDS kills these men in their sleep by way of massive,
sudden heart attacks, leaving the victims dead on their backs with a
look of horror on their faces. This frightening way of death has been
reported to affect young males in the Philippines since at least 1917,
and Filipinos have even developed a myth to explain these random
tragedies: They say the *bangungot* is a fat man who sneaks into bedrooms by the dark of night and sits on the heads of the unlucky ones.

Bon Appétit!

After Italy's battle of Marengo in 1800, when Napoleon's army
defeated the Austro-Hungarian army, the victorious leader was hungry.
The cook combined chicken, tomatoes, eggs, crawfish, and an onion,
and voila—chicken Marengo was born. Napoleon gave the dish its
name and thought it lucky—so much so that he refused even one
ingredient be altered at all whenever he ate it.

I Vant to Transfer Your Blood!

❖ ❖ ❖ ❖

Basically, a blood transfusion is the process of transferring blood from one person to another, and it's a life-saving procedure that is performed about every two seconds somewhere in the world. More than 4.5 million patients need blood transfusions each year in the United States and Canada. That's a lot of red stuff. Read on for some interesting facts about blood and the history of transfusions.

- One of the earliest recorded blood transfusions took place in the 1490s. Pope Innocent VIII suffered a massive stroke and his physician advised a blood transfusion. Unfortunately, the methods used were crude and unsuccessful; the Pope died within the year and so did the three young boys whose blood was used. But good effort!

- Women receive more blood than men: 53 percent of all transfusions go to women, while 47 percent to men.

- Richard Lower, an Oxford physician in the mid-1600s, performed blood transfusions between dogs and eventually between a dog and a human. The dog was kept alive via the transfusion, and the experiment was considered a success. Several years later, however, cross-species transfusions would be deemed unsafe.

- Donating blood seems to appeal to folks with a sense of civic duty: 94 percent of blood donors are registered voters.

- In 73 countries, many of which are undeveloped and have a great need for blood, donation rates are less than 1 percent.

- One unit of blood can be separated into several components: red blood cells, plasma, platelets, and cryoprecipitate, which is a substance helpful in the clotting process.

- If you're older than 17 and weigh at least 110 pounds, you may donate a pint of blood (the most common amount of donation) about every two months in the United States and Canada.

- If only 1 additional percent of Americans would donate blood, shortages would disappear.

- In 1818, British obstetrician James Blundell performed the first successful transfusion of human blood. His patient, a woman suffering postpartum hemorrhaging, was given a syringe-full of her husband's blood. The woman lived and Blundell became a pioneer in the study of blood transfusions.

- About one in seven people entering a hospital need blood.

- More than 85 million units of blood donations are collected globally every year. About 35 percent of these are donated in developing and transitional countries, which makes up about 75 percent of the world's population.

- Those with type O blood are considered "universal donors," which means their blood can be cross-matched with all blood types successfully.

- Only 38 percent of the U.S. population is eligible to donate blood and less than 10 percent actually do on an annual basis. There are 43,000 pints of blood used each day in the United States and Canada.

- Thirteen tests (11 of which test for infectious diseases) are performed on every unit of donated blood.

- In 1916, scientists introduced a citrate-glucose solution that allowed blood to be stored for several days. Due to this discovery, the first "blood depot" was established during World War I in Britain.

- If you need a blood transfusion, try not to need one in the summer or around the holidays. Shortages of all blood types happen during these times.

- The first screening test to detect the probable presence of HIV was licensed and implemented by blood banks in the United States in 1985. Since then, only two people have contracted HIV from a blood transfusion.

INSPIRATION STATION

A Risky Romance

Things were a little different in the 1970s: People snorted cocaine with little fear of becoming addicted, hitchhikers jumped into cars without fear of being murdered, and grown men dated teenage girls seemingly without fear of going to prison. In fact, sometimes those grown men even wrote hit songs about their jailbait lovers. That's exactly what Doug Fieger, the singer/guitarist of The Knack, did after falling hard for 16-year-old Sharona Alperin. "My Sharona" was released as a single in June 1979; it went all the way to the top of the Billboard Hot 100 and stayed there for six weeks. Sharona herself graced the cover of the single, braless in an almost-transparent undershirt. The song became popular once again in 1994 when it was used in the hip grunge film *Reality Bites.*

More Than Just a Cookbook

In hindsight, it's easy to say that Lizzie Black Kander, born May 28, 1858, would be inspired to become a pioneer in social work. Not only was she born into a liberal-minded, Reform Jewish-German family, but she was also born in Milwaukee, Wisconsin—a city that would soon become known for its progressive values and openness to new ideas.

By the time Kander graduated with top honors from Milwaukee East Side High School, she was already deeply involved in the movement to help European immigrants assimilate in the United States. She became president of the Milwaukee Jewish Mission and founded the first "settlement house" in Milwaukee, aptly named The Settlement. Watching the poor immigrant women who frequented The Settlement struggle to make ends meet, Kander realized that with better shopping habits, kitchen organization, and food storage, the women could economize and save more money. The book she wrote in 1901 to aid women in the kitchen, *The Settlement Cook Book: The Way to a Man's Heart* (generally known today as *The Settlement Cookbook*), is now recognized as more than just a collection of recipes. It is a historical document and a culinary work of art, and to date it has sold over two million copies.

Literary Superstar/Murderer

❖ ❖ ❖ ❖

Norman Mailer is widely held to be one of the 20th century's greatest (and most controversial) writers. But it was his involvement with criminal Jack Henry Abbott that wound up being one of the more contentious episodes of his career.

Author/Prisoner

Born on a U.S. Army base in Michigan in 1944 to a soldier and an Asian prostitute, Jack Henry Abbott bounced around foster homes as a young child. He became a regular attendee of juvenile detention centers, until finally entering a reformatory at age 16. Five years later, while in prison, he stabbed a fellow inmate to death. In 1971, he escaped lock-up and robbed a bank in Colorado. Abbott was recaptured and had additional years added on to his sentence.

In 1977, Abbott heard that famed author Norman Mailer was working on a book called *The Executioner's Song.* The plot was about convict Gary Gilmore, who was scheduled to be executed—the first example of capital punishment to occur in the United States in years.

Abbott began writing to Mailer, offering to help the writer understand the mind-set of a convict. In particular, Abbott—who had been in jail his entire adult life (save nine and a half months)—offered an insight into the mind of the "state-reared" long-term convict. "The model we emulate is a fanatically defiant and alienated individual," Abbott wrote, "who cannot imagine what forgiveness is, or mercy or tolerance, because he has no experience of such values."

Mailer, who admitted that he knew little about prison violence, began corresponding with Abbott. As the men communicated, Mailer realized that the convict was a powerful and entirely self-taught writer.

The Beast on Broadway

The Executioner's Song won the 1980 Pulitzer Prize for fiction. Mailer continued to correspond with Abbott. In June 1980, Mailer's friend Robert Silvers, editor of *The New York Review of Books,* published some of Abbott's letters. The missives created a sensation, and publisher Random House offered Abbott a $12,500 advance for a book. Titled *In the Belly of the Beast,* the book was to be published in the summer of 1981.

As the countdown to the book's release continued, a surprising thing happened: Its author came up for parole in late spring 1981. Despite Abbott's own admission that "I cannot imagine how I can be happy in American society," and even though he had spent virtually his entire adult life locked up, Abbott was indeed paroled. It's possible the parole board was influenced by a letter from Mailer offering Abbott a job as a research assistant at $150 per week. On June 5, Abbott flew to New York City where he met Mailer and moved into a halfway house.

"Exceptional Man"

In early July, *In the Belly of the Beast* was published to overwhelming acclaim. *The New York Times Book Review* found Abbott "an exceptional man." The convict had become a celebrity.

This lasted about three weeks. Little did anyone know that Abbott was rapidly spinning out of control. He hated the city, and he got increasingly paranoid. Even something as basic as buying toothpaste sent him into a panic. Mailer tried to get Abbott to hang on until August, when he could accompany the family to Maine. But it was not to be.

Early on the morning of July 18, Abbott went to a small café, where he argued with a 22-year-old waiter named Richard Adan. Abbott stabbed Adan to death with the knife that he had bought almost as soon as he had been paroled.

The next day, the Sunday *Times* unwittingly ran a glowing review of *In the Belly of the Beast.*

Afterword

Abbott fled the city, but he was eventually caught and brought back to stand trial for murder. The trial was stormy, with the press demonizing Mailer for his part in getting Abbott released, in particular Mailer's initial claim that "Culture is worth a little risk."

The jury didn't agree and convicted Abbott of manslaughter. In February 2002, Abbott hung himself in his prison cell.

Unusual Art Projects

❖ ❖ ❖ ❖

Artists are often known to "push the envelope." Whether they use paint, clay, or toy blocks, the art world wouldn't be the same if all those wacky artists didn't make some really wild art.

Ronnie Nicolino's Breasts

For a guy who claims he's not obsessed with female breasts, Ronnie Nicolino sure spent a lot of artistic energy on them. In March 1994, this California-based artist created a two-mile long sand sculpture of 21,000 size 34C breasts at Stinson Beach, near San Francisco. He also planned to string enough donated brassieres together to reach across the Grand Canyon, but despite collecting more than enough bras, Nicolino simply lost interest in the project.

Konzentrationslager

Polish artist Zbigniew Libera was known in Europe for his controversial video art in the 1980s, but in 1996, he gained notoriety on a larger scale when he created a concentration camp out of LEGO blocks. Libera often uses children's toys in his work to illustrate the ways kids learn about human suffering. Libera's LEGO set includes pieces such as gallows, inmates, and corpses.

The Wee World of Willard Wigan

You can't see the artwork of British artist Willard Wigan unless you happen to have a microscope handy. Wigan carves sculptures out of grains of sand, rice, or sugar, and paints them with hairs plucked from a housefly's back. Wigan has trained himself to work "between heartbeats," since working at that scale makes a trembling hand a disaster waiting to happen. Most of Wigan's sculptures fit on the head of a pin, but that doesn't mean they carry a small price tag. Much of his work is valued around $300,000 or more.

Marcel Duchamp's *Fountain*

No report on strange art projects would be complete without a nod to Marcel Duchamp's famous *Fountain*. In 1917, this famous French Dadaist placed a porcelain urinal on a pedestal, signed it, and called it art. Most people thought it was a total disgrace and denounced Duchamp's work. But the artist had a method to his madness: It was one of the first times "conceptual art" had come on the radar. He took a regular, nonart object and gave it artistic status. "I don't believe in art. I believe in artists," Duchamp said. This notion was outrageous, sure, but it caused a wave of change in the way people view art and the objects around them that still resonates.

Tracey Emin's Bed

In 1998, British artist Tracey Emin let the world in on a very private part of her life when she exhibited *My Bed,* an exact replica of, you guessed it, her bed. Emin took great pains to show her unmade bed exactly as it usually was, replete with rumpled, stained sheets, dirty clothes at the foot, prophylactic wrappers and liquor bottles strewn about, and dingy slippers nearby. The artwork offended many, especially one lady who reportedly came to the gallery with a bucket of cleaning materials, hoping to tidy up the work of art.

Damien Hirst's Shark(s)

In 1991, British art collector and gallery owner Charles Saatchi offered to fund whatever project Damien Hirst wanted to make. So Hirst had a 14-foot-long tiger shark caught and killed off the coast of Australia. He then had it shipped to London, where it sat floating in a giant tank filled with formaldehyde as the conceptual art piece, *The Physical Impossibility of Death in the Mind of Someone Living.*

But the shark wasn't preserved properly, and it eventually began to rot from the inside and the liquid grew murky. Attempts to fix the problem failed (including stretching the shark's skin over a fiberglass model), until in 2006, a billionaire funded a rehab that was rumored to have cost more than $100,000. This entailed catching, killing, and shipping another shark and injecting it with formaldehyde. But is it Art? And is it Art if the original art rotted and had to be replaced? Critics continue to debate the point.

The Tyler Tragedy

❖ ❖ ❖ ❖

John Tyler was sometimes called the "accidental" president since he only became America's Chief Executive because of the death of President William Henry Harrison. But once in office, Tyler was almost the victim of another accident that would have removed him from the presidency—and this world.

Technical Marvel

On February 28, 1844, U.S. President Tyler and a few hundred government officials, dignitaries, and invited guests—including Dolley Madison, widow of President James Madison—had gathered on board the warship USS *Princeton*. The ship was scheduled to take a leisurely journey up the Potomac River.

The *Princeton* was the pride of the U.S. Navy. It was one of the most technologically advanced ships in the world, a steam-powered frigate propelled by a screw propeller instead of a paddle wheel. Its engines were silent and smokeless, using high-grade anthracite coal for fuel. It carried many heavy-duty cannons and two massive guns named "Peacemaker" and "Oregon." The Peacemaker was the largest gun ever forged from wrought iron. It was able to fire a 212-pound projectile more than three miles, obliterating any target of metal and wood. Nothing could stand in its way.

Fateful Request

In the early afternoon of February 28, the Navy put the ship through its paces for the important people in attendance, including demonstrations of the Peacemaker's awesome firepower.

Later in the day, someone noticed that they were sailing past Mount Vernon. They asked for a final firing of the Peacemaker in honor of George Washington. *Princeton* Captain Robert Stockton refused, saying "No more guns tonight." However, Secretary of the Navy Thomas Gilmer, who was on board, overruled Stockton and asked that the gun be fired.

Everyone who had been down below partying raced up to the deck to see the impressive gun at work again. Meanwhile, Tyler, who had been below deck about to offer a toast, lingered there a moment longer to hear a song sung by his son-in-law William Waller. It was a decision that saved his life.

Carnage

The crowd watched from the deck as the Peacemaker's ease of movement was demonstrated. Senator Thomas Hart Benton moved to the right to get a better view and opened his mouth to try to protect his ears from the roar of the gun. He saw the gun's hammer pull back, heard a tap, and then saw a flash. A moment later he was lying on the deck, unconscious.

The Peacemaker had exploded with terrifying force, sending jagged pieces of iron hurtling into the assembled crowd. When Benton woke up he saw "two seamen, blood oozing from their ears and nostrils, rising and reeling." Captain Stockton, with his hat blown off and his face blackened by powder, was "staring fixedly upon the shattered gun."

"My God!" Stockton screamed. "Would that I were dead, too."

The deck was like a scene out of a slaughterhouse. Blood and body parts were strewn everywhere. Among the dead were David Gardiner, father of the woman Tyler was wooing, with his arms and legs blown off; Navy Secretary Gilmer, with a gaping head wound; Secretary of State Abel Upshur, his stomach torn open; retired diplomat Virgil Maxey; two seaman, a commodore, and Tyler's black slave, Henry. Others wandered around, dazed and bleeding.

Divine Retribution?

The explosion was seen by many anti-slavery advocates as divine retribution, for the deaths of Gilmer and Upshur eliminated two of the strongest advocates for annexing pro-slavery Texas into the Union.

The tragedy was unprecedented in American government at the time, but it was not Tyler's last brush with death. Several days later, returning from the burial services, Tyler's carriage horses inexplicably bolted, sending his coach careening at breakneck speed through the streets of Washington. Just when all seemed lost, an African American man stepped out and stopped the horses, saving the president's life.

ﾟ Behind the Films of Our Time

- The blood in *Psycho*'s famous shower scene is actually chocolate syrup.

- Big-budget films were nonexistent when *The Three Stooges* films were in their heyday. In the mid-1950s, a typical Stooges movie cost $16,000 to make, including salaries for all three stars.

- The 1997 movie *Titanic* was longer (3 hours 14 minutes) than the sinking of the actual RMS *Titanic* (2 hours 40 minutes).

- If Dustin Hoffman were a woman...well, who knows? But he did wear a size 36C bra for the part of Dorothy in *Tootsie*.

- No sounds of music in Seoul, Korea. One movie theater manager there thought *The Sound of Music* was too long, so he cut out all of the songs.

- The 2009 movie *Taking Woodstock* points out that a ticket to the famous Woodstock Music and Art Fair cost just $8. Today it costs at least that much just to see the film about the festival.

- During the rape scene in the X-rated movie, *A Clockwork Orange,* actor Malcolm McDowell sang the unlikely tune, "Singin' in the Rain"—just because he happened to know the lyrics.

- The badge number assigned to the character Dirty Harry in, well, *Dirty Harry,* is 2211. The role was offered to Frank Sinatra, John Wayne, and Paul Newman before Clint Eastwood accepted the offer in 1971.

- Bill Murray was bitten twice by his groundhog costar while filming *Groundhog Day.*

- Approximately 30 movies have been made about—or at—the Alcatraz prison in San Francisco Bay.

- *Midnight Cowboy*, which was considered pretty shocking in 1969, was the first and only X-rated movie to win an Oscar for Best Picture.

- Do you have the time? In the movie *Ben-Hur*, several of the chariot racers are shown wearing watches.

Say What?

"Right now I have enough money to last me the rest of my life—unless I buy something."

—Jackie Mason

"Money won't buy happiness, but it will pay the salaries of a large research staff to study the problem."

—Bill Vaughan

"He is so aware of being politically correct, he refers to a taco as Hispanic food."

—Wendy Morgan

"When I was a boy, I was told that anybody could become president. I'm beginning to believe it."

—Clarence Darrow

"Too bad all the people who know how to run the country are busy driving taxicabs and cutting hair."

—George Burns

"By working faithfully eight hours a day, you may eventually get to be a boss and work 12 hours a day."

—Robert Frost

"I don't like the fact that doctors are referred to as practicing."

—Janet Schwartz

"A male gynecologist is like an auto mechanic who has never owned a car."

—Carrie P. Snow

"My ancestors wandered lost in the wilderness for 40 years because, even in biblical times, men would not stop to ask for directions."

—Elayne Boosler

"I generally avoid temptation, unless I can't resist it."

—Mae West

"I wanted to become an atheist, but I gave it up. They have no holidays."

—Henny Youngman

"A joke is a very serious thing."

—Winston Churchill

Champagne and the Widow Clicquot

❖ ❖ ❖ ❖

*Raise a glass of bubbly to the woman who defied odds
to become the grande dame of champagne.* Santé!

Wining Widow

No one would have blamed Barbe-Nicole Ponsardin
Clicquot if she'd decided to quit the wine business.
She was, after all, only 27 years old and newly widowed
with a toddler. The wine business her husband had left
behind was failing miserably, and it was 1804—the well-
heeled women of France were not expected to be seen
outside of the nursery or the drawing room, much less
run a business. Clicquot convinced her father-in-law to
keep the wine business going. He agreed as long as she
worked with a partner of his choosing: Alexandre Jérôme
Fourneaux. Together they launched the company Veuve
Clicquot Fourneaux (*veuve* is French for "widow").

Though the business started to make a name for itself among a
small roster of Russian clients, Clicquot couldn't seem to outdo her
competition, Jean-Rémy Moët, whose champagne had the distinction
of being General Napoleon Bonaparte's personal favorite as well as a
popular choice among Russia's royals. Not that this last point mattered
for long: In 1806, Napoleon restricted trade with Russia and other
foreign markets, making it difficult for Clicquot to get a foothold
overseas.

In 1810, Fourneaux walked away from the struggling company,
leaving Clicquot on her own. The business experienced another
blow in 1812: France invaded Russia, who, quite naturally, began
boycotting French champagne. Still, Clicquot refused to give up.

Race to Russia

The following year proved pivotal for the widow. The harvest of
1811 had been a good one, and her bottled champagne was coming of
age just as the war between France and Russia was resolving.

The end of the war meant the end of the embargo was on its way—and Clicquot knew whoever arrived first on the Russian shore with a boatload of French champagne would have a major advantage. To beat the competition, she secretly commissioned a ship to leave before the ban was officially lifted; by the time Moët and others shipped their first load, Clicquot had a strong head start. The demand for her champagne was so great, her salesman in Russia sold out before he even left his hotel room.

La Grand Dame

The widow's second boost came in 1815 with her invention of *remuage sur pupitre,* or "moving by desk," as a better way to remove the debris from the fermenting champagne bottles. The previous process involved laying a bottle on its side and waiting for the sediment to collect, which took several months—a long time spent not making sales.

While her competitors, including Moët, searched for a more efficient process, Clicquot moved her desk into the wine cellar and asked for it to be riddled with slanted holes so the bottles could be stored upside down. Her vision cut the time down to six weeks; a mechanized version of this same process is still used today.

The widow Clicquot continued to build and expand her business, renamed Veuve Cliquot Ponsardin, until her death in 1866. It wouldn't be until 1996, however, that another woman would serve at the company's helm.

Did You Know...?

- *Until the mid-18th century, people considered bubbles a sign that the wine had gone bad—they actually called it "devil's wine."*

- *Even in France, champagne was just called "sparkling wine" until the 1860s.*

- *Early champagne was ten times sweeter than today's demi sec (half dry) and eaten frozen, like a slushie, for dessert.*

Critical Cruelty!

❖ ❖ ❖ ❖

When these film critics speak their minds, the results can be painful!

Paul Blart: Mall Cop: "Looks like something stubbed out in an ashtray."
—Wesley Morris, *The Boston Globe*

Miss March: "A sex comedy that appears to have been made by people who've never actually had sex."
—Ty Burr, *The Boston Globe*

The Women: "It's not every movie that makes you wish Vin Diesel would run in and start blowing stuff up."
—Rene Rodriguez, *The Miami Herald*

Saw V: "It's not a good sign when watching someone stick their hand into a table saw is easier than listening to them recite dialogue."
—Sam Adams, *Los Angeles Times*

College: "[This] film hasn't been made so much as excreted."
—Wesley Morris, *The Boston Globe*

Disaster Movie: "This carpet-fouling mongrel of a movie no more deserves release than do anthrax spores."
—Jim Ridley, *LA Weekly*

Star Wars: The Clone Wars: "A continuation of Lucas' experiments to see how much s°°t his dwindling supporters will take before finally saying 'enough' and moving on to adult pursuits."
— Peter Vonder Haar, *Film Threat*

College Road Trip: "Phi betta crappa."
—David Hiltbrand, *The Philadelphia Inquirer*

The Love Guru: "The most joy-draining 88 minutes I've ever spent outside a hospital waiting room."
—Dana Stevens, *Slate*

Deception: "A nonprescription alternative to Ambien."
—Lou Lumenick, *The New York Post*

HOW IT ALL BEGAN

When in Rome

Next time you enjoy a slice from a six-tiered mocha wedding cake with raspberry-almond icing, give a quick thank-you to the ancient Romans who started the tradition. Granted, their "wedding cake" was more of a barley loaf broken over the wife's head for luck. When the Romans invaded England in A.D. 43, they brought along this tradition, effectively laying the foundation for wedding cakes to come.

Pie in the Sky

In medieval England, guests stacked spiced buns in front of the bride for luck; if she and the groom could reach over them to kiss, it foretold a prosperous (and fertile) future.

The 17th century saw the rise of the "bride's pie"—an elaborately decorated pastry filled with a concoction of lamb testicles, oysters, cow innards, and spices. Other variations included the more palatable "matrimony pie" filled with dried fruit, and the "bride's cake," made of currants sandwiched between short bread and baked over a fire.

With the availability of sugar and home ovens in the 18th century, more contemporary-looking cakes began to emerge. But refined sugar was still pricey—a bride who had a cake with white icing clearly came from money. For everyone else, a simple plum cake or brandied fruitcake, which had a longer shelf life, was the wedding cake du jour. The brandied fruitcake followed the pilgrims to Plymouth Rock and remained a custom in America until 1840, when Queen Victoria and Prince Albert changed the face of wedding cakes on both sides of the Atlantic.

Tiers of a Crown

Covered in white icing, hence known as "royal icing," Vicky and Al's multi-tiered masterpiece set the precedent for generations of towering cakes. No matter that bakers hadn't yet figured out how to stack cakes—they just made the bottom layer actual cake, while the rest was just layers of icing.

Prince Leopold's 1882 wedding cake was the first to feature stacked cakes, a look achieved by allowing the icing in between each layer to harden. It wasn't until the 20th century that bakers employed the modern practice of using wooden pillars to support each tier. With refined sugar now a staple, the tiered cake became a wedding must-have for most of the 20th century.

Chile Essentials

❖ ❖ ❖ ❖

Like it hot? Read on for some chile facts and terms.

Capsaicin: This is the chemical that makes some chiles hot. In humans, it stimulates a pain response release of endorphin, which is the closest thing to morphine that is produced in the body. It also excites the trigeminal nerve that leads to an increased receptivity to the flavor of foods. Pure extracts have been known to help patients suffering from rheumatoid arthritis and multiple sclerosis as well as amputees and those undergoing chemotherapy.

Bhut Jolokia: This Indian pepper translates to "ghost chile." In 2007, researchers at the Chile Pepper Institute at the New Mexico State University declared this to be the hottest known chile.

Dorset Naga: Some chile fans argue this is the hottest pepper. Simply inhaling the vapors of this pepper makes the nose tingle, and touching it is painful (cooks must wear gloves when handling it). Dorset Naga is the only food product that Tesco, Britain's leading supermarket chain, will not sell to children.

Habanero Peppers: These are the hottest of the commonly consumed chiles in the United States.

Homo Sapiens: We're the only mammals that voluntarily eat chiles.

"Pink Fix": This is the habit of snorting a mixture of cocaine and chile powder. Ow.

Scoville Scale: This test was developed in 1912 by chemist Wilbur Scoville, to measure the heat of chiles. The scale is based on the dilution of the chile in sugar syrup to the point that the capsaicin is no longer noticeable to the taster. Measurements are in Scoville Heat Units (SHU). Here's how some chiles and peppers measure up:

- Pure capsaicin—15 or 16 million units
- Pepper spray used by police—2 million units
- Bhut Jolokia chile—more than 1 million units
- Dorset Naga chile—outcomes vary from 960,00 to 1.6 million units
- Habanero pepper—577,000 units (for the hottest variety)
- Jalapeño pepper—2,500 to 8,000 units

MYTH CONCEPTIONS

Myth: Twins skip a generation—if your grandmother had twins, so will you.
Fact: While twins can run in families, the whole "skip a generation" thing isn't true. Identical twins result from one fertilized egg randomly splitting, creating two siblings with identical DNA. But there is no known gene that influences this process, so it's really just a rare coincidence when a big family has more than one set of twins.

Myth: The chupacabra lives!
Fact: Sorry, folks, but there is simply no such animal known in Spanish as the *chupacabra*, or "goat sucker." This ferocious little animal, found in the American southwest, is a figment of over-active imaginations. While we're at it, there's no such thing as a jackalope, either.

Myth: Eating carrots will keep you from going blind.
Fact: While carrots contain a lot of Vitamin A, which is good for eyes, skin, teeth, and bones, eating carrots isn't going to keep you from needing glasses. This rumor came about during World War II and has stuck around ever since.

Myth: Eating turkey makes you sleepy.
Fact: Not quite. It's been proven that turkey, chicken, and minced beef contain nearly equivalent amounts of tryptophan, the chemical that gets blamed for the sleep-inducing factor of turkey. Other common sources of protein (like cheese, for example) contain more tryptophan per gram than turkey does.

Myth: Cracking your knuckles causes arthritis.
Fact: It's an annoying habit, but cracking your knuckles won't cause arthritis, which is more commonly caused by heredity, joint injury, obesity, or lack of exercise.

Myth: Coca-Cola is an effective contraceptive.
Fact: Please, do not try this at home—it won't work. Scientists studied the spermicidal properties of Coke in 1985, but their slim findings were refuted years later by another scientific team in Taiwan. Our question is, who decided to try this in the first place?

FLUBBED HEADLINES

"Plenty Do Do Here for Local 'Tourists'"
Sounds like a place to avoid, frankly.

"No Benefits for Ill Man: Agency Says Terminal Illness Not Severe Enough"
After all, terminal illness is the new life-threatening disease.

"Cemetery Residents Making a Comeback"
And thus began the Great Zombie War.

"Funeral Homes Bring Cheer to Senior Citizens"
Just wait until they find out what's going on at the graveyards.

"Teen Learns to Live With Stutttering"
C'mon—that third "t" in "stutttering" was really just twisting the knife.

"Most Doctors Agree That Breathing Regularly Is Good for You"
Shyeah. Like we're going to believe that kind of med school nonsense.

"Ex-Minister Breaks Silence, Says Nothing"
You should hear what happened when he ended his fast.

"Superintendent: If We Don't Change, We'll Remain the Same"
Speechwriting courtesy of George W. Bush.

"Texans Support Death Penalty, But Only for the Guilty"
Whew. That's a relief for us innocent citizens.

"Police Arrest Everyone on February 22"
Welcome to the annual city roundup!

"Health Officials Say Flammable Water Is OK to Drink"
If you don't mind spontaneously combusting, that is.

"Bladder Control Causes Sunset Beach Flooding"
Oh, stop judging. When you gotta go, you gotta go.

Carved in Stone: 11 Memorable Epitaphs

❖ ❖ ❖ ❖

They might be six feet under, but a good epitaph means they'll never be forgotten. Here are some of our favorite gravestone inscriptions.

1. Mel Blanc: "That's all folks!"
Arguably the world's most famous voice actor, Mel Blanc's characters included Bugs Bunny, Porky Pig, Yosemite Sam, and Sylvester the Cat. When Blanc died in 1989 at age 81, his epitaph was his best-known cartoon line.

2. Spike Milligan: *"Dúirt mé leat go raibh mé breoite."*
The Gaelic epitaph for this Irish comedian translates as, "I told you I was ill." Milligan, who died of liver failure in 2002 at age 83, was famous for his irreverent humor showcased on TV and in films such as *Monty Python's Life of Brian.*

3. Joan Hackett: "Go away—I'm asleep."
The actor, who was a regular on TV throughout the 1960s and '70s, appearing on shows such as *The Twilight Zone* and *Bonanza,* died in 1983 of ovarian cancer at age 49. Her epitaph was copied from the note she hung on her dressing room door when she didn't want to be disturbed.

4. Rodney Dangerfield: "There goes the neighborhood."
This comedian and actor died in 2004 from complications following heart surgery at age 82. Dangerfield, master of self-deprecating one-liners, has an epitaph that's entirely fitting.

5. Ludolph van Ceulen: "3.14159265358979323846264338327950288 ... "
The life's work of van Ceulen, who died in 1610 at age 70, was to calculate the value of the mathematical constant pi (π) to 35 digits. He was so proud of this achievement that he asked that the number be engraved on his tombstone.

6. George Johnson: "Here lies George Johnson, hanged by mistake 1882. He was right, we was wrong, but we strung him up and now he's gone."
Johnson bought a stolen horse in good faith but the court didn't buy his story and sentenced him to hang. His final rest ing place is Boot Hill Cemetery, which is also "home" to many notorious characters of the Wild West, including Billy Clanton and the McLaury brothers, who died in the infamous gunfight at the O.K. Corral.

7. John Yeast: "Here lies Johnny Yeast. Pardon me for not rising."
History hasn't recorded the date or cause of John Yeast's death, or even his profession. We can only hope that he was a baker.

8. Lester Moore: "Here lies Lester Moore. Four slugs from a 44, no Les, no more."
The date of birth of this Wells Fargo agent is not recorded, but the cause of his death in 1880 couldn't be clearer.

9. Jack Lemmon: "Jack Lemmon in..."
The star of *Some Like It Hot, The Odd Couple,* and *Grumpy Old Men* died of bladder cancer in 2001 at age 76. Lemmon's epitaph reads like a marquee right above his resting place.

10. Hank Williams: "I'll never get out of this world alive."
The gravestone of the legendary country singer, who died of a heart attack in 1953 at age 29, is inscribed with several of his song titles, of which this is the most apt.

11. Dee Dee Ramone: "OK...I gotta go now."
The bassist from the punk rock band The Ramones died of a drug overdose in 2002, at age 49. His epitaph is a reference to one of the group's hits, "Let's Go."

Behind the Music of Our Time

- Cartoonist R. Crumb only agreed to do the cover art for Big Brother & the Holding Company's album, *Cheap Thrills,* if he could pinch lead singer Janis Joplin's breast. Joplin held up her end of the deal.

- Bow Wow Wow, known best for their hit cover of "I Want Candy," was the first major band to release an album (*Your Cassette Pet,* 1980) on cassette but not on vinyl.

- The Beatles' 1967 hit "Strawberry Fields Forever" not only broke new ground musically, but also promotionally. The cover of the EP featured a unique picture, and a short film was made to accompany the song— one of the first "music videos."

- The Spice Girls' massive 1996 hit "Wannabe" was recorded in just 20 minutes. Zigazig-ah, indeed.

- The angelic organ solo in Procol Harum's 1967 slow-dance favorite, "A Whiter Shade of Pale," was inspired by Percy Sledge's "When a Man Loves a Woman."

- "Tie a Yellow Ribbon" by Tony Orlando and Dawn is the second-most covered song in pop history, following The Beatles' "Yesterday."

- The title of Buddy Holly's song "That'll Be the Day" was taken from a line spoken by John Wayne in the western film *The Searchers.*

- The first British group to top the U.S. chart was The Tornados, with their 1962 hit "Telstar."

- When Norman Greenbaum failed to chart another hit after his smash, "Spirit in the Sky," he retired from music and went into the dairy business.

- Phil Spector wrote The Teddy Bears' hit "To Know Him is to Love Him" after being inspired by the inscription on his father's tombstone.

- Freddie Mercury, lead singer of Queen and the otherworldly voice behind such iconic hits as "Bohemian Rhapsody" and "Somebody to Love," announced to the press that he had AIDS just one day before he died of the disease in 1991.

Greed Is Good

❖ ❖ ❖ ❖

For decades, the origins of the popular board game
Monopoly were hidden behind a myth propagated by
the toy company Parker Brothers. But the real story
reflects a dark truth about American business.

The goal of Monopoly is for players to get rich through
the ruthless acquisition of property at the expense of
the other players. Any player can acquire property and
win—no matter their station in life—as long as they
play shrewdly with cutthroat tactics. Small wonder
Monopoly became popular during the Great Depression and has remained so popular—it encapsulates the
American Dream.

Darrow's Our Hero

The Parker Brothers version of the origin of Monopoly is a tale of
one man's ingenuity and determination, with a self-deprecating poke
at themselves to make it seem plausible. As the legend goes, Charles
Darrow was an unemployed salesman in Germantown, Pennsylvania,
who was struggling to make ends meet during the Depression.
Thinking back to better days when he and his family spent summers
in Atlantic City, Darrow began drawing the streets of the East Coast
fun capital on the kitchen tablecloth. Then he added or built tiny
hotels and houses, eventually turning the set-up into a miniature
Atlantic City. Visiting friends and family gathered around the makeshift game board to buy, rent, and sell real estate with play money.

Darrow began making and selling the games for a few dollars
each, offering them to local department stores in Philadelphia. He
was so encouraged that he attempted to sell his brainchild to Parker
Brothers, one of America's premier game manufacturers. But they
turned him down claiming the game had "52 fundamental gaming
errors," including everything from overly complicated rules and a
dull central concept to an unusually long playing time.

Undaunted, Darrow produced 5,000 copies and began selling
them to FAO Schwartz and other toy stores. Eventually, one fell into

the hands of Sally Barton, the daughter of George Parker, founder of Parker Brothers. Parker Brothers bought the game from Darrow, giving him royalties on all games sold, and Darrow retired as a millionaire. The end.

Go Straight to Jail; Do Not Collect $200

In 1974, economics professor Ralph Anspach invented a game called Anti-Monopoly, which prompted the General Mills Fun Group, which then owned Parker Brothers, to sue for infringement of its trademark name "Monopoly." Anspach fought back, resulting in a ten-year court battle in which the real story of Monopoly was revealed.

The origins of the game go all the way back to 1904, when a Quaker woman named Elizabeth Magie-Phillips developed and patented The Landlord's Game to illustrate political economist Henry George's tax principles. George called for a single tax based on land ownership, because he felt it would encourage equal economic opportunities and discourage land speculation. Despite any similarities between Monopoly and The Landlord's Game, the goal of the latter was to criticize land acquisition—not celebrate it—by illustrating that landowners have all the financial advantages in our society.

As years passed, the game's popularity spread, with the rules evolving and the name changing from The Landlord's Game to such variations as Finance, Auction Monopoly, and finally Monopoly. At least eight different people or groups were associated with a Monopoly-type game, including a hotel manager named Charles Todd, who may have introduced it to Darrow.

Truth and Fables

The Parker Brothers' version is more of an all-American, pull-your-self-up-by-the-bootstraps story—but it's not the whole truth. Darrow may have added the chance cards and the railroads, but he did not invent the original game concept. In fact, after Parker Brothers bought Darrow's version of the game, they quietly settled with the inventors of the other versions of the game to protect their investment. Parker Brothers began to spread their revised origins story, which was so accepted that in 1970 Atlantic City erected a plaque near the corner of Park Place in Darrow's honor.

Fast Facts

- *Looking for meteorites? Check out Antarctica—it's one of the best places in the world to find fallen space debris.*

- *It has not rained in the dry valleys region of Antarctica in at least two million years. As a result, the region's climate is very much like that of Mars.*

- *The only insect found in Antarctica is the* Belgica antarctica, *a wingless insect that measures just a half-inch long.*

- *The deepest spot on Earth is the Mariana Trench, located in the Pacific Ocean. It is 36,201 feet deep.*

- *Measuring over two feet tall, four feet long, and weighing an average of 100 pounds, the South American capybara is the largest rodent in the world.*

- *Capybaras love the water and can remain submerged for up to five minutes.*

- *I'll be a monkey's uncle! Chimpanzees and humans are remarkably alike, sharing a DNA similarity of about 98.4 percent.*

- *Wolverines may look like small bears, but they're actually the largest species of weasel.*

- *Edward G. Robinson (known for his roles in gangster flicks in the 1930s and '40s) was originally slated to play Dr. Zaius in the movie* Planet of the Apes. *He bowed out, however, and the role then went to Maurice Evans.*

- *Before he became famous as the director of such films as* National Lampoon's Animal House *and* The Blues Brothers, *John Landis had a bit part in* Battle for the Planet of the Apes.

7 Outrageous Hollywood Publicity Stunts

❖ ❖ ❖ ❖

The movie industry isn't exactly shy about self-promotion. After all, the Academy Awards began in 1928 simply to generate press coverage for the movies and stars of the day. Here are some of the wildest feats in the long history of movie publicity.

1. *Gone With the Wind* (1939): The search for the actress to play Scarlett O'Hara in the screen version of Margaret Mitchell's novel created much hoopla as the casting director traveled the country holding open auditions. After three years of interviews and auditions with stars such as Katherine Hepburn, Paulette Goddard, and Lana Turner, the role went to Vivien Leigh, who had appeared in a few films, but remained largely unknown outside of Great Britain. Frankly, the public didn't seem to give a damn, and *Gone With the Wind* became the highest grossing film in movie history (adjusted for inflation). Its original release and seven rereleases over the years have raked in nearly $2.7 billion in today's figures.

2. *Down Missouri Way* (1946): This musical features an agriculture professor who secures a movie role for her trained mule, Shirley. To promote the film, a studio publicity man led Shirley, with an ad for the movie on her back, down Fifth Avenue in New York City, and into the restaurant overlooking Rockefeller Plaza's ice rink. Managers naturally refused to seat the animal. The press showed up to record the event, so it accomplished the publicist's mission…but it didn't appear to do much for the movie, which was not a box office smash.

3. *Teacher's Pet* (1958): Clark Gable and Doris Day star in this comedy about a newspaper editor. For publicity purposes, Paramount filmed 50 Hollywood newsmen sitting at desks and gave a few of them lines in the film. What better way to get reporters to focus on your movie than to put them in it? The buzz may have worked; the *New York Times* placed *Teacher's Pet* in its top ten of 1958, and the movie received two Oscar nominations.

4. *Mr. Sardonicus* (1961): Colombia Pictures executives told director William Castle to film an alternate, happy ending for this dark movie. Castle turned the episode into a publicity opportunity, giving audience members thumbs-up and thumbs-down cards to "vote" for the main character's fate. Castle apparently understood human nature well—there are no accounts of audiences wanting a happy ending.

5. *The Blair Witch Project* (1999): Producers intimated that this thriller's documentary style was authentic and implied that the footage making up the entire movie had been discovered after three student filmmakers searching for the so-called "Blair Witch" disappeared in the woods of rural Maryland. They even listed the film's lead actors (the supposed filmmakers) as "missing, presumed dead" on the Internet Movie Database before the movie's release. The stunt seemed to work: The movie made the *Guinness Book of World Records* for the highest box-office-proceeds-to-budget ratio in film history. It cost only around $35,000 to make but pulled in more than $140 million in the United States and more than $248 million worldwide.

6. *Office Space* (1999): The corporate "cube farm" is the target of both this cult classic—which follows coworkers who rebel against their less-than-rewarding work environment—as well as its publicity stunt. For a week, the studio had a man sit inside a Plexiglas work cubicle on top of an office building overlooking Times Square. Everyone from Howard Stern to nearby office workers expressed sympathy. The publicity helped promote the film, which ranked number 65 on Bravo's 2006 list of the 100 funniest movies of all time.

7. Borat (2006): As the title character, British actor Sacha Baron Cohen played Borat, a misspeaking journalist from Kazakhstan. In 2006, Secret Service officers prevented Cohen (dressed as Borat) from entering the White House where he hoped to invite "Premier George Walter Bush" to a screening of the film. His antics even prompted the Kazakh government to remind audiences that the obnoxious character does not properly represent the country's values. Whether due to Cohen's shenanigans, generally positive reviews, or word-of-mouth, the film made more than $248 million worldwide.

Leave It to Beavers

❖ ❖ ❖ ❖

They toil 365 days a year. If you knock down their
work, they rebuild in a matter of hours. They use just
about everything they can find to forge their structures.
Read on to learn more about these mad builders.

- Beavers are the largest rodents in the world after the South American capybara.

- Beavers can stay submerged in water for up to 15 minutes. Using their webbed feet for speed and their flat tail as a rudder, they can swim as fast as five mph.

- Overtrapping in the early part of the 19th century led beavers to near extinction. Today, these large rodents number 6 to 12 million in the United States—a remarkable comeback.

- Beavers construct dams in order to deepen shallow waterways. This in turn creates ponds, which is where beavers like to build their lodges.

- Their instinct is to stop the movement of water, which is fine for the beavers but an unnatural state of affairs for a stream. Their obsessive focus is a potentially disastrous one in streams that function as part of a community's storm water drainage system.

- Beavers are seriously resourceful. Though the majority of dams are made of mud and sticks, beaver dams have been found made of cornstalks, leaves, soybean plants, sand, and gravel. There are even tales of dams built within city limits  containing fence posts, lawn furniture, and hobbyhorses—even animal carcasses!

- One trapper found a dam made entirely of footwear. A shoe store had closed and the company apparently felt it would be a great idea to dump the leftover shoes into a nearby stream. Though this was clearly a bad idea, the beavers used the shoes to build their dam, which remained stable for years.

If You See Only Five...

War Movies

❖ ❖ ❖ ❖

Of the hundreds of war movies, here are five
classics that should top everyone's list.

1. *Glory* (1989): The Civil War has been the backdrop for many films, but *Glory* is unique for its focus on the 54th Regiment of Massachusetts Volunteer Infantry, an all-black regiment commanded by Colonel Robert Gould Shaw, who was white. The 54th was an experiment that everyone expected to fail, but it proved to be a formidable fighting force.

2. *All Quiet on the Western Front* (1930): Very few films can be classified as both a war movie and an anti-war movie. Based on the novel by Erich Remarque, *All Quiet on the Western Front* shows World War I from the perspective of Paul Bäumer, a German youth who enlists because he doesn't want to miss the spectacle of war. However, disillusionment, followed by sheer terror, sets in when Bäumer is sent to the front lines.

3. *Saving Private Ryan* (1998): On its surface, Steven Spielberg's *Saving Private Ryan* is a basic World War II-era rescue flick that follows a group of soldiers on a mission to locate and retrieve Private James Ryan (played by Matt Damon). This isn't your typical rah-rah war flick—it's noted for its stark realism, in particular the opening sequence, which shows the bloody mayhem of the D-Day landing.

4. *The Steel Helmet* (1951): This movie tells the story of a small band of American soldiers who set up an artillery observation post in a Buddhist temple as they await the enemy during the Korean War. Driven by character much more than action, like *M*A*S*H*, which is also set in Korea, *The Steel Helmet* offers far more than mindless jingoism.

5. *Platoon* (1986): In this Oliver Stone classic, Chris Taylor (Charlie Sheen, in a role that mirrors Stone's own Vietnam experiences), enlists in a war others are fleeing the United States to avoid. *Platoon* excels at showing the many horrors of war, especially the so-called "fog of battle," in which nothing is as it seems. *Platoon* can be a difficult movie to watch, but it perfectly captures the essence of Vietnam.

Fast Facts

- The finish between Johnny Beauchamp and Lee Petty at the first Daytona 500 on February 22, 1959, was so close that the winner was not announced until 61 hours after the race.

- Baby bats are known as pups.

- Some species of bats can live more than 30 years.

- A brown bat can eat up to 1,000 mosquitoes in a single hour.

- The smallest mammal in the world is the bumblebee bat, which is found in Thailand. It weighs only as much as a dime.

- What do Patti Davis, Farrah Fawcett, and Madonna have in common? They all appeared nude in Playboy magazine.

- Jazz trumpeter Miles Davis was the subject of Playboy magazine's first Playboy Interview. The interviewer was Alex Haley, author of Roots.

- It takes 50 tons of paint to cover the Eiffel Tower. The job is performed every seven years.

- What do Karl Marx, Marilyn Monroe, Shirley Temple, and Oscar Wilde have in common? They're just four of the many notable personalities featured on the cover of The Beatles' Sgt. Pepper's Lonely Hearts Club Band album.

- Abraham Lincoln was related by marriage to Paul Revere.

- To reach 50 million users, it took the radio 38 years, the television 13 years, and the Internet a mere 4 years. Facebook reached that many in 9 months.

A National Shame: Canada's Concentration Camps

❖ ❖ ❖ ❖

The American internment of thousands of Japanese Americans during World War II is common knowledge. But not as many people know that Canada also rounded up and imprisoned its own citizens.

Enemy Aliens

National concentration camps in Canada started with World War I; key to the establishment of these concentration (later called "internment") camps was the War Measures Act, passed on August 22, 1914. This law gave the Canadian government the authority to do whatever it deemed necessary "for the security, defense, peace, order and welfare of Canada," with little accountability to Parliament.

One of the Canadian government's first orders under the War Measures Act was the registration and, in some cases, the internment of aliens of "enemy nationality." This affected a lot of Canadians, including more than 80,000 people who had immigrated from the Austrian-Hungarian empire. All had to register as "enemy aliens" and report regularly to local authorities.

During World War I, 24 internment camps were constructed throughout Canada, eight of them in British Columbia. They were supposed to contain only individuals who ignored regulations or posed a security threat, but many Canadians were interred for reasons ranging from "acting in a very suspicious manner" to simply being poor and unemployed. Between 1914 and 1920, more than 8,500 Canadians were shipped to internment camps. Approximately 5,000 of these people were of Ukrainian descent. Of the total people in the camps, only 2,321 were actual prisoners of war; the rest were civilians.

Later, during World War II, the "enemy aliens" were defined as "all persons of German or Italian racial origin who have become naturalized British subjects since September 1, 1922."

All told, approximately 30,000 Canadians were affected by the order, which required them to register with the Royal Canadian Mounted Police and report back monthly. And in New Brunswick, more than 700 Jews who had fled the Holocaust in Europe were also interred in Canada—at the request of British Prime Minister Winston Churchill, who suspected that spies had infiltrated the group.

Life in the Camps

Living in an internment camp was a nightmare. Upon their arrest, the internees' private property, businesses, and personal possessions were taken by the government and sold. Inside the camps, the internees' correspondence was censored, and mistreatment by guards was common. Those who were able-bodied were forced to work maintaining the camps, on railway and road construction, or for private companies. This source of free labor proved so helpful and profitable for Canadian corporations that the internment program continued for two years after the war's end.

Following the bombing of Pearl Harbor on December 7, 1941, the Canadian government issued an order authorizing the removal of "enemy aliens" within a 100-mile radius of the British Columbian coast. Twenty-two thousand Japanese Canadians were given just one day to pack before being sent to internment camps. Women, children, and the elderly were sent to certain camps, while able-bodied men were sent to road construction camps. Those who complained or broke minor rules were sent to prisoner of war camps in Ontario. Conditions were notoriously poor in the camps. "I was in that camp for four years," remembered internee Hideo Kukubo. "When it got cold the temperature went down to as much as 60 below... We lived in huts with no insulation... I had to lie in bed with everything on that I had."

Picking Up the Pieces

At the end of the war, the government extended an Order in Council to force Japanese Canadians to either move to Japan and give up their Canadian citizenship or move to eastern Canada. In fact, it was illegal for Japanese Canadians to return to Vancouver until 1949.

It took the government nearly four decades to acknowledge the thousands of citizens who had been imprisoned under the War Measures Act. In 1988, an official apology was extended and the government admitted that many of its actions had been provoked by racial discrimination. A redress agreement provided $21,000 each to those affected, although it hardly compensated for the gross mistreatment they experienced.

Fast Facts

- John Lennon received his first guitar from his Aunt Mimi. But she warned him against a career in music, saying, "The guitar's all right as a hobby, but it won't earn you any money."

- The song "Lucy in the Sky with Diamonds" was inspired by comments made by John Lennon's 4-year-old son, Julian, regarding a painting he brought home from school.

- John F. Kennedy won a Pulitzer Prize in 1957 for his book, Profiles in Courage.

- In 1965, Richard Nixon was offered a position as a player's representative to the Major League Baseball Players Association. He declined, preferring instead to pursue his political career.

- In 1915, Woodrow Wilson became the first president to attend a World Series baseball game. He attended with his fiancée, Edith Gault, and insisted on paying for their tickets rather than getting in for free.

- Before stepping out onto the moon, Apollo 11 lunar module pilot Edwin "Buzz" Aldrin took Holy Communion using a small kit prepared by his pastor. In addition to a communion wafer, the kit included a tiny container of wine.

- The Apollo 11 astronauts left behind several mementos when they departed the moon, including a patch from the Apollo 1 mission, medals honoring Soviet cosmonauts Vladimir Komarov and Yuri Gagarin, goodwill messages from 73 world leaders, and a small gold pin shaped like an olive branch.

- At the time of the first moon landing, some scientists worried that the lunar surface was covered with a layer of dust thick enough to engulf anything that landed on it. Luckily, the dust proved to be just a few inches deep.

The Mystery of the Concrete Ship

❖ ❖ ❖ ❖

*That's right—a concrete ship. What, you've
never seen a floating cinder block?*

Are You Dense?

A floating cinder block seemingly goes against all logic, but that
didn't stop a Norwegian named N. K. Fougner from launching the
first oceangoing concrete ship on August 2, 1917, an 84-foot-long
boat named *Namsenfjord.* See, apparently if a piece of concrete
shaped like a ship contains enough air, its density will be less than the
water it displaces, allowing it to float. When it didn't sink like, well, a
concrete block, governments around the world took notice.

With steel in short supply because of World War I, the U.S.
government decided to build a fleet of 38 concrete ships, though in
the end, only 12 were built. Sailors took to calling the ships "floating
tombstones." Mercifully, before the United States had moved on to
ships made out of newspaper, the war had ended and steel was again
available.

S.S. *Atlantus*

One notable concrete ship was the S.S. *Atlantus,* which weighed
2,500 tons and was 250 feet long. It was launched on December 5,
1918, at Brunswick, Georgia, and it operated as a coal steamer in
New England. At war's end, however, the *Atlantus* was sent to
Norfolk, Virginia, to rot—or flake—away.

Enter Colonel Jesse Rosenfeld, who wanted to start a ferry service
between Cape May, New Jersey, and Cape Henlopen, Delaware. He
thought that the *Atlantus* would be great as part of a ferry dock, so he
towed the ship to Cape May in 1926 and moored it there.

Bad idea. On June 8, a storm hit and broke the ship free. It
drifted 150 feet and lodged into the sandy bottom off Sunset Beach.
It remains there to this day, a curious tourist attraction. It was
even used as a billboard space during the 1950s, advertising boat
insurance. Alas, the *Atlantus* continues to sink into the sand a little
more each year; today it's barely visible above the surface.

WORD HISTORIES

Fib: This word originated during the 15th century, and it was associated with the word *fable,* which could mean both an interesting story and a lie. A couple hundred years later, a small lie became commonly known as a "fibble-fable." The word eventually was shortened to fib—and that's no lie.

Lady: This term originally meant a woman who makes bread.

Idiot: The Greek word *idiotes* simply meant a private person or a common man. It later evolved into the Old French term *idiote,* meaning someone who was uneducated or ignorant person.

Manure: This word has taken on increased meaning over the years. In the 1300s, the French word *manouvrer* meant to work by hand, especially in terms of cultivating the soil. Nowadays we add a little "natural fertilizer" when we cultivate the soil: manure.

Umpire: This term derives from the 14th-century Middle English word *noumpere.* It evolved over the years to *oumpere* and finally to *nonper,* where the word breaks down into two parts: *non* for "not" and *per* for "equal." In short, the word meant "not an equal." It was used to describe the third man called in to settle disagreements. Interestingly, that is why there are an uneven number of umpires in sports—so someone always has the deciding vote.

Polka Dot: Back in the 1830s, a new dance from Bohemia was all the rage. Named the *polka,* or "Polish woman," people rushed to combine the name with everyday items. When a new fabric came out in the United States that featured round, evenly spaced dots, it was dubbed the polka dot. Connecting the fabric with the fad worked, and the name stuck.

Syllabus: This word actually originates from a printing error. In his *Ad Atticum,* the Roman philosopher Cicero had used the Greek word *sittubas* to refer to an index. In a 15th-century edition of Cicero's work, a printer mistakenly wrote "syllabos" instead. Over the years, the *o* changed to a *u,* and the word was accepted and adopted to mean not just an index, but also a list of subjects in a series of lectures.

Honeymoon: This word was first used to describe the love of a newly married couple—sweet as honey, but apt to wane like the moon sometime in the future. Sad but true.

A Pain in the Brain

❖ ❖ ❖ ❖

Neurologist and psychiatrist Walter Freeman believed that lobotomy was a cure-all for a wide variety of mental illnesses, and he wasn't afraid to dole them out. In fact, over a period of more than three decades, he scrambled the frontal lobes of more than 3,400 patients—sometimes with disastrous results.

Monkey Business

Walter Freeman became interested in the curative properties of lobotomy after attending a conference in which a colleague discussed how chimpanzees that suffered damage to their frontal lobes became docile and inactive. Freeman became particularly intrigued when Portuguese neurologist Egas Moniz started performing a procedure that replicated the frontal lobe damage found in the chimps on human patients with psychiatric illnesses.

Working with neurosurgeon James Watts at George Washington University Hospital, Freeman developed a technique that used an instrument called a *leucotome* to scramble the frontal lobes of the brain. In 1936, he performed his first lobotomy on a Kansas woman who was suffering from agitated depression. By all accounts, the procedure was successful in alleviating the woman's condition.

Honing His Craft

Initially, Freeman and Watts cored the frontal lobes through six holes drilled into the top of the skull. Later, the doctors replaced the leucotome with a device that resembled a butter knife, and they moved the entry holes from the top of the skull to the sides. Freeman eventually developed a procedure called transorbital lobotomy that allowed him to quickly and easily reach a patient's brain by driving an icepicklike device through the bone at the back of the eye socket.

Freeman was convinced that lobotomy was a quick and simple answer to a wide range of mental illnesses. He performed the procedure on patients young and old suffering from depression, manic depression, schizophrenia, obsessive-compulsive disorder, and a variety of undiagnosed conditions. Over the course of his career, he demonstrated the procedure at more than 55 hospitals in 23 states. More than a few of Freeman's colleagues questioned lobotomy's effectiveness, and many became incensed by his publicity mongering.

Not All's Well that Ends Well

Freeman touted lobotomy as effective in the majority of cases, but there was often a damaging downside to the procedure. Three percent of his patients died, and a large percentage of those who survived saw their emotions, inhibitions, and personalities subjugated. It wasn't uncommon for lobotomy patients to forget how to perform basic life functions such as dressing themselves and using the toilet; many would simply stare at the wall for hours. This suited officials at some mental institutions just fine—a gentle, dazed patient was certainly preferable to an aggressive one. One of the more famous of Freeman's patients—John F. Kennedy's sister Rosemary—was among the unfortunate. After she received a lobotomy for her mood swings, she became an invalid and needed full-time care for the next 64 years.

By the mid-1950s, tranquilizers had come into vogue as the treatment of choice for many of the psychiatric disorders for which Freeman was performing lobotomies. He moved to California and continued to perform lobotomies in his office and at state hospitals. He became known for his sense of showmanship. His records show that he lobotomized 3,439 patients during his career.

Leaving Lobotomy Behind

Freeman's practice came to an end in 1967 when he killed a patient by accidentally severing a blood vessel in her brain. His surgical privileges were revoked by the hospital where the procedure had been done, and Freeman performed no more lobotomies during the remaining five years of his life.

Today, lobotomy is pretty much a thing of the past. In the United States, fewer than 20 brain surgeries are performed annually for the treatment of psychiatric illness, with psychotherapy and drug therapy today's treatments of choice. However, researchers are investigating a futuristic approach to Freeman's work: an implantable device that uses electrodes to stimulate parts of the brain to help control conditions such as obsessive-compulsive disorder and Parkinson's disease. Any way you look at it, it's better than an ice pick through the eye.

Odd Ordinances

- Eating peanuts is forbidden in Boston churches.

- In Harper Woods, Michigan, it's illegal to sell sparrows painted as parakeets.

- You cannot cross the Minnesota state line with a duck on top of your head.

- In St. Cloud, Minnesota, it is illegal to eat a hamburger on Sunday.

- Don't even think about parking your elephant on Main Street in Virginia, Minnesota.

- In Tylertown, Mississippi, it is illegal to shave in the middle of Main Street.

- Disturbing a church service in Mississippi may result in a citizen's arrest.

- A milkman cannot run while on the job in St. Louis.

- Minors in Kansas City, Missouri, better have their own matches— it's legal for them to buy papers and tobacco, but not a lighter.

- It is a felony in Montana if a woman opens her husband's mail.

- Sports must not be big in Excelsior Springs, Montana—it is illegal to throw a ball within the city limits.

- In Montana, it is against the law for a sheep to ride in the cab of a truck without a chaperone.

- Mothers in Nebraska are prohibited from giving their daughters a perm without a state license.

- Doughnut holes cannot be sold in Lehigh, Nebraska. Now *that's* a crime.

- In Britain, you can receive a fine if anyone other than an electrician changes your lightbulb.

To the Moon!

❖ ❖ ❖ ❖

*Television and film star Jackie Gleason was fascinated
with the paranormal and UFOs. But he had no idea
that an innocent game with an influential friend
would lead him face-to-face with his obsession.*

Jackie Gleason was a star of the highest order. The rotund actor kept
television audiences in stitches with his portrayal of hardheaded but
ultimately lovable family man Ralph Kramden in the 1955 sitcom *The
Honeymooners.* He made history with his regularly aimed, but never
delivered, threats to TV wife Alice, played by Audrey Meadows: "One
of these days Alice, one of these days, pow, right in the kisser," and
"Bang, zoom! To the moon, Alice!"

But many fans didn't know that Gleason was obsessed with the
supernatural, and he owned a massive collection of memorabilia
on the subject. It was so large and impressive that the University
of Miami, Florida, put it on permanent exhibit after his death in
1987. He even had a house built in the shape of a UFO, which he
christened, "The Mothership." The obsession was legendary, and it
climaxed in an unimaginable way.

A High Stakes Game

An avid golfer, Gleason also kept a home close to Inverrary Golf and
Country Club in Lauderhill, Florida. A famous golfing buddy lived
nearby—U.S. President Richard M. Nixon, who had a compound
on nearby Biscayne Bay. The Hollywood star and the controversial
politician shared a love of the links, politics, and much more.

The odyssey began when Gleason and Nixon met for a golf
tournament at Inverrary in February 1973. Late in the day their
conversation turned to a topic close to Gleason's heart—UFOs. To
the funnyman's surprise, the president revealed his own fascination
with the subject, touting a large collection of books that rivaled
Gleason's. They talked shop through the rest of the game, but
Gleason noticed reservation in Nixon's tone, as if the aides and
security within earshot kept the president from speaking his mind.
He would soon learn why.

Later that evening around midnight, an unexpected guest visited the Gleason home. It was Nixon, alone. The customary secret service detail assigned to him was nowhere to be seen. Confused, Gleason asked Nixon the reason for such a late call. He replied only that he had to show Gleason something. They climbed into Nixon's private car and sped off. The drive brought them to Homestead Air Force Base in South Miami-Dade County. Nixon took them to a large, heavily guarded building. Guards parted as the pair headed inside the structure, Gleason following Nixon past labs before arriving at a series of large cases. The cases held wreckage from a downed UFO, Nixon told his friend. Seeing all of this, Gleason had his doubts and imagined himself the target of an elaborated staged hoax.

Leaving the wreckage, the pair entered a chamber holding six (some reports say eight) freezers topped with thick glass. Peering into the hulls, Gleason later said he saw dead bodies—but not of the human variety. The remains were small, almost childlike in stature, but withered in appearance and possessing only three or four digits per hand. They were also severely mangled, as if they had been in a devastating accident.

Returning home, Gleason was giddy. His obsession had come full circle. The enthusiasm changed in the weeks that followed, however, shifting to intense fear and worry. A patriotic American, Gleason couldn't reconcile his government's secrecy about the UFO wreckage. Traumatized, he began drinking heavily and suffered from severe insomnia.

The "Truth" Comes Out

Gleason kept details of his wild night with Nixon under wraps. Unfortunately, his soon-to-be-ex-wife didn't follow his lead. Beverly Gleason spilled the beans in *Esquire* magazine and again in an unpublished memoir on her marriage to Gleason. Supermarket tabloids ate the story up.

Gleason only opened up about his night with Nixon in the last weeks of his life. Speaking to Larry Warren, a former Air Force pilot with his own UFO close encounter, a slightly boozy Gleason let his secret loose with a phrase reminiscent of his *Honeymooners* days: "We've got 'em…Aliens!"

Queen of the Nile

❖ ❖ ❖ ❖

You've got to hand it to Cleopatra: The girl's got some serious staying power. One of the few figures from ancient history to still have a place in the modern cultural landscape, Cleopatra's story continues to fascinate. Here are some quick facts about this legendary queen.

- Born 69 B.C., Cleopatra (actually, she was Cleopatra VII) was the daughter of Ptolemy XII Auletes, the Macedonian king of Egypt. Cleopatra had several brothers and sisters, most notably her brother Ptolemy XIII. When her dad was dying, he bequeathed the throne to Cleopatra, then age 17 or 18, and Ptolemy XIII, age 12.

- It cannot be denied that Cleopatra was an exceptional young woman. She was extremely intelligent in the ways of business and politics and seriously ambitious to boot. She didn't take being ruler lightly and quickly went to work making sure everyone knew just who was in charge.

- Interestingly, one of Egypt's most famous rulers wasn't Egyptian at all—Cleopatra's family was Macedonian Greek in origin.

- Cleo decided early on to win a few points with the locals. Though her family had ruled Egypt for 300 years, they kept the Greek aristocracy firmly in place by speaking and acting Greek. Cleopatra was the first in her family to learn to speak Egyptian. She observed many of the Egyptian religious customs, too, making the Goddess Isis her patron deity.

- Cleopatra could speak nine languages.

- Her brother and his supporters kicked Cleo out of Egypt in 48 B.C., but then they lost Alexandria to Julius Caesar. According to lore, in order to gain access to the palace, the exiled queen had herself rolled into a large Persian rug to be given to Caesar as a gift. When the rug was delivered, she rolled out onto the floor. Caesar was smitten.

- In 47 B.C., Cleopatra had a son with Caesar named Caesarion. With Marc Antony she had fraternal twins named Alexander Helios and Cleopatra Selene, and later, she had another son, Ptolemy Philadelphos.

- After Caesar's death, Marc Antony entered the picture. The two met in 41 B.C. and they made political magic together, among other things. Antony married Cleopatra four years later.

- She lived a pretty lush lifestyle. Cleopatra was said to bathe daily in milk and had dozens of servants attending to her at every hour of the day.

- When things went downhill for Antony and Cleo, they went down fast. In 31 B.C., Antony and his troops defended Egypt against Roman attacks. It wasn't going so well. The following year, Antony mistakenly heard that his beloved was dead, and reportedly he killed himself in response. When Cleo heard what her husband had done, she killed herself.

- Cleo died as a result of poison. The exact story isn't verifiable, however: Some accounts say Cleopatra knowingly allowed an asp (or two) to bite her. Another version claims she poisoned herself the old-fashioned way—straight poison, no snakes needed.

- Cleopatra was the last of the Ptolemy dynasty and the last pharaoh in Egypt. Rome took over after her death on August 30.

- Most modern stories about Cleopatra cast her as a stunning beauty. Some of the world's most beautiful women (i.e. Theda Bara, Elizabeth Taylor) portrayed Cleopatra in well-known movie versions of her story. But was she really all that? It's hard to say, especially since ideals of beauty change over time. But consider that more than 2,000 years later, we're still mad about the girl.

Fumbling Felons

Better to Use OnStar

There must be a lesson here. If you drive a stolen car, don't ask police for roadside assistance. In 2007, Dean Gangl of Richmond, Minnesota, did just that. After the vehicle he stole went into a ditch, he flagged a passerby for help. Unfortunately for Gangl, the motorist passing by just happened to be an off-duty deputy sheriff. The officer recognized the car as one that had been reported stolen in St. Cloud a few hours earlier. Then during the routine arrest for auto theft, the deputy discovered Gangl was also in possession of a white crystal substance—methamphetamine.

This Crime Doesn't Add Up

The would-be robber who walked into a Fairfield, Connecticut, Dunkin' Donuts should have waited for a response from the cashier before acting on his own. The perp handed the clerk a note threatening that he had a bomb and a gun, and that he'd use both if he didn't get money right away. But apparently he got antsy, and without waiting for a reply, he grabbed what he thought was the cash register and ran from the store. Alas, no cash for him—the man took off with an adding machine.

Not For Sale

Have you ever gone to a garage sale and thought to yourself, "Oh, I have one of these I could sell"? Well, that happened to a woman in Severn, Maryland—literally. When she attended a yard sale three doors down from her home, she found almost $25,000 worth of stuff that previously had been stolen from her. She immediately called the police. When they arrived, they arrested David Perticone, who admitted that he had taken the items. His excuse: He needed money to purchase cocaine and heroine with his girlfriend. Oh, and he thought the house was abandoned, and that he may as well clear it out before the stuff was thrown in the dump. See? He was just trying to help!

Overdrawn Check

A Texan named Charles Fuller said he planned to start a record company when he tried to cash a personal check for $360 billion at a Fort Worth Bank. He said his girlfriend's mother had given him the check. She denied it. Guess who police believed?

The Times They Are A-Changin'

1972

- The RMS *Queen Elizabeth,* for many years the largest passenger liner ever built, is destroyed by fire in Hong Kong Harbor.

- Manned by U.S. astronauts Charlie Duke, Ken Mattingly, and John Young, *Apollo 16* lands on the moon.

- Antiwar protests break out in New York City, San Francisco, and Los Angeles in response to increased U.S. bombing in Vietnam.

- Nolan Bushnell and Ted Dabney found Atari Inc., which produces Pong and the Atari 2600. This marks the beginning of the video game generation.

- The Greenpeace Foundation is born after the Canadian environmental group, "The Don't Make a Wave Committee," officially changes its name.

- *The Godfather* hits American theaters and is nominated for 10 Academy Awards. It wins for Best Picture, Best Actor, and Best Screenplay.

- Frederick Smith founds Federal Express at age 27.

- The Watergate Scandal begins when five White House representatives are arrested for burglarizing the Democratic headquarters in Washington, D.C. It is the beginning of the political end for President Richard M. Nixon, who is caught on audiotape plotting to use the CIA to obstruct the FBI investigation and cover up the break-in.

- Hank Aaron becomes the first Major League Baseball player to sign a $200,000 contract.

- American Mark Spitz makes history, winning seven gold medals in swimming at the Summer Olympic Games in Munich, Germany.

- The Munich Massacre turns the Olympic Games into a tragedy. An eight-member Palestinian terrorist group called "Black September" attacks Israeli athletes, killing 11.

The Christmas Truce

❖ ❖ ❖ ❖

In December 1914, a war that everyone had expected would be over by Christmas had settled into a depressing trench warfare stalemate between Allied and German forces. But on Christmas Eve, the realities of war took a backseat to the realities of being human.

A Festive and Brief Affair

In August 1914, World War I broke out in Europe in an atmosphere of almost festival-like celebration. "Bring on the enemy, and we'll make short work of 'em," was the general consensus on both sides. But four months later, hundreds of thousands of men had been killed, wounded, or gone missing. Soldiers were floundering about in fetid trenches filled with putrid water. It was painfully clear that the festival had been canceled.

Pope Benedict XV suggested a Christmas cease-fire, but the idea was rejected as impossible by both sides. The Allied High Command had a better idea to lift the morale of the soldiers rotting in the trenches: an offensive. But it failed, and as Christmas approached, No Man's Land on the Western Front (roughly from the North Sea to the France/Switzerland border) became filled with bloated bodies.

Gifts from Home

Both sides received Christmas gifts from home to lighten their misery. The British received "Princess Mary boxes" containing candy, tobacco, and a picture card of Princess Mary, among other items. German troops received large meerschaum pipes from Kaiser Wilhelm II, while officers got boxes of cigars.

Perhaps it was the gifts that made the men wistful. The two sides began to communicate with each other through the trenches over distances sometimes as close as 30 or 40 yards. A week before Christmas, some Germans smuggled a chocolate cake into the British trenches, with a message that they wanted to have a concert that evening for their captain's birthday and invited the British to attend. That evening the concert was indeed performed, with the British applauding for every song. The Germans asked the English troops to join in on the chorus, but an English killjoy snapped, "We'd rather die than sing German."

"It would kill us if you did," responded a German affably.

Christmas Trees

On December 24, some German troops began placing small trees adorned with candles at the top of their trenches. Christmas trees were unknown in Britain at this time, and English soldiers crawled out of their trenches to ask the Germans about the curious sight. It was not a huge leap from there to an informal truce between both sides. "We all walked out and one of their officers came to meet us," remembered a British artilleryman. "We all saluted, shook hands, and exchanged cigarettes."

The two sides spontaneously came together at various places along the Western Front. Sometimes the gathering was playful, as when Germans and Scots kicked a soccer ball through a muddy field where they would have been shot dead just hours earlier. "Scots and Huns were fraternizing in the most genuine possible manner. Every sort of souvenir was exchanged, addresses given and received, photos of families shown, etc.," wrote a British officer.

Other meetings were grimmer. Sometimes the two sides got together to bury their dead comrades, who had been lying neglected in No Man's Land. Even so, the occasion could turn festive, as one Englishman remembered, "We gave [the Germans] some wooden crosses…which completely won them over, and soon the men were on the best terms and laughing."

The British High Command, toughing out the war in a luxurious château 27 miles behind the front, were horrified to learn about the truce, since they realized how hard it would be to make killers again of men who had become friends. But because so many officers took part in the truce, in the end very few were disciplined.

Eventually, the truce ended, and the two sides resumed shooting at each other—but perhaps with a little more reluctance.

Convict Corral

❖ ❖ ❖ ❖

At the Oklahoma State Penitentiary, hardened criminals—cowboy
convicts—risk life and limb while competing in a prison rodeo.

Spectator's Sport

Hotel rooms are hard to come by the weekend before Labor Day in
McAlester, Oklahoma (population 18,000). Masses of people visit the
town, or more precisely, the maximum-security Oklahoma State
Penitentiary, to watch an odd competition. Since 1940, the curious have
watched and cheered from behind a thick, razor wire–topped chain-
link fence within the prison's walls, as inmates from ten state prisons
compete in classic rodeo events such as steer wrestling and bull riding.

The top crowd-pleasers, though, are the prison's own signature
events. In the Money the Hard Way competition, inmates attempt
to grab a ribbon from between the horns of a 2,000-pound bull for a
prize of $100 (about ten times what they make in a month laboring
behind bars). In another event, four convicts sit around a card table
and wait for the bull to charge them. The last man sitting wins.

Dressed in borrowed Western wear and often lacking real-world
rodeo experience, the inmates compete in teams of ten, and only the
well behaved are eligible. Even so, armed guards stand at the ready in
watchtowers above the arena.

A Dangerous Game

Despite the convicts' checkered pasts, the real danger comes from
the livestock: Injuries range from minor scrapes to ruptured groins
and, yes, the occasional goring. Nevertheless, inmates clamor for the
chance to prove themselves on the back of a bronco. Afterward, they
share a celebratory meal of hamburgers and milkshakes before it's
time to return to their cells.

Oklahoma is said to have modeled its prison rodeo after that of
its neighbor and rival, Texas, which held the nation's first "behind the
walls" rodeo at Huntsville in 1931. A lack of funding forced that rodeo
to close down in 1986, leaving the Okie competition the distinction as
the world's only behind-the-walls prison rodeo.

Fast Facts

- One in eight married American couples currently say they met through online dating.

- The eye of an ostrich is bigger than its brain.

- Bible verse Isaiah 8:1 mentions the longest name you'll find in the entire book—Mahershalalhashbaz, son of Isaiah.

- A butterfly's ability to taste is located in its hind feet.

- Bartolomeo Cristofori of Italy created the first piano, called the fortepiano, in 1709.

- Golfer Jack Nicklaus is nicknamed the "Golden Bear."

- Mariah Carey was nicknamed "Mirage" in high school because she missed so many classes.

- Sloths, armadillos, and opossums are the laziest animals, sleeping 80 percent of the time.

- Charlie Brown's dad was a barber.

- A human body has 60,000 miles of blood vessels. If the vessels were laid end to end, it would be enough to circle the planet 2½ times.

- Animals won't eat another animal that was killed by lightning. Maybe they don't like their meat cooked?

- Chinese restaurant favorite dim sum may derive from the early Chinese custom of cooking bite-size pieces of food because fuel was at a premium and small pieces cooked faster. Also, wealthy Chinese often served as many as 32 different courses at a meal.

Alexander Hamilton: Suicide by Duel?

❖ ❖ ❖ ❖

The duel between Aaron Burr and Alexander Hamilton in Weehawken, New Jersey, is one of the most discussed events in American history. Yet many questions remain unanswered about the affair. Did Hamilton go to the duel determined to die?

The tension and the anger had been building for years. Accusations and insults were flung back and forth between former Secretary of the Treasury Alexander Hamilton and U.S. Vice President Aaron Burr. After Burr's stint with President Thomas Jefferson was finished, he ran for governor of New York in 1804. Hamilton did everything he could to undermine Burr's credibility in the race, and Burr was subsequently defeated. In April, the *Albany Register* published a (originally private) letter, in which it was reported that Hamilton had said some nasty things about Burr. Burr demanded an apology, but Hamilton danced around the matter.

Furious, Burr ultimately challenged Hamilton to a duel on July 11, 1804, which ended Hamilton's life and Burr's political career. Hurt feelings and honor aside, many historians consider the reasons for the duel flimsy at best and have debated for years over Hamilton's exact intentions for participating in it.

Wasted Shot

Some historians feel that Hamilton was depressed and suicidal, and that he goaded Burr so as to force the duel to occur. As writer and historian Henry Adams wrote, "Instead of killing Burr, [Hamilton] invited Burr to kill him." In Ron Chernow's 2004 biography of Hamilton, he cites four psycho-biographers who in 1978 concluded that the duel was a disguised form of suicide by Hamilton.

The reasons given for Hamilton's depression are several: His son Philip was killed in a duel in 1801; he realized that there was no place for him in national politics now that his rival Thomas Jefferson was president; and he had severely weakened the

Federalist political party, which he helped create, by attacking its candidate for president (John Adams) in 1800.

In the book *A Fatal Friendship: Alexander Hamilton and Aaron Burr,* author Arnold Rogow maintains that Hamilton was a manic depressive who was severely depressed over his own physical maladies and the death of George Washington in 1799, and that his deteriorating condition led him to push for the duel.

A reason often cited by "pro-suicidal" historians as proof of Hamilton's queasy mental state is that he decided before the duel to "throw away his fire," or waste his first shot. This is seen by many as an invitation by Hamilton to be killed by Burr.

A Gamble Lost

However, others say the duel was inevitable. They point out that although Hamilton was morally against dueling, he was also bound by 19th century codes of honor. He could not back out once Burr had challenged him. After all, he *did* attack Burr's character.

In a letter to his wife written the night before, Hamilton says that he did not want to fight: "If it had been possible for me to have avoided the interview, my love for you and my precious children would have been alone a decisive motive."

Chernow postulates that Hamilton gambled that Burr would not shoot to kill. Dueling was outlawed in the northern states, and both men knew that Burr would be labeled a murderer and politically destroyed if he killed Hamilton. In another letter written the night before his impending duel, Hamilton said, "I have resolved, if our interview is conducted in the usual manner, and it pleases God to give me the opportunity, to reserve and throw away my first fire, and I have thoughts even of reserving my second fire."

Perhaps Hamilton viewed the duel as nothing more than a dare and counter-dare. He had, after all, taken part in ten previous shotless duels.

Whether Hamilton went into the duel meaning to die or not, his death remains a cold hard fact. Burr's shot hit Hamilton in the abdomen, damaging his ribs and several internal organs. When Burr later heard of what Hamilton had written about wasting his shot, he reportedly responded, "Contemptible, if true."

FLUBBED HEADLINES

"Enraged Cow Injures Farmer with Ax"
Coming to a theater near you!

"Prisoner Serving 2,000-Year Sentence Could Face More Time"
They say that third thousand is the worst one.

"Blind Woman Gets New Kidney from Dad She Hasn't Seen in Years"
Oh, right. Because of the whole blindness thing.

"Panda Mating Fails; Veterinarian Takes Over"
How chivalrous!

"Two Sisters Reunited After 18 Years at Checkout Counter"
Now, *that's* one long checkout line.

"Police Begin Campaign to Run Down Jaywalkers"
Geez, what ever happened to issuing a warning?

"Iraqi Head Seeks Arms"
And legs, too.

"Stolen Painting Found by Tree"
The tree would accept an award for its heroic action, but it had to leaf.

"Red Tape Holds Up New Bridges"
Here's hoping that's some seriously strong adhesive.

"New Study of Obesity Looks for Larger Test Group"
Also, a larger lunch buffet. Those test subjects sure know how to put away the tacos.

Scenes from a Mall

❖ ❖ ❖ ❖

What's more American than baseball? Try shopping malls.
From Main Street to megaplex, and from city to suburb,
Americans have always heeded the call of the mall.

1920s: Starter Strip

The precursor to the modern mall debuted in 1922, courtesy of
J. C. Nichols and his Country Club Plaza in Kansas City. Built near
a residential development on the city's edge, the Plaza was the first
shopping district set away from a downtown area.

As automobile traffic and urban congestion continued to drive
families out of cities and into the suburbs, more shopping centers
popped up. They all followed the same "strip" format: A line of
convenience shops (anchored by a grocery or pharmacy) with a
single parking lot out front.

1930s–'40s: Main Street in a Box

With the decline of urban Main Streets—typically lined with specialty stores such as jewelers, clothiers, and cobblers—came the rise
of the department store, which housed all of these specialties under
one roof.

Meanwhile, shopping centers continued to evolve as surrogate
town squares, offering community activities and entertainment
such as firework displays and live music. In 1949, the Town and
Country Shopping Center in Columbus, Ohio, introduced nighttime
shopping with performances by Grandma Carver—a woman who
dove from a height of 90 feet into a small pool of flaming water.

1950s–'60s: A Mall Is Born

The post-World War II era saw the marriage of department stores
and strip centers (it sounds sexier than it actually was). In 1950,
Northgate in Seattle opened as the first shopping center to have two
parallel rows of stores facing each other with a pedestrian walkway
in between. These walkways were originally called "malls," hence
the name.

The following year, the first two-level shopping center opened in Framingham, Massachusetts. In 1956, an Austrian architect named Victor Gruen fully modernized malls with the opening of the first fully enclosed, two-level, climate-controlled shopping center in Edina, Minnesota—Southdale Center—which ultimately became the blueprint for all modern malls. By 1964, America was home to 7,600 of them.

1970s: Festival Fever and Vertical Velocity

By 1972, there were 13,174 suburban malls. Not to be "malled" by the competition, cities responded with their own take on the suburban staple. In 1976, two new models made the scene: Boston introduced Faneuil Hall Marketplace as the first "festival marketplace" (an historic site rehabbed into a shopping destination), while Water Tower Place in Chicago debuted as the first "vertical mall" (suburban sprawl squeezed into skyscraper form).

1980s–'90s: Malls Get Mega

Between 1980 and 1990, more than 16,000 new shopping centers cropped up from coast to coast. Also on the rise: factory outlet stores and "category killers"—big-box retailers such as Toys "R" Us and Office Depot that specialize in just one thing. The shopping mall took a serious hit in the '90s with the advent of the Home Shopping Network and the Internet. The solution? "Shoppertainment," which transformed shopping into a full-on "experience" with amusement parks, restaurants, movie theaters, miniature golf, and, oh yeah, stores. The first megamall, Mall of America in Bloomington, Minnesota, opened in 1992 and remains the nation's largest mall at 4.2 million square feet.

2000 and Beyond: A Return to Main Street

Today's mall is going back to where it started—only better. The latest trend combines the ambience of old-time Main Street with megamall experiences (restaurants and multiplexes) and strip-mall convenience (parallel layouts and out-front parking). Dubbed "lifestyle centers," the new malls promise to provide something for everyone. Perhaps it is a mall world after all.

Talk to the Expert

TATTOO ARTIST

Q: What got you interested in the tattoo business?
A: Growing up around tattoo parlors—my mom's heavily tattooed, and my uncle was a tattoo artist. So I was always raised around it.

Q: How do you practice?
A: The best practice is just draw, draw, draw. The apprenticeship generally lasts about a year of you learning all the techniques and skills the tattoo artist has to show you. And when you think you've got a good grasp of everything, you find yourself a client.

Q: So, what happens if you mess up on a client?
A: You don't.

Q: What's your favorite type of tattoo to do?
A: I love sailor-style traditional artwork. Just real bold, bright colors. A lot of swallow birds and anchors and pirate ships.

Q: What's the most common place to get a tattoo?
A: On women, it's generally the lower-back area. On men, it's usually the top of the arm.

Q: Any part of the body you won't tattoo?
A: I don't tattoo people's faces, unless you're in the [tattooing] industry. You've gotta think about your future. I don't tattoo hands or knuckles unless you're a certain age; I don't tattoo necks unless you're a certain age. You can't be 18 and getting your hands or your face tattooed. How are you going to work for the rest of your life?

Q: What are some of the most common tattoo requests?
A: Religious artwork. Or script—oh my gosh, I could do script with my eyes closed.

Q: Any advice for people considering their first tattoo?
A: Think! This is on you for the rest of your life. You're wearing a part of your life on your body. Make sure it's memorable.

Match the Measurements!

Most of us are familiar with units of measurement such as inches, gallons, pounds, and miles. But how well do you know old-fashioned units like the fingerbredd or the mutchkin?

If the answer is "not at all," don't feel bad—these are archaic forms of measurement, most of which disappeared from use following the adoption of more modern forms such as the metric system. Try your luck at matching the unusual and obscure measurements on this page with the correct definition on the opposite page. For good measure, check your answers at the bottom of the page!

1. acino
2. fingerbredd
3. barleycorn
4. Big Mac Index
5. elephant
6. baker's dozen
7. smidgen
8. braccio

9. mutchkin
10. millihelen
11. fortnight
12. jerk
13. zolotnik
14. cubit
15. butt

a) Measurement equal to half a pinch or $\frac{1}{32}$ of a teaspoon.

b) An archaic Russian unit of weight equaling one-sixth of an ounce.

c) Unit of distance used in biblical times, equal to 18 inches or the distance between a man's middle finger and his elbow.

d) Archaic unit of length equal to one-third of an inch.

e) The amount of beauty required to launch a single ship; humorous unit of measurement named after Helen of Troy (who had a face "that launched a thousand ships").

f) Means a single grape; an Italian unit of measurement for light weights.

g) Two weeks or 14 days; derived from the words "fourteen nights."

h) Measure of exchange rates between two currencies.

i) Old unit of volume equaling two hogsheads or 126 gallons.

j) The width of a finger (usually the middle finger); a Swedish unit of measurement.

k) Equal to 13.

l) Archaic unit of liquid measurement equal to three-quarters of an imperial pint.

m) Unit of paper measurement equaling 28 by 23 inches.

n) Measure of the rate of change of acceleration; equal to 0.3048 m/sec^3.

o) Means arm; an Italian unit of linear measurement equaling approximately half a meter.

Point, Counter-Point

Who was the inventor of the mechanical pencil? Well, it may be safe to say that it was invented twice. Japanese inventor Tokuji Hayakawa, founder of Sharp electronics, allegedly produced the first version from nickel in 1915. After an earthquake destroyed his factory in 1923, Hayakawa rebuilt his company in Osaka.

In the United States, the credit goes to Bloomington, Illinois, resident Charles Keeran, who patented and produced the popular sterling silver Eversharp in 1913. To keep up with production, Keeran tried to purchase machinery from the Chicago-based Wahl Company, but Wahl wanted its own contract to manufacture the pencils. Keeran finally agreed, and by 1916, Wahl was producing 1,000 pencils a day, eventually subsuming Keeran's Eversharp Company altogether. Though ousted from his own business, Keeran went on to sell his patent to other writing-utensil companies, such as Autopoint, Durolite, and Realite.

On a Roll

Fountain pens were cumbersome (and messy), so in 1938, Hungarian brothers Laszlo and Georg Biro patented a pen that used a ball bearing to apply ink—a faster-drying and neater alternative. The pen also didn't leak or explode at high altitudes, which is why the British government licensed them during World War II for its Royal Air Force. After the war, the Biros resettled in Argentina, where American pilots also encountered the pen. In May 1945, Eversharp purchased exclusive rights to produce the Biro pen in the United States.

Meanwhile, American businessman Milton Reynolds visited Argentina, also discovered the Biro pen, brought it home, and cobbled together some knock-offs—beating Eversharp to the market in November 1945 and selling out the Gimbels Manhattan location's supply of 10,000 pens (at $12.50 apiece) in just 6 hours. Although ballpoint pens remained popular for a while, the pens didn't perform well, so eventually consumers switched back to their trusty fountain pens.

Frenchman Marcel Bich, founder of Bic pens, is credited with single-handedly reviving the ballpoint-pen industry. His 1953 model was the first inexpensive ballpoint pen that actually worked. In 1958, Bic pens were introduced to American audiences. Today more than 100 billion Bic pens have been sold.

Stranger than Fiction:
Doppelgängers

❖ ❖ ❖ ❖

A perplexing number of people have reported
encountering their doppelgängers. Read on for some
of the more famous (and creepy) examples.

Haven't We Met Before?

According to many sources, *doppelgänger* is a German word meaning "double goer" or "double walker." Essentially, a doppelgänger
is defined as a person's twin, although not in a Doublemint Gum
sense. Rather, a doppelgänger is often described as a very pale,
almost bloodless version of the person. Its appearance usually
means impending danger or even death for its human counterpart,
although there have been instances in which the doppelgänger
foretold the future or simply showed up and didn't cause any
harm.

Interestingly, the doppelgänger is such a constant phenomenon
that Sigmund Freud tackled it in a paper titled "The Uncanny." In
it, he theorized that the doppelgänger is a denial of mortality by
people. Once they leave that denial behind, the double remains as
"the ghastly harbinger of death."

Deathly Dopplegängers

Many famous people have reported
seeing their doppelgänger, and most
of the time it wasn't a good thing.
One of the most famous instances
was U.S. President Abraham
Lincoln, who reported seeing his
doppelgänger in a mirror in 1860,
just after his election. As he supposedly described it to his friend Noah
Brooks, the double was "five shades"
paler than himself. Lincoln's wife

interpreted this as an omen that he would be elected to a second term but would not live through it. She was eerily on the mark.

At the very end of her long reign, Queen Elizabeth I of England reportedly saw a pale and wizened double of herself laid out on her bed. She died soon afterward in 1603. Renowned poet Percy Bysshe Shelley supposedly encountered his doppelgänger in Italy. The figure pointed toward a body of water. Shortly after, Shelley drowned while sailing on July 8, 1822.

In 1612, English poet John Donne was traveling abroad in Paris when suddenly appearing before him was the doppelgänger of his pregnant wife. Although the double was holding a newborn baby, she appeared incredibly sad. "I have seen my dear wife pass twice by me through this room, with her hair hanging about her shoulders, and a dead child in her arms," Donne told a friend. He later found out that at the precise moment the apparition appeared to him, his wife had given birth to a stillborn child.

Sometimes a person won't see his or her doppelgänger, but somebody else will, often with the same unfortunate result. That was the case with Pope Alexander VI who was a man given to murder, incest, and other manner of foul deeds. According to some stories, Alexander plotted to kill a church cardinal for his money. He brought poisoned wine to a dinner with the cardinal but forgot to bring an amulet he owned that he believed made him invulnerable to poison. According to lore, Alexander sent a church official back to get it. When the official entered Alexander's room, he saw a perfect image of the pope lying atop a funeral bier in the middle of the room. That night at dinner Alexander drank his own poison by mistake. He died a few days later on August 18, 1503.

Hello, It's... Me?

Not all doppelgängers sound Death's clarion call. In 1905, a severe influenza outbreak prevented a member of the British Parliament named Sir Frederick Carne Rasch from attending a session. However, during the session a friend, Sir Gilbert Parker, looked over and saw Rasch sitting there. Another member also reported briefly seeing Rasch, who, as it turned out, had never left his home. (When Rasch finally returned to Parliament, he became annoyed whenever someone poked him in the ribs to make certain it was really him.)

In 1771, while traveling to a city, Wolfgang von Goethe encountered himself, wearing unfamiliar clothes, heading in the opposite direction. Eight years later, Goethe found himself traveling the same road, heading in the same direction as his double had—and wearing the same clothes that before had seemed unfamiliar. Ninteenth-century French writer Guy de Maupassant once watched as his double sat down across from him and dictated what he was writing. De Maupassant's doppelgänger experiences became so common that he wrote about them in his short story *Lui*.

Twin Teachers

One of the most celebrated cases in doppelgänger lore occurred in 1845 in Latvia. Emilie Sagée was a popular French teacher at a school for upper-class girls. The students often talked about how Sagée seemed to be in two places at once: One student would report seeing her in a hallway, but another girl would shake her head and say no, she had just seen Sagée in a classroom.

One day, while Sagée was writing on the blackboard, her double appeared right beside her, moving its hand in exact unison with the teacher. Another time, as Sagée helped a young girl dress for a party, the girl looked in the mirror to see two Sagées moving in perfect harmony, working on the girl's dress.

Sagée's doppelgänger was resistant to touch at times, while at other times a person could walk right through it. Oddly, her double would appear healthy and energetic when Sagée was ill.

While reports like these and similar incidents involving Sagée didn't seem to distress the students, it freaked out their parents, who began pulling their children out of the school. According to some stories, the headmaster decided that he would have to let Sagée go. When told of this, the teacher reportedly lamented that she had lost nearly two-dozen teaching positions throughout her career for the same reason.

Say What?

"Advertisements contain the only truths to be relied on in a newspaper."
—*Mark Twain*

"When a man retires and time is no longer a matter of urgent importance, his colleagues generally present him with a watch."
—*R. C. Sherriff*

"Old age is when you know all the answers but nobody asks you the questions."
—*Laurence J. Peter*

"The cable TV sex channels don't expand our horizons, don't make us better people, and don't come in clearly enough."
—*Bill Maher*

"For birth control, I rely on my personality."
—*Milt Abel*

"I don't get too excited about the Olympics. In fact, I only watch about every four years."
—*Wendy Morgan*

"Certainly I believe in luck. How else do you explain the success of those you don't like?"
—*Jean Cocteau*

"We can't all be heroes, because someone has to sit on the curb and clap as they go by."
—*Will Rogers*

"My mother said, 'You won't amount to anything because you procrastinate.' I said, 'Just wait.'"
—*Judy Tenuta*

"If I only had a little humility, I'd be perfect."
—*Ted Turner*

"I never gossip, but I can give you the names of certain people who do."
—*Judy Hampton*

"It is almost impossible to find those who admire us entirely lacking in taste."
—*J. Petit-Senn*

The History of the Birthday Cake

❖ ❖ ❖ ❖

This ubiquitous candlelit confection has been a tradition in Western countries for centuries. Read on for the full scoop!

Whose Cake Is This?

The origin of the birthday cake is up for debate. Some scholars place its creation with the ancient Greeks, who made celebratory round honey cakes to offer up to the goddess Artemis; or with the Romans, who would make small savory cakes with honey, cheese, and olive oil. Other folks claim the birthday cake was born in the Middle Ages. At that time in Germany, sweet dough was formed into a petite cake to represent the baby Jesus wrapped in his swaddling clothes. The cake was eaten on Jesus's birthday (or rather, Christmas Day). Later, it became tradition for the cake to be given to children on their own birthdays.

Cake Customs and Custom Cakes

However the trend began, the birthday cake has been claimed by many birthday-celebrating cultures and cake customs have evolved over time. In England starting in the late 1600s, small charms were baked into birthday cakes; each charm foretold the recipient's future: If you bit into a coin, you'd be rich. Got the thimble? Be prepared to die lonely.

For many years, however, only the rich enjoyed birthday cakes. Before the industrial revolution (when cake mixes and home baking became more commonplace), frosted tiers of sugary cake were luxuries afforded only by the wealthy. These days, a birthday cake can be cheaply made at home or purchased at a bakery or grocery store.

Not everyone loves to celebrate their birthday, and plenty of cultures don't celebrate it at all. Jehovah's Witnesses believe the birthday celebration to be a pagan tradition and refuse to celebrate birthdays—no cake for them. Other people do celebrate the anniversary of their birth, but not with cake. In Korea, seaweed soup is the special birthday dish. In the Netherlands, birthdays are all about fruit tarts served with cream.

Fast Facts

- *The most a golf ball can weigh is 1.62 ounces.*

- *If a clock is included in an ad, it's usually set to 10:10.*

- *In 1987, American Airlines found a way to save $40,000— by eliminating one olive from each salad in a first class meal.*

- *A whopping 80 million Americans go on a diet each year.*

- *With all the flavors available these days, the best-selling ice cream is vanilla.*

- *July is the peak month for marital fights, riots, hasty legislation, and criminal violence.*

- *Founded in 1776, Phi Beta Kappa was the first Greek letter organization. Today it is an honorary fraternity.*

- *Tootsie Rolls were the first penny candy to be individually wrapped.*

- *Sweet or salty? There are 220 calories in 1.5 ounces of milk chocolate and 230 in 1.75 ounces of potato chips.*

- *The first American president to use a telephone was James Garfield.*

- *Gamma Phi Beta was the first women's organization referred to as a "sorority." Professor Frank Smalley coined the word to apply to the group at Syracuse University in 1874.*

- *Several species of snakes, including the spitting cobra, fake death by flipping over on their backs when threatened.*

That's No Way to Treat Lady Liberty!

❖ ❖ ❖ ❖

*The Statue of Liberty is one of the world's most iconic
figures. However, it wasn't always treated that way.*

Return to Sender?

The Statue of Liberty Enlightening the World (the Statue of Liberty's
full name) was the brainchild of French jurist and writer Édouard-René
Lefebvre de Laboulaye in 1865, who felt the gift would commemorate the democratic bond between France and America. The informal
arrangement was that France would pay for the statue, and America
would foot the bill for the pedestal.

However, fundraising for the pedestal didn't go as planned. By
March 1885, even as the completed statue was packed into 214 separate
boxes for its trip to the United States, work on the pedestal ground
to a halt for lack of funds. Cities such as Baltimore and San Francisco
expressed interest in having the statue if New York could not pay for it.
Frustrated, the French were uncertain if they should even send it.

To the Rescue

Into this situation stepped newspaper magnate Joseph Pulitzer, who
had bought the moribund *New York World* newspaper and sought a
popular cause to build its circulation. The pedestal campaign failure fit
the bill. In print he hammered the city's financial tycoons: "The dash of
one millionaire merchant's pen ought to settle the matter."

The nation's millionaires didn't fall for it, so when work on the
pedestal stopped, Pulitzer upped the ante. He called for the *World*'s
subscribers to raise the money for the pedestal. "Let us not wait for the
millionaires…Let us hear from the people," he wrote.

The people responded by sending in whatever amount they could,
from a few pennies to a dollar or more. Pulitzer printed every donor's
name in the paper next to a drawing of Uncle Sam holding out his hat
like a beggar. By August 1885, an overwhelming 120,000 subscribers
had donated $101,191—more than enough to complete the pedestal.
"The people have done their work well," wrote Pulitzer.

385

Just Powdering Their Noses

Many modern Americans would be shocked to know how prevalent
—and how respectable—cocaine use once was in this country. In
fact, one of the most all-American products, the Coca-Cola soft
drink, used cocaine in its recipe from 1886 until 1903 and even
took its name from the combination of coca leaves and kola nuts.
In the late 19th and early 20th centuries, there were no raised
eyebrows when doctors prescribed cocaine to patients as a treatment for everything from depression to asthma. The influential
psychologist Sigmund Freud made no secret of his own cocaine
use, and he urged his followers to try it as well. But after a few
decades, it became obvious that the drug led to addiction and
psychosis; in 1914, cocaine was outlawed with the passage of the
Harrison Tax Act.

You Drive Like a Girl

Ah, the Fifties. When "gals"
were still "sugar and spice and
everything nice," and corporations thought they could sell
women anything as long as they
slapped some pink paint on it. The most infamous example may
have been in 1955, when Dodge designed an automobile specifically for women. Yes, you guessed it—the Dodge La Femme was
pink, though they gave the color the fancy name "heather rose."
And just like a lady, the La Femme liked her accessories—
she came with a kit containing matching rain hat, umbrella,
purse, and cosmetics to wear while you drove the car and didn't
worry your pretty little head about anything.

Dodge stopped production of the La Femme after two
seasons. Arthur Liebler, the vice president of marketing and
communications at Chrysler, remarked years later, "I guess we
just didn't get it at the time." Now, that's an understatement!

Jeu de Paume, Anyone?

❖ ❖ ❖ ❖

Ever watch people playing handball and wonder, "Ow! Isn't that hell on their hands?" Well, it can be. That's why some players decided to take a different approach to handball, and used a racket instead. Here's more on the origins of tennis.

Tennis: Sport of Monks

Interestingly, no one is quite sure exactly when tennis was invented. Some folks believe it's an ancient sport, but there's no credible evidence that tennis existed before A.D. 1000. Whenever the time period, most people can agree that tennis descends from handball.

The first reliable accounts of tennis come from tales of 11th-century French monks who needed to add a little entertainment to their days spent praying, repenting, and working. They played a game called *jeu de paume* ("palm game," that is, handball) off the walls or over a stretched rope. The main item separating tennis from handball—a racket—evolved withinin these French monasteries. (The first rackets were actually used in ancient Greece, in a game called *sphairistike* and then in *tchigan,* played in Persia.) The monks had the time and means to develop these early forms of the tennis racquet: Initially, webbed gloves were used for hand protection, then paddles, and finally a paddle with webbing. The first balls were made from leather or cloth stuffed with hair, wool, or cork.

Banned by the Pope

Once outside the cloister, the game's popularity spread across the country with the speed of an Amélie Mauresmo backhand. According to some sources, by the 13th century, France had more than 1,800 tennis courts. Most of the enthusiasts were from the upper classes. In fact, the sport became such a craze that some leaders, including kings and the pope, tried to discourage or ban the game as too distracting. Not to be torn from their beloved game, the people played on.

It didn't take long for tennis to reach merry olde England. There the game developed a similar following, counting kings Henry VII and Henry VIII among its fans. Even The Bard, William Shakespeare, refers to the game in his play *Henry V.* At England's Hampton Court Palace, research suggests that the first tennis court was built there between 1526 and 1529. Later, another court was built, The Royal Tennis Court, which was last refurbished in 1628 and is still in use.

15-Love!

Those who believe that tennis originated in ancient Egypt argue that the word "tennis" derives from the Egyptian town of Tinnis. It is also possible that the term comes from the French cry of *"Tenez!"* which in this context could mean, "take this!" or "here it comes!" using the formal address. A similar version would be *"Tiens!"* As with any living language, French pronunciation has evolved, so it's difficult to know precisely whether the word came from French monastery trash-talk—but it's quite plausible.

Ever wonder what's up with tennis's weird scoring system? And what does any of it mean, anyway? Here are a few tennis pointers.

• The term "Love," meaning a score of zero, may descend from *"L'Oeuf!"* which means "the egg"—much like "goose egg" means zero in American sports slang.

• Evidently, the scoring once went by 15s (0, 15, 30, 45, and Game). But for some reason, it was decided that the numbers should have the same number of syllables. Hence, the "5" got dropped from the French word *quarante-cinq* (45), leaving just *quarante* (40), which is in use today.

• The term "Deuce" (when the game ties 40–40 and is reset to 30–30) likely comes from *"À Deux!"* which loosely translates as "two to win!" This is because in tennis, one must win by two.

The Worst of The Beatles

❖ ❖ ❖ ❖

*Ob-la-di, ob-la-*oh, no.

After their 1964 television appearance on *The Ed Sullivan Show,* it seemed everyone knew The Beatles. The quartet's influence on the world's youth was instant and profound, the reverberations of which echo to this day. That said, the Fab Four were human, and frankly, not everything among the nearly 200 recordings issued during their run was golden. Here are an album's worth of The Beatles' worst tracks, listed chronologically.

1. **"Love Me Do" (1962):** Their debut single put them on map, at least in their hometown. Producer George Martin was rightly underwhelmed by the early Lennon-McCartney songbook, but reckoned this bauble to be the best of the lot. Paul's nervousness at taking over the lead vocal (so John could play harmonica) was palpable, while newly seated drummer Ringo was demoted to tambourine. Martin hired a studio pro to play drums for the track, unwittingly seeding the canard that Ringo's percussive skills were sub-par.

2. **"Hold Me Tight" (1963):** A string of hits (including "She Loves You") mandated a quick return to the studio for another LP. The group quickly cranked out a mix of covers and originals for *With The Beatles,* including this placeholder. Their rushed execution resulted in out-of-tune and sloppy vocals, marring what wasn't any great shakes to begin with.

3. **"When I Get Home" (1964):** Similar to "Hold Me Tight," *A Hard Day's Night* is a doozy. Of the album's 13 original tracks, this hastily constructed tune bore silly lyrics ("I'm gonna love you till the cows come home") and an abrasive hook ("whoah, AHH!") that was mixed too loud. Forgettable.

4. **"Mr. Moonlight" (1964):** A busy year thoroughly exhausted the band. With new original material scarce, the Fab Four were forced to revisit the covers comprising their pre-fame club act to round out *Beatles For Sale.* This one, featuring an over-the-top

Lennon vocal intro and Hammond organ, routinely ends up on their "worst" list.

5. "Run For Your Life" (1965): Featuring classics like "In My Life" and "Michelle," *Rubber Soul* represented a major artistic leap forward. However, this closing rockabilly number later gave John, its author, some problems with its misogynistic lyrics ("I'd rather see you dead, little girl...").

6. "Dr. Robert" (1966): From the Lennon-McCartney pen came this tuneless paean to a New York City pill-pusher to the stars, blemishing the otherwise stellar *Revolver* album.

7. "Within You Without You" (1967): The much-acclaimed *Sgt. Pepper* album raised the game for rock bands the world over, presenting a seamless, eclectic collection of tunes that pushed the boundaries of the recording studio's capabilities. That said, George's excursion into Indian instrumentation, however adeptly arranged, wasn't to everyone's taste, resulting in what is for some people the album's most skipped-over track.

8. "Ob-la-di, Ob-la-da" (1968): Embodying what John and George regarded as Paul's "Granny music" tendencies, this bouncy trifle taxed his band mates' patience to the limit as McCartney led them through take after take. (Lennon's agitated piano intro made it to the issued recording.)

9. "Revolution #9" (1968): Thoroughly taken with the sound experiments of new girlfriend Yoko Ono, John offered up this sprawling *musique concrète* for what became known as "The White Album." To many listeners, the collage of found sound, running over eight minutes long, was alternately frightening and tedious.

10. "What's the New Mary Jane" (1968): Another "White Album" Lennon-Ono experiment, this charmless in-joke was dropped, only to resurface on *Anthology 3* for no good reason.

11. "Maxwell's Silver Hammer" (1969): Here we have yet another saccharine McCartney music hall offering. Paul's insistence that this lightweight ditty could be a hit drove a wedge between the foursome.

⚞ Behind the Films of Our Time

- Dogs rule. Terry the dog got $125 a week to play Toto in *The Wizard of Oz*. Meanwhile, the folks who played the Munchkins only received $50 a week.

- Director Steven Spielberg planned to use M&Ms as the candy that attracted the alien in the movie *E.T.*, but he couldn't get the rights from the company. Reese's Pieces went on to film fame as the replacement.

- Not only did Gary Cooper turn down the offer to play Rhett Butler in *Gone with the Wind*, but he was also very vocal in his feeling that the movie would be a flop. "I'm just glad it'll be Clark Gable who's falling on his face," he said, "not Gary Cooper." Of course, the movie went on to win the Oscar for Best Picture in 1939—and a Best Actor nomination for Gable, who played Rhett.

- Sarah Michelle Gellar and Freddie Prinze Jr. met on the 1997 set of *I Know What You Did Last Summer*. They were engaged by 2001, got married, had a child, and are still going strong.

- The phrase "Let's get out of here" may give you that déjà vu feeling. It's the line that has been used most often in films.

- Shiloh Jolie-Pitt, daughter of Brad Pitt and Angelina Jolie, appeared with her dad in *The Curious Case of Benjamin Button* as Benjamin and Daisy's daughter. She was 10 months old at the time.

- It may look gross in the movie, but the pile of human waste that Jamal jumps into in *Slumdog Millionaire* is actually made of peanut butter and chocolate.

- Would the horror movie *Halloween* been such a hit if it had been called by its original title, *The Babysitter Murders*?

- Heath Ledger posthumously won 32 Best Supporting Actor awards for his role as The Joker in *The Dark Knight*, including an Oscar, a Golden Globe, and a Critic's Choice Award.

- In *The Green Mile*, the prison guards are seen wearing uniforms, but guards didn't typically wear uniforms in 1935, when the movie was set.

Animal Cannibals

❖ ❖ ❖ ❖

Cannibalism, the act of consuming one's own species, is more common in the natural world than you might think. Read on for examples of animals and insects that take a bite out of their own kind.

Rats and Mice—When populations of mice and rats rise rapidly, there's less food to go around. And when this happens, the hungry and stressed survivors sometimes kill and eat their young. What's particularly interesting about rat cannibalism is that a lot of the time, it's the mama rat that does the eating. When a baby rat is sick or deformed, the mother may eat it because she knows it won't survive, and it will give her strength after labor.

Lions—An adult lion that wants to take over a pride will often kill the group's lion cubs. Basically, it's a way to ensure that there's no rivalry between the preexisting cubs and any that he may father. Sometimes the lions will also eat the cubs. An odd side benefit (for the lion, anyway): If her cubs are dead, a lioness will usually go into heat after two or three weeks, allowing the lion to mate with her sooner. Nice way to woo a lady.

Chickens—Chickens will eat a lot of funky stuff—including their own kin. Cannibalism occurs in chickens most often when they are kept in close captivity and mistake pecking their brethren for typical food foraging. It's also been suggested that some laying hens crave more protein and, er, get by with a little help from their friends.

Caterpillars—Before monarch and queen butterflies become beautiful winged creatures, they're less-than-adorable caterpillars that often eat the eggs of their own species. Hey, it takes a lot of energy to turn from a wormy-looking grub into a lovely butterfly, and they need the calories.

Baboons—The males of several primate species practice infanticide. Baboons have been known to kill and occasionally eat their young. Bands of male primates will attack a rival group and drive off any males. Like the lions, they then kill the offspring so they can mate with the females.

Seagulls—Perhaps a response to overcrowding and food scarcity, male gulls often make a lunch (or breakfast or dinner) of gull eggs and hatchlings.

Crows—It's not pretty, but it's effective: Sometimes a crow will eat the eggs and chicks of his rivals to ensure his own successful breeding.

Spiders—If you're going on any dates with a black widow spider in the near future, watch your back: These and other female arachnids are known to kill and eat their mates either before, during, or after intercourse. But why? There are many theories as to why the female does this, including nourishment or biological habit. As to why the males continue to let it happen, that's a mystery.

Mantid—Perhaps the most well-known cannibal in nature is the Chinese mantid, or praying mantis. The female eats her mate immediately after mating. In fact, it has been studied that more than 63 percent of a female mantis's diet is made up of her paramours.

Hippos—Hippos are one of the largest mammals in the world, able to grow 11 feet long and almost 5 feet tall. These animals eat grass for the most part, but there have been cases when, faced with starvation, hippos have committed cannibalism. Considering the average male hippo weighs between 3,500 and 9,920 pounds, that's a big meal.

Humans—Yes, it's true. See page 311 for an article about humans getting a taste of their own kind.

Sand Gobies—There are a lot of fish in the sea—and some of them eat their own species. The male sand goby tends the eggs, while the female goes off to mate again. If the eggs still haven't hatched after a long breeding season, sometimes the male goby will eat them.

Who Was Button Gwinnett?

❖ ❖ ❖ ❖

His invasion of Florida was a disaster and he may have plagiarized his most lasting composition, but Button Gwinnett still managed to get his signature on the Declaration of Independence.

From England to Georgia to Pennsylvania

In 1762, Button Gwinnett emigrated from England to the colonies, where he dabbled in trade before borrowing a large sum to establish a plantation. He served as a representative to the colony's House of Commons until 1773. After losing his land and slaves, Gwinnett allied himself with the burgeoning revolutionary cause, but his English birth made him politically unpopular, so Gwinnett's rival, Lachlan McIntosh, was given the honor of leading Georgia's Continental battalion. Denied the laurels of military leadership, Gwinnett went to Philadelphia as one of the state's representatives to the Continental Congress. It was in this role that he signed the Declaration of Independence in 1776.

Elected to the Georgia legislature, Gwinnett used a pamphlet given to him by John Adams as the basis for the new state's constitution. When the governor died in early 1777, Gwinnett was appointed to the post. At a time when the struggling nation could ill afford intrigue, he worked to undermine his old rival General McIntosh by spreading dissent among his officers, devising a questionable plan for invading Florida, and then appointing one of McIntosh's subordinates to lead the ill-fated expedition. After a mere two months in office, Gwinnett lost the governorship.

Lachlan's Loose Tongue

Like Gwinnett, McIntosh was a boastful man who delighted in the embarrassment of his rivals. In the days following Gwinnett's defeat, McIntosh publicly derided the ex-governor. Finally, Gwinnett challenged him to a duel. On May 16, 1777, the two Georgians stood 12 paces apart and discharged pistols. Both men were wounded; McIntosh survived, but Gwinnett succumbed to gangrene. He died days later at age 42.

Fast Facts

- A mayfly only lives one day. (In May, perhaps?)

- The first food available in a mix was the Aunt Jemima pancake mix, invented in 1889.

- Don't shake the vending machine! Toppling machines kill more than ten people each year.

- Kareem Abdul-Jabbar holds the record for the most fouls committed by a professional basketball player in his career: 4,657.

- Cy Young must have played a lot of baseball in his day. He holds the record for the most baseball games won (511) and also for the most games lost (316).

- Johnny Depp, star of the Pirates of the Caribbean movie series, may be the bravest pirate ever, but the actor suffers from coulrophobia—a fear of clowns.

- Many diehard Chicago Cubs fans believe in the "curse of the goat," which occurred during the 1945 World Series when Cubs owner P. K. Wrigley kicked fan William "Billy Goat" Sianis and his pet goat out of Wrigley Field. The Cubs haven't won a Series since.

- The 1995 Honda Civic is the most-stolen car in the United States.

- Elephants have no problem finding things to do—they spend as many as 16–20 hours eating each day.

- During the average human lifetime, a person could fill two swimming pools with their saliva. Gross.

- There are approximately 7,000 feathers on the average bald eagle.

When Nature Turns Mean!

❖ ❖ ❖ ❖

Man and nature are supposed to live in harmony, right?
But sometimes certain animals don't get the memo. The
following tales are incredible stories of man (and woman)
versus beast in a remarkable fight for survival.

Bearing Down

On November 1, 1999, hunter Gene Moe of Anchorage, Alaska, was dressing a freshly killed deer atop a mountain on Raspberry Island when an 8-foot-tall, 700-pound Kodiak bear attacked him. Armed only with a 3¾-inch-long hunting knife, Moe went toe-to-toe with the snarling behemoth in a terrifying battle to the death.

Moe first tried to shove his knife down the bear's throat but missed, allowing the bruin to tear away a large flap of flesh on his right arm. Moe repeatedly stabbed the animal in its neck and back each time it attacked, but the bear managed to get in a few more licks of its own, at one point mangling Moe's right leg with a vicious bite and slashing one of his ears. When the bear lunged at him a final time, Moe met the assault with a wild punch to the animal's face, a blow that managed to sever the bear's already damaged vertebra. With that, the beast fell dead at Moe's feet.

But Moe's ordeal wasn't over yet. Bleeding heavily and in excruciating pain, he crawled two miles down the mountain to where the rest of his party was waiting. In the hospital, Moe received more than 500 stitches. But he recovered well enough to go hunting again the following year.

A Game of Cat and Bicyclist

On January 8, 2004, Anne Hjelle of Mission Viejo, California, was riding her mountain bike with her friend, Debi Nicholls, at Whiting Ranch Wilderness Park when she was ambushed and knocked to the ground by a 110-pound mountain lion. When Nicholls arrived on the scene, the big cat had latched on to Hjelle's head with its powerful jaws and was trying to drag her into the brush. Nicholls's first instinct was to throw her bike at the animal, but it barely flinched.

She then grabbed Hjelle by the leg, engaging the lion in a life-or-death game of tug-of-war.

Nicholls struggled to keep the lion from dragging Hjelle down into the ravine, but the cat was strong and managed to pull both women about 30 feet into the brush before a group of other cyclists heard Nicholls's screams and rushed over. With Nicholls still clinging desperately to Hjelle's leg, the other cyclists threw rocks at the killer cat until it finally let go and slunk away into the underbrush.

Hjelle's left cheek was almost completely ripped off in the attack, and she suffered numerous other lacerations on her head and face. However, her plastic surgeons did a remarkable job of sewing her back up, and Hjelle was back riding her bike within a few months.

Honeymoon Surprise

In August 2001, Krishna Thompson of Central Islip, Long Island, took his wife, AveMaria, to Freeport, Grand Bahama, to celebrate their wedding anniversary. On their second morning there, a shark attacked Thompson while he was out for an early-morning swim in the ocean.

The shark grabbed Thompson's left leg and started to drag him out to sea. Once in deeper water, the shark submerged, taking Thompson with him. As the light above him grew dimmer, Thompson desperately reached down and tried to pull the shark's jaws apart. He lacerated his hands on its razor-sharp teeth, but finally succeeded in making it release him. Thompson then punched the shark several times, until it turned and swam away.

Thompson swam to shallow water, then hopped to the beach on his uninjured leg and screamed for help. A physician who was jogging nearby tended to Thompson until an ambulance could take him to the hospital. The lacerations on Thompson's left leg were so severe that the limb had to be amputated. Thompson was later fitted with a computerized prosthetic limb. Today, Thompson lectures as a motivational speaker.

The Secret Side of Elvis

❖ ❖ ❖ ❖

Being the King of Rock 'n' Roll is not all it's cracked up to be.

Sparkling white jumpsuit, shiny black pompadour, soulful eyes, and shimmying hips—that's the mythic image of Elvis Presley everyone knows and loves. But although he was a revolutionary recording artist and the King of Rock 'n' Roll, Elvis was also made of darker stuff. From his obsession with guns to his bizarre behavior regarding his mother's corpse and a long fascination with occult teachings, Elvis had a secret side that his publicists preferred to keep under blue suede wraps.

I Remember Mama

Born on January 8, 1935, in Tupelo, Mississippi, to Vernon and Gladys Presley, Elvis Aaron came into the world along with a stillborn twin brother, Jesse Garon. It was an early tragedy that haunted Elvis for most of his life. The family was poor—a situation made worse when Vernon was sent to prison for forging a check. At age three, Elvis was suddenly the man of the house.

After Vernon's release in 1948, the family moved to Memphis, Tennessee. Even as his recording career began to take off in the mid-'50s, Elvis and his mother remained incredibly close and devoted to one another. She lived with him at his Graceland estate until her death in 1958. To say Elvis did not take his mother's death well would be an understatement, and his grief morphed into often bizarre behavior. Family and friends worriedly noted that he seemed obsessed with his mother's corpse. Later, he talked at length to friends about the technical details of the embalming process.

When Gladys's glass-topped coffin was brought to lie in state at the Graceland mansion, Elvis threw himself on the corpse. Elvis also threw himself on her coffin as it was being lowered into the ground. Recording artist Barbara Pittman said he was screaming and had to be restrained. Afterward, he carried his mother's nightgown everywhere for more than a week.

Don't Be Cruel

When Elvis began dating 14-year-old Priscilla Beaulieu in 1959, he showed another strange side—the control freak. He asked her to dye her hair the same jet black as his own; the couple looked so similar that people thought they were twins. He chose her wardrobe and once became upset over an imperfect polish job on one of her toenails. He also required her to carry a concealed handgun.

Of course, Elvis sometimes carried as many as five guns himself, and was in the habit of shooting objects that irked him. A television with poor reception? *Blam!* Shattered console televisions were constantly dragged out of the Jungle Room at Graceland. Elvis once even shot his Ferrari after it stalled on the road.

Got My Mojo Workin'

Elvis continued to feel haunted by the loss of his brother and mother, and he grew desperate for some sort of spiritual answer. For a time, he sought solace in the beliefs of a hair stylist named Larry Geller. Elvis confessed to Geller that as a young child, he often heard a voice and wondered if it was his dead brother. Geller, something of a New Age mystic, introduced Elvis to metaphysical books and to his own philosophy that—as redundant as it sounds—the purpose of life was to find one's purpose in life. Presley staff member Alan Fortas said Elvis referred to Geller as his guru and to himself as "the divine messenger."

Elvis began carrying a numerology book with him that he consulted to help him decide which gifts to bestow on any given individual. His metaphysical journey ended after he tripped and hit his head in 1967, after which he was "de-programmed" by his manager Colonel Tom Parker. In the end, Elvis apparently had enough, and his collection of metaphysical books wound up in flames in a burn pit on the grounds of Graceland. But when Elvis was found dead in his bathroom on August 16, 1977, he was wearing the symbols of three religions: an Egyptian ankh, a Jewish Star of David, and a Christian crucifix.

FROM THE VAULTS OF HISTORY

Glad to Be Sad

Robert Burton, a vicar of St. Thomas Church at Oxford, made a giant leap in the understanding and treatment of mental illness when in 1621 he published *The Anatomy of Melancholy*. The popular book included such pithy observations as "Who cannot give good counsel? 'Tis cheap, it costs them nothing." But perhaps Burton's most interesting comment is one that has been rephrased many times by modern-day comedians such as Jim Carrey and Robin Williams: "Aristotle said...melancholy men of all others are most witty."

Kilt Complex

You don't see kilts worn much these days—though often the skirts that are seen are worn by Prince Charles and his sons while they're doing fabulous country things on their fabulous country estates. But the truth is that before 1745, Scottish aristocrats wouldn't have been caught dead in kilts. The plaid skirts were considered distinctly lower class, the uniform of tradesmen and farmers. In 1745, the kilt was banned by the British Parliament. Suddenly Scotsmen of all social classes decided that they just loved kilts. The fact that the kilt had actually been invented by an Englishman, Thomas Rawlinson, was conveniently ignored by everyone on both sides of the controversy.

Thanks, but I'll Pass

English history is fraught with centuries of backstabbing and machinations as royal children fought over the throne. That is, except for the sons of King George V, who died in 1936. A problem arose when the king's heir, Edward, abdicated the throne to run off with his divorced sweetheart, Wallis Simpson—his brother, Albert (who was next in line for the position), didn't want any part of it. Albert was happy living a quiet country life with his wife and children, and his shyness and stuttering made him dread ascending the throne. Unlike his brother, Albert eventually bolstered himself and did his duty as King George VI. He was much beloved by the British people for his courage during World War II.

Odd Amusements in Old Atlantic City

❖ ❖ ❖ ❖

Long before it was the home of glittering gambling dens, the Atlantic City Boardwalk was home to some of the oddest and most outrageous amusements ever to grace a coast. Here's a look at the boardwalk during its heyday, from about 1890 to 1940.

If You Build It...

The first boardwalk was built in Atlantic City, but not as an entertainment center—it was made for people to scrape the sand off their shoes before they entered the city's hotels. The boardwalk was constructed in portable sections so it could be stored away during the winter. However, it didn't take American capitalists long to realize that there was gold in them there boards. From the 1890s onward, the boardwalk became a permanent structure as well as a bustling bastion of business. As Atlantic City grew in popularity, it became America's playground—with an emphasis on *play.*

Around & Around

Before the Ferris wheel was invented in 1893, Atlantic City had the Epicycloidal Diversion in the 1870s. It consisted of four wheels, each about 30 feet in diameter, which rested on a 10-foot-high circular platform. Each wheel had cars for 16 people. Not only did the wheels turn up and down, but they also turned sideways in a circle. It must have seemed like a giant beater swirling back and forth.

Another popular attraction was the Haunted Swing, which appeared in the 1890s. Folks piled in the middle of what looked like a room in a normal house. In the middle of the room hung a large swing, where people sat down. The swing would then move back and forth at tremendous speed, until finally it flipped completely over as the objects in the room, including a chair, bureau, and rug, remained totally stationary. Only later did the riders realize that it was the room that was spinning around, while they stayed completely still in the swing.

Walk (and Dive) with the Animals

The Atlantic City Boardwalk was the place to see talented animals strut their stuff. For a price, you could see a chicken hit a home run (or possibly a *fowl* ball), watch the feline fur fly as two cats sitting on their hind legs slugged it out in a miniature boxing ring, or observe a man dancing with a tiger.

However, the most famous (and longest running, as it was showcased until the 1970s) animal act was the High Diving Horse, who jumped from a tower into a pool of water dozens of times daily. Some horses would stand at the top of the platform for minutes, gazing serenely around and building up unbearable suspense in the waiting crowd below. Others, however, would just climb to the top and immediately jump down. "You can lead a horse to water, but you can't teach him showmanship," explained one of the horse trainers.

Oddities Abound

Vacationing secretaries, erstwhile novelists, and people with sloppy handwriting hurried to the giant Underwood typewriter at Garden Pier. Built for $100,000 by the Underwood Corporation, the 14-ton machine was 1,728 times the normal size of a regular typewriter and had a ribbon one-mile long. Operated by using a normal-sized typewriter, the giant Underwood typed on a 9-foot by 12-foot–long piece of paper.

Odd personalities were drawn to the Atlantic City Boardwalk like narcissists to reality TV. The curious could visit the Wild Man of Borneo, who wore animal skins and chewed raw bones, and the aptly named "America's Luckiest Fool," Alvin "Shipwreck" Kelly, who sat for 49 days on a Steel Pier flagpole. (That's right: Flagpole sitting was a fad in the 1920s.)

Then there were the daredevils, who dived, dropped, and jumped from all manner of things into the Atlantic Ocean nearby. This became quite the rage until a sudden shift in the winds one day concluded the performance of one poor soul in shocking fashion by sending him into electrical power lines instead of the ocean.

Ah, the Atlantic City of old—a place where the Protestant work ethic took a good beating. As *The New York Times* noted, "...in New York, play is unfortunately adulterated with work. But in Atlantic City, work is not even a grim spectre in the background."

Behind the TV Shows of Our Time

- In the 1950s, movie-star-turned-TV sensation Loretta Young was famous for the grand, sweeping entrances she would make on her *The Loretta Young Show*. But at the height of her fame, she was hiding a secret: Her "adopted" daughter was really her biological daughter, who had been fathered by the very debonair (and very married) actor Clark Gable.

- The famous fireplace mantel of the little house on *Little House on the Prairie*, which was inscribed with the initials CI-CI (for the show's Pa and Ma characters, Charles Ingalls-Caroline Ingalls), was not made of wood but of Styrofoam.

- Telly Savalas's brother George chose to bill himself as "Demosthenes" Savalas for the first two seasons of *Kojak*. After that, he went back to plain ol' George.

- "You Look at Me" was the theme song for the *Happy Days* spin-off *Joanie Loves Chachi*. Stars Erin Moran and Scott Baio sang the tune. Unfortunately for them, no one looked at the show, and it was a flop.

- The Iolani Palace, which appeared as a government building in many episodes of *Hawaii Five-O*, once housed the Hawaiian Legislature.

- The same building that houses the set and offices of *Scrubs* was used in Britney Spears's movie, *Crossroads*.

- One of the most famous witnesses at the O. J. Simpson murder trial, Kato Kaelin, was nicknamed after a character played by Bruce Lee in the late-'60s crime drama *The Green Hornet*.

- Bette Nesmith Graham, the mother of *The Monkees'* Mike Nesmith, invented Liquid Paper.

- Bea Benaderet, who played Cousin Pearl Bodine on *The Beverly Hillbillies*, also provided the voice of Betty Rubble on *The Flintstones*.

- While actor Daniel Stern provided the voice-over narration for *The Wonder Years*, his brother, Dave Stern, was a writer on the show.

- The title of Diane's unbearably pretentious novel on *Cheers* was *Jocasta's Conundrum*.

The Brief Death of Sherlock Holmes

❖ ❖ ❖ ❖

*"I am in the middle of the last Holmes story," wrote Sir Arthur
Conan Doyle, author of the Sherlock Holmes series of mysteries,
to his mother in April 1893, "after which the gentleman vanishes,
never to reappear. I am weary of his name." Doyle was wrong—
Sherlock Holmes did not die then. It would take several more
months for the author to figure out a suitable demise for his world-
famous and wildly popular detective. But why kill Holmes at all?*

It's a Mystery

Ever since he first burst onto the literary scene in
1887, Holmes had become one of the most popular literary characters of all time. His popularity
enabled Doyle to achieve the financial and artistic
freedom to pursue whatever creative avenue
he chose. However, as the years went by, Doyle
began to feel strangled by his own creation.

It seems as if more theories have been
advanced about the decision to kill off Holmes, a fictional character,
than have been put forward for the demise of an actual person.
Some postulate that publishing deadlines were tight, and the
pressure of always having to come up with intricate plots was
wearing on Doyle and affecting his overall literary output. "The
difficulty of the Holmes work," Doyle wrote, "was that every story
really needed as clear-cut and original a plot as a longish book would
do. One cannot without effort spin plots at such a rate."

Another theory is that he was so busy living the life of a writer
and meeting deadlines for Holmes stories that he did not notice
the beginnings of an illness in his wife that eventually became
tuberculosis of the lungs. "As a doctor, [Doyle] should have
recognized her condition long before it developed advanced
symptoms," wrote biographer Martin Booth. The speculation is that
Doyle felt guilty for overlooking his wife's symptoms and blamed
Holmes. Perhaps killing the character was a form of revenge.

Whatever the reason, Doyle had been thinking about killing Holmes for quite some time. Toward the end of 1891, he mentioned to his mother his plans, and she frantically pleaded with him to change his mind. Doyle changed his mind, albeit briefly. "He still lives," he told his mother, "thanks to your entreaties."

Fearful Falls

Doyle knew that his creation, the ultimate detective, needed a proper death. "A man like that mustn't die of a pin-prick or influenza," he said. "His end must be violent and intensely dramatic."

In the summer of 1893, Doyle visited Switzerland and told Silas K. Hocking, an English cleric and novelist, of his plans to kill Holmes. "Why not bring him out to Switzerland and drop him down a crevasse?" Hocking said. "It would save funeral expenses."

Doyle laughed, but the conversation stuck with him. During the trip, he visited the famous Reichenbach Falls, and he decided the foaming waters there would be a suitable end for his detective. Doyle then set about writing *The Final Problem*, in which he created the criminal mastermind Professor Moriarty. At the end of the story, the two adversaries, locked in combat, apparently plunge into Reichenbach Falls.

"Killed Holmes," Doyle noted in his diary.

Or so he thought.

A Cry Heard Around the World

The death of Sherlock Holmes unleashed worldwide protest. *The Strand* magazine, publisher of the Holmes stories, lost 20,000 subscriptions. Doyle received thousands of hostile letters. People wore black mourning armbands in London. Even the British royal family was upset.

For eight years, Doyle resisted the pressure to bring back Holmes. Finally, in 1901, he published *The Hound of the Baskervilles*, but set it before Holmes's death. However, the public still wasn't satisfied. In 1903, Doyle relented and published *The Adventure of the Empty House*, which brought Holmes back safe and sound (turns out he never went into the falls at all). Ultimately, Doyle's creation had a life of its own, and he went on to write Holmes stories for another two decades.

INSPIRATION STATION

Song for a Lost Friend

After relocating to Los Angeles in the late 1960s when he was barely out of his teens, Canadian rocker Neil Young was shocked at the rampant substance abuse in the musical community—and especially at the toll heroin use was taking amongst his friends and acquaintances. He became even more concerned after learning that many of those closest to him, members of his band and road crew, were shooting up on a regular basis.

In frustration he wrote the song, "The Needle and the Damage Done," which appeared on his 1972 album *Harvest* and is widely considered to be one of the shining gems in a career full of masterful songwriting. Sadly, his musical warning did not save his friend (and guitarist in his band Crazy Horse) Danny Whitten, who died of a heroin overdose in 1972 at age 29. Whitten was hired to play on Young's upcoming tour, but was too high most of the time to make much of a contribution. Young fired him, giving him $50 for a plane ticket home. Whitten, unfortunately, spent it on the heroin that ultimately killed him. While saying he does not want to appear preachy, Young has nonetheless spoken out about the dangers of hard drugs ever since.

The Real Story of *Love Story*

Erich Segal was never a "preppy" like Oliver Barrett IV, the protagonist of his blockbuster novel, *Love Story* (that was made into an equally successful film starring Ryan O'Neal and Ali MacGraw). In fact, he grew up lower-middle-class in Brooklyn and attended public schools. But once he managed to get into Harvard, Segal met plenty of "Olivers"— including future vice president Al Gore, who got a lot of flack when he told *Time* magazine that he and his wife Tipper inspired the lovers Oliver and Jenny. But Gore wasn't completely off-base: Segal confirmed to *The New York Times* that Oliver's difficult relationship with his father was based on the one Gore had with his dad, but he strongly denied that Gore inspired the romantic side of Oliver. That honor goes to Segal's other Harvard pal, future Academy Award–winning actor Tommy Lee Jones.

Odd Ordinances

- In Iowa, one-armed pianists may not charge for their performances.

- Horses are not allowed to eat fire hydrants in Marshalltown, Iowa.

- If two trains come together in one spot on the same track in Kansas, neither one may proceed until the other has passed. So...how does that work?

- Preschoolers better do their learning during daytime hours in Topeka, Kansas, because singing the alphabet on the streets at night is forbidden.

- In Kansas, you may not shoot rabbits from a motorboat.

- Women in Owensboro, Kentucky, must have their husband's permission to buy a hat.

- Bank tellers in Louisiana have reason to feel safe: It is against the law to rob a bank and shoot the teller with a water pistol.

- It's illegal to tie animals to fire hydrants in Michigan.

- Prisoners in Louisiana could receive an additional two years in jail if they attempt to hurt themselves.

- It is against Maine law to step out of a plane while it's in flight.

- In Maine, you are open to getting a fine if you leave your Christmas decorations up after January 14.

- Ads are banned from cemeteries in Wells, Maine.

- Sorry, Simba: In Maryland, it's not legal to take a lion to the movies.

- It's illegal to swim in public fountains within the city limits of Rockville, Maryland.

- Massachusetts law prohibits giving beer to hospital patients.

- It's against the law to tickle a woman in Virginia.

The Great Beyond

❖ ❖ ❖ ❖

*"In this world," Benjamin Franklin once observed, "nothing is
certain but death and taxes." And both are equally mysterious to
the average person. Read on for some interesting burial traditions.*

All About Embalming

Embalming is currently the most widely accepted method of preparing a body for viewing and burial. The idea of preserving bodies
by pumping them full of chemicals gained acceptance during the
Civil War, when soldiers who died in combat were sent home for
burial—oftentimes many states away. The technique was improved
in the years that followed, and today many of those who die in the
United States are embalmed as a part of the funeral process.

Chemical embalming helps ward off the natural decomposition
that begins almost immediately upon death. A variety of bacteria
and enzymes start to break down the body once we leave this
mortal coil, and without embalming we would very quickly be very
unpleasant to be around. The chemicals used in the embalming
process—specifically formaldehyde—help kill the bacteria and
stop the enzymes from doing their job. Formaldehyde is also a
good embalming fluid because it is an effective disinfectant, and
it coagulates protein, which makes the body sturdier and easier to
work with.

The big question, of course, is how long do the effects of
embalming last? Many people believe that the process leaves
the body looking pretty practically forever, but that's not true.
No matter how talented the embalmer, sooner or later a body
will begin to decompose. A variety of factors play a role in
determining how long that might take, however. If embalming is
done immediately after death, the embalmer does a thorough job,
and the casket remains airtight, a body can remain in very good
condition for many, many years. However, if the body is exposed to
air in any way, decomposition will set in fairly quickly. In addition,
bodies interred in aboveground mausoleums tend to break down
faster than those interred in the ground.

Funereal Facts

- Interestingly, certain ancient techniques, such as mummification, have proved very effective at body preservation, sometimes even more so than modern embalming. Back in the day, mummification involved removing the brain and internal organs (with the exception of the heart); treating the body with a variety of preservative compounds, including a natural salt called "natron;" then wrapping it in linen. This process was so efficient that mummies thousands of years old have been found in astoundingly good condition.

- Burial ceremonies are as old as human civilization, and perhaps even older. Certain Neanderthal burial grounds dating back to 60,000 B.C. suggest that the prehistoric dead weren't simply stuck in the ground. Instead, they were sent on their way with meaningful rituals, which at times included placing animal antlers and flowers with the deceased.

- Many of today's common burial customs are actually based in pagan beliefs. Wearing special clothes, such as black, harkens back to the custom of donning a disguise to confuse returning spirits. Wakes stem from the ancient custom of keeping watch over a dead person in the hope that he or she might return to life.

- Over the years, a remarkable array of death rituals have been enacted by various civilizations and cultures. There are many who fear the spirits that were assumed to be after the deceased's soul, and so they took action to protect themselves. The Zulus of Africa, for example, burn all of a dead person's belongings to dissuade evil spirits from hanging around. Other tribes set up a ring of fire around dead bodies to singe the wings of the spirits and prevent them from attacking the living.

- In Tibet, the deceased undergoes a "sky burial." First, the body is dismembered by a *rogyapa,* or body breaker. Then it is dragged to a remote location and left out in the open to be eaten by wild animals and birds. The belief ties into the Tibetans traditional Buddhist beliefs that once a person dies, their body is simply a shell. Plus, it gives a meal to the native birds of prey.

Fast Facts

- The Superball was invented in the summer of 1965, and seven million balls were sold by Christmas. At 98 cents each, they were considered great stocking stuffers.

- News anchor Ted Baxter is the only WJM-TV employee who was not fired in the series finale of The Mary Tyler Moore Show.

- What color is an airplane's black box? Duh—it's orange.

- Of the 37 plays that William Shakespeare is known to have written, 14 are comedies, 11 are tragedies, and the rest are, pardon the pun, histories.

- The coldest temperature ever recorded in the United States was 80 degrees below zero Fahrenheit in Prospect Creek, Alaska, on January 23, 1971.

- The Peshtigo Fire in Wisconsin was actually the worst fire in U.S. history, killing 1,500 people. So why haven't you heard about it? It just so happened to break out the same day as the Great Chicago Fire of 1871.

- Brandy, rum, whiskey, and red wine cause more hangovers than any other alcohol.

- Early Americans weren't so straitlaced after all! Former presidents George Washington and Thomas Jefferson both grew marijuana plants on their land.

- If you truly eat like a bird, you might be a little on the plump side: Birds eat half their weight in food each day.

- Walking downhill puts pressure on your knees equal to three times your body weight.

Sponge Party

❖ ❖ ❖ ❖

Deep-sea sponges + fiber optics = undersea rave?

Deep-Sea Darkness

No one likes to be left in the dark—including giant sea sponges. Yet the bottom of the ocean, where these sponges are found, is a very dark place indeed. To deal with this problem, some massive deep-sea sponges have evolved fiber optic exoskeletons by which they illuminate their surroundings. These aren't sponges of the squishy, ideal-for-washing-dishes variety; they're sturdy sponges that produce reinforced glass tubes known as *spicules.* Although sponges are some of the world's most primitive creatures, these spicules are astoundingly intricate, growing up to about three feet in length and rivaling some of humanity's spiffier architectural designs.

Light Show

How does a sponge grow such an intricate exoskeleton? First, it spins silica from the ocean into microscopic bits of glass. It then adheres together these thin pieces of glass to form little fibers. The sponge arranges these fibers into a complex lattice, which it reinforces with a kind of glass cement. According to a report on NPR's *All Things Considered,* this lattice design resembles techniques used for building skyscrapers, such as the Swiss Tower in London or the Eiffel Tower in Paris. And just like these manufactured structures, the sponges light up.

The undersea light show occurs because the spicules behave like fiber-optic rods, enabling the sponge to transport light throughout its tissue. Many tiny life-forms live inside the sponge—such as green algae and glass shrimp—because these organisms need its light to survive. According to scientists, the spicules conduct light in such a way that they're more sophisticated than many human-made fiber-optic cables. Plus, they don't require the high temperatures needed for manufactured fibers. So if you ever find yourself on the ocean floor and in need of a light source, look for the sponges with spicules. It's where the little shrimp like to party!

Shoichi Yokoi: Lost Soldier, Found

❖ ❖ ❖ ❖

*Shoichi Yokoi fled from the Americans invading Guam in
1944 and was not captured until 1972. Repatriated to Japan,
he quickly became a sensation—for better or worse.*

On the night of July 21, 1944, Sergeant Shoichi Yokoi of the Japanese
Imperial Army was engaged in a desperate fight with advancing
Americans whose tanks were ripping apart his regiment. As the
situation became increasingly dire, Yokoi chose to flee rather than
be killed, or worse, captured alive. He was not alone: More than
1,000 Japanese soldiers were hiding in the jungles of Guam when
Americans secured the island; nearly all were killed or captured
soon afterward. Only Yokoi and eight other soldiers remained undis-
covered in the dense jungle.

By 1964, his companions had either surrendered or died, and
Yokoi was alone. He knew the war was over but he chose to remain
hidden. "We Japanese soldiers were told to prefer death to the
disgrace of getting captured alive," he later said. Certainly, Yokoi
had another strong motive for remaining hidden. The Japanese army
had been cruel to the native Guam population and Yokoi feared that
he would be killed in reparation. So he hid and survived alone for
another eight years—a remarkable 28 years total—before he was
discovered by hunters, captured, and taken into custody.

How Did He Do It?

Clothing: Before the war, Yokoi had been a tailor's apprentice.
Though his skills with fabric and thread were of no help against
American tanks, they proved immensely useful in the jungle. By
pounding the bark of the native pago tree, Yokoi was able to make
a durable fiber that he used to fashion three suits of clothes. He
reworked a piece of brass to make a sewing needle and he repur-
posed plastic from a flashlight to make buttons.

Food: While hiding in the jungles of Guam, Yokoi ate snails, rats,
eels, pigeons, mangoes, nuts, crabs, and prawns. Occasionally he'd
have wild hog. Although he boiled all the water he drank, and

cooked the meat thoroughly, he once became ill for a month after eating a cow.

Shelter: Surviving in the jungle for 28 years is one thing. Surviving *undetected* in the jungle is quite another. As such, Yokoi went to great lengths to disguise his shelters. His most permanent dwelling was a tunnel-like cave, painstakingly hand-dug using a piece of artillery shell. At one end of the three-foot-high shelter, a latrine emptied down an embankment into a river; at the other end a small kitchen contained some shelves, a cooking pot, and a coconut shell lantern.

"It is with much embarrassment that I have returned alive"

The Japanese word *ganbaru* refers to the positive character traits associated with sticking to one's task during tough times. For many Japanese who survived the war, Yokoi was the living embodiment of ganbaru. However, for the young people of Japan's increasingly Western, postwar culture, 56-year-old Yokoi was an embarrassing reminder of the previous generations' blind fealty to the Emperor that had caused Japan's disgrace. Though he longed to see the Emperor and wrote a letter to apologize for having survived the war, Yokoi was never granted an audience.

Reassimilation

Millions of television viewers across Japan watched Yokoi's return trip to his native village where a gravestone listed his death as September 1944. From those who considered him a hero, Yokoi received gifts of money totaling more than $80,000 and many marriage offers. He purchased a modest home and married Mihoko Hatashin, who he described as a "nice, old-fashioned" girl, unlike the modern Japanese girls whom he described as "monsters whose virtue is all but gone from them, and who screech like apes."

Though horrified by the Westernization of his homeland, Yokoi prospered as a lecturer on survival techniques. He unsuccessfully ran for Parliament on a platform that stressed simplicity and discipline and included such measures as enforced composting and converting golf courses into bean fields. On September 22, 1997, Yokoi died of heart failure at age 82.

Fumbling Felons

Click It and Ticket

If you're going to break the law by purse snatching, speeding, and leading the police on a high-speed chase, you may as well go all the way and break one more law by not wearing a seat belt. At least that's how Lawrence Neal of Detroit must have felt after his adventure. He committed the first three crimes, but it was the car seat belt that proved his undoing. During the chase, Neal tried to ditch the car on a front lawn and flee on foot, but got his foot tangled in the seat belt. He was dragged a few hundred feet and broke his leg in the process. Police caught up with him and brought him in on several charges.

Where Do You Find Emma Christ in the Bible?

Emma Kim-Tashis Harrison sometimes goes by her married name: Emma Christ. Or rather, Mrs. Jesus Christ, the name she recently used when attempting to buy a $70,000 car in Jacksonville, Florida. Apparently when you write a check that large, the car dealership feels obligated to run an inquiry on it right away. And surprise, the check and the names on it were bad. The sheriff was called in and charged her with three felonies, including organized fraud. Harrison said her husband, Jesus Christ, would be stopping by the next week to sign papers and pick up the car.

Shoplifting Seagull Chooses Chips

Here's one thief that's actually popular with the locals. His name is Sam—Sam the seagull. No one knows how he got started on his life of crime, but he has been seen (and videotaped) walking into RS McColl Newsagents in Aberdeen, Scotland, and snatching a bag of Doritos with his beak. There's no breaking and entering; the bird simply strolls into the store while the door is open. Maybe it's the proximity of that brand of "crisps," or perhaps it's the look of the bag, but Sam steals the same type of chips each time. He's a savvy little thief, waiting until the coast is clear to make the grab. Then he walks right out and shares his loot with his bird buddies. People are so amazed and entertained by the fowl convict that they have begun to pay the 55 pence for his treat.

The Times They Are A-Changin'

1982

- In a rare occurrence, all nine planets come into near-alignment on the same side of the sun.

- Barney Clark becomes the first person to receive a permanent artificial heart. The successful operation takes place at the University of Utah.

- An Air Florida jet crashes into the 14th Street Bridge in Washington, D.C., and plunges into the Potomac River, apparently due to improper de-icing of the aircraft. Five motorists and more than 74 passengers are killed in the tragedy.

- On February 10, Braemar in Aberdeen, Scotland, boasts the coldest temperature ever recorded in the United Kingdom when the mercury hits −16.96 degrees Fahrenheit.

- Stevie Wonder and Paul McCartney team up to release the hit, "Ebony and Ivory."

- Spain joins the North Atlantic Treaty Organization (NATO) as its 16th member, the first addition since West Germany in 1955.

- Elvis fans rejoice when Priscilla Presley opens Graceland for public viewing.

- Montreal hosts baseball's first Major League All-Star Game to take place outside the United States.

- Dozens of countries send representatives to Geneva, Switzerland, to discuss world trade and the possibilities of free trade.

- Walt Disney World in Florida goes educational with the opening of the EPCOT Center.

- The first execution by lethal injection in the United States is carried out in Texas.

- Michael Jackson releases his sixth studio album, *Thriller*. It's an instant hit, and in little more than a year, it becomes the best-selling album of all time.

The Bottled Water Craze

Bottled water is definitely trendy, but people have been hip to the healing powers of water from mineral springs since ancient times. By the late-18th century, European nobles regularly headed to spas to bathe in and drink from the powerful waters (though not at the same time). By the mid-19th century, railroads made it possible to ship bottled mineral water to middle-class consumers across Western Europe. In North America, Native Americans were sipping from springs in the mid-16th century. White settlers discovered the springs' waters and soon jugs of the stuff were loaded onto western-bound wagon trains.

But by the 20th century, municipal water systems had improved, thanks to the addition of chlorine, and bottled water fell out of fashion. That is, until the chairman of the French water company Perrier decided to try peddling his wares stateside in 1976.

Bottled Enthusiasm

Bruce Nevins was working for Pony athletic company when Perrier's Gustave Leven, an investor in Pony, suggested he sell the bottled carbonated water to U.S. consumers. Within two years, Nevins carved out a $20 million market for Perrier, emphasizing the water's exclusivity and, in particular, its healthfulness—a matter of interest to Americans in the 1970s and '80s.

Impressed with Perrier's success, French company Danone International (known stateside as yogurt company Dannon) introduced Evian to America in 1984 as a plastic-bottled, noncarbonated water targeted to the gym crowd. By the end of the decade, it was Madonna's drink of choice and the hottest accessory for supermodels to be seen toting off the runway, touting its benefits as a complexion clearer and appetite suppressant. The '90s health craze continued to keep the bottled water business afloat. Eventually, bottled water was everywhere from gas stations to gourmet restaurants as a portable—and potable!—cure-all.

Plastic Passion

The industry really took off, when—to counteract all the anti-soda health messaging—Pepsi and Coke jumped on the bandwagon, launching, respectively, Aquafina in 1994 and Dasani in 1999. Today, amid protests about the environmental waste of plastic water bottles, Americans collectively go through more than 25–50 million bottles of water a year.

Being Jeeves

❖ ❖ ❖ ❖

*Think being a butler is all bowing and opening doors? Here's
your chance to find out what it takes to be a butler.*

Do butlers do anything besides answer the door?
Butlers, also known as household managers, take care of everything
that's happening in and around the house, including tending to guests,
managing the budget, supervising other household personnel, organizing dinner parties, taking care of the silverware and other household
items, and organizing the wine cellar. Some butlers may also serve as
personal assistants, running errands, planning travel, and keeping the
family's schedule.

I graduated with a degree in psychology. Can I be a butler?
A good personality and manners are more important than a formal
education, so while the degree may come in handy (for deciphering the
needs of your employer, for instance), it's not necessary. Most employers do look for previous experience, however, so it might behoove you
to take a course at a school such as The International Butler Academy.

Do butlers make any money?
As with any job, your salary as a butler will depend on your location,
skills, and responsibilities. According to the Butlers Guild, a butler is
likely to make anywhere from $40,000 to $150,000 a year. And, the
job usually comes with a bevy of perks, including housing, food, and a
car. Sure, the money sounds smashing, but don't forget, you're on call
24 hours a day.

Are all butlers British?
No, but British butlers are usually what come to
mind when one thinks of the profession. The word
derives from the Old French term *bouteillier,* who
was the person who oversaw the wine cellars and
poured the booze. Servants such as butlers have
been used all over the world, but it was the British
that turned this everyday job into an art form.

The Curse of Camelot: The Kennedy Family

❖ ❖ ❖ ❖

*The Kennedys were as close as America got to royalty.
Educated, attractive, and about as well-placed in society and
politics as possible, the Kennedy family put the "A" in "A-list."
But all the beauty, brains, and big bucks in the world can't
keep a family safe from natural disaster, calamity, and
death—and the Kennedys have endured so much of all three
that some wonder if there's a curse on the whole crew.*

Incriminating Evidence

Okay, so maybe if this family had stayed away
from the White House and off of airplanes,
things would have worked out differently. But
for a family so heavily involved in world politics and jet-setting affairs, that has never really
been an option. As a result, the Kennedys have
seen a rather high number of family tragedies
in the sky and on the political road:

- President John F. Kennedy's brother Joseph
  Jr. and sister Kathleen both died in separate plane crashes in
  1944 and 1948, respectively.

- Another one of JFK's sisters, Rosemary, was institutionalized in a
  mental ward after a failed lobotomy when she was 23.

- America's 35th president, John F. Kennedy, was assassinated in
  1963 at age 46.

- JFK's brother Robert was assassinated in 1968.

- JFK's youngest brother, Senator Ted Kennedy, survived a plane
  crash in 1964. In 1969, he was driving a car that went off a bridge
  and caused the death of his companion, Mary Jo Kopechne.

- In 1984, Robert's son David died of a drug overdose. Another son,
  Michael, died in a skiing accident in 1997.

- In 1999, John F. Kennedy Jr., his wife, and his sister-in-law died when the small plane he was piloting crashed into the Atlantic Ocean.

In addition, JFK's wife, Jackie, suffered a miscarriage and had a stillborn baby during their marriage. When Jackie remarried, her stepson Alex Onassis died in a plane crash and stepdaughter, Christina, died in Argentina of a drug overdose. Several other Kennedy relatives have also died in plane crashes or were involved in deadly car accidents.

Is It a Curse or Bad Luck?

Unlike many rumored curses, there's no ancient origin of the Kennedy curse—no angry king, no agitated 16th-century wizard, no funky tribal hex. No, the Kennedy family's alleged curse seems to have been born out of a general dismay at all the awful things that seem to happen to them. One family couldn't possibly fall victim to that many tragedies; thus, they must be cursed!

It's more likely that the general public is more aware of these tragedies because the Kennedy family for generations has lived life in the public eye. Your Aunt Myrtle might've passed away from a strange Amazonian jungle disease on the same day your dog died, but no one's claiming your family is cursed. The Kennedys have lived under scrutiny for decades, which makes the public and media more apt to draw conclusions based on non-corollary information.

In addition, the Kennedy family is big—bigger than most (JFK was one of nine children, and Robert had 11 kids), which increases the likelihood of accidents. The more people there are, the more chance there is that someone's going to die in a remarkable way.

Furthermore, when your entire family spends a lot of time in private jets on international missions, in fast sports cars, and with high-rolling people who tend to live dangerously, the chances are much higher that some of you might perish in plane crashes, auto accidents, and drug overdoses.

Only time will tell if the next generation of the Kennedy clan will fare any better, or if the "curse" will prove to be more than just a popular myth.

Fast Facts

- When he died, George Washington had but a single real tooth left in his mouth.

- Calvin Coolidge liked having his head rubbed with Vaseline at breakfast.

- In 1930, Herbert Hoover predicted unemployment would be eliminated within 60 days.

- Almost as many Americans fought for the British during the American Revolution as fought against the British.

- In 1828, Philadelphia tried to sell the Liberty Bell for scrap.

- Despite popular belief, Confederate President Jefferson Davis was not wearing women's clothing when he was captured at the end of the Civil War.

- The first Emancipation Proclamation was not issued by Abraham Lincoln, but by British Royal Governor Lord Dunmore of Virginia in 1775.

- In early 1865, the Confederacy told England and France that it was willing to emancipate its slaves in return for recognition as an independent country.

- In 1659, the leaders of the Massachusetts Bay colony passed a law against celebrating Christmas.

- The Pilgrims first landed at Provincetown, Massachusetts—not Plymouth.

- During the Civil War, there were more Northern-born Confederate generals than Southern-born Union generals.

FROM THE VAULTS OF HISTORY

- In 1943, Nebraskan quilter Grace Snyder completed her quilt, "Flower Basket Petit Point," using 87,000 tiny triangles. Her design was based on a china pattern.

- The first man to die during planning and construction of the Hoover Dam was the father of the last man to die during its construction. J. G. Tierney, a Bureau of Reclamation employee who was part of the geological survey, drowned when he fell from a barge on December 20, 1922. Exactly 13 years later, in 1935, his son, Patrick W. Tierney, fell to his death from a dam intake tower.

- John Lennon's girlfriend at art school before meeting his first wife was named Thelma Pickles.

- Beethoven was rumored to be extremely particular about his coffee: He insisted on counting 60 beans per cup.

- A woman named Mary Anderson patented the windshield wiper in 1905.

- Only two people signed the Declaration of Independence on July 4, 1776: John Hancock and Charles Thomson. Most of the rest of the signatures came later, on August 2.

- As a child, Albert Einstein was diagnosed as dyslexic, because he couldn't speak properly until he was four years old and couldn't read until he was nine.

- Dr. William Semple first added sugar to chewing gum in the late 1800s. He also experimented with adding charcoal and powdered licorice root, believing these ingredients added to his (rubber) gum would help clean teeth.

- Mel Blanc, the voice of Bugs Bunny, also provided the rabbit's signature carrot-chomping sound. However, chewing and swallowing a carrot took too much time and effort, so during recording Blanc would bite into a carrot, chew a bit, then spit it out.

- Dr. Seuss pronounced his last name to rhyme with "rejoice."

- If Barbie's measurements were true to life size, she'd measure an impossible 39–23–33.

Losing Philip K. Dick's Head

❖ ❖ ❖ ❖

*Consider the sorts of things an air traveler might accidentally
leave in an overhead bin: a novel, a jacket, a laptop computer…
or perhaps the $750,000 android head of author Philip K. Dick.*

Meet David Hanson

In the world of robotics, David Hanson is known as the genius inventor of "frubber"—an uncannily authentic-looking synthetic skin. With
this breakthrough, Hanson has created robots modeled after popular
figures, anyone ranging from Albert Einstein to rocker David Byrne.
In 2004, his firm, Hanson Robotics, led a team of artists, scientists,
and literary scholars to create an android modeled after science fiction
writer Philip K. Dick, who died in 1982. To build the android's body
of synthetic knowledge, a team led by artificial intelligence (AI) expert
Andrew Olney scanned 20 of Dick's novels as well as interviews,
speeches, and biographical information into its computer brain.

After six months of work, the completed android was an impressive
achievement. Using a camera for its eyes, the android could follow
movement, make eye contact, and recognize familiar faces in a crowd.
The android's cutting-edge AI applications allowed it to respond to
queries using its inputted source material (though its replies were
often off-topic and bordered on the surreal—not unlike the real-life
Dick, according to friends). The team called him "Phil."

Meet Philip K. Dick

Hanson and his team chose an apt subject for their robot. Many of
Dick's stories are peopled with synthetic humans who call into question what qualifies as human. This theme is evident in several of the
films adapted from his works, including *Blade Runner* (based on
the novel *Do Androids Dream of Electric Sheep?*) and *Total Recall*
(based on *We Can Remember It for You Wholesale*). Hanson's team
was particularly inspired by Dick's novel *We Can Build You,* in which
two unsuccessful electric-organ salesmen construct a lifelike robot of
Edward M. Stanton, Secretary of War under Abraham Lincoln. The
competing needs of the human characters, coupled with the android's

increasing humanity, play out in a rich tale that challenges the reader's imagination. Little did Hanson's team realize that their robot would also become part of its own odd legend.

David Hanson Loses His Head

In June 2005, Phil made his debut appearance at Chicago's NextFest technology exhibition. He was a sensation. The technically minded marveled at the feat of engineering, the sci-fi fans thrilled at the wonderful irony of interacting with an android replication of their long-dead hero, and the merely curious were rewarded by the eerie sense of humanity that Phil inspired.

On the heels of this success, Hanson, juggling time between his growing firm and his doctoral work, carted Phil around the country. In Pittsburgh, Hanson received the Open Interaction Award for Robotics from the American Association for Artificial Intelligence. At the San Diego Comic Con, Phil took part in a panel discussing the upcoming release of *A Scanner Darkly* (based on the Dick novel of the same name). Phil was a sensation: Hanson and Phil made appearances in Memphis, New Orleans, and Dallas. There was talk of a tour to promote the movie, an appearance on the *Late Show with David Letterman,* and a stint in the Smithsonian Institute's traveling collection. It was awfully heady stuff for a head.

In early 2006, Phil was on his way to Mountain View, California. He was stored face down in Styrofoam, bundled in a gym bag, and stowed in the overhead bin on the plane. Hanson, bleary from sleep, changed flights in Las Vegas. Soon afterward, he realized that Phil was still on the plane. The airline confirmed that Phil had traveled with the plane to Orange County. The android was supposed to be put on a flight to San Francisco but never arrived. Phil has not been seen since.

All Is Not Lost

Though the unique Philip K. Dick head has vanished, Hanson's laptop, containing Phil's brain, is safe. Despite the heartbreaking loss, Hanson has indicated that he may build another head for Phil. A failed lawsuit against the airline, however, means that, ironically, like the real-life Philip K. Dick, Phil must wait for the two things most precious to a struggling writer: time and money.

INSPIRATION STATION

Heaven, Hell, and Everything in Between

No other book has ever affected the city of Savannah, Georgia, as much as *Midnight in the Garden of Good and Evil,* John Berendt's 1994 highbrow true crime story. Berendt's fascinating description of Savannah's eccentric characters and their unique manners and habits fueled a huge tourist boom for Savannah in the years to follow.

But perhaps just as intriguing as Berendt's writing is the cover photograph of the book, taken by Savannah photographer Jack Leigh. Inspired by the southern gothic ghoulishness of *Garden,* Leigh went to Bonaventure Cemetery and snapped the now-iconic photo of the *Bird Girl,* a 1936 bronze sculpture by Sylvia Shaw Judson. Wearing a long, simple dress and a peaceful (yet rather spooky) expression on her face, the Bird Girl holds up a plate in each hand, seemingly weighing the good and evil described in Berendt's title. So many fans of *Midnight in the Garden of Good and Evil* flocked to Bonaventure Cemetery to see her, that for her own safety she was finally moved to Savannah's Telfair Museum of Art.

Sweet as Candy

Most women can't even say they're the inspiration for even one song, but Candy Darling wasn't even a natural-born woman, and she was the muse for *three* tracks. Candy was a beautiful, blonde, male-to-female transsexual who ran with Andy Warhol's crowd in the late 1960s and early '70s.

She also starred in two of Warhol's films. As part of the New York scene, she came in contact with Lou Reed, the lead singer and guitarist of the psychedelic rock band The Velvet Underground. Though Candy was only one of Reed's many muses, she was captivating enough to inspire a couple of songs. First, with the Velvet Underground, he recorded "Candy Says," about Darling's struggle to become a woman and the effect female hormones had on her: "I've come to hate my body/ And all that it requires in this world." Later, as a solo musician, he wrote about Candy again in "Walk on the Wild Side," describing her as "everybody's darling." She also may have been the inspiration for the Kinks' hit, "Lola." Candy died of leukemia at the age of 29 on March 21st, 1974—still fabulous in full makeup.

Pepsi's Mad Scientists

❖ ❖ ❖ ❖

In their quest to unseat the cola giant, Coca-Cola, the folks at Pepsi Co. are continually hard at work to create the ultimate drink—resulting in some pretty bizarre beverages.

Crystal Pepsi
When Pepsi said they were going to release a caffeine-free "clear alternative" to other colas, they weren't kidding. In 1992, they released Crystal Pepsi, a colorless cola that confused the heck out of people. The enormous flop lasted only a year on the market.

Pepsi Blue
In 2002, Coca-Cola released Vanilla Coke. In an attempt to compete with this new taste sensation, Pepsi countered with their Pepsi Blue. This blue-tinted soda was said to contain "berry flavors," although just which berries was never specified. Despite massive advertising campaigns, Pepsi Blue tanked and left most markets by 2004.

Pepsi Fire and Pepsi Ice
In early 2005, fire and ice (in cola form) started appearing on grocery shelves all across Asia. Pepsi Fire had a taste not unlike that of hot cinnamon candies, while Pepsi Ice had a bizarre "minty aftertaste." Not surprisingly, teens dared each other to drink "fire and ice" concoctions.

Pepsi Ice Cucumber
In 2007, Pepsi released a new flavor that a spokespeople said was designed to make "people think of keeping cool in the summer heat." Apparently that meant Pepsi Ice Cucumber. For better or worse, the beverage does not contain any real cucumbers, but rather the "refreshing taste of a fresh cucumber."

Pepsi White
In 2008, a new flavor hit Japanese markets: Pepsi White. The bizarre drink's flavor was supposed to be a combination of Pepsi and yogurt. However, the milky white concoction didn't taste like either one. Pepsi White was soon labeled a "limited edition" and was gone by year's end.

Stealing the President

❖ ❖ ❖ ❖

*While he was alive, President Abraham Lincoln was loved
and admired by many. Perhaps his popularity was the
reason why in 1876, a group of men decided that people
would be willing to pay a lot of money to see the 16th
president of the United States—even if he was dead.*

Breaking Out Boyd

The plot was hatched in 1876, 11 years after
President Lincoln's assassination by John
Wilkes Booth. Illinois engraver Benjamin
Boyd had been arrested on charges of creating engraving plates to make counterfeit
bills. Boyd's boss, James "Big Jim" Kinealy,
a man known around Chicago as the King of
the Counterfeiters, was determined to get
Boyd out of prison in order to continue his
counterfeiting operation.

Kinealy's plan was to kidnap Lincoln's corpse from his
mausoleum at the Oak Ridge Cemetery in Springfield, Illinois,
and hold it for ransom—$200,000 in cash and a full pardon for
Boyd. Not wanting to do the dirty work himself, Kinealy turned to
two men: John "Jack" Hughes and Terrence Mullen, a bartender
at The Hub, a Madison Street bar frequented by Kinealy and his
associates.

Kinealy told Hughes and Mullen that they were to steal
Lincoln's body on Election Night, November 7, load it onto a
cart, and take it roughly 200 miles north to the shores of Lake
Michigan. They were to bury the body in the sand, to stow it until
the ransom was paid. The plan seemed foolproof until Hughes
and Mullen decided they needed a third person to help steal the
body—a fellow named Lewis Swegles. It was a decision Hughes
and Mullen would come to regret.

The Plan Backfires

The man directly responsible for bringing Boyd in was Patrick D. Tyrrell, a member of the Secret Service in Chicago. Long before their current role of protecting the president of the United States, one of the main jobs for members of the Secret Service was to track down and arrest counterfeiters. One of Tyrrell's informants was a small-time crook by the name of Lewis Swegles. Yes, the same guy who agreed to help Hughes and Mullen steal the president's body. Thanks to the stool pigeon, everything the duo was planning was being reported back to the Secret Service.

On the evening of November 7, 1865, Hughes, Mullen, and Swegles entered the Lincoln Mausoleum, unaware of the Secret Service lying in wait. The hoods broke open Lincoln's sarcophagus and removed the casket, and Swegles was sent to get the wagon. Swegles gave the signal to make the arrest, but once the Secret Service men reached the mausoleum, they found it to be empty. In all the confusion, Hughes and Mullen had slipped away, leaving Lincoln's body behind.

Unsure what to do next, Tyrrell ordered Swegles back to Chicago to see if he could pick up the kidnappers' trail. Swegles eventually found them in a local Chicago tavern, and on November 16 or 17 (sources vary), Hughes and Mullen were arrested without incident.

Lincoln Is Laid to Rest (Again)

With no laws on the books at the time pertaining to the stealing of a body, Hughes and Mullen were only charged with attempted larceny of Lincoln's coffin and a count each of conspiracy. After a brief trial, both men were found guilty. Their sentence for attempting to steal the body of President Abraham Lincoln: One year in the Illinois state penitentiary in Joliet.

As for Lincoln's coffin (and body), it was finally returned to its home in Oak Ridge Cemetery on September 26, 1901. This time, though, the Lincoln family took steps to ensure Abe's body could never be stolen: It was buried ten feet under the floor of the mausoleum, inside a metal cage, and under thousands of pounds of concrete.

Fast Facts

- *The first stop sign was erected in Detroit in 1914.*

- *Chrysler offered an in-dash record player as an option in 1956. It played special 16 ⅔ RPM records.*

- *In 1932, the United States became the world's first country to tax gasoline.*

- *The average person exerts between 125–150 pounds of pressure when biting or chewing. However, people with a condition known as bruxism may exert up to 250 pounds of pressure—enough to crack a walnut.*

- *Oil dropped to as low as three cents a barrel in 1901. This cheap oil made gasoline engines win out over other available sources of automotive power, such as electricity or steam.*

- *The smallest snake in the world is the Martinique thread snake, which measures only 4¼ inches long when full grown.*

- *As originally presented, the self-service laundry was called a "washateria."*

- *Disposable diapers—nick-named "nappies"—first appeared in Great Britain in 1949.*

- *The first drive-in restaurant, which opened in 1921, was called the Pig Stand.*

- *Renowned aviator Charles Lindbergh was asked to leave the University of Wisconsin because of poor grades. After he became the first person to fly solo across the Atlantic Ocean, the university awarded him an honorary doctorate.*

Errol Flynn and the Cuban Rebel Girls

❖ ❖ ❖ ❖

Flynn's last film is a peculiar screen epitaph of a Hollywood legend.

The final screen appearance of virile Hollywood leading man Errol Flynn is a shocker. It seems inconceivable that the man who had starred in *The Adventures of Robin Hood* and *The Sea Hawk* should place himself in a no-budget 1959 picture called *Cuban Rebel Girls*—co-starring his real-life teenage girlfriend, no less. Not to mention Flynn's physical condition in the movie is more than disquieting—at barely 50 years old, he was lined, faintly bloated, and visibly drunk.

Screen Idol
Errol Flynn played swashbuckling heroes many times, but nowhere as effectively as in real life. Tall, athletic, and dashingly handsome, he exuded an easy, irreverent charm that won him fans and friends. An accomplished yachtsman, Flynn also was a novelist, memoirist, inveterate womanizer, and Olympian drinker. He was married three times, and after he beat a statutory rape charge in 1943, Americans began using the expression, "In like Flynn," to signify a person who beat the system, someone too cool for words.

Politically, Flynn leaned to the left—no surprise for a man who reveled in excess and answered to no one. While traveling in Cuba in 1958, Flynn became enchanted with Fidel Castro—or perhaps with the *idea* of Castro—and the final push to oust U.S.-supported dictator Fulgencio Batista.

The Actor, the Girl, and the Guerrilla
Accompanying Flynn in Cuba was 16-year-old Beverly Aadland, a baby-faced blonde whom he had chatted up when he met her a year or two prior at the Hollywood Professional School. With Aadland and a small film crew in tow, Flynn ventured into the Sierra Maestra mountains, where he arranged a face-to-face meeting with Castro and filmed the leader and his rebels.

One result of this was a not-bad 50-minute documentary called *Cuban Story*. Since documentaries didn't exactly draw big crowds in 1958, Flynn reasoned that he could cover his travel and production expenses if he spliced some of the real-life footage into a new, fictional story: *Cuban Rebel Girls*.

The Creative Muse

A small cast of unknowns was assembled. Flynn selected Barry Mahon to direct and, nominally, produce the picture. In earlier years, Flynn had worked with some of the best directors in the world, but Mahon's only prior credit was a wretched sci-fi thriller called *Rocket Attack USA*. (Mahon's resume would later include such triumphs as *Pagan Island, Nudes Inc.*, and *Prostitutes' Protective Society*.)

Flynn plays himself in *Cuban Rebel Girls*, but not simply as a movie star with a vague political agenda—no, he's a globetrotting adventurer hired by a news service to cover the revolution. As he makes his way deep into the mountains in the opening of this 68-minute "epic," he encounters Castro, and he chronicles the guerrillas' daily activities via a blend of fact and fabrication. The Cuban rebel girls—including the very-blonde Aadland—are just as convincing as one might imagine.

Fade to Black

In the film's woeful highlight, Flynn takes a (fake) bullet in the leg and is bandaged by Aadland. Our hero is very obviously and very amiably drunk in these scenes, unsteady on his feet, and unable to focus on Aadland or anything else. But star power seldom dies out completely; although Flynn appeared older than his years, he still was a good-looking man who managed to summon an ounce of the old sparkle.

Flynn did not live to see the brief theatrical run of *Cuban Rebel Girls;* he died of heart failure in Vancouver on October 14, 1959. An autopsy revealed that more than just Flynn's heart was worn out: Most of the rest of his body—particularly his poor, beleaguered liver—was shot. The doctor remarked that, internally, Flynn's 50-year-old body was that of an elderly man.

In *The Filmgoer's Companion*, film historian Leslie Halliwell praised Flynn "for living several lives in half of one, and almost getting away with it."

We'll buy that.

MYTH CONCEPTIONS

Myth: Birth control pills don't work as well with antibiotics.

Fact: Medical scientists have officially concluded that common antibiotics don't affect the efficacy of birth control pills.

Myth: Humans use only about 10 percent of their brains.

Fact: Actually, scientists have proven that there is no part of the brain that is not active in some way.

Myth: Most of your body heat is lost through your head.

Fact: Sorry, there's nothing special about your noggin—at least when it comes to heat loss. You'll lose heat through any uncovered body part.

Myth: Marijuana use causes brain damage.

Fact: Modern brain-imaging techniques have found no signs of brain damage or killed brain cells in marijuana users, even in those who smoke multiple times per day. No widely accepted scientific studies have proven long-term damage resulting from marijuana use, either.

Myth: Crashing is the worst thing that can happen on a plane.

Fact: Not to be a downer here, but actually, in most airplane accidents, there's an on-board fire. And when there's a fire, the biggest threat is actually the toxic smoke, which can spread fast in a closed cabin, obstructing everyone's view of the emergency exits and making it difficult to breathe or speak.

Myth: It never snows in the desert.

Fact: Believe it or not, the largest desert in the world is Antarctica, where it snows a lot—the mean annual precipitation ranges from 5.9 to 10.2 inches. So why is Antarctica considered a desert? The definition of a desert is a region that receives very little rain. To be precise, a desert landscape exists where rainfall is less than 10 inches per year. Rain, of course, is needed to sustain certain types of plants and animals, but snow doesn't count as rain. So Antarctica is dry enough to be considered a desert and too dry for a person to survive without water.

Pirates? *Yar!*

❖ ❖ ❖ ❖

As long as cargo has been carried across the sea, there have been pirates who have tried to plunder the goods, or "booty." Learn more about what it meant to be a pirate in the good ol' days of privateering.

The Genuine Arrr-ticle

Most consider the golden age of piracy to be from the 16th to 18th centuries. Pirates at this time could be found primarily sailing their ships around the Caribbean Sea, off the coasts of Arabia and North Africa, and in the South China Sea. These were major sea trade routes at the time, and the huge cargo ships there routinely transported everything from gold and silver to ivory, spices, and slaves. Anything of worth was desirable to the pirate, who could either use what he stole or sell it at a profit wherever his ship landed next.

Worth the Risk?

Being a pirate was a big gamble. Piracy was illegal, and punishment often meant torture and death by hanging. Basically, if you were caught pirating, you were toast.

But if you could remain free, privateering was a better occupation than many available on land. You could say that pirates were equal opportunity employers: blacks, West Indians, Arabs, and everyone in between were welcome to "go on the account," in other words, to sign up to work a pirate ship. Discrimination was almost nonexistent: If you could sail, steal, and keep a secret, you were in. Many black men enlisted, since their only other option was often forced slavery in Europe and in America. Criminals on the lam, as well as people who opposed their government, found asylum on a pirate ship (which numbered around 100 men, depending on the size of the vessel). Piracy was a refuge for many, but remember, if they were caught, they faced death.

Another Day at the Office

Many jobs were onboard the ship. There was the role of the captain, who acted as the commander of his onboard army. Captains, while

indisputably in charge, were just as vulnerable as the rest of their men when it came to
justice. If one pirate ship attacked another,
the captain of the victorious fleet would
ask the captured crew if their captain was
a fair man. If he was, he lived. If not, he'd
likely be thrown overboard. Famous pirate
captains include "Black Sam" Bellamy and
Blackbeard,

For others, most of their time
privateering was spent like that of any
mariner. The daily grind of mending the ship's ropes and sails,
repairing rowboats, and swabbing the decks kept the sailors busy
between attacks. Life onboard was much more lenient than that of,
say, the British Royal Navy, but there was still a lot of work to be
done, and each man was expected to pull his own weight.

There were specialty jobs, too. A surgeon (or someone with at
least a little medical experience) was usually kept onboard, as well
as a quartermaster, who dealt with counting money and keeping
the peace. Other positions aboard a pirate ship included the cook,
master gunner (in charge of ammunition), and boatswain (head of
the cables, anchors, and such).

A Pirate's Life for Me

Food was scarce on the ship, though pirates tended to eat better
than most other sailors. Dolphin and tuna meat was supplemented
with yams, plantains, and other exotic fruits. Life onboard was
crowded, dirty, and smelly, but the pirates kept their sense of humor.
They were known to put on plays, play cards and dice, sing songs,
and dance all day long, reveling in the freedom they enjoyed. There
were even some crews that held mock trials, entertaining themselves
with hypothetical scenarios of being caught and put on trial.

But what about all that booty? The notion of buried treasure has
been debunked, unfortunately—when pirates had money, they spent
it. When on land, the crew of a pirate ship could be found carousing
in pubs and indulging in wine, women, and song until it was time to
board the ship and sail in search of more treasure.

Odd Ordinances

- In Nevada, camels are not to be driven on the highway.

- In Elko, Nevada, the law states that everyone must wear a mask while on the street. That must make it easy for bank robbers.

- It is against the law to lie down on a sidewalk in Reno, Nevada.

- Picking seaweed from the beach is not considered legal in New Hampshire.

- Farmers, do you know where your cows are? Any cattle crossing New Hampshire state roads must be wearing a device that collects their feces.

- In New Hampshire, you cannot pay off your gambling debts by selling the clothes you are wearing.

- It's illegal for a man in New Jersey to knit during the fishing season.

- In Cresskill, New Jersey, cats must wear not one but *three* bells so that birds are forewarned of their whereabouts.

- There's no steak tartare in Ocean City, New Jersey—the selling of raw hamburger is prohibited.

- In Newark, New Jersey, it's against the law to sell ice cream after 6 P.M.—unless the customer has a note from his or her doctor.

- Idiots are not allowed to vote in New Mexico.

- It is illegal to hunt in Mountain View Cemetery in Deming, New Mexico.

- New Yorkers can be fined $25 for flirting.

- Here's one that makes sense: The penalty for jumping off a building in New York is death.

- In New York, it's illegal to throw a ball at someone's head for fun. Spoilsports.

- It's perfectly legal to take home roadkill for dinner in West Virginia.

Cuckoo Collections

❖ ❖ ❖ ❖

Tired of the usual museum fare? Try these oddball collections!

Mr. Ed's Elephant Museum

If you still retain a pinch of youthful wonder, a love of kitsch, and don't have a peanut allergy, Mr. Ed's Elephant Museum in Orrtanna, Pennsylvania, is the place for you.

Ed Gotwalt's obsession with elephants began in 1967 when his sister-in-law gave him an elephant statuette as a wedding present. He opened his first elephant museum in 1975, and the present location started in 1984. The museum's 6,000 items include an elephant potty chair, an elephant pulling a 24-karat gold circus wagon, and Miss Ellie, a 9½-foot-tall fiberglass elephant that welcomes visitors from the side of the road.

Museum of Bad Art

The *Mona Lisa* and *The Birth of Venus* are so cliché. Good art is over-appreciated, which is why bad art deserves a second look. At the Museum of Bad Art (MOBA) in Massachusetts, visitors can visit two galleries that display overwhelmingly awful works of "art." Both spaces are housed next to the men's restroom—one at the Somerville Theatre in Somerville and the other at the Dedham Community Theater in Dedham; there, the MOBA Web site points out, the artwork is "appropriately lit by one large, humming fluorescent light fixture."

International Banana Club Museum

If you tell Ken Bannister he's totally bananas, he'll probably take it as a compliment. The International Banana Club Museum in Hesperia, California, started when Bannister handed out banana stickers purely for fun and received a bunch of banana-related items in return. Since 1976, this storehouse of all things banana has grown vast enough to be listed in *Guinness World Records.*

The museum showcases banana trees, pipes, pins, belts, charms, glasses, rings, clocks, software, cups, and lights. Wacky (well, *wackier*) items include a Michael Jackson banana, and a "petrified" banana, which is hard as rock and dates back to 1975.

The Enigma of the Crystal Skulls

❖ ❖ ❖ ❖

Once upon a time, a legendary set of crystal skulls was scattered across the globe. It was said that finding one of these skulls would bring the lucky person wealth ... or death. The story also goes on to say that if all the skulls were located and placed together, they would begin to speak and reveal prophecies, including the end of the world. Could these skulls really exist?

The History... Maybe

Admittedly, the background of the crystal skulls is a little patchy. According to the legend, either the Aztecs or the Mayas hid 13 crystal human-size skulls around the world (though the number varies story to story). The skulls are said to possess supernatural powers, including the ability to speak as well as to heal, so perhaps they were hidden to prevent them from falling into the wrong hands.

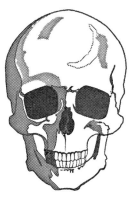

Incredibly, several crystal skulls do exist—you can see even them in respected museums such as the British Museum and the Smithsonian. However, there is no documentation to support that any of the skulls were found during an excavation, or how they were found at all, for that matter. So where did they come from?

Selling Skulls and Seeing Visions

In the late 1800s, Eugene Boban was enjoying a successful career as a world-traveling antiques dealer. Boban is believed to have owned at least three of the crystal skulls, although it is unclear where he acquired them. However, two of these Boban skulls would end up in museums—one in the British Museum and one in Paris' Musee de l'Homme.

But the most intriguing crystal skull is one that Boban did not own. This skull was discovered in 1924 by Anna Le Guillon

Mitchell-Hedges, the adopted daughter of famed British adventurer F. A. Mitchell-Hedges. Anna claimed she found the skull in what is now Belize, inside a pyramid. Interestingly, her father wrote several books, but he never once mentions his daughter finding a crystal skull. Professional jealousy or did he regard the skull as a sham? Regardless, Anna claimed that the skull had magical powers and that she once stared into the skull's eye sockets and had a premonition of President John F. Kennedy's assassination.

Putting the Skulls to the Test

Since the legends say that the skulls were handcarved, or a gift from the heavens (or aliens), scientists were eager to determine how they were formed. When the British Museum conducted tests on the two skulls they owned, they found marks that made it clear the skulls were carved using modern rotary tools. Likewise, Paris' Musee de l'Homme also found that their skull was created using modern tools. Both museums also discovered that the type of crystal used to form the skulls wasn't even available anywhere in the Aztec or Mayan empires.

At first, Anna Mitchell-Hedges was open to having the skull she found tested by the company Hewlett Packard (HP). They found that the skull was indeed crystal—and one solid block of crystal at that, which is incredibly difficult to carve, whether by hand or using modern machinery. Interestingly, Hewlett Packard also found that the quartz crystal is the same kind of crystal used in making computers.

The Legend Continues

Skeptics dismiss the crystal skulls as nothing more than a silly story. And it *is* an entertaining theory: Even director Steven Spielberg jumped on the bandwagon with his 2008 movie, *Indiana Jones and the Kingdom of the Crystal Skull.* True believers, on the other hand, firmly believe that just because the current skulls may be fakes, it doesn't mean the real skulls aren't still out there waiting to be found. And, say the believers, once all 13 are placed together in a room, the skulls will begin to speak, first to each other and then to anyone else who might be present. But until then, the crystal skulls are keeping their mouths shut.

FROM THE VAULTS OF HISTORY

Everyone Hates Galileo

It would be an understatement to say that the Catholic Church and Italian Jack of all science, Galileo Galilei, didn't get along very well. The Church didn't like Galileo putting all kinds of wild ideas into people's heads, such as the fact that the earth revolves around the sun and that objects of different weights fall at the same speed.

Under extreme pressure from the church, Galileo eventually recanted the scientific stuff and was forced to live in seclusion until his death in 1642. But all the blame can't be laid on the Catholics—there were plenty of Protestants who were happy to have the Catholic Church do all the dirty work. One of those Protestants was the German reformer Martin Luther, who called Galileo a "madman," and insisted, "Scripture tells us that Joshua bade the sun, and not the Earth, to stand still." See, but if the sun wasn't moving, Joshua couldn't have told it to stand still. So there!

Dissecting Geography

There's been many a child who has hated his or her geography lessons. Even John Spilsbury, an English mapmaker and engraver, recognized this way back in the 1760s. He decided that rather than bore children to tears with rote memorization, he would come up with an interesting and entertaining way to teach them the locations of the countries and territories of Europe and the wider world. Spilsbury used a fine saw to cut apart maps that were pasted onto wooden boards, inventing the first of what he called "dissected maps." They may not have been quite as exciting as episodes of *Where in the World Is Carmen Sandiego?*, but these large puzzles presumably made the subject of geography just a little more bearable for 18th-century children.

"War is God's way of teaching Americans geography."

—Ambrose Bierce

ANAGRAMS

An anagram is a word or phrase that exactly reproduces the letters in another word or phrases. The most interesting of them comment on the subject of the first.

Debit card—Bad credit

Noël Coward is—no Oscar Wilde

Dentist chair—I'd sit an' retch

Dinner date—End it, Andre

Relationship—I trip on leash

Literary agent—Try a great line

Youtube star—Rob? A tutu? Yes!

Chairman Mao—I am on a march

One night stand—Had, isn't no gent

Hair metal—Harem tail

Dormitory—Dirty room

Politician—A con, I lip it

Rolling Stones—I'll rest, no song

Cheerleader—Cad here leer

Alec Guinness—Genuine class

Simon Cowell—I'm lone scowl

Baseball Game—Gamble as able

M. Caine—Cinema

Cowboy Hat—Hot by Waco

Pantyhose—Nay, she opt

Summer Vacation—Car? Van? Use it, Mom.

The eyes—They see

The King Who Talked with Trees

❖ ❖ ❖ ❖

*Known as "Farmer George" for his love of rural life
and "America's Last King" for losing the Revolutionary
War, the unfortunate final nickname of King George
III could well have been "His Royal Madness-ty."*

A Fine Start

George III became King of England in 1760 at age 22, after his
grandfather, George II, died from
an aneurism that he suffered while
in his water closet. (Young George's
father, Frederick, who would have
been heir to the throne, had died
when the prince was age 12.)

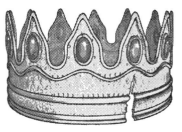

George III and his queen, Charlotte, produced 15 potential heirs
to the throne, and they became known for their model family life.
To the chagrin of family and other proper upper-class folks, George
enjoyed many hobbies considered eccentric for a royal. Keenly
interested in agriculture, he spent much time constructing and
supervising model farms. He collected books (approximately 65,250)
and tinkered endlessly with watches and other small gadgets. His
subjects found these common traits endearing. But neither they
nor the upper crust could have imagined the eventual fate of their
modest and generous leader.

Monarch Madness

Although he was a healthy devotee of exercise and simple food,
George had his first mental breakdown in the fall of 1788 when
a page observed him involved in a heated discussion with a tree.
Other times, George would incoherently and incessantly babble.
After he started foaming at the mouth, doctors bled him, put him in a
straitjacket, and covered him with smelly hot compresses designed
to draw out evil substances. Despite the archaic 18th-century medical practices, he miraculously recovered in about a year.

However, the illness returned in 1811 after the death of his favorite daughter, Amelia, who had succumbed to tuberculosis. Now age 72, George began acting with such "dreadful excitement" that the "mad doctor" had to be called back to the castle. The king continued to suffer frequent delusions, often declaring Princess Amelia was alive and living in Germany. Eventually his aides had to bring out restraints again; George barely escaped a proposed shock treatment of being doused with buckets of cold water. His son, the future George IV, ruled in his father's stead as official prince regent of Great Britain.

King George spent the last ten years of his life wandering in an enclosed area of Windsor Castle in a purple robe, blind and eventually deaf, his royal jewelry pinned to his chest. Some of his later delusions were that God had sent a second flood similar to Noah's, and that he, himself, was dead. Eventually, he was so far removed from reality that he never knew that his wife died in 1818. The king quietly passed away in his bed in 1820 at age 81.

Why the Weirdness

Two doctors, Ida Macalpine and Richard Hunter, published an article in 1966 claiming George III actually suffered from a complex of genetic disorders called porphyria, a medical condition that was not recognized in the monarch's time. Porphyria causes the blood to make too much red pigment, which affects the entire nervous system and brain and can cause a wide constellation of symptoms, including bizarre behavior.

In 2003, an envelope holding a few strands of hair of George III was found buried in a London museum. Specialists tested the hair; they found that the king's medicine contained high levels of arsenic—as much as 300 times the toxic level—that could have poisoned him and brought on the porphyric attacks. Ironically, the medicine was prescribed by the "mad doctor"—who was simply trying to cure the very illness he was creating.

Say What?

"No man living knows more about women than I do—and I know nothing."

—*Seymour Hicks*

"A woman has got to love a bad man once or twice in her life, to be thankful for a good one."

—*Marjorie Kinnan Rawlings*

"Television is called a medium because it is neither rare nor well-done."

—*Ernie Kovacs*

"Everything you read in the newspapers is absolutely true, except for that rare story of which you happen to have firsthand knowledge, which is absolutely false."

—*Erwin Knoll*

"Condoms aren't completely safe. A friend of mine was wearing one and got hit by a bus."

—*Bob Rubin*

"Anyone who goes to a psychiatrist should have his head examined."

—*Samuel Goldwyn*

"If a doctor treats your flu, it will go away in 14 days. If you leave it alone, it will go away in two weeks."

—*Gloria Silverstein*

"Smoking is one of the leading causes of statistics."

—*Fletcher Knebel*

"Smart women love smart men more than smart men love smart women."

—*Natalie Portman*

"Why don't they make the whole plane out of that black box stuff?"

—*Steven Wright*

"To err is human, but to really foul things up, you need a computer."

—*Paul Ehrlich*

"Analyzing humor is like dissecting a frog. Few people are interested and the frog dies of it."

—*E. B. White*

If You See Only Five...

Classic Horror Flicks

❖ ❖ ❖ ❖

*Horror has long been a cinema staple. These
five creepy classics are sure to please.*

1. Nosferatu (1922): Nine years before Bela Lugosi donned his
trademark tuxedo in *Dracula,* movie audiences thrilled to this unauthorized
German adaptation of Bram Stoker's novel. Directed by F. W. Murnau and
starring Max Schreck as the blood-sucking Count Orlok, the movie was
considered groundbreaking, and it continues to terrify nearly nine decades
later.

2. Cat People (1942): A modern variation on the classic werewolf theme,
Cat People revolves around Irena Dubrovna, who believes herself to be a
descendant of an evil tribe capable of transforming into panthers when
emotionally aroused. Director Jacques Tourneur reveals as little as possible,
preferring instead to let the audience's imagination do the heavy lifting.

3. Psycho (1960): Relating the story of creepy motel owner Norman
Bates and his murderous "mother," *Psycho* is one of director Alfred
Hitchcock's best-known films. *Psycho* also has an interesting pedigree: It's
based on the same-titled Robert Bloch novel, which in turn was inspired by
notorious real-life murderer and grave robber Ed Gein.

4. The Haunting (1963): Haunted house stories are a dime a dozen, but
few are as genuinely frightening as *The Haunting,* based on the novel *The
Haunting of Hill House* by Shirley Jackson. Julie Harris plays Eleanor "Nell"
Lance, an emotionally unbalanced woman who agrees to stay in a creepy
mansion as part of a study into the paranormal. This is another film that
often suggests more than it shows, with truly frightening results.

5. The Exorcist (1973): Based on the novel by William Peter Blatty, which
in turn was inspired by a real-life exorcism that occurred in the Washington,
D.C., area in 1949, *The Exorcist* made 13-year-old Linda Blair a star and
inspired a host of imitations. Once the demonic possession central to the
story kicks in, the movie grabs the viewer by the throat and doesn't let go.
More than thirty years later, *The Exorcist* still has the ability to disturb—
a sign of a truly great fright flick.

Fast Facts

- *Ruth Wakefield, owner of the Toll House Inn in Massachusetts, invented the Toll House chocolate chip cookie in 1933.*

- *The pop-top aluminum can was developed after one day in 1959, Ermal Cleon Fraze of Dayton, Ohio, forgot his can opener on a picnic and had to smash a regular can against the fender of his car to open it.*

- *When the first men's briefs were introduced in 1935, the manufacturer advised left-handers to wear the undies inside out.*

- *In 1905, Australian swimmer Annette Kellerman caused a sensation by wearing the first one-piece bathing suit on a California beach.*

- *The bikini was named after Bikini Atoll in the South Pacific. The United States had tested an atomic bomb there, and the suit was so-named because of its "explosive" impact on the world.*

- *Calvin Coolidge once made the following statement: "When more and more people are thrown out of work, unemployment results."*

- *The notorious Nazi Adolf Eichmann was originally a traveling salesman.*

- *A man named Plennie L. Wingo once walked from Santa Monica, California, to Istanbul, Turkey—backward. He covered over 8,000 miles altogether.*

- *In the 1970s, a Baptist minister named Hans Mullikin crawled from his home in Marshall, Texas, to Washington, D.C.*

- *William McKinley was the first American president to ride in an automobile.*

More Critical Cruelty!

❖ ❖ ❖ ❖

Even writers of the classics aren't immune to scathing criticism.
Here are a few more rejections received by
some now-very-famous writers.

The Diary of Anne Frank: "The girl doesn't, it seems to me, have a special perception or feeling which would lift that book above the 'curiosity' level."

***Bridge Over River Kwai* by Pierre Boulle:** "A very bad book."

***Animal Farm* by George Orwell:** "It is impossible to sell animal stories in the USA."

***And To Think That I Saw It On Mulberry Street* by Dr. Seuss:** "...too different from other juveniles [titles] on the market to warrant its selling."

***Lord of the Flies* by William Golding:** "An absurd and uninteresting fantasy which was rubbish and dull."

***The Spy Who Came In From The Cold* by John le Carré:** "You're welcome to le Carré—he hasn't any future." (note from one publisher to another regarding John le Carré's first novel)

***Catch-22* by Joseph Heller:** "I haven't the foggiest idea about what the man is trying to say. Apparently the author intends it to be funny—possibly even satire—but it is really not funny on any intellectual level."

***Lolita* by Vladimir Nabokov:** "Overwhelmingly nauseating, even to an enlightened Freudian. The whole thing is an unsure cross between hideous reality and improbable fantasy. It often becomes a wild neurotic daydream. I recommend that it be buried under a stone for a thousand years."

Maria Callas: Operatic Superstar

❖ ❖ ❖ ❖

In the history of modern opera, there have been a handful of
legendary performers even non-opera fans can name drop,
such as Luciano Pavarotti or Plácido Domingo. But perhaps
the most famous name of them all is Maria Callas.

Little Maria Anna Sophie Cecilia Kalogeropoulos

In 1923, Maria was born in New York City to unhappily married
Greek immigrant parents. It was also around this time that the
family's name was changed from Kalogeropoulos to the less wieldy
Callas.

Maria's mother, Evangelia, was a domineering and ambitious
woman. When she learned that her chubby youngest daughter,
Maria, could sing—and we mean *really* sing—she packed up her two
daughters and returned to Athens (sans husband). There, Evangelia
hoped to enroll Maria at the famous Athens Conservatoire. Maria
wasn't accepted, but she continued to train. She eventually landed
a spot at the Conservatoire, wowing the admissions committee with
her powerhouse style.

Hardest-Working Diva in the Business

Under the tutelage of tough but encouraging teachers, Callas
devoured librettos and scores for ten hours a day, not only learning her parts but the parts of the other singers, too. But this wasn't
entirely because of her insatiable interest in music—she was myopic
and seeing the conductor was difficult (and glasses definitely were
not considered an option). In order to be able to follow along and
not miss a beat, Callas had to know all the parts of every opera in
which she took part.

In 1940, Callas signed on at the Greek National Opera. Two
years later, the rising star landed a principal part in Eugen d'Albert's
Tiefland. Reviewers and audiences were unanimous: Maria Callas
was unlike anything they had ever seen. The emotion she brought to
the roles she played was raw and real—a powerful combo of virtuoso
voice and an extraordinary actress.

A Rise to Fame, Fortune—and Drama

By the time she left Greece in 1945 at the tender age of 21, Callas had given 56 performances in seven operas and had appeared in 20 recitals. Her teachers advised her to make a name in Italy, the center of the opera world. After making a short detour to the Metropolitan Opera in New York, she was under the guidance of Tullio Serafin, a maestro opera conductor whom Callas credited with launching her career. What was particularly amazing about her voice was her ability to sing dark, heavy roles and then jump to roles written for light, agile sopranos. Callas's abilities redefined the very concept of vocal range.

Her big break came when she stepped in as a replacement for another singer who fell ill before the opening of *I Puritani* in Venice. Never mind that she only had six days to learn the part and that she was already singing the large role of Brunnhilde in *Die Walkure.* It was a challenge she couldn't refuse.

Diets, Rumors, Heartbreak

Throughout the '50s, Callas dominated the Italian opera world, essentially launched the Chicago Lyric Opera with an inaugural performance of the lead in *Norma,* gave star turns in London, and was on the cover of *Time* magazine. But with increased exposure came more backlashes against Callas. She had always been a robust woman, but then she lost about 80 pounds mid-career. Rumors circulated that she had taken a tapeworm pill. There were stories of diva behavior after a string of cancelled performances, lawsuits, and contract troubles. True, Callas was a force to be reckoned with, but those close to her knew that many of the stories had been either embellished or totally fabricated

Whether it was the stress of being the world's most famous opera singer, the weight loss (some believed the diet contributed to her vocal decline), or simply the march of time, Callas's voice began to lose some of its luster throughout the '60s. Romantically, she had long been involved with shipping magnate Aristotle Onassis—she left her husband for him in 1959—but Onassis moved on to Jackie Kennedy. Callas was devastated.

In 1977, at age 53, Maria died in Paris of a heart attack. Since then, she's been named the greatest soprano of all time by the BBC, won a Grammy Lifetime Achievement Award, and her name still plays on the lips of anyone who is asked to name history's opera legends.

Fast Facts

- *In April, 1969, Bessans, France, recorded 68 inches of snow in just 19 hours.*

- *Contrary to popular belief,* The Great Train Robbery *was not the first western movie made. It was* Kit Carson, *made by the American Mutoscope and Biograph Company in 1903.*

- *While filming* City Lights, *Charlie Chaplin shot 342 takes of one scene.*

- *The original name of the Beatles' song "Yesterday" was "Scrambled Eggs."*

- *In the 1926 John Barrymore film,* Don Juan, *the actor averages one kiss every 53 seconds.*

- *In 1924, lawyer Thornton Jones dreamed that he had slit his own throat. He awoke to find that he had done exactly that. He died 80 minutes later.*

- *A Florida woman became obsessed with the idea that she had stomach cancer. To cleanse her body she went on periodic water fasts, during which she ate nothing but drank up to four gallons of water daily. Ultimately her kidneys were overwhelmed, and the excess fluid filled her lungs, drowning her.*

- *A 1902 issue of* Harper's Weekly *magazine predicted that roads built for "motor cars" would not happen in the near future.*

- *When Michael J. Fox was cast as Marty McFly in* Back to he Future (1985), *he was still working on the TV show* Family Ties. *To make it work, Fox slept only one to two hours a night and would drive straight to the movie set after the sitcom finished taping for the day. Most of the filming for* Future *took place between 6 P.M. and 6 A.M.*

Fumbling Felons

Thirsty Thief
Store employees caught a man stealing two bottles of liquor at a store in Boynton Beach, Florida. The workers called the police, and when officers arrived on the scene, the thief was guzzling alcohol out of one of the bottles. His explanation? He said if he had to go to jail anyway, he might as well drink.

Don't Hold the Ketchup
In 2009, a Surprise, Arizona, woman surprised a Kentucky Fried Chicken employee, resulting in her own arrest. Monique Aguet was upset when she didn't get condiments with her order at the KFC drive-through, so she took matters into her own hands. She walked into the store boiling mad and confronted an employee who asked the irate woman to leave. The employee even followed her out to the parking lot. Aguet may not have gotten the food her way, but she did get her way in the fight: She started her car and backed up over the startled employee. Aguet was arrested on suspicion of assault with a deadly weapon and disorderly conduct.

Kitty Porn
A Jensen Beach, Florida, man accused of downloading more than 1,000 pictures of child pornography has an unusual claim—he says his cat did it. Keith R. Griffin said that when he left his computer after downloading some music, the cat leaped onto the computer keyboard. Griffin returned to his computer with unusual images on the screen. Oddly enough, officers on the scene didn't buy his story. He was arrested with bail set at $250,000.

Crime Really Stinks
Some people steal money or jewelry or even electronics. A few criminals have even stolen pedigree dogs. But a skunk? That's what a Sarasota, Florida, couple took from the Animal Crackers Pet Store in 2009. It's bad enough that the pair stole the $400 baby animal, but the real kicker is that the man tried to return the skunk the next day. Suspicious employees called the police, who charged the man with grand theft and the woman with accessory to the crime.

The Mystery of the Lost Dauphin of France

❖ ❖ ❖ ❖

History is rife with conspiracy theories. More than 200 years later, the fate of the Lost Dauphin of France still baffles historians.

Little Boy Lost

Born in 1785, Louis XVII, son of King Louis XVI and Queen Marie Antoinette, was the heir apparent to the throne (giving him the title of *le Dauphin*). The young boy's destiny was unfortunately timed, however, coinciding with the French Revolution's anti-royalist frenzy that swept away the monarchy. His father met his end on the guillotine in January 1793; as next in the line of succession, little eight-year-old Louis XVII was a dead boy walking.

The family was imprisoned and stripped of their regalia. A few months later, on the night of July 3, 1793, guards came for Louis. Realizing that she would never see her son again, Marie Antoinette clung to Louis, and for the next two hours she pleaded for his life. She finally relented after the commissioners threatened to kill both her son and daughter. The boy was dragged crying and screaming from his mother.

To keep the monarchy from reestablishing, Louis was imprisoned in solitary confinement in a windowless room. Some reports state that the young boy was horribly starved and abused by his jailers. Less than two years later, on June 8, 1795, the ten-year-old Dauphin of France died. The official cause of death was tuberculosis.

But instead of ending the matter, the mystery of the true fate of Louis XVII had just begun.

Pretenders to the Throne

Rumors grew like wildfire that the body of Louis XVII was actually someone else. Like any good mystery, there were plenty of stories to fuel the flames of conspiracy:

- Louis's jailers were a husband and wife. Later, the aged wife told the nuns who were nursing her that she and her husband had once smuggled out the Dauphin. "My little prince is not dead," she reportedly said.

- A doctor who had treated the Dauphin died "mysteriously" just before the boy did. The doctor's widow suggested he had refused to participate in some strange practices concerning his patient.
- The Dauphin's sister was never asked to identify his body.
- In 1814, the historian of the restored French monarchy claimed that Louis was alive.
- In 1846, the mass grave where the Dauphin had been buried was exhumed. Only one corpse, that of an older boy, showed evidence of tuberculosis.

Contenders (or Pretenders?) to the Throne

With all of these doubts about what really happened to Louis, it's amazing that only about 100 people came forward throughout the years claiming to be the lost Dauphin and rightful heir to the throne. Among them were:

- **John James Audubon**—Many people thought the famous naturalist Audubon was Louis because he was adopted, was the same age as the Dauphin would have been, and spoke with a French accent. Audubon liked a good story and sometimes implied that he was indeed the Dauphin. In 1828, while visiting France, he wrote a letter to his wife that said, "...dressed as a common man, I walk the streets! I...who should command all!"

- **Eleazer Williams**—Although his father was a member of the Mohawk tribe, this missionary from Wisconsin somehow convinced people that he was the Lost Dauphin and became a minor celebrity for a few years.

- **Karl Wilhelm Naundorff**—Perhaps the most successful of all, this German clockmaker convinced both the Dauphin's nurse and the minister of justice under Louis XVI that he was indeed the lost heir. He was even recognized as such by the government of the Netherlands. DNA tests in the 1950s disproved his claim. Finally, in 2000, DNA tests confirmed that the boy who died in prison was indeed Louis XVII. Even so, as with many conspiracy theories, many people dispute the test's finding.

🎼 Behind the Music of Our Time

- "I Will Survive" was originally slated to be a B-side for Gloria Gaynor's single "Substitute."

- Dolly Parton and Sylvester Stallone teamed up in the epic flop film *Rhinestone*, but they also recorded a duet—"Stay Out of My Bedroom"—for the soundtrack.

- Stevie Wonder played harmonica on both Eurythmics' "There Must Be an Angel" and Elton John's "I Guess That's Why They Call It the Blues."

- Toni Tennille of Captain & Tennille sang backing vocals on Pink Floyd's *The Wall* album.

- The song "Killing Me Softly," which was a hit for both Roberta Flack and The Fugees, was cowritten by Lori Lieberman. She was inspired after she saw "American Pie" singer Don McLean in concert and was deeply touched by his performance.

- After Bananarama's 1984 hit "Robert De Niro's Waiting" rose on the UK charts, the Oscar-winning actor invited the band out for dinner and drinks.

- After the 9/11 terrorist attacks, the largest corporate owner of radio stations in America banned both Billy Joel's "Only the Good Die Young" and Jerry Lee Lewis's "Great Balls of Fire."

- Before Maya Angelou became a famous author/poet and one of Oprah's best pals, she recorded an album called *Miss Calypso* in the mid-1950s.

- The singer behind the cartoon group The Archies (famous for the hit "Sugar, Sugar") was a guy named Ron Dante, who went on to produce a string of hits for Barry Manilow.

- Sister Luc-Gabrielle, who was known as The Singing Nun and became internationally famous in 1963 with her hit "Dominique," committed double suicide with her lesbian lover in 1985.

- None of the Taylors in Duran Duran—Andy, John, and Roger—are related by blood.

The Real-Life Dead Zone

❖ ❖ ❖ ❖

The Dead Zone is a popular book (by Stephen King), movie, and television series. But it is also a terrifying reality. There are currently hundreds of dead zones in the world's oceans, which threaten marine life, and possibly, humanity as well. Unfortunately, this isn't a fictional horror story.

Death from Life

Dead zones are areas of bottom waters in oceans where the oxygen is too depleted to support most life. They first began being noticed in 1910, when four such zones were identified. As of 2008, that number had increased to a staggering 405, and current scientific studies suggest that dead zones may increase by a factor of ten or more by the year 2100. In a worst-case scenario, more than 20 percent of the world's oceans could one day turn into dead zones.

These zones are scattered up and down the eastern and southern coasts of the United States. They are also found in several West Coast river outlets. However, the problem isn't only domestic—dead zones are found throughout the world. In fact, the largest dead zone to date is in the vast expanse of the Baltic Sea— its bottom waters do not contain oxygen year round.

Agricultural fertilizer is the primary cause of dead zones. Fertilizer contains large amounts of nitrogen, which runs off of fields into rivers, and eventually finds its way into the ocean. Algae feed on this nitrogen. The algae die and sink to the bottom of the ocean, where they are eaten by microbes. And these microbes consume oxygen as they feed. So the more algae, the more microbes there are feeding, which robs more oxygen from the water.

Mobile fish and bottom-dwellers can escape this oxygen loss, but others that are not as quick-moving (such as clams) die off in massive numbers. Then the microbes that thrive in oxygen-free environments move in. They form vast bacterial mats, which produce the toxic gas hydrogen sulfide.

Comeback...and Disaster

Sometimes a dead zone can recover—just take a look at the Black Sea. Formally a dead zone, it recovered between 1990 and 2000, when fertilizer became extremely costly after the Soviet Union collapsed and took the planned agricultural economies of many central and eastern European countries with it.

Ironically, one of the most cataclysmic events in recent U.S. history—Hurricane Katrina—actually helped the local dead zone problem. The largest zone in the United States is at the mouth of the Mississippi River, measuring approximately 8,500 square miles (an area equivalent to the size of New Jersey).

When Katrina came along, it acted like a giant blender: The storm's awesome power mixed the oxygen-filled surface water with the oxygen-free water on the bottom. Hard on Katrina's heels came Hurricane Rita, which finished the job. This temporarily dissipated the dead zone in that area. But waiting for massive hurricanes to come along and repair dead zones is a poor way to solve the problem. Global warming also throws a wrench into the works. Since warmer water holds less oxygen than cooler water, global warming reduces the ocean's ability to store oxygen at the same time it decreases the amount of oxygen available in deeper water.

Recent computer simulations by Danish researchers indicate that dead zones caused by global warming will last for thousands of years. "They will be a permanent fixture [of the oceans]," said University of Copenhagen researcher Gary Shaffer.

Searching for a Solution

Scientists are currently scrambling for solutions to dead zones. One idea is to pump air into smaller areas of water and see what happens, much like a pond is aerated to prevent low oxygen. Ultimately, however, it may take massive revolutions in agriculture and human behavior to save the world's oceans from becoming a giant dead zone. And that's a future we don't want to see happen.

Fast Facts

- *It may be cute, but the world's dumbest dog is the Afghan hound.*

- *The United States has the highest minimum drinking age of any country in the world.*

- *Polls show that used car salesman is the least-admired job.*

- *Many insurance companies have blacklisted the Rottweiler and pit bull, deeming the pooches too dangerous. Some agencies won't write homeowner policies for people who own them.*

- *The White Castle chocolate shake has a whopping 1,600 calories.*

- *In 1962, astronaut John Glenn ate the first space food: pureed applesauce from a tube.*

- *The first Jelly Belly flavors were Very Cherry, Green Apple, Grape, Lemon, Licorice, Tangerine, and A&W Cream Soda and Root Beer.*

- *The modern piano has more than 11,000 parts.*

- *Betsy Ross had a full set of teeth when she was born.*

- *Whether you lick them or eat them whole, Oreos are the best-selling cookie. Americans have been eating them since 1912.*

- *When frying a doughnut, not all the dough cooks at the same speed. In 1847, a young baker's apprentice punched the soggy dough out of the center of a donut back, accidentally inventing the world's first ring doughnut.*

Poor Marie Prevost

❖ ❖ ❖ ❖

*"She was a winner/that became a doggie's dinner." So goes the
1980s pop song written about Marie Prevost, the silent film
star who once epitomized flapper chic. Prevost rose high and
fell hard in the early days of Hollywood—an It girl whose
only remaining legacy is her gruesome and untimely death.*

La Belle Canadienne

Before she was Marie Prevost, she was Mary Bickford Dunn: an
Ontario, Canada, native born on November 8, 1898, and educated
in a Catholic convent. After her father's death, 17-year-old Mary
moved with her mother and sister to Los Angeles, where the comely
Mary found work as a stenographer. At age 18, her secretarial aspirations took a star turn when she tagged along with a girlfriend to
meet producer (and fellow Canadian) Mack Sennett.

The curvy, dark-haired beauty captivated Sennett. He called her
the "exotic French girl" and cast her as one of his Bathing Beauties
under the stage name "Marie Prevost." As one of Sennett's Beauties,
Prevost joined future Tinseltown royalty Gloria Swanson and Carole
Lombard as the scantily clad eye candy in Sennett's silent slapstick
comedies.

Star of the Silent Screen

By 1921, Prevost had graduated from bathing beauty to flirty flapper.
Her looks were ideal: saucer eyes, trendy bob, and cupid's-bow lips.
Prevost signed a contract with Universal to play coy party girls in a
string of silent pictures.

Two years later, she abandoned Universal to become a leading
lady, starring in the Warner Bros. film adaptation of F. Scott
Fitzgerald's novel *The Beautiful and the Damned.* Fitzgerald
denounced the film as the worst garbage he'd ever seen, but
the movie proved box-office boon—due in no small part to the
smoldering on- and off-screen chemistry of Prevost and her co-star,
matinee hunk Kenneth Harlan. The two married soon afterward.

By 1926, Prevost had worked with nearly every big-name director of the day, including Frank Capra and Cecil B. DeMille. But at age 28, her career had already peaked; there was nowhere to go but downhill. Fast.

Beautiful and Damned, Indeed

That year, Prevost had just left Warner Bros. and was filming a new picture for Producers Distributing Corporation when she received word that her mother had been killed in a car accident. Prevost's marriage to Harlan was already on the skids after just two years; the tragedy pushed them over the edge, and they divorced the following year.

To cope, Prevost started hitting the bottle, which led to weight gain. At the same time, the movie business was undergoing a massive revolution, as "talkies" replaced silent films. Rumor has it Prevost's voice was nasal and unappealing for this new film format. True or not, by 1929, Prevost was overweight and out of work.

In the 1930s, Prevost slimmed down a bit thanks to a rigid alcohol-only diet, and she also had some success playing Rosie O'Donnell-type roles of the rotund, wisecracking friend. But parts were scarce: By now, Prevost was in her 30s; the best roles were going to the younger, fresher, and thinner talent. By 1936, her roles were reduced to uncredited parts with just a few speaking lines.

Dogged Demise

One night in January 1937, police were called to a dilapidated Hollywood apartment building after neighbors complained of a dog barking. Inside, they found Prevost dead, her arms and legs gnawed by her pet dachshund who'd tried to wake her. The cause of death was ruled a combination of malnutrition and starvation: Essentially, she had drunk herself to death.

Despite her early success, Prevost died with a paltry $300 to her name, which went to her sister and a friend. Fellow early flapper Joan Crawford allegedly paid for Prevost's no-frills funeral.

Today, most silent film histories neglect to mention Prevost, and those that do seem to focus only on her grizzly death. She is, of course, immortalized in a 1980s pop song called "Marie Provost" by Nick Lowe—which, ironically, doesn't even spell her name right.

Crossing Ed Sullivan

❖ ❖ ❖ ❖

Throughout the 1950s and '60s, a spot on The Ed Sullivan Show
*could be a career-maker—but if you angered the host, watch out.
Here are some famous folks who dared cross the mighty Ed Sullivan.*

Bo Diddley Beat

In November 1955, rock 'n' roller Bo Diddley was set to perform the
up-tempo song "Bo Diddley" on the show. Sullivan, however, didn't
like it. He told Diddley instead to play "Sixteen Tons" by Tennessee
Ernie Ford. Though the performer begrudgingly agreed, he instead
roared into "Bo Diddley." The result was a riotous number that
inspired a wave of future musicians from the Rolling Stones to Bruce
Springsteen—and a lifetime ban of Diddley from the show.

Incurring Sullivan's Wrath

In the early 1960s, Jackie Mason was a rising young comedian who
had already logged numerous appearances on *The Ed Sullivan Show.*
In October 1964, Mason was doing his bit on the show, when Sullivan
began gesturing frantically to Mason to wind up his routine. Sullivan
held up two fingers (for two minutes) and then one.

"They're giving me the finger," Mason reportedly said. "Well,
I've got some fingers for you—and you." He began making his own
exaggerated finger motions. Did he flip off Sullivan? Maybe yes, maybe
no. (Mason denies it.) But a furious Sullivan was certain he had, and he
began a campaign to destroy Mason's career. Mason filed suit against
Sullivan. Eventually the two reconciled.

For their 1967 performance, the Rolling Stones were told to
change their lyrics from "Let's spend the night together" to "Let's
spend some time together." Singer Mick Jagger did as he was told, but
he theatrically rolled his eyes while singing the censored version.

After being specifically told not to sing the lyric "Girl we couldn't
get much higher" (and then doing so anyway), the Doors were officially
banned from the show. And Elvis Presley wasn't totally banned from
the show—only certain parts of him. Sullivan didn't allow the singer's
gyrating hips to be shown.

More Northern Justice

❖ ❖ ❖ ❖

*Here are more examples of the weird ways
you can break the law in Canada.*

No Yellow Margarine

While the rest of Canada can enjoy yellow margarine with impunity, Quebec's dairy industry has successfully lobbied the provincial government to pass a law that all margarine sold to the public must be a color other than yellow (so that the consumer doesn't mistake it for butter). Plans for blue and pink bread spreads were quickly abandoned in favor of the blander-hued off-white.

The Cow: Queen of Beasts

Canada's animal cruelty laws impose a penalty of two years on anyone who tortures or mistreats any animal. But woe to the soul who abuses a cow—inflicting harm on Bessie can result in up to five years behind bars.

Trick, Treat, or Be Eaten

Polar bears may be an endangered species but not in the Far North town of Churchill, Manitoba. Visits from the snowy bruins present so much of a problem in this community (people must huddle in their houses as the large predators rumble through) that the municipal government has banned furry Halloween costumes for fear of attracting the bears.

Crime Comics

Canada has notoriously vague obscenity laws—one problematic prohibition takes a stand against images showing the "commission of crimes, real or fictitious." At least that stops super villains in Canadian comic books from dressing as polar bears or bothering cows.

Carousing in Calgary

Calgary, Alberta, is cracking down on horseplay after closing time, as shown in its new system of bylaws. Spitting can cause you to be $115 out of pocket, and relieving yourself in public carries a price tag of $300. Curiously enough, brawling and beating the wazoo out of one other will result in only a $250 penalty. Better to punch than to pee!

Simple Skill Testing Questions

No one can simply be given a prize in a Canadian raffle, draw, or sweepstakes. Instead, Canadians are required to "earn" the prize, usually by answering a "skill-testing question," which often takes the form of a simple arithmetic problem. So if you're not up on your basic math, there's a chance that jet-ski's not coming home with you.

Just Say "Boo!"

Canadian law specifically states that it is a criminal act to frighten a child or a sick person to death. Apparently, it's just peachy to pop out of a laundry hamper while wearing a hockey mask—as long as your victim is a healthy adult!

One in Five Songs

Non-Canadians have a difficult time understanding Canadian Content laws or "Can-Con," which require a substantial portion of television and radio programming be filled with homegrown Canadian talent. Basically, it's an attempt to keep Canadian culture from being overwhelmed by Hollywood and Nashville.

WORD HISTORIES

Vandal: The Vandals were a Germanic tribe that helped invade and destroy the Roman Empire in A.D. 455. While no worse than the other countries that did the same, *vandal* became the word used to describe someone who intentionally destroys or damages something.

Heirloom: The first instance of this word, as *ayre lome,* was recorded in 1472, in old England and perhaps Scotland. It later became the separate words "heir" and "loom." Interestingly, the latter didn't necessarily have to do with the textile business. *Loom* was a word that encompassed all implements, household items, tools, and other personal items.

Terrier: Here is a dog that is named for its behavior. From the Old French word *chien terrier,* which literally means "earth dog" or "burrowing dog." Tenacious terriers were known for chasing rabbits, foxes, and other animals into their burrows.

Churlish: The English had little respect for a *churl,* that is, a peasant or rude person. The word *churlish* takes that a step further, meaning someone who is vulgar or boorish.

Chestnut: Other than the nut itself, this word is also used to describe an oft-repeated joke or story. It came about as part of *The Broken Sword,* a popular play in 1816. In it, two characters banter back and forth, ending with one saying the answer is "chestnut"—that is, he knows because he's heard the story 27 times. By the 1880s, *chestnut* came to mean that very thing: a story told over and over again.

Weisure: When there's no clear line between work and leisure, we get *weisure,* or free time spent doing work. This is what workaholics do for fun.

Daisy: In Old English, the words *daeges eage* translated to the more modern "day's eye," used to describe the white petals of a daisy opening during the day to expose the yellow center.

Shilly-shally: Here's a case of a silly phrase becoming part of our language. In the 1700s, an indecisive soul may have queried, "Shall I, shall I?" The phrase morphed into "Shill I? Shall I?" And later it was simply *shilly-shally,* a term to describe indecision.

The Great Dwarf Wedding (of Peter the Great)

❖ ❖ ❖ ❖

If you've ever been in a wedding, spent time with someone who is about to be wed, or have gotten married, you know that the wedding process can be kind of a circus. But Russian Tsar Peter the Great took it to a whole new level.

Peter's Peculiar Pastimes

For 43 years beginning in 1682, Pyotr Alexeyevich Romanov (let's call him Peter for short) ruled the land of Russia. He took the tsarist empire into a new, expanded era, which resulted in more power and influence across the country and indeed around the world. It wasn't an easy task, and Peter wasn't a hero in everyone's eyes—millions of people died due to his actions. He's remembered not only for his strong-willed political victories but also for being a tyrant.

Perhaps all the pressure heaped on him is why the infamous leader had a fondness for spectacle and humor in his downtime— think practical jokes, elaborate gifts, and Peter's "monsters." This was a pre-PC time, and the tsar's "monsters" were dwarfs (what we'd now call Little People), giants, and malformed humans that Peter took to arranging in carnivalesque weddings and funerals.

Though it makes most people uncomfortable to think about today, in Peter's time the practice of putting dwarves on display or "keeping a buffoon" was considered typical entertainment. Peter took the pastime further than most, largely because he could afford it. He sent a decree across the land that anyone who sent a malformed human "marvel" to St. Petersburg would receive 100 rubles. With his ever-expanding cast of characters, Peter set about designing events to showcase them.

A Double Wedding

In 1710, Peter's niece Anna was wed to Frederick William, whose uncle was the Duke of Prussia. The wedding, like most at the time, was arranged for political reasons. Peter had a hand in organizing the wedding festivities, because he had a secret plan in mind: Several days after the feasting and celebrations for the happy couple were over, a second wedding was held, this one between two dwarfs. From the bride's dress and the food served, to the nuptials and the grounds decorations, all of it was modeled exactly after the wedding of Anna and Frederick.

More than 70 dwarves were gathered for the event. Peter himself presided over parts of the ceremony, and chairs were set up around the perimeter of the room for the court to watch. After the wedding (which was sped up, just as Anna and Frederick's had been), the audience watched the dwarfs enjoy a banquet. It was all very amusing to the crowd, especially since many of the dwarves were peasants and spoke in a coarse vernacular, or were hunchbacked from working in the fields all their lives. The dwarves got drunk and fights broke out. The guests spilled food and generally caused chaos. While all this was happening, Peter and his retinue looked on, laughing and applauding the ridiculous antics of the dwarves.

Commentary or Just Plain Creepy?

Looking at Peter's callous dwarf spectacles, a modern person's sensibilities are likely offended. But was Peter solely crass or was he making a comment on the largely out-of-touch lifestyle of the wealthy? Either the dwarf wedding was a big joke on the people watching and laughing, or it was a cruel display of a marginalized portion of 18th-century Russia. Perhaps it was purely a way to pass the time in between wars and political upheaval, or perhaps the tsar simply had too much money on his hands. It's probably safe to assume that for Peter the Great, one of history's most intriguing leaders, it was a little bit of everything.

Fast Facts

- *The vanilla bean comes from the edible fruit of a tropical orchid.*

- *Who posed for all those Roman statues? It doesn't matter—most of the statues had detachable heads that could be removed and changed.*

- *In her pre-TV days, Oprah Winfrey held the title of Miss Fire Prevention.*

- *Fingernails grow fastest on the hand a person uses most.*

- *South African surgeon Dr. Christiaan Barnard performed the first successful heart transplant in 1967. The patient lived another 18 days.*

- *A spoonful of sugar... is what McDonald's uses to make their fries a golden brown color. Burger King uses starch.*

- *Before 1937, the basketball referee tossed a jump ball after every basket. And you thought fouls make the play drag on.*

- *The first Harry Potter book and movie,* Harry Potter and the Sorcerer's Stone, *actually goes by the name* Harry Potter and the Philosopher's Stone *everywhere but in the United States. So every scene that mentions the stone had to be filmed twice—once with the actors using the word "philosopher's" and another where they say "sorcerer's."*

- *Outdoor filming for the movie* Fargo *had to be moved all over North Dakota, Minnesota, and Canada because the area was having the second-warmest winter in 100 years.*

- *The swimming naked-baby-turned-icon on the cover of Nirvana's debut album* Nevermind *is a boy named Spencer Elden.*

The Times They Are A-Changin'

1992

- The European Union is created.

- Euro Disney opens for business in Marne-la-Vallee, France. However, the French people aren't so enthusiastic about the spread of American pop culture, and the park's economy has been on shaky ground ever since.

- U.S. space shuttle *Endeavour* makes a successful maiden voyage, returning safely to the Kennedy Space Center Shuttle Landing Facility.

- Hurricane Andrew, the second most powerful hurricane of the 20th century, strikes the Bahamas, Florida, and Louisiana. It causes $26.5 billion in damages and 65 deaths.

- Johnny Carson hosts his last *Tonight Show* after 30 years behind the desk.

- The Church of England votes to allow women to serve as priests.

- Kent Conrad becomes the first U.S. senator to hold two Senate seats at the same time. North Dakota senior senator Quentin Burdick dies in September, and Conrad successfully runs for office to fill the empty seat. In December, Conrad is sworn in for the senior senator's seat, and that same day he resigns from his old seat in the Senate.

- Bill Clinton and his running mate, Al Gore, defeat incumbent President George H. W. Bush in their bid for the White House. Democrats also assume control of Congress.

- Prince Charles and Princess Diana of Wales formally announce their separation.

- Birth control options increase when the Food and Drug Administration (FDA) approves the hormone injection Depo-Provera for use as a contraceptive in the United States. The shot lasts three months and is considered 97–99 percent effective.

- Big Macs come to China when Beijing opens its first McDonald's restaurant.

Before They Were Billionaires

❖ ❖ ❖ ❖

*People like Warren Buffett and Bill Gates may seem like
they're made out of money, but they weren't born that
way. Here's a look at what some of the world's richest
people were doing before they were billionaires.*

Warren Buffett

With close to $40 billion in his back pocket, Warren Buffett prob-
ably doesn't dine at many buffets. (We suspect he gets room service
instead.) Buffett's empire has long landed him in the top couple of
spots on the *Forbes* list of the world's wealthiest folks. His fortune is
entirely self-made, too: Buffett grew up delivering newspapers in his
neighborhood and chasing lost golf balls at a Nebraska-area course.
He started toying with the stock market at the ripe old age of 11.

By high school, Buffett was making $50 per week with a pinball
business he'd created. Buffett's big fortune, however, came in the early
'60s, when he bought 5 percent of American Express's stock despite
the company's near-bankrupt state. He may have looked like a fool at
the time, but once American Express rebounded and his stock value
skyrocketed, Buffett was the one laughing—all the way to the bank.

Ted Turner

Mr. Television wasn't always a wealthy chap, either. Ted Turner
worked for his father's outdoor advertising company as a young man,
dutifully mowing around billboards and helping maintain ad-housing
properties. He worked his way through college and then got kicked
out of the Coast Guard before taking over the family business.

In 1970, things really turned around when Turner turned down
everyone's advice and decided to buy a tiny TV station in Atlanta.
That station eventually expanded into a broadcasting empire, with
networks such as TBS and CNN helping Turner earn billions.

Sam Walton

Wal-Mart founder Sam Walton used a small-town approach to create what's now one of America's biggest retail chains. Walton started
his career in sales at JCPenney, and later he decided to open his own

Ben Franklin craft store franchise. He soon oversaw 15 stores, all of which operated in relatively large cities.

Walton decided that the country's more rural areas were an untapped market and—not getting the support he wanted from Ben Franklin—opted to strike out on his own. The first Wal-Mart opened in Rogers, Arkansas, in 1962. As the chain grew, so too did Walton's worth: By the time of his death in 1992, his net worth was approximately $21–23 billion.

Michael Dell

Michael Dell clearly did something right. Consistently ranking on *Forbes's* richest-person list, Dell has billions of dollars and one of the world's biggest computer companies in his portfolio. And to think it all started with cashew chicken. Dell saved up dough working at a Chinese restaurant as a kid, and then he used his cash to buy valuable postage stamps from traders. He sold his stamp collection to buy a computer, used his computer to start a newspaper subscription business, and used the profits from that to buy a BMW. Sure, sounds easy!

In college, Dell continued his entrepreneurial streak by going door-to-door selling computers he'd refurbished. Once he'd made $180,000, he dropped out of school and started Dell.

Bill Gates

Wrestling with Warren Buffett for the title of *Forbes's* richest man, Bill Gates had an estimated $40 billion in 2009, down from $58 billion the year before. (Hey, even filthy rich people aren't immune to the slumping economy!) Microsoft's main man was making major money while still a teenager: Gates formed a programming club in his high school, and he helped build a traffic-monitoring program under the company name Traf-O-Data. The program brought in around $20,000 and gave Gates his first serious taste of success.

Gates started to study at Harvard as a pre-law student, but then he and programming pal Paul Allen saw a "window" of opportunity, you might say, and they left the scholastic world behind. The duo formed a little venture known as Microsoft and never looked back.

On the Cutting Edge

In 1920, Josephine Dickson was the young bride of Earle, who worked at Johnson & Johnson in New Jersey, a leading producer of surgical supplies. As the story goes, Earle would arrive home every day to find Josephine cut, burned, or bleeding from some kitchen mishap, so he'd get out the adhesive tape and gauze and bandage up his accident-prone wife.

After a while, it became clear that Josephine needed a way to quickly and easily bandage herself throughout the day, so Earle stuck several pieces of gauze onto individual strips of adhesive tape and covered them with crinoline to keep them secure. He took his idea to work, and the company loved it; in 1920, Johnson & Johnson began making Band-Aids. At first the bandages were quite large—18 inches by 2 inches—and were made by hand. But by 1924 the company had perfected a machine that made the bandages smaller and easier to make. Initially, the public wasn't too interested in Band-Aids. Then Johnson & Johnson launched a PR stunt to give free bandages to Boy Scouts across the country—and soon the sticky strips were a national sensation.

A Clear Winner

Speaking of sticky strips, the ever-useful Scotch tape owes its existence to a lab technician for the Minnesota Mining and Manufacturing Company (3M). Richard Drew had already developed a masking tape in 1925 to help body shops edge a paint job without tearing existing paint off the car. It worked, but it wasn't waterproof. In 1929, a client called asking for a waterproof adhesive to cover the insulation batting in refrigerated railroad cars.

Also new at this time was a waterproof product called cellophane. Drew ordered 100 yards of it to see if his theory was right and adhesive could be applied to cellophane. His theory was correct, but Drew's invention failed to meet the railroad client's needs. Nevertheless, he knew he was on to something. Drew learned that if a primer coat was applied to the back of cellophane, it would coat evenly, and special machinery could keep the cellophane from tearing. On September 8, 1930, the first roll of Scotch Cellophane Tape was given to a customer, who sent back rave reviews.

As for the name, it apparently comes from feedback that a 3M salesman received from a frustrated auto worker regarding an early version of Drew's masking tape: "Take this tape back to your stingy Scotch bosses and tell them to put more adhesive on it!"

If You See Only Five...

Gangsters Galore!

❖ ❖ ❖ ❖

These mob movies are sure to straighten out any wise guy.

Bad guys often make for very good movies, as illustrated by the plethora of gangster flicks that have come out of Hollywood. Here are five classic mob movies to satisfy the godfather within.

1. *Little Caesar* (1931): Directed by Mervyn LeRoy, *Little Caesar* helped make Edward G. Robinson a star and established the gangster movie as a legitimate film genre. Robinson is outstanding as Rico, aka Little Caesar, a two-bit hood who rises to the top of a ruthless gang, only to find that crime doesn't pay.

2. *The Godfather* (1972): This is the granddaddy of mob movies, and many think it is one of the best movies of any kind ever made. Based on the novel by Mario Puzo and directed by Francis Ford Coppola, the film tells the story of Vito Corleone (played by Marlon Brando), a powerful mafia don who finds himself in the middle of a gangland power struggle.

3. *Once Upon a Time in America* (1984): Italian director Sergio Leone is best known for his so-called "spaghetti westerns" starring Clint Eastwood. However, this epic film about gangster life in 20th century New York is not to be overlooked. Starring Robert DeNiro and James Woods, it's a deeply layered study of crime, family, and friendship spanning several decades.

4. *Goodfellas* (1990): This wasn't director Martin Scorsese's first foray into mob movies (see 1973's *Mean Streets*), but it's one of his best. Ray Liotta stars as real-life mobster Henry Hill, a lifelong criminal whose testimony ultimately brings down the gang for whom he worked.

5. *Casino* (1995): Also directed by Scorsese, *Casino* tells the true story of Sam Rothstein (Robert DeNiro), a casino operator in '70s-era Las Vegas whose mob connections and drug-addicted wife (Sharon Stone) bring him nothing but grief. Everyone shines in this Oscar-nominated film, particularly Joe Pesci as out-of-control mobster Nicky Santoro.

Down Under

❖ ❖ ❖ ❖

When the going gets rough, these cities have
managed to rise above—literally.

Seattle

You may think that Seattle was built on Microsoft, but it was actually built on something quite a bit softer—mud. In 1852, the first neighborhood of Seattle was settled in an area known today as Pioneer Square. Even though the builders brought in fill from surrounding areas, the city's sea-level status still posed some problems. When the tide came in, the streets would fill with mud, and the toilets would turn into gushing fountains. Sounds pleasant!

The fire of 1889 destroyed the young city, and a new Seattle was built on top of the old. The city planners knew that this was their chance to fix the mistakes of the past, so with the relief money they received, they built retaining walls on the sides of the existing streets, filled the space, and raised the streets eight feet more than they previously were.

Eventually, sidewalks were built between the new streets and the second stories of the surrounding buildings. In effect, the first (that is, original) floors of stores and homes became the underground. Today, humorous tours are available to those looking to explore Seattle's underside.

Edinburgh

Take a tour of Edinburgh's underground, and you'll find plenty of fables and good-old fashioned scares, but the history of the Scottish underground is not quite so lighthearted. In Edinburgh's early days, the rich and the poor shared space. But as Old Edinburgh became overcrowded in the 18th century, the more fortunate folk moved to the north and south ends of the city. The North and South bridges were built to link the two wealthy areas. The South Bridge was built over a large ravine, and the area below the bridge was excavated. Rooms and chambers were made, which became known as the Edinburgh Vaults. The area was used primarily for storage, but over the years, it became home to a number of businesses.

When the bridge began to leak, the businesses moved out, and the underground became home to the city's poorest and most destitute residents, including a gravedigger and his family, and a girl whose family had died of the plague. In fact, victims of the bubonic plague lived in the vaults. The vaults eventually were filled and forgotten, but they were rediscovered in 1985. Today, visitors can take tours of the vaults.

Rome

Visitors to this ancient city are familiar with the typical haunts: the museums, the Coliseum, and the Pantheon. But below the well-known attractions lies a labyrinth of catacombs, roads, temples, and houses that date back to the fall of the Roman Empire. Because of frequent floods, the citizens of Rome started building upwards and continued to do so for some 3,000 years, covering previous cities as well as their own history. Though a few archeologists have explored the underground in hopes of finding clues about the powerful ancient city, much of it has remained untouched. According to *National Geographic* writer Paul Bennett, you can dig a hole just about anywhere within the walls that once surrounded the city and find something of historical significance. In fact, many of the discoveries to date have been made by accident. In 2008, while a modern rugby stadium was being renovated, an ancient cemetery built to resemble a city was found underneath it.

Cappadocia

Now known as Turkey, this ancient region features a number of cities that sit atop buried historic towns. In all, there are thought to be 150 underground dwellings lurking beneath the rocky landscape. Perhaps the most well known of these, Derinkuyu, is eight stories deep, measuring about 279 feet. The dwellings served as hiding places for early Christians escaping persecution from Romans and Muslims, although these underground cities were thought to have been originally dug out upwards of 2,000 years ago. Many of these refuges feature churches, trapdoors, and remnants of kitchens and shops, and were large enough to hold thousands of people. Today, a handful of the subterranean cities have been turned into swanky hotels and homes for affluent Turks.

Fast Facts

- *Peanut butter and jelly sandwiches are a staple in many households, with most kids eating 1,500 by the time they graduate from high school.*

- *In order to complete his visits on Christmas Eve, Santa Claus would have to stop at 822 houses per second, traveling at a speed of 650 miles per second. Let's hope he doesn't get pulled over.*

- *The "S.O.S" written in the handy steel wool pads stands for "Save Our Saucepans." You can tell the difference between this and the universal call for help because S.O.S pads have no period after the second S.*

- *The holes in ice cream sandwiches are called* docker pinholes. *They're there to ensure even baking of the cookie parts.*

- *The first Christmas card was sent in 1843.*

- *The most expensive Super Bowl ticket in 1967 cost $12.*

- *The first computer banner ads were launched in 1994.*

- *The Whopper cost 37 cents when Burger King started selling it in 1957.*

- *In the* Harry Potter *books, there are 142 staircases at the Hogwarts School for Witchcraft and Wizardry.*

- *In* Star Trek, *Mr. Spock's mother's name is Amanda.*

- *Women blink twice as often as men.*

Pearls of Wisdom

❖ ❖ ❖ ❖

*Always wanted to try slurping down an oyster, but didn't know
what you were doing? Read on for some oyster pointers.*

How Do I Eat This Thing?

1. Pluck the oyster from its bed of crushed ice and seaweed. If you
   like, dribble a bit of lemon juice or Worcestershire sauce on it.
2. Lift the shell to your lips and slurp the juices and the oyster into
   your mouth.
3. Wait a few heartbeats to experience the sensation described by
   the poet Léon-Paul Fargue as "like kissing the sea on the lips."
4. Resist the temptation to swallow the oyster whole. Instead, gently
   tenderize the oyster with your molars before letting it glide down.
5. Take a drink from your beverage of choice—we suggest a dry
   white wine.
6. Repeat.

What the Heck Did I Just Eat?

Good question. There are five main species of edible oysters:

Ostrea edulis (aka Belons, European Oyster, Galway, Mersey Flats)
Native to Europe, these are the most regular in appearance; salty
and sometimes metallic in taste.

Crassostrea virginica (aka Eastern or Atlantic Oysters) Native to
North America's East Coast, varieties can be found from Prince
Edward Island in Canada to the Gulf of Mexico. The highest con-
centrations are in Maryland's Chesapeake Bay region, where they
constituted the most commercially viable resource as early as the
Civil War. Flavor ranges from very briny (Malpeques) to sweetly
bland (Apalachicola).

Crassostrea gigas (aka Pacific, Japanese) Found throughout the
world in many varieties. Typically sweet with cucumber or mineral
touches.

Crassostrea sikaema (aka Kumamoto Oysters) Originated in Japan but are now grown along North America's West Coast as well. Crisp texture with a taste similar to melons or cucumbers.

Ostrea lurida (aka Olympia Oysters) Found only along the West Coast; small in size but strong in flavor with the sweet taste of earth and grass.

Bold Souls

- Though exceptionally fond of oysters, British writer Jonathan Swift once stated, "He was a bold man that first ate an oyster."

- Sergius Orata, a Roman engineer, cultivated oysters on rock piles in southern Italian lakes. It was rumored that Orata was capable of growing oysters on the roof of his home.

- New York, London, and Paris are all located near perfect estuaries where oysters once thrived. Of the three, Paris is the only metropolis that still produces its own oysters.

- While living in Illinois, Abraham Lincoln frequently threw oyster parties at his home.

Wait, What Month Is It?

Contrary to folk wisdom, it is not unhygienic to eat oysters harvested during their summer spawning months; rather, the energy required to spawn depletes the oyster's flavor. As one female commentator wryly observed: "Oysters, like all men, are somewhat weaker after they have done their best at reproducing."

Why Are They Called "Ocean Cleaners"?

Oysters eat plankton by sucking in seawater and expelling everything that is not plankton. During this process they turn nitrogen into solid waste pellets which then decompose and return to the atmosphere. A single oyster can filter up to 50 gallons of water per day!

Going, but Not Gone

When Captain John Smith first sailed into the Chesapeake Bay, he observed that the oysters "lay thick as stones." Today, no thanks to overharvesting and runoff pollution, the Bay's oyster population is just 1 percent of what it was.

Talk to the Expert

IMPROV COMIC

Q: Life is basically one big improvisation—completely unscripted—and yet so many people are uncomfortable with the thought of doing improv. Why is that?
A: It's hard for a lot of people to step out of reality, and that's what improv is. You're using reality, but you're stepping out of it, you're stepping out of yourself, and that's very uncomfortable. Comedy's scary as it is, never mind making it up as you go and hoping the people that paid $22 like it.

Q: Do you think anyone can do improv?
A: I think anyone can do it, but not everyone can do it *well*.

Q: So much of doing improv relies on audience suggestions. What have been some of your most and least favorites?
A: My least favorites are the ones we are able to name before they happen. Like when somebody [famous] dies, we know we're going to get that. When something happens in the news, we know we're going to get that. I've been in more improv "Laundromats" than actual Laundromats. And inevitably, if we're asking for a celebrity who's dead, we'll get Elvis.

Q: Do you always have to take the first suggestion you hear?
A: No, you don't. If I ask for a dead celebrity and someone says Elvis, I'll say "Elvis isn't dead," and everyone giggles enough not to care. And then there's nothing wrong with going, "You know, we get JELL-O all the time here. Let's try to be a little more creative. You're a smarter audience than that." I don't think there's anything wrong with trying to tell your audience you want to give them something you haven't done a thousand times before.

Q: Improv comics often say nothing makes them laugh anymore. Is that true?
A: You really have to catch me off guard to make me laugh. But then again, the people I perform with do that constantly.

The Tunguska Event

❖ ❖ ❖ ❖

What created an explosion 1,000 times greater than the atomic bomb at Hiroshima, destroyed 80 million trees, but left no hole in the ground?

The Event

On the morning of June 30, 1908, a powerful explosion ripped through the remote Siberian wilderness near the Tunguska River. Witnesses, from nomadic herdsmen and passengers on a train to a group of people at the nearest trading post, reported seeing a bright object streak through the sky and explode into an enormous fireball. The resulting shockwave flattened approximately 830 square miles of forest. Seismographs in England recorded the event twice, once as the initial shockwave passed and then again after it had circled the planet. A huge cloud of ash reflected sunlight from over the horizon across Asia and Europe. People reported there being enough light in the night sky to facilitate reading.

A Wrathful God

Incredibly, nearly 20 years passed before anyone visited the site. Everyone had a theory of what happened, and none of it good. Outside Russia, however, the event itself was largely unknown. The English scientists who recorded the tremor, for instance, thought that it was simply an earthquake. Inside Russia, the unstable political climate of the time was not conducive to mounting an expedition. Subsequently, the economic and social upheaval created by World War I and the Russian Revolution made scientific expeditions impossible.

Looking for a Hole in the Ground

In 1921, mineralogist Leonid A. Kulik was charged by the Mineralogical Museum of St. Petersburg with locating meteorites that had fallen inside the Soviet Union. Having read old newspapers and eyewitness testimony from the Tunguska region, Kulik convinced the Academy of Sciences in 1927 to fund an expedition to locate the crater and meteorite he was certain existed.

The expedition was not going to be easy, as spring thaws turned the region into a morass. And when the team finally reached the area of destruction, their superstitious guides refused to go any further. Kulik, however, was encouraged by the sight of millions of trees splayed to the ground in a radial pattern pointing outward from an apparent impact point. Returning again, the team finally reached the epicenter where, to their surprise, they found neither a meteor nor a crater. Instead, they found a forest of what looked like telephone poles—trees stripped of their branches and reduced to vertical shafts. Scientists would not witness a similar sight until 1945 in the area below the Hiroshima blast.

Theories Abound

Here are some of the many theories of what happened at Tunguska.

Stony Asteroid: Traveling at a speed of about 33,500 miles per hour, a large space rock heated the air around it to 44,500 degrees Fahrenheit and exploded at an altitude of about 28,000 feet. This produced a fireball that utterly annihilated the asteroid.

Kimberlite Eruption: Formed nearly 2,000 miles below the Earth's surface, a shaft of heavy kimberlite rock carried a huge quantity of methane gas to the Earth's surface where it exploded with great force.

Black Holes & Antimatter: As early as 1941, some scientists believed that a small antimatter asteroid exploded when it encountered the upper atmosphere. In 1973, several theorists proposed that the Tunguska event was the result of a tiny black hole passing through the Earth's surface.

Alien Shipwreck: Noting the similarities between the Hiroshima atomic bomb blast and the Tunguska event, Russian novelist Alexander Kazantsev was the first to suggest that an atomic-powered UFO exploded over Siberia in 1908.

Tesla's Death Ray: Scientist Nikola Tesla is rumored to have test-fired a "death ray" on June 30, 1908, but he believed the experiment to be unsuccessful—until he learned of the Tunguska Event.

Okay, but What Really Happened?

In June 2008, scientists from around the world marked the 100-year anniversary of the Tunguska event with conferences in Moscow. Yet scientists still cannot reach a consensus as to what caused the event. In fact, the anniversary gathering was split into two opposing factions—extraterrestrial versus terrestrial—who met at different sites in the city.

Fast Facts

- *Forget fingerprints—everyone has a different tongue print.*

- *The bones in your hands and feet make up more than half the bones in your body.*

- *In an unusual case, in 1985 an organist was ejected from a baseball game in Florida after he played "Three Blind Mice," following an unpopular call by the umpire.*

- *The first football huddle was formed to accommodate a deaf player who used sign language. The team wanted to keep the calls a secret from the opposition.*

- *President Rutherford B. Hayes introduced the first White House Easter Egg Roll in 1878.*

- *The first Olympic Games to take place in the United States were held in St. Louis, Missouri, in 1904.*

- *Baseball players didn't use gloves until the 1870s. Ouch.*

- *Each year, 10 percent of all the salt mined worldwide is used to de-ice American roads.*

- *Christmas didn't become an official U.S. holiday until 1870, when it was signed into law by President Ulysses S. Grant. It wasn't until 1890 that every state followed suit and declared it a holiday.*

- *The first White House was actually gray. It was painted white after the War of 1812 to cover smoke stains sustained when the building was burned by Canadian troops.*

Hair, There, and Everywhere

❖ ❖ ❖ ❖

Amaze your friends with these follicle facts.

- If you're an average nonbalding person, you have approximately 100,000 hairs on your head.

- The amount of hair varies based on natural color: Blondes have the most, with about 140,000 hairs; dark-haired folks have about 110,000; and redheads have only a meager 80,000–90,000 strands attached to their noggins.

- Most people normally shed about 50 to 100 hairs a day.

- More than half of all men start going bald by the time they're 50. But they'll have lost at least 50 percent of the hair on their heads before it even becomes noticeable.

- The Guinness World Record holder for longest hair is a Chinese woman named Xie Qiuping, whose hair measures a whopping 18.5 feet long. That's a lot of brushing!

- Most hair grows about six inches per year, and men's hair tends to grow faster than women's.

- Hair is actually made of keratin, a kind of dead protein. It's the same stuff that makes up your fingernails.

- Your hair follicles determine whether your locks are straight, curly, or wavy: Flat follicles produce curls, while oval-shape follicles lead to waves. Round follicles make for straight strands.

- A single strand of hair can support up to 100 grams of weight, or just under a quarter of a pound.

- Using that calculation, your entire head of hair could support more than 22,000 pounds, or 10–15 tons, of weight. That'd be the weight equivalent of 85 Arnold Schwarzeneggers (during his bodybuilding heyday). We don't recommend testing this in an experiment, however.

FROM THE VAULTS OF HISTORY

Nothing New Under the Sun

We live in an age in which a celebrity scandal is reported on the Internet almost while it's happening, and sex tapes leak out the moment the camera is turned off. Frankly, paper tabloids are beginning to look downright quaint and old-fashioned. But famous people behaved just as badly in the 19th century as they do today—and non-famous people simply had to wait for the dish. One celebrity owned a newspaper, so when she reported a sex scandal, it was easy to give the affair her own spin. Her name was Victoria Woodhull, and the newspaper was called *Woodhull & Claflin's Weekly*. Woodhull believed that women should have the same sexual freedoms as men, so in 1872, after she exposed the affair between prominent minister Henry Ward Beecher and his best friend's wife, she wrote him up as a married hypocrite who had taken up with yet another lover. The scandal also hurt Woodhull, who was running for president at the time (the first woman to do so), but she never expressed an ounce of regret.

Save the Caganers

Spain, being a largely Catholic country, is of course partial to nativity scenes during the Christmas season. In the region of Catalonia, however, nativity scenes traditionally include a figure that is shocking to Christians in other parts of the world: the caganer. The word literally means "pooper," and yes, the little fellow is pulling his pants down and taking care of business. Sure, he might be squatting discreetly over in the corner of the stable, but still—he's clearly doing Number Two in the presence of the Baby Jesus. Caganers have been a fixture of southwestern European nativity scenes since at least the 17th century, but in 2005, the city council in Barcelona commissioned a nativity scene and tried to quietly leave out the caganer. They claimed it had nothing to do with political correctness and that they were merely trying to show support for a new anti-public defecation law, but Barcelonans weren't buying it. They demanded their caganer back—and in 2006, he returned.

Superheroes Unmasked!

Even non-comic book readers know that Superman's alter ego is mild mannered reporter Clark Kent and that Batman is, in truth, millionaire playboy Bruce Wayne. Can you match these superheroes to their alter egos?

1. The Flash
2. Spider-Man
3. Green Lantern
4. Wonder Woman
5. Incredible Hulk
6. Iron Man
7. Captain Marvel
8. Plastic Man
9. The Thing
10. Daredevil
11. Green Arrow
12. Supergirl
13. Hawkman
14. Black Canary
15. Invisible Woman
16. Aquaman
17. Captain America
18. She-Hulk
19. Storm
20. Wasp
21. Wolverine
22. Atom
23. Martian Manhunter
24. Huntress
25. Metamorpho
26. Swamp Thing

a. Sue Richards
b. Steve Rogers
c. Peter Parker
d. Ben Grimm
e. Janet Van Dyne
f. James Howlett
g. Ororo Munroe
h. Arthur Curry
i. Ray Palmer
j. Dinah Lance
k. Billy Batson
l. Eel O'Brian
m. Barry Allen
n. Oliver Queen
o. Hal Jordan
p. Carter Hall
q. Helena Bertinelli
r. J'onn J'onnzz
s. Rex Mason
t. Diana Prince
u. Bruce Banner
v. Matt Murdock
w. Alec Holland
x. Kara Zor-El
y. Jennifer Walters
z. Tony Stark

ANSWERS

1. m; 2. c; 3. o, 4. t; 5. u; 6. z; 7. k; 8. l; 9. d; 10. v; 11. n; 12. x; 13. p;
14. j; 15. a; 16. h; 17. b; 18. y; 19. g; 20. e; 21. f; 22. i; 23. r; 24. q;
25. s; 26. w.

481

What's Eating You?

❖ ❖ ❖ ❖

There are more than 130 parasites that can inhabit the human body. While it might be a bit creepy to think of all those critters wriggling inside you, just think of it this way: At least you'll never be lonely! Here are some freaky (and intensely gross) facts about human parasites. Warning: Don't eat while reading this list.

- Researchers suspect that instances of Crohn's disease, a once-rare inflammatory intestinal disorder, may be on the rise because of the lack of intestinal parasites in much of the first-world population.

- Demodex mites are also called "face mites," because they live on human hair follicles, eyelashes, and nose hairs.

- As they're only 0.0118 inch long, as many as 25 Demodex mites can live on a single hair follicle.

- There are more than 3,000 species of lice in the world.

- Head lice are parasites that live on human hair, gripping the shafts with their claws and drinking blood from the scalp.

- Although head lice only live for a month in your hair, each one can lay up to 100 eggs during that time.

- Leeches can suck ten times their body weight in blood.

- Tapeworms can grow to more than 60 feet long in human intestines.

- The tapeworm's segmented tail contains eggs. This is so that when the segments break off and are expelled from the host's body, the eggs can move on to another animal.

- Instead of a head, the tapeworm has a hooked knob that it uses to cling to the intestinal walls as it sucks nutrients off the surface.

- Tapeworms can only reproduce in humans. When the eggs are eaten by another animal, they reside in the animal's muscle tissue until that flesh is consumed by a human as under-cooked meat.

- Upon attaching to a human host, a chigger (also called red bugs or harvest mites) uses an enzyme to dissolve the flesh at the bite, and then it consumes the liquefied tissue.

- Mosquitoes help transmit botfly eggs to humans, where they hatch and burrow into the skin. To remove them, lay a slice of raw meat on the skin. The maggots will leave the body and enter the meat instead.

- When bathing in the Amazon, men and women always cover their genitals with one hand to prevent the parasitic candiru fish from swimming into their urethra.

- Roundworms grow to 15 inches long and lay as many as 200,000 eggs daily.

- Roundworms are the most common form of intestinal parasite, with an estimated one billion hosts worldwide.

- Rather than feeding on the material found in human intestines, hookworms attach themselves to feed on the blood and intestinal tissue.

- Occasionally, a whipworm infection is discovered when a worm crawls out of the anus or up through the throat and out through the nose or mouth.

- Whipworms can cause the loss of approximately one teaspoon of blood per day.

- After entering the human body in larval form, the two-foot-long adult Guinea worm exits by creating a hole in the flesh of the leg.

- Giardiasis is caused by a one-celled parasite found in dirty water; noticeable symptoms include sulfurous belches and flatulence.

- One out of every three people worldwide is hosting an intestinal parasite.

- Mosquitoes that harbor the malarial parasite plasmodia bite more people per night and live longer than uninfected mosquitoes, but they lay fewer eggs.

Behind the Music of Our Time

- Harry Belafonte was the first black male singer to top the British music charts.

- The Bellamy Brothers' country hit, "If I Said You Had a Beautiful Body (Would You Hold It Against Me)" was based on a quip from comedian Groucho Marx.

- Marvin Gaye's hit single, "I Heard It Through the Grapevine," is a cover—Smokey Robinson and the Miracles recorded it first.

- In the late '70s, many unlikely rock groups caved into pressure from their record companies and recorded a disco song—even hippie icons The Grateful Dead. Their dance track "Shakedown Street" was recorded for an album of the same name that went gold in 1978.

- The best-selling pop duo in history is Hall & Oates, whose hits include "Rich Girl," "Kiss on My List," and "Private Eyes."

- Nick Lowe's 1979 hit "Cruel to Be Kind" coincidentally peaked at No. 12 on four music charts around the world—the United States, the United Kingdom, Canada, and Australia. Think of the odds!

- In 1997, Hanson's debut single, "MMMBop," went to the top of the charts in both the United States and Britain in the same week.

- One of the biggest rock groups ever to come out of Europe is The Scorpions, who have sold more than 100 million albums worldwide.

- When asked about Nirvana's influences after the release of *Nevermind,* Kurt Cobain said, "We sound like The Knack and The Bay City Rollers being molested by Black Flag and Black Sabbath."

- Screamin' Jay Hawkins made a major music blunder when he decided to follow up his million-selling hit "I Put a Spell on You" with a song called "Constipation Blues." Many radio stations refused the track simply because of its title.

- The name of the band Everything but the Girl, who had a big hit with "Missing" in 1995, came from the sign outside a furniture store in Hull, England: "For your bedroom needs, we sell everything but the girl."

Unwanted Visitors!

❖ ❖ ❖ ❖

You don't have to go globe hopping to see the world's wildest flora and fauna. Just visit South Florida.

Vacation Destination

Since the 1950s, a menagerie of nonindigenous mammals, birds, fish, reptiles, and amphibians, and an arboretum's worth of foreign plants have invaded the Sunshine State. And thanks to Florida's subtropical climate, wildlife biologists report that these newcomers have become so well established that it's practically impossible to get rid of them.

It's an eclectic mix of critters, too. Flocks of colorful parrots from South America, Asia, and Africa cause a ruckus on South Florida's golf courses. Fire ants from Brazil build mounds in homeowners' backyards. Walking catfish from Thailand meander in search of a new pond to call home. Football-size *Bufo marinus* toads steal pet food from back porches.

Coming to (North) America

These unwanted visitors came to Florida in a variety of ways. Some, such as pythons and boa constrictors, were discarded pets that grew too large or ornery to keep at home. With plentiful food and South Florida's warm temperatures very much like that of their native South America, the giant snakes quickly became a dominant species in an ecosystem that had never seen anything like them before.

Others, such as the various types of parrots, escaped from local zoos following a hurricane. And a handful of species simply fled into the wild when no one was looking, such as the nine-banded armadillo, a native of South and Central America. Though common to the southwestern states since the 1880s, armadillos were unknown to Florida until 1922, when a man named Gus Edwards added a few of the armored animals to his 15-cent zoo in Cocoa Beach. The crafty critters escaped within days and skedaddled into the Florida wilderness, where they continued to breed until the state was practically knee-deep in 'dillos.

The Bad, the Ugly, and the Bitey

The nine-banded armadillo calls Florida home because of a stupid mistake. Other nonindigenous species, however, were intentionally introduced into the state, with unforeseen consequences. The water-sucking melaleuca tree, for example, was imported from Australia as a windbreak and swamp drainer. But there was just one problem: Melaleuca trees are practically impossible to kill. They spread with alarming speed, and now the trees threaten to overrun the Everglades. Worse, the tree's bark is like paper, which makes forest fires especially nasty.

The warty, irascible muscovy duck, a native of South America, is another example of do-goodery gone wrong. Introduced as colorful additions to municipal ponds, the ducks began breeding like crazy and now pose a serious risk to indigenous waterfowl.

Indeed, the dangers posed by the growing number of non-native species in South Florida are many. Some, like the fire ant, can give a painful bite or sting, or, like the *Bufo marinus* toad, emit a dangerous toxin when touched. Others can have a devastating effect on native species and/or ecosystems, sometimes years or decades after their initial introduction.

Luckily for Floridians, truly dangerous species have, so far, been unable to get a foothold. Piranhas, the meat-eating scourge of the Amazon River, have been caught a handful of times by local fishermen. Biologists investigated the area each time a piranha was hooked and determined that they were individual releases, meaning there were no breeding schools—good news for water skiers and swimmers.

Spiny catfish and other unusual fish have also been caught on occasion, and wildlife officials in Miami have stopped more than one electric eel from entering the country and, quite possibly, local waters.

These days, most Floridians have come to accept the finned, feathered, and furry invaders that have taken over their yards. After all, there's little that can be done now to eradicate them. So the next time you're vacationing in sunny Miami and see something straight out of a television nature series, just remember that it's probably an international visitor who decided to stay.

The Necessities of Survival

❖ ❖ ❖ ❖

When rock climber Aron Ralston's arm was pinned by a boulder while out on a climbing trip, he did the unthinkable in order to survive.

In 2003, Aron Ralston went on a hiking trip in Utah's Blue John Canyon. Feeling confident and adventurous, Ralston, an experienced mountain climber, set out on the solo trip, neglecting to tell anyone he was leaving. The trip began perfectly: nice hike, beautiful day. Then, as Ralston tried to negotiate a narrow opening in the canyon, an 800-pound boulder fell and pinned his right forearm, completely crushing it.

It looked like there would be no escape. Ralston was completely trapped under the boulder and his hand and arm were deadened due to the pressure of the blow. For the next five days, Ralston concentrated on staying alive, warding off exhaustion, hypothermia, and dehydration. He knew no one would be looking for him, since no one knew of his trip. Assuming the worst, he carved his name into the rock that held him down, along with what he thought would be his death date. Using a video camera he had packed with his supplies, he taped goodbyes to his friends and family.

On the sixth day of being trapped, delirious and starving, Ralston made a hellish decision: He would cut off his own arm to escape. Bracing his arm against a climbing tool called a chockstone, Ralston snapped both his radius and ulna bones and applied a tourniquet with some rags he had on hand. Using the knife blade of his multi-tool, he then cut through the soft tissue around the broken bones and tore through tendons with the tool's pliers. The makeshift operation took about an hour.

After he was loose, Ralston still had to rappel down a 65-foot-tall cliff, then hike eight miles to his parked truck. Dehydrated and badly injured, he walked to the nearest trail and was finally discovered. A helicopter team flew Ralston to the nearest hospital where he was stabilized and sent immediately into surgery to clean up and protect what was left of his arm. He later received a prosthetic limb.

Once the press caught wind of his story, Ralston became a celebrity. These days, Ralston works as a motivational speaker, and he still goes on climbing trips, regularly setting new records.

Don't Believe Everything You Read!

❖ ❖ ❖ ❖

Hitler's diaries, Howard Hughes's autobiography, the astounding story of a young Holocaust survivor who lived with a pack of wolves—great stories, but none of them are true.

In 2006, the literary world reeled when it learned that writer James Frey's heart-wrenching memoir, *A Million Little Pieces,* was more fiction than fact. But literary hoaxes are nothing new. Over the years, dozens of books published as nonfiction have turned out to be nothing more than literary lies. Here are some of the most famous.

The Hitler Diaries: In 1983, *Stern,* a respected German magazine, made headlines around the world when it reported that it had come into possession of 62 diaries supposedly penned by der Fuehrer himself. After the diaries had been "authenticated," and a bidding war ensued for the international publishing rights, it was revealed that the diaries were actually the work of forger Konrad Kujau.

The Autobiography of Howard Hughes: Con artists Clifford Irving and Richard Suskind almost hit the big time in 1971 when they penned the "memoirs" of the world's most famous recluse, allegedly based on interviews between Howard Hughes and Irving. Just months before the book's scheduled release, Hughes came out of hiding to denounce the work as a fraud.

Misha: A Mémoire of the Holocaust Years: Belgian writer Misha Defonseca (real name: Monique de Wael) alleged in her 1997 best-selling autobiography that as a child she had escaped the horrors of the Holocaust by trekking across Europe, protected by a pack of wolves. In 2008, she admitted that neither that story, nor her claim of being Jewish, was true.

The Amityville Horror: A True Story: In 1977, George and Kathy Lutz fast-talked writer Jay Anson into penning this book about their terrifying experiences while living in a supposedly haunted house in the Long Island town of Amityville. Brimming with all manner of evil goings-on, the Lutz's story continues to be debated: Was it a clever hoax or a terrifying truth? Nevertheless, the experience was the subject of nine Amityville movies.

Angel at the Fence: The True Story of a Love That Survived: Herman and Roma Rosenblat convinced the world that they met and fell in love while Herman was a prisoner in a German concentration camp during World War II. Oprah Winfrey twice had the couple on her talk show and called their tale "the single greatest love story" that was ever told on her show. But, in 2008, Berkley Books cancelled *Angel at the Fence* at the last minute when it was revealed that their love story was pure fiction. In truth, the Rosenblats met on a blind date in New York after the war.

The Heart Is Deceitful Above All Things: This 2001 book spun the troubled life of author JT LeRoy, an HIV-positive former drug addict and two-bit hustler. Its popularity even led to a 2004 movie based on the book. In reality, "LeRoy" was New York writer Laura Albert. After the ruse was discovered, in 2007, Albert was convicted of fraud and ordered to pay reparations.

I, Libertine: Some literary hoaxes are done not so much to scam as to make a point. In this case, humorist Jean Shepherd wanted to prove that bestseller lists were compiled based not only on actual sales figures but also on requests at bookstores. In 1956, Shepherd encouraged his radio show listeners to visit their local bookshops and request the nonexistent book *I, Libertine* by Frederick R. Ewing. When shops actually became interested in carrying copies of *I, Libertine,* publisher Ian Ballantine hired science fiction author Theodore Sturgeon to write the book based on Shepherd's outline. Sturgeon churned out the manuscript in one exhausting session, with Ballantine's wife, Betty, penning the final chapter after Sturgeon fell asleep. Proceeds from the book were donated to charity.

Fast Facts

- *Maine is the only one-syllable state.*

- *Ever wondered how the powers that be in the airline industry managed to come up with ORD as the abbreviation for Chicago's O'Hare Airport? It comes from its original name: Orchard Field.*

- *The Atlantic Ocean is saltier than the Pacific, but the water in the Great Salt Lake is the saltiest.*

- *No two cows have the same spot patterns.*

- *Just one little brown bat can catch 1,200 mosquitoes per hour.*

- *Does your dog cock its head at the end of The Beatles' song "A Day in the Life"? If so, it's because Paul McCartney recorded a whistle call that can only be heard by dogs.*

- *Even though the character was a girl, the star of Lassie was played by several male dogs.*

- *If you shaved a tiger, you'd discover striped skin under its fur. Not that we recommend you shave a tiger.*

- *Mary Queen of Scots, one of the first woman golfers, called her bag carriers "cadets" back in 1552. The name stuck and was eventually shortened to "caddy."*

- *Rubber bands will keep longer if they're stored in the refrigerator.*

- *The first telephone was invented in 1876.*

- *Bill Gates's home was partially designed on a Mac computer.*

Vodka: The Water of Life

❖❖❖❖

Plain or flavored, straight or mixed, vodka has a unique flavor and an interesting history. Wet your whistle with some of these facts.

- What do screwdrivers and Bloody Marys have in common? Vodka, of course! This colorless alcohol hails from Russia, where its original name, *zhiznennaia voda,* means "water of life."

- To make vodka, vegetables (such as potatoes or beets) or grains (barley, wheat, rye, or corn) are put through a process of fermentation, distillation, and filtration. Grain vodkas are considered to be of the highest quality.

- The most expensive vodka in the world is Diaka, which comes in a crystal bottle that also contains crystals (much like the worm in some tequilas). The makers of Diaka attribute the vodka's exclusivity to its unique filtration process: through 100 diamonds up to a carat in size.

- Vodka seems to have provided a distraction for a couple of notorious Russian czars. In 1540, Ivan the Terrible stopped fighting long enough to establish the country's first vodka monopoly, and in the late 17th century, Peter the Great explored improved methods of distillation and means of export.

- During the reign of Peter the Great, it was customary that foreign ambassadors visiting the court consume a liter and a half of vodka. Lightweight ambassadors began to enlist stand-ins to drink so that the official could discuss important matters with a clear head.

- The Russian phrase *na pososhok* is a toast to the last drink given to a departing guest. It derives from the tradition that visitors traveling from afar would often facilitate their trip with a walking stick called a *pososh,* which had a hollowed-out hole on top. At the end of the visit, a glass of vodka was placed in the hole, and if the visitor could drink the vodka without touching the glass, he was likely able to get home on his own. Otherwise, it was the couch and a banging headache in the morning.

Say What?

"Anyone can do any amount of work provided it isn't the work he is supposed to be doing at the moment."

—*Robert Benchley*

"I am free of all prejudice. I hate everyone equally."

—*W. C. Fields*

"If you don't go to other men's funerals, they won't go to yours."

—*Clarence S. Day*

"When I was born I was so surprised I didn't talk for a year and a half."

—*Gracie Allen*

"I'd hate to drown. You look so awful afterward."

—*Alan Ayckbourn*

"No one really listens to anyone else, and if you try it for a while, you will see why."

—*Mignon McLaughlin*

"There is only one way to find out if a man is honest—ask him. If he says 'yes,' you know he's a crook."

—*Groucho Marx*

"A filing cabinet is a place where you can lose things systematically."

—*T. H. Thompson*

"The reports of my death have been greatly exaggerated."

—*Mark Twain*

"There is nothing safer than flying; it's crashing that is dangerous."

—*Theo Cowan*

"Kindly inform troops immediately that all communications have broken down."

—*Ashleigh Brilliant*

"Remember that happiness is a way of travel, not a destination."

—*Roy Goodman*

The Worst Team in Baseball History

❖ ❖ ❖ ❖

*Most teams experience an off-season. But in 1899, the
Cleveland Spiders couldn't be more off their game.*

Who was the worst team in major league baseball history? The 1962
New York Mets and their record of 40–120? Ha! The 42–112 Pittsburgh
Pirates of 1952? Please. The 2003 Detroit Tigers, who went 43–119?
C'mon.

No, the worst team in professional baseball history was the 1899
Cleveland Spiders, whose record of 20–134 gave them a scintillating
.130 winning percentage. They were good (or bad) enough to finish a
mere 84 games out of first place. Yet just four years prior the Spiders
had been the best team in baseball. What happened?

Along Came Some Spiders

The Cleveland Spiders, so called because of the skinny appearance of
many of their players, began life in baseball's National League in 1889.
In 1892, led by future pitching great Denton True "Cy" Young (who
was bought by the team for $300 and a new suit), the Spiders finished
second in the league. In 1895, the Spiders won the Temple Cup, the
forerunner to the World Series.

However, despite the large crowds that would attend Sunday
games, playing baseball on that day was still controversial. In 1897, the
entire Spiders team was thrown into the pokey for playing baseball on
the Sabbath. The following season, Cleveland was forced to shift most
of their Sunday games to other cities. Attendance suffered, and the
team stumbled to a record of 81–68.

Web Spinning

One other factor contributed to the Spiders' demise: Syndicate baseball. This meant that it was acceptable for owners of one National
League team to own stock in another. Inevitably, the team with the
better attendance and players drew most of the owner's attention and
finances, while the lesser team suffered.

Syndicate baseball arrived in Cleveland in early 1899, when owner Frank Robison bought the St. Louis Browns at a sheriff's auction. He decided that St. Louis was a better market than Cleveland, and so he shipped all of the best Spiders there and renamed the new group— in case anyone missed the point—the Perfectos. Meanwhile, the absent Spiders were replaced by, well, anybody.

Robison's brother Stanley was put in charge of Cleveland. Stanley started off on the wrong foot with Cleveland fans by stating that he intended to operate the Spiders "as a sideshow." Faced with that encouraging news, less than 500 fans turned out for Cleveland's Opening Day double-header. Not surprisingly, the Spiders lost both games. The rout had begun.

And what a rout it was! After the first 38 games, the Spiders had 30 losses. Deciding that third baseman/manager Lave Cross was the problem, Robison sent him to St. Louis (which actually was a reward). With virtually no one showing up for the games, Stanley locked the Cleveland ballpark and announced that the Spiders would play their remaining "home" games on the road.

Woebegone Wanderers

The dismal team—now dubbed the "Wanderers," "Exiles," and "Foresakens"—won just 12 more games the entire season. At one point they lost 24 games straight, which is still a record. They were so bad that after the Spiders beat the Baltimore Orioles, the Orioles' pitcher was fined and suspended. In the midst of all this, Cleveland sportswriter Elmer Bates compiled a tongue-in-cheek list of reasons to follow the Spiders. Among them:

1. There is everything to hope for and nothing to fear.
2. Defeats do not disturb one's sleep.
3. There is no danger of any club passing you.
4. You are not [always] asked . . . "What was the score?" People take it for granted that you lost.

On the last day of the season, a 19-year-old cigar stand clerk pitched for the Spiders; the team lost 19–3. After the game, the Spiders presented the team travel secretary with a diamond locket because, as the dedication said, he "had the misfortune to watch us in all our games." The following year Cleveland was dropped from the National League.

INSPIRATION STATION

Guernica: A Powerful Tool

On April 26, 1937, German and Italian planes bombed the town of Guernica, in the Basque region of Spain. The attack was at the behest of Generalisimo Francisco Franco and his fascist Nationalist army, as a strike against civilians who were perceived to be supporters of the autonomous, left-leaning Basque Government. Hundreds of men, women, and children who were going about their business at an open-air market were killed in the bombing.

At the request of the Spanish Republican government, which also opposed Franco, the artist Pablo Picasso painted *Guernica*, a work that depicted the suffering and deaths of both humans and animals. The large mural (11' 6" by 25' 8") was exhibited around the world during the next few years. It remains a powerful anti-war and anti-fascism statement and is one of Picasso's most well-known paintings. Picasso would not allow *Guernica* to return to Spain while Franco's government was in power, but it is now housed at the Museo Reina Sofia in Madrid. Sadly, Picasso died before Spain became a republic once again. According to one anecdote, while Picasso was in Paris during WWII, a German officer examined the artist's apartment. Upon noticing a photograph of *Guernica*, he asked, "Did you do that?"

"No, you did," replied Picasso.

A Vision Made Visual

On January 6, 1941, President Franklin D. Roosevelt addressed Congress and the American people with a speech now known as the "Four Freedoms speech." Roosevelt knew that World War II was inevitable, and he knew he had to prepare the citizens of the United States for the sacrifices that must be made to preserve the liberties they held dear. One of the millions of Americans listening to Roosevelt's speech that night was the artist Norman Rockwell, best known for the folksy, all-American covers he painted for *The Saturday Evening Post*. Rockwell was so moved by the president's words that he began painting *The Four Freedoms:* Freedom of Speech, Freedom of Worship, Freedom from Want, and Freedom from Fear. *The Four Freedoms* series was used very successfully on posters promoting U.S. war bonds, and they may have been Rockwell's most famous paintings in a career chock-full of famous paintings.

Terror by Night!

❖ ❖ ❖ ❖

Life during the Blitz was a constant struggle for millions of Britons.

After France, Poland, and other nations had fallen before the German blitzkrieg at the onset of World War II, Hitler turned his attention to Great Britain. But the Nazis were unable to gain air superiority over the British during the Battle of Britain, so Hermann Göring, head of the German Luftwaffe, authorized a sustained, punishing air assault that came to be known as the Blitz.

Bombs over London

The goal of the Blitz was to terrify and demoralize the British government and its citizenry into surrendering without the need for an invasion. So rather than attack Royal Air Force bases, the bombings focused on British cities, particularly London.

The first intentional wave of bombings over London occurred on the afternoon of September 7, 1940, and continued for 57 consecutive nights. By the time the Blitz came to an end in May 1941, more than 40,000 civilians had been killed (more than half of them in London) and one million homes had been destroyed. Smaller attacks over the course of the war brought the civilian death total to over 51,500.

Surviving the Blitz

Life during the Blitz was a constant struggle for Londoners and those living in other targeted cities. Because the aerial assaults occurred primarily at night, blackout rules were strongly enforced. Families were required to cover their windows with black material to make it more difficult for German pilots to find their targets. Street lamps were also extinguished and automobiles were required to drive with their headlights off, which made road and pedestrian travel perilous. Traffic accidents were common, and several people drowned after accidentally walking off bridges.

When German bombers were spotted, air raid sirens sounded to warn the populace. Many families hunkered in their basements or in specially constructed bomb shelters on their property. Those who didn't have a home shelter sought refuge in municipal bomb shelters or underground subway stations. However, even these ready-made shelters were not entirely safe. In January 1941, a bomb fell directly above the Bank subway station, killing 111 people. The bombs fell, loud and frightening. Jack Court was a young paperboy at the time. "It was always a great shock to anyone experiencing the blitz for the first time," he recalled for the BBC. "The great, great, noise, the never before heard of sounds, the echoes that hurt the chest."

Once air raid wardens gave the "all clear," people would emerge from their shelters. Many returned to find their homes destroyed, and family members and neighbors dead or missing. A common peril was unexploded ordnance, which required special disposal. "Unexploded bomb" signs were common throughout the devastated cities as people did their best to go about their daily lives.

At the war's start, some London families sent their children to the country, where they were safer from German bombs. For many city youngsters, it was an eye-opening experience as they saw farm animals and fresh produce for the very first time.

Rationalizing Rations

During the Blitz and throughout the war, rationing was a common part of daily life for all Britons. Three major commodities were rationed throughout much of the conflict: food, clothing, and gasoline. Food, in particular, became increasingly sparse, because England was forced to import what it could not raise or grow on its own. Other nations, especially the United States and Australia, were willing to help, but German U-Boats destroyed many supply ships before they could reach their destination. As a result, food was heavily rationed and meat became a rare luxury.

Gasoline was another coveted commodity throughout the war. The lion's share went to power Britain's war machines—trucks, tanks, and planes. As a result, the majority of people came to rely on public transportation, such as buses and the subway, to get around.

The Blitz took a heavy toll on everyone in Britain, but it ultimately failed in its intended goal of demoralizing the British people into submission. In fact, the effect was just the opposite, instilling in all Britons a deep resolve that carried them through the war. Germany was able to conquer almost all of Europe, but it found in the British a strength and perseverance that could not be defeated.

FLUBBED HEADLINES

"Utah Poison Control Center Reminds Everyone Not to Take Poison"
Bless those hard-working poison control experts. How would we ever stay safe without them?

"Wood: 'I Feel Great'"
Some pickup lines are simply destined to fail.

"A-Rod Goes Deep, Wang Hurt"
Baseball has always had the whole sexual "bases" connotation, but this might be taking things too far.

"Alton Attorney Accidentally Sues Himself"
Let's be honest: This guy deserves whatever judgment he gets.

"Meeting on Open Meetings Is Closed"
The meeting on closed meetings, however, is now open.

"Federal Agents Raid Gun Shop, Find Weapons"
In other news, federal agents discovered cases of hoagies at the local delicatessen. A full investigation is now underway.

"Local Child Wins Gun From Fundraiser"
If it came from the aforementioned gun shop, there's going to be trouble.

"Ruler Can't Measure Johnson's Impact"
See? It's not only the size that counts.

"Puerto Rican Teen Named Mistress of the Universe"
Her phone has been ringing off the hook ever since.

"Police: Crack Found in Man's Buttocks"
Something about this headline just doesn't smell right.

"Midget Sues Grocer, Cites Belittling Remarks"
You know, remarks like someone referring to him as a "midget."

"FEMA Probe Reveals Rain Caused Floods"
That's your taxpayer dollars at work right there, folks.

"Lobbyists Offer Legislators Cash at Ethics Session"
Well, no one ever explicitly said that sort of thing was frowned upon.

🎥 Behind the Films of Our Time

- The cover of the novel *Twilight* shows a close-up of what appears to be Edward's hands holding an apple. The filmmakers wanted to duplicate that for the movie version, so Bella drops an apple, and Edward picks it up and gently holds it in his hands, offering it to her. According to the director, the scene took 13 takes to get right.

- Fifty-one-year-old Gary Cooper wore very little, if any, make-up in the 1952 movie *High Noon,* to better show the worry lines on his face.

- Four Academy Award–winning movie titles contain animal names, but the movies aren't about those animals. They are *One Flew Over the Cuckoo's Nest* (1975); *The Deer Hunter* (1978); *Dances With Wolves* (1990); and *The Silence of the Lambs* (1991).

- John Travolta's white disco suit in 1977's *Saturday Night Fever* later sold for $145,000.

- The 1996 horror movie *Scream* was the unlikely setting for a romance between costars Courtney Cox and David Arquette. They did two sequels to the movie, got married in 1999, and have a daughter together.

- *The Dark Knight* is the first Batman film that didn't have the name "Batman" in the title.

- For the women who think Sean Connery was the sexiest spy: You might be surprised to learn that Connery wore a toupee in all of his James Bond movies, even the 1962 hit, *Dr. No.*

- The first movie directed by a woman to gross over $100 million in the United States was *Big,* directed by Penny Marshall in 1988.

- Finding a backer in 1981 for *A Nightmare on Elm Street* was a nightmare. The show's original investor backed out days before filming, and two weeks in, the producers had run out of money. Line producer John Burrows used his credit card to float the show until new backers were found.

- Brooke Shields was taller than her costar Christopher Atkins in *The Blue Lagoon,* so the director frequently had her walking and standing in a trench so that she would appear shorter.

Nancy Drew and the Hardy Boys: The Mystery of the Ghostwriters

❖ ❖ ❖ ❖

Nancy Drew and the Hardy Boys may be aces at uncovering secrets, but the real secret lies in the origins of these teen detective novels. The credited authors—Carolyn Keene and Franklin W. Dixon—are as fictitious as the teen sleuths themselves. And all are the brainchildren of early 20th-century children's literature magnate Edward Stratemeyer.

Fiction Factory

Edward Stratemeyer was a successful juvenile fiction writer—so successful that he didn't have time to finish all of the books assigned to him. So he assembled a group of ghostwriters to help, and around 1904–1906 (sources vary), Stratemeyer Syndicate was born.

The process functioned like an assembly line: Stratemeyer developed the outlines and character descriptions, farmed them to ghostwriters who worked under the pseudonym assigned to each series, and then he edited each story to ensure consistency across the series. The ghostwriters received a meager $75 to $150 and gave up "all right, title and interest" as well as "use [of] such pen name in any manner whatsoever."

Mystery Makers

Following the syndicate's first successful ventures—the Bobbsey Twins and Tom Swift—Stratemeyer masterminded what would become his greatest legacies.

In 1927, mystery-solving teen brothers Frank and Joe Hardy, aka the Hardy Boys, debuted, authored primarily by Canadian writer Leslie McFarlane under the pseudonym Franklin W. Dixon. Two years later, all-American girl sleuth Nancy Drew hit the scene, written mostly by Mildred Wirt under the pen name Carolyn Keene.

Unfortunately, Stratemeyer would not live to see the success of Nancy Drew; he died just two weeks after the first books, *The Secret of the Old Clock, The Hidden Staircase,* and *The Bungalow Mystery,* hit stands in April 1930.

Initially, Stratemeyer's daughters, Edna and Harriet, hoped to sell the syndicate, but it was the height of the Great Depression, and buyers were scarce. So the two sisters—primarily Harriet—took over the business. They managed the ghostwriters and, above all, endeavored to keep their authors' identities secret.

Ghostbusters

In 1958, the syndicate's publisher, Grossett & Dunlap, requested an update of the books for contemporary audiences. Harriet, who had severed the syndicate's ties with Mildred Wirt five years earlier, assumed the rewriting of Nancy Drew herself and even added new titles to the series. Suddenly, despite her previous reticence, Harriet began claiming publicly that she was the real Carolyn Keene and always had been.

In 1980, Harriet sold the Nancy Drew series to Simon & Schuster, who made national fanfare over the series' 50th anniversary, touting Harriet as the originator. Wirt, along with Grossett & Dunlap, promptly sued—and promptly lost. The media had a field day with the "real" Carolyn Keene.

Simon & Schuster subsumed the entire syndicate following Harriet's death in 1982. Despite evidence to the contrary, her obituary lamented the passing of the real Carolyn Keene. Twenty years later, Mildred Wirt's did the same.

- Stratemeyer initially named his heroine Stella Strong, with alternate suggestions of Diana Drew, Diana Dare, Nan Nelson, Nan Drew, and Helen Hale. Not a fan of the name Stella, Grosset & Dunlap chose Nan Drew and lengthened it to Nancy.

- The original rules for the series included "no smooching." Neither Frank, Joe, nor Nancy enjoyed so much as a peck until the 1980s, after Simon & Schuster took over. However, Nancy does faint into "the strong arms" of her boyfriend, Ned Nickerson.

- In 1959, Nancy's car was updated from a roadster to a convertible. Today, she drives a hybrid.

Fumbling Felons

Give Her a Break
Ohio police pulled over 42-year-old Nancy M. Lang's van after they noticed her driving erratically. They suspected that she might be driving under the influence, so they submitted her to the usual sobriety tests. Lang couldn't stand on one leg or walk in a straight line when asked, but she voluntarily performed several jumping jacks and a cartwheel to show she could still drive. Lang was charged with a DUI, driving with an expired registration, and driving with a suspended license. Her excuse? According to police reports, she offered, "Please, give me a break. I'm drunk."

Burglary and Ethics
Two burglars in North Yorkshire, England, committed a crime when they stole a laptop computer owned by 24-year-old Richard Coverdale. All went well until the pair took a look at the computer. They were surprised to see videos and pictures of child abuse and pornography disturbing enough that they decided to turn it over to the police. Coverdale confessed to several counts of sexual offenses and was sentenced to 3½ years in jail. The original perpetrators got a little leniency for their belated honesty: They both got one year of community service.

It's Not a Field Trip
An undercover policeman in Toronto, Canada, was a little surprised when a suspected drug dealer met him for an arranged drug deal—with his five children in tow. That's right: The guy brought along his two teenagers, a 10 year old, an 11 year old, and a toddler while he sold cocaine. After buying the drugs, the detective followed the man back to his car where he found additional cocaine and two knives. The dad was arrested and charged with selling cocaine, possession with the intent to sell, and possession of a weapon. The Children's Aid Society took the kids into protective custody. Apparently, this was not an appropriate way to participate in Bring Your Kids to Work Day.

Fast Facts

- *No wonder cats hear so well—they have 32 muscles in each ear.*

- *Goldfish only have a memory of three seconds. Perhaps that's why they keep swimming in circles.*

- *The average weight of each stone in the Great Pyramid is 2.5 tons. However, some larger stones weigh up to 50 tons.*

- *Why are the drug companies selling so many sleep aids when the average person falls asleep in seven minutes?*

- *If you want to make good use of the English alphabet, try writing or saying, "The quick brown fox jumps over the lazy dog." It uses all 26 letters.*

- *Here's a disgusting thought: Over the course of his or her life, the average person eats eight spiders while they're sleeping.*

- *Frank J. Zamboni, inventor of the ice-resurfacing machine of the same name, has been inducted into the World Figure Skating Hall of Fame, the National Inventors Hall of Fame, and the United States Hockey Hall of Fame.*

- *Jim Morrison wanted to put 30 dogs on the cover of The Doors' album* Strange Days *because "dog is God spelled backwards." The idea was ultimately nixed, however.*

- *Guinness is big business in Ireland. Seven percent of the country's barley crop is used to make the world-famous beer.*

- *The Guinness Book of World Records began in 1955 when an employee at the Guinness Brewery in the UK decided to create a book of records to settle pub disputes.*

Whatever Happened To...?

❖ ❖ ❖ ❖

*On June 25, 2009, the world was shocked to learn that pop superstar
Michael Jackson had died. As weeks went by, rumors of drug
abuse, including a nightly intravenous drip of the potent anesthetic
propofol, and other mysterious circumstances began filtering
out. Perhaps we'll never fully know what happened to Jackson.
However, it certainly seems the King of Pop has joined the ranks
of Hollywood celebrities who have suffered mysterious deaths.*

The Fatal Match

In the early 1930s, Russ Columbo was a singer whose popularity
rivaled Bing Crosby's. But his bizarre early death took care of that.

On September 2, 1934, Columbo went to see a photographer
friend named Lansing V. Brown Jr. The two were talking and
examining Brown's collection of Civil War dueling pistols. Brown
reportedly struck a match on one of the pistols, which unbeknownst
to him was loaded. The action caused the weapon to discharge; a
bullet ricocheted off a desk and hit Columbo in the left eye, fatally
wounding him.

But this weird story gets even stranger: Just before he died,
Columbo's mother suffered a heart attack. The family knew that
word of her son's death might be enough to kill her, so a story was
concocted that Columbo had married frequent pal Carole Lombard,
and that the two had run off together. For the next ten years, the
family wrote letters supposedly from "Russ & Carole" to his mother.
They also gave her monthly checks from "Russ" that were actually
from his insurance policies.

In 1954, Columbo's cousin Alberto was found murdered gangland-
style. This has led to speculation that there was more to Columbo's
odd death than "meets the eye."

Death of the Tenor

Many people still recognize the name of singer and movie star Mario
Lanza, but few know the the controversy surrounding his death.

Despite his fame and devoted legions of fans, Lanza had an
up-and-down career in Hollywood and was known to be in a

constant battle with his weight (at one time he was on a "diet" of grapefruit and alcohol). According to lore, in 1959, while living in Italy, Lanza became friends with big-time gangster Lucky Luciano, who "suggested" that Lanza sing at a charity affair in Naples. Lanza apparently agreed, but he skipped the scheduled rehearsal, at which point two thugs allegedly visited Lanza and told him he'd better show up at the affair.

Rather than perform as told, Lanza got indignant. As the story goes, the singer left for Rome, where he checked into a clinic to try a new weight-loss plan. On October 7, 1959, Lanza died of an apparent heart attack, his third one (and he was only 38 years old). His wife, Betty, died six months later at their home in California—some say of a broken heart. Fans and family dispute this story, saying Lanza never had any mob ties, but the tale persists.

Left Hanging

David Carradine was best known for his starring role on the television series *Kung Fu* as a character who dispensed wisdom about life. However, there was little wisdom in how he died.

In June 2009, Carradine was in Thailand to shoot a movie. On June 4, the actor was found hanging naked inside a closet in his hotel room in Bangkok. His hands were reportedly tied above his head. According to a report in a local newspaper, one end of a shoelace had been tied around his penis, and the other end tied around his neck.

Theories of both suicide and murder floated about, but in the days and weeks after his death, reports of Carradine's fascination with self-bondage and autoerotic asphyxiation came out, leading to the conclusion that his death was a bondage experiment gone horribly wrong.

Monkey Business, Indeed

The "Ice Cream Blonde," Thelma Todd, was one of Hollywood's brightest stars in the late 1920s and early '30s. She is best known today for her roles in two classic Marx Brothers films, *Monkey Business* and *Horse Feathers.* Her untimely death remains one of Hollywood's most mysterious cases.

On December 16, 1935, Todd was found dead in the front seat of a Packard convertible at a house belonging to film director Roland

West. The car had been running inside the garage, filling it with deadly exhaust fumes. Most people considered it a suicide.

But was it? A replacement porcelain tooth had been knocked out of Todd's mouth. Blood was found on her clothing. An autopsy revealed that she had suffered a broken nose, some broken ribs, and bruises.

An immediate suspect in her death was film director West, who also happened to be Todd's lover and business partner. But a stronger suspect emerged in gangster Lucky Luciano. Todd (along with West) had opened a joint called Thelma Todd's Roadside Rest Café. Organized crime was just beginning to penetrate California, and Luciano visited Todd's café with a proposition: He wanted to turn the top floor into a secret gambling casino. All Todd had to do was to keep the food and drink flowing on the bottom floor and look the other way.

Todd, however, turned him down flat; this led to speculation that she had been killed for her refusal. Her lawyer was so certain of this that he got the district attorney to schedule a second inquest and investigate this lead. But other Hollywood types, fearful of Luciano, got the D.A. to reconsider and close the case for good. Today the restless ghost of Thelma Todd is reported to haunt the building where her café once stood.

And Let's Not Forget...

- **George Reeves**—The former Superman was found shot under mysterious circumstances. Some say suicide, others say murder.

- **Bob Crane**—The *Hogan's Heroes* star was found bludgeoned to death in bed. Was he murdered because of his vigorous sex life and habit of taping his sexual conquests?

- **James Whale**—The director of *Frankenstein* was found floating in his pool. Was it suicide or murder?

- **Marilyn Monroe**—This material girl died of an overdose of sleeping pills. Was it suicide or murder by (take your pick) the mob, the Kennedys, or some combination thereof?

Odd Ordinances

- It is illegal to drive while sleeping in Tennessee.

- In Danville, Pennsylvania, all fire hydrants must be inspected one hour before a fire.

- It is illegal to throw pickle juice on a trolley in Rhode Island.

- It's not legal to wear transparent clothes in Providence, Rhode Island. Spoilsports.

- A Spartanburg, South Carolina, law forbids people from eating watermelon in the Magnolia Street Cemetery.

- No runaway grooms: If a man promises to marry a woman in South Carolina, he is bound by law to do so.

- You cannot fire a missile without a permit in South Carolina.

- It is against the law to lie down and go to sleep in a cheese factory in South Dakota.

- Movies that depict police officers as being beaten or treated badly are banned in South Dakota.

- It is not legal to use a lasso to catch a fish in Tennessee. Though good luck trying.

- In Memphis restaurants, no pie may be taken home or given to fellow diners.

- Shooting a buffalo is prohibited from the second story of a hotel in Texas.

- Criminals in Texas must give their victims written or verbal notice 24 hours in advance, explaining what crime is about to be committed.

- You may not dust any public place with a feather duster in Clarendon, Texas.

- Snowball throwers can expect a $50 fine in Provo, Utah.

Watch What You Say!

❖ ❖ ❖ ❖

*These common American gestures can
get you in hot water overseas!*

When "OK" Is Not Okay

The next time you're visiting Brazil, refrain from giving the traditional "OK" sign by touching the tips of your thumb and forefinger. In South America's largest nation, that all-American gesture is considered obscene.

That's just one example of how body language can get you into trouble when traveling overseas. International travel experts note that a run-of-the-mill gesture in the United States often has a completely different meaning in other parts of the world.

Take, for example, the "V for victory" sign, which is made by raising the index and middle finger of one hand, palm facing out. (Since the '60s, this has also become known as the peace sign.) This gesture is perfectly acceptable in the United States. But not in England—if the palm faces inward, it means a resounding "up yours."

Depending on what country you're visiting, the "thumbs up" gesture also has several different connotations. In the United States, it typically means that something is met with approval. In Australia, however, if you make a slight jerk upward with the extended digit, it means "up yours." The gesture is also an insult in Nigeria, so keep that in mind when hitchhiking there.

And then there's the common gesture of rotating a finger around one's ear, which in the United States usually signifies that someone is crazy. Not in Argentina, however. There, the gesture means you have a telephone call.

Don't Get Me Wrong...

Two potentially problematic gestures are nodding and shaking your head. In the United States, of course, a nod means yes and a shake means no. One would think this is universal, but in Bulgaria, parts of Greece, Yugoslavia, Turkey, and Iran, the reverse is true—a shake of the head means yes, and a nod means no.

Personal contact can be a particularly touchy issue when traveling abroad. In the United States, we're taught to give each other a little space when conversing, usually an arm's length. But in densely populated Japan, where personal space is appreciated and touching of any kind is considered taboo, the distance between two conversing individuals is typically greater.

Making Friends in the Middle East

Interestingly, the opposite is true in many Middle Eastern countries, where it's not uncommon to see two conversing people stand literally toe to toe as they talk, and even touch each other's arms or bodies in the process. In the Middle East, it's also perfectly acceptable for two men to walk hand in hand in public. The gesture has no particular sexual connotation, it's just a sign of friendship.

When visiting the Middle East, one should also refrain from inadvertently showing others the soles of your shoes by crossing your legs. The gesture is considered extremely insulting because the soles of your shoes are viewed as the dirtiest part of the body. Public displays of affection between men and women are also frowned upon, and in some very strict Muslim nations it can even land you in jail. In addition, get used to using your right hand for everything, including eating, presenting gifts, and touching others. In Middle Eastern culture, the right hand is the "clean" hand, while the left hand is considered "unclean" and is used primarily for bodily hygiene. Sorry, southpaws.

World travel can be enlightening and a lot of fun, but make sure you are well versed in the local customs of the regions you visit. Otherwise, an innocuous hand gesture could result in a punch in the nose!

Fast Facts

- The microwave was invented by accident. In 1945, scientist named Percy Spencer walked past a radar tube and was surprised to find that the chocolate candy in his pocket melted. From there he deduced that microwave waves could be used to cook food.

- Wrigley's gum was the first product to have a barcode.

- It costs an average of $6,400 to raise a medium-sized dog to age 11.

- Superman's pet dog is named Krypto.

- The phrase "Goodnight, sleep tight" originated in the 1500s when mattresses were made with a rope bottom. Each night the ropes were tightened to make the mattress sag less.

- Kite flying is a professional sport in Thailand.

- Get out the sunblock: Pigs, light-colored horses, and walruses can get sunburned.

- Doughnuts got their name from their original description: a sweet treat made from raised dough with a nut baked in the center.

- The first pre-sliced bread was Wonder Bread.

- In a box of Animal Crackers, you'll find one buffalo, one lion, two monkeys, two sheep, two tigers, three rhinos, four camels, five bears, and six gorillas.

- In the first few years of the 20th century, Thomas Edison designed and manufactured a battery for an electric car. But by the time it came to market in 1909, the internal combustion engine was too well established for the electric car to catch on.

Murphy's Law

❖ ❖ ❖ ❖

Perhaps you've heard of "Murphy's Law," which basically means, "If anything can go wrong it will." It's a simple adage that seems to perfectly sum up so many situations in our topsy-turvy lives.

Ah, Murphy, dear Murphy. Your failures have served as such a global inspiration. Murphy likely had no idea his name would become synonymous with screw-ups when he uttered that now infamous phrase. Although, to be fair, the phrase we know isn't *exactly* what he said. Here's the story.

Meet Murphy

As the tale goes, there once was a U.S. Air Force captain named Edward A. Murphy. Back in 1949, Captain Murphy was working on a military air test at Edwards Air Force Base, trying to figure out how much force a human body could tolerate during a plane crash.

It's probably no surprise that things didn't go as planned. After the test, Murphy and his crew realized all of the sensors they'd installed on the test subjects—the devices that, after the experiment ended, should have allowed them to get the data they needed—failed to work.

Days later, the captain held a news conference at which he inadvertently cemented his place in history. "If there are two or more ways to do something and one of those results is a catastrophe," he was quoted as saying, "then someone will do it that way." Thus, Murphy's Law was born.

Murphy's Law in Action

Whether it's the traffic lane next to yours always moving faster, the dropped piece of bread always landing butter-side down, or a single sock always disappearing during laundry, the law is still used as the all-purpose scapegoat. But not everyone agrees with the origins of Murphy's Law—some folks swear Murphy mistakenly received credit for the creed. If so, the fact that its true creator was cheated out of the glory is, one might say, a perfect example of Murphy's Law in action.

Trashing the White House

❖ ❖ ❖ ❖

When did democracy come to America? Many historians say
that winning the American War of Independence introduced
democracy to the country. Others, however, may point to an
incident that occurred during the inauguration of Andrew Jackson
as the true birth of democracy: the trashing of the White House.

Man of the People

As simply put by the government's own Web site, Andrew Jackson
"More nearly than any of his predecessors . . . was elected by popular
vote; as President he sought to act as the direct representative of the
common man."

Jackson was a popular figure and a war hero. In 1824, he was
one of four candidates who sought the presidency. He won the most
popular votes, but because no candidate won a majority of Electoral
votes, the election went into the House of Representatives. There,
presidential candidate Henry Clay threw his support to fellow
contender John Quincy Adams, supposedly in return for a promise
to be named Secretary of State. Adams became president and did
indeed name Clay his Secretary of State. This "corrupt bargain"
infuriated Jackson and his supporters, who campaigned vigorously
against it for four years. In 1828, they were rewarded when Jackson
overwhelmed Adams in a rematch to become the seventh President
of the United States.

On March 4, 1829, Jackson was inaugurated president. A crowd of
15,000–20,000 people swarmed around the Capitol building and the
surrounding streets to see and hear their hero take the oath of office.
After he did, the enthusiastic crowd burst through a chain holding
them back and mobbed around Jackson, congratulating him. Jackson
was barely able to get away, and he was spirited into the building.

King Mob

Jackson exited from the Capitol and mounted a white horse for the
trip to the White House, where a public reception had been planned.
"As far as the eye could reach," said an onlooker, "the side-walks of

the Avenue were covered with people on foot, and the centre with innumerable carriages and persons on horseback." This massive throng—country boys, dandies, ladies and gentlemen of all races— moved en masse with Jackson to the White House. The Man of the People had won the election, and the people intended to celebrate.

When Jackson arrived at the Executive Mansion, its lower floor was filled with a teeming mass of humanity from all classes and walks of life. "I never saw such a mixture," said a witness. "The reign of KING MOB seemed triumphant."

Melee!

Waiters opened the White House doors to bring barrels of orange punch outside. Bad move. The crowd rushed forward and plowed into the waiters like a flying wedge in football. Waiters, glasses, pails of liquor, and guests collided, sending people and implements flying.

The free-for-all was underway. Men in muddy boots tramped onto satin-covered chairs to get a better look at Jackson. People surged into the building through the doors or leaped in through open ground-floor windows. Expensive china and glasses were broken and the pieces crushed underfoot. The mob flowed throughout the White House, unrestrained and unfettered. One senator called it a "regular Saturnalia."

"Ladies fainted, men were seen with bloody noses," said one stunned participant. "A rabble scrambling, fighting, romping ... " Most folks could only escape by jumping back out of the windows.

Everyone wanted a piece of Jackson, the opportunity to shake his hand, touch his sleeve, congratulate him, or shout words of encouragement. Eventually Jackson, who was still in mourning because of the recent death of his wife, became exhausted and was taken away by several aides. The crowd only left the White House when punch tubs were placed on the lawn.

Amidst the confusion, a small girl disappeared. Her parents later found her jumping up and down on a sofa in Jackson's private quarters. "Just think, mama!" she yelled. "This sofa is a millionth part mine!"

Ah, democracy.

Behind the TV Shows of Our Time

- Both Leif Garrett and Willie Aames portrayed Felix Unger's son, Leonard, on *The Odd Couple*.

- *Seinfeld's* Soup Nazi was based on a real New York City soup vendor named Al Yegeneh.

- Little Joey Stivic of *All in the Family* was played by adorable infant twins Jason and Justin Draeger. The character became so popular that the Ideal Toy Company released a Joey doll. But the doll was a bit controversial because it had a penis.

- The estate of gangster Al Capone sued the producers of the early-'60s crime drama *The Untouchables* for $1 million for using Capone's name and likeness without their permission.

- Before creating and hosting *The Twilight Zone,* Rod Serling was most famous as a writer on prestigious drama series such as *Playhouse 90,* for which he wrote the critically acclaimed episode "Requiem for a Heavyweight."

- When ABC tried to copy NBC's *Laugh-In* with a clone show called *Turn-On* in 1969, the result was an absolute disaster that was so tasteless many network affiliates refused to air it. It was cancelled immediately after one episode was aired.

- The names of 1950s sitcoms can seem delightfully quaint and innocent to us now. One short-lived NBC offering was called *Too Young to Go Steady*.

- In 1976, in an effort to save the faltering *Tony Orlando and Dawn* variety show, its name was changed to *The Tony Orlando and Dawn Rainbow Hour*. It didn't help, and the show was cancelled.

- The uvula is the little thing that dangles in the back of the throat, but many people don't know what it's called. *Saturday Night Live* took advantage of this ignorance in a 1977 sketch in which Gilda Radner repeated the word "uvula" over and over, suggesting that it was some kind of "feminine" organ.

The Times They Are A-Changin'

2002

- The unstoppable basketball phenom Michael Jordan, originally of the Chicago Bulls (then with minor league baseball's Birmingham Barons, back to the Bulls, and later with the NBA Washington Wizards), plays his first game in Chicago since returning to professional basketball.

- Funeral services for Her Majesty Queen Elizabeth of the United Kingdom are held at Westminster Abbey in London.

- Former President Jimmy Carter is awarded the Nobel Peace Prize. He is the third U.S. president to receive the coveted award. The others are Woodrow Wilson and Theodore Roosevelt.

- A suicide bomber kills 28 people on Passover in Netanya, Israel.

- NASA's space probe, *Mars Odyssey,* finds that ice exists beneath the surface on Mars—enough to fill Lake Michigan twice.

- The U.S. Congress officially recognizes that Italian inventor Antonio Meucci, of Staten Island, was the first inventor of the telephone. Meucci had succeeded in producing a method of voice communication in 1871, but he couldn't afford to renew the $10 patent when it expired in 1874. Alexander Graham Bell entered the scene with his telephone transmission in 1876.

- Nine coal miners are trapped in the Quecreek Mine when it floods in Somerset, Pennsylvania. They are finally rescued after 77 hours underground.

- The United States government raises the Homeland Security Advisory System's terror alert to Orange, or High, for the first time in response to threats that coincide with the anniversary of the September 11, 2001, attacks.

- French scientist and Clonaid CEO Brigitte Boisselier reports that a baby clone named Eve was born, prompting a deluge of scientific and ethical questions.

- *Spiderman* is the movie blockbuster of the year, grossing $406 million.

World's Weirdest Sea Creatures

❖ ❖ ❖ ❖

From creatures that look like rocks to fish that are blind from constant darkness to those that make their own light, the sea is filled with things you definitely don't want to encounter while swimming!

Sea Horse

Sea horses are weird in so many ways. For instance, they travel less than one foot per minute, are monogamous, and have prehensile tails. They also do not have teeth or a stomach, and the males are the ones who become pregnant and give birth. Come to think of it, sea horses should have their own reality show.

Deep Sea Anglerfish

Living more than 3,000 feet underwater, deep-sea anglerfish don't see much light. Instead, they create their own. The female grows a bioluminescent "fishing rod" to attract and distract prey. When some species of anglerfish mate, the male uses his mouth to permanently attach himself to the female's body; from that point forward, they share circulatory and reproductive systems.

Cone Shell

The cone shell is a sea snail that slowly and methodically hunts and tracks its prey. When the victim is within range, the cone shell fires a tiny poisonous harpoon at it. After the prey is paralyzed, the cone shell pulls it to its mouth by the thread that attaches the harpoon to its body.

Stonefish

The stonefish bears the dubious honor of being the most poisonous fish in the world. Although treatable if caught in time, its venom can kill a human within hours or at least require the amputation of a limb. Stonefish are found in shallow waters where waders can easily step on the fish's spiny, venomous dorsal fins. To make matters worse, they are nearly impossible to spot, as their camouflage renders them invisible against the ocean floor.

Caligula and Incitatus

❖ ❖ ❖ ❖

Caligula (A.D. 37–41) *is the poster child for depraved Roman emperors, and not without reason. An oft-repeated story about his life says that he appointed his horse a consul of Rome. It makes a great tale, but there's no evidence that it's true.*

Both surviving ancient accounts of Caligula's reign, Suetonius's *Lives of the Twelve Caesars* and the papers of historian Cassius Dio, were written long after Caligula's death. These chroniclers agreed that "Little Boot" (in Latin, "Caligula"; his proper name was Gaius) was touchy, boorish, unpredictable, dangerous—and rather fond of his horse Incitatus. It's said that Caligula went so far as to handpick and purchase a "wife" for Incitatus, a mare named Penelope.

For the Love of a Horse

According to Dio, Caligula had Incitatus over for dinner, toasted his health, fed him gold-flecked grain, appointed him a priest, and promised to make him a consul. Dio believed it was a serious vow. Suetonius wrote that Caligula gave Incitatus a luxurious stable with an ivory feed trough, lavish purple blankets, jeweled collars, and attendants. On evenings before races, the emperor forbade any noisemaking that might agitate Incitatus. Suetonius also mentioned the plans of consular promotion.

Not Out of the Question

No ancient source says the horse was ever actually consul. Priest, maybe, if you believe Dio. Historians now have the consular list from 37–41, and Incitatus isn't on it. Both Dio and Suetonius convincingly describe him as a pampered pet; only one feels Rome might have had a neigh-saying consul had Caligula lived longer. Both describe Caligula as someone descending into lunacy, capable of any number of mad deeds. Had he lived, we might today gaze upon Roman coins bearing Incitatus's horsey countenance. Perhaps, near the end of the sordid reign of Caligula, Incitatus was the only creature his master truly liked and trusted.

Fast Facts

- *Despite its name, the 1969 Woodstock Festival was not held in the town of Woodstock, New York. It actually took place on a dairy farm in nearby Bethel.*

- *Two deaths and two births were reported to have taken place at Woodstock during the three-day festival.*

- *Musician Bob Dylan was scheduled to appear at Woodstock but was unable to make it because one of his children was in the hospital that weekend.*

- *When food ran short at Woodstock, a local Jewish community center made sandwiches from 200 loaves of bread and 40 pounds of cold cuts.*

- *Liberace's last meal was Cream of Wheat with brown sugar.*

- *When the London* Daily Mirror *accused Liberace of being gay, he sued and won. The paper was forced to pay him damages totaling $22,400.*

- *When the* Titanic *sank on April 14, 1912, it took with it 3,000 bags of mail and an automobile.*

- *A first-class ticket on the* Titanic *cost $4,350.*

- *One of the amenities aboard the* Titanic *was a heated swimming pool—the very first ever installed on a ship.*

- *The nine-banded armadillo is the only mammal known to always give birth to four identical young.*

- *Warning! It is illegal to own an armadillo in the state of Maine.*

Who Was Davy Crockett?

❖ ❖ ❖ ❖

Just who exactly was Davy Crockett? Was he a rough-and-tumble pioneer, a man whose fearless exploits helped tame the wilderness? Or was he an ambitious and self-promoting politician, made famous by a well-orchestrated public relations campaign and a little help from Hollywood?

A Man from Tennessee

Some aspects of David "Davy" Crockett's life are not in dispute, though much of it is. We know that he was born on August 17, 1786, in eastern Tennessee. His first wife was Mary "Polly" Finley, who died in 1815. He soon remarried, taking the widow Elizabeth Patton to be his bride.

Crockett was an excellent hunter. Often his rifle enabled him to provide food for his wife and five children. But he wasn't entirely an outdoorsman: He was elected to the Tennessee legislature in 1821, then the United States House of Representatives in 1827. For the next decade he was in and out of Congress, and when he found himself in a hard-fought battle for the Congressional seat in 1835, he threatened that if he lost the election he would tell his constituents "to go to hell" and move to Texas. He lost the vote and kept his word, departing to Texas, where he met his end at the Alamo on March 6, 1836.

Two Men the Same—Two Men Different

Crockett is always lumped together with Daniel Boone as one of the two premier American frontiersmen, blazing trails through untamed wilderness. Without question, Boone was the real deal. He explored Kentucky when it was populated almost primarily by Native Americans, built the Wilderness Road to provide greater access to the region, led settlers into Kentucky when it was just a howling wilderness, and narrowly escaped death numerous times.

Crockett's life followed a different path. Bitten by the political bug upon his first foray into elected office, he progressed from justice of the peace to U.S. Congressman in a remarkably short time, particularly because political campaigns then—as now—cost money, and Crockett's low-budget campaigns would have embarrassed a shoestring.

Crockett was a natural for politics. Independent-minded and loyal to his backwoods constituents, he was also gregarious, quick-witted, and personable. Once, a flock of guinea hens showed up at an outside political debate and squawked so loudly that his opponent was completely unnerved. Crockett, however, joked that the birds had actually been chanting "Crockett, Crockett, Crockett," which is why the other candidate was spooked. He won the debate and the election.

Contrast that with the stoic and reclusive Boone, who probably would have preferred to swim the entire length of the Mississippi River rather than hobnob and glad-hand. As one story has it, Boone once welcomed a visitor to his cabin and in conversation asked where the man lived. When informed that he resided about 70 miles from Boone's home, Boone turned to his wife and said, "Old woman, we must move, they are crowding us."

A Lion with a Touch of Airth-Quake

Crockett enjoyed his reputation as a humble backwoodsman in sophisticated Washington, D.C. This reputation was spread even further by the wildly popular 1831 play *The Lion of the West.* The main character, obviously based on Crockett, is a Congressman from Kentucky named Nimrod Wildfire, who boasts that he's "half horse, half alligator, a touch of the airth-quake, with a sprinkling of the steamboat." Beginning in 1835, with the publication of the so-called *Crockett Almanacs,* he was portrayed in an even more sensational light—as biographer Mark Derr calls him, a "comic Hercules."

Thanks to Walt Disney in the mid-1950s, Crockett became one of the first media sensations of the modern age. By the time Disney was finished with his legend, people everywhere were singing about Tennessee mountaintops and wearing coonskin caps (which Crockett never wore). From then on, Crockett's image as an authentic American hero was set.

A Little of This, a Little of That

So who was Davy Crockett? Like all of us, he's hard to pin down—a combination of different factors that make a characterization difficult. Part frontiersman and part politician mixed with a keen wit, unabashed honesty, and a friendly nature, Davy Crockett in the end was 100 percent uniquely American.

HOW IT ALL BEGAN

Prints Charming

Hollywood's world-famous Grauman's Chinese Theatre was the brainchild of former newspaper salesman turned mega movie-palace designer Sid Grauman. Envisioned as part theater, part museum of Chinese art and history, the Chinese Theatre opened in 1927 on Hollywood Boulevard, just blocks from Grauman's Egyptian Theatre, built a few years prior.

The Chinese Theatre's fame undoubtedly centers on its "forecourt," featuring the hand- and footprints of Hollywood legends, but sources differ on how this tradition began. One story claims silent-screen star Norma Talmadge started it when she stumbled onto the wet sidewalk and left her footprints. In a photo dated April 1927, screen stars Mary Pickford, Douglas Fairbanks, and Sid Grauman are shown in what the theater calls the "very first footprint ceremony."

Allegedly, Grauman intended the prints to be just a gag among a select group of friends, but the movie studios eventually pressured him to allow their big-name stars to leave prints behind as well. Today, a little more than the original 200 empty squares remain, so you have to be a major deal (and a major moneymaker) to get one.

Star Path

Inspired by Grauman's forecourt, Hollywood Chamber of Commerce President E. M. Stuart devised the Walk of Fame in 1955 to help bring the buzz back to Hollywood Boulevard—something that had notably diminished with the advent of television.

In 1956, the chamber green-lighted the $1.25 million-dollar project (paid for by merchants lucky enough to share sidewalk space with the Walk). The plans included 2,518 coral terrazzo stars set in bronze running down five acres of Hollywood Boulevard and a mass dedication ceremony for the Walk of Fame, honoring eight screen actors including Joanne Woodward, Burt Lancaster, and Edward Sedgwick.

The Walk's official groundbreaking took place in early February 1960, and within 16 months 1,558 stars were claimed. Today, each candidate faces a rigorous nomination process as well as a $25,000 price tag for the honor, usually paid for by the honoree's "people." The next star was dedicated eight years later to studio executive Richard Zanuck, and since then about 24 stars are added each year.

Famous Hypochondriacs

❖ ❖ ❖ ❖

*If you've ever had a cold and thought you were dying of pneumonia
or had a sore back and were sure you had meningitis, you
might be a hypochondriac. But you're in good company—read
on for some famous folks who were also hypochondriacs.*

Hypochondriacs are individuals who are abnormally anxious about
their health. What is a normal ache and pain for one person is a catastrophe for a hypochondriac, and often, the hypochondriac will imagine
symptoms that were never there in the first place. Chronic hypochondriacs struggle their whole lives in fear and doubt, and ironically, they
are often in poor health.

Howard Hughes
As a boy, Howard Hughes—movie mogul, captain of industry, pilot,
and ladies man—suffered from an undiagnosed affliction that caused
minor hearing loss. His mother doted on him as a result, and Hughes
came to associate being sick with being loved and cared for, so he was
"sick" quite a bit. As an adult, Hughes's hypochondria was made worse
by his legendary obsessive-compulsive disorder and his generally poor
mental health. Hughes died in the mid-1970s, a recluse in terrible
physical condition.

Adolf Hitler
The cruel and neurotic dictator was known for his aversion to germs
and illness. Hitler did suffer from various conditions, including paranoia, halitosis (bad breath), and flatulence (gas). He would examine his
own feces on a regular basis to check for consistency and eventually
took on Dr. Morell, a quack doctor who put Hitler on a steady regimen
of amphetamines. The drugs did nothing but make an already jumpy,
crazed leader all the more unwell—and unpredictable.

Hans Christian Andersen
Danish writer of beloved fairytales such as "The Little Mermaid,"
Andersen was said to be self-obsessed and a super-sensitive hypo-
chondriac. He was so terrified of being buried alive that on his travels

through Europe, he slept with a note that read, "I only seem dead" so that no one might mistake him for a corpse.

Charles Darwin

Author of *The Origin of the Species* Charles Darwin was kind of a mess health-wise. It's still unknown what exactly he suffered from, but he was ill most of his life. Indigestion, stomach problems, fatigue, nervousness, and nausea, among other symptoms, plagued Darwin at one time or another. Many believe today that while Darwin was probably suffering from at least one affliction, his hypochondria made him sicker and further prevented him from getting well.

Florence Nightingale

For 53 years, starting when she was 37 years old, Red Cross founder Florence Nightingale lived the life of a bedridden, almost agoraphobic invalid. But was she actually sick? Some have diagnosed Nightingale as suffering from an organic disease, likely chronic brucellosis, which causes joint and muscle pain. Others believe she was a hypochondriac who used physical symptoms to manipulate people. Recent evidence suggests that she suffered from bipolar disorder.

Sara Teasdale

Poet Sara Teasdale was born to a severely overprotective mother who would send her daughter to bed with the slightest cough or sniffle. By the time Sara was nine years old, she was thoroughly convinced she was simply a sickly person. Nearly every year, she would take a "rest" and convalesce at home, surrounded by medicine, blankets, and, if she was feeling up to it, her writing materials.

Tennessee Williams

Shy and equally afraid of both failure and success, legendary playwright Tennessee Williams was a serious hypochondriac obsessed with his own sickness and death. Convinced he was slowly losing his sight, he had four eye operations for cataracts. Worried his heart would stop beating, he drank and took pills in great quantities to both head off impending disease and calm his nerves, neither of which worked. Williams died in 1983 as a result of choking on the cap of an eye drop bottle, though drugs and alcohol may have been involved as well.

Fast Facts

- Armadillos are commonly used in leprosy research

- The great Incan empire lasted just 90 years.

- The Mayan "long count calendar" ends on December 21, 2012. Some have theorized that it heralds the end of the world, but thankfully, most academics disagree.

- Charlie Chaplin's body was stolen three months after his death in an attempt to extort money from his estate.

- Charlie Chaplin's middle name was Spencer.

- The North American beaver can weigh up to 60 pounds.

- Peter the Great, who ruled Russia from 1682 to 1725, instituted a tax on beards.

- A tornado is only a tornado if it touches the ground. Otherwise, it's just a funnel.

- Smile! One in four people older than age 60 has lost all of his or her teeth.

- The Fujita scale gauges the strength of a tornado by measuring the amount of damage it does to buildings. The scale ranges from 0 to 5, with 5 being the most destructive.

- The role of the wizard in The Wizard of Oz was originally written for comedian W. C. Fields.

Dem Bones, Dem Bones

❖ ❖ ❖ ❖

Do you think bones are only good for keeping vertebrates from being shapeless lumps of goo? There's far more to it than that! Bones get pressed into use as art, medicine, weapons, and furniture. Bones tell tales dead men can't. Sometimes, bones even go bump in the night. Here are some fast facts about all things osseous.

- At birth, human babies have more than 300 bones, but adults have only 206. Some of the bones fuse together as we grow.

- The human femur (thighbone) is stronger than concrete.

- In 2006, an Indian yogi was arrested for using ground-up human bone in his homemade impotence medicine.

- Although Westerners usually think of vampires as "bloodsuckers," in African cultures, vampires are believed to eat bones.

- Drink your milk! Ninety-nine percent of the calcium within the human body is contained in the bones.

- The entire human skeleton is replaced with new bone matter every 10 to 25 years.

- Like all other cells, your bones "breathe" by consuming oxygen and releasing carbon dioxide.

- Most mammals, including raccoons, horses, walruses, gorillas, and whales, have a *baculum,* or penis bone.

- In the Ozark Mountains, raccoon penis bones are used as love amulets and toothpicks.

- Bone china dishes are actually a type of porcelain that is made from powdered clay and stone mixed with bone ash. *Bon appétit!*

- The phrase "to make no bones about" means tackling a difficulty with little hesitation. It mostly derives from the ease of eating stew without bones.

- In parts of Africa, "throwing the bones" is a form of divination.

- Singer Louis Prima did not coin the phrase "closest to the bone, sweeter is the meat." It actually was a saying back in the 14th century.

- The bones from more than 40,000 human skeletons have been turned into chandeliers, sculptures, religious vessels, and decorations at the Kostnice Ossuary in Sedlec, Czech Republic.

- Human bones can be owned, bought, or sold legally in most parts of the United States, except Tennessee and Georgia.

- The easiest way to clean large quantities of bones is to employ a colony of flesh-eating dermestids, otherwise known as "museum beetles."

- Embedded in the ethmoid bone, located between the eyes, humans have a sliver of magnetite, which acts as a small compass.

- Evidence of human skulls being used as bowls, cups, and lamps has been found in Scandinavia, parts of Western Europe, Peru, Mexico, Great Britain, and Asia.

- The Hopewell Native Americans are known to have carved human bones into rattles and whistles, which they decorated with paint or copper.

- In 1987, India (formerly the world's largest supplier of bones) banned the sale of human remains. Now China claims the distinction.

- The *tibia,* or shinbone, was named for the Latin word for flute, as instruments were commonly made out of deer bones.

- Measuring only one-tenth of an inch, the stapes, or stirrup bone located inside the inner ear, is the smallest bone in the human body.

FROM THE VAULTS OF HISTORY

- Isaac Asimov is the only author to have a book in every Dewey Decimal category.

- During his stint in Alcatraz, Al Capone was inmate No. 85.

- Isaac Newton was elected Member of Parliament for the University of Cambridge to the Convention Parliament of 1689 and sat again from 1701 to 1702. Funny job for a guy who contested so much conventional wisdom.

- President Warren G. Harding is often labeled as one of the worst U.S. presidents ever. His gambling, womanizing, and laziness are legend, but perhaps not as bad as his bribing and corruption. "Never before, here or anywhere else," declared the *Wall Street Journal*, "has a government been so completely fused with business."

- The first lock and key system was a 4,000-year-old Egyptian creation. The first serious attempt to improve on the idea was made in England by Robert Barron, who patented a double-acting tumbler lock in 1778.

- In one theory of the origin of the nursery rhyme "Jack and Jill," Jack represents French King Louis XVI, who "broke his crown" in the French Revolution. Jill, who came "tumbling after," was Marie Antoinette, and the tumble was likely a reference to her head.

- Scarlett O'Hara, the heroine of *Gone With the Wind,* was originally named Pansy.

- In England during World War I, many families with German names and titles changed them to more English-sounding monikers. The royal family from Saxe-Coburg-Gotha changed their name to Windsor. Kaiser Wilhelm II once jokingly said that he was off to see a performance of *The Merry Wives of Saxe-Coburg-Gotha.*

- American legend Benjamin Franklin is credited with charting the course of the Gulf Stream.

- Coin collectors may be interested to know that Canada's 1911 Silver Dollar is now worth at least $1 million. Only two were minted and the Canadian Currency Museum is tight-fistedly hanging on to one of them. The other is in the hands of an American coin collector.

You Can't Take Down a Bull Moose

❖ ❖ ❖ ❖

During a 1912 Milwaukee political speech, Teddy Roosevelt took a lickin' (or rather, a bullet) but kept on tickin'.

A Four-Way Race

American politics were in a state of chaos during the presidential election season of 1912. Ex-President Theodore Roosevelt had broken with the Republicans and established the Progressive Party, which then nominated the "Bull Moose" himself as its candidate. Incumbant President (and Republican) William Howard Taft was running for a second term, Woodrow Wilson waged a high-minded campaign on behalf of the Democrats, and Eugene Debs was running as a Socialist. Roosevelt needed every vote in this contentious four-way race. In particular, he needed to win over Progressives allied with Wisconsin senator Bob LaFollette, who had expected to receive the Progressive party's nomination and was increasingly critical of Roosevelt. To this end, Roosevelt included Milwaukee at the end of an extensive speaking tour.

Milwaukee Turns Deadly

On the evening of October 14, a large crowd gathered to see the Bull Moose leave from his Milwaukee hotel for a speech at the auditorium. Roosevelt stepped into a waiting car where Henry F. Cochems, Chairman of the National Speakers' Bureau of the Progressive party, was seated. As Roosevelt stood waving to the crowd from the open car, John Schrank, a New York City saloonkeeper who had followed Roosevelt across the country, stepped forward and fired a Colt revolver into Roosevelt's chest.

Roosevelt's stenographer leapt upon the shooter. The Bull Moose's knees buckled at first, but he straightened and raised his hat to the crowd. Roosevelt barked to a crowd of people looking to do harm to Schrank, "Don't hurt him; bring him to me here!" Schrank, still struggling for possession of the weapon, was dragged to Roosevelt who studied him while Cochems secured the revolver. Later Roosevelt admitted that he had no curiosity concerning

Schrank: "His name might be Czolgosz or anything else as far as I'm concerned," he said referring to the assassin who felled President McKinley in 1901 (giving Vice President Roosevelt the presidency). Later, Schrank said he was convinced by a dream that Roosevelt was responsible for McKinley's death, and that he believed no president should be allowed to serve three terms.

Saved by a Speech (and Some Suspenders)

Though he was bleeding steadily from a hole below his right nipple, Roosevelt refused to be taken to the hospital. He could tell that the bullet, slowed first by his heavy overcoat, then his folded 50-page speech, his metal glasses case, and finally his thick suspenders, had not penetrated his lung. At the auditorium, in front of a crowd of 9,000–12,000 people, Roosevelt's first words were: "Ladies and gentlemen, I don't know whether you fully understand that I have just been shot; but it takes more than that to kill a Bull Moose." Someone yelled, "Fake!" but Roosevelt smiled and opened his vest to reveal his bloodstained shirt. The room went silent.

Roosevelt vs. LaFollette

Instead of collapsing, Roosevelt spoke for 90 minutes. When aides tried to cut short his speech, he quipped: "I am all right and you cannot escape listening to the speech either." When a woman near the stage said, "Mr. Roosevelt, we all wish you would be seated;" the candidate quickly replied: "I thank you, madam, but I don't mind it a bit." LaFollette supporters yelled protests at each mention of their beloved senator's name, but Roosevelt ignored their outbursts.

After speaking, Roosevelt was rushed to the hospital where exploratory surgery revealed that the bullet was inoperable. Roosevelt later admitted that he never believed the wound fatal. "Anyway.. if I had to die," he laughed, "I thought I'd rather die with my boots on." During his weeklong hospital recovery, both Wilson and Taft suspended their campaigns. Still, Schrank got his wish in the end: Although Roosevelt's Milwaukee speech was sensational, it failed to impress the LaFollette Progressives who voted overwhelmingly against Roosevelt, denying him the third term.

Behind the Films of Our Time

- Linda Fiorentino played the female lead in *Men in Black*, after winning the role—and $1,200—in a poker game against director Barry Sonnenfeld.

- Would the Rodgers and Hammerstein musical *Oklahoma!* have been as popular with its original name, *Away We Go*?

- In *Forrest Gump*, the background music that's playing while Forrest is in the bathroom at the Kennedy White House is the theme from *Camelot*, in reference to the name often used to describe President John F. Kennedy's life and administration.

- The characters' names in *WALL-E* have real meaning: WALL-E stands for "Waste Allocation Load Lifter Earth-class," and EVE stands for "Extraterrestrial Vegetation Evaluator."

- Phillip Alford, who played Jem Finch in the 1962 classic *To Kill A Mockingbird*, didn't really want to try out for the part, but his mom told him he could miss a half-day of school if he went to auditions.

- When Brad Pitt chipped a tooth filming *Fight Club*, he waited until the movie was completed before getting it capped, thinking the chipped tooth would better fit the part.

- Watch out for the fruit! When you see an orange in the *Godfather* movies, it means someone is about to die, or at least have a close call.

- Although Mega City in *The Matrix* is not real, the street references are of real streets in Chicago, hometown of the writers, the Wachowski Brothers.

- The 1994 film *The Shawshank Redemption* was only a minor hit at the box office, but was one of the best moneymaking videos of all time. It was voted the number-one Must See Movie of All Time by Capital FM in London and took top spot in the IMDb Top 250 movies as voted by viewers.

- The props department built a door that could be easily broken for the set of *The Shining*. Unfortunately, Jack Nicholson, who once had worked as a volunteer fire marshal, didn't know his own strength. The door broke much too easily and one that held up a little longer had to be constructed.

Fast Facts

- *Donald Duck had a sister named Dumbella.*

- *Although the Declaration of Independence was signed in 1776, all of its signers weren't identified until months later.*

- *Thomas Jefferson, one of the most scientific men of his time, refused to believe in meteorites, reportedly saying: "I would rather believe that two Yankee professors would lie than believe that stones would fall from heaven."*

- *Benjamin Franklin considered the eagle a bird of "bad moral character." He wanted the turkey to be America's national symbol.*

- *Albert Einstein's last words were in German; unfortunately, they are thus lost to the world because his nurse did not speak German.*

- *Thomas Edison did not invent the phonograph for its entertainment value. He was more interested in its educational uses, such as playing recordings for the blind.*

- *Edison liked to use Braille to read, even though he was not blind.*

- *The height of the Eiffel Tower can vary by as much as six inches from one day to the next, depending upon the outside temperature.*

- *Chinkiang, a Chinese city 150 miles inland, was once a seaport.*

- *In 1884, Theodore Roosevelt's first wife and mother both died on the same day—February 14.*

- *Ironically, the movie* Paris, Texas, *was banned in the town of Paris, Texas.*

Maass-ively Brave

❖ ❖ ❖ ❖

*Today the name Clara Maass is not well known. But at
the turn of the century, practically everyone in the United
States knew her as the nurse who risked her own life
to help defeat the dreaded yellow fever epidemic.*

Young Girl Grows Up

Clara Louise Maass was born in East Orange, New Jersey, on June
28, 1876. She was the daughter of German immigrants who quickly
discovered upon their arrival in America that the streets were not
paved with gold. The family was just barely getting by.

Clara began working while she was still in grammar school. At
around age 16, she enrolled in nursing school at Newark German
Hospital in Newark, New Jersey. Graduating from the rigorous
course in 1895, she continued working hard; by 1898, she was the
head nurse at Newark German.

Yellow Jack War

The Spanish-American War began on February 15, 1898. As wars
go, the war was more period than paragraph, lasting just four short
months. However, there was something more deadly to American
troops than Spanish bullets: yellow fever.

Since its arrival in America in the summer of 1693, yellow
fever had ravaged the country. For two centuries, "Yellow Jack,"
as the disease was dubbed, killed randomly and indiscriminately.
The disease would devastate some households, while those next
door would go untouched. One in ten people were killed by
yellow fever in Philadelphia in 1793. The disease caused President
George Washington and the federal government (Philadelphia was
then the U.S. capitol) to flee the city. In 1802, Yellow Jack killed
23,000 French troops in Haiti, causing Napoleon to abandon the
New World (and eventually agree to the Louisiana Purchase).
An 1878 outbreak in Memphis killed 5,000 people there, and
20,000 total died in the Mississippi Delta. No one knew what caused
yellow fever or how to stop it.

The Experiments

In April 1898, Maass applied to become a contract nurse during the Spanish-American War; in Santiago, Cuba, she saw her first cases of yellow fever. The next year she battled the disease in Manila, as it ravaged the American troops there.

No one knew why Maass kept going to these danger zones when she could have remained safely at home nurturing her burgeoning nursing career. Yet when Havana was hit by a severe yellow fever epidemic in 1900, Maass once again answered a call for nurses to tend the sick.

In Havana, a team of doctors led by Walter Reed was trying to find the cause of yellow fever. They had reason to support a controversial theory that mosquitoes were the disease carrier, but they needed concrete proof. Desperate, they asked for human volunteers, offering to pay them $100—and another $100 if they became ill. Maass volunteered for the tests, though no one is sure why she put herself up to it. Possibly she hoped that contracting a mild case of the disease would give her immunity to it and allow her to better treat patients.

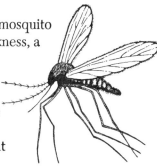

On August 14, 1901, after a previous mosquito bite had produced just a mild case of sickness, a willing Maass was bitten once again by an *Aedes aegypti* mosquito loaded with infectious blood. This time the vicious disease tore through her body. She wrote a feverish last letter home to her family: "You know I am the man of the family but pray for me..."

On August 24, Maass died. Her death ended the controversial practice of using humans as test subjects for experiments. But it also proved, beyond a doubt, that the *Aedes aegypti* mosquito was the disease carrier—the key to unlocking the sickness that scientists had been seeking for centuries. Yellow fever could finally be conquered, in part because of Maass's brave sacrifice.

The next day, a writer for the *New York Journal* wrote, "No soldier in the late war placed his life in peril for better reasons than those which prompted this faithful nurse to risk hers."

INSPIRATION STATION

From Beautiful Poem to Beautiful Painting

She sits so still in the small boat, one hand grasping a thin chain, a soft breeze blowing her long hair from her face—a face that, while beautiful, has a definite look of dread. This lady is the focus of John William Waterhouse's 1888 painting, *The Lady of Shalott*, one of the best-known and most-beloved paintings of the Pre-Raphaelite art movement. Waterhouse was inspired by Lord Alfred Tennyson's 1833 poem of the same name. It describes a fair maiden living under a curse in a tower, who one day catches sight of Sir Lancelot riding past on his horse. Deciding to follow him to Camelot, she abandons the tower and attempts to sail to the mythical city on a boat. Sadly, the Lady of Shalott dies before her boat reaches the shore, but even in death she impresses Lancelot with her beauty. Both Tennyson's poem and Waterhouse's painting are typical of their romantic, sentimental times and genres. Interestingly, the painting (along with other Pre-Raphaelite works) seems to have come back into fashion as the perfect type of art to match with "shabby chic" and French country interior decor.

Rhymes with Witch

When Clare Booth Luce decided to write a play about wealthy, catty, backstabbing women, she didn't have to look far for inspiration. A Manhattan socialite who had worked on the staffs of both *Vogue* and *Vanity Fair* magazines, Luce knew the sophisticated world she was writing about inside and out. She called her play simply *The Women*, and though men are obsessed over constantly, not a single Y-chromosome character is seen or heard throughout the entire thing. Instead the audience is treated to some of the funniest, wittiest, bitchiest, most sarcastic dialogue ever put on paper. *The Women* opened on Broadway on December 26, 1936, and in 1939 it was made into a critically acclaimed and very successful film starring Norma Shearer, Joan Crawford, and Rosalind Russell. The movie is now considered a camp classic, and devotees love to quote Crawford's quick-witted line, "There is a name for you, ladies, but it isn't used in high society... outside of a kennel."

Pinball Wizardry!

❖ ❖ ❖ ❖

Fun facts about America's favorite table game.

Before the advent of video games, pinball was the activity of choice for people with a few minutes to kill and some change in their pocket. For many aficionados, the caroming steel ball, flashing lights, and dizzying sounds had an almost hypnotic effect as players competed for high score.

Genuine pinball games are increasingly difficult to find in arcades and bars, but it didn't used to be that way. In fact, from the 1930s through the '80s, pinball was ubiquitous. Wherever people congregated, the flashy machines were soon to follow.

In the Beginning
The basic concept of pinball dates back to the 1700s and a popular French table game called Bagatelle, which featured a ball, fixed pins, and holes for the ball to fall into. The game produced numerous variations and improvements over the years; in the 1930s, the first coin-operated "marble games" or "pin games" were introduced, which became pinball as we know it today. The first truly popular pinball game was Baffle Ball, introduced in 1931 by David Gottlieb. For a penny, players got to try their luck with five to seven balls—a real bargain during the Great Depression, when inexpensive fun was at a premium.

Pinball and the Law
As pinball became more popular, it didn't take long for the law to ruin everyone's fun. Some cities considered pinball a game of chance and either regulated the machines or banned them outright.

New York City instituted a pinball ban in the early 1940s. For game buffs, a day that will truly live in infamy is January 21, 1942. That's when the city conducted a sweep and confiscated an estimated 3,525 pinball machines. Within weeks, hundreds more were located and destroyed, their wooden legs used to make police night sticks and their metal components—nearly five tons of the stuff, including 3,000 pounds of steel balls—were donated to the war effort. It wasn't until 1976 that pinball was officially declared legal again in New York City.

Play Ball!

As a game, pinball is both very simple and quite complicated. It must be fun and easy enough that beginning players don't become frustrated, but not so easy that it ceases to be challenging to hard-core players. According to manufacturers, the average game should last between two and three minutes, and the player should receive a free game for every four games he or she plays.

The "tilt" function, which penalizes players for trying to finesse the ball by physically moving the machine, was first instituted in 1932 in a Bally pinball game called Advance. Interestingly, its inventor, Harry Williams, originally called the function "The Stool Pigeon." One day while watching players try their hand on the first prototypes, Williams overheard one unlucky guy exclaim, "Damn, I tilted it!" The rest, as they say, is history.

The cost of pinball, and the number of balls allotted per game, has greatly evolved over the years. In 1931, players received seven balls for a penny. Then it was ten balls for a nickel. In 1933, when steel balls replaced glass marbles, players received between five and seven balls for a nickel. By the late 1960s, players got three five-ball games for a quarter. A decade later, it was two five-ball games for a quarter.

Pinball and Popular Culture

Pinball quickly ingratiated itself into American popular culture. Writer William Saroyan featured the games in two of his works, including the 1939 stage play *The Time of Your Life.*

Pinball has also been featured in song and motion pictures. For example, the classic rock opera *Tommy* by The Who is about a messiahlike figure who can play pinball better than anyone, despite being deaf, mute, and blind. Just check out the bedazzled Elton John singing "Pinball Wizard" in the film version of *Tommy.* And in the 1978 movie *Tilt,* Brooke Shields played a young pinball champion who enters a tournament to help her musician boyfriend.

Fast Facts

- Science Digest *predicted in 1948 that landing on and moving about the Moon were such serious problems that it could take science another 200 years to solve them. Twenty-one years later, an American man successfully landed on the Moon.*

- *The large knobs between sets of escalators have no other purpose than to stop people from sliding down the flat space between the escalators.*

- *The famous St. Andrews golf course in Scotland originally had 22 holes.*

- *During the filming of* Julie & Julia, *tricks were used to make the 5'6" Meryl Streep appear taller (the real Julia Child was 6'2"). Countertops were lowered, Streep wore very high heels, different camera angles were used, and the majority of the extras hired for the film were short.*

- *Clocks run "clockwise" because they mimic sundials from the northern hemisphere, which in turn mimicked the direction that shadows moved. If clocks had been built to mimic sundials from the southern hemisphere, it's possible clockwise would be the opposite direction.*

- *The term "hat-trick" in sports comes from English cricket. It describes a bowler's taking three wickets on successive balls. At one time, the reward for this was a new hat.*

- *The initials "M&M" of the popular chocolate candy stand for Mars & Murrie.*

- *Goofy's original name was Dippy Dawg.*

- *Bagels have holes because they were originally shaped to resemble the stirrups of King Sobiesky, who fought on horseback to save Vienna from the Turks.*

The Potsdam Giants

❖ ❖ ❖ ❖

Ever heard of a Napoleon complex? Well, this short-statured Prussian king took a unique approach to building himself up.

It makes sense that the king of Prussia should want a decent military. And you can't really blame a guy for having specific tastes when it comes to soldiers. But you can definitely accuse Prussian King Frederick William I (also known as Fredrich Wilhelm) of being a little weird and a little too, well, *particular.*

Assembling an Army

Prussia was a former kingdom of north-central Europe including present-day northern Germany and Poland. The state became a republic in 1918 and was formally abolished after World War II. But prior to that, Frederick took the Prussian throne in 1713. His first order of business was to improve his military forces. He increased his military numbers from 38,000 men to an army of 83,000 strong. He outfitted them with better weapons and insisted they train harder or face harsh consequences. Satisfied with his army, the king could move onto beefing up his own personal regiment—and that's where things got a little strange.

How's The Weather Up There?

Convinced that a tall soldier was a better soldier, the small-size king (he stood at about 4'11") began to recruit men with above-average height for his group of "Grand Grenadiers of Potsdam." He set a height requirement at 5'11", which in the 18th century was seriously tall (the average height for a European man at the time was 5'6"). Most of the men were at least six feet tall and many were nearly seven feet tall. Frederick became obsessed with "collecting" tall soldiers and was known to actually have grown men kidnapped that he felt fit the bill. Stories of Irish longshoremen being thrown into boxes and Austrian diplomats being snatched off the street were common.

Word got out about Frederick's need for hundreds of tall men. Neighboring countries would send their tallest male citizens (often against their wills) as gifts to keep relations open and friendly with the king. Frederick demanded that his army of giant men marry tall women in hopes of breeding tall children. According to writer Stephan S. Hall, one medical historian noted that Frederick's Potsdam Giants were "The tallest men ever assembled until the birth of professional basketball."

Unfortunately, the Potsdam Giants weren't actually fit for battle. Many of them were mentally disabled or somewhat mentally handicapped as a result of their gigantism. Most of them never used the weapons the king provided. Even if they were able to fight, a lot of them wouldn't have wanted to. Living conditions in their camp were atrocious. Food and shelter shortages were common and over 200 of the Giants mutinied every year. The ones that were caught after they escaped had their noses and ears cut off before being thrown in jail. Frederick loved his soldiers—that is, as long as they were simply tall and not opinionated.

What Goes Up Must Come Down

In 1740, Frederick died and with him his dream of an infantry of tall soldiers he had so brutally created. The crown prince, Frederick II, took the throne; interestingly, Frederick II was a small, sickly child, which had been quite a source of consternation with his father. Despite this tense relationship, Frederick II grew up to be a natural leader and became known as Frederick the Great. One of his first acts as king was to disband the Potsdam Giants. According to one biography of Frederick the Great, contemporary sources claim that after the Giants were released, "the roads to Paris were littered with half-wits trying to find their way back home."

❖ ❖ ❖ ❖

"If you aren't in over your head, how do you know how tall you are?"

—*T. S. Eliot*

The Road to Nowhere

❖ ❖ ❖ ❖

A dark, abandoned portion of the Pennsylvania Turnpike
has become a curious destination for thrill-seekers.

In October 1940, a toll road unlike any other in America was opened
to the public. Connecting the expanse between Harrisburg and
Pittsburgh, the 160-mile-long Pennsylvania Turnpike made history
when it became America's first bona fide superhighway. Seven long
tunnels were built to sidestep the pesky mountains that stood in the
way of the highway, offering drivers super-fast passage across the
state. "The Tunnel Highway," as the turnpike was dubbed, was a
success and eventually became the prototype for America's Interstate
Highway system.

Everything moved swiftly until the 1960s, when increased
usage placed a greater demand on the turnpike. Backups became
commonplace, particularly at those points where the roadway
narrowed to pass through tunnels. After a 1968 decision was made
to bypass the Ray's Hill and Sideling Hill tubes, the 12 total miles
of roadway were abandoned in favor of a new "cut" through the
mountains.

Forty-odd years is a long time to neglect a highway. Yet aside from
overgrowth, the abandoned portion of the Pennsylvania Turnpike,
including its tunnels, appears eerily intact. The abandoned section
of turnpike still sees its share of visitors, mostly hikers, bicyclists,
and urban explorers, despite the risk of a trespassing violation. Since
nothing can be seen for miles except the pockmarked roadway,
walking along its path, one feels like the only person left on Earth.

The abandoned tunnels have been the scenes of some odd
happenings, from an ambush training session for the U.S. Army to
a church choir that enjoyed a tunnel's acoustics. Plans are currently
afoot to turn an eight and a half-mile portion of the roadway
(including both tunnels, which will be brightly lit) into a bicycle trail.
If this happens, some of the roadway's mystique and scariness will be
lost. On the other hand, it's not every day that people can gleefully
ride their Schwinns down the middle of our nation's first superhighway and come back in one piece.

PALINDROMES

A palindrome is a phrase that reads the same in both directions. The word is derived from the Greek palíndromos, *which means running back again* (palín = *again;* drom-, drameîn = *to run).*

I won, Karen, an era know I

He stops spots, eh?

Golf? No sir, prefer prison flog

Did I draw Della too tall, Edward? I did?

Del saw a sled

A dank, sad nap. Eels sleep and ask nada

Strap on no parts

Tuna nut

Won't cat lovers revolt? Act now!

Oh, no! Don Ho

Cain: A maniac

Desserts, I stressed

Lee had a heel

Man, Eve let an irate tar in at eleven AM

Mr. Owl ate my metal worm

Top step's pup's pet spot

'Tis Ivan on a visit

Straw warts

Roy, am I mayor?

I, man, am regal—a German am I

Evade me, Dave

Bombard a drab mob

Riding with the Pony Express

❖ ❖ ❖ ❖

*Neither rain, nor sleet, nor dark of night could keep the
Pony Express from running mail across the Wild West.*

Prior to the Pony Express, it took weeks upon weeks to deliver mail
throughout the West, and that was done either by boat or stagecoach. Three men—William H. Russell, Alexander Majors, and
William B. Waddell—believed that with the Pony Express, they
could reduce the delivery time down to a mere ten days.

Planning the Route

In early 1860, the men began by picking locations to serve as "hubs"
for the Pony Express: Sacramento, California, and St. Joseph, Missouri. Mail would arrive at each of these locations either by boat
(Sacramento) or train (St. Joseph), where it would be handed off to
the Pony Express riders to deliver. All in all, the total one-way mail
route would run approximately 2,000 miles.

While researching the route, it was determined that a pony at
full gallop could travel approximately ten miles a day. Pony Express
stations were constructed every ten miles or so along the route
between the two hubs. An estimated 119 to 153 stations were
built (sources vary), where riders could get fresh ponies. Between
400 and 500 ponies were purchased by the Pony Express Company.
Now all that remained was to hire riders willing to make the trek.

Finding the Right Men

In the spring of 1860, posters went up in Sacramento and St. Joseph
that read:

> **Wanted:** Young, skinny, wiry fellows not over 18.
> Must be expert riders, willing to risk death daily.
> Orphans preferred.
> Wages $25 per week

In order to keep the load as light as possible, potential
applicants also couldn't weigh more than 125 pounds. Most of
the weight would come from the mail, which was carried in the

pockets of a *mochila* (Spanish for "pouch"). The mochila could be filled and placed over the horse's saddle.

Once the mochila was in place, riders would be expected to travel alone, day and night, regardless of the weather. Every ten miles, the riders could stop at one of the Pony Express stations to switch ponies and get water. But only after traveling 75–100 miles could the rider switch out with another rider and rest.

Since the riders would be traveling alone, they were subject to the elements and attacks from wild animals, Native Americans, and even bandits. Originally, the riders were armed with several guns. But eventually most of the weapons were taken away from the riders in a continual attempt to lighten the load and increase speed.

The First Trip

For the opening day of the Pony Express, April 3, 1860, two riders left their stations—one traveling west from St. Joseph and one traveling east from Sacramento. It was approximately midnight on April 13 when the first Eastern mail arrived in Sacramento. The following day, the Western mail arrived in St. Joseph. All total, the first westbound trip was made in 9 days and 23 hours; the eastbound journey took 11 days and 12 hours.

The End of the Pony Express

Incredibly, even after the success of the first run, the Pony Express never really caught on. In fact, stagecoaches were still used to carry the bulk of the mail throughout the East Coast and central United States. Then the Civil War broke out in 1861, which also put a damper on things.

On October 24, 1861, the transcontinental telegraph connected the cities of Sacramento, California with Omaha, Nebraska, thereby joining the Midwest with the West. Two days later, the Pony Express officially went out of business. During their 18 months, the Pony Express made approximately $90,000. Their net losses, however, were more than double that.

Say What?

"The pen is mightier than the sword—and considerably easier to write with."

—*Marty Feldman*

"Who invented the brush they put next to the toilet? That thing hurts."

—*Andy Andrews*

"Do you know the difference between a kayak and a college student? A kayak tips."

—*Chad Morgan*

"I've noticed the customers in health food stores. They are pale, skinny people who usually look half dead. In a steak house, you see robust, ruddy people. They're dying, of course, but they look terrific."

—*Bill Cosby*

"I'd like to start a family, but you have to have a date first."

—*Larry David*

"There are three signs of old age: loss of memory...I forget the other two."

—*Red Skelton*

"For those who like this sort of thing, this is the sort of thing they will like."

—*Max Beerbohm*

"Be smart, but never show it."

—*Louis B. Mayer*

"Comedy has to be based on truth. You take the truth and you put a little curlicue at the end."

—*Sid Caesar*

"I like long walks, especially when they are taken by people who annoy me."

—*Noël Coward*

"A man wrapped up in himself makes a very small bundle."

—*Benjamin Franklin*

"I have never killed a man, but I have read many obituaries with a lot of pleasure."

—*Clarence Darrow*

"I hate quotations. Tell me what you know."

—*Ralph Waldo Emerson*

Drama in Government: 10 Actors Turned Politicians

❖ ❖ ❖ ❖

*Government's nothing if not drama-filled. Who better, then,
to lead us than someone straight out of Hollywood?*

Arnold Schwarzenegger

Perhaps the biggest actor (literally) to transition into politics, Arnold Schwarzenegger raised more than a few eyebrows—and punch lines—when he announced his run for governor of California in 2003. Going up against such reputable contenders as porn star Mary Carey and actor Gary Coleman, Schwarzenegger quickly moved to the head of the pack. When the results rolled in, then-current governor Gray Davis was out and the "Governator" was in.

Al Franken

Saturday Night Live alum Al Franken started making real headlines when he ran for a Senate seat against Minnesota incumbent Norm Coleman in 2008. A too-close-to-call race led to a seemingly endless string of recounts and court challenges. Franken finally won the seat on June 30, 2009.

Fred Thompson

Law & Order vet Fred Thompson tossed his hat into the ring for the 2008 presidential election. (If we have to tell you that he didn't win, you're probably reading the wrong book.) Thompson had previously dabbled in politics, too: He served in the U.S. Senate from 1993 to 2003.

Ronald Reagan

Ronald Reagan progressed from president of the Screen Actors Guild to president of the United States. Reagan's early career saw him appearing in dozens of films and television shows. In 1966, he made it to the California governor's mansion, paving the way for his two terms in the White House during the 1980s.

Jesse Ventura

Known to wrestling fans as "The Body," Jesse Ventura brought his bulk to the Minnesota governor's office for one term in 1998, sailing past more traditionally qualified candidates to win the election and get the gig.

Sonny Bono

Cher's former partner-in-crime started his political career in 1988 when he was elected mayor of Palm Springs, California. From there, Bono served in the House of Representatives, where he worked for two terms as a U.S. Congressman before his death in 1998.

Alan Autry

Alan Autry did it all: He played in the NFL, played Captain Bubba Skinner in TV's *The Heat of the Night,* then played politics for the state of California. He was elected mayor of Fresno and served two terms starting in 2001.

Shirley Temple Black

Former child star Shirley Temple Black lost her 1967 run for a Congressional seat in California, but she didn't let that hold her back from her political aspirations. Black went on to hold numerous diplomatic posts as an adult, including delegate to the United Nations and U.S. Ambassador to Ghana and Czechoslovakia.

Ben Jones

Who would have thought a guy known as "Cooter" could become a member of Congress? Ben Jones, the actor made famous for his role as the mechanic in *The Dukes of Hazzard,* served two terms after being elected in Georgia.

Clint Eastwood

This cowboy wrangled his way into the political arena for a brief stint as mayor of Carmel, California. Eastwood ran for office in 1986 when the city's planning board prevented him from remodeling a piece of his property. Once mayor, Eastwood fired the board members who voted against his proposal. Now, that's how you take care of business, Dirty Harry–style.

Odd Ordinances

- North Carolina law forbids the use of elephants to plow cotton fields.

- Possessing a lottery ticket in North Carolina is illegal, resulting in up to $2,000 in fines. You'd need to have a winning ticket to pay it off.

- Shooting a Native American on horseback in North Dakota is legal only if you are in a covered wagon.

- Women may not wear patent leather shoes in public in Ohio.

- In Bexley, Ohio, it is illegal to install and use a slot machine in an outhouse.

- You'd better grocery shop on Saturday in Columbus, Ohio, because it is against the law to sell corn flakes on Sunday.

- Oklahoma law prohibits anyone from taking a bite from another person's hamburger.

- You may not read a comic book while driving a car in Oklahoma.

- In Wynona, Oklahoma, birdbaths are off-limits to mules.

- Oregon fish have discriminating palates—you may not use canned corn as bait.

- Sorry, but there's no juggling without a license in Hood River, Oregon.

- Pennsylvania law puts unusual restrictions on appliances—you may not sleep on top of a refrigerator outdoors.

- "Swept under the rug" is more than just a saying in Pennsylvania. Housewives are actually banned from hiding dirt and dust under a rug in a residence.

- It's only the best for convicts in Wisconsin, where butter substitutes are prohibited in state prisons.

- Store windows in La Crosse, Wisconsin, may not display a naked mannequin.

- Lollipops are banned in Washington State.

A Trek of No Return

❖ ❖ ❖ ❖

Many people attempt to climb Mount Everest—
and many never return.

It's no secret that ascending Everest, the tallest mountain in the world, is a risky feat. It's also no secret that some climbers die trying: In fact, more than 200 people have perished in their attempt to summit the 29,035-foot-tall peak. But did you know that many of these dead bodies remain on the mountain, never to receive a proper burial? There are many explanations as to why climbers die on Everest and why their bodies are left behind, yet the issue remains steeped in ethical debate.

The Death Zone

Among the dangers of climbing Mount Everest are avalanches, falling ice, fierce winds, the possibility of falling in a crevasse, severe cold, inadequate equipment, and lack of physical preparation. The majority of deaths, however, are caused by high-altitude sickness. This occurs where the technical climbing begins, far above the final base camp at 26,000 feet. The area is known as the "Death Zone," because the conditions here—specifically the amount of oxygen—cannot sustain human life.

A 2008 study conducted by a group of researchers from Massachusetts General Hospital found that most deaths on Everest were associated with "excessive fatigue, a tendency to fall behind other climbers, and arriving at the summit later in the day." The limited oxygen in the Death Zone contributes to confusion, disorientation, and a loss of physical coordination. Most of the climbers who die do so after reaching the summit, on their way down the mountain.

Frozen in Time

Because of the severe conditions in the Death Zone, most of the dead bodies are left behind. It would be extremely dangerous to attempt to take them off Everest, and there's really nowhere to bury them on the icy upper slopes. In other words, as climbers ascend, along the way they pass the frozen forms of those who have made the trek before them—sometimes decades prior.

Among those frozen in time is George Mallory, who attempted to summit Everest in 1924 but never returned from his climb. When asked why he wanted to climb the tallest mountain on the planet, he famously responded, "Because it's there." In May 1999, Mallory's body was found below the summit at 27,200 feet, a climbing rope still cinched around his waist. To this day, no one knows if Mallory and his climbing partner Andrew Irvine arrived at the summit before they died. If they had, they would have been the first to do so, preceding Sir Edmund Hillary and Tenzig Norgay's ascent in 1953.

In May 1996, eight climbers lost their lives in a sudden storm on their return from the summit. Two bodies from the expedition were never found. In 1998, Francys Arsentiev collapsed and died on her descent from the summit. For years her body lay close to the trail, in full view of climbers on their way up the mountain. A mountaineer named Ian Woodall, who was unable to help her as she neared her death, returned to Everest in 2007 to bury her in an American flag. Alas, he and his climbing partner were met with harsh weather conditions and only had time for a brief ceremony before dropping her body over the edge of the North Face. Some climbers criticized Woodall for initially abandoning Arsentiev, so perhaps this burial was a gesture of putting the controversy to rest.

Some of the most skilled climbers, the local sherpas, make it a point to avoid corpses. Teams from China have planned a cleanup of the mountain, which has been called "the world's highest garbage dump." In addition to picking up oxygen canisters, camping gear, and other materials discarded on the northern side of Everest, the crew intends to bring back any bodies that can be safely transported.

Behind the TV Shows of Our Time

- Because of contract disputes over money, co-stars Redd Foxx and Demond Wilson missed so many episodes of *Sanford and Son* that the writers were forced to work around them and create episodes around minor characters such as Grady. This led to the show's eventual cancellation in 1977.

- Mary Tyler Moore is often thought of as TV's first "independent woman," but that honor actually goes to Marlo Thomas of *That Girl*, who in 1965 was the first woman on television—as actress and model "Ann Marie"—to live alone and support herself.

- In 1983, Leonard Nimoy made a guest appearance on his pal William Shatner's police drama *T. J. Hooker* as a cop driven mad by his daughter's rape.

- One of the most expensive failures in television history was 1979's *Supertrain*, a *Love Boat* rip-off that spent millions of dollars on sets and promotions, and then flopped after nine episodes.

- Before getting his own late-night talk show on NBC, Conan O'Brien was a writer for both *The Simpsons* and *Saturday Night Live*.

- Bill Macy, who played husband Arthur on *Maude*, was in the original cast of *Oh! Calcutta*, the first Broadway show to feature full frontal nudity.

- Before he went on to superstardom in the movies, Richard Dreyfuss was a guest star on many television series during the '60s, including *Bewitched*, *Gunsmoke*, and *The Mod Squad*.

- The character of Cliff was not created by the writers of *Cheers*, but was suggested to them by John Ratzenberger after he auditioned for—and lost to George Wendt—the role of Norm.

- Before getting his own sitcom, Jerry Seinfeld had a small role as a comedy writer on *Benson* starring Robert Guillaume.

- Justin Fargas, the former starting running back for the Oakland Raiders, is the son of actor Antonio Fargas, most famous for his role as the flamboyant informant Huggy Bear on the police drama *Starsky and Hutch*.

Edward Hyde: Cross-dresser or Double-crossed?

❖ ❖ ❖ ❖

Edward Hyde, Viscount Cornbury, Third Earl of Clarendon, was governor of New York and New Jersey from 1701 to 1708, yet his legacy is one that politicians wouldn't want to touch with a ten-foot pole. Aside from doing a generally terrible job, rumors of Hyde's cross-dressing ways landed him a sullied spot in the annals of political history.

Here, Have a Job!

As the story goes, being of noble English lineage, Edward Hyde was able to buy an officer's commission in the British army. While in that position, he helped overthrow his commander (and uncle), King James II. The king who replaced James was William III, who was quite pleased with Hyde's assistance in getting him the throne, so in 1701, William made Hyde governor of New York as a way of saying thanks. Later, William's successor (and Hyde's first cousin), Queen Anne, also threw in the governorship of New Jersey for Hyde. Suddenly, a woefully underqualified guy from England was in charge of two of the most prominent colonies in the New World.

Corruption, Colonial Style

When Hyde arrived in New York in 1703 to assume his new post, he didn't make a very good impression with the struggling, toiling colonists. His luxurious house was filled with sumptuous linens, curtains, silverware, furniture, and art. To make matters worse, he soon found it necessary to divert public defense funds toward his new country house on what was then christened "Governor's Island."

It didn't take long for the bribery to start. At first, Hyde reportedly turned down a bribe from a New Jersey proprietor, but it appears he only passed because the bribe wasn't big enough. The man, hoping to get preferential treatment of some kind, then upped the ante. Hyde accepted the bribe the second time around and did the businessman's bidding. Soon, a group of the governor's favorites controlled tax and rent collections across the area. The bribes were constant, and the governor sank deeper and deeper into corruption. He was described at one point as "a spendthrift, a grafter, a bigoted oppressor and a drunken vain fool."

By 1707, a desperate New Jersey assembly wrote to Queen Anne to take Hyde back to Britain. One assembly member, Lewis Morris, made a list of Hyde's crimes and added a juicy bit: He claimed the corrupt governor was fond of dressing in women's clothing. That item of gossip didn't sit well with the queen, and Hyde lost his job. What isn't often mentioned is that Hyde, thrown into disgrace (and into debtor's prison) for some time, actually rallied later in life and held office in England where he was a respected diplomat of the Privy Council.

Right This Way, Mrs. Hyde?

The question remains whether Hyde really was a cross-dresser or just the victim of a rumor drummed up by his enemies to help push him out of office. One story tells of Hyde costumed as Queen Anne in order to show deference and respect—but could that really be true?

According to certain historians, there is no hard evidence that Hyde was fond of wearing dresses. Only four contemporary letters contain any information pertaining to his cross-dressing, and they don't include eyewitness accounts. Experts maintain that if the governor of New York and New Jersey really did don full petticoats and silk taffeta, it would have been plastered across every newspaper in the Western Hemisphere—people in the 18th century loved a scandal as much as people do now.

Still, the rumors persisted for years and stories of his behavior grew—there is even a period portrait of a scruffy man in women's clothing that is said to be Hyde. Yet, art historians say there's no proof that the painting is of anyone other than an unfortunate-looking young woman.

Fast Facts

- The Wonderful Wizard of Oz *author L. Frank Baum came up with the name for the magical city of Oz from the labels on his office filing cabinets. The first was labeled A–M, the other O–Z. Luckily, he went with the second one.*

- *Diamonds come in a variety of colors, known in the biz as "fancies."*

- *Most diamonds are more than 3 billion years old.*

- *Diamonds make great scalpels because their sharp edges never dull, and their hydrophobic surfaces ensure that wet tissue never sticks to them during surgery.*

- *You can walk 150 feet on the calories contained in a single chocolate chip.*

- *Warning: Chocolate is poisonous to dogs! It contains the chemical theobromine, which can adversely affect a dog's central nervous system.*

- *You would have to eat a dozen chocolate bars to consume the amount of caffeine found in just one cup of coffee. Not that we recommend you scarf down a dozen chocolate bars or anything.*

- *Thomas Jefferson died on July 4, 1826—the 50th anniversary of the signing of the Declaration of Independence.*

- *The Library of Congress's vast collection started with the purchase of Thomas Jefferson's sizable personal library.*

- *Marlon Brando and Robert De Niro are the only actors to win an Academy Award for playing the same character—gangster Vito Corleone. Brando won for* The Godfather (1972) *and De Niro for* The Godfather Part II *(1974).*

Like Money from Heaven

❖ ❖ ❖ ❖

Money may not grow on trees, but it does occasionally fall from the sky. Welcome to the strange but lucrative market in space rocks (and the objects they impact).

Heads Up!

Every day the Earth is bombarded by meteorites. Most originate in our solar system's asteroid belt, some are pieces of passing comets, and others originate from the Moon or Mars. On a clear dark night it's possible to observe as many as a few per hour; during a meteor shower the count may rise to as many as 100 per hour.

Despite the large numbers of meteorites, most of them burn up upon hitting the Earth's atmosphere. Of those that survive, most fall into an ocean; the meteorites that fall on land are typically the size of a pea or smaller.

Aside from the few kilograms of moon rocks retrieved from various *Apollo* and *Luna* space missions, meteorites are the only extraterrestrial artifacts on the planet. Not only does this make them valuable to scientists seeking knowledge about other planets, but it also makes them valuable to collectors seeking rarities and oddities. As such, finding a bona fide meteorite is a rare and potentially lucrative event.

Watch the Skies...for Cash!

In 2007, a small meteorite from Siberia sold for $122,750 at an auction in New York City. In 1972, a cow in Valera, Venezuela, was hit by a falling meteorite. Tiny fragments of the stone that hit the beast are worth more than $1,000. (Unfortunately, the cow was eaten—perhaps its carcass could have fetched a good deal more. "Space steaks," anyone?)

Looking to get married? As of 2009, you can purchase a custom wedding ring made from fragments of the Gibeon Meteorite that hit Africa more than 30,000 years ago (after spending 4 billion years hurtling through space) for as little as $195. If you'd rather save some money, a dime-size sliver of Mars goes for about $100 online.

Lucrative Destruction

Interestingly, the most sought-after meteorite fragments are those that hit other objects. These meteorites are called "hammers," and the smaller the object they hit the better. Even more valuable than hammer meteorites, however, are the objects themselves.

While many people would order their meteorite off the Internet, one woman had hers delivered in a more direct manner. On the evening of December 10, 1984, Carutha Barnard of Claxon, Georgia (who was not a meteorite collector at the time), received a surprise package when a small stone slammed into the back of her mailbox and thudded into the ground below. Though the box itself was knocked from its post, the outgoing mail flag intrepidly remained in the upright position. In October 2007, the mailbox, without the accompanying meteorite, sold for a whopping $83,000 at auction.

The Most Valuable Chevy on Earth

On October 9, 1992, thousands of people across the Mid-Atlantic States witnessed one of the most spectacular meteor showers on record. Glowing brighter than a full moon, and breaking into more than 70 fragments as it arched through the heavens, the meteorite was recorded by more than a dozen video cameras.

In Peekskill, New York, Michelle Knapp was startled by a loud noise outside her home and emerged to find the rear end of her red 1980 Chevy Malibu badly damaged. The police were soon on the scene and filed a criminal report, not realizing that the perpetrator was still on the premises. The smell of leaking gasoline, however, brought the fire department, which discovered the fallen meteorite fragment in the Malibu's gas tank. Knapp sold the car and rock to collector R. A. Langheinrich for an estimated $30,000. Since then, the car has traveled the world as a display piece to places such as New York, Paris, Tokyo, and Munich.

Fumbling Felons

Printer Theft Leads to Sentence

Sometimes people aren't entitled to tech support on their electronics. Perhaps they didn't buy the warranty or register the equipment. Or in the case of Timothy Scott Short, maybe he stole the machine. Shortly after a printer that was used to make driver's licenses was stolen from the Missouri Department of Revenue in 2007, Short called the printer company's tech support wondering whether it was possible to buy a new part for it. A voice message and the suspect's phone number led police back to Short, who was charged with the felony of possessing document-making implements and theft.

No Dancing Matter

It all began on Andrew Singh's 2009 wedding day in Preston, Lancashire, England. A coach bus from Manchester was hired to transport three loads of wedding guests to the ceremony. On the way there, a car swerved into the bus causing a small collision. Oddly, the groom decided this was the perfect opportunity to come away with a bit of cash. He and his family sued the motor coach company, claiming that they had suffered injuries such as bruising and whiplash. But the case had no legs: It was soon discovered that Andrew and his father were not actually passengers on the bus during the accident. A judge threw out their claim, and a police investigation was launched. The final straw was a video taken at the wedding reception, showing Andrew, his family, and festive wedding guests dancing, clapping, and cheering—and not looking very injured at all. The groom and his parents were convicted of conspiracy to defraud and perjury, and they were sentenced to a year in jail. Wisely, the bride ditched them all. Who's dancing now?

Con Man Quickies

In November 2006, a jail inmate in Austria climbed into a cardboard box and mailed himself to freedom. Two months later, a prison inmate in neighboring Germany did the same.

In 2008, Reginald Peterson called 911 to lodge a complaint. The charge? Apparently, a Jacksonville, Florida-based Subway sandwich shop employee left the sauce off his spicy Italian sub. In fact, he called 911 twice—first to complain about the lack of sauce and later to complain that police were slow in responding.

Index

❖ ❖ ❖ ❖

Contributing Writers

❖ ❖ ❖ ❖

Jeff Bahr has contributed to a number of books in the Armchair Reader™ series, including *The Gigantic Reader; Weird, Scary & Unusual,* and *The Book of Myths & Misconceptions.* With this offering he has increased that number by one—a Mammoth one.

Fiona Broome is a highly respected ghost hunter with more than 20 years of experience as a paranormal researcher. As the founder and lead investigator of HollowHill.com, she has also written several books, is a popular guest at annual conferences such as Dragon°Con, and has appeared on numerous TV and radio shows.

Robert Bullington is a writer, editor, and educator based in Richmond, Virginia.

Eric Erickson is a writer and founder of Temple of the Cave Productions. His work has appeared in the *Chicago Tribune, Chicago Sun-Times,* and numerous other news and media outlets. He is also the author of several plays and stage works as well as a contributor to the Armchair Reader™ series.

Mary Fons-Misetic is a professional freelance writer and performer living in Chicago. Read Mary's blog, PaperGirl, and find out more at maryfons.com.

Erika Cornstuble Koff is a freelance writer whose work includes three Armchair Reader™ books and a slew of interesting assignments for corporate and creative clients. Erika holds a B.S. in Speech from Northwestern University and an M.A. in Writing from DePaul University. She lives with her husband and twin daughters in suburban Chicago.

Shanon Lyon is a Seattle-based freelance writer specializing in game content and trivia. Her most recent projects include a themed edition of Trivial Pursuit and a board game celebrating 35 years of *Saturday Night Live.* She's the author of *Gifts with Meaning,* and her work has appeared in a number of national publications, including *Kiwi, ID, Natural Health,* and *American Girl.*

Susan McGowan is a poet and software tester in Columbus, Ohio, where she lives with her husband, fierce pirate daughter, wee bean of a son, a redundant array of orange cats, and two pets named Murph. In her free time, she knits poorly and travels the world.

Laura Pearson is a Chicago-based freelance writer and editor specializing in arts and culture reporting. She has contributed to other Publications International titles and especially enjoys writing for the Armchair Reader™ series, as her love of random trivia is truly *mammoth.*

JR Raphael is a syndicated writer and world-renowned armchair aficionado. His work regularly appears in such publications as *PC World, The Washington Post,* and MSNBC.com. JR also runs eSarcasm.com, voted 0.2 time as the best geek-humor Web site in the world. Come say hello at facebook.com/The.JR.Raphael.

Jason Rip works extensively as a playwright, actor, and periodical writer. An anthology of his darker works, *Middlesex & Violence,* was published early in 2009, and he has also written plays about Fatty Arbuckle and Arthur Rimbaud. He lives in London, Ontario, Canada.

Russell Roberts has been a freelance writer for 25 years. He has published more than a dozen books for adults, several dozen for children, hundreds of articles, and dozens of pieces of fiction. He resides in New Jersey with his family, including a wily calico cat.

Sue Sveum is an author and freelance writer with a journalism degree from the University of Wisconsin-Madison. She has coauthored two nonfiction books and contributed to many others, including four in the Armchair Reader™ series. Sue currently lives in Madison with her family—all Badger fans.

Wesley Treat has spent the last decade seeking unusual roadside attractions in an effort never to squander another summer waiting in theme-park lines while holding an $8 lemon slushie. A Dallas native, he works as a photographer, author, and graphic designer to support his ongoing search.

Donald Vaughan has been a professional writer for more than 30 years. During that time, he has written hundreds of articles for scores of magazines, including *Military Officer Magazine, Filmfax, Cat Fancy, MAD Magazine,* and the *Weekly World News.* When not writing, Donald enjoys baseball, autograph collecting, and correcting misspelled signs.

James A. Willis is the founder and director of the paranormal research organization The Ghosts of Ohio and has spent more than 25 years seeking out all things strange and spooky. He has also coauthored or been a contributing author to ten books, including four in the Armchair Reader™ series. He currently resides in Columbus, Ohio, with his wife, parrot, and three narcoleptic cats.

Kelly Wittmann is the author or coauthor of nine books. She lives in Chicago.

Anna Zaigraeva was born in Russia, back when it was still the USSR. After being tossed hither and thither by winds of fate, she found harbor in Chicago, where she now dwells with her husband and cat. When she is not writing or translating, she studies Finnish and Wing Chun kung fu.